Lecture Notes in Artificial Intelligence 11755

Subseries of Lecture Notes in Computer Science

Series Editors

Randy Goebel
University of Alberta, Edmonton, Canada
Yuzuru Tanaka
Hokkaido University, Sapporo, Japan
Wolfgang Wahlster
DFKI and Saarland University, Saarbrücken, Germany

Founding Editor

Jörg Siekmann
DFKI and Saarland University, Saarbrücken, Germany

More information about this series at http://www.springer.com/series/1244

Gloria Corpas Pastor · Ruslan Mitkov (Eds.)

Computational and Corpus-Based Phraseology

Third International Conference, Europhras 2019
Malaga, Spain, September 25–27, 2019
Proceedings

Springer

Editors
Gloria Corpas Pastor
University of Malaga
Malaga, Spain

Ruslan Mitkov
University of Wolverhampton
Wolverhampton, UK

ISSN 0302-9743 ISSN 1611-3349 (electronic)
Lecture Notes in Artificial Intelligence
ISBN 978-3-030-30134-7 ISBN 978-3-030-30135-4 (eBook)
https://doi.org/10.1007/978-3-030-30135-4

LNCS Sublibrary: SL7 – Artificial Intelligence

This Springer imprint is published by the registered company Springer Nature Switzerland AG
The registered company address is: Gewerbestrasse 11, 6330 Cham, Switzerland

Preface

Computational and Corpus-Based Phraseology

Language is phraseological and phraseology is the discipline which studies phraseological units (PUs) and their related concepts referred to (and regarded largely synonymous) by scholars as multiword units, multiword expressions (MWEs), fixed expressions, set expressions, formulaic language, phrasemes, idiomatic expressions, idioms, collocations, and/or polylexical expressions. PUs or MWEs are ubiquitous and pervasive in language. They are a fundamental linguistic concept which is central to a wide range of natural language processing and applied linguistics applications, including, but not limited to, phraseology, terminology, translation, language learning, teaching and assessment, and lexicography. Jackendoff (1997) observes that the number of MWEs in a speaker's lexicon is of the same order of magnitude as the number of single words. Biber et al. (1999) argue that they constitute up to 45% of spoken English and up to 21% of academic prose in English. Sag et al. (2002) comment that they are overwhelmingly present in terminology and 41% of the entries in WordNet 1.7 are reported to be MWEs.

It is not only in the computational treatment of natural language that PUs play a crucial role. Terms are often MWEs (and not single words), which makes them highly relevant to terminology. Translation and interpreting are two other fields where phraseology plays an important role, as finding correct translation equivalents of PUs is a pivotal step in the translation process. Given their pervasive nature, PUs are absolutely central to the work carried out by lexicographers, who analyse and describe both single words and PUs. Last but not least, PUs are vital not only for language learning, teaching, and assessment, but also for more theoretical linguistic areas such as pragmatics, cognitive linguistics, and construction grammars. All the aforementioned areas are today aided by (and often driven by) corpora, which makes PUs particularly relevant for corpus linguists. Finally, PUs provide an excellent basis for inter- and multidisciplinary studies, fostering fruitful collaborations between researchers across different disciplines. While there are some exceptions (e.g. Corpas Pastor and Colson 2019/forthcoming; Granger and Meunier 2008; Mitkov et al. 2018), such collaborations are still generally largely unexplored.

This volume features a selection of regular papers accepted after rigorous reviewing and presented at the international conference "Computational and Corpus-based Phraseology" (Europhras 2019). The conference was jointly organised by the European Association for Phraseology (EUROPHRAS), the University of Malaga (Research Group in Lexicography and Translation), Spain, the University of Wolverhampton (Research Group in Computational Linguistics), United Kingdom, and the Association for Computational Linguistics, Bulgaria, and was sponsored by EUROPHRAS, the Sketch Engine, the University of Malaga, and the University of Wolverhampton. Europhras 2019 provided the perfect opportunity for researchers to present their work, fostering interaction and interdisciplinary collaboration. The papers in this volume cover a number of topics including general corpus-based approaches to phraseology, phraseology in translation and cross-linguistic studies, phraseology in language teaching and learning, phraseology in specialised languages, phraseology in lexicography, cognitive approaches to phraseology, the computational treatment of multiword expressions, and the development, annotation and exploitation of corpora for phraseological studies. We have deliberately not grouped the contributions around specific topics – as many of them cut across more than one of the above listed topics – but have instead opted for presenting the papers alphabetically according to the (first) family name of the (first) author.

Every submission to the conference was evaluated by three reviewers. The reviewers were either members of the Programme Committee, consisting of 56 scholars from 24 different countries, or one of the 16 additional reviewers from 3 countries, who were recommended by the Programme Committee. The conference contributions were authored by a total of 150 scholars from 27 different countries. These figures attest to the truly international nature of Europhras 2019.

We would like to thank all colleagues who made this wonderfully interdisciplinary and international event possible. We would like to start by thanking all colleagues who submitted papers to Europhras 2019 and travelled to Malaga to attend the event. We are grateful to all members of the Programme Committee and the additional reviewers for carefully examining all submissions and providing substantial feedback on all papers, helping the authors of accepted papers to improve and polish the final versions of their papers. A special thanks goes to the invited speakers, namely the keynote speakers of the main conference (Sylviane Granger, Miloš Jakubíček, Natalie Kübler, Kathrin Steyer, and Aline Villavicencio), the invited speakers of the accompanying workshop on Multiword Units in Machine Translation and Translation Technology (Jean-Pierre Colson and Aline Villavicencio), and the tutorial speakers from Lexical Computing. Words of gratitude go to our sponsors: EUROPHRAS, the Sketch Engine, the University of Malaga, and the University of Wolverhampton.

Last but not least, we would like to use this paragraph to acknowledge the members of both the Organising Committee and Programme Committee, who worked very hard during the last 12 months and whose dedication and efforts made the organisation of this event possible. All those who have contributed are listed (in alphabetical order) on the following pages. We would like to single out several colleagues for competently carrying out numerous organisational and reviewing-related tasks and being ready to step in and support the organisation of the conference both on weekdays and during the weekends – in fact, whenever needed. Our big 'thank you' goes out to Rocío Caro Quintana, Maria Kunilovskaya, Francisco Javier Lima Florido, Desiré Martos García, Tharindu Ranasinghe Hettiarachchige, and Shiva Taslimipoor.

September 2019   Gloria Corpas Pastor
                                                          Ruslan Mitkov

References

Biber, D., Finegan, E., Johansson, S., Conrad, S. and Leech, G. 1999. *Longman Grammar of Spoken and Written English*. Longman, Harlow.

Corpas Pastor, G. and J.P. Colson (Eds). 2019/forthcoming. *Computational Phraseology*. Amsterdam and Philadelphia: John Benjamins.

Granger, S. and Meunier, F. 2008. Disentangling the Phraseological Web. In Granger, S., & Meunier, F. (Eds.), *Phraseology. An interdisciplinary perspective*. Amsterdam: John Benjamins publishers.

Jackendoff, R. 1997. *The Architecture of the Language Faculty*. Cambridge, MA: MIT Press.

Mitkov, R., Monti, J., Corpas Pastor G. and Seretan, V. (Eds). 2018. *Multiword Units in Machine Translation and Translation Technology*. John Benjamins.

Sag, I. A., Baldwin, T., Bond, F., Copestake, A. and Flickinger, D. 2002. 'Multiword Expressions: A Pain in the Neck for NLP'. In *Proceedings of the third international conference on intelligent text processing and computational linguistics (CICLING 2002)* (pp. 1–15). Mexico City, Mexico.

Organisation

Europhras 2019 was jointly organised by the European Association for Phraseology (Europhras), the University of Malaga (Research Group in Lexicography and Translation), Spain, the University of Wolverhampton (Research Group in Computational Linguistics), United Kingdom, and the Association for Computational Linguistics, Bulgaria.

Conference Chairs

Gloria Corpas Pastor	University of Malaga, Spain
Ruslan Mitkov	University of Wolverhampton, UK

Programme Committee

Mariangela Albano	University Dokuz Eylül of Izmir, Turkey
Verginica Barbu Mititelu	Romanian Academy Research Institute for Artificial Intelligence, Romania
Farouk Bouhadiba	University of Oran 2, Algeria
Nicoletta Calzolari	Institute for Computational Linguistics, Italy
María Luisa Carrió Pastor	Polytechnic University of Valencia, Spain
Sheila Castilho	Dublin City University, Ireland
Cristina Castillo Rodríguez	University of Malaga, Spain
Ken Church	Baidu, China
Jean-Pierre Colson	Université Catholique de Louvain, Belgium
Anna Čermáková	Charles University, Czech Republic
María Sagrario del Río Zamudio	University of Udine, Italy
Dmitrij Dobrovolskij	Russian Language Institute, Russia
Peter Ďurčo	University of St. Cyril and Methodius, North Macedonia
Jesse Egbert	Northern Arizona University, USA
Natalia Filatkina	University of Trier, Germany
Thierry Fontenelle	Translation Centre for the Bodies of the European Union, Luxembourg
José Enrique Gargallo	University of Barcelona, Spain
Sylviane Granger	Université Catholique de Louvain, Belgium
Kleanthes Grohmann	University of Cyprus, Cyprus
Miloš Jakubíček	Lexical Computing, Czech Republic
Simon Krek	University of Ljubljana, Slovenia
Natalie Kübler	Paris Diderot University, France
Alessandro Lenci	University of Pisa, Italy

Elvira Manero	University of Murcia, Spain
Carmen Mellado Blanco	University of Santiago de Compostela, Spain
Flor Mena Martínez	University of Murcia, Spain
Pedro Mogorrón Huerta	University of Alicante, Spain
Johanna Monti	L'Orientale University of Naples, Italy
Sara Može	University of Wolverhampton, UK
Michael Oakes	University of Wolverhampton, UK
Inés Olza	University of Navarra, Spain
Petya Oscnova	Sofia University, Bulgaria
Stéphane Patin	Paris Diderot University, France
Alain Polguère	University of Lorraine, France
Encarnación Postigo Pinazo	University of Malaga, Spain
Carlos Ramisch	Laboratoire d'Informatique Fondamentale de Marseille, France
Rozane Rebechi	Federal University Rio Grande do Sul, Brazil
Mª Ángeles Recio Ariza	University of Salamanca, Spain
Irene Renau	The Pontifical Catholic University of Chile, Chile
Omid Rohanian	University of Wolverhampton, UK
Ute Römer	Georgia State University, USA
Leonor Ruiz Gurillo	University of Alicante, Spain
Agata Savary	François Rabelais University, France
Miriam Seghiri Domínguez	University of Malaga, Spain
Julia Sevilla Muñoz	Complutense University of Madrid, Spain
Kathrin Steyer	Institute of German Language, Germany
Joanna Szerszunowicz	University of Bialystok, Poland
Shiva Taslimipoor	University of Wolverhampton, UK
Yukio Tono	Tokyo University of Foreign Studies, Japan
Cornelia Tschichold	Swansea University, UK
Agnès Tutin	University of Stendhal, France
Aline Villavicencio	Federal University of Rio Grande do Sul, Brazil, and University of Essex, UK
Tom Wasow	Stanford University, USA
Eric Wehrli	University of Geneva, Switzerland
Juan Jesús Zaro Vera	University of Malaga, Spain
Michael Zock	French National Centre for Scientific Research, France

Additional Reviewers

Rocío Caro Quintana	University of Wolverhampton, UK
Souhila Djabri	University of Alicante, Spain
Anna Feherova	University of Wolverhampton, UK
Emma Franklin	Lancaster University, UK
Le An Ha	University of Wolverhampton, UK
Patrick Hanks	University of Wolverhampton, UK
Maria Kunilovskaya	University of Wolverhampton, UK
María Araceli Losey León	University of Cadiz, Spain

Carmen Merino Ferrada   University of Cadiz, Spain
Emad Mohamed   University of Wolverhampton, UK
Carmen Noya Gallardo   University of Cadiz, Spain
Encarnación Núñez   University of Wolverhampton, UK
Alistair Plum   University of Wolverhampton, UK
Maria Stasimioti   Ionian University, Greece
Victoria Yaneva   University of Wolverhampton, UK
María Ángeles Zarco Tejada University of Cadiz, Spain

Keynote Speakers Main Conference

Sylviane Granger   Université Catholique de Louvain, Belgium
Miloš Jakubíček   Lexical Computing and Masaryk University,
                              Czech Republic
Natalie Kübler   Paris Diderot University, France
Kathrin Steyer   Institute of German Language, Germany
Aline Villavicencio   Federal University of Rio Grande do Sul, Brazil,
                              and University of Essex, UK

Invited Speakers of the MUMTTT 2019 Workshops

Jean-Pierre Colson   Université Catholique de Louvain, Belgium
Aline Villavicencio   Federal University of Rio Grande do Sul, Brazil,
                              and University of Essex, UK

Organising Committee

Rosario Bautista Zambrana   University of Malaga, Spain
Rocío Caro Quintana   University of Wolverhampton, UK
Isabel Durán Muñoz   University of Malaga, Spain
Sandra Elfiky   University of Wolverhampton, UK
Javier Alejandro Fernández University of Malaga, Spain
  Sola
Mahmoud Gaber   University of Malaga, Spain
Rut Gutiérrez Florido   University of Malaga, Spain
Carlos Manuel Hidalgo   University of Malaga, Spain
  Ternero
Suman Hira   University of Wolverhampton, UK
Pavlina Krasteva   University of Wolverhampton, UK
Maria Kunilovskaya   University of Wolverhampton, UK
Francisco Javier Lima   University of Malaga, Spain
  Florido
Gema Lobillo Mora   University of Malaga, Spain
Araceli Losey León   University of Malaga, Spain
Desiré Martos García   University of Malaga, Spain
Luis Carlos Marín Navarro   University of Malaga, Spain

Juan Pascual Martínez Fernández	University of Malaga, Spain
Sara Može	University of Wolverhampton, UK
Míriam Pérez Carrasco	University of Malaga, Spain
Alistair Plum	University of Wolverhampton, UK
Tharindu Ranasinghe Hettiarachchige	University of Wolverhampton, UK
Fernando Sánchez Rodas	University of Malaga, Spain
Anastasia Taramigou	University of Malaga, Spain
Shiva Taslimipoor	University of Wolverhampton, UK
Gergana Zyumbilska	University of Wolverhampton, UK

Association for Computational Linguistics (Bulgaria)

Nikolai Nikolov
Ivelina Nikolova

Sponsors

EUROPHRAS

EUROPHRAS

EUROPÄISCHE GESELLSCHAFT FÜR PHRASEOLOGIE

Sketch Engine

University of Wolverhampton

UNIVERSITY OF
WOLVERHAMPTON

University of Malaga

Antequera

Málaga Convention Bureau

Contents

Contents

The Grammatical Environment of Intensifier-Noun Collocations: Insights from Lexical Priming Theory

Moisés Almela-Sánchez[1(✉)] and Pascual Cantos-Gómez[2]

[1] Depto. Fil. Inglesa, Fac. Letras, University of Murcia, 30001 Murcia, Spain
moisesal@um.es
[2] University of Murcia, Murcia, Spain
pcantos@um.es

Abstract. A recurrent topic in collocational research is the idiosyncratic distribution of intensifiers with nearly equivalent meanings. So far, this phenomenon has been mostly investigated from the perspective of the control exerted by the lexical context. In the case of adjective–noun collocations, this implies an almost exclusive focus on the nominal head. In this paper, we draw the attention towards the role that *colligation* –i.e. preferences for particular grammatical contexts– exerts on the selection of intensifying adjectives. Drawing on insights from Hoey's lexical priming theory –in particular, the concept of *nesting*–, we conducted two corpus-based case studies involving collocations of intensifying adjectives with two different nouns in English (*attention* and *fear*). The results suggest that the selection of intensifier is sensitive to the interplay of lexical collocation and grammatical context.

Keywords: Collocations · Lexical priming · Intensifiers

1 Introduction

Hoey's theory of *lexical priming* underlines the importance of cumulative loading of contextual information associated with word usage in accounting for phenomena of naturalness and fluency in language production and comprehension [1–3]. The theory is informed by a neo-Firthian approach to language, and it is empirically underpinned by converging evidence from corpus linguistics and psycholinguistic research. Like other neo-Firthian developments in modern linguistics –notably the *idiom principle* [4] and *pattern grammar* [5] – the theory of lexical priming favours a *phraseological view* of language, as it emphasizes the structural impact of item-specific combinatory preferences and subtle –often subliminal– formulaic patterns.

In this study, we will apply the analytical apparatus of lexical priming theory to the collocational behaviour of intensifying adjectives. These elements belong to one of the most frequently investigated types of collocations (see [6–9], among others). Previous studies of this type of collocational patterns reflect the diversity of conceptions of the notion of collocation, in particular, the distinction between the semantically oriented approach of the *Continental tradition*, on the one hand, and the statistically oriented

© Springer Nature Switzerland AG 2019
G. Corpas Pastor and R. Mitkov (Eds.): Europhras 2019, LNAI 11755, pp. 1–14, 2019.
https://doi.org/10.1007/978-3-030-30135-4_1

approach of the Firthian (or *British contextualist*) tradition, on the other. The former has been mainly inspired by the work of Hausmann and Mel'čuk (see [6, 10–15]), while the leading figure in the development of the modern, neo-Firthian approach to collocation has been Sinclair (see [4, 16, 17]). In the Hausmann/Mel'čuk approach, the concept of collocation denotes a phraseological expression with an asymmetrical semantic structure, which consists of a semantically dependent lexeme and a semantically autonomous lexeme. The Sinclairian approach adopts a broader conception of collocation, which includes any word co-occurrence pattern that occurs with statistical significance in a corpus (the question of how to measure such significance and in what search space is, in turn, another object of discussion in the literature: [18–22]). For a detailed explanation of differences between the two approaches, the reader is referred to the abundant literature on the topic (see [23–28], among others).

However, beyond the diversity of theoretical and methodological perspectives that inform these two approaches, studies dealing with collocations of intensifying adjectives and nouns show two main points of common ground: first, they provide extensive descriptions of differences in the syntagmatic behaviour of near-synonyms; second, they focus the analysis of co-textual dependency on the lexical level, specifically on the head noun. The framework provided by lexical priming theory is compatible with these two observations, but additionally, it facilitates the account of more idiosyncratic features involved in the distributional differences among near-synonymous intensifiers. In particular, the focus of the present paper is on differences in the *colligational primings* (i.e., preferences for particular grammatical contexts) of collocations formed with different intensifying adjectives.

The paper is organized as follows. First, in the next section, we will offer a brief explanation of those descriptive categories and tenets of lexical priming theory which bear direct relevance to our object of study. Section 3 will be devoted to the clarification of methodological issues, particularly about the techniques employed for extracting patterns of lexico-grammatical attraction from corpora. Then, the theoretical and methodological framework described in these sections will be applied to two different case studies in Sect. 4, each of them focusing on a different set of grammatical categories (syntactic functions and phrase structure, respectively). The discussion of implications drawn from these case studies is addressed in Sect. 5.

2 Theoretical Background

The theory of lexical priming is at the crossroads of psycholinguistic and corpus-based research. This crossing of boundaries across disciplines is not at odds with current trends in linguistics. Though not exempt from controversy, the convergence of psycholinguistic theorizing and corpus-based studies represents a growing tendency [29, 30]. Regarding collocational research, which is the main object of our study, the connection between corpus evidence and psycholinguistic reality finds a strong empirical support in the results of an experiment conducted by Ellis et al. [31], in which corpus data on collocational patterns were compared with response times by participants in lexical decision tasks. The findings indicate that words that tend to occur together also tend to be processed faster.

There are mainly two concepts from psycholinguistics which have been set in direct relationship with the phenomenon of collocation. One is *word associations*, and the other is, precisely, the concept of *priming*. Word associations consist of *cue-response* pairs. These pairs are obtained from experiments in which participants are asked to provide words which come to their mind (response words) given another word (the cue word or stimulus word) [32–34]. The relationship between the concepts of word association and collocation has been approached from two main angles. Firstly, it has been observed that one of the most common types of link between stimulus words and responses involves relations between words that tend to be found together [32]. From this standpoint, collocation corresponds to a specific type of the diverse linguistic phenomena that underlie word association.

Another approach to the relationship between word associations and collocation was introduced by Church and Hanks, who suggested that collocation extraction can be used as part of a methodology for obtaining norms of word association. Although the standard procedure for obtaining aggregated data on word associations is to collect responses by thousands of participants (for a recent study, see [33]), Church and Hanks argued that such norms could be estimated directly from corpora using association measures [35]. In particular, the statistics they proposed to use was *mutual information*, which is now widely used as a lexical association measure. At present, the term *lexical association* has become specialized in the statistical, corpus-based description of syntagmatic associations between words [20], while the term *word association* has retained its original reference to cue-response pairs obtained from psycholinguistic experiments [33, 34].

Like word associations, the notion of *priming* is applied to relations between words in the mental lexicon, but the method for obtaining such relations is different. In psycholinguistic experiments, a word *a* is said to prime a word *b* if the presence of *a* facilitates the processing of *b* [32]. Recognition time is interpreted as a clue for this relationship. Thus, if the priming word is related to the target, the listener will recognize the target word faster than if they had been given an unrelated priming word.

Hoey adapts the psycholinguistic notion of *priming* and applies it to the analysis of corpus data. This adaptation implies a shift in focus: instead of focusing on the relationship between the priming item and the target word in the mental lexicon, the notion of *lexical priming*, as conceived by Hoey, lays special emphasis on the relevance of co-textual information for our knowledge of the lexical properties of the item investigated [1]. In this theoretical framework, collocation represents one of the four main layers of contextual information which is cumulatively loaded in the usage record of a word. The other three main layers of lexical priming are *semantic association, colligation*, and *pragmatic association* [1–3]. As explained by Hoey, this fourfold classification is only partially equivalent to the four descriptive categories (collocation, colligation, semantic preference, semantic prosody) used by Sinclair in his account of the notion of *extended lexical items/units of meaning* [36, 37].

The four descriptive categories adopted by Hoey inform the first four hypotheses of lexical priming theory (Hoey formulates a total of ten *priming hypotheses*, of which the first five will bear direct relevance to the present study). Thus, the first priming hypothesis states that every word is primed for use in combination with particular other words (its *collocates*). The following three hypotheses make analogous claims about the priming for occurrence in combination with particular semantic sets (the semantic associations), in association with particular pragmatic functions (these are the pragmatic associations of the word), and in particular grammatical positions and functions (these are its colligations) [1].

It is essential to add that priming phenomena can have a positive and a negative dimension. The positive dimension refers to those linguistic features with which the word under scrutiny is primed to occur, whereas the negative dimension refers to those linguistic features which the occurrences of the word tend to repel. The exact original formulation of the fourth hypothesis includes these two dimensions: there, words are claimed to *occur in* or to *avoid* certain grammatical positions and functions. Hoey offers examples of positive and negative colligational primings of the word *consequence* in a journalistic corpus. According to his results, *consequence* is primed to occur in the functions of complement and adjunct, but it tends to avoid (i.e., is negatively primed for use with) the object function.

Another fundamental characteristic of primings has to do with their possibilities for recursivity. The products of primings (for instance, particular collocations or colligations) can, in turn, be primed for occurrence with particular words, semantic sets, pragmatic functions, or grammatical contexts [1, 38]. Hoey describes this property of priming as *nesting* [1].

Nestings can combine properties from different structural levels. A case in point is *wouldn't say a word against* [1, 2]. As explained by Hoey, this sequence can be analyzed as a product of successive layers of priming involving the four descriptive categories: the word group *a word against* is primed for co-occurring with words from the semantic set 'sending/receiving communication' (SEND/RECEIVE + *a word against*); in turn, combinations resulting from this priming, such as *say a word against* or *hear a word against*, have their own colligates, namely, modal verbs (e.g. *wouldn't say a word against*). Furthermore, Hoey also observes that for most speakers, the combination SEND/RECEIVE + *a word against* has a pragmatic association with DENIAL. Hoey suggests that the complexity of the primings thus formed can even be extended to include typical properties of the subject and the prepositional object. The example provided by Hoey illustrates the flexibility of the nesting and combinatory possibilities of primings. In the case studies conducted in Sect. 4, we will analyze some nesting properties of primings which manifest themselves in the behaviour of collocations with intensifying adjectives. For the sake of focus, our analysis will concentrate on the interplay of collocations and colligations.

3 Methodology

The study of complex patterns formed by collocational and colligational patterns can take advantage of methodological advances made in corpus linguistics over the last decades. The seminal article on *collostructional analysis* published by Stefanowitsch and Gries in 2003 [39] paved the ground for a new line of research dealing with the question of which techniques are more suitable for measuring the association between lexical items and grammatical constructions. Schmid and Küchenhoff [40] discuss four of these techniques (Fisher Exact test, Attraction and Reliance, Delta P, and Odds Ratio).

In this study, we will apply Delta P (DP, hereafter). To the best of our knowledge, this measure has not been used yet in the lexical priming literature, but it suits the goals of the present study. DP combines the use of conditional probabilities and 2×2 contingency tables. It has been used both as a measure of lexical association, i.e., as collocation statistics [41], and as a measure of lexico-grammatical attraction [40]. In the latter use, DP calculates the probability of a lexical item (or a word group) in a given construction, and vice versa, but subtracts from it the probability of other constructions occurring with the same lexeme/sequence and –in the opposite direction– the probability of other lexemes/sequences occurring with the same construction. This measure offers two important advantages. First, it avoids p-values and does not have to rely on the questionable assumption that linguistic data could be randomly distributed. This is important in our study because we will use an extensive corpus, and it has been pointed out that sample size tends to reduce p-values [40]. Second, DP does not conflate the two directions of association (from the lexical expression to the construction, and the other way round) but offers a different score for each of them (i.e., it is a bi-directional measure). DP scores oriented from the lexical item to the grammatical context are termed *DP Reliance*; those oriented from the grammatical context to the lexical item are termed *DP Attraction* [40].

DP scores range between a minimum of –1 and a maximum of 1. Positive values of DP Attraction are interpreted as indicating the capacity of the grammatical context for attracting the selection of the lexical target (conversely, negative values suggest that the grammatical environment under scrutiny repels the word). Positive values of DP Reliance indicate the potential of the lexical item for predicting its occurrence in the grammatical context considered; conversely, negative values of reliance indicate the tendency of the lexical item for avoiding the grammatical context analyzed. This means that DP scores can give us useful information for detecting not only cases of positive priming, but also negative priming.

The application of DP to our research objective is implemented as follows (see Tables 1 and 2). The grand total represents the frequency of the node word in the corpus. In our case studies, this will be a noun modified by the intensifying adjectives. Cell 1 represents the frequency with which a given collocation (consisting of the node and each of the intensifying adjectives analyzed) occurs in a specified grammatical context. In the table, *nw* stands for *node word* and *cc* for *collocate*. The grammatical context can be a particular position, a syntactic function, or a sequence involving a specific grammatical category (for instance, the presence of a possessive determiner in the same noun phrase). Any such feature (relative position, function, category) treated as an element of colligational priming will be referred to as a *colligate* (abbreviated to *cg*). Thus, the figure in Cell 1 may stand, for instance, for the frequency with which the collocation *big mistake* occurs in a subject noun phrase, or for the frequency with which *full attention* is preceded by a possessive determiner in the same noun phrase, etc. Cell 2 represents the frequency with which the same colligate occurs with other lexical co-occurrences of the same node word, and Cell 3 stands for the frequency with which the same node-collocate pair occurs in contexts from which the colligate is absent (e.g. occurrences of *big mistake* in non-subject noun phrases, or of *full attention* not preceded by a possessive determiner). Finally, Cell 4 stands for the frequency with which the same node occurs in other grammatical contexts and in absence of the collocate in question in the modifier position. Given this data structure, the scores of DP Attraction and Reliance are calculated using the following formulae (see [40]):

Table 1. Contingency table.

	b	¬b	Totals
a	Cell 1	Cell 3	Row total
¬a	Cell 2	Cell 4	Row total
Totals	Column total	Column total	Grand total

DP Attraction:

$$DP(cc|cg) = \frac{Cell1}{Cell1 + Cell3} - \frac{Cell2}{Cell2 + Cell4} \tag{1}$$

DP Reliance:

$$DP(cg|cc) = \frac{Cell1}{Cell1 + Cell2} - \frac{Cell3}{Cell3 + Cell4} \tag{2}$$

The data used for the two cases studies are all drawn from the enTenTen15 corpus (also known as English Web 2015). This is a vast web corpus of English, containing 15,703,895,409 words. The corpus is accessible through the Sketch Engine corpus query system, and it has been annotated by the English TreeTagger tool using a part-of-speech tagset with modifications developed by Sketch Engine [42]. The extraction of the data for this study was carried out using a combination of tools from the said corpus query system, including frequency information from Word Sketches (i.e., grammatically categorized lists of collocates), and concordance filtering using Corpus Query Language (CQL). The CQL is a programming language which allows the user to define highly refined queries, such as the search for modifiers in noun phrases with subject or with object function, or sequences of a possessive determiner followed by a modifier of a noun, among other possibilities. The results obtained automatically from the system were supervised and checked for annotation errors. Where necessary, the retrieved output was corrected through successive filtering (this was especially necessary for calculating the frequency of verb-object combinations, given that the initial output retrieved from the system included predicative noun phrases erroneously parsed as object-of relations).

The co-occurrence patterns analyzed consist of combinations of intensifying adjectives with the nouns *attention* and *fear*. The selection of the target adjectives was based on lexicographic information from entries in the Oxford Collocations Dictionary (OCD) [43]. This dictionary does not provide glosses or semantic definitions, but collocates with a similar semantic relation to the lemma are grouped together, separated from other groups of collocates by vertical bars. For this study, we selected all the

Table 2. Contingency table cross-tabulating frequency scores of collocations and colligations.

	Colligate: present	Colligate: absent	Totals
Collocate: present	$(nw + cc)_{cg}$	$(nw + cc)_{\neg cg}$	$nw + cc$
Collocate: absent	$(nw, \neg cc)_{cg}$	$(nw, \neg cc)_{\neg cg}$	$(nw, \neg cc)$
Totals	$(nw)_{cg}$	$(nw)_{\neg cg}$	nw

members of collocate sets with a semantic function of intensification, and then we applied to each of them the measure of association between collocations and grammatical contexts. Each case study focuses on a different group of potential colligates (i.e., of grammatical contexts for which the target collocate could be primed). The first case study will focus on features of phrase structure –particularly on the presence or absence of determiners– while the second case study will focus on the syntactic function of the noun phrase.

4   Results and Analysis

4.1   Case Study 1: Intensifier + *Attention*

In the OCD, the entry for *attention* contains two groups of collocates which express an intensification of the meaning of the head noun. The first group includes *careful, close, meticulous, scrupulous,* and *serious*; the second group is formed by *full, rapt,* and *undivided*. There is a subtle difference in meaning between the two groups. In another collocation dictionary, the Macmillan Collocations Dictionary (MCD) [44], we are given explicit information about this difference: the semantic contribution of collocates of the first group is described with the gloss 'careful', while the gloss used for the second group is 'complete'. In any case, both meanings convey a sense of intensification of the meaning of *attention*, so the two sets must be taken into account here.

The target colligates for this case study are centred on structural properties of the noun phrase, specifically on the determiners. We have distinguished three main possibilities: possessive determiner (Colligate 1), definite article (Colligate 2), and absence of any determiner (Colligate 3). Since *attention* is uncountable, the indefinite article was not considered as a target colligate. Some occurrences of *attention* with the indefinite article are attested (e.g. *...a close attention to the geography of Mars; ...a close attention to detail; ...an uninterrupted full attention to one another*), but they are relatively rare and were not considered here as potentially significant.

The scores for DP Attraction and Reliance are shown in Tables 3, 4 and 5. The collocates are arranged in order of decreasing DP Attraction scores. The data structure of these tables is explained as follows. The first column provides the joint frequency of the collocation and the colligate, i.e. the number of occurrences of each intensifier-noun collocation within the specified grammatical context (this corresponds to Cell 1 in Tables 1 and 2); the second column indicates the frequency of the collocation, i.e. of the combination of each intensifying adjective with the head noun, regardless of the presence or absence of the colligate (this corresponds to the first row total in Tables 1 and 2). This second column contains the same information for all the tables containing the same set of intensifier-noun collocations. Additionally, there are two frequency values which are used for calculating the DP scores and which remain constant for all the cells of each table (these are given in brackets in the table captions). The first of these constant values corresponds to the frequency of the node word (nw), which here is the noun *attention*; the second one is the joint frequency of the node word and the colligate ($[nw]_{cg}$), regardless of the presence or absence of the intensifier or any other possible collocate.

Table 3. DP Attraction/Reliance between intensifier + *attention* and POSSESSIVE DETERMINER (constant values: F(nw) = 2,110,071; F($[nw]_{cg}$) = 327,391)

	$(nw + cc)_{cg}$	nw + cc	DP Attraction	DP Reliance
full	6,569	11,785	0.01714	0.40451
undivided	2,351	4,237	0.00612	0.40052
scrupulous	31	309	−0.00006	−0.05484
meticulous	260	2,178	−0.00028	−0.03582
rapt	161	2,363	−0.00074	−0.08712
serious	151	5,421	−0.00250	−0.12763
careful	356	10,330	−0.00451	−0.12129
close	452	30,394	−0.01542	−0.14234

The results shown in Tables 3, 4 and 5 can be summarized in two main points. The first one is that all the collocations analyzed tend to repel the use of the definite article in the same noun phrase (Table 4). Expressions such as *the very close attention, the closest attention, the necessary close attention, the full attention, the same careful attention*, etc., constitute possible but not typical grammatical realizations of this set of intensifier-noun collocations. The presence of the definite article in combination with these collocations is indeed licensed by the grammar but not privileged by priming phenomena.

The second aspect to be highlighted here lies in the comparison of Tables 3 and 5. This comparison points towards a complementary distribution between *full/undivided* and the other collocates. The collocations with *full* and *undivided* are the only ones that are primed to occur with the possessive determiner, and they are also the only ones that are primed to avoid phrases with no determiner. This means that expressions such as *their full attention, our full attention, her undivided attention*, etc., constitute more typical grammatical realizations of these lexical combinations than other expressions which contain the same sequence of attributive adjective and noun but no determiner (e.g. *...and need full attention; ...devote full attention to...; ...minutes of undivided attention*). All the other collocations analyzed in this subsection (*careful/close/ meticulous/rapt/scrupulous/serious + attention*) show the reverse pattern: they are negatively primed for the possessive determiner and positively primed for phrases with no determiner. This suggests that expressions such as *our close attention* and *their careful attention*, although possible, do not represent prototypical grammatical realizations of the collocational pattern under scrutiny. Their counterparts with no

Table 4. DP Attraction/Reliance between intensifier + *attention* and DEFINITE ARTICLE (constant values: F(nw) = 2,110,071; F([nw]$_{cg}$) = 329,273)

	(nw + cc)$_{cg}$	nw + cc	DP Attraction	DP Reliance
scrupulous	25	309	–0.00008	–0.07515
meticulous	188	2178	–0.00055	–0.06980
rapt	218	2363	–0.00054	–0.06386
undivided	543	4237	–0.00043	–0.02795
serious	282	5421	–0.00203	–0.10430
full	1,335	11,785	–0.00181	–0.04301
careful	698	10,330	–0.00329	–0.08891
close	470	30,394	–0.01538	–0.14264

Table 5. DP Attraction/Reliance between intensifier + *attention* and ZERO DETERMINER (constant values: F(nw) = 2,110,071; F([nw]$_{cg}$) = 1,196,256)

	(nw + cc)$_{cg}$	nw + cc	DP Attraction	DP Reliance
close	27,584	30,394	0.01998	0.34560
careful	8,612	10,330	0.00532	0.26807
serious	4,024	5,421	0.00184	0.17582
rapt	1,758	2,363	0.00081	0.17724
meticulous	1,487	2,178	0.00049	0.11593
scrupulous	218	309	0.00008	0.13860
full	3,482	11,785	–0.00618	–0.27299
undivided	1,143	4,237	–0.00243	–0.29776

determiner (e.g. *...are paying close attention to...; ...we should pay close attention to...; ...give careful attention to...*) seem to be more representative of how these collocations are used, based on our results.

4.2 Case Study 2: Intensifier + *Fear*

The group of intensifiers analyzed in this section comprises 11 adjectives: *big, deep, deep-seated, genuine, great, intense, overwhelming, pure, real, terrible, utter*. All of them express intensification, and they are all grouped within the same set of collocates in the OCD entry for fear. To offer a variety of features of colligational priming, the target colligates, in this case, are centred on the syntactic function of the noun phrase rather than on its internal structure. We have compared here four different slots: object function (Colligate 1), subject of the verb *be* (Colligate 2), and subject of verbs other than *be* (Colligate 3). This list of colligates does not exhaust all the possible syntactic functions of intensifier-*fear* collocations, but it allows us to focus on specific slots with a strong potential for colligational priming. The scores of association between collocations and grammatical contexts are shown in Tables 6, 7 and 8 (the value of F(nw) here corresponds to the frequency of *fear* as noun). The data structure of these tables is analogous to that of Tables 3, 4 and 5. The only difference resides in the target collocates and colligates.

Table 6. DP Attraction/Reliance between intensifier + *fear* and OBJECT (constant values: F (nw) = 1,068,626; F([nw]$_{cg}$) = 233,766)

	(nw + cc)$_{cg}$	nw + cc	DP Attraction	DP Reliance
real	1,562	3,045	0.00491	0.29506
great	2,251	7,485	0.00336	0.08256
deep	1,053	2,556	0.00270	0.19368
genuine	421	799	0.00135	0.30839
intense	444	1,286	0.00089	0.12666
deep–seated	190	427	0.00053	0.22630
terrible	176	416	0.00047	0.20440
overwhelming	142	472	0.00021	0.08213
big	1,060	4,862	−0.00002	−0.00074
pure	39	225	−0.00006	−0.04543
utter	11	113	−0.00008	−0.12142

These tables offer several contrasting patterns among intensifying collocates. In this case, there seems to be no division between subsets of collocates with a tendency towards complementary distribution. However, a detailed analysis of individual cases reveals subtle differences. Consider, for instance, the distribution of *big*. This adjective is primed for occurrence in only one of the syntactic contexts considered, namely, in subject noun phrases with the verb *be*, for example: *A big fear for me is "the unknown"; Our big fear is that the US will intervene...; ...her biggest fear had been that her group...; ...my biggest fear was actually finding the courage to start*, etc. The collocation *big fear* shows a very high score of reliance on this syntactic context, and the attraction which this context exerts on the selection of *big* –instead of other modifiers of *fear*– is also very strong (both scores are at the top of Table 7). Additionally, one can also observe that many of the examples analyzed show the use of this lexical collocation in conjunction with a preceding possessive article and the superlative form of the adjective (*my/her/our biggest fear* + BE). The analysis of this possible element of colligational priming lies not within the scope of the present subsection, but it can be conducted in future research using the same methodology.

The preferences of *big fear* stand in sharp contrast with, for instance, those of *intense* and *overwhelming*. Unlike *big*, the collocations of *attention* with *intense* and *overwhelming* are positively primed for occurrence with object function, and when they occur in the subject slot, their preference is not for copular constructions with the verb *be* (e.g. *...the overwhelming fear ate him from inside for too long; ...intense fears can develop and persist to the extent that...*). The implication is that *intense/overwhelming fear* are more strongly associated with transitive and intransitive complementation patterns than *big fear*.

Table 7. DP Attraction/Reliance between intensifier + *fear* and SUBJECT OF *BE* (constant values: F(nw) = 1,068,626; F([nw]$_{cg}$) = 37,683)

	(nw + cc)$_{cg}$	nw + cc	DP Attraction	DP Reliance
big	1,758	4,862	0.04364	0.32781
great	1,394	7,485	0.03108	0.15204
real	230	3,045	0.00337	0.04039
deep	158	2,556	0.00187	0.02662
utter	0	113	−0.00011	−0.03527
pure	0	225	−0.00022	−0.03527
overwhelming	5	472	−0.00032	−0.02468
deep–seated	2	427	−0.00036	−0.03059
terrible	1	416	−0.00038	−0.03287
genuine	13	799	−0.00042	−0.01901
intense	14	1,286	−0.00086	−0.02441

Table 8. DP Attraction/Reliance between intensifier + *fear* and SUBJECT OF NOT *BE* (constant values: F(nw) = 1,068,626; F([nw]$_{cg}$) = 56,410)

	(nw + cc)$_{cg}$	nw + cc	DP Attraction	DP Reliance
great	414	7,485	0.00035	0.00254
overwhelming	34	472	0.00017	0.01925
intense	76	1,286	0.00015	0.00632
terrible	27	416	0.00009	0.01212
pure	13	225	0.00002	0.00499
utter	4	113	−0.00004	−0.01739
deep–seated	19	427	−0.00007	−0.00829
genuine	24	799	−0.00034	−0.02277
deep	101	2,556	−0.00063	−0.01330
big	195	4,862	−0.00115	−0.01274
real	87	3,045	−0.00138	−0.02429

5   Conclusions and Reflections for Further Research

In this study, we have focused on a neglected aspect of a frequently investigated phenomenon. The idiosyncratic distribution of adjectival collocates with an intensifying function has been a common object of study in the literature on collocation, but the account of their syntagmatic behaviour had been almost exclusively analyzed from the point of view of the lexical control exerted by the nominal head they modify (i.e. the item that functions as *base* of the adjective-noun collocation, in the Hausmann/Mel'čuk nomenclature). The results from this study suggest the existence of other factors that may also play a significant role in the combinatory behaviour of these collocates. In particular, we have observed that different intensifiers are primed to occur in different grammatical environments with the same head noun. The implication is that, in order to account for the peculiar combinatory behaviour of this type of collocates, it is necessary to consider not only the lexical context provided by the noun but also the colligational preferences of the lexical collocation in which they participate. Or, to put it in more simple terms: nesting phenomena are part of what makes the selection of intensifiers so unpredictable.

At this point, we can apply this conclusion only to the two case studies investigated here. In future research, a similar methodology can be applied to a broader range of collocational patterns with other nouns. This should help us to determine the extent to which the interactions of collocational and colligational patterns observed here may be symptomatic of a more general phenomenon.

Another issue to be addressed in future research is a possible refinement of the method applied here, especially in order to demarcate non-compositional and compositional aspects of *nesting* (i.e. to determine which aspects of the primings attributed to the collocation are not deducible from the primings of the individual words). For instance, we have found that *big fear* is primed to occur as a subject of *be*, but at present we cannot determine whether this priming is an exclusive feature of the collocation as a whole, or whether it is also consistent with a tendency of this adjective to occur in this syntactic context when it is used as an intensifier. Similarly, we may wonder whether the priming of *full/undivided attention* for co-occurring with a possessive determiner may not be related to a similar individual priming of these adjectives. To answer these and other related questions in future research, it might be necessary to modify or expand the methodology applied here, possibly by including comparisons of scores of DP Attraction/Reliance at different levels (i.e. at the level of the collocation and at the level of individual words). Pursuing this objective is beyond the scope of the present paper, but it is a direction towards which its findings are pointing.

References

1. Hoey, M.: Lexical Priming. A New Theory of Words and Language. Routledge, London (2005)
2. Hoey, M.: Corpus-driven approaches to grammar: the search for common ground. In: Römer, U., Schulze, R. (eds.) Exploring the Lexis–Grammar Interface, pp. 33–47. John Benjamins, Amsterdam (2009)
3. Pace-Sigge, M., Patterson, K.J.: Introduction. In: Pace-Sigge, M., Patterson, K.J. (eds.) Lexical Priming. Applications and Advances, pp. 11–23. John Benjamins, Amsterdam (2017)
4. Sinclair, J.: Corpus, Concordance, Collocation. Oxford University Press, Oxford (1991)
5. Hunston, S., Francis, G.: Pattern Grammar. A Corpus-driven Approach to the Lexical Grammar of English. John Benjamins, Amsterdam (2000)
6. Hausmann, F.J.: Collocations in the bilingual dictionary. In: Hausmann, F.J., Riechmann, O., Wiegand, H.E., Zgusta, L. (eds.) Wörterbücher, Dictionaries, Dictionnaires: Ein internationales Handbuch zur Lexikographie/An International Encyclopedia of Lexicography/Encyclopédie internationale de lexicographie, vol. 3, pp. 2775–2778. Walter de Gruyter, Berlin (1991)

7. Partington, A.: Patterns and Meanings. Using Corpora for English Language Research and Teaching. John Benjamins, Amsterdam (1998)
8. García-Page, M.: Cuestión capital, error garrafal, fe ciega, etc. El intensificador en las colocaciones léxicas N + A. Verba. Anuario galego de filoloxía, Anexo, vol. 48, pp. 156–170 (2001)
9. Koike, K.: Colocaciones léxicas en el español actual: estudio formal y léxico-semántico. Universidad de Alcalá/Takushoku University (2001)
10. Hausmann, F.J.: Un dictionnaire des collocations est-il possible? Travaux de Linguistique et de Littérature Strasbourg **17**(1), 187–195 (1979)
11. Hausmann, F.J.: Was sind eigentlich Kollokationen? In: Steyer, K. (ed.) Wortverbindungen – mehr oder weniger fest (Jahrbuch des Instituts für Deutsche Sprache), pp. 309–334. Walter de Gruyter, Berlin (2004)
12. Hausmann, F.J.: Lexicographie française et phraséologie. In: Haag, E. (ed.) Collocations, phraséologie, lexicographie: Études 1977–2007 et Bibliographie, pp. 121–153. Shaker, Aachen (2007)
13. Mel'čuk, I.: Collocations and lexical functions. In: Cowie, A.P. (ed.) Phraseology. Theory, Analysis and Application, pp. 23–53. Clarendon, Oxford (1998)
14. Mel'čuk, I.: Lexical functions. In: Burger, H., Dobrovol'skij, Kühn, P., Norrick, N.R. (eds.) Phraseology. An International Handbook of Contemporary Research, vol. 1, pp. 119–131. Walter de Gruyter, Berlin (2007)
15. Mel'čuk, I., Clas, A., Polguère, A.: Introduction a la lexicologie explicative et combinatoire. Duculot, Louvain-la-Neuve (1995)
16. Sinclair, J., Jones, S., Daley, R.: English lexical studies: report to OSTI on project C/LP/08; final report for period January 1967-September 1969. Department of English, University of Birmingham (1970)
17. Jones, S., Sinclair, J.: English lexical collocations. A study in computational linguistics. Cahiers de lexicologie **24**, 15–61 (1974)
18. Mason, O.: Parameters of collocation: the word in the centre of gravity. In: Kirk, J.M. (ed.) Corpora Galore. Analyses and Techniques in describing English, pp. 267–280. Rodopi, Amsterdam (2000)
19. Evert, S.: Corpora and collocations. In: Lüdeling, A., Kytö, M. (eds.) Corpus Linguistics. An International Handbook, vol. 2, pp. 1212–1248. Walter de Gruyter, Berlin (2009)
20. Pecina, P.: Lexical association measures and collocation extraction. Lang. Resour. Eval. **44**, 137–158 (2010)
21. Uhrig, P., Proisl, T.: Less hay, more needles – using dependency-annotated corpora to provide lexicographers with more accurate lists of collocation candidates. Lexicographica **28**, 141–180 (2012)
22. Uhrig, P., Evert, S., Proisl, T.: Collocation candidate extraction from dependency-annotated corpora: exploring differences across parsers and dependency annotation schemes. In: Cantos-Gómez, P., Almela-Sánchez, M. (eds.) Lexical Collocation Analysis. QMHSS, pp. 111–140. Springer, Cham (2018). https://doi.org/10.1007/978-3-319-92582-0_6
23. Alonso Ramos, M.: Hacia una definición del concepto de colocación: de J. R. Firth a I. A. Mel'čuk. Revista de lexicografía **1**, 9–28 (1994–1995)
24. Corpas Pastor, G.: Manual de fraseología española. Gredos, Madrid (1996)
25. Bartsch, S.: Structural and Functional Properties of Collocations in English: A Corpus Study of Lexical and Pragmatic Constraints on Lexical Co-occurrence. Gunter Narr, Tübingen (2004)
26. Hausmann, F., Blumenthal, P.: Présentation: collocations, corpus, dictionnaires. Langue Française **150**, 3–13 (2006)

27. Sánchez Rufat, A.: Apuntes sobre las combinaciones léxicas y el concepto de colocación. Anuario de Estudios Filológicos **33**, 291–306 (2010)
28. Siepmann, D.: Collocation, colligation, and encoding dictionaries. Part I: lexicological aspects. Int. J. Lexicogr. **18**(4), 409–443 (2005)
29. Tummers, J., Heylen, K., Geeraerts, D.: Usage-based approaches in cognitive linguistics: a technical state of the art. Corpus Linguist. Linguist. Theory **1**(2), 225–261 (2005)
30. Arppe, A., Guilquin, G., Glynn, D., Hilpert, M., Zeschel, A.: Cognitive corpus linguistics: five points of debate on current theory and methodology. Corpora **5**(1), 1–27 (2010)
31. Ellis, N.C., Frey, E., Jalkanen, I.: The psycholinguistic reality of collocation and semantic prosody (1): lexical access. In: Römer, U., Schulze, R. (eds.) Exploring the Lexis-Grammar Interface, pp. 89–114. John Benjamins, Amsterdam (2009)
32. Aitchison, J.: Words in the Mind. An Introduction to the Mental Lexicon. Blackwell, Oxford (1994)
33. De Deyne, S., Storms, G.: Word associations: norms for 1,424 Dutch works in a continuous task. Behav. Res. Methods **40**(1), 198–205 (2008)
34. De Deyne, S., Storms, G.: Word associations: network and semantic properties. Behav. Res. Methods **40**(1), 213–231 (2008)
35. Church, K.W., Hanks, P.: Word association norms, mutual information, and lexicography. Comput. Linguist. **16**(1), 22–29 (1990)
36. Sinclair, J.: The search for units of meaning. In: Sinclair, J., Carter, R. (eds.) Trust the Text. Language, Corpus and Discourse, pp. 24–48. Routledge, London (2004)
37. Sinclair, J.: The lexical item. In: Sinclair, J., Carter, R. (eds.) Trust the Text. Language, Corpus and Discourse, pp. 131–148. Routledge, London (2004)
38. Cantos-Gómez, P., Almela-Sánchez, M.: Colligational effects of collocation: lexically conditioned dependencies between modification patterns of the noun cause. In: Pace-Sigge, M., Patterson, K.J. (eds.) Lexical Priming. Applications and Advances, pp. 231–249. John Benjamins, Amsterdam (2017)
39. Stefanowitsch, A., Gries, S.: Collostructions: investigating the interaction of words and constructions. Int. J. Corpus Linguist. **8**(2), 209–243 (2003)
40. Schmid, H.-J., Küchenhoff, H.: Collostructional analysis and other ways of measuring lexicogrammatical attraction: theoretical premises, practical problems and cognitive underpinnings. Cogn. Linguist. **24**(3), 531–577 (2013)
41. Gries, S.: 50-something years of work on collocations… what is or should be next. Int. J. Corpus Linguist. **18**(1), 137–165 (2013)
42. Sketch Engine. https://www.sketchengine.eu/ententen-english-corpus/
43. MacIntosh, C. (ed.): Oxford Collocations Dictionary for Students of English. Oxford University Press, Oxford (2009)
44. Rundell, M. (ed.): Macmillan Collocations Dictionary for Learners of English. Macmillan, Oxford (2010)

Towards a Typology of Microsyntactic Constructions

Tania Avgustinova[1](✉) and Leonid Iomdin[2](✉)

[1] Department of Language Science and Technology, Saarland University,
66123 Saarbrücken, Germany
avgustinova@coli.uni-saarland.de
[2] Institute for Information Transmission Problems,
Russian Academy of Sciences, 103051 Moscow, Russia
iomdin@iitp.ru

Abstract. This contribution outlines an international research effort for creating a typology of syntactic idioms on the borderline of the dictionary and the grammar. Recent studies focusing on the adequate description of such units, especially for modern Russian, have resulted in two types of linguistic resources: a microsyntactic dictionary of Russian, and a microsyntactically annotated corpus of Russian texts. Our goal now is to discover to what extent the findings can be generalized cross-linguistically in order to create analogous multilingual resources. The initial work consists in constructing a typology of relevant phenomena. The empirical base is provided by closely related languages which are mutually intelligible to various degrees. We start by creating an inventory for this typology for four representative Slavic languages: Russian (East Slavic), Bulgarian (South Slavic), Polish and Czech (West Slavic). Our preliminary results show that the aim is attainable and can be of relevance to theoretical, comparative and applied linguistics as well as in NLP tasks.

Keywords: Microsyntax · Typology · Comparative linguistics ·
Multilingual resources · Slavic languages · Russian · Bulgarian · Polish · Czech

1 Background

Written and spoken communication relies on a large amount of "prefabricated language"[1]. Many elements of this prefabricated language belong to what can be called syntactic idioms (Jackendoff 1997), the domain of microsyntax (Iomdin 2006, 2017; Apresjan et al. 2010). These microsyntactic elements can neither be handled within the lexicon alone nor interpreted compositionally by standard grammar rules. The syntactic behavior of phraseological units in a sentence, their lexical combinatorics, the communicative interaction with other elements of the discourse and even the used prosodic pattern can be very specific. No wonder: phraseology is the fragment of language in which ancient, long-established elements – syntactic constructions, lexical units, and grammatical forms come into close contact with modern language use, sometimes

---

[1] This term has been actively used since 1970s in language learning studies, e.g. (Hakuta 1974).

© Springer Nature Switzerland AG 2019
G. Corpas Pastor and R. Mitkov (Eds.): Europhras 2019, LNAI 11755, pp. 15–30, 2019.
https://doi.org/10.1007/978-3-030-30135-4_2

forming combinations so intricate that they can confuse not only a foreigner brilliantly speaking the language in question but also a well-educated native speaker. Moreover, it is not just the fact of a unit belonging to phraseology that makes it peculiar with regard to a free word combination but the fact that practically every such unit proves to be syntactically unique.

On the practical side of idiomaticity description (as seen from the viewpoint of text generation), we need to know what linguistic situations and phenomena may be conveyed by standard expressions, although alternatives are normally available, and to know what these alternatives are and which are preferable – regular or idiomatic. As stated by (Warren 2005) following (Sinclair 1991), language users have at their disposal a number of more or less pre-constructed phrases, so that the production of texts involves alternation between word-for-word combinations (open choice principle) and pre-constructed multi-word combinations (idiom principle). For the open choice principle, syntax is there to specify the slots into which memorized items – normally single words – can be inserted, while the idiom principle highlights the availability of memorized semi-pre-constructed combinations as single choices, even though they might appear to be analyzable into segments. What is more, (Mel'čuk 1996) suggests that memorized expressions outnumber single words. (Langacker 1998) makes a distinction between stored low-level patterns, many of which incorporate particular lexical items, and high-level schemas, which are general and productive patterns, but suggests that the low-level structures "do much, if not most of the work in speaking and understanding". Native speakers obviously know more than words and rules of how to put them together because of frequency effects: we naturally memorize what is repeated. Moreover, retrieving more or less ready-made combinations of words requires less mental effort than composing an utterance word for word (Wray 2002) – which, by the way, foreign language learners have to resort to.

The idiomaticity under investigation here goes beyond plain single-word cross-linguistic correspondences and takes various forms of semantic non-compositionality. The classical examples are quite heterogeneous – from regular form-meaning pairings (including proverbs, allusions and clichés) over so-called formal idioms (or partially lexicalized constructions with idiosyncratic meaning) to collocations (realizing combinatorial potentials of words). We accept a working definition proposed by (Čermák 2007): "The idiom is such a unique and fixed combination of at least two elements for which it holds that at least some of these do not function, in the same way, in any other combination or combinations of the kind, or occur in a highly restricted number of them, or in a single one only".

Thus, traditionally studied idioms can be functionally equivalent to major word classes like verbs (*rub someone's nose in it, change horses in midstream*), nouns (*skeleton in the cupboard, an Indian summer*) or adverbs (*with hands down, in the middle of nowhere*). Other grammar idioms are equivalent to grammar words and used in the same function, e.g. English, Czech, or Russian prepositions (like *with regard to, in view of,* Ru. *в свете* 'in the light of', *за неимением* 'for want of', *Cz. na úkor '*at the expense of', *s výjimkou* 'with the exception of'); conjunctions (Ru. *как будто* 'as though', *будь то ... или* '≈ be it... or'; Cz. *i když* 'even though'), particles (Ru. *только что* 'just now', *разве что* '≈ if any', Cz. *jen jestli* 'only if', *co kdyby* 'what if'), pronouns (Ru. *что бы то ни было* 'whatsoever', Cz. *kdokoliv který* 'whoever') etc.

In the class of multiword prepositions, Čermák further distinguishes two types: (a) non-paradigmatic multiword prepositions, formed irregularly with the help of words belonging to various parts of speech, for which corpus-based lists can be created (e.g. Ru. *что касается* 'as concerns', *один на один с* 'one-on-one with', Cz. *co do* 'as for', *počínaje od* 'beginning with', *spolu s* 'together with', *vzhledem k* 'in view of', *tváří v tvář* 'face to face' – as in *tváří v tvář ženě* 'in the presence of the woman'), and (b) paradigmatic multiword prepositions, a potentially open class formed regularly with highly frequent nouns following a unified pattern [P N^{abstr} (P)] – e.g. Ru. [P N_{LOC}] *в интересах* 'in the interests of', [P N_{DAT} P] *по сравнению с* 'as compared to', [P N_{ACC} P] *в отличие от* 'in contrast to', Cz. [P N_{GEN}] *z hlediska* 'from viewpoint of', [P N_{ACC}] *pro případ* 'in case of', [P N_{LOC}] *v oblasti* 'in the field of'; [P N_{INSTR}] *pod vlivem* 'under the influence of'; [P_1 N P_2]: *na rozdíl od* 'unlike', *s ohledem na* 'with regard to', *ve srovnání s* 'in comparison with', etc.

As argued in (Sag et al. 2002), the enormous variety of multiword expressions (MWE) call for distinct treatment including (i) listing words with spaces, (ii) hierarchically organized lexicons, (iii) restricted combinatorial rules, (iv) individual lexical selection, (v) idiomatic constructions and (vi) simple statistical affinity. For the analyzed English data, the classification in Fig. 1 has been proposed.

Lexicalized MWE have at least partially idiosyncratic syntax or semantics and, with regard to "decreasing lexical rigidity" can be further broken down into fixed (i.e. fully lexicalized and undergoing neither morphosyntactic variation nor internal modification), semi-fixed (undergoing some degree of lexical variation) and syntactically-flexible expressions (exhibiting a much wider range of syntactic variability). Institutionalized MWE are syntactically and semantically compositional but "statistically idiosyncratic", occurring with "markedly high frequency" in certain contexts. Importantly, the conclusion drawn in Sag's work is relevant for the purpose of this paper: "Scaling grammars up to deal with MWEs will necessitate finding the right balance among the various analytic techniques. Of special importance will be finding the right balance between symbolic and statistical techniques".

The creation of multilingual microsyntactic resources can be useful in a variety of research and development projects, from computer-assisted language learning tools to cross-linguistic studies including typological and cross-cultural dimensions. One important project that could benefit from such resources is Universal Dependencies community (http://universaldependencies.org) especially if – as required by (Croft et al. 2017) – typological research on language universals is systematically considered and dependencies are based on universal construction types over language-specific strategies. Hence, a universal annotation scheme would be able to use a classification of constructions as its universal foundational layer, avoiding solutions reliant on language-specific strategies while capturing the most commonly occurring strategies, too.

On a deeper systematic level, the formalism of lexical functions and paraphrasing rules (Melčuk 1998; Wanner 1996) is worth considering for certain classes of phenomena, too. The lexical functions cover both semantic-derivation relations (synonyms, antonyms, conversives, nominalizations, verbalizations, actant names,

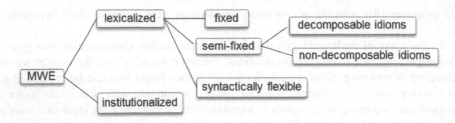

Fig. 1. Classification of multiword entities

adjectives characterizing actants, etc.) and collocational relations (intensifiers, positive and negative evaluators, light verbs, realization verbs, etc.). Paraphrasing rules, as understood by the Meaning-Text Theory, are formulated in terms of lexical functions and are applicable both within a language and between languages, i.e. as intra-lingual and inter-lingual paraphrasing. In particular, paraphrasing rules may be very convenient for rule-based machine translation systems.

There have been relatively few studies specifically devoted to the typology of MWE units so far, even though certain aspects of this typology (or, at least, comparison of two or more languages) were considered in a number of research studies, starting from (Blanco 1997), who discusses the typology of translation divergence in compound nouns between French and Spanish), and in a computer-assisted language learning project CALLLex, where the formalism of lexical functions was used to compare multiword entities involving lexical functions in Russian, German, French, and, later, Spanish (Apresjan et al. 2002; Boguslavsky et al. 2006).

The project considered here, however, is the first attempt at creating a typology of microsyntax (i.e. nonstandard syntactic constructions and syntactic idioms) for a number of Slavic languages.

2   Microsyntax Cross-Linguistically

Multi-component units are characterized by language-specific idiomaticity involving various degrees of non-compositionality due to the grammaticalization and/or lexicalization of the respective expression. The easily observable fact that cross-linguistic equivalents of such units belonging to a particular language usually appear as multi-component units in other languages, too, suggests that microsyntactic phenomena are cross-linguistically comparable, especially when closely related languages are considered.

Microsyntactic units defy uniform interpretation while exhibiting little freedom in formation and pronounced anomaly in structure. Yet, as far as cross-linguistic comparison is concerned, many of the peculiarities of microsyntactic units of one language are, at least partially, reproducible in cognate languages. This fact makes it a feasibly task to build a typology of microsyntactic phenomena starting from a particular language, for which the classification has been (more or less) established, and finding the equivalents of these phenomena in other languages and, possibly, subgroups of languages. Specifically, we start with Russian, for which microsyntactic research has been going on for almost two decades and the respective microsyntactic dictionary and corpus resources have been developed, and build our typology for several Slavic languages, taking Russian as the pivot language. Altogether, we focus on four Slavic languages representing the three main sub-groups of the language family – Russian (East Slavic), Bulgarian (South Slavic), Polish and Czech (both West Slavic). This language selection provides us with the required typological variability in grammar. In addition, all four languages are well-resourced: large-scale national corpora are available as well as parallel multilingual data and dedicated query tools. For an adequate comprehensive analysis of microsyntactic phenomena from a typological perspective we employ both symbolic and statistical techniques.

By methodically studying and elaborating the inventory of constructions established on the basis of Russian, we aim at a fine-grained and cross-linguistically applicable hierarchy of microsyntactic phenomena. Lexical, grammatical and constructional information about the monolingual microsyntactic units has to be captured in a modular way in order to enable their language-family oriented interpretation. Cross-linguistic correspondences of microsyntactic phenomena need to be found, investigated and accordingly classified. These include bilingual correspondences between Russian and another Slavic language, as well as multilingual correspondences. Our objective is to design a comprehensive typology resource encompassing the multitude of conventionalized multi-word combinations cross-linguistically in the form of a core Slavic micro-syntactic database to be used for educational purposes and in language-technology applications.

The central linguistic resource we use is the Russian National Corpus (RNC), in particular, its main sub-corpus (over 600,000,000 tokens), the parallel corpus with counterparts of Russian texts in five Slavic languages, i.e. Belarussian (9,500,000 tokens), Bulgarian (3,800,000 tokens), Czech (1,500,000 tokens), Polish (6,300,000 tokens) and Ukrainian (9,300,000 tokens), as well as the syntactically annotated sub-corpus (1,200,000 tokens). Two different interfaces of the main RNC sub-corpus and the parallel corpora are freely available through any web browser at http://ruscorpora.ru and http://corpus.leeds.ac.uk/ruscorpora.html. The former interface provides access to the whole array of the main RNC sub-corpus, while the latter provides access to a 50,000,000-token fragment of this sub-corpus and some other sub-corpora but it also enables searching other Russian corpora, the internet, or performing a combined search. Additionally, in the newest version of the syntactically annotated aub-corpus SynTagRus, over 10,000 sentences have microsyntactic tags annotations, and the inventory of microsyntactic elements present in SynTagRus counts about 1,100 items.

We started with the collections of multiword expressions provided at the RNC website (http://www.ruscorpora.ru/obgrams.html), which were selected from RNC frequency collocation database and supplemented with the data from the Malyj Akademičeskij Slovar' (MAS 1999) and a collocation dictionary (Rogozhnikova 2003):

  (i)   Prepositions (http://ruscorpora.ru/obgrams-PR.html)
 (ii)   Adverbial and Predicatives (http://ruscorpora.ru/obgrams-ADV.html)
(iii)   Parenthetical expressions (http://ruscorpora.ru/obgrams-PARENTH.html)
 (iv)   Conjunctions (http://ruscorpora.ru/obgrams-CONJ.html)
  (v)   Particles (http://ruscorpora.ru/obgrams-PART.html)

These inventories are used for finding translational equivalents in parallel and multilingual sub-corpora.

3 Empirical Foundation

Based on the Russian data, three major types of microsyntactically relevant material can be preliminarily distinguished and will be referred here – for the sake of illustration – as lexically idiomatic Type A, syntactically idiomatic Type B and constructionally idiomatic Type C.

3.1 Lexically Idiomatic Cross-Slavic Correspondences (Type A)

Type A contains lexicalized multi-component units with an idiosyncratic meaning and word-like status, e.g., compound prepositions (*в отличие от* 'unlike', *на тему* 'on the subject of', *по причине* 'due to'), or closed-class combinations of pronominal and function words (*как будто* 'as though', *будто бы* 'as if', *разве что* 'perhaps only', *только что* 'just now', *что за* 'what the', *не прочь* 'don't mind'), as well as parenthetical expressions (*стало быть* 'so then', *была не была* 'nothing to lose', *между прочим* 'by the way') or semi-lexicalized patterns (*кто/.../что угодно* 'whatever/whoever', *чёрт/.../бог знает кто/.../зачем* 'Devil/.../God knows why'). Three subtypes of Type A constructions are distinguished:

Type A1: Multiword Idiomatic Prepositions
Typically the pattern [P_1 N^{abstr} (P_2)] is followed, as summarized in Table 1. Multilingual correspondences are illustrated in Table 2.

Table 1. Russian idiomatic multiword prepositions

P_1	$N^{abstract}$	(P_2)	N_{case}	English equivalent	Available alternatives	Examples of alternative implementations
в	связи	с	N_{instr}	with regard to	*в DEM связи*	*в этой связи* 'in this regard'
в	отличие	от	N_{gen}	unlike, in contrast to		
в	адрес		N_{gen}	in/to the address of	*в INT/POSS адрес*	*в мой адрес* 'to my address, toward me'; *в чей адрес* 'to whose address'
во	время		N_{gen}	at the time of	*в DEM время*	*в то же время* 'at the same time'
по	причине		N_{gen}	because of, due to	*по DEM/INT причине*	*по какой причине* 'for what reason'
в	соответствии	с	N_{inst}	in accordance with		
на	тему		N_{gen}	on the topic of	*на DEM/INT тему*	*на какую тему* 'on which subject'

For some of the compound prepositions, alternative realizations exist, involving demonstrative (DEM), interrogative (INT) or possessive (POSS) modifiers of the nominal component (cf. Type A1). There are obvious parallels to what (Čermák 2007) considers as grammar idioms which are equivalent to grammar or auxiliary words and therefore used in the same function.

Table 2. Cross-lingual correspondences to Russian idiomatic multiword prepositions

Russian	Bulgarian	Polish	Czech
в связи с	във връзка с	w związku z	v souvislosti s
в отличие от	за разлика от	w przeciwieństwie do	na rozdíl od
в адрес	на адреса на	na adres	na adresu
во время	по време на	w czasie	během
по причине	поради	z powodu	z důvodu
в соответствии с	в съответствие със	zgodnie z	v souladu s
на тему	на тема	na temat	na téma

Alternative implementations, e.g. Polish constructions allowing for modifiers like *w tym związku* 'in this respect', *na pański adres* 'to your address', *z jakiego powodu* 'for which reason', *na ten temat* 'on this topic', have to be included into the database with details of their syntactic and semantic behavior too.

Type A2: Combinations of Closed Class Pro-forms and Function Words
The examples are given in Table 3. Again, the intended multilingual output is illustrated in Table 4. For brevity, only several examples are given.

Table 3. Russian syntactic idioms acting as function words

adv/prep/prt	aux$_1$	pron/conj	prt	adv/A/N^{abstr}	aux$_2$	English equivalents
		как	бы 1			'as if, like, sort of' (particle): *Он как бы играл* 'he sort of played'
		как	бы 2			'lest' (conjunction):*Я боюсь, как бы он не опоздал* 'I fear lest he should be late'
		всё	же			'all the same'
только		что				'just now'
		тем	не	менее		'however', 'yet'
между		тем				'meanwhile'
между				прочим		'by the way'
		как	буд-то			'as though'
		что	ли			'or something'
		что	за			'what kindof a'

(continued)

Table 3. (*continued*)

adv/prep/prt	aux₁	pron/conj	prt	adv/A/N^{abstr}	aux₂	English equivalents
		тот	*же*			'same as'
пока		*что*				'as yet'
разве		*что*				'perhaps only'
		тем		*более*		'especially'
			не	*прочь*		'don't mind'
		то	*и*	*дело*		'every now and then'
		так	*и*		*быть*	'so be it'
		всё		*равно*		'just the same'
		как		*раз*		'just, exactly'
не		*тут-*	*-то*		*было*	'nothing of the kind'
	будь	*что*			*будет*	'whatever happens'
	была		*не*		*была*	'I'll risk it; nothing to lose'
	стало				*быть*	'hence'

Table 4. Cross-lingual correspondences to Russian syntactic idioms acting as function words

Russian	Bulgarian	Polish	Czech
как бы 1	*като че ли*	*jakby*	*jakoby*
всё же	*все пак*	*jednak*	*přesto, stejně*
только что	*току-що*	*dopiero*	*zrovna, právě*
тем не менее	*въпреки това*	*tym niemniej, mimo wszystko*	*nicméně, presto*
между тем	*същевременно*	*tymczasem*	*mezitím*
между прочим	*между другото*	*nawiasem mówiąc, przy okazji*	*mimochodem*

The result of a sample search for the grammar (conjunction-like) idiom *как будто* ('as though') in the four selected languages is provided below to exemplify the procedure. It includes translations of a sentence from Mikhail Bulgakov's *Master and Margarita* into the three Slavic languages. The English equivalent of the sentence is *He looked Berlioz up and down **as though** he were measuring him for a suit.*

Ru: *Он смерил Берлиоза взглядом, **как будто** собирался сшить ему костюм*
Bg: *Той измери Берлиоз с поглед, **като че ли** му взимаше мярка за костюм*
Pl: *On zmierzył Berlioza spojrzeniem, **jakby** zamierzał uszyć mu garnitur*
Cz: *Změřil si ho pátravým pohledem, **jako by** se mu chystal šít oblek*

Type A3: Semi-lexicalized Patterns with Constant and Variable Parts
These are syntactic idioms in which some parts are fixed whilst others may vary: the extent of variation can be different and sometimes extremely difficult to generalize. So, in the two examples given in Table 5, one part is represented by an interrogative pronoun while another is instantiated by a concrete word (*угодно* ≈ 'ever' in (a) and *знает* 'knows' in (b), to account, respectively, for expressions like *Поеду куда угодно*

'I'll go anywhere' and *Чёрт знает, что он замышляет* 'The devil only knows what he is up to'.

Table 5. Russian semi-lexicalized patterns

	N^{variable}	V^{constant}	Interrogative pro-form	Adv^{constant}	English equivalent
(a)			*кто/что/где/зачем/куда*	*угодно*	'wh-ever'
(b)	*чёрт/бес/бог*	*знает*	*кто/что/где/зачем/куда*		'God knows'

The syntactic idiom (b) allows for a lexical variation with the noun being *чёрт* 'devil', *бес* 'demon', but also *бог* 'God', *Аллах* 'Allah', as well as several other names for devils and deities (but not all!) and bizarrely enough, *пёс* 'dog'. Note that cross-linguistic typological research of such patterns is quite demanding with regard to time, effort, and qualification.

3.2   Syntactically Idiomatic Cross-Slavic Correspondences (Type B)

A separate class consists of syntactic idioms that have neither structural transparency nor word-like status. One of their key features is that they acquire valence properties as a unit, cf. (a) *как быть* (as in *Как быть профессору* [X] *со студентами* [Y] *на экзамене* [Z], *если они списывают?*) 'What should the professor do (about the students if they cheat in the exam?), and (b) *то ли дело,* constructing a contrapositive "*не V$_{fin}$ ..., то ли дело* X" (*Он не любит делать уроки, то ли дело мультики смотреть* 'He does not like doing homework – how much better is watching cartoons'; *С детьми ты не играешь, то ли дело одноклассники в интернете.* 'You don't play with the kids, but with classmates on the internet it's a different story'). This class further includes (c) the transitive use of the finite forms of the verb БЫТЬ 'be' (only in the indicative future: *буду, будешь,* etc.), selecting a complement with food/drink/smoking semantics in a situation of immediacy and service (*буду только чай* 'I'll have just tea', *торт не буду* 'I don't want cake', *Он будет прямо из бутылки* 'he'll drink straight from the bottle', *Будешь сигарету?* 'Will you have a cigarette'). Valence structures of Type B syntactic idioms are summarized in Table 6.

The number of weakly lexicalized syntactic idioms of this type is much smaller than that of lexicalized ones of Type A1, and we expect them to be more language specific and not always allow for close equivalents even in related languages. The outcome of a sample search for the syntactic idiom (a) in available Slavic languages is illustrated in Table 7 to give us an idea of the nature of the variation we are confronted with. Only one of the three Russian translations of Lewis Carroll's *Alice in Wonderland* (Russian_2, by Vladimir Nabokov) uses this syntactic idiom, and there is no equivalent of the verb *быть* in the other Slavic translations, which is not surprising since all translations were made from the English original, rather than Russian. A quick search through Russian-Polish parallel corpus of RNC for the equivalents of *как быть* reveals a similar result. There is only one occurrence of the Polish verb *być* in the pair Pl. *A co będzie z tymi, co już byli?* – Ru. *А как быть с теми, кто был раньше?*, which

Table 6. Russian syntactic idioms

(a)

как быть	X_{dat}	$Y_{[with]}$	$Z_{[situation]}$
'what to do about'	профессору	со студентами	на экзамене
	'professor'	'with students'	'at examination'

(b)

не V_{fin} ...,	*то ли дело*	X
(negated proposition)		(non-negated proposition)

(c)

[situation: immediacy + service] **BE-auxiliary**[future] [transitive]	$X_{[food/drink/tobacco]}$
буду/будешь/будет/будем/будете/будут	*чай*
'will have'	'tea'

however has a notable difference in meaning: the Polish sentence simply asks what will happen to those who were before, while the Russian translation asks what the protagonist should do about these people. The Russian/Bulgarian and Russian/Czech parallel corpora provided no such results, either. Yet the two East Slavic languages showed a very close correspondence for this syntactic idiom: *як быць* in Belarussian and *як бути* in Ukrainian in almost all cases.

Table 7. Cross-lingual correspondences to Russian syntactic idioms

English	Alice had no idea what to do,
Russian	Алиса растерялась.
Russian_2	Аня не знала, как ей быть.
Russian_3	Бедная Алиса не знала, что ей делать;
Ukrainian	Аліса не знала, що робити;
Belarussian	Алеся ня мела ніякага ўяўленьня, што рабіць.
Polish	Alicja nie wiedziała, jak wybrnąć z tej sytuacji.
Polish_2	Zupełnie nie wiedząc, co począć,
Czech	Alenka nevěděla, co počít,
Slovak	Alica raz nevedela, čo robiť;
Slovene	Alica sploh ni vedela, kaj naj stori;
Croatian	Jadna Alica! Šta će sad? Ne znajući kako da se izvuče iz neprilike
Serbian	Алиса није имала појма шта да ради.
Macedonian	Алиса воопшто не знаеше што да прави,
Bulgarian	Алиса не знаеше какво да стори

3.3   Moderately Transparent Cross-Slavic Correspondences (Type C)

The number and the variety of moderately transparent non-standard syntactic constructions are quite impressive (Fig. 2). In many cases they have no counterparts even in closely related languages.

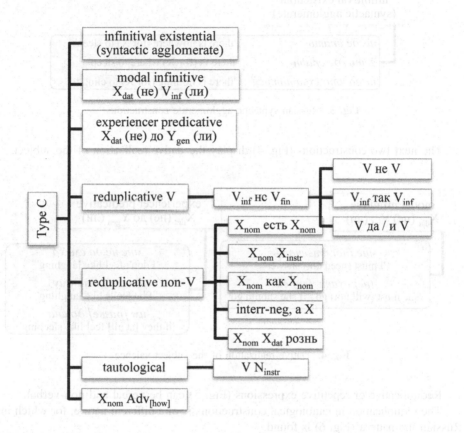

Fig. 2. Russian moderately transparent non-standard syntactic constructions

Relevant examples include the modal infinitive with a dative subject (мне скоро улетать 'I'm leaving [lit. flying away] soon'), reduplicative/repetitive expressions (знать не знаю, но… 'as for knowing, I don't know, but…'; люди как люди 'just the usual people [lit. people like people]'; гулять так гулять 'let's celebrate properly [lit. celebrate so celebrate]'), expressions with constant and variable parts (какой-никакой, а X – cf. Здесь я какой-никакой, а герой 'Here I'm a hero in any case'; or X-у не до Y-а – as in Им не до сна 'They have more important things than sleeping, they don't feel like sleeping').

The syntactic agglomerate construction (Fig. 3) has been first studied by (Apresjan and Iomdin 1989) and later formalized in (Avgustinova 2003). It poses a theoretical challenge to lexicon and grammar. The respective equivalents from a cross-linguistic perspective are quite diverse in lexical realization and with regard to structure.

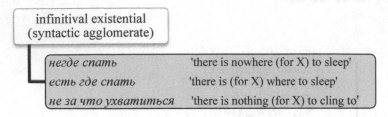

Fig. 3. Russian syntactic agglomerate constructions

The next two constructions (Fig. 4) display the dative realization of the subject.

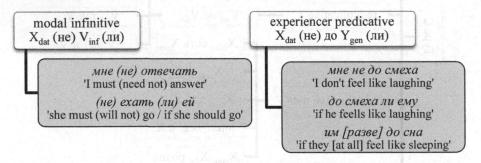

Fig. 4. Dative realization of the subject valence

Reduplicative or repetitive expressions (Fig. 5) can be verbal and non-verbal.

The reduplication in tautological constructions is of a different nature, for which in Russian the pattern (Fig. 6) is found.

Finally, colloquial expressions relating to personal circumstances follow the pattern in (Fig. 7).

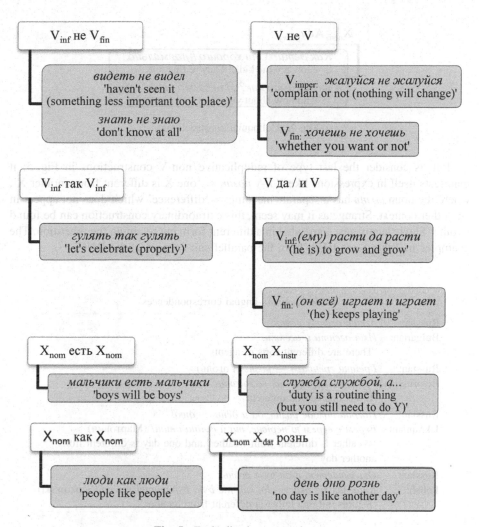

Fig. 5. Reduplicative expressions

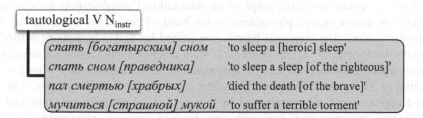

Fig. 6. Tautological constructions

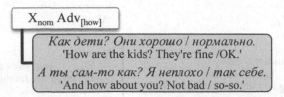

Fig. 7. Colloquial constructions

Let us consider the last type of reduplicative non-V constructions in Fig. 5: it manifests itself in expressions like *X X-у рознь* ≈ 'one X is different from another X', where the noun *рознь* has a separate meaning ≈ 'difference' which does not appear in any other context. Strange as it may seem, this extraordinary construction can be found in other Slavic languages, somewhat in a different form but retaining the repetition. The examples in Table 8 are taken from the parallel sub-corpora of the RNC.

Table 8. Cross-lingual correspondences

Russian:	*Агент агенту рознь.*
Bulgarian:	*Има агенти и агенти.*
	'There are different sorts of agents'
Russian:	*Грешки грешкам — рознь* (Гоголь)
Belorussian:	*Грашкі на грашкі ня выходзяць.*
	'Little sins can be different'
Russian:	*Погода погоде рознь, да и день — дню!*
Ukrainian:	*Верем'є верем'ю нерівне, та й днина дині!* (Мартович)
	'Weather is different from weather, and one day is different from another day'
Russian:	*Оказывается, пуля пуле рознь.*
Polish:	*Kula, jak się okazywało, kuli nie była bynajmniej równą* (Sapkowski)
	'It turns out one bullet is different from another'

4   Conclusion

We have presented the initial stage of an international collaboration for creating a typology of microsyntactic phenomena on the basis of contrastive syntactic and lexicographic studies. The empirical base is constituted by Slavic languages as they are mutually intelligible to various degrees. In such a setup, monolingual idiomaticity of microsyntactic constructions can be approximated cross-linguistically from the perspective of its comprehensibility to speakers of closely related languages. The presented approach can be instrumental in the creation of monolingual, bilingual and multilingual resources that deal with non-standard syntactic phenomena and thus promising in improving natural language processing applications.

Acknowledgements. The authors are grateful to the Russian National Foundation (grant No. 16-18-10422-P) and the German Science Foundation (DFG, grant within the Collaborative Research Centre SFB 1102) for their partial support of this research.

References

Apresjan, J.D., Boguslavsky, I.M., Iomdin, L.L., Sannikov, V.Z.: Theoretical problems of russian syntax. Interaction of the grammar and the lexicon. [Teoretičeskie problemy russkogo sintaksisa]. In: Apresjan, J.D. (ed). Jazyki slavjanskix kultur Publishers, Moscow, 408 p. (2010). ISBN 978-5-9551-0386-0. (in Russian)

Apresjan, J.D., Boguslavsky, I.M., Iomdin, L.L., Tsinman, L.L.: Lexical functions in NLP: possible uses. Computational Linguistics for the New Millennium: Divergence or Synergy? Festschrift in Honour of Peter Hellwig on the occasion of his 60th Birthday, Peter Lang, pp. 55–72 (2002)

Apresjan, J.D., Iomdin, L.L.: The construction of the NEGDE SPAT' type: syntax, semantics, lexicography. [Konstrukcija tipa NEGDE SPAT': sintaksis, semantika, leksikografija]. Semiotika i informatika, pp. 34–92. Vsesojuznyj institut nauchnoj i texnicheskoj informacii, AN SSSR, Moscow (1989). (in Russian)

Avgustinova, T.: Russian infinitival existential constructions from an HPSG perspective. In: Kosta, P. et al. (eds.) Investigations into Formal Slavic Linguistics. Contributions of the Fourth European Conference on Formal Description of Slavic Languages, pp. 461–482. Peter Lang Europäischer Verlag der Wissenschaft (2003)

Boguslavsky, I., Dyachenko, P., Barrios Rodríguez, M.A.: CALLEX-ESP: a software system for learning Spanish lexicon and collocations. In: Current Developments in Technology-Assisted Education. Badajos (Spain): FORMATEX, vol. 1, pp. 22–26 (2006)

Čermák, F.: Grammatical Idioms. Philologica Pragensia, XVII, vol. 2, pp. 75–90 (2007)

Croft, W., Nordquist, D., Looney, K., Regan, M.: Linguistic typology meets universal dependencies. In: Proceedings of the 15th International Workshop on Treebanks and Linguistic Theories (TLT15), pp. 63–75 (2017)

Hakuta, K.: Prefabricated patterns and the emergence of second language acquisition. Lang. Learn. **24**(2), 287–297 (1974)

Iomdin, L.L.: Polysemous syntactic idioms: between the vocabulary and the syntax [Mnogoznačnye sintaksičeskie frazemy: meždu leksikoj i sintaksisom]. In: Computational Linguistics and Intellectual Technologies. Proceedings of the International Conference "Dialog-2006", Moscow, RGGU Publishers, pp. 202–206 (2006). (in Russian)

Iomdin, L.: Between the syntactic idiom and syntactic construction. Nontrivial cases of microsyntactic ambiguity. [Meždu sintaksičeskoj frazemoj i sintaksičeskoj konstruktsiej. Netrivial'nye slučai mikrosintaksičeskoj neodnoznačnosti]. In: SLAVIA, časopis pro slovanskou filologii, ročník 68, sešit 2–3, pp. 230–243 (2017). (in Russian)

Jackendoff, Ray: Twisting the night away. Language **73**, 534–559 (1997)

Langacker, R.W.: Indeterminacy in semantics and grammar. Paper presented to the Estudios de Lingüística cognitiva, 1998 (1998)

MAS: The Small Academic Dictionary of Russian in 4 volumes, A. P. Evgenyeva, ed. [Slovar' russkogo jazyka v 4-x tomax, MAS, Malyj Akademičeskij Slovar. Russkij Jazyk Publisher, Moscow (1999). http://feb-web.ru/feb/mas/mas-abc/default.asp

Mel'čuk, I.: Lexical functions: a tool for the description of lexical relations in a lexicon. In: Lexical Functions in Lexicography and Natural Language Processing, vol. 31, pp. 37–102 (1996)

Mel'čuk, I.: Collocations and lexical functions. In: Phraseology. Theory, Analysis, and Applications, pp. 23–53 (1998)

Rogozhnikova, R.P.: An Explanatory Dictionary of Collocations Equivalent to Words [Tolkovyj slovar sočetanij, ekvivalentnyx slovu]. Moscow, Astrel, 414 p. (2003). (in Russian.)

Sag, I.A., Baldwin, T., Bond, F., Copestake, A., Flickinger, D.: Multiword expressions: a pain in the neck for NLP. Paper presented to the International Conference on Intelligent Text Processing and Computational Linguistics (2002)

Sinclair, J.: Corpus, concordance, collocation. Oxford University Press (1991)

Wanner, L.: Lexical functions in lexicography and natural language processing. John Benjamins Publishing (1996)

Warren, B.: A model of idiomaticity. Nordic J. Engl. Stud. **4**, 35–54 (2005)

Wray, A.: Formulaic language in computer-supported communication: theory meets reality. Lang. Awareness **11**, 114–131 (2002)

'*Alla finfine sono daccordo*': A Corpus-Based Case Study on Italian Adverbial Phrases Grammaticalization

Lucia Busso[1](✉) and Margherita Castelli[2]

[1] Università di Pisa, Pisa, Italy
lucia.busso90@gmail.com
[2] Università degli Studi di Perugia, Perugia, Italy

Abstract. We present results of a corpus-based synchronic study on the grammaticalization of Italian adverbial phrases. In particular, we claim that spelling irregularities of adverbial constructions provide evidence of ongoing grammaticalization processes. Adverbial phrases are hence already decategorized analytic constructions that are undergoing paradigmaticization and subsequently lexicalization. We selected 40 adverbial phrases of different length (2–5 constituents) at different stages of the process: from completely non-alternating structures to phrases with two (or more) accepted standard spellings. By means of a corpus-based analysis we considered several properties of those constructions (i.e. frequency) and tested their significance with mixed effect modelling analysis. Specifically, we model the presence of spelling irregularities, its measure (i.e. partial or total univerbation), and frequency of irregular forms. Results of such a corpus-based statistical analysis, albeit preliminary, yield several interesting considerations on synchronic factors that facilitate or hinder processes of grammaticalization, especially the role of frequency and number of construction constituents. Findings support current usage-based literature on grammaticalization as constructionalization.

Keywords: Grammaticalization · Italian · Adverbs · Usage-based linguistics

1 Introduction

Grammaticalization is the linguistic process by which a lexical item with a full referential meaning (i.e. an open-class element) turns into an item with grammatical meaning (i.e. a closed-class element) [1, 2]. Traditionally, the process of grammaticalization of a linguistic item is represented using a *cline* [3–5]: *content item > grammatical word > clitic > inflectional compound*.

Hence, grammaticalization starts from a free combination of lexical elements in discourse which are gradually – over the course of time – converted into an analytic construction, where some of the lexemes assume grammatical functions.

Grammaticalization works along several recognized principles of language change. Since this is not the place for an in-depth discussion on different perspective in the literature on mechanisms of language change, we will only briefly outline them.

G. Corpas Pastor and R. Mitkov (Eds.): Europhras 2019, LNAI 11755, pp. 31–45, 2019.
https://doi.org/10.1007/978-3-030-30135-4_3

Reanalysis and Analogy. Reanalysis is the principal mechanism of language change – in general – and grammaticalization – more specifically. It modifies underlying grammatical and semantic representations without affecting the form (e.g. [Hamburg] + [er] 'item (of food) from Hamburg' → [ham] + [burger] → [] [burger]) and brings about rule change. On the other hand, analogy only affects surface manifestations, and happens paradigmatically, whereas reanalysis works at the syntagmatic level. Analogy is particularly important in grammaticalization processes as it is often the first visible proof of undergoing reanalysis, and even though it does not affect directly language change, it can be of crucial importance in the diffusion and paradigmaticization of such change.

Desemantization, Decategorization, and Phonetic Reduction. These mechanisms account for the gradual loss of analyzability and a parallel gain in autonomy, leading to a reduction in constituent structure [6]. *Desemanticization*, (or semantic bleaching) is the loss of semantic lexical content undergone by a linguistic element, while its grammatical content is retained [7]. Once the sign is desemanticized, the grammaticalizing element undergo a process of d*ecategorization*, i.e. a change in category which usually results in the loss of morphological and syntactic constituents [8, 9]. Phonetic reduction (or erosion) is the gradual loss of phonetic substance in patterns that are often produced together. Since these chunks are claimed to be stored and processed together [10, 11], neuromotor activity becomes more efficient with repetition, leading to a reduction in the individual articulatory gestures and an increase in temporal overlap [12, 13].

Paradigmaticization levels differences of grammaticalized items to integrate them into the new 'paradigm' [14, 15]. Paradigmaticization is signaled by increasing irregularity, since spelling becomes less semantically motivated and increasingly arbitrary. At the very end of the process, *morphologization* further reduces the analytic construction to a synthetic one (i.e. univerbation); lexicalization 'tightens' the newly formed word changing its morphological status from agglutinative to flexional [14, 16].

Grammaticalization is traditionally studied from a diachronic perspective, even in computational or corpus-based approaches [17]. Nevertheless, a growing body of literature has started to explore language change synchronically [18, 19], using cues of ongoing change in contemporary language.

1.1 Grammaticalization, Usage-Based Theory and Frequency Effects

Research on grammaticalization is arguably the area of study in linguistics that mostly benefits from taking a usage-based perspective on language – i.e. a model claiming that language structure emerges from usage events – since language change describes small gradual shifts occurring in actual usage-events [6, 10, 20–23][1].

Since usage shapes language structure (and change), a crucial aspect to be considered is the effect of frequency. The importance of frequency effects in language has been widely investigated by many scholars [3, 24–26]. For instance, several

---

[1] See [6] for a systematic account of usage-based theory and grammaticalization.

quantitative studies have shown a link between phonetic reduction and token frequency in grammaticalization [e.g. 27, 28], and that collocational frequency correlates to reduction [29]. However, high frequency is also been found to yield the opposite effect: since high frequent patterns are deeply entrenched, a phraseological unit may resist to be grammaticalized [26]. It has also been claimed that low-frequency phrasal patterns grammaticalize by analogy to more frequent parallel structures [30].

Another crucial concept in usage-based theory is the notion of constructions, i.e. "learned pairings of form with semantic or discourse function" [31, p. 5] that in Construction Grammar are held to be the basic units of language, autonomous and entrenched in the speaker's knowledge about language [31, 32]. These larger, phraseological patterns have recently been studied from a grammaticalization perspective [9, 23, 33–35]. In constructionist approaches, language change is re-conceptualized in terms of shifts that affect the *constructicon* as a whole, i.e. the structured network of constructions that represent speakers' knowledge of language. The emergence of new nodes in the network is called *constructionalization* [35] [2]. Namely, a linguistic unit represents a new node in the network if it shows not only a new morphosyntactic structure, but also a new meaning since constructions are pairings of form and function.

Another interesting approach to grammaticalization and frequency effects is put forward by [34], which combines insights from various usage-based works on language change. The author propose the *Upward Strengthening Hypothesis*, which argues that: "whereas in grammaticalization the experience of a linguistic unit leads to the progressive entrenchment of a more schematic construction, situated at a higher level in the constructional network, constructional change can manifest itself in the strengthening of several more specific sub-schemas, at lower levels of the constructional network" [34, p. 6].

In the present work, we will argue for the usage-based perspective concisely outlined above and use constructionist insights for our case-study on Italian adverbial phrases. Before turning to describing materials and analyses, we will first briefly describe the category of adverbs, with special regard to Italian.

1.2   Adverbs and Adverbial Phrases

"Pars omnium proprium tandem si perderit actum,
Istius in vasta gurgite mersa iacet,
Adgregat ut pelagus partes sorbendo marinum,
Et violenter eas ad sua iura trahit[3]"

Despite being traditionally recognized as one class, adverbs are a very heterogeneous category, since many grammaticalizing decategorized elements are included in the category of adverbs [38, 39]. Given this heterogeneity, adverbs are best conceived as a

---

[2] Even though the two notions are not entirely overlapping, for the purposes of this work we will use the terms interchangeably.

[3] "If in the end the parts of speech lost their own proper function, they would lie drowned in the vast whirlpool of adverbs. The adverb draws to itself parts of speech, like the all-absorbing sea, and violently forces them to obey its laws" (Smaragdus, IX cent. AD. Translated by [36] as cited in [37]).

prototype-like structure. Although members of the class cannot be reduced to a unique prototype [40–42], a range of core elements can be identified for operational reasons, by considering a twofold formal and functional perspective: "formally, adverbs are invariable and syntactically dispensable lexemes (…). Functionally, adverbs are modifiers of predicates, other modifiers or higher syntactic units" [43, p. 187].

In Romance languages and in English, functional and formal prototypes often match: many prototypical adverbs are also mono-morphological, opaque and/or universated. For instance, the Latin NP *hoc die* ('in this day') is not immediately recognizable in the Italian or Spanish lexicalized forms *oggi* and *hoy* ('today'). In fact, the two adverbs – as many other core adverbs – represent the final stage of a continuum from full lexicality to full grammaticality. English forms *tomorrow* and *yesterday,* or the Italian *chiaramente,* or *insomma* are instead intermediate steps, since univerbation does not render the form completely opaque.

At the 'fuzzy boundaries' of the category of Italian adverbs we find non-prototypical forms of analytic adverbial constructions (henceforth: AdvCs). These structures are fixed phrases that perform the same function, and occupy the same paradigmatic position as proper adverbs [43] (see 1)[4].

1. *Gli ingegneri cancelleranno mano a mano parte dei dati* (Engineers will gradually erase part of the data)

AdvCs are often transparent and compositional but tied by very strong syntagmatic bonds, which render them full-fledged phraseological units. We claim that such analytic constructions are at different levels of the grammaticalization cline: once fully lexical collocations, they are gradually becoming routinized chunks and reanalysed as analytic adverbial constructions by decategorization, desemanitcization and (sometimes) erosion. Paradigmaticization of these structures causes spelling irregularities, since their constituents are often no longer perceived as independent lexemes.

Based on these premises, we propose a corpus-based quantitative case study of Italian AdvCs. Namely, we investigate possible synchronic factors that either contribute or hinder the paradigmaticization and lexicalization of AdvCs.

2   Spelling Irregularities as a Sign of Grammaticalization

Italian displays a wide range of adverbs which have been completely grammaticalized and lexicalized. For example, the original lexical collocation *sopra tutto* ('above everything', (2a)) is now completely lexicalized in the mono-morphological adverb *soprattutto* ('especially, primarily', (2b)).

2. a. *Grande è il Signore, il nostro Dio sopra tutti gli dei* (Great is the Lord, our God above all other gods)
   b. *Previsto un forte aumento degli alunni disabili, soprattutto alle superiori* (Asignificant increase in disabled students is expected, especially in high school)

---

[4] All following examples are taken from the *ItWac* corpus.

We hypothesize that an analogous process of grammaticalization and lexicalization is still ongoing in contemporary Italian, and that cues of this phenomenon can be found by looking at spelling uncertainties of analytical AdvCs. For example, the Italian AdvC *d'accordo* ('agreed, OK'), which originally means "to be in agreement with [someone]" is today an analytic AdvC, and at sub-standard levels is starting to lexicalize in the univerbated form *daccordo* (3a–b).

3. a. *Io non potrò mai essere d'accordo con una proposta del genere.* (I could never agree with such a proposal).
   b. *Mi è venuta un'idea, sempre se tu sei daccordo.* (I got an idea, if you agree)

However, it is not automatic that all AdvCs undergo subsequent phases of grammaticalization. The aim of this paper is specifically to investigate which – if any – properties of AdvCs significantly correlate with spelling alternations and irregularities.

3 Materials and Methodology

40 Italian AdvCs of varying length (2 to 5 constituents) were selected based on their frequency (checked on the corpus *ItWac* [44]) and their familiarity (based on native speaker knowledge and intuition by the two authors). The resulting list includes highly common and familiar phrases, both of high and low token frequency (see the Appendix for a complete list of the stimuli and of their frequency per million word).

Each AdvC was queried in the corpus *ItWac* using *CQL* language and regular expressions, to achieve maximum precision and recall. For every AdvCs a number of parameters were extracted from the corpus:

- the token frequency of AdvCs[5];
- the alternative irregular spellings;
- the relative token frequency of the irregular forms;
- the type frequency of the AdvCs open-class constituents (henceforth: OCC) (e.g.: "d'accordo": accordo, noun).

We chose to include type and type frequency of OCCs since highly frequent – and thus entrenched – constituents could yield a conserving effect on further steps of grammaticalization[6]. Furthermore, more grammatical elements (i.e. adverbs) could facilitate the process of paradigmaticization.

Besides the corpus-based parameters, we also considered other features of AdvCs that we hypothesize could influence grammaticalization. Length of the AdvCs was also considered, as a reasonable assumption is that longer forms could be more difficult to lexicalize. We further disentangled this notion into two separate factors: number of syllables and number of constituents. In presence of an alternate (or more) irregular

---

[5] All frequencies were normalized per million words.

[6] A few OCCs in Italian AdvCs are linguistic fossils (as is the N "canto" in the sense of "location" in the AdvC "d'altro canto"). However, we had too few data points to statistically account for these elements. We reserve a more in-depth account of such cases for future work.

spelling(s), we distinguished between partial and total univerbation. If all the constituents in the constructions are fused together, we have a total univerbation (*d'altro canto* → *daltrocanto*, 'on the other hand') whereas if only a part of the construction is univerbated, the process is considered partial (*d'altrocanto* → *daltro canto*). Univerbation is also considered partial when reanalysis and decategorization have 'transformed' one of the constituents of the AdvC. For instance, this is the case of the AdvC *un po'* (a bit), where the apostrophe signals an apocope of the last syllable of the adjective *poco*. The reanalysed form *un pò*, or *un po* (without the apostrophe) is fairly common in substandard written language, indicating that the constituent *po'* is losing all semantic relations with its original form *poco*. Several of the irregular spellings for AdvC are no longer considered errors in standard Italian, but rather spelling varieties; this fact signals that some AdvCs are thus further along in the grammaticalization cline, and it is plausible to assume that acceptability results in higher frequency of alternating spelling. To account for such a fact, we included the binary factor of acceptability (yes/no). Table 1 below summarizes all the parameters that were considered.

Table 1. Parameters of AdvCs

Parameters of AdvCs	
Presence of irregular forms (yes/no)	
Partial/Total univerbation	
Number of constituents	
Length (i.e. number of syllables)	
Open-class constituents	
Frequency of AdvC	
Frequency of irregular form	
Frequency of open-class element	
Acceptability	

Based on the above listed factors, we adopt mixed modelling to statistically assess the significance of such parameters in predicting the presence of the irregular spelling, its measure (i.e. partial/total) and the frequency of the irregular form.

4   Statistical Analyses

As already mentioned, we wanted to understand the effect of the predictors in Table 1 on 3 different variables: the presence or absence of a spelling irregularity, the measure (partial or total) of the univerbation process in those AdvCs that do show alternations in spelling, and the attested frequency in the corpus of the irregular form.

From a visual inspection of the data, some preliminary consideration may already be made. Below, we can see an effect of length (Fig. 1) on spelling irregularities (either the presence or absence of a spelling irregularity, or partial versus total univerbation of the AdvC). It appears as though both length in syllables and number of constituents affect spelling irregularities: the longer an AdvC, the fewer the irregularities. In Fig. 2

the trend of the inverse relation irregularity/length is confirmed: namely, the plots display how AdvCs with more constituents (and hence with a higher number of syllables) are less prone to irregularity with respect to shorter ones.

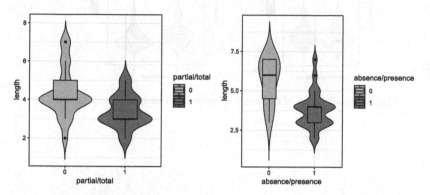

Fig. 1. Relation of length, partial vs total univerbation and absence or presence of irregularities

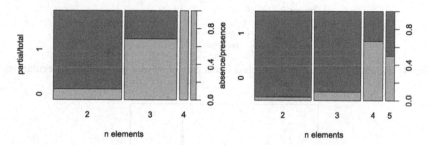

Fig. 2. Relation of number of constituents, partial vs total univerbation and presence vs absence of spelling irregularities

However, type frequency of OCCs does not seem to yield a particular effect on spelling irregularities, as it can be seen from Fig. 3 below[7]. Token frequency of AdvCs' irregular forms also appears to be correlated inversely with token frequency of open class items occurring in them (Fig. 4): alternating AdvCs tend to have lower-frequency items, whereas higher-frequency constituents are so entrenched as independent units that they do not trigger any form of decategorization or semantic bleaching.

Additionally, acceptability too appears to influence the frequency of irregular forms, as we had assumed (Fig. 5).

---

[7] Frequencies were logarithmically transformed for visualization purposes for all charts.

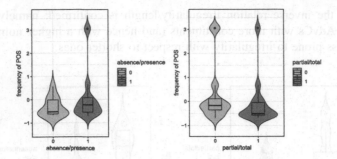

Fig. 3. Relationship of frequency of open class item and irregular AdvC

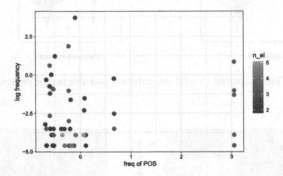

Fig. 4. Relation frequency of open-class items part of speech and spelling irregularities

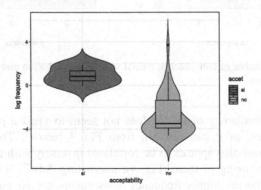

Fig. 5. Relationship frequency and acceptability

Three models were built to statistically asses the influence of the parameters outlined in Sect. 3 on spelling irregularities of AdvCs[8]. We opted for linear and logistic mixed effect modelling as they have been proved to be preferable for corpus data [46, 47]. In the following paragraphs, we present the results and discuss our findings.

---

[8] We performed all following analyses in the statistical computing environment *R* [45].

4.1 First Model: What Factors Influence the Presence of Spelling Irregularities?

Firstly, we used logistic mixed effect modelling to asses which constituents are statistically significant in determining the presence or absence of alternating spelling (and hence of grammaticalization). For model selection, we followed an automatic stepwise procedure via Likelihood-Ratio Test [48], as implemented in the R package *afex* [49]. The final model in (1) includes as predictors number of constituents ($\chi^2 = 9.6$, $p < .005$), frequency of AdvC ($\chi^2 = 9.6$, $p < .005$) and of open class items ($\chi^2 = 0.07$, $p > .5$). The random structure comprises intercept for items. All numerical predictors were centred.

$$Irregularity(yes/no) \sim num.el + freq.AdvC + freq.\ open\ class\ element + (1|item) \quad (1)$$

Table 2. Fixed effects of the first model

Fixed effects, model 1				
Predictors	Estimates	Odds ratios	Std. error	p
(Intercept)	232.7	47.23	6.34	**<0.001*****
Num. constituents	−28.1	0.4	6.1	**<0.001*****
Freq. AdvC	6.18	484.6	12.8	**<0.001*****
Freq. POS	0.89	3.27	10.7	.91

The results in Table 2 above show that all predictors except type frequency of open class constituents are significant. Namely, while higher frequency of AdvC positively correlates with the presence of alternating spelling, a higher number of constituents has a negative impact, confirming our assumption that longer phraseological units are more difficult to decategorize.

4.2 Second Model: What Factors Influence the Measure of the Irregularity?

Frequent and short AdvCs are hence the constructions more subject to be decategorized and to spelling irregularities. But can the different level of univerbation (partial vs total) be at least partially explained by synchronic factors? To test for this hypothesis, we built a second logistic model following the methodology outlined above. The final model in (2) includes as predictors number of constituents ($\chi^2 = 14$, $p < .0005$), length ($\chi^2 = 2.9$, $p < .05$), and frequency of AdvC ($\chi^2 = 3.5$, $p < .05$). We added the parameter of length since in partially or totally univerbated strings further phonetic erosion may depend on the number of syllables and – consequently – from phrasal or lexical accent position (Table 3).

Table 3. Fixed effects for the second model

Fixed effects, model 2				
Predictors	Estimates	Odds ratios	Std. error	p
(Intercept)	12.72	201688.42	3.8	**0.002*****
Num. constituents	−3.0	0.04	0.93	**0.001*****
Length	−1.19	0.38	0.63	0.1
Frequency of AdvC	−0.79	0.49	0.4	**0.06+**

$$Measure\ (partial\ vs\ total) \sim num.\ elem. + length + freq.\ AdvC + (1|item) \quad (2)$$

Two main observations can be made from the results of the model: first, no effect of syllable length is present, whereas number of constituents of the AdvC remains a highly significant predictor. Additionally, the effect of frequency – which is only marginally significant – is opposite with respect to the first model (see Table 2). That is, highly frequent AdvCs are more likely to undergo a process of decategorization and paradigmaticization – which leads to the presence of spelling irregularities; however, high-frequency decategorized items show a marginal tendency to remain in analytical form, whereas more low-frequency constituents tend to lexicalize completely. In Fig. 6 effect plots of the predictor of AdvC token frequency visually shows the trend.

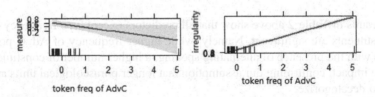

Fig. 6. Effect plots of the predictor AdvC frequency, respectively from model 2 and 1

4.3 Third Model: What Factors Affect Frequency of Irregularities?

Having found the factors that influence both the presence and the measure of spelling irregularities, we turn to the effect of our parameters on frequency of irregular AdvCs[9].

To test for effects on frequency, we used linear mixed effect modelling. The final model in (3) includes acceptability ($\chi2 = 13.6$, $p < .001$), frequency of AdvC ($\chi2 = 4$, $p < .05$), number of constituents ($\chi2 = 1.9$, $p = .17$) and OCC ($\chi2 = 10.4$, $p < .005$) in interaction terms ($\chi2 = 10$, $p < .005$). Random intercept for item was used as random structure. The factor of OCC was sum coded, as we are not interested in having a specific reference level. Table 4 reports fixed effects for the model.

---

[9] The dependent variable (token frequency of irregularly spelled AdvCs) was log-transformed.

Table 4. Fixed effects of model 3

Fixed effects, model 3			
Predictors	Estimates	Std. error	p
(Intercept)	−1.77	1	**0.08+**
Acceptability (yes)	−3.46	0.96	**<0.001*****
Freq. AdvC	0.56	0.3	**0.06+**
Num. constituents	−0.43	0.34	0.2
Noun	3.3	1.3	**0.01***
Adverb	−3.7	1.4	**0.01***
Adjective	0.4	1.5	0.8
Num. el x Noun	−1.28	0.5	**0.01***
Num. el x Adverb	1.37	0.5	**0.005****
Num. el x Adjective	−0.09	0.4	0.83

$$frequency \sim acceptability + freq.\ AdvC + num.\ constituents * OCC + (1|item) \quad (3)$$

Results show that – as we assumed – acceptability hinders unacceptable forms and significantly favors acceptable ones. Frequency of AdvC is only marginally significant, as high frequency of non-lexicalized forms is clearly directly proportional to the frequency of irregular spellings.

Notably, frequency of irregularities is not directly affected by their length, but by the interaction of length and OCE. That is, longer irregular AdvCs with nouns as OCC are significantly less frequent than irregularities with adverbs (see Fig. 7). We interpret this finding as corroborating our hypothesis; namely, an AdvC containing an already grammatical element tends to display spelling irregularities more frequently, as paradigmaticization into the "all-absorbing sea" of the category of adverbs is facilitated.

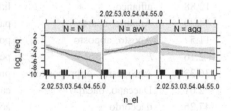

Fig. 7. Effect plot of the interaction of OCC and number of constituents

5 Conclusions

We have presented an innovative quantitative and corpus-based study on Italian AdvCs aimed at individuating facilitating factors for grammaticalization in synchronic language. In fact, we claim that such structures are undergoing grammaticalization, and that spelling irregularities are to be considered signs of ongoing language change, as suggested by the literature.

Results of the analysis show that token frequency and number of constituents of the AdvC affect the presence of spelling irregularities; these factors also influence the measure of the irregularity (i.e. if the alternate form is partially or totally lexicalized). In this latter case frequency is shown to have negative correlation with measure of irregularity, a finding that we suggest correlates with entrenchment. Finally, frequency of irregular forms is significantly affected by acceptability, frequency of AdvCs, and by the interaction of OCCs and length.

Our findings are consistent with the usage-based account on grammaticalization presented above (Sect. 1.1): Italian AdvCs constitute analytical phraseological units that are undergoing a process of grammaticalization (or constructionalization), since their repeated occurrence strengthens a more abstract node in the network of constructions [34]. More specifically, we have claimed that a twofold process is currently ongoing and can be investigated via spelling irregularities: paradigmaticization into the class of adverbs and subsequent univerbation and lexicalization, as their syntagmatic bonds become less and less semantically motivated. Effects of frequency [24], number of constituents, and OCC of the AdvC on spelling irregularities and their token frequency were also shown.

Much additional work is certainly required for a full understanding of the problem.

Nevertheless, we hope that the present paper will contribute to the growing interest on synchronic corpus-based accounts on grammaticalization phenomena, which we believe can provide interesting insights for the understanding of constructional change.

Appendix

AdvC	Freq. pm	Irregular spelling	OCC	POS
a caso	21.12	/	caso	N
a fianco	12.88	affianco	fianco	N
a parte	44.20	Apparte, aparte	parte	N
a posto	11.5	Aposto, apposto	posto	N
a malapena	2.16	/	pena	N
a proposito	36.33	Aproposito, approposito	proposito	N
da capo	2.61	Daccapo, dacapo	capo	N
d'accordo	47.26	daccordo	accordo	N
di nuovo	0.50	dinuovo	nuovo	agg
di sopra	54.29	disopra	sopra	avv
fin qui	9.69	finquì	Fin, qui	avv
in effetti	34.28	ineffetti	effetti	N
nient'affatto	1.9	nientaffatto	Niente, affatto	avv
per caso	19.21	percaso	caso	N
per favore	9.68	perfavore	favore	N

(continued)

(*continued*)

AdvC	Freq. pm	Irregular spelling	OCC	POS
per niente	9.71	perniente	niente	avv
tutt'altro	12.04	tuttaltro	altro	agg
un po'	252.60	Unpò, un pò	poco	agg
a meno che	15.26	/	meno	avv
al di là	37.94	Aldilà, al dilà	là	avv
al di sopra	9.87	al disopra, aldisopra	sopra	avv
alla fin fine	1.27	alla finfine	fine	N
d'altra parte	8.22	daltra parte, d'altraparte	parte	N
d'altro canto	6.98	Daltrocanto, d'altrocanto	canto	N
di buon'ora	0.5	di buonora	ora	avv
per di più	8.14	per dipiù, perdipiù	più	avv
per lo meno	5.36	per lomeno, perlomeno	meno	avv
per lo più	14.25	Perlopiù, perlo più	più	avv
più o meno	14.25	piu o meno	Più, meno	avv
su due piedi	0.47	/	Due, piedi	N
a colpo d'occhio	0.31	/	ocehio	N
a mano a mano	2.51	/	mano	N
dall'oggi al domani	0.32	/	Oggi, domani	avv
di punto in bianco	0.44	/	Punto, bianco	N
di tanto in tanto	4.48	di tanto intanto	tanto	agg
di volta in volta	11.63	di volta involta	volta	N
d'ora in poi	4.12	dora in poi	ora	avv
in quattro e quattr'otto	0.2	in quattro e quattrotto	Quattro, otto	agg
per filo e per segno	0.4	/	Filo, segno	N

References

1. Kuryłowicz, J.: The evolution of grammatical categories. Diogenes **13**(51), 55–71 (1965)
2. Meillet, A.: L'évolution des formes grammaticales. Scientia **XII**(XXXVI), 6 (1912)
3. Hopper, P.J., Traugott, E.C.: Grammaticalization. CUP, Cambridge (2003)
4. Norde, M.: Degrammaticalization. OUP, Oxford (2009)
5. Protopopescu, D.: The Morphologization Of Adverbs – An Instance of Grammaticalization. Studii şi cercetări lingvistice (2011)
6. Bybee, J.L.: Usage-based theory and grammaticalization. In: Heiko, N., Heine, B. (eds). The Oxford Handbook of Grammaticalization. OUP, Oxford (2011)
7. Heine, B.: Auxiliaries: Cognitive Forces and Grammaticalization. OUP USA, New York (1993)
8. Bybee, J.L., Torres, R.: Phonological and grammatical variation in exemplar models. Stud. Hisp. Lusophone Linguist. **1**(2), 399–414 (2008)
9. Torres Cacoullos, R., Walker, J.A.: Collocations in Grammaticalization and Variation. OUP, Oxford (2011)

10. Bybee, J.L.: From usage to Grammar: the mind' s response to repetition. Language **82**(4), 711–733 (2005)
11. Ellis, N.C.: Second language acquisition. In: Gass, S., Mackey, A. (eds) The Routledge Handbook of Second Language Acquisition (2013)
12. Browman, C.P., Goldstein, L.: Articulatory phonology: an overview. Phonetica **49**(3–4), 155–180 (1992)
13. Mowrey, R., Pagliuca, W.: The reductive character of articulatory evolution. Ital. J. Linguist. **7**, 37–124 (1995)
14. Lehmann, C.: Thoughts on Grammaticalization, 3rd edn. Language Science Press (2015)
15. Norde, M.: Lehmann's parameters revisited. In: Grammaticalization and Language Change: New Reflections, pp. 73–109 (2012)
16. Givon, T.: On Understanding Grammar. John Benjamins, Amsterdam (1979)
17. Lindquist, H., Mair, C. (eds.): Corpus Approaches to Grammaticalization in English. Benjamins, Amsterdam (2004)
18. Hildebrand-Edgar, N.: Disentangling frequency effects and grammaticalization, p. 23 (2016)
19. Renzi, L.: Come cambia la lingua. L'italiano in movimento. Mulino, Bologna (2012)
20. Barlow, M., Kemmer, S.: Usage Based Models of Language. CSLI, Chicago (2000)
21. Beckner, C., Bybee, J.: A usage-based account of constituency and reanalysis. Lang. Learn. **59**, 27–46 (2009)
22. Bybee, J.: Language. Usage and Cognition. CUP, Cambridge (2010)
23. Hopper, P.J.: Emergent grammar. In: PrOCEedings of the Thirteenth Annual Meeting of the Berkeley Linguistics Society, Berkley, CA, pp. 139–157 (1987)
24. Bybee, J.L.: Frequency of Use and the Organization of Language. OUP, Oxford (2006)
25. Bybee, J.L.: Usage-based theory and exemplar representation. In: Hoffman, T., Trousdale, G. (eds.) The Oxford Handbook of Construction Grammar, pp. 49–69. OUP, Oxford (2013)
26. Bybee, J.L., Hopper, P.J. (eds.): Frequency and the Emergence of Linguistic Structure. Benjamins, Amsterdam (2001)
27. Shank, C.: Grammaticalization, complementization and the development of an epistemic parenthetical: a diachronic analysis of the verb feel. Int. J. Lang. Linguist. **3**(3), 19–33 (2016)
28. Thompson, S.A., Mulac, A.: A quantitative perspective on the grammaticization of epistemic parentheticals in English. In: Traugott, E.C., Heine, B. (eds.) Typological Studies in Language, pp. 313–339. John Benjamins, Amsterdam (1991)
29. Lorenz, D.: From reduction to emancipation: Is gonna a word? In: Hasselgård, H., et al. (eds.) Studies in Corpus Linguistics, pp. 133–152. John Benjamins, Amsterdam (2013)
30. Hoffmann, S.: Grammaticalization and English Complex Prepositions: A Corpus-based Study. Routledge, London/New York (2007)
31. Goldberg, A.E.: Constructions at Work: The Nature of Generalization in Language. OUP (2006)
32. Hilpert, M.: Construction Grammar and its Application to English. Edinburgh University Press, Edinburgh (2014)
33. Coussé, E., et al.: Grammaticalization meets Construction Grammar. John Benjamins Publishing Company (2018)
34. Hilpert, M.: From hand-carved to computer-based: noun-participle compounding and the upward strengthening hypothesis. Cogn. Linguist. **26**(1), 113–147 (2015)
35. Traugott, E.C., Trousdale, G.: Constructionalization and Constructional Changes. OUP, Oxford, New York (2013)
36. Michael, I.: English Grammatical Categories. CUP, Cambridge (1970)
37. Hopper, P.: The paradigm at the end of the universe. In: Ramat, A., Hopper, P. (eds.) Limits of Grammaticalization, pp. 147–158. John Benjamins, Amsterdam (1998)

38. Payne, T.: Describing Morphosyntax: A Guide for Field Linguists. CUP, Cambridge (1997)
39. van der Auwera, J.: Adverbial Constructions in the Languages of Europe, 2nd edn. de Gruyter, Berlin (2011)
40. Hummel, M., Valera, S. (eds.): Adjective Adverb Interfaces in Romance. John Benjamins Publishing Company, Amsterdam (2017)
41. Ramat, P., Ricca, D.: Prototypical adverbs: On the scalarity/radiality of the notion of adverb. Rivista di Linguistica **6**, 289–326 (1994)
42. Rauh, G.: Adverbs as a linguistic category (?). In: Pittner, K., Elsner, D., Barteld, F. (eds.) Adverbs. Functional and Diachronic Aspects, pp. 19–45. John Benjamins, Amsterdam (2015)
43. Ramat, P., Ricca, D.: Sentence adverbs in the languages of Europe. In: Auwera, J. (ed) Adverbial Constructions in the Languages of Europe, pp. 187–275. de Gruyter, Berlin (1998)
44. Baroni, M., et al.: The WaCky wide web: a collection of very large linguistically processed web-crawled corpora. Lang. Resour. Eval. **43**(3), 209–226 (2009)
45. R Development Core Team: R: A language and environment for statistical computing. R Foundation for Statistical Computing, Vienna, Austria. http://www.R-project.org
46. Barth, D., Kapatsinski, V.: Evaluating logistic mixed-effects models of corpus-linguistic data in light of lexical diffusion. In: Speelman, D., Heylen, K., Geeraerts, D. (eds.) Mixed-Effects Regression Models in Linguistics. QMHSS, pp. 99–116. Springer, Cham (2018). https://doi.org/10.1007/978-3-319-69830-4_6
47. Gries, S.: The most under-used statistical method in corpus linguistics: multi-level (and mixed-effects) models. Corpora **10**(1), 95–125 (2015)
48. Baayen, R.H., Davidson, D.J., Bates, D.M.: Mixed-effects modeling with crossed random effects for subjects and items. J. Mem. Lang. **59**(4), 390–412 (2008)
49. Singmann, H., et al.: afex: Analysis of Factorial Experiments. R Package Version (2017)

On the Structural Disambiguation
of Multi-word Terms

Melania Cabezas-García[(⊠)] [iD] and Pilar León-Aráuz[(⊠)] [iD]

University of Granada, Granada, Spain
{melaniacabezas,pleon}@ugr.es

Abstract. Multi-word terms pose many challenges in Natural Language Processing (NLP) because of their structure ambiguity. Although the structural disambiguation of multi-word expressions, also known as bracketing, has been widely studied, no definitive solution has as yet been found. Although linguists, terminologists, and translators must deal with bracketing problems, they generally must resolve problems without using advanced NLP systems. This paper describes a series of manual steps for the bracketing of multi-word terms (MWTs) based on their linguistic properties and recent advances in NLP. After analyzing 100 three- and four-term combinations, a set of criteria for MWT bracketing was devised and arranged in a step-by-step protocol based on frequency and reliability. Also presented is a case study that illustrates the procedure.

Keywords: Multi-word term · Structure ambiguity · Bracketing

1 Introduction

The creation of multi-word expressions is a frequent word-formation mechanism. When they belong to a specialized domain, they are known as 'multi-word terms' (MWTs) and usually specify a broader concept (e.g. *timing belt*, which is a type of belt that controls the opening and closing times of an engine's valves). MWTs are often composed by more than two elements when even more characteristics of the concept are conveyed (e.g. *permanent magnet synchronous generator*).

Surprisingly, studies that specifically address these longer combinations, characterized by their structural ambiguity, are fewer in number than those focusing on two-term MWTs [1–5]. In these MWTs a dependency analysis must be performed, which has cognitive implications since it is the basis for an accurate semantic analysis of the MWT and its subsequent applications (i.e. translation). This structural disambiguation, often known as 'bracketing' [6], involves the grouping of the dependent elements so that the MWT is reduced to its basic form of modifier+head, as in [*permanent magnet*] [*synchronous generator*].

Natural Language Processing (NLP) has particularly focused on multi-word expression bracketing because of its inherent difficulties for NLP systems [1, 2, 5, 7, 8]. However, problems that have still not been solved include MWTs formed by more than three elements. In fact, the more constituents an MWT has, the more difficult its bracketing. In addition, other areas such as Terminology or Translation Studies have

© Springer Nature Switzerland AG 2019
G. Corpas Pastor and R. Mitkov (Eds.): Europhras 2019, LNAI 11755, pp. 46–60, 2019.
https://doi.org/10.1007/978-3-030-30135-4_4

not addressed this phenomenon despite its relevance for MWT description in knowledge bases or the establishment of interlingual equivalences of MWTs. Since terminologists or translators do not usually resort to NLP systems to analyze MWT structures by means of algorithms, they require manual solutions.

This paper describes a series of steps for the bracketing of MWTs, based on the linguistic properties of these terms and recent advances in NLP. For this purpose, a corpus of English specialized texts on wind power was used to extract candidate MWTs and perform CQL queries based on a dataset to clarify dependences. Our goals included the following: (i) to devise a set of criteria for the manual bracketing of MWTs; and (ii) to propose generalizations to make the inference of bracketing structures easier. This proposal facilitates MWT disambiguation by terminologists, translators or any linguist, who do not have access to advanced NLP systems. In addition, it can also be used to enrich NLP algorithms for this task.

2 Structural Ambiguity in Multi-word Terms

MWTs are sequences of two or more elements that designate a specialized concept. For instance, the term that designates SOLAR PANEL is *solar panel* in English, *panel solar* in Spanish, *panneau solaire* in French, and *Solarmodul* in German. Since these terms usually have a nominal head, they are known as complex nominals, noun compounds or nominal compounds. These compounds can be endocentric or exocentric. Endocentric complex nominals have a head and a modifier, and specify a broader concept (*solar generator* is a type of *generator*), whereas exocentric complex nominals lack a head and, thus, are not subtypes of any of their constituents (*saber tooth* is not a hyponym of either *saber* or *tooth* because it designates a *saber-toothed tiger* by means of metonymy) [3]. The most frequent MWTs in specialized texts are endocentric complex nominals, which are the specification of a hypernym.

MWTs do not usually allow the insertion of elements [9], namely those modifying their conceptual content (*wind generator* can become *wind turbine generator*, but not **wind small generator*). They are a well-known term formation procedure, because they allow meaning condensation by means of the deletion of some elements, i.e. the semantic relation held by the constituents and, often, even some MWT constituents. MWTs are formed by a slot-filling mechanism. For example, WIND TURBINE can be specified depending on the orientation of its rotation axis (*horizontal/vertical axis wind turbine*), its location (*offshore/onshore wind turbine*), its number of blades (*two-/three-bladed wind turbine*), etc. Accordingly, these slots allow the formation of sets of MWTs [10].

As previously stated, two-term combinations have been the main focus in MWT research, whereas longer sequences have received less specific attention. However, when dependencies are not analyzed, the interpretation of longer MWTs can be erroneous. For instance, in *offshore wind turbine*, *offshore* modifies *wind turbine*. The bracketing would thus be *offshore* [*wind turbine*], and not [*offshore wind*] *turbine*. In fact, incorrect assumptions regarding this MWT can lead to translation errors. For example, translating *offshore wind turbine* into Spanish as *turbina de viento marino* would imply that *offshore* modifies *wind*. The correct translation would be *aerogenerador marino*, which conveys that it is the *turbine* that is located *offshore*. Bracketing is thus a complex process that requires linguistic knowledge, world knowledge, as well as manual or computational techniques. An example of the complexity of this analysis are the MWTs *offshore* [*wind power*] and *wind* [*power output*], where the same combination (*wind power*) participates in two different bracketing structures.

NLP has proposed two models for the bracketing of three-term MWTs: the adjacency model and dependency model. The adjacency model [11, 12] takes an MWT p1p2p3 and compares if p2 is more related to p1 or p3. For that purpose, the number of occurrences of p1p2 and p2p3 are compared. For instance, in *renewable energy technology* there are more occurrences of *renewable energy* than of *energy technology*. Thus, a left-bracketing structure is adopted, and the system interprets the MWT as [*renewable energy*] *technology*. The dependency model [1] also takes an MWT p1p2p3 and compares whether p1 is more strongly associated with p2 or p3. Therefore, the analysis does not start from the central term, as in the adjacency model, but rather from the first one to the left. When p1 is more strongly associated with p2 than to p3, there is a left bracketing ([*tip speed*] *ratio*). In contrast, when p1 is dependent on p3, there is a right bracketing (*mean* [*wind speed*]).

In the same line, [13] states that these types of term are usually characterized by an internal structure that joins words in a binary branching dependency tree. The author adds that these structures govern how the terms can be abbreviated: "*civil rights activist* can be bracketed as [*civil rights*] *activist*, which can be shortened to *rights activist* but not to *civil activist*. On the other hand, *Yale medical library* is properly bracketed as *Yale* [*medical library*] which can then be reduced to *Yale library* or *medical library*, but not to *Yale medical*" [13, p. 65].

However, following both models the two possible combinations may have a similar frequency. Especially in four-term combinations, this criterion may not be as straightforward. Moreover, in the case of having a small or unbalanced corpus, frequency cannot be the single disambiguating rule. For this reason, the structural disambiguation proposed by these models should rely on additional factors.

Apart from frequency, [7, pp. 19–21] point out other signs that can clarify the dependencies in English MWTs. These include the identification of term variants on the web. If they have the following characteristics (see Table 1), they point to an internal group. [7] also suggest that paraphrases are useful for identifying internal dependencies in MWTs. For instance, *health care reform* is left-bracketed because paraphrases separating those groups can be found, as in "reform *in* health care". The bracketing indicators in [7] are very useful for the disambiguation of English MWTs. However, they may not apply to other languages, such as those not having the possessive genitive or internal inflection.

Additional clues to the structure of MWTs are offered in [5], one of the few studies addressing the bracketing of multi-word expressions of more than three constituents. They argue that internal dependencies are based on relational, coordinating or lexical links. Their proposal is characterized by the use of Wikipedia, as a term and named entity list, and as a corpus merging the information in all its pages [5, p. 72].

To initially determine that certain constituents are linked by a semantic relation, [5] rely on the use of prepositions. For instance, they search for n1 *for* n2 in the corpus. If

Table 1. Bracketing signs in [7, pp. 19–21].

CN to be disambiguated	Term variant	Bracketing indicator	Bracketing structure
cell cycle analysis	cell-cycle analysis	hyphen	[cell cycle] analysis
brain stem cell	brain's stem cell	possessive genitive	brain [stem cell]
plasmodium vivax malaria	Plasmodium vivax Malaria	internal capitalization	[plasmodium vivax] malaria
leukemia lymphoma cell	leukemia/lymphoma cell	slash	leukemia [lymphoma cell][a]
growth factor beta	growth factor (beta)	brackets	[growth factor] beta
tumor necrosis factor	tumor necrosis factor (NF)	abbreviation	tumor [necrosis factor]
health care reform	healthcare reform	concatenation	[health care] reform
adult male rat	male adult rat	change of order	adult [male rat][b]
tyrosine kinase activation	tyrosine kinases activation	internal inflection	[tyrosine kinase] activation

[a]The authors argue that there is right bracketing because the terms separated by a slash are alternatives [7, p. 20].

[b]The authors defend that there is right bracketing because the two first terms separately modify the head.

occurrences are found, n1 and n2 are said to encode a semantic relation and are thus bracketed. Nevertheless, this criterion cannot be applied to specialized discourse, where all MWT constituents usually belong to a concept system, and thus encode different semantic relations.

Therefore, in MWTs such as *offshore wind industry*, there are semantic relations between all of its constituents: industry *located* offshore, industry *uses_resource* wind, and wind *located* offshore. In this sense, further studies could be undertaken to address this issue by establishing a prioritized order in which semantic relations apply in the dependency link. Additionally, [5] argue that the existence of coordinating elements prevents their dependency. Thus, they look for the conjunctions *or, and,* and *nor* to ascertain whether two constituents are coordinated. For example, *cotton* and *polyester* are coordinated, because both terms are usually linked by those conjunctions. Consequently, in *cotton polyester shirt* those elements are not bracketed. This example is similar to the change of order mentioned in [7] (e.g. *adult male rat*, which is right-bracketed, see Table 1).

Although both studies highlight that the modifiers of these examples individually complement the head, which is undoubtedly true, in our opinion, these modifiers should be bracketed since none of the modifiers is more closely linked to the head than the other. That is why none of them should primarily be grouped with the head. Furthermore, bracketing is an internal grouping mechanism that facilitates analysis. For this reason, we argue that modifiers should be bracketed in this case, representing thus a coordinate MWT (*cotton polyester*) inside a broader MWT ([*cotton polyester*] *shirt*).

Finally, [5] search for determinants and plural uses of the elements to ascertain their lexical links. In *cotton polyester shirt*, for example, a large number of occurrences of *the cotton shirts* was found. The fact that considerably fewer occurrences of *the cotton polyesters* were retrieved suggests that *cotton* and *polyester* separately modify the head *shirt*. Accordingly, they relied on the presence of the possible combination of these elements in a lexical resource, i.e. Wikipedia. However, this criterion does not appear to be as useful for all MWTs since lexical resources can lack many terms. Moreover, in the same way as frequency, we can also find entries for the different possible combinations.

In short, more than twenty years after the development of bracketing models, structural disambiguation still remains problematic. In particular, this applies to combinations of more than three elements, which apart from [5], have not been studied in any depth. A list of bracketing indicators is also necessary for MWTs in specialized texts, formed by three or more constituents. In specialized discourse, these complex terms have specific characteristics that complicate their dependence analysis, such as the formation of long MWTs and the deletion of some constituents. Still another factor is their internal semantic relation, which can be domain specific (*uses_resource*). Bracketing trends should also be explored. In addition, bracketing is also useful for terminologists, translators and other linguists that rarely have access to NLP systems. Thus, manual techniques are a viable solution for these professionals.

3   Materials and Methods

For the purposes of this research, a corpus on wind power of approximately 3 million words was manually compiled. It consisted of specialized texts, such as scientific articles and PhD dissertations, originally written in English. The corpus was analyzed in Sketch Engine (https://www.sketchengine.eu/) [14], a corpus analysis tool that can generate concordance lines, wordlists, and word sketches (frequent word combinations), among many other utilities. We performed the following CQL (Corpus Query Language) queries to extract three- and four-term MWTs, respectively:

$$[tag="N.*|JJ.*|RB.*|VVN.*|VVG.*"]\{2\}[tag="N.*"]$$
$$[tag="N.*|JJ.*|RB.*|VVN.*|VVG.*"]\{3\}[tag="N.*"]$$

On the rightmost part of the queries, a nominal head is specified as [tag="N.*"], which can be preceded by nouns (N.*), adjectives (JJ.*), adverbs (RB.*), past participles (VVN.*) or present participles (VVG.*) on the order of two for three-term MWTs ({2}) (first CQL query) and three in the case of four-term MWTs ({3}) (second CQL query). This query was based on the different elements that have been found to premodify[1] nouns in English MWTs, which have been analyzed in previous work. We selected three-term MWTs because bracketing is necessary for this number of

---

[1] Although MWTs can also be postmodified (*angle of attack*), premodification is the preferred MWT formation pattern [3, 15, 16].

constituents. In addition, they are the most frequent MWTs of those that require bracketing. Four-term MWTs were also addressed because of their greater difficulty, since more patterns are possible. However, our results showed that the more constituents an MWT has, the fewer occurrences are found.

After verifying the terms in concordance lines, those MWTs that had been erroneously extracted were rejected. Examples of discarded MWT candidates were *axis wind turbine*, which always appeared as *horizontal/vertical axis wind turbine* (thus, they were included in the list of four-term MWTs), or *different wind penetration level*, which was a three-word term modified by an adjective. In contrast, there are other apparently similar MWTs that were nonetheless selected because the adjective modifying the head was not only an attribute but also conveyed specialized knowledge. For example, *large wind farm* was considered a concept because *large* actually points to power capacity, as in "In North America, typically, wind farms are larger than 50MW, with some projects of up to 200MW".

Other MWTs, in particular those referring to named entities, were also rejected, since these concepts will be addressed in future work. In the end, we focused on a set of 100 MWTs composed of the 50 most frequent three- and four-term MWTs (Table 2). As can be observed, four-term MWTs suffered a drastic reduction of frequency, which complicated the extraction of results.

Table 2. Sample of most frequent three and four-term MWTs in the corpus

Three-term MWTs	Freq.	Four-term MWTs	Freq.
Offshore wind farm	1024	Horizontal axis wind turbine	129
Tip speed ratio	445	Wind power generation system	105
Wind power plant	419	Installed wind power capacity	101
Wind power generation	374	Doubly feed induction generator	84
Wind power capacity	333	Vertical axis wind turbine	68
Mean wind speed	311	Offshore wind power plant	58
Wind power production	298	Annual mean wind speed	56
Average wind speed	284	Design tip speed ratio	55
Offshore wind turbine	281	Variable speed wind turbine	50
Renewable energy source	265	Wind power forecast error	48
Offshore wind power	264	Large offshore wind farm	46
Offshore wind energy	213	Annual average wind speed	46
Wind energy system	211	Squirrel cage induction generator	43
Small wind turbine	210	Blade root bending moment	39
High wind speed	199	Wind power output fluctuation	38
Variable-speed wind turbine	184	Micro hydro power plant	36
Rated wind speed	183	Permanent magnet synchronous generator	33
Large wind farm	179	Wind energy conversion system	30
Onshore wind farm	177	PMSG wind turbine system	29
Wind turbine blade	170	Optimum tip speed ratio	25
Wind power output	165	Hub height wind speed	25

(continued)

Table 2. (*continued*)

Three-term MWTs	Freq.	Four-term MWTs	Freq.
Low wind speed	157	Wind power penetration level	24
Wind turbine rotor	156	Small signal stability analysis	24
Large wind turbine	149	Gross final energy consumption	24
Wind energy converter	148	Wound rotor induction generator	22
Wind turbine system	147	Axial flow induction factor	22
Installed wind power	145	Wind turbine drive train	21
Wind turbine design	144	Wind turbine control system	21
Wind penetration level	144	Wind speed time series	21
Wind speed data	138	Power factor correction capacitor	21
Novel wind turbine	134	Short-term wind speed forecasting	20
Domestic hot water	127	Offshore wind supply chain	19
Power generation system	126	Average wind power density	19
Offshore wind market	125	Offshore wind energy resource	17
Renewable energy technology	121	Average annual wind speed	17
Wind power penetration	120	Optimal tip speed ratio	16
Wind power forecast	120	Wind energy penetration level	15
Wind power development	117	Wind turbine power curve	14
Total installed capacity	115	Wind farm power output	14
Conventional power plant	115	Free stream wind speed	14
Power system reliability	113	Fixed speed wind turbine	14
Offshore wind project	113	Wind turbine power production	13
Wind turbine model	111	Total wind power capacity	13
Power electronic converter	111	Offshore wind power development	13
Wind turbine generator	108	Insulated gate bipolar transistor	13
Sound pressure level	108	Hourly mean wind speed	13
Wind turbine manufacturer	106	Constant tip speed ratio	13
Wind energy project	105	Wind power grid integration	12
Wind power fluctuation	76	Short-term mean wind speed	12
Heat transfer medium	74	Network impedance phase angle	12

After extracting the list of terms to be analyzed, new queries were performed in order to disambiguate all possible groupings. These queries were aimed at researching different occurrences and frequencies based on the bracketing models described in the literature and our own observations:

1. Based on [9], we checked whether all adjacent groupings were found in the corpus intersected by external elements: $p1 * p2 + p3$; $p1 + p2 * p3$ (in the case of three-term MWTs) and $p1 * p2 + p3 + p4$; $p1 + p2 * p3 + p4$; $p1 + p2 + p3 * p4$; $p1 * p2 * p3 + p4$; $p1 * p2 + p3 * p4$; $p1p2 * p3 + p4$ (added in the case of four-term MWTs).
2. In contrast, we checked whether all adjacent groupings, while sticking together, were combined with other modifiers and/or heads: $*p1 + p2$; $p1 + p2*$; $*p2 + p3$;

p2 + p3∗; ∗p1 + p2∗; ∗p2 + p3∗ (in the case of three-term MWTs) and ∗p1 + p2; p1 + p2∗; ∗p2 + p3; p2 + p3∗; ∗p3 + p4; p3 + p4∗; ∗p1 + p2∗; ∗p2 + p3∗; ∗p3 + p4∗; ∗p1 + p2 + p3; p1 + p2 + p3∗; ∗p2 + p3 + p4; p2 + p3 + p4∗; ∗p1 + p2 + p3∗; ∗p2 + p3 + p4∗ (added in the case of four-term MTWs).

3. According to the adjacency model [11, 12], for three-term MWTs, we checked and compared the occurrence and frequency of the following combinations in the corpus: p1 + p2; p2 + p3. Evidently, in the case of four-term MWT, the searches were: p1 + p2; p2 + p3; p3 + p4; p1 + p2 + p3; p2 + p3 + p4.

4. According to the dependency model [1], for three-term MWTs, we checked and compared the occurrence and frequency of p1 + p3 and p1 + p2; whereas for four-term MTWs, we compared p1 + p2; p2 + p3; p1 + p4; p1 + p3; p2 + p4; p1 + p2 + p3; p1 + p2 + p4;p1 + p3 + p4.

5. According to the shortening model [13], we checked and compared the occurrence and frequency of p2 + p3 and p1 + p3 (for three-term MWTs) and p3 + p4; p1 + p4; p2 + p4; p2 + p3 + p4; and p1 + p3 + p4 (for four-term MWTs).

6. Based on the bracketing signs of [7], together with synonymic and antonymic patterns, we checked whether all possible groupings showed any variants or antonyms in the corpus (e.g. p1+p2 *also known as* x).

These queries are illustrated and discussed in more detail in Sect. 4.

4 Experiments and Discussion

4.1 Bracketing indicators

The analysis of the terms in Table 2 and the queries described in Section 3 produced the following list of indicators to perform MWT structural disambiguation tasks in a prioritized order. Unfortunately, to the best of our knowledge, there is no baseline available on specialized terms with which to compare the precision of our method. Therefore, the verification of our results relies on the specialized knowledge acquired during the development of EcoLexicon, a terminological knowledge base on the environment [17, 18].

This first indicator is most often sufficient to infer the bracketing, especially in three-term combinations. However, since specialized corpora are not always available or are sufficiently representative, the rest of the indicators can also be used to confirm the results of the first one. Furthermore, in MWTs consisting of more than three terms more disambiguation steps may be required, since when there are more possible combinations, the results are also more contradictory.

Therefore, for a combination of two or more elements to be grouped together (e.g. *large [wind farm]*), the candidate MWT should comply with at least two of the following requirements in the following order:

Step 1: Adjacent Groupings Within the MWT Appear as Independent Terms in the Corpus. MWTs formed by more than two components are usually the combination of other (shorter) MWTs (*wind power + power output = wind power output*). Thus, these MWTs integrate different concepts combined in a single more complex concept

[15]. Adjacency models are based on this MWT property, which constitutes the main criterion for structural disambiguation (e.g. lexical links in [5]). However, very often, because of the effects of compositionality in specialized language, all possible adjacent combinations appear in the corpus. However, a significant frequency difference among the results can resolve the ambiguity.

In this step, the identification of all possible groupings in the corpus is performed through a query that searches for each adjacent grouping with no other elements susceptible of forming larger compounds. In this way, the starting MWT or other MWT consisting of more than two components are excluded. This is exemplified in the following queries for the MWT *offshore wind turbine*, which search for *offshore wind* and *wind turbine* isolated from other elements, on the left ([tag!="JJ.*|N.*|RB.*|VVG.*|VVN.*"]) and on the right ([tag!="N.*|JJ.*"])..

    [tag!="JJ.*|N.*|RB.*|VVG.*|VVN.*"][lemma="offshore"][lemma="wind"][tag!="N.*|JJ.*"]
    [tag!="JJ.*|N.*|RB.*|VVG.*|VVN.*"][lemma="wind"][lemma="turbine"][tag!="N.*|JJ.*"]

In the case of four-term MWTs the same types of queries are performed. This involves adding or reducing lemmas for all possible combinations, which can consist of two or three elements. For example, in *power factor correction capacitor*, all possible combinations are *power factor*, *factor correction*, *correction capacitor*, *power factor correction* and *factor correction capacitor*. Thus, five different queries need to be made.

If only one of the combinations is found in the corpus, the bracketing is straight-forward. For instance, for *rated wind speed* two queries searched for *rated wind* (with no results) and *wind speed* (with 1,974 occurrences). Therefore, the bracketing is undoubtedly *rated [wind speed]*. In addition, if one of the combinations is clearly more frequent than the other, the most frequent combination drives the bracketing. For example, for *wind turbine system*, *wind turbine* shows 4,567 results and *turbine system* 10. The resulting bracketing is thus *[wind turbine] system*.

Nevertheless, if the corpus is not sufficiently large or representative, and especially in the case of four-term MWTs, new indicators should be sought. In the same way, when frequency differences are not significant, further queries should be made. For instance, the queries for *offshore wind power plant* do not show conclusive results (Table 3), since different groupings show similar results. Thus, it is still unknown whether the bracketing is *[offshore wind] [power plant]*, *offshore [wind power plant]* or *[offshore wind power] plant*.

Table 3. Frequencies of possible bracket groupings in *offshore wind power plant*

Offshore wind power plant	Freq.
Offshore wind	426
Wind power	2568
Power plant	226
Offshore wind power	104
Wind power plant	262

Something similar can also occur with a particular type of MWT, such as *power generation system*. In this type of MWTs the middle word is the nominalization of a predicate that explicitly codifies the semantic relation between the other two components. In this case, the system *generates* power. Therefore, both structures (*power generation* and *generation system*) can be expected to be equally frequent and other criteria should be applied for disambiguation.

Step 2: The Most Frequent Adjacent Grouping is Still More Frequent Than Other Dependencies. This is in consonance with the dependency model and uses the same types of query in the corpus. For example, in order to corroborate that *wind turbine system* is bracketed as [*wind turbine*] *system*, *wind turbine* should again show more occurrences (4,567) than *wind system* (146), which is the case. A variant of the original dependency model is the shortening technique as mentioned above in the words of [13], which in the case of *wind turbine system* would involve comparing the results of *wind system* (146) and *turbine system* (10). As in the case of *civil rights activist*, if the bracketing is [*wind turbine*] *system*, the term could be shortened to *turbine system* and not *wind system*, since *turbine* is the head of the bracketed nominal group. However, the results point in the wrong direction, contradicting the two previous indicators (Table 4).

Table 4. Adjacency, dependency and shortening indicators for *wind turbine system* and *wind power output*

Wind turbine system			
Adjacency	wind turbine (4,567)	turbine system (10)	[wind turbine] system
Dependency	wind turbine (4,567)	wind system (146)	[wind turbine] system
Shortening	wind system (146)	turbine system (10)	wind [turbine system]
Wind power output			
Adjacency	wind power (2,568)	power output (421)	[wind power] output
Dependency	wind power (2,568)	wind output (10)	[wind power] output
Shortening	wind output (10)	power output (421)	[wind power] output

In our study, this last model was not worth including in the protocol, since most of the time, the results led to more confusion than clarification. There were certain MWTs that comply with all of these three criteria, such as *wind power output* (Table 4), but most of them were not helpful. Therefore, this indicator should be included, if at all, in the protocol, as a last resort, and only in combination with others. Further studies will explore whether the MWTs, for which the shortening technique does not work, are different those to which the three criteria apply (*wind turbine system* vs. *wind power output*).

Step 3: Bracketing Groupings Do Not Allow the Insertion of External Elements Modifying Their Meaning. This determines its lexical unit [9] and its "concepthood", since there are a few cases where external elements can be inserted but no meaning change occurs in the combination. For example, in *wind power plant*, occurrences of *wind power generation plant* were not regarded as insertions since meaning is not affected. In fact, *power plant* could still be a bracket grouping because *generation* is a frequently omitted component of term that makes the relationship between power and plant explicit. In contrast, MWTs such as *low wind speed* are found to be "broken" in examples such as *low average wind speed* or *low cut-in wind speed*, where *low* and *wind* can already be ruled out from the bracketing.

In order to find possible insertions among the elements, we apply the following queries, exemplified with the MWT *offshore wind farm*:

> [lemma="offshore"][]{1,3}[lemma="wind"][lemma="farm"] within <s/>
> [lemma="offshore"] [lemma="wind"] []{1,3}[lemma="farm"] within <s/>

[]{1,3} identifies possible insertions of one to three words among the elements of the MWT; within <s/> is included to make sure that all occurrences are extracted within the same sentence. If only one of the possible groupings complies with this rule, the bracketing is solved. For instance, in *large wind farm*, the distinction between [*large wind*] *farm* and *large* [*wind farm*] is clear when no elements are found between *wind* and *farm* and several elements are found between *large* and *wind*: *large offshore wind farm*, *large onshore wind farm*, *large commercial wind farm*, etc.

If more than one possible grouping complies with the rule, or none of them complies with it, other criteria should also be applied. This indicator is very reliable, but it is not the first one because very often no external elements can be found among the components of the MWT, which indicates the fixed degree of lexicalization of many idiomatic specialized terms.

Step 4: Bracketing Groupings are Found Combined With Other Elements. This indicator is the opposite of the previous one, as it shows how a bracketing grouping represents a concept and can thus be combined with other modifiers and heads. This means that the relation with the rest of the MWT is not necessary, marking the boundaries of the bracketing. This also represents the previously mentioned slot-opening mechanism.

The following queries were performed, exemplified with the MWT *high wind speed*:

> [lemma="high"][lemma="wind"][tag="N.*" & lemma!="speed"]
> [tag="JJ.*|N.*|RB.*|VVG.*|VVN.*"][lemma="high"][lemma="wind"][lemma!="speed"]
> [lemma!="high"][lemma="wind"][lemma="speed"][tag="N.*"]
> [tag="JJ.*|N.*|RB.*|VVG.*|VVN.*" & lemma!="high"][lemma="wind"][lemma="speed"]

In the first query, *high wind* is searched for followed by any other noun than speed ([tag="N.*" & lemma!="speed"]) in order to extract other MWT where *high wind* is combined with different heads. In the second query, *high wind* is searched for in combination with new modifiers and, again, a different head. The other two queries do the same with *wind speed*. For four-term MWT, the same queries are used, expanding or reducing the number of lemmas according to all possible combinations. For example, in *optimum tip speed ratio*, one of the possible groupings is *tip speed ratio*. Therefore, the first query is the following:

[lemma!="optimum"][lemma="tip"][lemma="speed"][lemma="ratio"][tag="N.*"]

If only one of the possible groupings appears to be combined with other elements, or if frequency figures differ in a meaningful way, the bracketing is solved. For instance, in *wind turbine system*, *wind turbine* appears integrated within a total of 6,509 other MWTs: *wind turbine access*, *wind turbine aerodynamics*, *wind turbine airfoils*, *wind turbine blade*, *wind turbine certification*, etc. and *synchronous wind turbine generator*, *DIG-based wind turbine*, *fixed-speed with turbine*, etc. In contrast, *turbine system* only appears within other MWTs in 10 occurrences (e.g. *shrouded turbine system's performance*, *turbine system model* and *horizontal axis turbine system*, *air-driven turbine system*).

If all possible groupings, or none of them, can be integrated with other MWTs, the next indicators should be applied. For example, all the possible groupings of *offshore wind energy resource*, can be combined within other MWTs. Moreover, contradictory groupings show very similar frequencies (e.g. *offshore wind* and *wind energy*) (Table 5).

Table 5. Possible groupings in *offshore wind energy resource* and other combinations

Offshore wind energy resource		
Possible groupings	Integration within other MWTs	Frequency
Offshore wind	-offshore wind plant/industry/technology -installed offshore wind capacity/global offshore wind market	3345
Wind energy	-wind energy capacity/development -available/land-based wind energy	2292
Energy resource	-energy resource availability/development -renewable/clean energy resource	133
Offshore wind energy	-offshore wind energy potential/project -future/global offshore wind energy market/plant	96
Wind energy resource	-wind energy resource assessment/study -onshore/European/future wind energy resource	50

Step 5: Bracketing Groupings Have Synonyms or Antonyms. This indicator also highlights the "concepthood" of the groupings, since many concepts show denominative variations (e.g. *wind energy*, *wind power*) or antonyms (*horizontal axis wind turbine* vs. *vertical axis wind turbine*) that reinforce the conceptual nature of the possible combinations. It is related to term-formation mechanisms (different concepts emerge by opposition: *small* [*wind turbine*], *large* [*wind turbine*]) and to slot filling (*power* in this case).

According to [7], some of these variants could include the possessive genitive, slashes, hyphens or acronyms, and monolexical variants would be the most reliable proof of the concepthood of one of the possible groupings. For example, in *insulated-gate bipolar transistor* and *power factor correction (PFC) capacitor*, the hyphen and the acronym disclose the bracketing mechanism. The following sentence extracted from the corpus reveals *wind turbine* to be the bracket grouping in most of the MWTs where it takes part, since it has a monolexical variant (*aerogenerator*): "Wind turbines or aerogenerators transform the kinetic energy of the wind into electrical energy".

Therefore, apart from searching for possible punctuation-related issues that could unfold [7]'s variants, synonyms in the corpus were also searched through queries based on the knowledge patterns that usually convey synonymy in real texts:

[tag="RB.*"]?[word="known|called|referred"][tag="RB.*"]?[word="to"]?[word="as"]? [tag="N.*"]
[be]?[]{0,3}[lemma="synonym"] [word="of|for|to"] [tag="N.*"]
[tag="N.*"] []{1,3} [word="spelling"] [word="of"] []{0,3}

If only one of the possible groupings shows synonyms or antonyms, bracketing is solved. For instance, from all possible groupings in *offshore wind power plant*, *wind power plant* is related to a synonym in the corpus (*wind power station*), as codified in the pattern *also known as*: "Wind turbines can be installed as individual units or grouped in wind power stations, also known as wind power plants". Therefore, the bracketing *offshore* [*wind power plant*] is chosen. Regarding antonyms, in *reactive power compensation*, one of the possible groupings (*reactive power*) has an antonym (*active power*), which means that the bracketing is [*reactive power*] *compensation*.

This indicator is quite reliable but is suggested as the last step because explicit synonymy or antonymy are not as frequent as other phenomena in specialized corpora. The queries could thus be complemented with the consultation of external terminological resources.

4.2   Case study: *Wind Farm Power Output*

In order to illustrate the application of the previous indicators in a protocol-like manner (on the analysis of the same MWT), we present the example of *wind farm power output*. The possible combinations were the following:

[*wind farm*] [*power output*]
wind [*farm power*] *output*
[*wind farm power*] *output*
wind [*farm power output*]

After applying the first and second indicators, i.e. adjacency and dependency rules, the four possibilities were reduced to two: [*wind farm*] [*power output*] (whose groups had respectively 2,498 and 421 occurrences) and [*wind farm power*] *output* (*wind farm power* having 3 occurrences). This criterion initially seemed to be conclusive. However, we carried out the remaining steps of the procedure for further confirmation.

The third indicator, i.e. the impossibility for external elements to be inserted in the possible combination, also pointed to this organization. External elements were found between *wind farm* and *power output*, which were of the order of 13, as in *wind farm electrical power output* and *wind farm average power output,* or propositional examples such as *wind farm ramps its power output up* and *wind farm will produce similar power output.* On the contrary, external elements were not found between *wind farm power* and *output* in the other possible structure: [*wind farm power*] *output.* This suggested that *power output* should not be separated.

The fourth indicator, i.e. the formation of other MWTs, was also conclusive since the two groups in [*wind farm*][*power output*] formed many more MWTs than the grouping in [*wind farm power*] *output.* In particular, *wind farm* formed 3,786 MWTs (e.g. *wind farm design, commercial wind farm*) and *power output* was present in 489 MWTs (e.g. *power output fluctuation, real power output*), while *wind farm power* formed 13 MWTs (e.g. *wind farm power prediction, real wind farm power curve*). The preferred structure was again [*wind farm*][*power output*].

Finally, according to the fifth indicator, we searched for synonyms or antonyms of the possible combinations, especially monolexical variants. Although no synonyms or antonyms were found for *power output* (supporting the structure [*wind farm*][*power output*]) nor for *wind farm power* (in the structure [*wind farm power*] *output*), synonyms of *wind farm* were retrieved (e.g. *wind power plant, wind power station*). These highlighted the conceptual link of these elements and confirmed the validity of the structure [*wind farm*][*power output*].

5 Conclusions

In this paper, we have addressed the structural disambiguation of MWTs based on the information extracted from a specialized corpus on wind power. We have extracted and analyzed a set of 100 MWTs. This has led us to study the most frequent bracketing structures as well as the most reliable methods to perform disambiguation. Based on these methods, we devised a set of indicators and steps in order to disambiguate the structural dependencies of all possible combinations.

As a future line of research, we plan to enhance these structural indicators with more semantic-oriented criteria, since the relation held between the components of an MWT could also enrich the protocol. Moreover, the combination of structural and semantic criteria would lead to a more accurate interpretation of MWTs since semantic elicitation depends on bracketing, and bracketing can also benefit from semantic-based indicators. Other lines of research will also include the testing of the protocol in other languages and types of multiword expressions.

Acknowledgements. This research was carried out as part of project FFI2017-89127-P, Translation-Oriented Terminology Tools for Environmental Texts (TOTEM), funded by the Spanish Ministry of Economy and Competitiveness. Funding was also provided by an FPU grant given by the Spanish Ministry of Education to the first author.

References

1. Lauer, M.: Designing statistical language learners: experiments on noun compounds. Ph.D. Macquarie University, Australia (1995)
2. Girju, R., Moldovan, D., Tatu, M., Antohe, D.: On the semantics of noun compounds. Comput. Speech Lang. **19**(4), 479–496 (2005)
3. Nakov, P.: On the interpretation of noun compounds: syntax, semantics, and entailment. Nat. Lang. Eng. **19**(03), 291–330 (2013)
4. Kim, S.N., Baldwin, T.: A lexical semantic approach to interpreting and bracketing English noun compounds. Nat. Lang. Eng. **19**(3), 385–407 (2013)
5. Barrière, C., Ménard, P.A.: Multiword noun compound bracketing using Wikipedia. In: Proceedings of the First Workshop on Computational Approaches to Compound Analysis, Dublin, Ireland, pp. 72–80 (2014)
6. Marsh, E.: A computational analysis of complex noun phrases in navy messages. In: Proceedings of the 10th International Conference on Computational Linguistics, Standford, CA, pp. 505–508 (1984)
7. Nakov, P., Hearst, M.: Search engine statistics beyond the n-gram: application to noun compound bracketing. In: Proceedings of the Ninth Conference on Computational Natural Language Learning, CoNLL 2005, Ann Arbor, MI, pp. 17–24 (2005)
8. Utsumi, A.: A semantic space approach to the computational semantics of noun compounds. Nat. Lang. Eng. **20**, 185–234 (2014)
9. Johnston, M., Busa, F.: Qualia structure and the compositional interpretation of compounds. In: Viegas, E. (ed.) Breadth and Depth of Semantic Lexicons, pp. 167–187. Springer, Dordrecht (1999). https://doi.org/10.1007/978-94-017-0952-1_9
10. Cabezas-García, M., Faber, P.: A semantic approach to the inclusion of complex nominals in english terminographic resources. In: Mitkov, R. (ed.) EUROPHRAS 2017. LNCS (LNAI), vol. 10596, pp. 145–159. Springer, Cham (2017). https://doi.org/10.1007/978-3-319-69805-2_11
11. Marcus, M.: A Theory of Syntactic Recognition for Natural Language. MIT Press, Cambridge (1980)
12. Pustejovsky, J., Anick, P., Bergler, S.: Lexical semantic techniques for corpus analysis. Comput. Linguist. **19**(2), 331–358 (1993)
13. Grefenstette, G.: Explorations in Automatic Thesaurus Discovery. Kluwer Academic Press, Boston (1994)
14. Kilgarriff, A., et al.: The sketch engine: ten years on. Lexicography **1**(1), 7–36 (2014)
15. Levi, J.: The Syntax and Semantics of Complex Nominals. Academic Press, New York (1978)
16. Sager, J.C., Dungworth, D., McDonald, P.F.: English Special Languages. Principles and Practice in Science and Technology. Brandstetter Verlag, Wiesbaden (1980)
17. Faber, P.: A Cognitive Linguistics View of Terminology and Specialized Language. De Gruyter Mouton, Berlin/Boston (2012)
18. San Martín, A., Cabezas-García, M., Buendía, M., Sánchez-Cárdenas, B., León-Araúz, P., Faber, P.: Recent advances in EcoLexicon. Dictionaries: J. Dictionary Soc. North Am. **38**(1), 96–115 (2017)

Phraseology in Specialised Language:
A Contrastive Analysis of Mitigation
in Academic Papers

María Luisa Carrió-Pastor(✉) ⓘ

Universitat Politècnica de València, Camino de Vera, 14, 46022 Valencia, Spain
lcarrio@upv.es

Abstract. The hypothesis of this paper is that writers with different academic backgrounds employ different mitigation devices and use phraseological units in a particular way in English research papers. The main objective of this study is therefore to analyse whether mitigation devices are used with different frequencies in the specific fields of engineering, medicine and linguistics. The corpus of this study consisted of academic papers published in international research journals devoted to these three disciplines. Mitigation devices were then detected and analysed in context with METOOL, a tool designed to identify metadiscoursal devices (research project reference FFI2016-77941-P). The data obtained revealed that there were in fact differences in the use of the phraseological units associated to mitigation devices by writers that belong to different specific fields, even though in theory they share the same genre and academic style.

Keywords: Mitigation · Specialized languages · Academic English

1 Introduction

In this paper, the pragmatic aspects of language and, specifically, metadiscourse are taken into account as the starting point. Metadiscourse can be defined as the study of the strategies that speakers of a language use to explain ideas in a coherent way and to interact with the reader or listener. In this sense, language is analysed from a functional point of view, taking into account its role in communication rather than its grammatical form.

Thompson (2001: 59) differentiated two main types of interaction in written texts: textual metadiscourse categories, that is, "[…] these primarily involve the management of the flow of information and thus serve to guide readers through the content of the text", and interpersonal metadiscourse categories, that is, "[…] these are aspects which aim to involve readers in the argument or ethos of the text". Here, I focus on the latter, the interactive metadiscourse categories, and more specifically on hedges.

Hedges can be defined as language devices that are used to mitigate propositions and to hide the speaker's face. They have been of interest to researchers such as Hyland (1998), Abdi (2011), Hu and Cao (2011), Alonso Almeida (2012) and Carrió-Pastor (2014, 2016a, b), who have referred to them as one of the different metadiscoursal

© Springer Nature Switzerland AG 2019
G. Corpas Pastor and R. Mitkov (Eds.): Europhras 2019, LNAI 11755, pp. 61–72, 2019.
https://doi.org/10.1007/978-3-030-30135-4_5

strategies that play a key role in knowledge construction and allow academic writers to express their ideas humbly in an objective, systematic and precise way. It should be taken into account that, since hedges are textual variables (Crompton, 1998) a contextual analysis is needed to identify instances of hedging. Crompton (1997, 1998) questions the definition of hedges and focuses his analysis on the different taxonomies of hedges suggested by several researchers such as Skelton (1988), Myers (1989), Salager-Meyer (1994) and Hyland (1994). Taking into account previous studies, Crompton (1997: 281) also proposes a definition of hedges: "an item of language which a speaker uses to explicitly qualify his/her lack of commitment to the truth of a proposition he/she utters". He (1997: 282) also suggests a simple test for determining whether a proposition is hedged: "Can the proposition be restated in such a way that it is not changed but that the author's commitment to it is greater than at present? If 'yes' the proposition is hedged". To this definition, it should be added that the meaning of commitment may vary depending on the writer's background, as sometimes the academic and/or cultural backgrounds of writers favour the use of hedging devices. In this vein, Yang (2013: 33) explains "While the Chinese academic community favours a more authoritative and assertive way of presenting scientific claims […] the English-medium journals encourage the use of hedges to mitigate knowledge claims or author commitment towards the statements". Thus, it seems that the use of hedges is sometimes contextually dependent – the writer should choose a linguistic form that shows (or not) his/her commitment to the proposition. Although Lyons (1968: 413) indicates that "meaningfulness implies choice", linguists should identify the causes and characteristics of this choice in order to understand linguistic patterns.

Focusing on taxonomies of hedges, Crompton (1997, 1998, 2012) identifies a classification based on Hyland's (1998, 2005) proposal. He distinguishes different kinds of hedges taking into account their syntactic nature: modal verbs, adverbials, lexical verbs, nouns and adjectives. Crompton (2012: 60), expanding the definition of hedges indicated above, explains: "As other researchers have noted, (a) hedges may take many forms and cannot be reduced to a finite set of linguistic items and (b) linguistic items frequently identified as being hedges cannot be assumed to be serving as hedges: analysis of the co-text is therefore required". He (2012: 56) adds that "Research that compares native English speaker (NES) academic writing and non-native English speaker (NNES) writing also consistently finds that NNES writers hedge differently from and usually less than their NES peers, and on this account suggests a role for pedagogic intervention". It can be observed that he expands his initial definition of hedges, strengthening the position that hedges are context-dependent.

I believe that there are still some aspects of hedging that should be studied in depth, such as the identification of devices that act as hedges taking into account their specific context and the phraseological units that are associated to these hedges. This could be useful to identify the connections between linguistic patterning and specialized contexts of academic discourse. It could also be beneficial for educational purposes, by making it possible to identify phrases in academic papers that can potentially be of use for pedagogical purposes such as being included in textbooks to show the collocations or bundles of the most frequent hedges.

Focusing on collocations, phraseology is an area of research that has been of interest to a number of researchers over the last thirty years, as stated by the studies of

Hunston (2002), Granger and Paquot (2008), Charles (2006, 2011), Durrant (2009, 2016), Durrant and Mathews-Aydınlı (2011), Vincent (2013), Brett and Pinna (2015), Le and Harrington (2015), Grabowski (2015), John, Brooks and Schriever (2017), Cunningham (2017), Fiedler (2017) and Kim and Yeates (2019). In this analysis, I follow the distributional or corpus-driven approach, which has been used by researchers such as Hunston and Francis (2000), Scott and Tribble (2006), Saber (2012), Cortes (2013) and Carrió-Pastor (2017). Corpus studies have focused on identifying the most common phrases in academic English and this fact may be helpful to determine the patterns followed by language users, as it provides long lists of formulaic phrases and represents academic English. Nevertheless, one of the well-known problems of using corpus techniques and retrieving individual items is that language patterns may not be identified, resulting in a fragmented analysis of discourse (Charles 2011). This is the reason why I have applied here a phraseological analysis of hedges, performed in order to have a wider view of discourse patterns and identify differences in the use of certain structures. Therefore, this paper takes an integrative corpus and discourse approach, showing how hedging devices use different phraseological units to signal specific fields in academic writing. As Vincent (2013: 44) explains, "Findings have consistently shown that phraseology is register specific", but in this study my interest lies in demonstrating that hedging phraseology is also specific to different fields of knowledge in a given genre.

In this paper, my main objective is to identify the phraseological units associated to mitigation or hedging devices. It presents some of the results of a research project (reference FFI2016-77941-P, Spanish Ministerio de Economía y Competitividad) in which metadiscoursal devices are detected with a tool specifically developed to identify and calculate the occurrences of metadiscoursal categories: METOOL. The hypothesis of this paper is that writers with different academic backgrounds use different mitigation devices and use phraseological units in a particular way in English research papers. Hence, this study sets out to analyse whether mitigation devices are used with different frequencies in the specific fields of engineering, medicine and linguistics.

This paper is organized as follows. First, the Introduction provides a general overview of the theoretical background of the study and the objectives have been stated. Second, the section 'Corpus and Method' describes the different academic papers compiled and the procedure used in the study. Third, the quantitative results are shown and some examples from the corpus are discussed in the section 'Results', and finally the conclusions are drawn in the last section.

2 Corpus and Method

The corpus used in this study was composed of academic papers devoted to the study of linguistics, medicine and engineering. The papers were compiled from international research journals published during the period 2016–2019. The nationality of the researchers (from English-speaking countries) was determined considering their affiliation and an e-mail was sent to the authors to determine their mother tongue. In research papers written by several authors, only papers of which at least 60% of the authors were native English writers were compiled. The papers compiled and the total number of tokens can be seen in Table 1:

Table 1. Number of texts and tokens of the corpora.

Corpora	No. texts	No. tokens
Engineering	65	653,787
Medicine	67	454,573
Linguistics	80	636,620
Total	212	1,744,980

The occurrences were processed automatically with METOOL, a program developed at the University of Wolverhampton (Research Institute for Information and Language Processing) that allows the semi-automatic identification of metadiscourse devices. The interface of the tool can be seen below in Fig. 1:

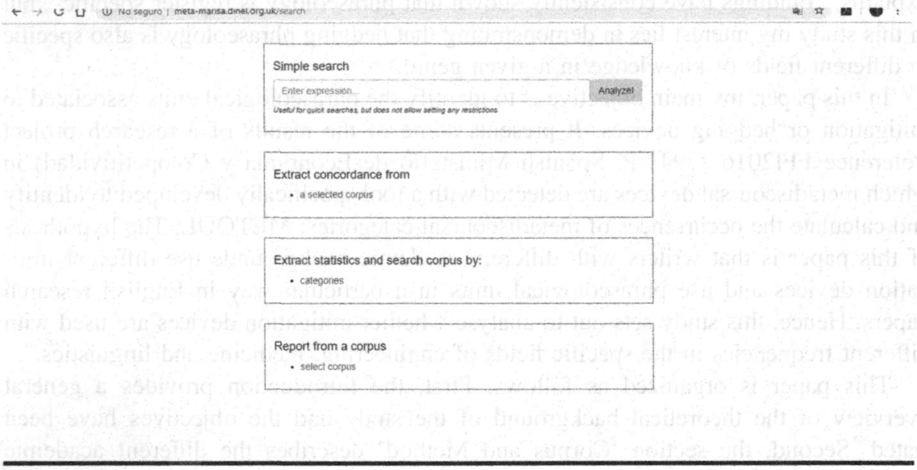

Fig. 1. Interface of METOOL.

The criteria used to identify hedges in the corpus were based, on the one hand, on considering the mitigation devices detected in previous studies (Hyland 2005; Mur Dueñas 2011) and identified by METOOL and, on the other hand, some hedges were also included after the manual tagging of the corpus. Thus, the hedges included in this study were identified automatically and manually, and those devices that could potentially be hedges but were not in context were removed.

The aim of this data-driven methodology was to perform a quantitative analysis of the frequencies of use of hedges by native speakers of English. The occurrences found were classified, following Crompton's proposal (2012), into modal verbs, adverbials, lexical verbs, nouns, adjectives and phrases. This classification was considered the most appropriate for this analysis as the results might also be applied to teach students how to use hedges and the phraseology associated to hedges in academic discourse. The phraseological units were detected with METOOL and the most frequent ones were identified, as shown in Fig. 2:

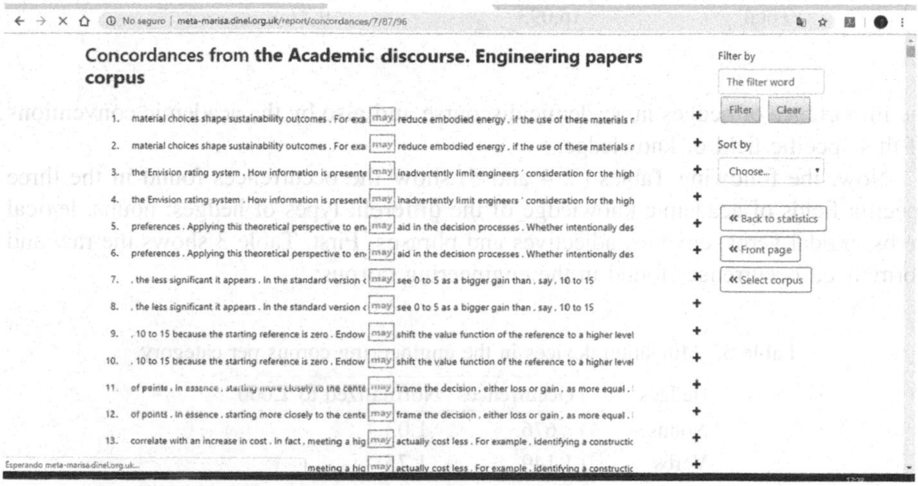

Fig. 2. Concordances in engineering academic writing (METOOL).

The results were noted in tables and the frequencies were contrasted. The results were normalized to 1,000 words, given the different numbers of tokens in the three corpora. Then I additionally read the three sets of corpora manually to check that all hedges and their phraseological units had been detected correctly, given that the interpretation of hedges is context dependent. Some examples of the hedges that were used in the three specific fields of knowledge in the corpora were discussed to indicate the possible causes of the variation found in the data. In this sense, the data obtained revealed that there were in fact differences in the use of the phraseological units associated to mitigation devices by writers that belong to different specific fields, even though in theory they share the same genre and academic style. Finally, the results were discussed and conclusions were drawn.

3   Results

The results extracted from the analysis are shown below. Table 2 shows all the mitigation devices found in the corpus. The data are shown in raw occurrences and in normalized results, given that the number of tokens was dissimilar in the three corpora analysed:

It can be observed in the general results that linguists used more mitigation devices than engineers and medical doctors. This may have been caused by the awareness of

Table 2. Mitigation devices in the corpora.

Fields of knowledge	Occurrences of hedges	Normalized to 1,000
Engineering	6,664	10.19
Medicine	2,127	4.67
Linguistics	7,302	11.46
Total	16,093	9.22

the importance of hedges in academic discourse and also by the academic conventions of this specific field of knowledge.

Now, the following Tables (3, 4 and 5) show the occurrences found in the three specific fields of academic knowledge of the different types of hedges: nouns, lexical verbs, modal verbs, adverbs, adjectives and phrases. First, Table 3 shows the raw and normalized occurrences found in the engineering corpus:

Table 3. Mitigation devices in the engineering corpus per category.

Hedges	Occurrences	Normalized to 1,000
Nouns	676	1.03
Verbs	1,149	1.75
Modal verbs	2,606	3.98
Adverbs	870	1.33
Adjectives	1,237	1.89
Phrases	126	0.19
Total	6,664	10.19

As can be seen, in the engineering corpus the most frequently used category is modal verbs. The categories of nouns, verbs, adjectives and adverbs are the categories that are also quite frequent in this corpus. This is in line with the results obtained in other previous studies (Hyland 2005; Carrió-Pastor 2016a).

Table 4 shows the raw and normalized occurrences of the hedges identified in the medicine corpus:

In the specific field of medicine, modal verbs are the most frequent mitigation devices, and are used to soften the propositions of the authors. The second most used category is adjectives, followed by adverbs, verbs and nouns. Finally, Table 5 illustrates the raw and normalized occurrences found in the field of linguistics:

In the linguistics corpus, the most utilized category is modal verbs (3.59), followed by adjectives, verbs, adverbs and nouns. Figure 3 shows a global comparison of the normalized occurrences of hedges in the three corpora:

In Fig. 3 it can be seen that modal verbs are the most frequently used mitigation devices in the three corpora, followed by adjectives, verbs and adverbs. It should also be noticed that the normalized data confirms that linguists used more mitigation devices than engineers and medical doctors.

Table 4. Mitigation devices in the medicine corpus per category.

Hedges	Occurrences	Normalized to 1,000
Nouns	186	0.40
Verbs	288	0.63
Modal verbs	769	1.69
Adverbs	309	0.67
Adjectives	493	1.08
Phrases	82	0.18
Total	2,127	4.67

Table 5. Mitigation devices in the linguistics corpus per category.

Hedges	Occurrences	Normalized to 1,000
Nouns	1,077	1.69
Verbs	1,269	1.99
Modal verbs	2,287	3.59
Adverbs	1,169	1.83
Adjectives	1,334	2.09
Phrases	161	0.25
Total	7,302	11.46

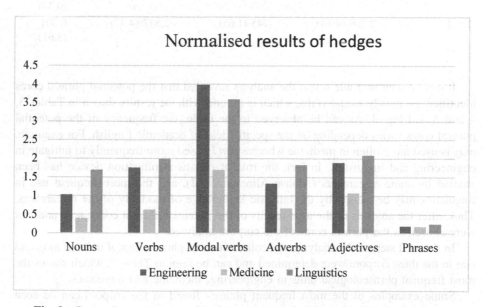

Fig. 3. Comparison of the use of hedges per syntactic category in the three corpora.

After obtaining the results of the different categories of hedges, the most frequent hedges were then extracted to identify potential phrasal cores that could be useful for academic writers, translators and language learners. The most frequent hedges found in the three corpora are detailed in Table 6 (frequencies normalized to 1,000 are shown in brackets):

Table 6. Most frequent mitigation devices in the corpus per specific field.

Most frequent hedges	Engineering occurrences	Medicine occurrences	Linguistics occurrences	Total
May	804 **(1.22)**	266 **(0.58)**	624 **(0.98)**	1,694 **(0.97)**
Can	951 **(1.45)**	173 **(0.38)**	1,174 **(1.84)**	2,298 **(1.31)**
Might	98 (0.14)	65 (0.14)	276 (0.43)	439 (0.25)
Could	278 (0.42)	99 (0.21)	283 (0.44)	660 (0.37)
Probability	181 (0.27)	4 (0.00)	35 (0.05)	220 (0.12)
Potential	208 (0.31)	93 (0.20)	95 (0.14)	396 (0.22)
Possible	189 (0.28)	45 (0.09)	360 (0.56)	594 (0.34)
Total	2,709 (4.14)	745 (1.65)	2,847 (4.47)	6,301 (3.61)

It can be seen in Table 6 that the analysis revealed that the potential phrasal cores identified are mostly modal verbs, which is in tune with the results shown in Tables 3, 4 and 5 and Fig. 3. As can be observed in the table, the frequency of the potential phrasal cores varies depending on the specific field of academic English. For example, *may* is used more often in medicine whereas *can* is used more frequently to mitigate in engineering and linguistics. In fact, the role of *can* as a mitigation device has been studied by some researchers (Alonso-Almeida 2012), and the more frequent use in linguistics may be caused by the intrinsic knowledge of modality of the researchers. Thus, after the analysis of the total results of the potential phrasal cores, *may* and *can* were chosen as the phrasal cores of the corpora analysed.

In the next step of the analysis, the collocations or phraseological units of *may* and *can* in the three corpora were determined and can be seen in Table 7, which shows the most frequent phraseological units in engineering, medicine and linguistics:

Some examples of the most frequent phrases found in the corpora can be seen below in examples [1–9]:

1. Engineering: "This analysis *may lead to* a better understanding of how often and when...".

Table 7. Most frequent phraseological units of phrasal cores.

Phrasal cores	Engineering	Medicine	Linguistics
MAY	Noun + may + reduce	That + may + account	Noun + may + appear
	Noun + may + actually	Noun + may + increase	Noun + may + differ
	Noun + may + have	Noun + may + be +adj.	Noun + may + be +adj
	Noun + may + be + past participle	Noun + may + be + past participle	Noun + may + be + past participle
	Noun + may + apply	Noun + may + benefit	Noun + may +in fact + V
	Noun + may + also + V	Noun + may + not be	Noun + may + also + V
	Noun + may + allow	Noun + may + mitigate	Noun + may + not + V
	Noun + may + lead to	Noun + may + lead to	Noun + may + not
	Noun + may + not + be as	Noun + can + be + ing	necessarily + V
CAN	Noun + can + affect	Noun + can + be + past participle	Noun + can + account
	Noun + can + be + past participle	Noun + can + cause	Noun + can + be + past participle
	Noun + can + also + be	Noun + can + have	Noun + can + also + be
	Noun + can + have	Noun + can + lead	Noun + can + have
	Noun + can + result	Noun + can + help	Noun + can + appear
	Noun + can + help	Noun + can + only + verb	Noun + can + estimate
	Noun + can + provide		Noun + can + only + verb

In this example, the authors use *may* to hide their face and to suggest the importance of their findings.

2. Engineering: "…this decision point, the impact of the intervention *can be measured* more effectively".

   Can is, in general, a mitigation device that can be interpreted in different ways as a hedge. It can be used to hide the face of the writer, to show a lack of commitment on the part of the author or to mitigate an assertion. In this example, the authors hide their face and this fact is reinforced with the use of the passive voice.

3. Engineering: "So, the assessment of prioritization *may not be as* robust as it should be…".

   Mitigation is expressed in this example with the use of *may* next to *not*. The authors soften the negative meaning of the proposal with the modal verb.

4. Medicine: "…hypothesis that pre-transplant treatment of HCV *may mitigate* risk of liver-related mortality".

   The authors hedge the risk of liver-related mortality with the use of the modal verb *may* and the verb *mitigate*, stressing the intention to soften the risk of suffering a mortal illness.

5. Medicine: "…on children, observational scales *can be used* to evaluate pain, the most common of…".

   In this sentence, the author uses *can* to mitigate an assertion (i.e. are used), indicating that there are other possibilities with the use of the modal verb *can*.

6. Medicine: "…newborns after a vaginal birth is disturbing because E coli *can cause* septicemia, meningitis, urinary tract infection".

In this example, *can* is used to show a lack of commitment on the part of the authors. The authors mitigate the enumeration of the different illnesses caused by E coli.

7. Linguistics: "…and when it does apply, the displaced pronoun *may appear* in a range of positions".
May indicates that the author is not sure about the statement – in this case, the author transmits vagueness in order not to explain the different positions of the displaced pronoun.

8. Linguistics: "High intensity of actualization *can also be discerned* in correlative constructions".
The author of the research paper uses the modal verb *can* to mitigate the possibility of discerning a high intensity of actualization. The author could have avoided the use of *can* (i.e. is also discerned) in the sentence but prefers to show lack of commitment.

9. Linguistics: "The spatial relation expressed in (1) *can* be expressed in the Bantu language Mushunguli".
The author mitigates the proposition, that is, the expression of spatial relation, with the modal *can*, thereby lowering the strength of the statement.

In the examples, it can be observed that the verbs used after the phrasal cores depend on their field of knowledge and on the aspects that the writers preferred to highlight in their research. For example, medical doctors prefer the use of *cause* and engineers *measure*. This phraseological choice was due to the specificity of the researchers' discipline.

4 Conclusions

The conclusions of this analysis have highlighted that there are in fact differences in the way academic writers use mitigation devices and their phraseological units in research papers. The identification and examination of the phrasal cores can help tell us whether the phrase of which it forms part occurs more frequently and so several patterns have been identified. These data could be interesting for academic writers as well as for teachers of academic English since they can show their students real examples. Specifically, the identification of *can* and *may* as the most frequent phrasal cores to mitigate in academic English is a finding that has been suggested by several researchers (Hyland, 2005; Mur Dueñas, 2011; Carrió-Pastor, 2014) but has been demonstrated in this paper.

Furthermore, the variants of a phrase have been identified in the different specific fields of knowledge. For example, in the three corpora analysed it can be observed that the combinations of the most frequently used phraseological units vary and this should be taken into consideration (see Table 7). In this paper, it is suggested that the academic writer should take into account the most frequent mitigation devices and then check in an academic corpus whether they are representative of his/her field of knowledge.

I am aware that the frequency of such phrases is not considered in itself and that the three corpora should incorporate more academic texts. Nevertheless, this paper offers some results and examples that could raise awareness of the importance of phraseological units in academic English and in its specific fields of knowledge.

References

Abdi, R.: Metadiscourse strategies in research articles: a study of the differences across subsections. J. Teach. Lang. Skills 3(1), 1–16 (2011)

Alonso Almeida, F.: An analysis of hedging in eighteenth century English astronomy texts. In: Moskowich, I., Crespo, B. (eds.) Astronomy "playne and simple": The Writing of Science between 1700 and 1900, pp. 199–220. John Benjamins, Amsterdam/ New York (2012)

Brett, D., Pinna, A.: Patterns, fixedness and variability: using PoS-grams to find phraseologies in the language of travel journalism. Procedia Soc. Behav. Sci. 198, 52–57 (2015)

Carrió-Pastor, M.L.: Verbal phraseology: an analysis of cognitive verbs in linguistics, engineering and medicine academic papers. In: Mitkov, R. (ed.) EUROPHRAS 2017. LNCS (LNAI), vol. 10596, pp. 325–336. Springer, Cham (2017). https://doi.org/10.1007/978-3-319-69805-2_23

Carrió-Pastor, M.L.: A contrastive study of the hedges used by English, Spanish and Chinese researchers in academic papers. In: Almeida, F.A., et al. (eds.) Input a Word, Analyze the World: Selected Approaches to Corpus Linguistics, pp. 477–492. Cambridge Scholars, Newcastle upon Tyne (2016a)

Carrió-Pastor, M.L.: A contrastive study of interactive metadiscourse in academic papers written in English and in Spanish. In: Almeida, F.A., Cruz García, L., González Ruiz, V. (eds.) Corpus-Based Studies on Language Varieties. Peter Lang, Bern (2016b)

Carrió Pastor, M.L.: Cross-cultural variation in the use of modal verbs in academic English. Sky J. Linguist. 27, 23–45 (2014)

Cortes, V.: The purpose of this study is to: connecting lexical bundles and moves in research article introductions. Engl. Acad. Purp. 12(1), 33–43 (2013)

Charles, M.: Adverbials of result: phraseology and functions in the problem-solution pattern. J. Engl. Acad. Purp. 10, 47–60 (2011)

Charles, M.: Phraseological patterns in reporting clauses used in citation: a corpus-based study of theses in two disciplines. Engl. Specif. Purp. 25, 310–331 (2006)

Crompton, P.: Hedging in academic writing: some theoretical problems. Engl. Specif. Purp. 16(4), 271–287 (1997)

Crompton, P.: Identifying hedges: definition or divination? Engl. Specif. Purp. 17(3), 303–311 (1998)

Crompton, P.: Characterising hedging in undergraduate essays by middle-eastern students. Asian ESP J. 8(2), 55–78 (2012)

Cunningham, K.J.: A phraseological exploration of recent mathematics research articles through key phrase frames. J. Engl. Acad. Purp. 25, 71–83 (2017)

Durrant, P.: Investigating the viability of a collocation list for students of English for academic purposes. Engl. Specif. Purp. 28, 157–169 (2009)

Durrant, P.: To what extent is the academic vocabulary list relevant to university student writing? Engl. Specif. Purp. 43, 49–61 (2016)

Durrant, P., Mathews-Aydınlı, J.: A function-first approach to identifying formulaic language in academic writing. Engl. Specif. Purp. 30, 58–72 (2011)

Fiedler, S.: Phraseological borrowing from English into German: cultural and pragmatic implications. J. Pragmat. **113**, 89–102 (2017)

Grabowski, L.: Keywords and lexical bundles within English pharmaceutical discourse: a corpus-driven description. Engl. Specif. Purp. **38**, 23–33 (2015)

Granger, S., Paquot, M.: Disentangling the phraseological web. In: Granger, S., Meunier, F. (eds.) Phraseology: An Interdisciplinary Perspective, pp. 27–49. John Benjamins, Amsterdam (2008)

Hu, G., Cao, F.: Hedges and boosting in abstracts of applied linguistics articles: a comparative study of English and Chinese medium journals. J. Pragmat. **43**, 2795–2809 (2011)

Hunston, S.: Corpora in Applied Linguistics. Cambridge University Press, Cambridge (2002)

Hunston, S., Francis, G.: Pattern Grammar: A Corpus-Driven Approach to the Lexical Grammar of English, vol. 4. John Benjamins, Amsterdam (2000)

Hyland, K.: Metadiscourse: Exploring Interaction in Writing. Continuum, London (2005)

Hyland, K.: Hedging in academic writing and EAP textbooks. Engl. Specif. Purp. **13**, 239–256 (1994)

Hyland, K.: Hedging in Scientific Research Articles. John Benjamins, Amsterdam/Philadelphia (1998)

John, P., Brooks, B., Schriever, U.: Profiling maritime communication by non-native speakers: A quantitative comparison between the baseline and standard marine communication phraseology. Engl. Specif. Purp. **47**, 1–14 (2017)

Kim, S., Yeates, R.: On the phraseology of the linking adverbial besides. J. Engl. Acad. Purp. (2019, in press). https://doi.org/10.1016/j.jeap.2019.05.006

Le, T.N.P.. Harrington, M.: Phraseology used to comment on results in the discussion section of applied linguistics quantitative research articles. Engl. Specif. Purp. **39**, 45–61 (2015)

Lyons, J.: Introduction to Theoretical Linguistics. Cambridge University Press, Cambridge (1968)

Mur-Dueñas, P.: An intercultural analysis of metadiscourse features in research articles written in English and in Spanish. J. Pragmat. **43**, 3068–3079 (2011)

Myers, G.: The pragmatics of politeness in scientific articles. Appl. Linguist. **10**(1), 1–35 (1989)

Saber, A.: Phraseological patterns in a large corpus of biomedical articles. In: Boulton, A., Carter-Thomas, S., Rowley-Jolivet, E. (eds.) Corpus-Informed Research and Learning in ESP: Issues and Applications, pp. 45–81. John Benjamins, Amsterdam (2012)

Salager-Meyer, F.: Hedges and textual communicative function in medical English written discourse. Engl. Specif. Purp. **13**(2), 149–170 (1994)

Scott, M., Tribble, C.: Textual Patterns: Key Words and Corpus Analysis in Language Education, vol. 22. John Benjamins, Amsterdam (2006)

Skelton, J.: The care and maintenance of hedges. ELT J. **41**, 37–43 (1988)

Thompson, G.: Interaction in academic writing: learning to argue with the reader. Appl. Linguist. **22**(1), 58–78 (2001)

Yang, Y.: Exploring linguistic and cultural variations in the use of hedges in English and Chinese scientific discourse. J. Pragmat. **50**, 23–36 (2013)

Vincent, B.: Investigating academic phraseology through combinations of very frequent words: a methodological exploration. J. Engl. Acad. Purp. **12**, 44–56 (2013)

"Sword" Metaphors in Nikita Khrushchev's Political Rhetoric

Elena V. Carter(✉)

Saint Petersburg Mining University, Saint Petersburg 199106, Russia
elena.carter@hotmail.com

Abstract. There is no doubt that paremias are not only ubiquitous but also all-inclusive in their comments on the multifaceted aspects of the human condition. The proverbial wisdom of the world is well aware of the interrelationships of war and peace over the countries, and paremias have long been employed during the times of tension. "Sword" metaphors from the worldwide scene of proverbs have found repetitive use in the verbal arguments against aggression and warfare. The paper deals with the repertoire of proverbial texts with the symbolic component "sword" utilized in Nikita Khrushchev's public speeches and writings (in Russian as well as in their English translations) made during the Cold War period between the United States of America and the Soviet Union. The system of metaphorical conceptions for *sword* revealed within selected contexts is scrutinized. The comparative analysis is aimed at identifying common and specific features in the constituent element of the Russian and English phraseological units.

Keywords: Comparative research · Nikita khrushchev · "Sword" metaphors

1 Introduction

Tensions, attitudes, and symbols are embedded in the language. A lot of emphasis is placed upon finding differences among peoples, although a certain uniformity of human nature seems to spell itself out in proverbs.

Naturally, every language has numerous paremias[1] that deal with the obvious relationship between war and peace [26: 94–95], as well as between the means of warfare and the ways of creating peaceful coexistence. One of the military arms is a sword, an "ancient weapon consisting of a handle and a metal blade with a sharp point and one or two cutting edges" [40: 1058]. It gained its symbolic meaning in antiquity and it occurred in the works of classical authors. The sword symbolizes strength, power, dignity, leadership, light, courage, and vigilance. These meanings of the sword as a symbol of culture have appeared over time, receiving new semantic shades, though

---

[1] A *paremia* is a Greek term for a *proverb* that is "a short, generally known sentence of the folk which contains wisdom, truth, morals, and traditional views in a metaphorical, fixed and memorizable form and which is handed down from generation to generation" [27: 21]. A proverbial expression is a conventional saying related to a paremia. The difference is that proverbs are complete thoughts that can stand by themselves, while proverbial phrases are "allegoric sayings expressing an incomplete statement" [35: 7], and they must be integrated into a sentence.

© Springer Nature Switzerland AG 2019
G. Corpas Pastor and R. Mitkov (Eds.): Europhras 2019, LNAI 11755, pp. 73–85, 2019.
https://doi.org/10.1007/978-3-030-30135-4_6

the phraseology seems to reflect its general symbolic meaning: the universality of the image of the sword as an object of justice and punishment for wrong deeds. The fact that quite a number of proverbial texts with the symbolic component "sword" were loan translated into various European languages apparently allows to recognize the international character of this phraseological phenomenon [4].

2 Previous Research

Proverbs in actual use are verbal strategies for dealing with social situations. To understand the meaning of proverbial texts in actual speech acts, they must be viewed as part of the entire communicative performance and the entire cultural background, against which a speech-event has to be set [41: 27]. This is true for proverbs used not only in oral speech, but also in their frequent employment in literary works. Moreover, only the analysis of the application and function of paremias within particular contexts can determine their specific meanings. In fact, proverbs in collections are almost dead, but they become significant and alive once they are employed as a strategic statement that carries the weight of traditional wisdom. Paremias thus exhibit different semantic possibilities due to their various functions and situations [2: 597].

One of the most powerful and the most frequently-used expressive means for creating images is the metaphor. The metaphor is a complicated psychological phenomenon for human perception. However, the image based on metaphorical comprehension is close to people. It brings them associations that are directly connected with their life and culture. People have a metaphorical vision of the world around them. They are surrounded by metaphors, sometimes even not realizing it.

The metaphorical level is the symbolism, expressing the nature of the relationship between interlocutors, their ontological status, as well as their desires, thoughts, and feelings. The metaphorical language represented in folk speech makes people's interaction more open. The metaphor is directly related to the image, and it is important for the pragmatic effect of communication. It should be noted that the image in the phraseological unit is always reduced. Though it cannot be called a "mirror" image of the situation, it certainly highlights a particular specific feature of it due to the peculiarity of human perception to capitalize on the essence, i.e. the main meaning of the language unit stored in the human's mental lexicon [1]. In order to recognize a pragmatic code and an adequate perception of a metaphor, speakers and their communicative partners need to have common cultural background knowledge [38: 18].

In recent research, much attention is being given to comparative studies conducted both in sister languages as well as in unrelated languages.[2] Some linguists have attempted to address the issue of universal and specific features based on the main

---

[2] See, for instance, Bezkorovainaya [4] and Isaeva [11].

concept spheres in phraseology. As it turned out, the frontal interlingual comparison makes it possible to weed out subjective "nationalized" interpretations of some proverbial texts. However, there is still a great deal of debate over it.

It appears that it is exactly the intangible nature of proverbial texts that leads to their continued and effective use in all modes of communication. And it is definitely true in relation to political discourse that can be defined as "the totality of all speech acts used in political discussions, as well as the rules of public policy consecrated by tradition and tested by experience" [3: 6].

One of the features that determines politicians' manner in which they make speeches and create a certain emotional background is the aphoristic character (i.e. idioms, proverbs, metaphors, etc.) which is notable for the novelty and originality of thought. Internationally acknowledged paremiologist Wolfgang Mieder questioned the assumption that paremias are more applicable for common parlance of everyday communication than for any formal setting. In a number of celebrated books and enlightening articles, the scholar provided much evidence that some well-known erudite public figures were masterful employers of proverbs in their political speeches as well as in their writings.[3] There is some scholarship on the use of proverbs by such Soviet/Russian leaders as Vladimir Lenin, Joseph Stalin, Nikita Khrushchev, and Mikhail Gorbachev.[4]

While Nikita Khrushchev's inclination towards the employment of proverbs and proverbial expressions has been noticed and paid some attention to,[5] there is merely a very short study that refers to his use of a variety of proverbial phrases illustrated by textual examples,[6] and the metaphorical matters with a special focus on the concept "sword" have not been scrutinized yet. Thus, the paper provides a comparative cross-linguistic analysis of the contextualized references of the phraseological group with the symbolic component "sword" which are taken from Nikita Khrushchev's public speeches made during his two visits to America in 1959–1960 as well as from his Russian memoirs.

---

[3] For the use of proverbs in the political rhetoric of American presidents, see Mieder [25–27].

[4] For the discussion of the employment of proverbial texts by Soviet/Russian leaders, see Wein [43]; Zhigulyov [45]; Morozova [34]; Meščerskij [24]; Mokienko [31]; McKenna [19]; Reznikov [37].

[5] For example, in his article in *The New York Times* (September 13, 1959), Horace Reynolds wrote that "'One cannot live without proverbs' is one of several Russian sayings that praise the proverb. As all the world knows, Premier Nikita S. Khrushchev is a devoted subscriber to this adage" [36: 28]. This is in line with Kevin McKenna's view that this Soviet leader "showed a thorough appreciation for the usage and rhetorical effect of Russian proverbs and proverbial expressions" [19: 218]. See also Burlatsky [5]; Dautova [10]; Taubman [39].

[6] See Carter [6–9].

3 Corpus and Methodology

In the present research, metaphors for *sword* were examined in the parallel corpus, i.e. "a corpus that contains source texts and their translations" [18: 20], which includes 28 Russian speeches by Soviet leader Nikita Khrushchev[7] delivered in different settings in the USA[8] and his memoirs along with their translations in the English language.[9] According to McEnery and Xiao [18: 18], such corpora can give new insights into the languages compared – insights that are not likely to be noticed in studies of mono-lingual corpora; they can be used for a range of comparative purposes and can increase our knowledge of language-specific, typological and cultural differences, as well as universal features.

After compiling a parallel corpus, the original texts and their translations were searched for the target phraseological units with the symbolic component "sword." Then the subcorpus of text fragments with the phraseological forming symbol was compiled, and each example was analyzed in terms of conceptual metaphors and their possible linguistic equivalents.

4 Analysis

In Nikita Khrushchev's Russian speeches made in America and in his memoirs, the lexeme "sword" in all its grammatical and derived formed appears 9 times, and all these instances have been translated into English.

The Bible was one of Nikita Khrushchev's favorite repositories of quotable material [9]. It is well-known that there are quite general statements based on Biblical laws of life, but the Soviet leader usually connected these bits of wisdom more directly with the concerns and issues of his time.

---

[7] Khrushchev, Nikita Sergeevich (1894–1971), Soviet Premier, 1958–64. As a loyal Stalinist during the great purges of the 1930s he managed the Communist Party in the Ukraine. During World War II he was a political adviser in the army, defending Stalingrad. When Josef Stalin died in March 1953, Khrushchev became a member of the Soviet Union's 'collective leadership,' taking over as first secretary of the Central Committee. His famous 'secret speech' of 1956, attacking Stalin, inaugurated the policy of the 'de-Stalinization,' and by 1958 Khrushchev had made himself both premier and party head. During his rule Khrushchev traveled extensively, addressing the UN General Assembly in New York in 1959 on disarmament, and meeting with President Kennedy in Vienna in 1961. His main setback in foreign policy came in 1962, when the United States forced him to withdraw Soviet missiles secretly installed in Cuba. This crisis, his rift with the People's Republic of China, and repeated crop failures led to his removal from power [40: 508].

[8] See Khrushchev [14, 15]; as well as [12, 13].

[9] The first complete four-volume Russian edition of N.S. Khrushchev's memoirs ("Vremia. Liudi. Vlast"; lit. "Time. People. Power") was produced by the Moscow News Publishing Company in 1999. It is based on the transcripts of all the tape recordings dictated by N.S. Khrushchev from 1966 to 1971 and translated into English ([21–23]). The analyzed passages are from the second complete two-volume Russian edition appeared in 2016 ([16, 17]). It includes the full text of memoirs as well as the set of unique photographs from the family archive and brief biographies of numerous participants of the events mentioned in the narration.

The Bible offers a truly magnificent proverbial metaphor to illustrate what could be done to overcome the seemingly eternal cycle of wars. The proverbial expression "to beat swords into plowshares" is a most appropriate image for world peace, where all military arms can be transformed into useful tools to feed and sustain the world's population. In his speech at the luncheon in Pittsburgh on September 24, 1959, Nikita Khrushchev employed the biblical proverbial text "to beat swords into plowshares" [44: 419]/ "перековать мечи на орала" [33: 400] twice: while describing one of the most famous Russian statues made by the sculptor Yevgeny Vuchetich,[10] and later, making a point that nonviolence was the only way to stop wars and all the ills of violent mistreatments of others in the future. Undoubtedly, he made these references to emphasize the necessity for all countries to renounce the Cold War and to place their relations on a peaceful basis:

There is a distinguished sculptor in our country, Yevgeny Vuchetich. He has made a moving statue, called "Let's Beat Swords into Plowshares." It is a fine piece of work that deservedly attracts everyone's attention. It represents the figure of a blacksmith hammering a plowshare out of a sword. If any of you visited our exhibition in New York, you must have seen that gifted work of art. The sculptor has succeeded in embodying in bronze what millions upon millions of people are thinking and dreaming of today [12: 169].

В нашей стране есть известный скульптор Евгений Вучетич. Он создал волнующую скульптуру "Перекуем мечи на орала". Очень хорошая скульптура, заслуженно привлекающая внимание каждого человека. Она представляет собой фигуру кузнеца, превращающего меч в плуг. Если кто-либо из вас был на нашей выставке в Нью-Йорке, он мог видеть это талантливое произведение. Скульптор удачно воплотил в бронзе то, о чем думают и мечтают сейчас миллионы и миллионы людей [14: 249].

The surest way of avoiding such unenviable prospects is to destroy the means of waging war, that is, "to beat swords into plowshares." We propose that cold war be outlawed everywhere and for all time [12: 169].

Самый верный путь избежать подобной незавидной перспективы – уничтожить средства ведения войны, именно – "перековать мечи на орала". Мы предлагаем объявить вне закона "холодную войну" – повсюду и навсегда [14: 250].

In his speech at the session of the UN General Assembly on September 18, 1959, relying on the proverbial wisdom of Jesus, Nikita Khrushchev found a perfect metaphor to refer to the ruthless and merciless wars of the Middle Ages. The Soviet leader cited a slightly varied proverbial phrase from the New Testament "wipe with fire and sword"/"искоренять огнем и мечом" (the standard form is "to put to fire and sword" [30: 140]/"предать огню и мечу" [32: 340])[11] as a metaphorical sign of violence. Obviously, he made this comparison to strengthen the point that instead of undertaking

---

[10] For the use of this proverbial expression as "the metaphorical motto for peace of the United Nations," see Wolfgang Mieder's intriguing article "'Beating Swords into Plowshares': Proverbial Wisdom on War and Peace" [26].

[11] The proverbial phrase *Ferro ignique vastare* (Latin) dates back to classical antiquity. It was loan translated into various European languages: Russian (*предать огню и мечу*); English (*to put to fire and sword*); German (*Mit Feuer und Schwert verwüsten*); Italian (*Mettre a ferro e fuoco*); Spanish (*Poner a hierro y fuego*); and French (*Mettre à feu et à sano*) [30: 140].

new destructive crusades, all countries should find a common language on the question of peaceful coexistence:

In international affairs success in solving controversial problems is possible provided the states concentrate on what brings states closer together rather than on what divides the present-day world. No social or political dissimilarities, no differences in ideology or religious beliefs must prevent the member-states of the United Nations from reaching agreement on the main thing: that the principles of peaceful coexistence and friendly cooperation be sacredly and unswervingly observed by all states. If, on the other hand, differences and social dissimilarities are pushed to the fore, it is bound to doom to failure all our efforts to preserve peace. In the twentieth century one cannot undertake crusades to wipe out unbelievers with fire and sword, as the fanatics of the Middle Ages did, without running the risk of confronting humanity with the greatest calamity in its history [12: 69].

В международных делах, в решении спорных проблем успех возможен, если государства будут ориентироваться не на то, что разделяет современный мир, а на то, что сближает государства. Никакие социальные и политические различия, никакие расхождения в идеологии и религиозных убеждениях не должны мешать государствам – членам ООН договориться о главном – о том, чтобы принципы мирного сосуществования и дружественного сотрудничества свято и неукоснительно соблюдались всеми государствами. Если же выдвигать на первый план разногласия и социальные различия, то это наверняка обречет на неудачу все наши усилия по сохранению мира. В двадцатом веке нельзя, подобно фанатикам средневековья, предпринимать походы для искоренения огнем и мечом иноверцев, не рискуя поставить человечество перед величайшей в его истории катастрофой [14: 144–145].

Again and again the Soviet leader draws on the proverbs of the Bible to lend authority and traditional wisdom to his arguments. The Biblical adage "He who lives by the sword shall perish by the sword"[12] is the ultimate warning against anybody's

---

[12] On the use of the Biblical proverbial texts "He who lives by sword shall perish by the sword" and "to beat swords into plowshares" by such politicians as Frederic Douglas, Martin Luther King, Dwight D. Eisenhower, Winston Churchill, Harry S. Truman, see Mieder [25]; [27] as well as Mieder and Bryan [28]; [29].

Of special interest is Kevin McKenna's seminal article "Proverbs in Sergei Eisenstein's *Aleksandr Nevsky*" [20]. The author explores the use of the paremias in Sergei Eisenstein's (1898–1948) film masterpiece, "Aleksandr Nevsky," produced by Mosfilm in 1938, and, notably, the Biblical proverb "He who lives by sword shall perish by the sword": "Perhaps anticipating a future admonition to the rapidly-expanding German armed forces, Eisenstein directs his hero – Prince to stand before his people and utter a grim and prophetic warning to all those who would think to invade Russia that 'Если кто с мечом к нам войдет, от меча и погибнет'/ 'He who comes to us with a sword in hand, will perish by that sword.' Eisenstein clearly succeeds in enhancing the gravity of the ominous warning through the medium of the famous Biblical proverb, taken from the Book of Revelations: 'He that leadeth into captivity shall go into captivity: he that killeth with the sword must be killed by the sword.' Judging from the intent facial expression of Nevsky as he utters his famous injunction, the Russian director creatively transforms the final sentence of verse ten from peaceful note, 'Here is the patience and the faith of the saints,' to a grave and determined warning slowly and intently pronounced for the benefit of a twentieth-century German audience. The grave admonition provides an effective close to Eisenstein's patriotic film about the threat of medieval Teutonic knights, and leaves no room for misunderstanding on the part of future German invaders in the twentieth century, as well" [20: 94].

malicious plans to unleash a new war on the sovereign territory of any country.[13] In his book of memoirs, Nikita Khrushchev employed this proverbial text as a moral metaphor brought to life by the victory of the Soviet people in the Great Patriotic War:

And so we came to the culmination of a great epic – the war of the peoples of the USSR against Hitler's invasion. Joy at the destruction of our enemy was combined with a tremendous feeling of moral satisfaction at our victory. A passage from the Holy Scriptures came to me, one that was repeated by Aleksandr Nevsky: "All they that come against us with the sword shall perish with the sword." That saying was on everybody's lips, and at last it had come true in the form of our victory. When I heard that Germany had surrendered, the joy I felt was unbelievable [21: 633].

Когда завершилась великая эпопея войны народов СССР против гитлеровского нашествия, смешались воедино радость от уничтожения врага и высокое чувство морального удовлетворения от нашей победы. Фраза из Священного писания, когда-то повторенная Александром Невским: "Кто с мечом к нам придет, от меча и погибнет" – в то время была у всех на устах и наконец-то воплотилась в жизнь в результате нашей победы. Когда я узнал, что Германия капитулировала, радость моя была невероятной [16: 457].

The phraseological unit "the sword of Damocles" comes to be used as a symbol of impending danger [42: 68]. According to Greek mythology, Damocles, a sycophant of Dionysius of Syracuse, declared that the latter was the happiest man on the earth. He was taught the insecurity of happiness by being made to sit through a banquet with a sword suspended over his head by a single hair. Due to the fact that this proverbial phrase goes back to antiquity, it exists in translation in other languages as well.[14] In his memoirs, Nikita Khrushchev used this phrase twice as a clear metaphor for the horrors of Stalin's persecutions when the whole nation was under suspicion and the threat of being arrested and killed:

Here's how the Uspensky case started. Stalin telephone me one day and told me that there was evidence on the basis of which it was necessary to arrest Uspensky. [Because of the poor phone connection] it was hard to hear, and it sounded as though he had said not Uspensky, but Usenko. Usenko was the first secretary of the Central Committee of the Ukrainian Young Communist League. There was testimony against him, and the Damocles sword of arrest was already hanging over his head [21: 168].

Дело Успенского началось так. Однажды мне звонит по телефону Сталин и говорит, что имеются данные, согласно которым надо арестовать Успенского. Слышно было плохо, мне послышалось не Успенского, а Усенко. Усенко был первым секретарем ЦК ЛКСМУ, на него имелись показания, и над ним уже висел дамоклов меч ареста [16: 141].

---

[13] There are equivalents in various languages: Latin (*Qui gladio ferit, gladio perit*); Russian (*Взявши меч, от меча и погибнет*); English (*He that strikes with the sword by the sword shall perish*); German (*Wer das Schwert nimmt, der soll durchs schwert umkommen*); Italian (*Chi di spade ferisce, di spade prisce*); and Spanish (*Todos los que tomen espada, a espada pereceran*) [30: 312].

[14] There are equivalents in Latin (*Periculum imminens*); Russian (*Дамоклов меч*); English (*the sword of Damocles*); German (*Damoklesschwert*); Italian (*La spade di Damocle*); Spanish (*La espada de Damocles*); and French (*L'épée de Damoclès*) [30: 313].

Malinovsky told me about other events in his life. He said: "The fact that I had been in the Russian expeditionary corps in France was like a cloud that hung over my head." I can't remember now exactly what he told me, but I know from history that the expeditionary corps had great difficulty returning to Russia. It seems it was sent back from France in such a way that the soldiers ended up on the territory occupied by the Whites. Malinovsky had to travel a long road before he found himself with the Red army. The episode in question is important for an understanding of the atmosphere of the Stalin era. There always hung over Malinovsky, like the sword of Damocles, the fact that he had been in the expeditionary corps, in France on the territory held by the Whites before he joined the Red Army [21: 489].

Малиновский рассказывал мне и о других событиях своей биографии. "Очень, – говорит, – тяготило надо мной, что я находился в составе экспедиционного корпуса". Сейчас я не могу точно припомнить, что он мне рассказывал, но знаю из истории, то этот корпус с большими трудностями возвращался в Россию. Кажется, его послали оттуда так, чтобы его солдаты попали на территорию, которую занимали белые. Малиновский прошел длинный путь, прежде чем очутился в Красной Армии. Данный эпизод важен для понимания духа сталинского времени. Над Малиновским висело как дамоклов меч обвинение, что он был в составе экспедиционного корпуса во Франции и на территории, занятой белыми, до того, как вступил в Красную Армию [16: 358].

The lexeme "sword" got its negative connotation in the 20th century. The sovietism "the sword of the party" as a designation of the agencies of state security (i.e. the instrument of defense and punishment, and the use of force) appeared in the era of Stalinism. Actually, it is a metaphorical phrase of the euphemistic character [4]. While reflecting on the role played by NKVD (the People's Commissariat for Internal Affairs), Nikita Khrushchev applied the metaphorical name "the sword of the revolution" to characterize one of NKVD's original functions, that is, the struggle with the enemies of the revolution. However, everything seems to indicate that, in fact, the author wanted to reveal one "new" ominous function of this "sword" and underscore its responsibility for the mass extrajudicial executions of untold numbers of Soviet citizens:

How many collective farm chairmen, specialists in animal husbandry, agronomists, livestock experts, and scientists in general might have laid down their lives as "Polish-German agents"! How many of them might have perished! Later I remembered the Kharkov professor and the director of the institute who had been shot, and thought: "How could this be? What's going on? It's clear to everyone now that these people were not guilty, and yet they confessed." Apparently I found some sort of explanation for this at the time; I don't recall what it was. I could not then have supposed that it was a hostile act on the part of the agencies of the NKVD; such a thought I could not have admitted. Was it negligence? Yes, it might have been negligence. The NKVD "organs" were considered infallible; they were called the sword of the revolution, which was directed against our enemies [21: 168].

Сколько председателей колхозов, животноводов, агрономов, зоотехников, ученых сложили головы как "польско-немецкие агенты", сколько их погибло! Я вспоминал потом о харьковском профессоре, о директоре института, которые тоже были расстреляны, и думал: "Как же так? Как же это могло быть?

Люди, теперь всем ясно, не виноваты, а сознались?" Видимо, я тогда нашел этому какое-то объяснение, не помню, какое. Я не мог тогда и предположить, что это был вражеский акт со стороны органов НКВД, я и мысли такой не допускал. Небрежность? Да, небрежность могла быть. Органы эти считались безупречными, назывались революционным мечом, направленным против врагов [16: 140].

Preoccupied with the proverbial wisdom, Nikita Khrushchev employed a number of other "sword"- phrases. Thus, remembering the events of 1957 (the planned invasion of Syria by the military coalition of the USA, Iraq, Iran, and Turkey), the Soviet leader used the expression "to raise the sword"/"занести меч" to unveil the destructive policy of the capitalist countries:

The Soviet leadership celebrated because we had succeeded in staying the hand of the imperialists without firing a shot. They had raised their sword over the Syrian republic, but bloodshed had been prevented [23: 869].

Советское руководство торжествовало в связи с тем, что удалось без выстрела остановить руку империалистов, которая занесла меч над Сирийской республикой, и предотвратить кровопролитие [17: 384].

These are the last two examples from Nikita Khrushchev's arsenal of "sword" metaphors. In his speech at the closed session of the 20th Party Congress on February 25, 1956, the Soviet leader denounced Joseph Stalin, describing the damages done by his Personality Cult and the repressions known as the Great Purge that killed millions and traumatized many people in the Soviet Union. Later, in his memoirs, Nikita Khrushchev reflected on the causes and the effects of Stalin's dictatorship. It is interesting to note that while in the former passage, the author employed the proverbial phrase "to turn the sword"/"направить меч" to blame Stalin for his atrocities, in the latter text, he used it to do justice to the dictator's ability to be a good leader:

Enemies of the people! Wreckers! He kept frightening and intimidating people who believed in him unconditionally, believed he was doing everything for the good of the party and the people. Of course, it was hard to sort it all out. After all enemies of the revolution, enemies of the working people, wreckers, and saboteurs, had actually existed earlier. But it was not against those people that he turned the sword, thereby weakening the country, the party and the army, giving the enemies a chance to do enormous harm to the Soviet Union [22: 157].

Враги народа! Вредители! Он запугал и запутал людей, которые беспредельно верили ему, верили, что он делает все на благо партии и народа. Конечно, трудно было разобраться. Ведь раньше действительно существовали и враги революции и враги трудового народа, и вредители. Но это были не те люди, против которых он направил меч и тем самым ослабил страну, партию и армию, дав возможность врагу нанести огромный урон Советскому Союзу [16: 609].

I was then confronted with the question: How could all this have happened? Everyone knew about Stalin's important role as an individual, his revolutionary qualities, his services to the country, and the other qualities for which he was celebrated in the party. He had full justification for aspiring to a special position, because he really did stand out from those around him, both by his ability to organize and by his intelligence. He stood head and shoulders above the others. And even today, despite my irreconcilable feelings towards the methods of operation and his abuse of power, I will acknowledge this. However, if he were still alive today, for example, and a vote were held on the question of this responsibility for what was done, I would take the position that he should be put on the trial. Nevertheless, we should grant him his due. He was not just a man who came to us with a sword and won over hearts and minds by force. No, he showed his superiority in life itself, his ability to lead the country, his ability to subordinate others to himself, to promote people, and other qualities necessary for a leader on the grand scale [22: 204].

Тогда передо мной встал вопрос: как это могло произойти? Все знали о роли Сталина, его личности, его революционности, его заслугах перед страной и качествах, которые были отмечены партией. Он имел полное право претендовать на особую роль, потому что действительно выделялся из своего круга и умением организовать дело, и умом. Он действительно стоял выше других. И даже сейчас, несмотря на мою непримиримость, относительно его методов действий и его злоупотреблений, я признаю это. Однако если бы сейчас, например, он был еще жив, и состоялось бы голосование по вопросу о его ответственности за содеянное, я занял бы ту позицию, что его надо судить. Но следует и отдать ему должное. Этот человек не просто пришел к нам с мечом и завоевал наши умы и тела. Нет, он проявил в жизни свое превосходство, умение руководить страной, умение подчинять себе людей, выдвигать их и прочие качества, необходимые руководителю крупного масштаба [16: 640–641].

5   Conclusions

In light of the research on the phraseological units with the symbolic component "sword" employed in Nikita Khrushchev's political rhetoric, it seems safe to conclude that this core lexeme reveals a commonality of associations. Our analysis of Biblical phraseologisms shows the international character of the Biblical phraseology in general. The common concept base proves the universality of the symbol "sword" as the weapon of destruction and the object punishing for wrong-doings both in Russian and in English. The evidence indicates the international character of the antique phraseology as well. This is convincingly illustrated by a number of equivalents of the proverbial expressions with the "sword" component as the symbol of danger and cruelty. Judging by the findings, such proverbial texts contain wisdom that has been recognized in the world for many centuries and that still holds true today. However, a case should be made in relation to the Soviet times when the sword specifically symbolized a punitive instrument, the "state weapon of persecution." Thereby, such observations strongly suggest that, by studying linguistic cultural equivalency in phraseology, we acquire rich material for understanding culture, mentality, and language structure of different nations from the point of view of the real world coding.

References

1. Aitchison, J.: Words in the Mind: An Introduction to the Mental Lexicon. Blackwell, London (2003)
2. Folklore, American: An Encyclopedia. Garland, New York (1996)
3. Baranov, A.N., Kazakevich, E.G.: Parlamentskiye debaty: traditsii i novatsii [Parliamentary Debates: Traditions and Innovations]. Znaniye, Moskva (1991)
4. Bezkorovaynaya, G., Lomakina, O., Makarova, A.: Obshchee i natsyonalno-spetsyficheskoye (na materiale frazeologizmov s komponentom-simvolom mech/sword/le glaive v russkom, angliiskom i frantsuzskom yazykhah) [Linguistic and Cultural Potential of Phraseology: Common and Nationally Specific Features (Based on the Phraseologisms with the Symbolic Component sword/le glaive in Russian, English and French]. In: Filologicheskiye nauki. Lingvistika, vol. 4(50) (2017). https://cyberleninka.ru/article/n/lingvokulturol ogicheskiy-potentsial-frazeosimvola-obschee-i-natsionalno-spetsificheskoe-na-materiale-fraz eologizmov-s-komponentom. Accessed 25 Mar 2019
5. Burlatsky, F.M.: Khrushchev i jego sovetniki – krasnyje, chjornyje, belyje. [Khrushchev and His Advisers – Red, Black, White]. Sobranije, Moskva (2008)
6. Carter, E.V.: "With an Open Heart": Somatic Idioms in Nikita Khrushchev's Political Discourse in America. In: Szerszunowicz, J., Nowowiejski, B. (eds.) Linguo-Cultural Research on Phraseology, pp. 347–360. University of Bialystok Publishing House, Bialystok (2015)
7. Carter, E.V.: He who lives in a glass house should not throw stones: Nikita Khrushchev's proverbial speeches at the United Nations. In: Mieder, W. (ed.) Proverbium: Yearbook of International Proverb Scholarship, pp. 63–82. The University of Vermont, Burlington, Vermont (2015)
8. Carter, E.V.: Melting the ice of the cold war: Nikita Khrushchev's proverbial Rhetoric in America. In: Soares, R.J.B., Lauhakangas, Q. (eds.) Proceedings of the 8th Interdisciplinary Colloquium on Proverbs, 2–9 November 2014, Tavira, Portugal, pp. 184–198. Tipografia Tavirense, Tavira (2015)
9. Carter, E.V.: "God knows": Nikita Khrushchev's use of biblical proverbs in America. In: Soares, R.J.B., Lauhakangas, Q. (eds.) Proceedings of the 9th Interdisciplinary Colloquium on Proverbs, 1–8 November 2015, Tavira, Portugal, pp. 145–156. Tipografia Tavirense, Tavira (2016)
10. Dautova, R.V.: N. S. Khrushchev i zarubezhnaya zhurnalistika [N. S. Khrushchev and Foreign Journalism]. Vestnik Udmurckogo Universiteta. Istoriya i filologiya 1, 116–123 (2011)
11. Isaeva, E. M.: Obshchee i spetsyficheskoye v avarskikh, russkikh i angliiskikh poslovitsakh o vsesilnoy lyubvi: lingvokulturologicheskii aspekt [Common and Nationally Specific Features in Avar, Russian and English Proverbs about Omnipotent Love: Lingual and Cultural Aspects]. In: Philology and Culture, vol. 3(49) (2017). https://cyberleninka.ru/article/n/ obschee-i-spetsificheskoe-v-avarskih-russkih-i-angliyskih-poslovitsah-o-vsesilnosti-lyubvi-lingvokulturologicheskiy-aspekt. Accessed 30 Apr 2019
12. Khrushchev in America. Crosscurrents Press, New York (1960)
13. Khrushchev in New York. Crosscurrents Press, New York (1960)
14. Khrushchev, N.S.: Mir bez oruzhiya – mir bez voiny [World without Weapon – World without War]. Gosudarstvennoye Izdatel'stvo Politicheskoy Literatury, Moskva (1960)
15. Khrushchev, N.S.: O vneshnei politike Sovetckogo Soyuza. 1960 god. [About Public Affairs of the Soviet Union. 1960]. Gospolitizdat, Moskva (1961)

16. Khrushchev, N.S.: Vospominaniya. Vremya. Lyudi. Vlast. [Reminiscences. Time. People. Power]. V 2 kn. Kn. 1. Veche, Moskva (2016)
17. Khrushchev, N.S.: Vospominaniya. Vremya. Lyudi. Vlast. [Reminiscences. Time. People. Power]. V 2 kn. Kn. 2. Veche, Moskva (2016)
18. McEnery, A., Xiao, R.: Parallel and comparable corpora: what is happening? In: Rogers, M., Anderman, G. (eds.) Incorporating Corpora: The Linguist and the Translator. Multilingual Matters, Clevedon (2007)
19. McKenna, K.J.: Propaganda and the Proverb: "Big Fish Eat Little Fish" in Pravda political cartoons. In: Mieder, W. (ed.) Proverbium: Yearbook of International Proverb Scholarship, pp. 217–242. The University of Vermont, Burlington (2000)
20. McKenna, K.: Proverbs in Sergei Eisenstein's *Aleksandr Nevsky*. In: Russkie Poslovitsy: Russian Proverbs in Literature, Politics, and Pedagogy, pp. 84–99. Peter Lang, New York (2013)
21. Memoirs of Nikita Khrushchev. Volume 1. Commissar [1918–1945]. The Pennsylvania State University Press, Province, Rhode Island (2004)
22. Memoirs of Nikita Khrushchev. Volume 2. Reformer [1945– 964]. The Pennsylvania State University Press, Province, Rhode Island (2006)
23. Memoirs of Nikita Khrushchev. Volume 3. Statesman [1953–1964]. The Pennsylvania State University Press, Province, Rhode Island (2007)
24. Meščerskij, N.A.: Traditionell-buchsprachliche Ausdrücke in der heutigen russischen Literatursprache (anhand der Werke V. I. Lenins). In: Jaksche, H., Sialm, A., Burger, H. (eds.) Reader zur sowjetischen Phraseologie, pp. 131–143. Walter de Gruyter, New York (1981)
25. Mieder, W.: Proverbs are the Best Policy. Folk Wisdom and American Politics. Utah State University Press, Logan (2005)
26. Mieder, W.: "Beating Swords into Plowshares": proverbial wisdom on war and peace. In: Soares, R.J.B., Lauhakangas, Q. (eds.) Proceedings of the 5th Interdisciplinary Colloquium on Proverbs, 6–13 November 2011, Tavira, Portugal, pp. 92–120. Tipografia Tavirense, Tavira (2012)
27. Mieder, W.: Behold the Proverbs of a People: Proverbial Wisdom in Culture, Literature, and Politics. University Press of Mississippi, Jackson (2014)
28. Mieder, W., Bryan, B.G.: The Proverbial Wisdom S. Churchill. An Index to Proverbs in the Works of Sir Winston Churchill. Greenwood Press, Westport (1995)
29. Mieder, W., Bryan, B.G.: The Proverbial Harry S. Truman: An Index to Proverbs in the Works of Harry S. Truman. Peter Lang, New York (1997)
30. Mnogoyazychniy slovar' sovremennoi frazeologii [Multilingual Dictionary of Modern Phraseology]. Flinta, Moskva (2012)
31. Mokienko, V.M.: Die russische Geschichte des Amerikanismus "Wir sitzen alle in einem Boot." In: Mieder, W. (ed.) Proverbium: Yearbook of International Proverb Scholarship, pp. 231–245. The University of Vermont, Burlington (1997)
32. Mokienko, V.M., Lilich G.A., Trofimkina, O.I.: Tolkovy slovar' bibleyskikh vyrazheniy i slov [Dictionary of Biblical Expressions and Words]. AST: Astrel', Moskva (2010)
33. Mokienko, V.M., Nikitina, T.G.: Bol'shoy slovar' russkikh pogovorok [Great Dictionary of Russian Proverbial Expressions]. OLMA media grupp, Moskva (2008)
34. Morozova, L.A.: Upotreblenie V. I. Leninym poslovits [V.I Lenin's Use of Proverbs]. Russkaya Rech 2, 10–14 (1979)
35. Pemyakov, G.L.: From Proverb to Folk-Tale: Notes on the General Theory of Cliché. "Nauka" Publishing House, Moscow (1979)

36. Reynolds, H.: A proverb in the hand – is often worth a thousand words: herewith an examination of homely literature (1959). In: Mieder, W., Sobieski, J. (eds.) "Gold Nuggets or Fool's Gold?": Magazine and Newspaper Articles on the (Ir)relevance of Proverbs and Proverbial Phrases, pp. 28–30. The University of Vermont, Burlington, Vermont (2006)

37. Reznikov, A.: "Separating cutlets and flies": political clichés in the Russian language of today. In: Mieder, W. (ed.) Proverbium: Yearbook of International Proverb Scholarship, pp. 315–320. The University of Vermont, Burlington, Vermont (2005)

38. Slepushkina, E.V.: Frazeologiya russkogo i angliiskogo yazykov v zerkale natsyonal'nogo mentaliteta [Phraseology of the Russian and English Languages in the Mirror of National Mentality]. Ph.D. The Pyatigorsk State Linguistic University, Pyatigorsk (2009)

39. Taubman, W.: Khrushchev: The Man and His Era. W.W. Norton & Company, New York (2003)

40. The New Webster's International Encyclopedia: Trident Press International. Naples, Florida (1994)

41. Ullmann, S.: Semantics. An introduction to the science of meaning. In: Readings in Modern English Lexicology, pp. 25–34. Prosveshcheniye, Leningrad (1975)

42. Walshe, I.A., Berkov, V.P.: Russko-angliiskii slovar' krylatykh slov [Russian-English Dictionary of Wing Words]. Russkii yazyk, Moskva (1988)

43. Wein, G.: Die Rolle der Sprichwörter und Redensarten in der Agitation und Propaganda. Sprachpflege 12, 51–52 (1963)

44. Wilkinson, P.R.: Thesaurus of Traditional English Metaphors. George Routledge, London (1993)

45. Zhigulyov, A.M.: Poslovitsy i pogovorki v bol'shevitskikh listovkakh [Proverbs and Proverbial Expressions in Bolshevik leaflets]. Sovetskaya Etnografia 5, 124–131 (1970)

Multiword Units and N-Grams Naming FEAR in the Israel-Corpus

Carolina Flinz[✉]

University of Milan, Milan, Italy
carolina.flinz@unimi.it

Abstract. Emotions play a special role in the Israel-Corpus (a corpus consisting of 274 recordings of narrative autobiographical interviews with emigrants from German-speaking regions of Central Europe created under the direction of Anne Betten between 1989 and 2012). The connection between narrative representation and the expression of one's own and the feelings of others is of central importance: the central questions posed by the interviewers take the interviewees on a journey into the past (Leonardi 2016: 2) and lead them to stories and reports about dramatic and difficult experiences, so that not only emotions of the past are awakened when they are related and remembered, but also new emotions arise in the narrative process itself. The aim of the paper is to analyze emotions (emotion denominations and expressions) using a quantitative-qualitative approach. Corpuslinguistic studies that focus on emotions in the whole Israel-Corpus or in only one of the subcorpora (IS, ISW or ISZ) are still pending even though they would have been advantageous: they can highlight significantly occurring emotive signs and patterns of language use (Bubenhofer 2009) in the underlying discourse. In the following paper I will concentrate only on the emotion FEAR (in German *ANGST*) analyzing the lexemes and the multiword expressions which name and express it in the subcorpus ISW.

Keywords: Emotions · Israel-Corpus · N-Grams

1 Introduction

The Israel-Corpus is a corpus created under the direction of Anne Betten between 1989 and 2012, consisting of 274 recordings of narrative autobiographical interviews with emigrants from German-speaking regions of Central Europe to Palestine in the Thirties. The corpus, which can be retrieved and searched in the DGD[1], has already been researched to investigate various scientific questions: grammatical (syntactic-stylistic)

---

[1] The DGD (*Datenbank für Gesprochenes Deutsch*) is a Database for Spoken German, hosted at the Leibniz-Institut für Deutsche Sprache in Mannheim (https://dgd.ids-mannheim.de/dgd/pragdb.dgd_extern.welcome).

The name 'Israel-Corpus' is not the official name of the corpus, but this term was designated over the course of time.

© Springer Nature Switzerland AG 2019
G. Corpas Pastor and R. Mitkov (Eds.): Europhras 2019, LNAI 11755, pp. 86–98, 2019.
https://doi.org/10.1007/978-3-030-30135-4_7

analyses and sociolinguistic approaches determined the publications in the period 1995–2005 (Betten 1995; Betten and Du-nour 2000, 2004). Subsequently the corpus was examined under various linguistic approaches, including dialogue and narrative analysis (Thüne 2009; Thüne and Leonardi 2011 and the essays in the publication Leonardi et al. 2016).

Emotions play a special role in the Israel-Corpus: the connection between narrative representation and the expression of one's own and the feelings of others is of central importance, since not only past events and the emotions associated with them are awakened during narration and remembering, but also new emotions arise in the narrative process (Leonardi et al. 2016). The aim of the paper is to analyze emotions (emotion denominations and expressions) using a quantitative-qualitative approach. In particular I will investigate the lexicon, in order to see what kind of multiword expressions name and convey the emotion FEAR. Corpus analyses are particularly relevant for these kinds of investigations, as they can highlight significantly occurring emotive signs and patterns of language use (Bubenhofer 2009) and thus focus on stereotypical perceptions, attitudes and evaluations of the underlying discourse. In addition, for the first time the Israel-Corpus has been investigated as a corpus, i.e. as 'a collection of written or spoken utterances in one or more languages in digital form' (Lemnitzer and Zinsmeister 2015: 39). Previous studies have focused on individual interviews or only small groups of interviews, but never the corpus or one of the sub-corpora.

2 Research Overview: Emotions as Research Object in the Israel-Corpus

Emotions are constitutive for human life and experience (Schwarz-Friesel 2013: 1) and determine states of consciousness as well as thought and action processes. Nevertheless, they remained unnoticed for a long time in linguistic and cognitive studies and it is only in recent years that neuroscientists and psychologists have demonstrated with empirical studies (Schwarz-Friesel 2011: 130) their indispensability for understanding human cognition and consciousness. After the so-called 'emotional turn', emotions were able to arise from their 'Cinderella' status and linguistic studies that deal with the question of how linguistic expressions can provide information about the inner emotional states and processes of humans (Schwarz-Friesel 2007: 279) were finally published: they focused especially on lexical and metaphorical expressions, as well as the functional and pragmatical relevance of the social manifestation and interaction forms of emotions in different contexts (among others Fiehler 2002; Drescher 2003). With Schwarz-Friesel (2013) the interaction of cognition and emotion (also from the point of view of theory formation) became for the first time the subject of investigations.

In the Jungle of Emotional Literature (James 1890: 1064) it is noticeable that emotions are described differently depending on the approach (Kleinginna and Kleinginna 1981 have identified more than 92 definitions and 11 different descriptive dimensions). For the present study, the distinction between emotion and feeling will be relevant (1) as well as the distinction between emotion thematization (emotion naming and emotion description) and emotion expression (2):

1. According to Schwarz-Friesel (2013: 144), emotions represent knowledge and evaluation systems that take physical, mental and affective states into account and can have a conscious and unconscious effect on the human organism. Feelings, on the other hand, are specifically experienced emotions that represent consciously felt states. The feeling of fear, which can be experienced consciously and cognitively, is the subjective experience of the emotional state FEAR (*ANGST* in German) which also has unconscious and physical components (Schwarz-Friesel 2011: 131). The present study will focus in particular on lexemes that refer to emotional states and forms of experience (Schwarz-Friesel 2013: 144);
2. "Emotional thematization" is understood to mean the local establishment of an overall shared relevance perspective: 'eine übergreifende gemeinsame Rele- vanzperspektive' (Fiehler 1990: 114), while "emotional expression" is understood to mean all behaviors within the framework of an interaction that are manifested and interpreted in connection with emotions (Fiehler 1990: 100). The present study will focus on the emotional thematization concentrating in particular on the procedures of naming (i.e. the emotion vocabulary) and of describing emotions (i.e. the description of a specific experience, as e.g. with the statement '*es war wirklich ein sehr schwerer Schlag*'[2] (ISW-_E_00009).

The interviews recorded by Anne Betten and her team with German-speaking Jewish emigrants who escaped the Nazi violence are suitable documents for the analysis of emotional thematization: the text type 'autobiographical narrative interview' (Betten et al. 2016: VII) is clearly defined with regard to the topics and, despite the differences, the three sub-corpora (cf. 3.1) can be assigned to a common discourse, even if the interviews were conducted in different years and with different generations of Jewish emigrants (first and second generation[3]). The central questions posed by the interviewers take the interviewees on a journey into the past (Leonardi 2016: 2) and lead them to stories and reports about dramatic and difficult experiences, so that not only emotions of the past are awakened when they are told and remembered, but also new emotions arise in the narrative process itself. Studies investigating emotions in the Israel-Corpus have focused on different language levels: the lexical level (among others Koesters Gensini 2016), grammatical and syntactic characteristics (among others Leonardi 2016), prosodic characteristics (among others Schwitalla 2012; Thüne 2016) as well as the expression of emotions in metaphorical phrases (among others Leonardi 2016, 2019; Thüne and Leonardi 2011). However, corpuslinguistic studies[4] that focus emotions in the whole Israel-Corpus or in only one of the sub-corpora (IS, ISW or ISZ - cf. 3.1), are still pending, even though they would have been advantageous: they can highlight significantly occurring emotive signs and patterns of language use (Buben- hofer 2009), pointing out stereotypical perceptions, attitudes and evaluations in the underlying discourse (Rothenhöfer 2015: 250).

---

[2] In English: it was really a very severe blow.

[3] Among others Betten (1995), Betten and Du-nour (1995, 2000), Betten (2017).

[4] The only two studies, which analyze a consistent group of interviews from a qualitative perspective, are Koesters Gensini (2016) and Antonioli (2015).

3 Research Questions and Methods

3.1 Corpus, Methods and Tools

The aim of the intended study is to examine emotions in the corpus ISW[5] (considered the corpus of investigation) with a quantitative-qualitative approach focusing on the lexical level. The Israel-Corpus consists of three sub-corpora (Table 1):

Table 1. Information on the Israel-Corpus.

Corpus	Audio and video recording	Transcripts: corrected and available	Transcripts: uncorrected, on request
Emigrantendeutsch in Israel (IS)[a]	176 (audio files), 2 (video files)	22 (302.140 Tokens)	82
Emigrantendeutsch in Israel: Wiener in Jerusalem (ISW)[b]	28 (audio files)	20 (444.564 Tokens)	8
Zweite Generation deutschsprachiger Migranten in Israel (ISZ)[c]	67 (audio files), 1 (video files)	–	64

[a]In English: German of emigrants in Israel.
[b]In English: German of emigrants in Israel: Viennese in Jerusalem.
[c]In English: Second generation of German-speaking migrants in Israel.

With the DGD, the corpora can be searched both exploratively and in detail with a focus on specific research objects. With both options the relationship between the different data types is always maintained: the metadata of the interviewees and the audio file can both be retrieved from the transcript. Form-determined questions, which have the use of a linguistic form as the aim of the investigation, are ideal candidates for the machine search (cf. the analysis of *das heißt* in Deppermann and Schmidt 2014: 8), while formal-abstract and interpretative phenomena are less suitable and are possible with greater effort: the cases are to be searched, then sampled and evaluated manually, or only indicators for the specific phenomenon can be searched for (Deppermann and Schmidt 2014: 9). Both possibilities are of interest for the present study, since emotion names belonging to the FEAR frame are ideal candidates for the machine search, while the expression of emotions and the identification of examples of metaphorical expressions can also be based on indicators and require manual qualitative work. The approach is therefore quantitative-qualitative (Lemnitzer and Zinsmeister 2015: 37).

---

[5] The choice of the ISW-Corpus as the investigation corpus was determined from the fact that it is the only corpus which is nearly complete: with the exception of the interview with Ari Rath, all other interviews are transcribed and uploaded in the DGD.

In the present corpus-controlled procedure ISW is the study corpus, but in highlighting if there are significantly occurring emotive signs and patterns of language use other corpora play a central role:

- the corpus FOLK (also in the DGD), which has been selected as a reference corpus. FOLK will serve as a universal reference corpus;
- the corpus IS, which has been selected as a comparable corpus.

In addition to the functionalities of the DGD for the intended investigation other tools such as Sketch Engine and Lexpan are of importance:

- Sketch Engine[6] (Kilgarriff et al. 2004: 108–112), which can extract word lists using different parameters (among others absolute and relative frequency, lemma-form etc.), co-occurrences, word profiles on the basis of syntactic criteria and N-Grams;
- Lexpan[7] (Lexical Pattern Analyzer, cf. Steyer 2013: 110f.), which is used to explore syntagmatic structures focusing on strength, variance, slot occupancy and contextual embedding patterns. The exploratory possibility of Lexpan is particularly suitable for the inductive determination of patterns.

3.2   Research Questions

On the basis of the theoretical approach presented in Sect. 2, I will concentrate on the emotion FEAR (*ANGST* in German), considered from the perspective of Nazi victims as an expectation-founded emotion (Rothenhöfer 2015: 264), investigating the emotion names and descriptions used to thematize the emotion in the ISW-Corpus, in an attempt to see if there are differences to the IS-Corpus and to the reference corpus FOLK. In particular I will answer the following questions:

1. What are the most frequent and typical lexemes of the corpus ISW belonging to the word field '*Furcht/Schrecken*'[8] (Dornseiff 2004)?
2. What are the most significant linguistic patterns (3/4-Grams) used to thematize the emotion in the corpus ISW?
3. Concentrating on the lexeme '*Angst*'[9]: What are the typical slot fillers of the pattern *Angst vor* $X_{Dat\text{-}NP}$?

The corpus-controlled procedure used to answer the questions is schematized in Fig. 1:

---

[6] Sketch Engine is a commercial tool based on morphosyntactic annotations in the respective language. For German, the recommended German RFTagger 4.1 was used for the development of the word profile (Word Sketch).

[7] Lexpan is an analysis program independent of a single language, which was developed in the project "Usuelle Wortverbindungen" of the Institut für Deutsche Sprache (http://www1.ids-mannheim.de/lexik/uwv/lexpan.html).

[8] In English: fear/scare.

[9] In English: fear.

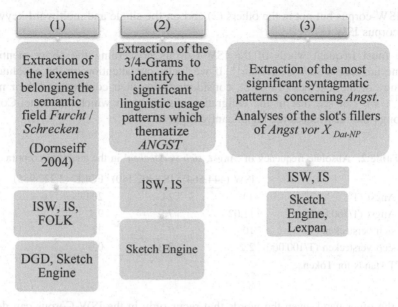

Fig. 1. Structure of the analyses, used corpora and tools

4   Results

4.1   The Most Frequent and Typical Lexemes of the Corpus ISW

The absolute and relative frequency can deliver interesting information, not only about the recurrence of the most used lexemes belonging to the word field '*Schrecken/Furcht*' (Dornseiff 2004), but also about the lexemes that can be considered the keywords of the investigated corpus. So, in this paragraph I will focus my attention on the words of the word field FEAR (among others *Angst, Auswegslosigkeit, Gänsehaut, Todesangst, Schreck*[10] etc.) (Fig. 2) that recur more than 10 times (1), on the words that occur only

Fig. 2. Lexemes belonging to the word field '*Schrecken/Furcht*'

---

[10] In English: anxiety; hopelessness; fear; goose bumps; fear of death; shock.

in the ISW-corpus but not in the others (2) and on the single and multiword keywords of the corpus ISW (3):

1. The most frequent words of the ISW-Corpus concerning the above-mentioned frame are *Angst, sich verstecken*[11]. If we focus our attention on the absolute frequency of the lexemes (Table 2), considering also their contexts and their meaning[12], we can see that in the emigration discourse to which the Israel-Corpora belongs the recurrences are significantly higher:

Table 2. Absolute frequency of '*Angst, sich verstecken*' in the analyzed corpora

	ISW (444.564)	IS (302.140)	FOLK (2.222.985)
Angst (T[a])	49	24	204
Angst (T/100.000)	11,02	7,9	9,1
sich verstecken (T)	10	7	22
sich verstecken (T/100.000)	2,2	2,3	0,9

[a]T stands for Token.

2. On the other hand, even the words that recur only in the ISW-Corpus can deliver interesting information (Table 3):

Table 3. Words that are recurrent in ISW but not in the other corpora

	ISW	IS	FOLK
Entsetzen (Engl. 'horror')	2	0	0
misstrauisch (Engl. 'suspicious')	2	0	0
verängstigt (Engl. 'scared')	2	0	0
Graus (Engl. 'horror')	0	1	0
blass (Engl. 'pale')	0	1	0
bleich (Engl. 'pallid')	0	1	0
haarsträubend (Engl. 'hair-raising')	0	1	0
scheuen (Engl. 'shy away')	0	1	0

With the above-mentioned lexemes, the people interviewed talk about themselves or other persons naming the emotion or thematizing it through physical aspects and behaviors (*blass*/pale, *bleich*/pallid, *stumm*/dumb).

---

[11] In English: fear; hide.

[12] I counted only the occurrences of the lexemes in which the seeds of fear ('threatened', 'oppression', https://www.duden.de/rechtschreibung/Angst) are dominant. Especially in the corpus FOLK the words are also used in contexts, with a more general meaning: *ich hab angst, dass ich was verpasse* (FOLK_E_0002), in which the seeds of 'apprehension' replace the one of 'threatened'.

3. The analyses of the keywords (Table 4) shows that the typical single and multi-words units[13] that thematize fear are all connected to the German Nazis and this terrifying historical moment:

Table 4. Keywords (single and multiwords units) that name or cause fear

Keywords	Freq. ISW	Freq. IS
Saujud (Engl. 'pig Jew')	8	0
Hakenkreuz (Engl. 'swastika')	8	0
großer Schock (Engl. 'big shock')	3	0
fürchterliche Sache (Engl. 'terrible thing')	3	0

They are all connected to powerful events, for example when the interviewees were addressed on the street as 'bastard Jews' (ISW-_E_00016), were accused of hiding things and removing their personal possessions (ISW-_E_00006) or when their houses and possessions were destroyed (ISW-_E_00004). Sometimes also the 'simple' sight of German Nazis marching through the streets (ISW-_E_00011) could be the cause of this emotion. But fear is also thematized when talking about another situation, for example when they were forced to escape, leaving their homes (ISW-_E_00014), their possessions, their families and starting a new life in a new country (ISW-_E_00004).

4.2 The Most Significant Linguistic Patterns (3/4-Grams) of the Corpus ISW

3/4-Grams analysis[14] can also deliver information on the typical usage patterns that thematize FEAR (Table 5). We notice that particular patterns, like *ich weiß nicht, in der Schule, und so weiter, da hab ich, und ich hab, und das war* and *und wir haben*[15] are present in both corpora. In particular we can see that two patterns (*ich weiß nicht* and *und so weiter*) are connected to the fact that those interviewees cannot or do not want to give information about certain events and wish to press on with the interview; the other three (*da hab ich*[16], *und ich hab, und wir haben*) show the reaction of the protagonists and his/her family to certain situations. *Und das war* gives instead evaluations to particular situations (*nicht leicht, sehr verwirrend*)[17], while *in der Schule* refers to events that happened in that place. In particular the emotion of FEAR seems to be prototypically connected to particular places, such as the school (*in der Schule*), the journey to school (*in die Schule*) and the street (*auf der Straße*):

---

[13] Keywords (single and multiple) were automatically extracted (Sketch Engine calculates the keyness score).

[14] To N-Grams in discourse analyzes see Bubenhofer 2017.

[15] In English: I don't know; at school; and so on; then I've; and I have; and that was; and we have.

[16] Verbs that complete this N-Gram are *beschlossen/gedacht/gesagt* (in English: so I decided; so I thought; so I said).

[17] In English: it wasn't easy; it was very confusing.

Table 5. N-Grams (3–4) in ISW and IS

N-Gram (3–4) ISW	Frequency	N-Gram (3–4) IS	Frequency
ich weiß nicht	144	und so weiter	226
in der Schule	92	ich weiß nicht	90
und so weiter	79	da hab ich	82
da hab ich	73	im Grunde genommen	68
und ich hab	59	und ich hab	63
und das war	57	ah äh äh	55
und er hat	48	und das ist	55
das erste Mal	46	das hab ich	54
in die Schule	45	das ist ein	51
Und das war	43	und das war	50
und für sich	42	und äh ich	47
an und für sich	41	hier im Lande	47
und wir haben	40	das ist eine	47
und da hat	39	in Tel Aviv	43
ich kann mich	39	und äh äh	41
das war ein	38	in der Schule	41
auf der Straße	38	vor allen Dingen	40
in der Schweiz	37	und äh die	39
nach dem Krieg	36	und wir haben	39
das war eine	35	dann hab ich	39

Inside the schools Jewish pupils had so much fear, that they avoided being seen together (ISW-_E_00016); they walked the streets with the oppressive thought, that they could be arrested or even beaten to death (ISW-_E_00016).

An interesting pattern which is connected to the description of fear experienced a long time ago, but in a certain way felt again in the moment of the interview, is the following: *ich kann mich*[18]. The trigram is often completed with the verb *erinnern/* remember and the adverbs *noch heute*/still today, *bis heute*/to this day and refers to powerful events that are the cause of fear, like an arrest (ISW-_E_00023), the attempt to cross the borders (ISW-_E_00023) or simply an episode in childhood that has left an impression (Witch of the Hansel and Gretel fairy tale in ISW-_E_00005).

4.3   The Typical Patterns of *Angst*

Considering that *Angst* is the most recurrent lexeme that names the emotion FEAR, I decided to extract the typical patterns[19] in which the word recurs[20] to see if they have

---

[18] In English: I can + myself.

[19] For the present study the valency is not relevant.

[20] *Angst vor X* (22); *Angst etwas zu machen* (7); *Angst, dass* (6); *Angst um X* (4). In English: fear from something; fear to do something; fear, that; fear about X.

specific characteristics in common. It turned out for example that they mostly refer to past events; when they are used to talk about present events, they are rather used by the interviewers to consider what is happening nowadays in Austria (1):

(1) *Aber es gibt schon eine verbreitete Angst, weil viele Österreicher der unteren Schicht Angst um ihren Arbeitsplatz haben im Moment*[21] (ISW-_S_00005).

The most frequent verb collocator is *haben*/have, only in one case can we find *bekommen*/become scared a verb, which highlights the unexpectedness of the event. The noun *Angst* is mostly accompanied by adjective collocators like *groß*/big (2) or intensifiers, like *genug*/enough (3):

(2) *sie hatten große Angst, vor dem vor diesem Lande, Sprache und äh Klima und alles*[22] (ISW-_E_00010);
(3) *ich hatte genug Angst vor den Deutschen*[23], (ISW-_S_00007).

The persons who thematize the emotion FEAR are in the majority of cases the interviewee and his/her family signalized with the pronoun 'we' (4), his/her parents (5), or an indefinite group of people, highlighted by the indefinite pronoun *man*/one, as to avoid admitting to a personal experience of emotion (6):

(4) *wir haben natürlich Angst gehabt vor den Deutschen*[24] (ISW-_S_00002);
(5) *und da hat sie [meine Mutter] Angst bekommen, was wird mit der Pension*[25] (ISW-_S_00007);
(6) *man hatte ja Angst, dass die Invasion auch hier sein wird, ja? Es war hier nicht weit in der Wüste*[26] (ISW-_S_00004).

In some cases, the interviewee refers also to Jews as a single entity that has lived for a long time (and still lives) in FEAR (7):

(7) *weil diese Angst der Juden*[27] (ISW-_S_00024).

The emotion FEAR seems a permanent emotion, that characterizes their lives, as belonging to the historical and collective subconsciousness. But what do the interviewees fear? The Germans, the Nazis, but also the future, the new lives (place, work, people) they are going to start.

Focusing the attention on the most frequent pattern *Angst vor X_{Dat-NP}*[28], we see the typical fillers of the conceptual slot for an anxiety-triggering event are usually nouns, like *den Deutschen*/the Germans, as the people who prototypically cause fear, *dem Land*/the land (Israel) and *der Sprache*/the language (Hebrew), as the symbols for a newly enforced life. Only in one case can we find the pronoun *mir*/me (8):

---

[21] In English: But there is already a widespread fear because many Austrians from a lower social class are afraid for their jobs at the moment.

[22] In English: They were very afraid of the country, language and the climate and everything.

[23] In English: I was scared enough of the Germans.

[24] In English: Of course we were afraid of the Germans.

[25] In English: And there she got scared– what about the pension?.

[26] In English: They were afraid the invasion would be here too, right? It wasn't far in the desert here.

[27] In English: Because this fear of the Jews.

[28] [no] fear from X. For the concept of patterns see among others, Steyer 2013.

(8) *die Leute Angst vor mir, weil Dolmetsch der Gestapo* (ISW-_E_00025)

In this example the interviewee is in an inverted situation (he is the one causing fear in other people because they think he is a Nazi) and feels the fear of the others, who had *Herzklopfen*/palpitations (as an expression of fear) when seeing Nazis walking on the street.

5 Conclusions

During the interview not only emotions associated with the past are awakened, but also new emotions arise in the narrative process. With the chosen quantitative-qualitative corpus controlled procedure it was possible to highlight the frequent and typical lexemes of the focus corpus, the multiword expressions and N-grams thematizing the emotion FEAR. In summary, it can be stated that:

- the most frequent lexemes of the ISW belonging to the word field *Furcht/Schrecken* are *Angst* and *sich verstecken* (the first one naming the emotion, the second one expressing it);
- the preference for certain lexemes (for example *Entsetzen, verängstigt* in the corpus ISW and *blass, bleich* in IS) and the avoidance of others that could be brought to the hypothesis, that had to be verified with further investigations involving other linguistic levels of analyses, that in the corpus ISW the interviewees prefer naming while in IS expressing the emotion FEAR;
- the single keywords are lexemes that are the cause of the emotions; the multiwords expressions instead evaluate the situation that has been narrated before or are to be narrated after;
- the extracted N-Grams show that the interviewees sometimes avoid speaking about certain events, but in some cases, they also give explicit evaluations. The naming of the emotions seems to be connected to particular places like the school, the journey to school and the street;
- the patterns of *Angst* show that the interviewees often prefer to talk about fearful events using the collective pronoun 'we'. In some cases, the emotion FEAR is also stated as the subconscious, historical emotion of the Jews. Fear-trigger events or persons are usually the Germans, but also the new land, which will be their new home.

This experiment showed that quantitative-qualitative corpus analyses are a helpful instrument to highlight significantly occurring emotive signs and patterns of language use in a discourse, completing the qualitative analyzes already done for this research object. In the future further investigations will focus on other types of emotions (also positive ones) and other linguistic levels, like the grammatical (intensificators) and prosodic ones, in order to analyse if there are interrelations.

References

Antonioli, G.: Konnektoren im gesprochenen Deutsch. Eine Untersuchung am Beispiel der kommunikativen Gattung autobiographisches Interview. Lang, Frankfurt a.M. (2015). (in German)

Betten, A. (Hrsg.): Sprachbewahrung nach der Emigration - Das Deutsch der 20er Jahre in Israel. Teil I: Transkripte und Tondokumente. Phonai, Bd. 42 und 1 CD, Niemeyer, Tübingen (1995). (in German)

Betten, A., Du-nour, M. (Hrsg.): Sprachbewahrung nach der Emigration - Das Deutsch der 20er Jahre in Israel. Teil II: Analysen und Dokumente. Phonai, Bd. 45 und 1 CD, Niemeyer, Tübingen (2000). (in German)

Betten, A., Du-nour, M. (Hrsg.): Wir sind die Letzten. Fragt uns aus. Gespräche mit den Emigranten der dreißiger Jahre in Israel. Neuauflage Gießen 2004 (1–3. Auflage Gerlingen 1995ff.). (in German)

Betten, A.: Sprachbiographien der 2. Generation deutschsprachiger Emigranten in Israel. Zur Auswirkung individueller Erfahrungen und Emotionen auf die Sprachkompetenz. In: Zeitschrift für Literaturwissenschaft und Linguistik, December 2010, vol. 40, pp. 29–57 (2017). (in German)

Bubenhofer, N.: Sprachgebrauchsmuster. Korpuslinguistik als Methode der Diskurs- und Kulturanalyse. De Gruyter (Sprache und Wissen), Berlin (2009). (in German)

Bubenhofer, N.: Kollokationen, n-Gramme, Mehrworteinheiten. In: Roth, K., Wengeler, M., Ziem, A. (Hrsg.) Handbuch Sprache in Politik und Gesellschaft, Handbücher Sprachwissen, pp. 69–93. De Gruyter, Berlin (2017). (in German)

Deppermann, A., Schmidt, T.: Gesprächsdatenbanken als methodisches Instrument der Interaktionalen Linguistik - Eine exemplarische Untersuchung auf Basis des Korpus FOLK in der Datenbank für Gesprochenes Deutsch (DGD2). In: Mitteilungen des Deutschen Germanistenverbandes, Jg. 61, H. 1, pp. 4–17 (2014). (in German)

Dornseiff, F.: Der deutsche Wortschatz nach Sachgruppen. De Gruyter, Berlin (2004). (in German)

Drescher, M.: Sprachliche Affektivität. Darstellung emotionaler Beteiligung am Beispiel von Gesprächen aus dem Französischen. Tübingen: Niemeyer. (2003). (in German)

Fiehler, R.: Kommunikation und Emotion. Theoretische und empirische Untersuchungen zur Rolle von Emotionen in der verbalen Interaktion. De Gruyter, Berlin (1990). (in German)

Fiehler, R.: How to Do emotions with words. emotionality in conversations. In: Fussell, S.R. (Hrsg.) The Verbal Communication of Emotion. Interdisciplinary Perspectives, pp. 79–106. Lawrence Erlbaum, Hillsdale (2002)

James, W.: The Principles of Psychology, vol. II. Macmillian, New York (1890)

Kilgarriff, A., et al.: The sketch engine. In: Williams, G., Vessier, S. (Hrsg) Proceedings of the 11th EURALEX International Congress, Lorient, France, 6–10 July. Bd. 1, pp. 105–115. Université de Bretagne Sud, Lorient (2004)

Kleinginna, P., Kleinginna, A.: A categorized list of emotion definitions, with suggestions for a consensual definition. Motiv. Emot. 5, 345–379 (1981)

Koesters Gensini, S.E.: Wörter für Gefühle. Der lexikalische Ausdruck von Emotionen im Israelkorpus. In: Leonardi, S., Thüne, E.-M., Betten, A. (Hrsg.) Emotionsausdruck und Erzählstrategien in narrativen Interviews. Analysen zu Gesprächsaufnahmen mit jüdischen Emigranten, pp. 123–170. Königshausen u. Neumann, Würzburg (2016). (in German)

Lemnitzer, L., Zinsmeister, H.: Korpuslinguistik. Eine Einführung. 3. Aufl. Narr, Tübingen (2015). (in German)

Leonardi, S.: Erinnerte Emotionen in autobiographischen Erzählungen. In: Leonardi, S., Thüne, E.-M., Betten, A. (Hrsg.) Emotionsausdruck und Erzählstrategien in narrativen Interviews. Analysen zu Gesprächsaufnahmen mit jüdischen Emigranten, pp. 1–46. Königshausen u. Neumann, Würzburg (2016). (in German)

Leonardi, S.: Metaphern und Identität in biographischen Interviews mit deutsch-jüdischen Migranten. In: Metaphorik.de 29/2019. (in German). https://www.metaphorik.de/de/journal/29/metaphern-und-identitat-biographischen-interviews-mit-deutsch-judischen-migranten-israel.html. Accessed 10 June 2019

Leonardi, S., Thüne, E.-M., Betten, A. (Hrsg.): Emotionsausdruck und Erzählstrategien in narrativen Interviews. Analysen zu Gesprächsaufnahmen mit jüdischen Emigranten. Würzburg: Königshausen u. Neumann (2016). (in German)

Rothenhöfer, A.: Gefühle zwischen Pragmatik, Grammatik und Idiomatik. Ein Beitrag zur Methodologie einer emotiven Diskursgrammatik. In: Kämper, H., Warnke, I.H. (Hrsg.) Diskurs – interdisziplinär. Zugänge, Gegenstände, Perspektiven. (= Diskursmuster - Discourse Patterns 6), pp. 245–280. De Gruyter, Berlin (2015). (in German)

Schwarz-Friesel, M.: Sprache, Kognition und Emotion: Neue Wege in der Kognitionswissenschaft. In: Kämper, H., Eichinger, L.M. (Hrsg.) Sprache – Kognition – Kultur. Sprache zwischen mentaler Struktur und kultureller Prägung. Jahrbuch des Instituts für Deutsche Sprache. De Gruyter, Berlin (2007). (in German)

Schwarz-Friesel, M.: Dem Grauen einen Namen geben? Zur Verbalisierung von Emotionen in der Holocaust-Literatur – Prolegomena zu einer Kognitiven Linguistik der Opfersprache. In: Germanistische Studien. Jubiläumsausgabe Nr. 10, Sprache und Emotionen, pp. 128–139 (2011). (in German)

Schwarz-Friesel, M.: Sprache und Emotion. Francke, Tübingen (2013). (in German)

Schwitalla, J.: Raumdarstellungen in Alltagserzählungen. In: Kern, F., Morek, M., Ohlhus S. (Hrsg.) Erzählen als Form – Formen des Erzählens, pp. 161–200. De Gruyter, Berlin (2012). (in German)

Steyer, K.: Usuelle Wortverbindungen. Zentrale Muster des Sprachgebrauchs aus korpusanalytischer Sicht. Narr, Tübingen (2013). (in German)

Thüne, E.-M.: Dinge als Gefährten. Objekte und Erinnerungsgegenstände in Bettens Israel-Korpus der ersten Generation. In: Dannerer, M., et al. (Hg.) Gesprochen – geschrieben – gedichtet. Variation und Transformation von Sprache. [Festschrift für Anne Betten zum 65. Geburtstag], pp. 189–204. ESV, Berlin (2009). (in German)

Thüne, E.-M.: Abschied von den Eltern. Auseinandersetzungen mit dem Tod der Eltern im Israelkorpus. In: Leonardi, S., Thüne, E.-M., Betten, A. (Hrsg.) Emotionsausdruck und Erzählstrategien in narrativen Interviews. Analysen zu Gesprächsaufnahmen mit jüdischen Emigranten, pp. 123–170. Königshausen u. Neumann, Würzburg (2016). (in German)

Thüne, E.-M., Leonardi, S.: Wurzeln, Schnitte, Webemuster. Textuelles Emotionspotenzial von Erzählmetaphern am Beispiel von Anne Bettens Interviewkorpus "Emigrantendeutsch in Israel". In: Kohlross, C., Mittelmann, H. (Hg.) Auf den Spuren der Schrift. Israelische Perspektiven einer internationalen Germanistik, pp. 229–246. De Gruyter, Berlin (2011). (in German)

Slovene Multi-word Units: Identification, Categorization, and Representation

Polona Gantar[1(✉)], Jaka Čibej[2(✉)], and Mija Bon[1(✉)]

[1] Faculty of Arts, University of Ljubljana, Slovenia, Ljubljana, Slovenia
{apolonija.gantar,mija.bon}@ff.uni-lj.si
[2] Jožef Stefan Institute, Ljubljana, Slovenia
jaka.cibej@ijs.si

Abstract. In this paper, we present the results of a manual annotation of a Slovene training corpus with multi-word units (MWUs) relevant for inclusion in a lexicon of Slovene MWUs. We analyze the annotations in terms of (a) the frequency with which a string has been identified as a MWU, (b) the degree to which the annotators agree on the category of the identified MWU, and (c) the degree to which the annotators agree on the range of the MWU in terms of its lexicalized elements. The results of the analysis will be useful in different stages of the compilation of a Slovene MWU lexicon. The list of dictionary-relevant MWUs obtained in the annotation task will be used to enrich the lexicon and to train models for the automatic identification of MWUs in running text. The findings will also help revise the criteria for the identification and categorization of dictionary-relevant MWUs in relation to free phrases, as well as more clearly define the distinction between the lexicalized elements of MWUs and the more or less stable elements of their textual environment, which will be useful when determining the canonical forms of MWUs in the lexicon on one hand and their relation to their variable elements and syntactic conversions on the other.

Keywords: Multi-word units · Slovene · Identification · Categorization · Multi-word lexicon

1 Introduction

Identifying multi-word units (MWUs) in running text is a task predominantly tackled by automatic extraction models that aim to identify a certain string of words in a sentence as a MWU and label it with a predefined category.

Because of their characteristics, such as multiwordness, idiosyncratic meaning, lexical and syntactic variability, and deviation from general language rules, MWUs are problematic in natural language processing (cf. Sag et al. 2002). As presented in this paper, MWU identification in running text is not a trivial task even in manual annotation.

To identify MWUs in authentic texts (either automatically or manually), it is crucial that their characteristics are as clearly defined as possible in order to distinguish between MWUs and non-MWUs, to correctly categorize identified MWUs, and to identify their lexicalized elements (particularly because MWUs also occur as non-

© Springer Nature Switzerland AG 2019
G. Corpas Pastor and R. Mitkov (Eds.): Europhras 2019, LNAI 11755, pp. 99–112, 2019.
https://doi.org/10.1007/978-3-030-30135-4_8

contiguous strings with various degrees of variability) that need to be distinguished from their (typical) context.[1]

We tackled this issue by conducting an annotation task in which annotators identified MWUs in running text, labeled them with categories based on linguistic criteria, and annotated the range of their lexicalized elements. The main purpose of the study presented in this paper is to analyze the annotations and use the findings to discover (a) the degree to which a certain string in text was identified as a MWU, (b) the degree to which the annotators agreed that an identified MWU falls into a predefined category, and (c) the degree to which the annotators agreed on the lexicalized elements of the MWU. It should be noted that we view MWUs primarily from the point of view of their inclusion in dictionaries. Our categorization was based on the definition used in the compilation of the Slovene Lexical Database (Gantar and Krek 2011), which describes a MWU as a dictionary unit with e.g. its definition and/or the information on its syntactic function and pragmatic role.

The paper is structured as follows: we first describe the annotation task and the criteria for the identification and categorization of dictionary-relevant MWUs. We continue by describing the training corpus, the annotation tool, and the quantitative results of the annotation task. This is followed by an analysis of the manual identification and categorization of MWUs. In a separate subsection, we analyze the annotation of range of MWUs in terms of their lexicalized elements. We conclude the paper with a summary of the main findings and describe how they can be taken into account in the compilation of a lexicon of Slovene MWUs.

2   Annotation Task

The goal of the task was to annotate a training corpus with MWUs based on the criteria described in Sect. 2.1. The Slovene training corpus ssj500k v2.1 (Krek et al. 2018) has previously already been annotated with verbal MWUs as defined within the PARSEME COST Action (Gantar et al. 2017, 2019). Although verbal MWUs represent a significant part of MWUs in a person's mental lexicon, they do not cover examples in which the verb is not the syntactic head of the unit. These include phrases such as *deževni gozd* 'rainforest', *kristalno čist* 'crystal clear', and *tukaj in zdaj* 'here and now'. In addition, the PARSEME MWU categories do not cover non-verbal units characterized by a more or less crystallized form and a high degree of semantic transparency. These can have a pragmatic function in the text and can act as connectors or discourse organizers. In the training corpus, we wanted to complement the existing annotations of verbal MWUs[2] with other types of MWU that require a dictionary description.

---

[1] In this case, lexicalized elements refer to the elements that must be present in each occurrence of the MWU and must always be realized by the same lexeme.

[2] For a detailed description, see Gantar et al. (2017, 2019).

2.1   Definition of MWU Categories

We view MWUs as (a) phrases of at least two words that can be identified in language as (b) units with their own meaning and/or (c) syntactic function. The definition is similar to the one used by Atkins and Rundell (2008: 166): "all different types of phrases that have some degree of idiomatic meaning or behaviour", but emphasizing an independent syntactic function allows it to cover MWUs that play a pragmatic or connecting role in the text. Examples include prepositional phrases (*in spite of*), phatic phrases (*have a nice day*), and sentence-like units such as greetings and routine formulas (*good morning, how do you do*). We distinguish MWUs from free phrases, which are formed on the fly in accordance with the purpose of communication. The annotation task also excluded collocations,[3] which are considered as semantically transparent Atkins and Rundell (2008: 223), but are useful from a lexicographic point of view for achieving (native-like) proficiency in language learning, illustration of typical word use, and semantic disambiguation (Sinclair 1987, 1991; Hunston and Francis 2000). The reason for excluding collocations from the task lies in the fact that models for the automatic extraction of Slovene collocations from corpora using the Word Sketch Grammar in the SketchEngine tool (Kilgarriff et al. 2004) have already been successfully implemented to compile the database of the Collocations Dictionary of Modern Slovene (Krek et al. 2016; Kosem et al. 2018), which is freely available online.[4]

The typology of MWUs used to annotate the training corpus (Fig. 1) was developed during the compilation of the Slovene Lexical Database (Gantar and Krek 2011; Gantar 2015) and distinguishes two types of MWUs: (a) lexical units, which require an explanation, and (b) lexico-grammatical units, which are semantically relatively transparent. The latter are characterized by the fact that they complement or disambiguate the sense description of a headword (e.g. collocations) or that they play a role of syntactic connectors or discourse organizers in language.

Multi-word Lexical Units
The general criterion to follow when identifying MWUs is to identify the integral meaning of the phrase that is more than the sum of the meanings of its parts. For the annotation, lexical units were further divided into (a) fixed expressions (FE; *varnostni trikotnik* 'warning triangle'), and (b) phraseological units (PU; *kaplja čez rob* 'the last straw'). FEs differ from PUs by the fact that FEs as units do not carry any metaphorical or expressive meaning.

Fixed Expressions – FE
Typically, FEs[5] belong to the discourse found in a certain expert field and have a concrete or abstract referent, e.g. *rdeči križ* ('the red cross' - institution), *črna luknja* ('black hole' - a phenomenon in space). FEs vary in the degree of their

---

[3] Collocations were also excluded from the PARSEME Shared Task annotation campaign.

[4] https://viri.cjvt.si/kolokacije/eng/.

[5] In related work on English MWUs, these expressions are usually called compounds. See Atkins and Rundell (2008: 171) for detailed classification.

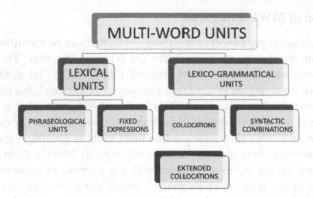

Fig. 1. The categorization of MWUs in terms of lexicographic relevance.

terminologicalness and are sometimes difficult to recognize in terms of their semantic independence, which makes them difficult to distinguish from collocations. In terms of their syntactic structure, most FEs are nominal phrases, e.g. *modre čelade* 'blue helmets', *blagovna znamka* 'trademark'. Some are adjectival, e.g. *funkcionalno nepismen* 'functionally illiterate'. The annotation instructions covered the following subcategories:

(a) foreign language phrases (such as *persona non grata* and *déjà vu*).
(b) phrases that denote generic names of institutions, documents, and events, e.g. *filozofska fakulteta* 'faculty of arts', *ustavno sodišče* 'constitutional court', *potni list* 'passport'. These were included because they are often culturally specific expressions with no direct translation equivalents in other languages.
(c) abbreviations such as *d. o. o.* (*delo z omejeno odgovornostjo* 'limited company') when denoting common nouns.

Phraseological Units – PU
Phraseological units (PUs) show at least some degree of fixedness in terms of structure and semantic idiomaticity. Unlike FEs, they typically express metaphorical (*princ na belem konju* 'knight in shining armor') or pragmatic meaning because their use depends on extralinguistic circumstances. PUs cover the following subcategories:

(a) Idioms and conversational formulas: *leta tečejo* 'years go by', *če verjameš ali ne* 'believe it or not'.
(b) Foreign language expressions with a metaphorical meaning (*per aspera ad astra*).
(c) Light verb constructions with non-compositional meaning (*imeti prav* 'to be right', *narediti sceno* 'to make a scene').
(d) Phrases with a pragmatic meaning, such as phrases used to express the attitude towards what is being communicated (*Spila sva eno pivo in to je to* 'We had one beer and that's that'), solicit confirmation or indicate reservations towards it (*Midva sva prijatelja, a ne da?* 'We're friends, aren't we?').

In ambiguous cases, annotators were instructed to consult the corpus and follow the rule of thumb to take into account the entire context of the phrase. Sometimes, the same phrase can be free in one sentence (example 1) and a PU in another (example 2):

(1) Naslov filma se mi zdi pomemben. 'I think the movie title is important.'
(2) Kje boš za novo leto? Doma, se mi zdi. 'Where are you spending New Year's Eve? At home, I think.'

Lexico-Gramatical Multi-word Units. Unlike lexical units, lexico-grammatical units have no lexical meaning, but are nevertheless relevant for lexicographic description because of their role as adverbials, sentence connectors, and discourse organizers. They frequently occur in certain (particularly prepositional) syntactic structures and open up syntactic slots in their textual environment. The most typical group of lexico-grammatical units are *syntactic combinations – SC*,[6] which include the following subcategories:

(a) Phrases that denote different types of circumstances: place (*na prostem* 'in the open'), time (*za zdaj* 'for now'), manner (*v skladu z/s* 'in accordance with'), quantity (*do te mere* 'to such a degree'), and reason (*iz maščevanja* 'out of vengeance'). Phrases with adjectival or numeral elements can also play adjectival roles, e.g. *eden od* 'one of', *vsak drugi* 'every other'.
(b) Phrases that act as discourse markers, which often include deictic expressions such as demonstrative pronouns, e.g. *v tem primeru* 'in this case', *in tako naprej* 'and so on'. This category also included abbreviations in this role, such as *ipd.* (*in podobno* 'and similar') and *itd.* (*in tako dalje* 'and so forth').
(c) Phrases that act as text organizers and connectors, particularly between sentence parts or sentences, e.g. *med drugim* 'among other things', *po eni strani - po drugi strani* 'on one hand - on the other hand'.

In language, syntactic combinations are usually very frequent and sometimes overlap with automatically extracted word-level n-grams, which do not necessarily play a specific syntactic role while semantically overlapping with pragmatic phraseological units.

2.2 Training Corpus and Annotation Tool

MWUs were annotated in the Slovene training corpus ssj500k v2.1 (Krek et al. 2018), which was sampled from the FidaPLUS corpus (Arhar Holdt and Gorjanc 2007). The corpus consists of 27,829 sentences containing a total of 586,248 tokens. The entire ssj500k corpus is manually tokenized, segmented into sentences, POS-tagged, and lemmatized. Various portions of the corpus also contain other manual annotations, e.g. syntactic dependencies, named entities, semantic role labels, and verbal multi-word expressions as part of the PARSEME annotation task (Gantar et al. 2017). As part of the endeavor presented in this paper, the first 6,500 sentences were additionally annotated with non-verbal MWUs. A custom-developed tool was used to annotate

---

[6] This category of MWUs has also been called compound prepositions (*in spite of*), MWUs with syntactic function (*with regard to*), prepositional phrases (*in bed, in jail*), complex prepositions (*on top of*), etc. For a more detailed overview, see Gantar et al. (2019).

MWUs within each sentence. The tool allows for a customizable annotation scheme and supports both contiguous and non-contiguous multi-layer annotations.

The 6,500 sentences were annotated by 10 annotators in total. The first 500 sentences were annotated by all 10 annotators as a test phase, while the remaining 6,000 sentences were divided in 12 parts (500 sentences each), which were annotated by a group of 3 annotators. The annotation was carried out in several phases and the annotators were re-distributed into groups of three in each phase.

The annotators, all students of linguistics at the Faculty of Arts of the University of Ljubljana, were familiarized with the criteria for the identification of MWUs. The annotation instructions contained examples for each category, including lists of representative MWUs, the criteria for dictionary relevance, and additional explanations for borderline cases. In case of doubt, the annotators were instructed to consult the Gigafida corpus of Slovene[7] and the Collocations Dictionary of Modern Slovene (Kosem et al. 2018)[8].

The annotation process resulted in a total of 15,727 annotations, with an average of approximately 350 annotations made by each annotator in an individual 500-sentence part, which translates into approximately 0.7 MWUs per sentence.

Aggregating annotations proved to be a complex task for several reasons: (a) a single sentence can include multiple MWUs, (b) not all MWUs are necessarily annotated by all annotators, (c) even if a MWU is identified by all annotators, the annotations may differ in the number of elements included; and (d) the same MWU can be annotated with different categories by different annotators. In order to aggregate the annotations, compare them, and define the actual number of identified MWUs in the corpus, the annotations were first grouped into batches within individual sentences using the following rule-based approach:

(1) Take all the annotations (made by all annotators) within a sentence.
(2) Add the first annotation to the first batch.
(3) For each subsequent annotation, check if it shares at least one token ID[9] with each annotation in any of the previous batches.
   (a) If it does, the annotation is added to that batch.
   (b) If it does not, it starts a new batch.

This allowed for differentiation between multiple MWUs in a single sentence and the comparison of annotations within the sentence. A total of 6,387 different strings were annotated in the corpus.

Because a MWU can occur multiple times in multiple sentences (and in multiple forms depending on capitalization, cases, tenses, and other inflectional categories used), an additional clustering approach was required. In the second phase, the batches within individual sentences were further aggregated into clusters using the following approach:

---

[7] http://gigafida.net.

[8] https://viri.cjvt.si/kolokacije/eng.

[9] Each token in the ssj500k v2.1 corpus has a unique ID. We used IDs instead of word forms or word lemmas to join batches to avoid introducing noise in case the same form/lemma occurred multiple times in the sentence.

1. Take all the different annotated strings in the corpus.
2. Add the first string to the first cluster.
3. For each subsequent string, check each batch to see if the string's alphabetical lemmatized form occurs in it.[10]
   a. If it does, check if the alphabetical lemmatized form also occurs in any of the previous clusters. If it does, add all the strings occurring in that batch to the same cluster.
   b. If it does not, start a new cluster and add the string to it.

The final number of clusters achieved this way amounted to 5,465. Table 1 shows three examples of clusters obtained.[11]

Table 1. Examples of MWU clusters.

Cluster	MWU (basic form)	Translation
operacijskega sistema operacijski sistem operacijskemu sistemu	operacijski sistem	operating system
za razliko od Za razliko od	za razliko od	as opposed to
Vzemite si čas Vzela si čas	vzeti si čas	to take one's time

Approximately half of the clusters (54%) contain only a single annotation. 20% and 10% contain 2 and 3 annotations, respectively, while the last 16% contain more than 3 annotations.

Table 2 shows the 3 clusters with the greatest number of annotations in the corpus.

Table 2. The top 3 clusters with the most annotations in the corpus.

Cluster	MWU (most frequent form)	Translation	Number of annotations
NAJ BI | NAJ NE BI | naj ne bi | naj bi | naj bi bil | Tako naj bi | naj bo | Rešitev bi se skrivala | bi naj | pa bi se naj | naj bi bila | torej naj bi	naj bi	should, is supposed to, is said to	352
bistveno več kot | več kot le | po več kot | trikrat več kot | več kot očitno | za pol več | nekaj več kot | torej celo več kot | več kot | Več kot	več kot	more than	149
od glave do peta | prodajalci od vrat do vrat | od države do države | Od do | od vrat do vrat | od do | premeril od glave do peta | OD DO	od [...] do [...]	from [...] to [...]	135

---

[10] The lemmatized form sorted in alphabetical order was used in order to aggregate strings that were essentially the same, but differed inflectionally, e.g. *ustavno sodišče* ('constitutional court' - nominative), *ustavnega sodišča* ('constitutional court' - genitive).

[11] For the sake of conciseness, each different form in the cluster is only shown once although it may actually appear multiple times.

3 Analysis and Findings

In this section, we analyze the annotations from three perspectives: (a) how often a certain phrase was identified as a MWU, (b) whether the identified MWU was correctly categorized, and (c) the range of the elements within the annotated MWU as the first step towards determining its representative form in the lexicon.

3.1 Identification

Among the 5,465 identified MWU clusters, a total of 2,971 (54%) were identified by a single annotator, which shows that despite the exhaustive annotation guidelines, the annotators were in disagreement on whether a phrase is a MWU in approximately half of the examples.

3.2 Categorization

In all three categories, between 46% and 52% of examples were annotated only once. A more detailed analysis of individual examples show that the majority of one-annotation phrases are not MWUs. However some examples (such as *na stroške* 'at the cost of', *živo srebro* 'quicksilver', *na vsakem koraku* 'at every step') fit the MWU criteria.

The analysis also shows that the annotators had the most difficulties identifying FEs and distinguishing them from collocations and free phrases. In certain cases, the annotators might not have checked the phrase in the Collocations Dictionary, either because the process is too time-consuming or because they did not feel it was required.

In some examples, the incorrect identification of a phrase as a MWU can be attributed to the fact that one of the elements in the phrase carries a metaphorical meaning (e.g. *prespati življenje* 'to sleep through life') or is rare, new or stylistically marked (e.g. *rana mladost* 'early youth', where 'rana' is archaic).

Furthermore, we looked into the degree to which the annotators agree on the category of the MWU in the examples that have been annotated more than once, as well as the percentage of examples in which the annotators were in complete agreement.

As shown in Table 3, the most agreed upon category in multiple annotation clusters is FE, followed by SC and PU. 142 clusters were ambiguously categorized (see Table 4).

According to the distribution of ambiguous clusters, the annotators had the most doubts distinguishing PUs and SCs. An analysis of these examples shows that they predominantly involve a prepositional phrase or a phrase that is structurally and semantically similar to a SC, but also plays a pragmatic role in the sentence, which according to the guidelines makes it a PU, e.g. *za vsako ceno* 'at any cost', *pod nobenim pogojem* 'under no circumstances'. The annotators also had doubts in examples where the discourse-organizing role was difficult to distinguish from the pragmatic or evaluating role, e.g. *kakorkoli že* 'in any case', *eno ali drugo* 'one or the other'.

Table 3. Number of MWU clusters per category and percentages of MWU clusters with complete agreement on the category.

MWU category[a]	Number of MWU clusters predominantly classified in the category	Number of MWU cluster with complete agreement on the category	%
PU	498	396	79.5
FE	1,074	1,026	95.5
SC	780	643	82.0
Ambiguous	142	–	–
All multiple annotation examples	2,494	–	–

[a]PU – phraseological unit, FE – fixed expression, SC – syntactic combination.

Table 4. Number of ambiguously categorized clusters.

MWU category	Number of clusters
PU/SC	53
PU/FE	57
PU/FE/SC	2
FE/SC	30
Total	142

The clusters that were ambiguously categorized as FEs and PUs involved MWUs that refer to a concrete referent and have no metaphorical meaning, but were formed in a metaphorical manner. We assume this was the reason why the annotators viewed the entire MWU as metaphorical, which was the criterion to categorize a MWU as a PU instead of a FE. Examples include *močnejši spol* 'the stronger sex' in the sense of 'men', *otroci cvetja* 'flower children' in the sense of 'hippies', and *življenjska pot* 'life path' in the sense of 'life'.

The SC/FE examples are mostly miscategorized FEs, particularly in the cases where FEs occur in the sentence along with a preposition, e.g. *(ob) koncu tedna* '(at) the end of the week', *(v) človekovi naravi* '(in) man's nature'.

3.3 Representation: Identification of Lexicalized MWU Elements

A corpus approach to the analysis of MWUs shows that the realizations of MWUs in authentic texts can be variant and flexible and feature different conversion options (Moon 1998; Gantar 2007). However, they also consist of a relatively fixed part (the phraseological core) that expands into the co-text based in accordance with certain patterns (Gantar 2007: 253). Some elements of the MWU are lexicalized, while others are predictable syntax- or valency-wise. On one hand, the aim of our analysis was to determine which categories and elements of the phrase were the one with the most overlap between the annotators, and, on the other hand, which elements represent typical additions to the MWU in terms of its morphosyntactic structure.

Table 5 shows the number of MWU clusters in which the annotators were in complete agreement in terms of their range, compared to the number of all multiple-annotation MWU clusters in the category[12]. Excluding the 3,325 single-annotation clusters, the annotators were in complete overlap in 1,202 clusters (57% of all multiple-annotation clusters). The most overlap can be observed in the FE category (74% of examples). The percentage of clusters with complete overlap ranges from 40% to 60% in the SC, PU, PU/FE, and PU/SC categories, and is somewhat lower in the FE/SC category (27%). No overlap was observed in the most ambiguous cases, i.e. PU/FE/SC.

Table 5. Clusters with complete overlap of lexicalized elements per category.

Category	Number of multiple-annotation clusters	Number of clusters with complete overlap	Percentage of clusters with complete overlap
FE	910	670	74%
SC	595	240	40%
PU	480	232	48%
PU/FE	54	30	56%
PU/SC	49	23	47%
FE/SC	26	7	27%
PU/FE/SC	2	0	0%
Total	2,116	1,202	57%

Table 6 shows the most frequent morphosyntactic structures of the annotated MWUs (excluding single-annotation examples). Patterns occurring with a frequency of less than 46 (i.e. less than 2% of all different multiple-annotation MWUs) were aggregated in the Other category (37%).

Table 6. The most frequent morphosyntactic patterns of the annotated MWUs.

Morphosyntactic structure[a]	Examples	Number of different MWUs	Percentage
A N	osnovna šola 'elementary school', delovno mesto 'work position'	899	37
S N	v resnici 'in truth', po ocenah 'according to estimates'	269	11

(continued)

---

[12] 24 clusters were excluded from the analysis either because of clustering errors (see Sect. 2.2) or because the annotator incorrectly included two MWUs in a single annotation or annotated only a single element of an otherwise correctly identified MWU.

Table 6. (*continued*)

Morphosyntactic structure[a]	Examples	Number of different MWUs	Percentage
V S N	*iti na živce* 'get on (someone's) nerves', *stati ob strani* 'be at one's side'	81	3
N N	*fitnes center* 'fitness center', *banana republika* 'banana republic'	80	3
S P N	*na vsak način* 'in any way', *za vsako ceno* 'at any cost', *v vsakem primeru* 'in any case'	50	2
S P	*kljub temu* 'despite this', *po mojem* 'in my opinion'	46	2
V N	*služiti kruh* 'to earn (one's) bread', *bog ve (God knows)*	46	2
Other	–	938	37
Total	–	2,409	100

[a]A – adjective, N – noun, S – preposition, V – verb, P – pronoun, R – adverb, M – numeral, C – conjunction, Q – particle.

The analysis of multiple-annotation MWUs in the corpus shows noticeable differences between the annotators' decisions on the range of the lexicalized elements of the MWU. In most cases, discrepancies between annotators most frequently stem from the incorrect annotation of obligatory syntactic slots within the MWU as lexicalized elements (e.g. *mi je šlo na živce* 'it was getting on my nerves'), or the inclusion of elements that typically occur within the range of the MWU in running text. The analysis shows the following frequently co-occurring elements (underlined):

(a) personal pronouns filling an open (but obligatory) slot that represents the agent/patient in a non-nominative case (cf. Gantar 2007: 106): *nama vlivajo moči* 'it gives us strength'
(b) general pronoun *vse* 'all, everything': *vse v najlepšem redu* 'everything in perfect order', *spričo vsega tega* 'based on all this'
(c) demonstrative pronouns in the S P N pattern: *v tem smislu* 'in that sense'
(d) possessive pronouns filling an obligatory slot that can be filled by other elements, e.g. S P N: *po njegovem mnenju* 'in his opinion'[13]
(e) adjectives in the S A N and V A N patterns: *v formalnem smislu* 'in the formal sense', *igrati pomembno vlogo* 'to play an important role'
(f) adjectives in the examples where the annotation encompasses either an extended collocation or the collocational environment of a FE: *poceni delovna sila* 'cheap labor force', *priporočena zgornja obrestna mera* 'recommended maximum interest rate'

---

[13] In some cases, the possessive pronoun can also be lexicalized, e.g. *proti svoji volji* 'against his/her/their own will'.

(g) verbs in obligatory syntactic slots that can be filled by other elements, particularly in PUs and when the verb frequently occurs with the MWU: _iti na vse ali nič_ 'to go for all or nothing'

(h) an auxiliary or light verb (_biti_ 'to be', _imeti_ 'to have'): _imeti/biti na voljo_ 'to be/have at one's disposal'

(i) nouns in annotations of extended collocations or the collocational environment of a FE with an A N or M N structure: _generalni direktor policije_ 'general director of the police'

(j) nouns filling an obligatory slot that can be filled by a wide range of nouns (particularly in PUs), especially when corpus examples show that the noun frequently occurs with the MWU, e.g. so _pogajanja_ v teku 'the negotiations are in motion'

(k) particles: _le s težavo_ 'only with effort'

(l) negative particle _ne_ (according to the guidelines, the particle is annotated only if the MWU does not exist without it): _ne biti v interesu_ 'to not be in the interest of'

(m) adverbs such as _čisto, kar, kako_: _bog ve kako_ 'God knows how', _čisto po nesreči_ 'completely by accident'

(n) conjunctions such as _pa, da, kakor, kot_: _znano je, da_ 'it is known that'

4 Discussion and Conclusion

One of the main criteria used to identify MWUs as lexical units is their integral meaning: a phrase is deemed a MWU and treated accordingly in the dictionary if the lexicographer surmises that the phrase as a unit requires an explanation. However, determining the semantic integrality of a phrase compared to the meanings of its elements is almost impossible. Corpus linguists and lexicographers agree that "many if not most meanings require the presence of more than one word for their normal realisation" Sinclair (1998: 4), and that "such patterns are found for many expressions that intuitions alone might encourage us to classify as fixed" (Hanks et al. 2018: 95).

In light of this, it is not surprising that our findings show that more than half of the annotated examples in our training corpus show no agreement between annotators on whether the annotated phrase is a MWU. The analysis of single-annotation examples has shown that most examples are not MWUs based on the guidelines, which raises the question of the reliability of the intuitive manual identification of MWUs in running text, and the degree to which this can be improved by linguistic definition of identification criteria.

The analysis has also shown that identifying MWUs in running text is difficult even for native speakers, as the task consisted not only of discovering (potential) MWUs and discriminating them from free phrases and collocations, but also categorizing them. Because the majority of single-annotation examples are in fact collocations (and present in e.g. the Collocations Dictionary of Modern Slovene), we can also conclude that manual annotation of collocations is less reliable compared to statistical methods used in the compilations of the Collocations Dictionary of Modern Slovene. The results have also shed light on the weak points of the annotation guidelines: the annotators require more detailed criteria to determine the terminological value (especially when discriminating between collocations and FEs) or the metaphorical meaning of the phrase compared to the metaphorical value of its elements (especially when discriminating between FEs and PUs). Although annotators show high agreement in multiple-annotation examples (between 80% and 95%), some ambiguous categorization (particularly FE and SC) can be attributed to the fact that numerous SCs, in addition to acting as connectors, also play a pragmatic role. As such, they fit in both categories.

The results of the analysis of disagreement in the lexicalized elements of the MWU are somewhat expected. The MWU patterns containing lexicalized verbal elements typically open up syntactic slots in the form of pronouns, which the annotators identified as a lexicalized element (e.g. *mi je šlo na živce* 'it was getting on my nerves'). Adjectives occurring in nominal structures were also frequently annotated when the adjective is an optional, but lexically typical element (e.g. *v bližnji prihodnosti* 'in the near future'). With PUs, verbs were also problematic, particularly in cases where the structurally fixed MWU core typically co-occurs with a variable verb (e.g. *pomagati po svojih močeh* 'to help as best one can'). In terms of determining the representative form of a MWU in a lexicon, it is also interesting to note the findings on pronominal and deictic elements of MWUs, which usually fill slots that have multiple syntactic realizations in the text, e.g. *po (njegovem) mnenju* 'in (his) opinion', *po mnenju (koga)* 'in the opinion of (someone)'. The annotators were also in doubt when identifying an auxiliary or semantically vague verb as a lexicalized element of the MWU (e.g. *biti pod nadzorom* 'to be under control').

The findings show that determining the representative forms of MWUs in the lexicon should also take into account phrases with extended elements and phrases with a variable element. The examples with deictic elements show that MWUs in the lexicon require a clear link between their various realizations (e.g. po (njegovem) mnenju, po (mnenju) koga). In addition, the difference between examples of use and the canonical MWU form must be established, e.g. *iti na živce* ('to get on one's nerves', canonical form), *mi je šlo na živce* ('it was getting on my nerves', realization in text).

Acknowledgments. The study presented in this paper was conducted within the New Grammar of Modern Standard Slovene: Resource and Methods project (J6-8256), which was financially supported by the Slovenian Research Agency between 2017 and 2020. The authors also acknowledge the financial support from the Slovenian Research Agency (research core funding *No. P6-0411 - Language Resources and Technologies for Slovene* and *No. P6-0215 - Slovene Language - Basic, Contrastive, and Applied Studies*). The authors would also like to thank the annotators: Anna Maria Grego, Tjaša Jelovšek, Tajda Liplin Šerbetar, Pia Rednak, Jana Vaupotič, Zala Vidic, Karolina Zgaga, and Kaja Žvanut.

References

Arhar Holdt, Š., Gorjanc, V.: Korpus FidaPLUS: nova generacija slovenskega referenčnega korpusa. Jezik in slovstvo **52**(2), 95–110 (2007)

Atkins, B.T.S., Rundell, M.: The Oxford Guide to Practical Lexicography. Oxford University Press, New York (2008)

Gantar, P.: Stalne besedne zveze v slovenščini. Založba ZRC, ZRC SAZU, Ljubljana (2007)

Gantar, P., Krek, S.: Slovene lexical database. In: Majchráková, D., Garabík, R. (eds.) Proceedings of the Natural Language Processing, Multilinguality: Sixth International Conference, Modra, Slovakia, 20–21 October 2011, pp. 72–80. Tribun EU, Brno (2011)

Gantar, P.: Leksikografski opis slovenščine v digitalnem okolju. Znanstvena založba Filozofske fakultete UL, Ljubljana (2015)

Gantar, P., Krek, S., Kuzman, T.: Verbal multiword expressions in Slovene. In: Mitkov, R. (ed.) EUROPHRAS 2017. LNCS (LNAI), vol. 10596, pp. 247–259. Springer, Cham (2017). https://doi.org/10.1007/978-3-319-69805-2_18

Gantar, P., Colman, L., Parra Escartín, C., Martínez Alonso, H.: Multiword expressions: between lexicography and NLP. Int. J. Lexicogr. 32(2), 138–162 (2019). https://doi.org/10.1093/ijl/ecy012

Hanks, P., El Marouf, I., Oakes, M.: Flexibility of multiword expressions and corpus pattern analysis. In: Sailer, M., Markantonatou, S. (eds.) Multiword Expressions: Insights from a Multi-lingual Perspective, pp. 93–119. Language Science Press, Berlin (2018)

Hunston, S., Francis, G.: Pattern Grammar: A Corpus-Driven Approach to the Lexical Grammar of English. John Benjamins, Amsterdam (2000)

Kosem, I., et al.: Collocations Dictionary of Modern Slovene (2018). https://viri.cjvt.si/kolokacije/eng/

Kosem, I., Krek, S., Gantar, P., Arhar Holdt, Š., Čibej, J., Laskowski, C.: Kolokacijski slovar sodobne slovenščine. In: Proceedings of the Conference on Language Technologies & Digital Humanities, Ljubljana, pp. 133–139 (2018)

Kilgarriff, A., Rychly, P., Smrz, P., Tugwell, D.: The sketch engine. Inf. Technol. 105, 116–127 (2004)

Krek, S., Gantar, P., Kosem, I., Gorjanc, V., Laskowski, C.: Baza kolokacijskega slovarja slovenskega jezika. In: Proceedings of the Conference on Language Technologies & Digital Humanities, Ljubljana, pp. 101–105 (2016)

Krek, S., et al.: Training corpus ssj500k 2.1, Slovenian language resource repository CLARIN.SI (2018). http://hdl.handle.net/11356/1181

Moon, R.: Fixed Expressions and Idioms in English. A Corpus-Based Approach. Clarendon Press, Oxford (1998)

Sag, I.A., Baldwin, T., Bond, F., Copestake, A., Flickinger, D.: Multiword expressions: a pain in the neck for NLP. In: Gelbukh, A. (ed.) Proceedings of the 3rd International Conference on Intelligent Text Processing and Computational Linguistics (CICLing 2002), pp. 1–15 (2002)

Sinclair, J. (ed.): Looking Up: An Account of the COBUILD Project in Lexical Computing and the Development of the Collins COBUILD English Language Dictionary. Collins, London and Glasgow (1987)

Sinclair, J.: Corpus, Concordance, Collocation. Oxford University Press, Oxford (1991)

Sinclair, J.: The lexical item. In: Weigand, E. (ed.) Contrastive Lexical Semantics, pp. 1–24. John Benjamins Publishing Company, Amsterdam/Philadelphia (1998)

Weighted Compositional Vectors for Translating Collocations Using Monolingual Corpora

Marcos Garcia[1,2]([✉]) [iD], Marcos García-Salido[1] [iD],
and Margarita Alonso-Ramos[1,2] [iD]

[1] Grupo LyS, Departamento de Letras, Universidade da Coruña,
Campus da Zapateira, 15071 Coruña, Galicia, Spain
{marcos.garcia.gonzalez,marcos.garcias,margarita.alonso}@udc.gal
[2] CITIC, Universidade da Coruña,
Campus de Elviña, 15701 Coruña, Galicia, Spain

Abstract. This paper presents a method to automatically identify bilingual equivalents of collocations using only monolingual corpora in two languages. The method takes advantage of cross-lingual distributional semantics models mapped into a shared vector space, and of compositional methods to find appropriate translations of non-congruent collocations (e.g., *pay attention–prestar atenção* in English–Portuguese). This strategy is evaluated in the translation of English–Portuguese and English–Spanish collocations belonging to two syntactic patterns: *adjective-noun* and *verb-object*, and compared to other methods proposed in the literature. The results of the experiments performed show that the compositional approach, based on a weighted additive model, behaves better than the other strategies that have been evaluated, and that both the asymmetry and the compositional properties of collocations are captured by the combined vector representations. This paper also contributes with two freely available gold-standard data sets which are useful to evaluate the performance of automatic extraction of multilingual equivalents of collocations.

Keywords: Multilingual collocations · Distributional semantics · Compositional semantics

This research was supported by a 2017 Leonardo Grant for Researchers and Cultural Creators (BBVA Foundation), by Ministerio de Economía, Industria y Competitividad (FFI2016-78299-P), and by the Galician Government (ED431B-2017/01). Marcos Garcia has been funded by a Juan de la Cierva-incorporación grant (IJCI-2016-29598), and Marcos García-Salido by a post-doctoral grant from Xunta de Galicia (ED481D 2017/009). We gratefully acknowledge the support of NVIDIA Corporation with the donation of the Titan Xp GPU used for this research.

© Springer Nature Switzerland AG 2019
G. Corpas Pastor and R. Mitkov (Eds.): Europhras 2019, LNAI 11755, pp. 113–128, 2019.
https://doi.org/10.1007/978-3-030-30135-4_9

1   Introduction

Bilingual models of distributional semantics have been used to automatically find word translations from both parallel and comparable corpora between several languages [8,10,32]. Besides, and also using parallel and comparable corpora, several attempts have been made to identify translations of different types of multiword expressions (MWEs), using external resources such as bilingual dictionaries or cross-lingual models of distributional semantics [2,11,15,34,38]. Most of these approaches, however, often consider the semantic load of each MWE component as similar, so that they obtain candidates in the target languages as word-to-word translations, which are then filtered and ranked using different metrics. For instance, the decomposition of the French MWE *examen clinique* may first generate different English candidate translations (*clinic inspection*, *clinical test*, *clinical review*, etc.), among which the most probable translations are then selected (e.g., *clinical examination*) [30].

Even if these strategies are well suited for some types of collocations (e.g., those in which the translation of each component is predictable), they fail to capture other cases where the meaning of one of their components is not a direct translation in the target language, that is, it is not a congruent equivalent. In this respect, we follow [31] and consider congruent equivalents those where a word-to-word translation generates sound combinations in both languages (e.g., English–Portuguese *formulate [a] hypothesis–formular [uma] hipótese*), and non-congruent those cases where this definition does not apply, such as the English–French translation *take [a] walk–faire une promenade* (where *faire* 'to do' is not the literal translation of *to take*). This is the case of some collocations, which are asymmetric combinations of two lexical units, where one of them (the *base*) is freely selected by the speaker due to its meaning, while the other (the *collocate*, whose selection is restricted by the base) conveys a particular meaning in this specific combination [24,25]. In the previous examples, *hypothesis/hipótese* and *walk/promenade* are the bases, while *to formulate/formular* and *to take/faire* are the collocates. From this point of view, the bases are often defined as *autosemantic* and the collocates as *synsemantic* [19].

For non-congruent collocations, finding the appropriate collocates in the target language is a challenging task both using bilingual dictionaries or distributional semantics models, since the source and the target words may not be semantically related except in that particular combinations.

In the field of distributional compositional semantics, several studies have proposed different methods to obtain vector representations of large expressions such as phrases and sentences [3,28,29,33]. These approaches vary from vector multiplication and addition to the creation of contextualized representations for each component word, later combined in compositional vectors which produce better representations of words in a particular context [42].

With that in mind, this paper explores the compositionality of collocations in distributional semantics by using compositional weighted vectors to translate this type of MWEs in English, Portuguese, and Spanish. For a given collocation in the source language, we obtain a compositional vector which allows us to identify candidate collocates which are semantically similar to the whole combination, but not necessarily related to the source collocate. Thus, the proposed strategy is able to find both non-congruent and congruent candidate collocates, used to create equivalent collocations in the target language. Aimed at having a better view of the compositional properties of these expressions, we evaluate the impact of different weights to construct the compositional vector, by giving more relevance to the base than to the collocate, and vice versa.

To evaluate our approach, we manually created test sets in English–Portuguese and English–Spanish of two types of collocations (based on syntactic dependencies): *adj-noun* (e.g., *fresh water*), and *verb-obj* (e.g., *pay attention*). For each relation and language we selected 50 input collocations, obtaining a final resource of 200 inputs with 365 possible translations. The results of several tests, using only cross-lingual word embeddings trained on monolingual corpora, improve previous translation methods, and confirm both the compositional character of collocations as well as their internal asymmetry, whereby collocates convey a particular meaning in each specific combination.

The rest of this paper is organized as follows. Section 2 presents some related work about the different tasks carried out in our study. Then, in Sect. 3 we introduce the proposed method to translate collocations using monolingual corpora. The experiments to evaluate our approach are addressed in Sect. 4, while Sect. 5 concludes this work.

2   Related Work

This paper deals with different tasks to perform unsupervised translation of collocations. Thus, this section briefly presents representative studies about bilingual collocation extraction, distributional compositional semantics as well as cross-lingual vector spaces.

The first approaches to identify bilingual equivalents of multiword expressions took advantage of parallel corpora and statistical measures to find translations of noun phrases or collocations [18,21,36]. Other strategies using bilingual corpora make use of syntactic information to identify predefined MWEs patterns [35,43]. More recently, [34] presented a system to extract collocation equivalents from parallel or comparable corpora using bilingual dictionaries and WordNet, while [39] uses a non-compositional approach by training cross-lingual distributional models in which collocations are treated as single units.

Grefenstette [17] describes a method which performs a word-to-word translation of MWEs using bilingual dictionaries, as well as ranking approach which relies on web frequency. Other works use comparable as well as unrelated corpora to extract MWEs equivalents between two languages [2,7,38]. They first identify the MWEs in a source language using pattern-based approaches and statistical metrics. Then, they generate candidate translations by applying a word-to-word approach, or extracting MWEs in the target data which are ranked using bilingual dictionaries or cross-lingual distributional models [15,30]. Cross-lingual models were also exploited in recent studies to find bilingual equivalents both using single-word vectors [41] and contextualized representations [12,13]. In general, most of these studies select candidate MWEs in the target languages using bilingual dictionaries or vectors representing single words, which make difficult to correctly identify non-congruent translations.

Regarding compositionality in distributional semantics, classical methods combine the vectors of syntactically related words using algebraic operations such as addition or multiplication [28,29]. Other approaches obtain the compositional representation of a given expression using a functional approach, where the semantic arguments are represented by vectors while functional words (including verbs) are functions operating on those vectors [4,5].

Finally, our work also takes advantage of cross-lingual distributional semantics models which map in the same vector space representations of different languages. Apart from bilingual models trained in parallel corpora [40], both count-based techniques [9,32] and recent neural network algorithms [1,22,27] obtain high quality bilingual models using comparable and unrelated corpora.

The method proposed in this paper follows the phraseological perspective about the internal properties of collocations [24], and takes advantage of weighted additive models [29] to find candidate collocates in the target language for a given source combination. This strategy allows us to evaluate non-congruent combinations where the components of each MWE are not word-to-word translations nor distributionally similar to the source ones. It is worth noting that this paper deals only with collocation-to-collocation equivalents, so other translations (e.g., *obtain [a] doctorate–doutorar-se*, in English–Portuguese) are not addressed.

3   Compositional Distributional Semantics for Collocations

In this section we first discuss some particular issues that should be taken into account when dealing with multilingual collocations equivalents, and then we present the method proposed to tackle those questions.

3.1   Multilingual Collocation Equivalents

As several studies have shown, the word-to-word approach for selecting candidate collocations (and other MWEs) in a target language obtains good results in different languages and morphosyntactic patterns [15,30,38]. One of the reasons of this success is that a considerable part of compositional MWEs are to some extent congruent in several language pairs (e.g., *deep analysis–análise profunda*, in English–Portuguese, or *jefe de policía–police chief* in Spanish–English), so bilingual dictionaries or distributional models, in combination with statistical filters are suitable to avoid many incorrect translations which do not occur in the target language. As an example, the English verb *to fill* is usually translated as *encher* (in Portuguese) when collocates with physical objects (*encher o copo*, 'fill the glass'), but as *preencher* in figurative contexts (*preencher um relatório*, 'fill a report'). In Spanish, these translations are similar (*llenar* and *rellenar*), but the latter is also used as equivalent to *refill* (*rellenar un vaso*, 'refill the glass'). These examples show the importance of considering the conventionality of these combinations even in those cases in which the candidate translations are relatively easy to find using word-to-word approaches.

A different case is the above mentioned non-congruent equivalents, in which the candidate collocates are not found using standard techniques. In this respect, the heads of light verb constructions (LVCs) such as in *take [a] picture*, or in *have breakfast* are often not semantically similar (when isolated) to their translations in the equivalent collocations in other languages (e.g., *tirar [uma] fotografia*, 'take a picture' in Portuguese, or *tomar [el] desayuno* 'have breakfast' in Spanish). Nevertheless, as these collocates are frequent support verbs in various languages, filtering strategies may help to find appropriate translations. However, other less frequent cases such as *pay attention* (where *to pay* is translated as *prestar*—literally 'to lend'—in both Portuguese and Spanish) are more difficult to identify, since the support verb has in most contexts a full meaning which is different than the one in that particular combination.

Similarly, many *adj-noun* collocation equivalents are non-congruent in several language pairs: for example, in *fresh water*, the adjective is usually translated as *doce* (Portuguese) or *dulce* (Spanish) (literally 'sweet' in both languages). In this respect, bilingual dictionaries (except those with collocational information) do not include *doce* or *dulce* as translations of *fresh*. Also, in standard cross-lingual distributional models the similarity between these words is close to 0.5, so it would be hard to select *água doce* or *agua dulce* as candidate collocations using word-to-word approaches.

These examples allow us to have a better view about some relevant properties concerning multilingual collocation equivalents, and also to note the importance of the idiosynchratic character of these expressions. Moreover, it is worth remembering that, although collocations are compositional, collocates often have particular meanings, in contrast to the bases (except, for obvious reasons, in polysemous words).

3.2 Weighted Compositional Vectors

To obtain a compositional vector of a given collocation, we follow [29] by using the *weighted additive models*. However, as we are focusing on the semantic properties of a base–collocate pair instead of the syntactic roles of a head–dependent relation,[1] we define a compositional vector v as the addition of the base and collocate weighted vectors b and c:

$$v = \alpha b + \beta c \tag{1}$$

where $\beta = 1 - \alpha$ (so that $\alpha + \beta = 1$). Thus, variations in α and β make the compositional vector asymmetric, allowing to better represent the semantic load

---

[1] In this regard, note that in an *adj-noun* collocation, the syntactic head is occupied by the base, while in *verb-obj* collocations the syntactic head is the collocate.

of both the collocate and the base. Therefore, if we set $\alpha = 0.2$ and $\beta = 0.8$, the collocate will contribute more to the compositional vector, and vice versa.

Taking the above into account, we define the method to identify bilingual collocations as follows: we use cross-lingual word embeddings to search for both base and collocate candidates in the target languages. For the bases, we simply use the source vector to retrieve the n most similar words (e.g., between 3 and 5) with the same PoS-tag. To search for candidate collocates we use the weighted compositional vectors described in Eq. 1, which allow us to find collocate candidates (e.g., 10, also with the same PoS-tag) whose meaning is closer to the one of the whole combination than to the collocate alone. Then, both base and collocate candidates are combined to generate collocations in the target language, with the same pattern as the source one. For each of these collocation candidates, we also obtain the weighted average vector in order to compute its translation confidence (in terms of cosine similarity) with respect to the input collocation. This confidence value is used to rank the target collocations with regard to the source one. Optionally, we use a corpus-based filter method to remove unconventional combinations in the target language.

Table 1. Collocate candidates (top) and extracted collocations (bottom) in Portuguese from the English input *pay attention*. Differences between using the vector of the *pay* and the weighted additive vector of *pay+attention* (0.5/0.5) to select collocate candidates in Portuguese. *Filter* means filtering out collocation candidates with frequency lower than 10 in the reference corpus. Floating-point numbers (in brackets) are the cosine distance between the source and target vectors, while ordinal numbers are the rank position in each list of candidates.

Input vector	Collocate candidates
pay	pagar (0.9), cobrar (0.7), custear (0.7), desembolsar (0.7), quantiar (0.7) [...], **prestar (0.5) (37th)**
pay+attention	pagar (0.7), cobrar (0.6), investir (0.6) [...], **prestar (0.6) (7th)**

Input vector	Extracted collocations
pay (no filter)	pagar atenção (0.9), cobrar atenção (0.8), pagar repercussão (0.8), custear atenção (0.8) [...]
pay (filter)	∅
pay+attention (no filter)	pagar atenção (0.9), pagar elogio (0.8) pagar repercussão (0.8), cobrar atenção (0.8) [...] **prestar atenção (0.7)**
pay+attention (filter)	**prestar atenção (0.7)**

Table 1 shows an example of the proposed approach to generate the Portuguese translation of the English collocation *pay attention* (using the models and data described in Sect. 4). First, top rows contain the collocate candidates selected using the vector of the collocate *pay* as well as the weighted additional vector of *pay+attention* (α and β were set to 0.5 in this example). On one hand, it can be seen that most similar verbs to *pay* in Portuguese have economical or financial meanings, and that *prestar* appears as the candidate 37th. On the other hand, the compositional vector reduces the load of its "economical meaning" (e.g., *pagar* 'to pay' drops from 0.9 to 0.7 of cosine similarity) and promotes *prestar* to a higher position (7th position).

Second, bottom rows display the selected collocation candidates from each set of collocates (generated using the top 10 and the top 5 candidates for the collocate and the base, respectively). The combinations created with the vector of *pay* do not include the correct translation *prestar atenção*, and none of the candidates passed the frequency filter ($f > 10$), so this method did not extract a suitable translation of *pay attention*. The compositional approach, however, generated the translation *prestar atenção* as one of the collocation candidates. This combination was the only one which passed the frequency filter and therefore was correctly selected as the Portuguese equivalent of *pay attention*.[2]

4   Experiments

In this section we carry out a set of experiments to evaluate the presented compositional approach using different weights for both the base and the collocate. This weighted model is compared to the following methods, all of them using the same cross-lingual models to select the translation candidates:[3] (i) baseline (*bas*), which creates a collocation selecting the most similar equivalents of both the base and the collocate in the target language (it is therefore a similar approach to those presented in [15,30]); (ii) addition (*add*), which generates at most 100 collocation candidates from the top 10 bases and collocates in the target language, and rank them by cosine similarity of the source and target compositional vectors $v = b + c$; (iii) multiplication (*mult*), the same as *add* but obtaining the collocation vectors by multiplication instead of addition ($v = b \cdot c$). Furthermore, we also evaluated a *non-compositional* strategy (*ncp*, explained below) which learns single vector representations for a given MWE. However, this method should not be directly compared to the other approaches, since the MWEs were added to the model from the gold-standard data sets (and not automatically selected). The frequency filter (applied to every model except for the baseline and non-compositional ones), selects only those collocations with a frequency $f > 10$ (using lemmas in the same dependency relation) in the 250M corpora used to train the distributional models (see below).

---

[2] It is worth noting that the candidate *cobrar atenção*, which exists in Brazilian Portuguese with a slightly different meaning, could be selected if we had used more resources from this variety and from other typologies. In our data, mostly composed of corpora from Portugal (besides the Wikipedia, with mixed varieties), this combination has a frequency of only 1.

[3] Both the gold-standard data as well as the output of each system can be downloaded at https://github.com/marcospln/bilingual_collocations.

4.1 Test Data

To evaluate the different methods we created two new gold-standard data sets as follows: First, we randomly extracted 100 English collocations (50 *adj-noun* and 50 *verb-obj*) from an annotated corpus [16]. Then, we manually translated these 100 examples into the most natural collocations in Portuguese and Spanish, obtaining a total of 365 equivalents, 227 in Portuguese and 138 in Spanish (as said, this paper is focused on collocation-to-collocation equivalents).[4] The Portuguese data set has more translations mainly because we have added spelling variants with regard to the Orthographic Agreement of Portuguese Language[5] and to the Brazilian orthography (e.g., *actual/atual* or *crónico/crânico*).

4.2 Distributional Models

To create the monolingual distributional models we compiled three corpora (for English, Portuguese, and Spanish) with 250 million tokens and similar properties: each of them is composed by 200 million tokens from Wikipedia, 20 millions from Europarl [20], 20 millions from news and web pages, and 10 million tokens from OpenSubtitles [23]. The sentences of each corpus were randomly selected, so the degree of comparability is low. Except for Wikipedia (which often contains mixed varieties), the European varieties (from UK, Portugal, and Spain) were preferred.

The texts were processed with LinguaKit [14] to convert them into *lemma_PoS-tag* corpora. They were also parsed with UDPipe [37] to obtain dependency triples used for the frequency filter. Then, the *lemma_PoS-tag* corpora were used to learn monolingual models using *word2vec* [26] (with the skip-gram algorithm, 300 dimensions, a window of 5 tokens, and a frequency threshold of 5). Finally, the monolingual models were mapped into a shared vector space with the semi-supervised mode of *vecmap* [1]: we used 100 numbers (0 to 99) and 300 randomly selected words (100 adjectives, 100 nouns, and 100 verbs) automatically translated and then reviewed by the authors.

For the *ncp* method we used the same lemmatized corpora (without PoS-tags) representing the gold (source and target) collocations as single tokens (e.g., *fresh_water*), and trained *word2vec* models with them. For non-adjacent collocations—linked by a dependency relation—we replaced the first element by the whole combination and removed the intermediate lemmas (e.g., "to take a brief walk" → *take_walk*). To map the models we used the same bilingual pair words as well as 10 additional bilingual collocation equivalents (e.g., *take_walk-dar_passeio* in English–Portuguese), different from those of the gold-standard.

---

[4] This gold-standard includes an average of 3.65 translations for each collocation, but, as discussed in Sect. 4.4, there may be more suitable equivalents for some of them.

[5] https://en.wikipedia.org/wiki/Portuguese_Language_Orthographic_Agreement_of_1990.

4.3   Results

For each run we computed precision, recall, and f-score values for the top-1 and top-3 candidates. For the proposed compositional approach we evaluated 9 different weight ratios of the bases (α) and collocates (β): from $\alpha = 0.9, \beta = 0.1$ (90), to $\alpha = 0.1, \beta = 0.0$ (10).

Table 2. Average precision, recall, and f-score using the top-1 translations (top), and the top-3 (bottom) in English-Portuguese and English-Spanish. Each column of *weighted vectors* shows the results of the proposed strategy using different base/collocate ratios (from 90/10 to 10/90). *mult* and *add* methods use multiplication and addition to obtain compositional vectors, while the baseline (*bas*) uses selects the most similar base and collocate from the source collocation. *ncp* (non compositional) learns a single vector for each source and target collocation.

		Weighted vectors									*mult*	*add*	*bas*	*ncp*
		90	80	70	60	50	40	30	20	10				
top-1	Precision	0.05	0.10	0.22	0.40	0.49	0.49	**0.50**	0.47	0.36	0.28	0.41	0.43	*0.95*
	Recall	0.03	0.07	0.16	0.33	0.42	**0.44**	**0.44**	0.42	0.32	0.28	0.41	0.43	*0.46*
	F-score	0.04	0.08	0.19	0.36	0.45	**0.47**	**0.47**	0.44	0.34	0.28	0.41	0.43	*0.61*
top-3	Precision	0.11	0.17	0.32	0.48	0.61	**0.63**	**0.63**	0.61	0.57	0.34	0.53	0.43	*0.98*
	Recall	0.08	0.12	0.23	0.39	0.53	**0.56**	**0.56**	0.53	0.50	0.34	0.53	0.43	*0.50*
	F-score	0.09	0.14	0.27	0.43	0.57	**0.59**	**0.59**	0.57	0.53	0.34	0.53	0.43	*0.65*

Table 2 displays the top-1 and top-3 results of each weighted model together with the other evaluated systems (average values of English–Portuguese and English–Spanish translations). In general, the weighted method achieved the best results both in top-1 and in top-3 translations (except for the non-compositional model, which obtained high precision values between 0.95 and 0.98).

About the base–collocate weights, the results show that to select collocate candidates for a given collocation the base should not contribute more than 30% or 40% to the compositional vector, being about 60% or 70% obtained by the collocate. With higher weights of the base, the performance is dramatically lower, while increasing the contribution of the collocate involves smaller drops.

The baseline achieved better results than *mult* (top-1 and top-3), and also than the *add* models (in the top-1 evaluation). Between these two compositional approaches, the addition method was better than *mult* in every scenario (in contrast to the results of other studies—not dealing specifically with collocations—such as [29]).

With regard to the different collocation patterns, Figs. 1a and b plot the f-score values (top-3) of the translation of *verb-obj* and *adj-noun* collocations in English–Portuguese and English–Spanish, respectively. In the first case, *adj-noun* collocations were better translated than *verb-obj*, while in English–Spanish the results of both types were very similar. Also, in English–Portuguese, the baseline

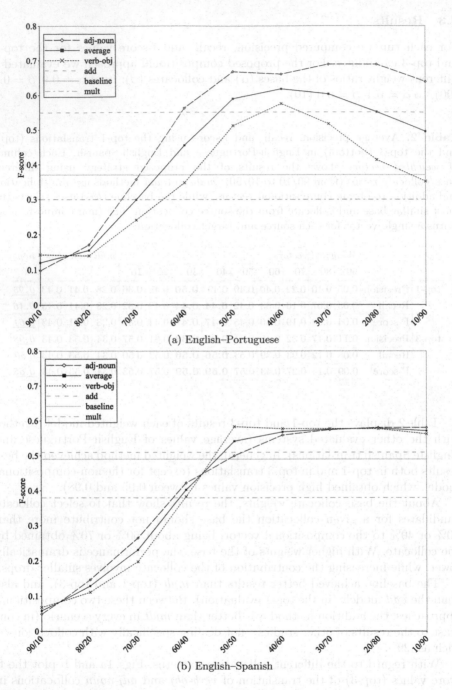

Fig. 1. F-score (top-3 results) *versus* base/collocate weight of the compositional vectors (from 90/10 to 10/90) for each collocation pattern in English–Portuguese (top) and English–Spanish (bottom) translations.

obtained noticeably worse results than both the weighted and the additive methods. If we look at the data, some of these differences in the English–Portuguese pair have arisen due to the incorrect translation of the support verb *to have* (e.g., *have [a] drink*) as *possuir* 'to own', thus generating incorrect combinations of LVCs using an incorrect collocate. These *verb-obj* results also involve a drop in the English–Portuguese values with collocate ratios of 70% and higher, which did not occur in the other language pair.

Finally, it is important to mention that, even if we should not compare the non-compositional approach to the compositional ones, the high precision achieved by this method suggests that this is a promising research line to translate both non-compositional and compositional (specially non-congruent) MWEs.[6] To make a fair comparison, we should have identified the source collocations using automatic methods, which will extract thousands of candidate collocations (many of them incorrect), thus introducing a lot of noise in the final models.

4.4 Error Analysis

In order to have a better view of the performance of our method, we have carried out a brief error analysis of the translations of the weighted models with the best average results (top-3 outputs with a 30%/70% base/collocate ratio). They had a total of 65 errors with respect to the gold-standard data, which were classified into the following 4 groups (see Table 3 for the percentage of each type):

1. Distributional model: the most frequent error type was caused by the distributional method, which represents with very similar vectors word pairs such as antonyms. For example, *put spell* was translated to Spanish as *deshacer [el] hechizo* 'break [the] spell'.
2. Compositional method: the weighted compositional method produced ≈22% of the errors. Some of them appeared due to a non-optimal weight ratio, such as the English–Portuguese *make [a] step→fazer [um] passo* instead the correct *dar [um] passo*, which was selected by the models with a higher weight of the base ($b > 0.3$). Some other mistranslations were produced because the weighted vectors (with any base/collocate ratio) could not find a proper collocate candidate among the top 10 selected.
3. Filter: few errors (4) were due to the frequency filter method, which removed several good translations with low frequency in our corpora. Thus, the English collocation *excellent mother* was translated to Spanish as *buena madre* instead of *madre excelente* because the correct equivalent only appears once in the corpus. Similarly, *dark sorcerer* was translated to Portuguese as *feiticeiro escuro* since *feiticeiro negro* also has a frequency of 1 in the corpus.
* Disagreement between the gold-standard: the second most frequent source

---

[6] Note that the high precision of the non-compositional method is an evidence of the good performance of the distributional approach and of the cross-lingual mapping, but it does not necessarily imply that collocations are non-compositional.

of errors is actually formed by suitable translations which differ from those of the gold-standard, so that they are not really mistranslations. For instance, *meet [the] requirement* was correctly translated as *reunir [el] requisito* in Spanish (instead of the gold *cumplir [el] requisito*), and *loud noise* produced the proper equivalent in Portuguese *barulho ensurdecedor* (but not *ruído alto* or *barulho alto*, the two translations present in the gold-standard).

Table 3. Percentage of each error type of the weighted additive model with a 30/70 base/collocate ratio (average results). *Disagreement* are not actual errors, but correct translations not found in the gold-standard.

	Distrib. model	Composit. method	Filter	Disagreement
Percentage	36.9	21.5	6.2	*35.4*

On one hand, these results indicate that out of 65 errors, 24 were actually good translations which differ from those in the gold-standard. This fact also helps us to understand why the results of our evaluations are lower than others in the literature, which were obtained by manually classifying the output of the systems instead of using gold-standard data sets. In this regard, the average precision results of the analyzed model would approximately increase from 0.63 to 0.75. On the other hand, the analysis sheds some light on some disadvantages of the proposed approach. Thus, the issues caused by the distributional method (which are frequent in these types of strategies) may be reduced by using contextualized models. Besides, the compositional method could be improved by dynamically adapting the weights of the additive models using unsupervised approaches which predict the compositionality of a given combination [6]. Also, it could be interesting to use different weight ratios for selecting collocate candidates and for computing the similarity between two combinations. With respect to the non-compositional model, it seems a good alternative for some combinations which are not well captured by the weighted additive models. Finally, the errors produced by the filter method were due to the relatively small size of the corpora. Further experiments are necessary to verify whether using large resources actually improves the accuracy of the filter.

5   Conclusions and Further Work

This paper has presented a compositional distributional semantics strategy to find bilingual equivalents of collocations using only monolingual corpora. The method consists of learning monolingual word embeddings and map them into a bilingual space using an (almost) unsupervised approach. To find the collocation equivalents in the target language, we first obtain a weighted compositional vector of the source collocation, which allows us to select only those collocates which are similar to the whole combination. Both to weigh the components of each collocation and to filter out unconventional combinations, we follow a phraseological approach which states that collocations are syntactically related and lexically restricted combinations of two lexical units.

Different experiments using two collocation patterns in English–Portuguese and English–Spanish have shown that a ratio of about 35%/65% (base/collocate) in the compositional vector achieves the best results in most scenarios. Besides, the evaluations have shown that the proposed method works better not only for non-congruent combinations, but also for other collocations which are also well covered by word-to-word approaches. These results confirm both the compositionality and the asymmetry of collocations, where the meaning of the collocate depends on the particular combination in which it occurs. Apart from that, we have also implemented a non-compositional strategy which obtained high precision values, being a promising method to translate compositional and non-compositional MWEs such as idioms.

In further work we plan to combine the weighted strategy with contextualized models of distributional semantics, such as the use of selectional preferences to represent the lexical units [13]. We believe that these approaches obtain more accurate distributional representations of words, so this may be an interesting line for further research, together with the referred non-compositional method. Besides, it would be interesting to separately evaluate the translation of congruent and non-congruent collocations (and eventually of non-compositional expressions) in order to identify the best method for each type, or whether simple approaches could deal with different sorts of MWEs.

Finally, it is worth mentioning that this study also contributes with two new freely available data sets for evaluating the translation of *adj-noun* and *verb-obj* collocations in English–Portuguese and English–Spanish.

References

1. Artetxe, M., Labaka, G., Agirre, E.: A robust self-learning method for fully unsupervised cross-lingual mappings of word embeddings. In: Proceedings of the 56th Annual Meeting of the Association for Computational Linguistics (Volume 1: Long Papers), pp. 789–798 (2018)
2. Baldwin, T., Tanaka, T.: Translation by machine of complex nominals: getting it right. In: Second ACL Workshop on Multiword Expressions: Integrating Processing, pp. 24–31. ACL, Barcelona (2004)
3. Baroni, M.: Composition in distributional semantics. Lang. Linguist. Compass **7**(10), 511–522 (2013)
4. Baroni, M., Zamparelli, R.: Frege in space: a program of compositional distributional semantics. LiLT (Linguist. Issues Lang. Technol.) **9**, 241–346 (2014)
5. Coecke, B., Sadrzadeh, M., Clark, S.: Mathematical foundations for a compositional distributional model of meaning. Linguist. Anal. **36**, 345–384 (2010)
6. Cordeiro, S., Villavicencio, A., Idiart, M., Ramisch, C.: Unsupervised compositionality prediction of nominal compounds. Am. J. Comput. Linguist. **45**(1), 1–57 (2019)
7. Delpech, E., Daille, B., Morin, E., Lemaire, C.: Extraction of domain-specific bilingual lexicon from comparable corpora: compositional translation and ranking. Proc. COLING **2012**, 745–762 (2012)

8. Fung, P.: A statistical view on bilingual lexicon extraction: from parallel corpora to non-parallel corpora. In: Farwell, D., Gerber, L., Hovy, E. (eds.) AMTA 1998. LNCS (LNAI), vol. 1529, pp. 1–17. Springer, Heidelberg (1998). https://doi.org/10.1007/3-540-49478-2_1

9. Fung, P., McKeown, K.: Finding terminology translations from non-parallel corpora. In: Fifth Workshop on Very Large Corpora, pp. 192–202. ACL (1997)

10. Fung, P., Yee, L.Y.: An IR approach for translating new words from nonparallel, comparable texts. In: Proceedings of the 36th Annual Meeting of the Association for Computational Linguistics and 17th International Conference on Computational Linguistics, Volume 1, pp. 414–420. ACL (1998)

11. Gamallo, P.: Comparing explicit and predictive distributional semantic models endowed with syntactic contexts. Lang. Resour. Eval. **51**(3), 727–743 (2017)

12. Gamallo, P.: The role of syntactic dependencies in compositional distributional semantics. Corpus Linguist. Linguist. Theory **13**(2), 261–289 (2017)

13. Gamallo, P., Garcia, M.: Unsupervised compositional translation of multiword expressions. In: Proceedings of the Joint Workshop on Multiword Expressions and WordNet (MWE-WN 2019). ACL, Florence (2019)

14. Gamallo, P., Garcia, M., Pineiro, C., Martinez-Castaño, R., Pichel, J.C.: LinguaKit: a big data-based multilingual tool for linguistic analysis and information extraction. In: Proceedings of the Fifth International Conference on Social Networks Analysis, Management and Security (SNAMS), pp. 239–244. IEEE (2018)

15. Garcia, M., García-Salido, M., Alonso-Ramos, M.: Using bilingual word-embeddings for multilingual collocation extraction. In: Proceedings of the 13th Workshop on Multiword Expressions (MWE 2017), pp. 21–30. ACL (2017)

16. Garcia, M., García-Salido, M., Sotelo, S., Mosqueira, E., Alonso-Ramos, M.: Pay attention when you pay the bills. A multilingual corpus with dependency-based and semantic annotation of collocations. In: Proceedings of the 57th Annual Meeting of the Association for Computational Linguistics (ACL 2019). ACL, Florence (2019)

17. Grefenstette, G.: The world wide web as a resource for example-based machine translation tasks. In: Proceedings of the ASLIB Conference on Translating and the Computer, vol. 21 (1999)

18. Haruno, M., Ikehara, S., Yamazaki, T.: Learning bilingual collocations by word-level sorting. In: Proceedings of the 16th Conference on Computational Linguistics. COLING 1996, vol. 1, pp. 525–530 (1996)

19. Hausmann, F.J.: Le dictionnaire de collocations. In: Hausmann, F.J., Reichmann, O., Wiegand, H., Zgusta, L. (eds.) Wörterbücher: ein internationales Handbuch zur Lexikographie. Dictionaries. Dictionnaires, pp. 1010–1019. Mouton De Gruyter, Berlin (1989)

20. Koehn, P.: EuroParl: a parallel corpus for statistical machine translation. In: Proceedings of the 10th Machine Translation Summit, Phuket, pp. 79–86 (2005)

21. Kupiec, J.: An algorithm for finding noun phrase correspondences in bilingual corpora. In: Proceedings of the 31st Annual Meeting on Association for Computational Linguistics (ACL 1993), pp. 17–22. ACL (1993)

22. Lample, G., Conneau, A., Denoyer, L., Ranzato, M.: Unsupervised machine translation using monolingual corpora only. In: Proceedings of the Sixth International Conference on Learning Representations (ICLR 2018) (2018)

23. Lison, P., Tiedemann, J.: OpenSubtitles2016: extracting large parallel corpora from movie and TV subtitles. In: Calzolari, N., et al. (eds.) Proceedings of the 10th International Conference on Language Resources and Evaluation (LREC 2016), pp. 923–929. European Language Resources Association (ELRA) (2016)

24. Mel'čuk, I.: Collocations and lexical functions. In: Cowie, A.P. (ed.) Phraseology. Theory, Analysis and Applications, pp. 23–53. Clarendon Press, Oxford (1998)
25. Mel'čuk, I.: Phraseology in the language, in the dictionary, and in the computer. Yearb. Phraseol. **3**(1), 31–56 (2012)
26. Mikolov, T., Chen, K., Corrado, G., Dean, J.: Efficient estimation of word representations in vector space. In: Workshop Proceedings of the International Conference on Learning Representations (ICLR 2013) (2013). arXiv preprint arXiv:1301.3781
27. Mikolov, T., Le, Q.V., Sutskever, I.: Exploiting similarities among languages for machine translation. CoRR abs/1309.4168 (2013)
28. Mitchell, J., Lapata, M.: Vector-based models of semantic composition. In: Proceedings of ACL 2008: HLT, pp. 236–244. ACL (2008)
29. Mitchell, J., Lapata, M.: Composition in distributional models of semantics. Cognit. Sci. **34**(8), 1388–1429 (2010)
30. Morin, E., Daille, B.: Revising the compositional method for terminology acquisition from comparable corpora. In: Proceedings of COLING 2012, Mumbai, India, pp. 1797–1810 (2012)
31. Nesselhauf, N.: The use of collocations by advanced learners of English and some implications for teaching. Appl. Linguist. **24**(2), 223–242 (2003)
32. Rapp, R.: Automatic identification of word translations from unrelated English and German corpora. In: Proceedings of the 37th Annual Meeting of the Association for Computational Linguistics (ACL 1999), pp. 519–526. ACL (1999)
33. Reddy, S., Klapaftis, I., McCarthy, D., Manandhar, S.: Dynamic and static prototype vectors for semantic composition. In: Proceedings of 5th International Joint Conference on Natural Language Processing, pp. 705–713. Asian Federation of Natural Language Processing (2011)
34. Rivera, O., Mitkov, R., Pastor, G.: A flexible framework for collocation retrieval and translation from parallel and comparable corpora. In: Proceedings of the Workshop on Multi-word Units in Machine Translation and Translation Technology, pp. 18–25 (2013)
35. Seretan, V., Wehrli, E.: Collocation translation based on sentence alignment and parsing. In: Actes de la 14e conference sur le traitement automatique des langues naturelles, TALN 2007, pp. 401–410. IRIT Press (2007)
36. Smadja, F.: How to compile a bilingual collocational lexicon automatically. In: Proceedings of the AAAI Workshop on Statistically-Based NLP Techniques, pp. 57–63. AAAI Press (1992)
37. Straka, M., Straková, J.: Tokenizing, POS tagging, lemmatizing and parsing UD 2.0 with UDPipe. In: Proceedings of the CoNLL 2017 Shared Task: Multilingual Parsing from Raw Text to Universal Dependencies, pp. 88–99. ACL, August 2017
38. Tanaka, T., Baldwin, T.: Noun-noun compound machine translation a feasibility study on shallow processing. In: Proceedings of the ACL 2003 Workshop on Multiword Expressions: Analysis, Acquisition and Treatment, pp. 17–24. ACL (2003)
39. Taslimipoor, S., Mitkov, R., Corpas Pastor, G., Fazly, A.: Bilingual contexts from comparable corpora to mine for translations of collocations. In: Gelbukh, A. (ed.) CICLing 2016. LNCS, vol. 9624, pp. 115–126. Springer, Cham (2018). https://doi.org/10.1007/978-3-319-75487-1_10
40. Upadhyay, S., Faruqui, M., Dyer, C., Roth, D.: Cross-lingual models of word embeddings: an empirical comparison. In: Proceedings of the 54th Annual Meeting of the Association for Computational Linguistics (Volume 1: Long Papers), pp. 1661–1670 (2016)

41. Vargas, N., Ramisch, C., Caseli, H.: Discovering light verb constructions and their translations from parallel corpora without word alignment. In: Proceedings of the 13th Workshop on Multiword Expressions (MWE 2017), pp. 91–96. ACL (2017)
42. Weir, D., Weeds, J., Reffin, J., Kober, T.: Aligning packed dependency trees: a theory of composition for distributional semantics. Am. J. Comput. Linguist. **42**(4), 727–761 (2016)
43. Wu, C.C., Chang, J.S.: Bilingual collocation extraction based on syntactic and statistical analyses. In: Proceedings of the 15th Conference on Computational Linguistics and Speech Processing, pp. 1–20. Association for Computational Linguistics and Chinese Language Processing (2003)

Phraseological Variation in Spanish Academic Writing

Marcos García Salido(✉) (iD)

Grupo LyS, Departamento de Letras, Universidade da Coruña,
Campus da Zapateira, 15071 A Coruña, Spain
marcos.garcias@udc.es

Abstract. Research on lexical bundles has shown that a considerable part of discourse relies on a set of routinised lexical combinations. This has had implications both for descriptive research and for lexicographic applications. Thus, from a descriptive perspective, considerable attention has been paid to the description of lexical bundles in terms of their structure and functions and to the different preferences of bundles' use from different genres. As for lexicographic applications, lexical bundles have been integrated in dictionaries and writing aids. This paper analyses to what extent a cross-disciplinary set of lexical bundles can be identified for academic writing in Spanish and to what extent the use of these bundles varies depending on the scientific domain considered.

Keywords: Lexical bundles · Academic writing · Cross-disciplinary variation

1 Introduction

To a considerable extent, discourse is not assembled on the fly by combining lexical units according to general syntactic rules, but speakers have at their disposal repositories of conventional ways for phrasing meanings. Corpus linguistics research provided evidence in this respect since its inception [18] and, more recently, there has been a number of studies confirming to what extent this assumption holds by studying recurrent lexical combinations often termed as *lexical bundles* [3,5,13].

Lexical bundles are recurrent n-grams (i.e. combinations of contiguous words, usually with a minimum length of three words), defined by their frequency[1] and dispersion. Structurally, lexical bundles are often fragmentary units in terms of their syntax [3]. They are also difficult to classify from a phraseological perspective—if phraseology is to be defined in terms of compositionality and/or the free combinatorial possibilities of lexical units [16]. Biber et al. [3] note that few bundles are idiomatic and the majority of them are compositional. They are,

---

[1] A common frequency threshold is 10 occurrences per million words.

G. Corpas Pastor and R. Mitkov (Eds.): Europhras 2019, LNAI 11755, pp. 129–143, 2019.
https://doi.org/10.1007/978-3-030-30135-4_10

however, prone to be grouped according to their discourse function and several classifications of this type have been proposed (cf. [3,13], among others).

Coxhead and Byrd [7] have emphasised the importance of lexical bundles in language instruction: they assume that these routinised combinations make the writing process easier, due to their ready-made character, and that, due to their frequent use, they act as markers of academic style. Academic discourse in particular has been one domain where the study of lexical bundles has thrived.

Although lexical bundles are recurrent and widespread across different texts, there seem to be partially different repertoires of lexical bundles depending on the text genre considered. Thus, Biber et al. [3] studied lexical bundles' variation in spoken and written modes. Cortés [5] focused on differences between published writers and students and, later on, on differences between academic styles in different languages [6]. Furthermore, a considerable amount of attention has been paid to differences between academic disciplines [8,11,13].

On account of his own findings, Hyland [13] emphasised the dissimilar occurrence patterns and values of lexical bundles across genres and was sceptical about the existence of a common core of academic vocabulary—either in terms of single words (see [14]) or combinations thereof. This view was challenged by Simpson-Vlach and Ellis [17], who proposed a list of academic formulas of English. Simpson-Vlach and Ellis also pointed out another limitation of using lexical bundles extracted on the basis of frequency and dispersion alone for teaching purposes: their unequal psycho-linguistic salience. Fragmentariness and redundancy (i.e. the fact that a given bundle is included in other of different length) have been also singled out as problematic aspects of bundle lists and several measures have been proposed to obtain more refined repertoires [2,9].

The aim of this paper is to establish to what extent a cross-disciplinary set of lexical bundles can be proposed for academic writing in Spanish and how the use of these bundles varies depending on the scientific domain considered. In this study, the scientific domains compared are established following an approach recently proposed by Durrant [8]: instead of dividing the corpus according to external criteria, the texts are grouped after their similarity in the use of n-grams.

The remainder of the paper is organised as follows. Section 2 presents the corpus from which the bundle candidates were extracted, the method used for its division into sections, and the criteria used to identify and classify lexical bundles. In Sect. 3, the division of the corpus based on the degree of overlap between the n-grams of each text is explained. Then the core academic bundles identified are described, as well as those with a markedly different distributions across subcorpora. These results are discussed in Sect. 4 and, finally, I briefly present the conclusions of the research.

2   Method

This section describes the corpus used in this study, the method to establish different sub-corpora and to identify lexical bundles shared across such sub-corpora and those with different patterns of use. Finally, it presents summarily a functional classification of bundles originally proposed by Hyland [13] that will be applied to the extracted bundles, with some modifications.

2.1   The Corpus

The corpus used here is part of the HARTA novice corpus [21]. This consists of BA and Master theses coming from four domains, established according to the degree of the author in question: Arts and Humanities, Biology and Health Sciences, Physical Sciences and Social Sciences. The theses were publicly available at the repositories of their respective universities in pdf format. Those files were then exported to xml and revised in order to guarantee the integrity of the texts (i.e., avoiding OCR misreadings, incorrect sentence splitting, etc.). For the present study, only texts with different authors were preserved, so that each author is represented only once in the corpus. This led to a sample of 166 texts, amounting to a total of 2,150,374 words.

To establish the internal divisions of the corpus, the method proposed in Durrant [8] was used. From each text, a list of its four-grams was extracted and then a matrix was built to reflect the distance between the whole set of texts. This was done by calculating the shared four-grams for each two texts, according to the formula proposed by Durrant [8]:

$$overlap = \frac{n1 + n2}{l1 + l2} \tag{1}$$

Given two texts in the corpus, $n1$ represents the total of four-grams from the first text that are found also in the second text; $n2$ the number of four-grams of the second text found in the first; $l1$ is the total of four-grams of the first text and $l2$ the same measure for the second text.[2]

If this matrix is submitted to a cluster analysis, the result is the one seen in Fig. 1 and commented in Sect. 3.1 below.[3]

2.2   Identification of Bundles and Distributional Differences

Lexical bundles are n-grams characterized by their recurrence and dispersion, so that frequency and distribution thresholds are their defining traits. Following Durrant [8], I set a dispersion threshold whereby, in order to be considered a lexical bundle, an n-gram should be used by at least 20% authors of each of the compared sub-corpora. This in itself led to a minimum frequency of 20 in the whole corpus (i.e. ca. 10 occurrences per million words).

To establish which elements from this set of academic lexical bundles was used differently across the sections of our corpus, the bundles in question must occur almost twice in a given section with respect to another (in terms of its normalized frequency).

---

[2] Only four-grams with a minimal frequency of 2 ware taken into account.

[3] The cluster analysis was performed with the factoextra package of R (available at https://github.com/kassambara/factoextra), used also to obtain the dendrogram representation.

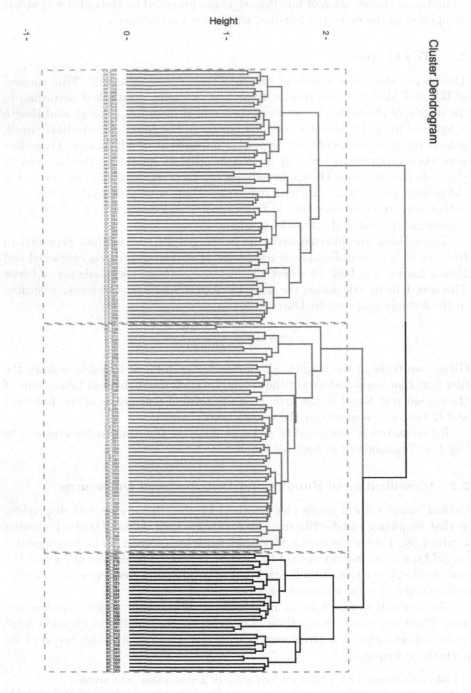

Fig. 1. Dendrogram of a cluster analysis of the corpus' texts (Color figure online)

2.3   Bundles Functional Classification

Hyland's proposal [13] was used to classify lexical bundles according to their function. Hyland establishes three main groups of functions related to systemic grammar's three metafunctions: ideational, textual and interpersonal. Hyland's first group covers research-oriented bundles that can express location, procedure and quantification, that are used to describe or are related to the particular topic of the text. To this group I added the category *agentive* and borrowed from Tracy-Ventura et al. [19] the category of *structural only* bundles. The former covers the cases of a complex preposition introducing agents and the latter includes instances of bundles made-up of functional words, which are hard to assign a unique function. Text-oriented bundles express additive and contrast relations (*transitions*), causal relations (*resultative*), give indications about textual organization (*text-structuring*), or "situate arguments in limiting conditions" [13, p. 14] (*framing*). Finally, Hyland proposes a third group with participant-oriented bundles, which is replaced here by the hallidayan label *interpersonal*. In this study, only one example of the interpersonal functions originally proposed by Hyland was found. To this, I added bundles introducing a source, given the usual inclusion of evidential markers within the interpersonal metafunction [12, p. 387].

3   Results

This section presents first the results of grouping the corpus texts in clusters according to their similarity in terms of shared n-grams. Then, the n-grams that met the requirements to qualify as lexical bundles are described in terms of their function and structure. Finally, I examine those bundles that have markedly different distributions in the sub-corpora.

3.1   Corpus Sections

As can be seen in Fig. 1, the texts have been grouped into three main clusters. These clusters are built bottom up, that is, the groups at the bottom contain texts more closely related than those in higher positions. A previous version with four big clusters yielded the same groupings, but the one in yellow was subdivided into two further clusters. A three-way division yields a more balanced division in terms of the number of texts included in each cluster, but the third one is still smaller than the other two clusters.

The initial branching corresponds to the traditional hard- and soft sciences division. This initial branching seems related to Biglan [4] paradigmatic vs. non paradigmatic dimensions, understanding paradigms à la Kuhn as specifications of "the appropriate problems for study and the appropriate methods to be used" [4, p. 195]. The rightmost branch is in turn subdivided into a medicine-dominated branch and one that combines mostly Medicine, Biology, Physical Sciences and Engineering texts. It is difficult to establish a correspondence between this subdivision of the hard-science texts and Biglan's dimensions. An examination of the research topics dealt with in the Medicine-only sub-cluster suggests that these texts focus mostly on health-care delivery. In contrast, the Medicine texts in the more heterogeneous Cluster 2 deal with a larger variety of topics (Neurophysiology, Pharmacology, etc.).

This division based on the overlap of lexical combinations of different texts diverges in some respects from the classification of texts based on external criteria that was originally applied in the compilation process. Thus, there are some texts belonging to the Humanities or Social Sciences within hard-science dominated clusters and some hard-science theses within the soft-science dominated cluster. As for the inclusion of texts belonging to disciplines traditionally conceived of as soft-sciences within Cluster 2, it probably has to do with the methodological approach of the studies in question. Two studies in Linguistics include experimental designs and techniques characteristic of psycho- and neurolinguistic research (reading speed measurements and event-related potentials). The case of two studies initially classified in the field "Education" is similar. Both include meticulous experimental designs—one of them uses also reading speed measures, among other standardized tests.

With respect to the inclusion of Biology, Physics and Geology texts in the soft-sciences cluster, it can be due to several reasons. Four of the Geology studies in this cluster (CS_030, CS_031, CS_032, CS_033) adopt a socio-historical perspective (three of them study climate evolution through time and the other climate in urban contexts). It is harder to explain the grouping of BC_001 (a study of birds from a particular region), BC_048 (about waste composting), AH_027 (on the curation of a fabric museum), CF_012 (a study on the dangers caused by floods) and CF_032 (about wildfires). The grouping of CF_006, CF_021, CF_023, CF_025 probably has to do with the topic of three of them (some aspects of light), but it is hard to see why were they included in the soft-science cluster.

All in all, it seems that not only topic, but also methodology, are decisive as to the similarity of word sequences present in the texts, and their consequent clustering.

For the rest of the study, given the markedly different size of the three clusters, the sections compared in terms of their use of lexical bundles are the ones resulting from the first branching: the cluster in blue, dominated by soft-sciences texts, and the one grouping the other two clusters, predominantly belonging to hard-sciences (Table 1).

3.2   Core Academic Lexical Bundles

The list of bundles that reach the frequency and dispersion thresholds includes 103 items (displayed on Table 3 in Appendix). This set represents, then, a repertoire of routinised sequences spread across a relatively wide variety of disciplines. They are described more thoroughly below in terms of their structure and discourse functions, according to the three big groups established in Sect. 2.3. With respect to discourse function, it must be noted that several of them have been given more than one. For instance, *a partir de el/la/etc.* ('starting from') can be used both to indicate an initial point in time (Example 1) and to introduce

Table 1. Correspondence between clusters and external classification

CLUSTER	Discipline	No. of texts
CLUSTER 1 1,305,895 words	Economics and Business	14
	Library Science	10
	Literature	8
	Linguistics	8
	Sociolocy	6
	Geology	6
	History and Culture	5
	Education	3
	Art	3
	Engineering	2
	Physics	2
	Biology	2
	Chemistry	1
CLUSTER 2 570,493 words	Biology	17
	Chemistry	15
	Medicine	11
	Geology	9
	Engineering	3
	Linguistics	2
	Computer Science	2
	Education	2
	Economics and Business	2
CLUSTER 3 273,986 words	Medicine	33

a source of information (Example 2). Similarly, *al inicio de* ('at the beginning of') can express temporal location (Example 3) or can refer to other parts of the text (Example 4):

Example 1. [...] a partir de la década de 1920, algunos cantones suizos empezaron a copiar estas prácticas [...]
'From the decade of 1920, some Swiss cantons started to copy these practices'

Example 2. [...] redactando por escrito cada uno de los diferentes apartados que comprenden el presente trabajo, a partir del material anteriormente mencionado [...]
'writing each of the different sections that make up this piece of research from the above mentioned material'

Example 3. [...] hay un millón y medio menos de activos menores de 30 años que al inicio de la crisis [...]

'There is a million and a half of employed people younger less than 30 years than at the beginning of the crisis'

Example 4. La discriminación es un tema, como se comenta al inicio del trabajo, importante de hoy en día [...]
'Discrimination is an important matter today, as said at the beginning of the text'

Research-Oriented Bundles. Most bundles fulfil research-oriented functions and, among these, those related to procedures are the most numerous. Some of them are non-compositional complex prepositions that convey either a sense of finality (*con el fin de, con el objetivo de* 'with the purpose of') or an instrumental meaning (*a través de DET* 'through DET'). Other are nominalizations, inserted or not in prepositional phrases, that refer to the research process or development (*el desarrollo de el* 'the development of', *en el desarrollo* 'in the development'). Finally, some of the few verbal bundles identified are included in this group (*ha llevado a cabo* 'has undertaken', *se lleva a cabo* 'is undertaken') and convey activity meanings.

Bundles conveying quantity are the second most numerous group with a research-oriented function: they are either imprecise quantifiers (*la mayoría de, la mayor parte de,* 'most of') or distributive ones (*cada uno de los,* 'each of the').

Location bundles tend to be complex prepositions (*a partir de* 'from') or prepositional phrases (*en los últimos años* 'in the last few years, lately'). Those with the structure of noun phrases tend to be fragments of prepositional phrases: thus the bundle *lo largo de* is always preceded by the preposition *a* in the corpus and *el ámbito de* follows the preposition *en* in 151 out of 170 occurrences.

Descriptive bundles are mostly used to ascribe an entity to a category (*de el tipo de* 'of the X type', *es uno de los* 'is one of the', *se trata de un* 'is a', etc.). The label *Topic* covers those bundles containing specific content words that are difficult to assign to the other functions. The two categories added to Hyland's original five are the least productive. However, the agentive category was included because *por parte de DET* is clearly a complex preposition that introduces agents in passive or middle constructions or nominalizations and did not seem to fit into the rest of ideational categories. The structural only bundles, in turn, are difficult to classify given their lack of lexical content.

Text-Oriented Bundles. Among the group of text-oriented bundles, those classified as framing signals are the most numerous. Most of them, when used clause-initially are topic markers, and, when used in non-initial positions, they act as prepositional phrases delimiting the applicability of the element they modify:

Example 5. Con respecto al lenguaje, las regiones cerebrales que abarcan estas funciones se corresponden con las siguientes áreas de Brodmann [...]
'As for language, the brain regions covering these functions correspond to the following Brodmann areas'

Example 6 (...). el resultado no sólo no mejora sino que claramente empeora con respecto al de la Fig. [...]
[...] the result not only does not improve, but is clearly worse as compared to that in Fig. [...]

This group of bundles also include those expressing condition (*en función de* 'as a function of'). An interesting case of framing signals is the bundle *desde el punto de vista*, which here appears fragmented (*desde el punto de*, *el punto de vista*). This bundle seems to be mostly used to shift topics or to delimit the domain of applicability of a statement, much in the same way as c*on respecto a DET* or *en cuanto a DET*:

Example 7. Desde el punto de vista de la comunicación, la conectividad permanente del móvil es su característica más relevante para diferenciarlo [...]
'With respect to communication, mobile phones' permanent connectivity is the most relevant characteristic to distinguish them [...]'

Example 8. '[...] las posibilidades de aprovechar estas ventajas en sectores poco estructurados, desde el punto de vista de los derechos de los trabajadores, son ínfimas [...]'
'the possibilities of profiting from those advantages in little structured sectors, in terms of workers' rights, are minimal [...]'

These uses also illustrate the lack of compositionality of this particular bundle: it is evident that communication or workers' rights are not capable of cognition, which is the domain to which dictionaries relate the expression *punto de vista* (the *Diccionario de la lengua española* [DLE][4] defines it as "[c]ada uno de los modos de considerar un asunto" 'way of considering a subject'). On the contrary, *desde el punto de vista*+PP/adjective conveys a procedural indication either in order to make clear text structure or to introduce restrictions to the propositional content conveyed by the modified clause.

The three remaining groups of text-oriented bundles have fewer instances. The transition signals, as proposed by Hyland, include addition (*al igual que* 'as well as', *al mismo tiempo* 'at the same time', *tal y como se* 'as REFL') and contrast markers (*a pesar de que* 'in spite of'). Three of them are included in the DLE as idioms ("locuciones conjuntivas").

Interpersonal Bundles. Lastly, in the case of interpersonal bundles, none of the strings meeting the frequency and dispersion criteria enter into the stance category proposed by Hyland. *Tener en cuenta que* 'take into account that' has been classified as an engagement feature. It occurs mostly in obligative verbal periphrases[5] (36 instances with *haber* 'have to' and 18 instances with *deber*

---

[4] Accessible at https://dle.rae.es.
[5] This is the traditional label for compounds of auxiliary plus auxiliated verbal forms, where the auxiliar conveys aspectual or modal senses.

'must' out of 84 instances). In such cases it directs the reader's attention to a particularly important point.

The function *Source* has been added to Hyland's original classification basically to account for some uses of the variants of *a partir de+DET*, which also convey locative meanings (see Example 1).

3.3   Variation Across Domains

Out of the 103 lexical bundles just described, only a relatively low percentage have distributions markedly different in the hard- and soft-sciences sections (i.e., they occur twice as much in one of the sections): 12 out of 103 (i.e., some 12%). These are displayed in Table 2.

Table 2. Key bundles in hard- and soft-sciences (the latter are given in boldface).

Discourse function		Bundle	Freq. in SoftS	Freq. in HardS
Research-ortd.	Location	*a el final de*	42.9	101.8
	Procedure	*el objetivo de este*	15.3	35.5
		para la realización de	29.1	60.4
		la realización de este	14.5	34.3
	Description	***es el caso de***	71.2	30.8
	Topic	*de la calidad de*	19.9	49.7
Text-ortd.	Resultative	*por lo que es*	17.6	35.5
		se basa en la	18.4	37.9
		y por lo tanto	37.5	99.5
	Text-struct	*en el presente trabajo*	37.5	99.5
	Framing	***desde el punto***	101.8	34.3
		el punto de vista	101.3	36.7

Out of these bundles, most are *key* to the hard-science sub-corpus and recurrently belong to the discourse functions *Procedure* and *Resultative*. By contrast, the bundles markedly more frequent in the soft-science sub-corpus perform describing and framing functions.

4   Discussion

The results reviewed so far can provide the answer to questions asked at the beginning of this paper: to what extent a cross-disciplinary set of lexical bundles can be proposed for academic Spanish and how they vary depending on the scientific domain considered. Both a set of common markers of academic writing and variation patterns across scientific disciplines have been identified. This could lead to tools that satisfy students' needs in writing both with general and specific academic purposes.

With respect to variation, the findings on the distributional differences of academic bundles are in accordance with some previous observations made in the case of English by authors such as Hyland [13] or Durrant [8]. Thus, both note the more prominent use of framing signals in the Humanities, and the more prevalent use of procedure-related bundles in the hard sciences. With respect to the latter, Hyland points out a desire of conveying the experimental basis of research and an emphasis on empirical over interpretive aspects. Durrant, in turn, notes the association between procedure-related bundles and the construal of objects as instruments or the conveying of the tight control exerted over processes.

Although in our study, the evidence in this respect is somewhat more scarce, some research-oriented bundles seem also to be associated with the fact that experimental designs are more prominent in hard-sciences texts. Some instances of *para la realización de* 'for the undertaking of', which combines procedural with purpose indications, appear in connection with the use of materials or the design of experiments.

Example 9. El material inventariable que se utilizará para la realización del estudio será el siguiente [...] (BC_063)
'The equipment that will be used to carry out the study'

Example 10. La información será utilizada única y exclusivamente para la realización del estudio (BC_042)
'The informantion will be used solely to carry out the study'

A difference between soft- and hard-sciences also apparent in Durrant's data is the more prominent use of resultative signals in the latter disciplines. This fact could be in contradiction with Hyland's perception of the lesser importance given to interpretation in hard-science—given that discovering causal relations requires interpretation. However, it cannot be discarded that soft-sciences exploit different means of conveying these cause-and-effect relations (less conventionalized ones, or not meeting the formal characteristics of the sequences studied here).

In any case, and according to our data, variation in lexical bundles between hard- and soft-sciences is not so prominent as to make impossible the identification of a core repertoire of academic combinations. In fact, in the corpus analysed only about 12% of the lexical bundles had markedly different distributions in the two sections compared, which indicate that the academic community rely on a shared repertoire of this type of combinations.

A different matter is whether this repertoire of lexical bundles (i.e. recurrent and spread n-grams) is of the same utility for writers. As pointed out in the introduction, Simpson-Vlach and Ellis [17] note that frequency and dispersion thresholds alone do not guarantee the same psycho-linguistic salience for every lexical bundle. In this respect, the so-called structural-only bundles come to mind. Those seem to be a particular feature of Spanish—or at least, to be absent from English four-word bundles—thence the incorporation of this category by Tracy-Ventura et al. [19] and by Cortés [6] afterwards.

Other problematical candidates are fragments and redundant bundles [2,9]. A case in point is *desde el punto de vista*. This six-word bundle occurs split in two different fragments in our set of candidates (*desde el punto de, el punto de vista*), which overlap themselves. Furthermore, one of these two fragments would have probably a different function (and meaning) outside this particular context (as said, the prepositional phrase is used mostly as a framing device that has lost the mental sense conveyed by the noun phrase alone).

These results have some implications for teaching and lexicography. As said, Simpson-Vlach and Ellis [17] compiled a list of English academic formulas with pedagogical aims by refining lexical-bundle extraction techniques. Other researchers and lexicographers have followed suit and integrated lexical bundles into lexicographical works [10,15,20]. Judging after the results of this study, it seems feasible to use bundle extraction to obtain a core set of academic formulas common to hard- and soft-sciences in Spanish, even though, there is probably a need of research on further refining of identification techniques in order to integrate the outcome of such extraction in user-oriented reference works.

5   Conclusion

This paper has studied whether a set of cross-disciplinary lexical bundles can be identified in academic texts and to what extent these vary across different disciplines. With such a view, I have used a corpus academic texts divided into sections, not by means of external criteria, but by their similarity in the use of four-grams. Lexical bundles are just a tiny subset of those four-grams that met certain frequency and dispersion criteria. Our results suggest that Spanish academic writing indeed possesses such a core repertoire of lexical bundles.

Within this set of core academic lexical bundles a few instances show differences in their distribution between hard- and soft-sciences texts. Such differences could correspond to discrepancies in research methods and aims between fields. There are also intriguing parallels between what can be observed for Spanish and what other studies have found in English academic writing. However, some caution is advisable, since most studies have focused on four-word bundles—this paper is no exception in this respect— and it cannot be known whether the same tendencies are present in lexical combinations of different lengths.

Finally, as other studies before [6,17], the results presented here open up new possibilities for the inclusion of this type of lexical combinations in teaching and lexicographic resources [1,10], but this is left for further research. What seems clear so far is that, whereas bundles identified on the bases of frequency and dispersion are useful for descriptive studies, their presentation to lay users would require further refinement.

Acknowledgments. Supported by Xunta de Galicia, through grant ED481D 2017/009.

Appendix: Cross-disciplinary Lexical Bundles

Table 3. Cross-disciplinary lexical bundles

Research-oriented	
Location	*a el final de, a el inicio de, a el mismo tiempo, a lo largo de, a partir de el, a partir de la, a partir de las, a partir de los, el ámbito de la, el inicio de el, en el interior de, en el momento de, en los últimos años, lo largo de el, lo largo de la*
Procedure	*a el uso de, a la hora de, a través de el, a través de la, a través de las, a través de los, a través de un, con el fin de, con el objetivo de, de el proceso de, de llevar a cabo, el análisis de la, el análisis de los, el desarrollo de el, el desarrollo de la, el estudio de el, el objetivo de este, el uso de el, en el desarrollo de, en el proceso de, ha llevado a cabo, la realización de este, para el desarrollo de, para la realización de, para llevar a cabo, se lleva a cabo*
Quantification	*cada una de las, cada uno de ellos, cada uno de los, de cada una de, de cada uno de, de el número de, en la mayoría de, la mayor parte de, la mayoría de las, la mayoría de los*
Description	*de el tipo de, de este tipo de, el aumento de la, el caso de las, el caso de los, en este tipo de, es el caso de, es una de las, es uno de los, las características de el, se trata de un, se trata de una*
Topic	*a la falta de, de la calidad de, de la universidad de, el estudio de el, el estudio de la, el hecho de que, en el estudio de, la base de datos*
Agentive	*por parte de los*
Structural only	*en el que se, en la que se, en las que se, en los que se*
Text-oriented	
Transition	*a el igual que, a el mismo tiempo, a pesar de que, tal y como se*
Resultative	*por lo que es, por lo que la, por lo que no, por lo que se, se basa en la (?), y por lo tanto*
Text-struct.	*a el final de, a el inicio de, el inicio de el, en el presente trabajo, tal y como se*
Framing	*con respecto a el, con respecto a la, desde el punto de, el ámbito de la, el campo de la, el caso de el, el caso de la, el caso de las, el caso de los, el caso de que, el punto de vista, en cuanto a el, en cuanto a la, en cuanto a las, en cuanto a los, en el ámbito de, en el caso de, en este tipo de, en función de el, en función de la, en relación a el*
Interpersonal	
Engagement	*tener en cuenta que*
Source	*a partir de el, a partir de la, a partir de los, a partir de las*

References

1. Alonso-Ramos, M., García-Salido, M., Garcia, M.: Exploiting a corpus to compile a lexical resource for academic writing: Spanish lexical combinations. In: Kosem, I., et al. (eds.) Proceedings of 2017 eLex Conference, pp. 571–586. Lexical Computing CZ, Brno (2017)
2. Appel, R., Trofimovich, P.: Transitional probability predicts native and non-native use of formulaic sequences. Int. J. Appl. Linguist. **27**, 1–20 (2017). https://doi.org/10.1111/ijal.12100
3. Biber, D., Conrad, S., Viviana, C.: If you look at... Lexical bundles in university teaching and textbooks. Appl. Linguist. **25**, 371–405 (2004)
4. Biglan, A.: The characteristics of subject matter in different academic areas. J. Appl. Psychol. **57**(3), 195–203 (1973). https://doi.org/10.1037/h0034701
5. Cortes, V.: Lexical bundles in published and student disciplinary writing: examples from history and biology. Engl. Specif. Purp. **23**(4), 397–423 (2004). https://doi.org/10.1016/j.esp.2003.12.001
6. Cortes, V.: A comparative analysis of lexical bundles in academic history writing in English and Spanish. Corpora **3**(1), 43–57 (2008). https://doi.org/10.3366/e1749503208000063
7. Coxhead, A., Byrd, P.: Preparing writing teachers to teach the vocabulary and grammar of academic prose. J. Second Lang. Writ. **16**(3), 129–147 (2007). https://doi.org/10.1016/j.jslw.2007.07.002
8. Durrant, P.: Lexical bundles and disciplinary variation in university students' writing: mapping the territories. Appl. Linguist. **38**(2), 165–193 (2017). https://doi.org/10.1093/applin/amv011
9. Grabowski, Ł., Juknevičienė, R.: Towards a refined inventory of lexical bundles: an experiment in the Formulex method. Stud. Lang. **29**, 58–73 (2017). https://doi.org/10.5755/j01.sal.0.29.15327. http://www.kalbos.ktu.lt/index.php/KStud/article/view/15327
10. Granger, S., Paquot, M.: Electronic lexicography goes local: design and structures of a needs-driven online academic writing aid. Lexicographica: Int. Ann. Lexicogr **31**(1), 118–141 (2015). https://doi.org/10.1515/lexi. http://hdl.handle.net/2078.1/166516
11. Groom, N.: Pattern and meaning across genres and disciplines: an exploratory study. Engl. Acad. Purp. **4**(3), 257–277 (2005)
12. Halliday, M.: Functional Grammar. Routledge, London (2004). https://doi.org/10.1023/A:1021717531970
13. Hyland, K.: As can be seen: lexical bundles and disciplinary variation. Engl. Specif. Purp. **27**(1), 4–21 (2008). https://doi.org/10.1016/j.esp.2007.06.001
14. Hyland, K., Tse, P.: Is there an "academic vocabulary"? TESOL Q. **41**(2), 235–253 (2007). https://doi.org/10.1002/j.1545-7249.2007.tb00058.x
15. Kübler, N., Pecman, M.: The ARTES bilingual LSP dictionary: from collocation to higher order phraseology. In: Electronic Lexicography, pp. 187–210. Oxford University Press (2012). https://doi.org/10.1093/acprof:oso/9780199654864.003.0010
16. Mel'čuk, I.: Phraseology in the language, in the dictionary, and in the computer. Yearb. Phraseol. **3**, 31–56 (2012). https://doi.org/10.1515/phras-2012-0003
17. Simpson-Vlach, R., Ellis, N.C.: An academic formulas list: new methods in phraseology research. Appl. Linguist. **31**(4), 487–512 (2010). https://doi.org/10.1093/applin/amp058

18. Sinclair, J.: Corpus, Concordance, Collocation. Oxford University Press, Oxford (1991). https://doi.org/10.2307/330144
19. Tracy-Ventura, N., Cortes, V., Biber, D.: Lexical bundles in speech and writing. In: Working with Spanish Corpora, pp. 217–231. Continuum, New York (2007)
20. Verdaguer, I., et al.: Scie-Lex. A lexical database. In: Verdaguer, I., Laso, N.J., Salazar, D. (eds.) Biomedical English: A Corpus-Based Approach, pp. 21–38. John Benjamins, Amsterdam (2013)
21. Villayandre Llamazares, M.: "HARTA" de noveles: un corpus de español académico. CHIMERA: Revista de Corpus de Lenguas Romances y Estudios Lingüísticos 5(1), 131 (2019). https://doi.org/10.15366/chimera2018.5.1.011

Identifying Lexical Bundles for an Academic Writing Assistant in Spanish

Marcos García Salido[1](✉)(iD), Marcos Garcia[1,2](✉)(iD),
and Margarita Alonso-Ramos[1,2](✉)(iD)

[1] Grupo LyS, Departamento de Letras, Fac. de Filoloxía, Universidade da Coruña,
Campus da Zapateira, 15071 A Coruña, Spain
{marcos.garcias,marcos.garcia.gonzalez,marcogarita.alonso}@udc.es
[2] CITIC, Universidade da Coruña, Campus de Elviña, 15071 A Coruña, Spain

Abstract. This paper presents the process of identifying recurrent multi-word expressions (i.e. lexical bundles) relevant for a writing-aid of academic texts in Spanish. It also proposes a repertory of discourse functions that enables the classification of the candidate word-strings as well as their onomasiological retrieval. This classification into discourse functions is also key in the process of selecting candidates, as those that do not fit in any function will predictably be of little interest in the context of the mentioned writing aid. Through the examination of the resulting data, the study explores the correlation between candidate selection by lexicographers and several association measures proposed in the literature to obtain high-quality lexical bundles, with a view to assess the feasibility of automating this process.

Keywords: Lexical bundles · Academic writing · Discourse functions

1 Introduction

Research on large amounts of textual data has revealed the existence of recurrent lexical combinations in all types of discourse [3,22]. Scientific or academic discourse is no exception in this respect, although each discipline seems to have its particular preferences [12]. These recurrent multi-word expressions, which usually go by the name of *lexical bundles*, cover a larger ground than phraseological units as conceived of in more traditional terms. With respect to idioms (i.e. non-compositional combinations of words, such as *en cuanto a* 'as for'), Biber et al. [3] and Hyland [12] have claimed they represent a more or less small set of the total amount of bundles a corpus can yield. As for compositional phraseological units, we do not have such estimations, but it seems reasonable to expect that compositional phrasemes, such as collocations (e.g. _hacen referencia a_, 'make reference to') and clichés (*en otras palabras* 'in other words'; cf. Mel'čuk [14]) will also represent a substantial share of the bundles of a corpus.

Although one of the most attractive aspects of lexical bundles to linguistic research has been their variation across academic disciplines [4,6,12], Simpson-Vlach and Ellis [21] have argued that it is possible to identify a core set of

© Springer Nature Switzerland AG 2019
G. Corpas Pastor and R. Mitkov (Eds.): Europhras 2019, LNAI 11755, pp. 144–158, 2019.
https://doi.org/10.1007/978-3-030-30135-4_11

academic bundles. It is evident that cross-disciplinary repertories of these routine lexical combinations are of great interest for the creation of lexicographic resources and, as a matter of fact, they have been incorporated in a number of tools aiming at helping students to write academic texts [10,13,23]. However, two problems arise when it comes to including lexical bundles in this type of resources: on one hand, determining which bundles are worth including in such a resource, and, on the other, planning how they are accessed by the final user.

Even though the defining traits of lexical bundles (i.e. frequency and dispersion) can be a good starting point to identify some types of phraseological multi-word expressions, additional filters are probably necessary in order to obtain lexical combinations that are relevant for lexicographic purposes. In this respect, some authors have voiced their reservations as to the interest of bundles identified by means of frequency and dispersion alone, and have proposed several criteria for obtaining more relevant multi-word sequences.

Thus, for instance, Grabowski and Juknevičienė [9] consider that the fragmentary character of many lexical bundles and the redundancy of sequences of different lengths are problematic and propose a method for getting rid of redundant combinations. Likewise, frequency and dispersion thresholds alone do not always guarantee bundles' psychological validity or pedagogical interest [2]. To solve this, both Simpson-Vlach and Ellis [21] and Salazar [20] have combined frequency with (pointwise) mutual information (MI), a statistical association measure. According to Simpson-Vlach and Ellis, high MI scores tend to correspond to bundles conveying "distinctive functions or meanings (p. 493)" [21], which is not always the case with frequent strings.

Appel and Trofimovich [2] determine the formulaic nature of multi-word sequences by means of transitional probability, a measure used in research on word segmentation. In this field, it has been observed that high transitional probabilities between syllables are found within words, whereas low transitional probabilities are associated to word boundaries. When applied to multi-word sequences, the authors find that high transitional probabilities are characteristic of relatively complete structures, thus avoiding the overlapping and fragmentariness of sequences retrieved by frequency alone.

With respect to the presentation of lexical bundles to users of lexicographic resources, onomasiological retrieval through discourse functions has been employed in several resources, such as ARTES [13] or the Louvain English for Academic Puroposes Dictionary (LEAD) [10]. Notwithstanding, there is not a fixed set of discourse functions and the different proposals vary in several respects. Hyland's proposal [12] has revealed itself useful for the classification of bundles in corpus studies, but probably lexicographic interfaces require more learner-oriented classifications—in this respect, ARTES [13] offers the user one of the most detailed taxonomies.

Whereas research in Spanish linguistics has not been alien to the above-mentioned interest in academic discourse, proposals within this area have been until recently more concerned with the rhetorical steps involved in the composition of a text [15], rather than with developing writing assistants. The first attempts in this direction that we know of are very recent (Estilector[1] [8] and arText[2] [5]). The latter seems to share the above-mentioned "superstructural" approach (guiding the division of the text in sections), which is combined with the proposal of style recommendations to the user (grammar, orthography, etc.). In both resources, lexical recommendations—including those on discourse markers—are given mostly as a means to enhance lexical richness and avoid repetition and verbosity. Likewise, in the spirit of Hyland, arText for the moment centers on three well-delimited disciplines.

This paper takes a different approach by focusing exclusively on some phraseological features of academic writing and examines two aspects mentioned above: namely, the identification of lexical bundles relevant for a writing-aid of academic Spanish [1], and their classification according to discourse function in order to enable the onomasiological retrieval of such bundles. Both aspects are related, since the fact that a given bundle can receive a discourse function is determinant with respect to its onomasiological retrieval and, as a consequence, its inclusion in the tool. The study also examines the relation between the choices of annotators and association measures, with a view to exploring the possibility of automating the process of identifying academic bundles in Spanish in future research. Even though there are several proposals in this regard, the performance of association measures in identifying phraseological word-combinations seems to vary depending on several factors (corpus size; the type of the multi-word expressions considered—i.e. n-grams, lemmas within a given syntactic relation, word-forms within a given span; possibly language; etc.; see [7]). It is therefore interesting to test the application of some of the measures proposed in the literature for identifying interesting bundles in the literature to data of academic Spanish.

The remainder of the paper is organised as follows. Section 2 describes candidate extraction and the system of discourse functions we employed to classify them. Section 3 presents and evaluates the results of the proposed methods, which are discussed in Sect. 4. Finally, the conclusions (Sect. 5) reflect briefly on the identification of academic lexical bundles and new venues of research.

2   Candidates Identification and Classification

The candidates to academic lexical bundles were extracted from a corpus containing 413 research articles and ca. 2 million tokens. About half of the corpus came from the Spanish part of the Spanish-English Research Articles Corpus (SERAC) [19], which includes research articles published in indexed and peer-reviewed journals. This database was improved by complementing it with other texts of the same type in order to obtain a more balanced sample in terms of the size of the four main domains of the corpus (see breakdown in Table 1).

---

[1] http://www.estilector.com/.
[2] http://sistema-artext.com/.

Table 1. Corpus breakdown.

Domain	Discipline	No of texts	Words
Arts & Humanities	Library Science	22	128,616
	Linguistics	30	204,245
	Literature	22	172,840
Total			505,701
Biology & Health Sciences	Biology	46	206,011
	Medicine	98	296,591
Total			502,602
Physical Sciences & Engineering	Physics/Chemistry	45	139,366
	Geology	28	154,967
	Engineering	54	212,311
Total			506,644
Social Sciences	Economy	22	138,366
	Education	25	154,868
	Sociology	22	216,911
Total			510,145
Corpus total			2,025,092

2.1 Candidates Extraction

From the corpus just-described we extracted n-grams with the following characteristics:

i. **Length of the string:** for the present study we have considered strings from two to four tokens,[3] i.e., bi-grams, tri-grams and four-grams. Bi-grams are not usually treated in studies on lexical bundles, but this set of sequences includes interesting candidates for our purposes, such as phrases with prepositional or conjunctional uses, sometimes performing discourse marker functions, e.g. *sin embargo*, 'however', *no obstante*, 'notwithstanding', etc.

ii. **Frequency and dispersion thresholds:** all candidates had to reach a frequency threshold of 10 occurrences per million words and should occur in the four domains of the corpus.

iii. **Pre-processing:** before assigning discourse functions to candidates, we discarded structures unlikely to be of interest for our purposes. In the case of bi-grams we eliminated those made up exclusively of grammatical elements (e.g. *de el* 'of the.MASC', *de la* 'of the.FEM', *ello se* 'it itself', etc.) and those beginning by determiners, since we assumed that these noun phrases would be mostly referring devices to entities of domain specific topics, hardly fulfilling textual or interpersonal functions (e.g. *el sistema* 'the system', *la media*

---

[3] The corpus was tokenized with Freeling [16].

'the average'). In the case of tri-grams, we discarded also completely grammatical bundles and strings with a clear fragmentary character, for instance
those ending either in articles or clitic pronouns (*lo que le(s)*, *lo que la*). In
the case of four-grams we considered this pre-processing phase unnecessary.

iv. **Manual selection:** Two annotators selected manually those candidates
that they judged were relevant for the academic writing aid among the pool
of n-grams that met the above-mentioned criteria. Decisive in this respect
was the possibility of a candidate to receive a discourse function from the
repertory described below (Sect. 2.2), so that candidates that could not be
assigned one of these functions were eventually discarded.

2.2 Discourse Functions

A set of discourse functions was devised to classify the candidates extracted from
the corpus. The definitive repertory is the product of combining top-down and
bottom-up approaches: we started adapting previous proposals and discarded
or added functions depending on corpus data. Thus, the threefold division into
research-oriented, text-oriented and interpersonal bundles is similar to those of
Biber et al. [3][4] or Hyland [12]—the latter has been adopted in later studies
[6,20]. However, our repertoire of lexical functions is somewhat more detailed,
with a view to facilitating bundle retrieval by users. For instance, Hyland's [12]
transition and structuring signals correspond in our classification to at least
seven functions, namely, expressing cause, consequence, addition, opposition,
condition, exception and alternative (in this regard, we are closer to the fine-
grained classification of ARTES [13]).

Below we present a summary of the discourse functions assigned to the
selected bundles:

Research-Oriented Bundles. We have included in this group bundles related
to the research process and other notions relative to representations of the
extralinguistic world, which in turn can be grouped as follows:

– *Bundles Related to the Research Process.* These are distributed across five
functions namely (1) *Present the topic of research*, e. g. *[X] se centra en* '[X]
focuses on', (2) *Present the objectives*, e.g. *el objetivo de este trabajo es* 'the
purpose of this study is', (3) *Present the methodology.* e.g. *para llevar a cabo*
'in order to undertake', (4) *Present data*, e.g. *basándose en* 'based on' and (5)
Present the conclusions, e.g. *podemos concluir que* 'we may conclude that'.
– *Descriptive Bundles.* Descriptive bundles are covered by three functions,
namely (1) *Naming* (e.g. *se conoce como* 'is known as'), (2) *Describing* (*se
caracteriza por* 'is known for') and (3) *Grouping* (*de este tipo* 'of this type').

---

[4] In Biber et al. [3] they are called "stance" and "referential expressions" and "discourse organizers", to which a fourth category of "special conversational" functions
is added.

– *Quantification Bundles.* This category is again covered by three functions: (1) *Express quantity* (e.g. *buena parte de* 'good amount of'), (2) *Express frequency* (e.g. *a menudo* 'often') and (3) *Express time* (e.g. *a largo plazo* 'in the long term').

Text-Oriented Bundles. This is the largest set of functions. They can be grouped into the following categories:

– *Ordering Bundles.* This function covers bundles such as *a continuación* 'below', *en primer lugar* 'first', *en segundo lugar* 'second', etc.
– *Bundles for Cross-reference.* These are dsitributed across three functions, namely (1) *Refer to the text itself*, e.g. *el presente trabajo* 'this paper', (2) *Refer to other sections*, e.g. *en la introducción* 'in the introduction', (3) *Refer to non-textual elements*, e.g. *en la figura 1* 'in Fig. 1', etc.
– *Framing Bundles*, either for (1) *(Re-)introducing a topic*, e.g. *con respecto a*, or (2) for *Delimiting* the applicability of the sentence at hand (often the same bundles serve the two functions, depending on their position in the sentence).
– *Bundles Expressing Logical Relations between Propositions*, such as cause, consequence, addition or opposition, e.g.*a causa de* 'because of', *de esta manera* 'so that', *de igual manera* 'likewise' or *en cambio* 'in contrast'.[5]
– *Rephrasing Bundles.* This category cover the functions (1) *Precise* (e.g. *en concreto* 'in particular'), (2) *Exemplify* (e.g. *por ejemplo* 'for example') and (3) *Rephrase* an idea (e.g. *más bien* 'rather').

Interpersonal Bundles. This category includes expressions conveying epistemic, deontic and evaluative meanings, under functions such as *Atenuate* (e.g. *tal vez* 'perhaps'), *Express necessity* (e.g. *es necesario que* 'it is necessary that), *Evaluate* (e.g.*es muy importante* 'it is very important') etc. It also accounts for bundles referring sources of information (*Quote/Indicate source*, e.g. *según datos* 'after data', *de acuerdo con* 'in accordance with').

Those bundles that did not receive a function were eventually discarded.

2.3   Association Measures

Although for this study all candidates resulting from applying the filters described at the beginning of this section were revised manually, it is interesting to explore the relation between those that were eventually selected by the annotators and the association between their components as measured in statistical terms.

There is a plethora of statistical association measures that have been used to retrieve collocations understood as binary word combinations within a given span of text [17] or related by a syntactic dependency [7]. Lexical bundles are in this respect structurally different from collocations (they are continuous strings

---

[5] For the sake of brevity, we do not give all the names of this group of functions.

made up of a variable number of words), so that not every measure used for binary strings can be applied for their selection. For the present study we chose three association measures that have been recently put forward for identifying phraseologically relevant bundles.

The first two measures come from Appel and Trofimovich [2], who have proposed using transitional probability as a means to refine bundle identification (see Sect. 1 above). They define backward transition probability (BTP) as the probability of X given Y:

$$BTP(X|Y) = \frac{XY}{Y} \tag{1}$$

where X is the first segment of the string (e.g., _a través de_, 'through').

In turn, the forward transition probability (FTP) is the probability of Y given X:

$$FTP(Y|X) = \frac{XY}{X} \tag{2}$$

where Y is the last segment of the strings, (e.g., _a través de_).

Likewise, several studies have proposed the use pointwise mutual information (MI) or variants thereof as a means of refining repertoires of lexical bundles [20,21]. Here we use MI for bi-grams and the adaptation proposed by Wei and Li for larger strings [24]:

$$MI(W_1, W_2, \ldots, W_n) = log_2(\frac{P(W_1, W_2, \ldots, W_n)}{WAP}) \tag{3}$$

where WAP stands for Weighted Average Probabilities and is obtained through the formula

$$WAP = \sum_{i=1}^{i=n-1} P_{[P(W_1, \ldots, W_i) \cdot P(W_{i+1}, \ldots, W_n)]} \cdot [P(W_1, \ldots, W_i) \cdot P(W_{i+1}, \ldots, W_n)] \tag{4}$$

3 Evaluation and Results

Below we present the results of the study, beginning by accounting for the proportion of bundles selected by the annotators and their classification into discourse functions. After that, we focus on the relation between the three association measures examined and the annotators' choices.

Table 2 displays the number of n-grams that reached the frequency and dispersion thresholds to be considered lexical bundles and the quantity and percentage thereof that have been manually selected on account of their relevance for an academic writing aid. As can be seen in the table, only a small set of the combinations that quantitatively qualified as bundles (between 10 and 23%) were manually selected as worthy of being included in the writing aid[6].

---

[6] A sample of the most frequent bundles selected can be seen in the Appendix, Table 5. For the sake of space, we only give the 35 most frequent ones.

Table 2. Selected bundles

	Bundles	Selected	%
bi-grams	2,816	286	10
tri-grams	2,282	435	19
four-grams	418	96	23

As for their classification, the manually selected bundles are more or less equally distributed across research-oriented and textual functions, while the proportion of interpersonal bundles is substantially lower, as shown in Table 3.

Table 3. Selected bundles across discourse function

	Selected	%
Research-oriented	364	45
Textual	355	44
Interpersonal	98	11

With regard to the relation between association measures and candidates selection, we have examined precision and recall values for raw frequency, MI, BTP and FTP (Fig. 1).[7] BTP seems the better performing association measure in the case of bi-grams, whereas frequency, MI and FTP have similar precision rates irrespective of the recall rate considered—their curves are therefore almost flat. In the case of tri-grams, in contrast, MI performs better, despite some drops corresponding to high values of this measure.

With respect to four-grams the situation is somewhat less clear. BTP has steadily higher precision rates than the other measures until it drops steeply at a precision level of 0.8. Frequency, in turn, starts out as the measure with the best precision, but drops under BTP at a precision rate of ca. 0.2 and under MI a little after.

Pecina and Shlesinger [18] and Evert et al. [7] propose using the average precision corresponding to recall rates equal or higher than 0.5 (AP50) as a summarizing value of precision/recall graphs. Table 4 displays AP50 values for the measures tested in our data. According to these, BTP is the best measure for bi- and four-grams, and MI is the winner in the case of tri-grams.

These data confirm the conclusions we tentatively drew from the exam of precision-recall curves.

4   Discussion

Our results suggest that, while the defining traits of lexical bundles—i.e. frequency and dispersion thresholds—may be a good starting point to extract

---

[7] For this, we used R's PRROC package [11].

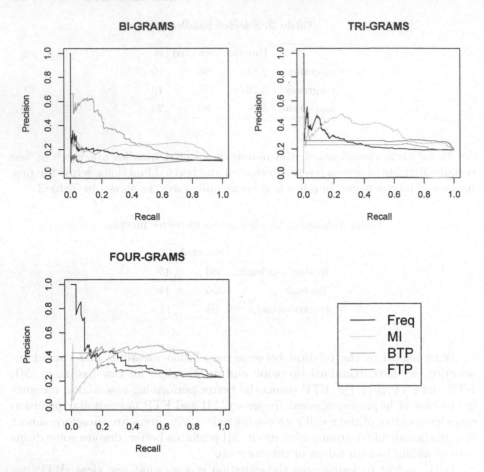

Fig. 1. Precision and recall per length and association measure

cross-disciplinary routine combinations, not every lexical bundle offers the same
lexicographic interest. In fact, among those strings that met our frequency and
dispersion thresholds, only a small set was selected by annotators (see again
Table 2).

In this respect, discourse functions have been useful as a criterion for selecting interesting lexical bundles and will allow users to retrieve them through a
lexicographic interface. From our results it is apparent that the three sets of
functions have different degrees of productivity. Thus, while research- and text-
oriented bundles take the lion's share of the selected candidates, interpersonal
bundles constitute a much more limited repertoire in our corpus. This may have
to do, at least partially, with the fact that the number of interpersonal functions
is lower than those in the other two sets, but the academic character of the corpus could also explain the more discrete presence of interpersonal expressions.
In any case, this aspect should be addressed in future research, along with the

Table 4. AP50 per bundle length and association measure

	bi-grams	tri-grams	four-grams
Frequency	20	32	45
MI	21	40	30
BTP	35	23	47
FTP	9	27	32

possible differences in use of bundles across the different academic domains of our corpus.

Although the process of selection described here has been manually performed, the review of quantifiable features of bundles can be used for the automation of similar processes in future research. One of these features is string length. This seems a decisive factor in terms of the lexicographical validity of bundles, since the proportion of selected candidates increases along with the number of words in the string. In this respect, it should be noted that most studies only consider three-word or longer strings as lexical bundles. For this reason, and given the interest offered by some two-word strings, we applied more aggressive pre-processing filters to this type of candidates (see Sect. 2). In spite of that, the proportion of selected two-word bundles was considerably lower than that of longer strings. In any case, these group of candidates produced some relevant academic combinations (e.g. *a continuación* 'below', *más adelante* 'below', *en concreto* 'in particular', etc.).

Association measures can also speed up the process of identifying phraseological combinations. A substantial number of association measures has been tested on binary word combinations—collocations—(cf. [7,17]). Here, we have examined three association measures that can be applied to n-grams of different lengths: the adaptation of MI proposed by Wei and Li [24] and BTP and FTP as applied by Appel and Trofimovich [2]. String length seems to interact with the different association measures tested, as we saw in Fig. 1. Thus, BTP has the best results in the case of two-word and four-word bundles, in line with the results of Appel and Trofimovich [2].

MI performs well in the case of tri-grams, but with all three types of bundles it exhibits a peculiar pattern: precision-recall curves display sharp drops in precision associated with very high MI scores. A qualitative examination suggests that these low precision rates correspond to phraseological combinations that could not be assigned a discourse function. Thus, the idiom *punto de vista* 'point of view' or participial forms of the complex verb *llevar a cabo* 'to undertake' are phraseological expressions appearing among the three-word bundles with the highest MI values, but cannot be associated with a given discourse function, and have therefore been discarded. This is due to the fact that discourse functions are relatively independent from the phraseological character of a given string. In fact, the elements in question have been assigned functions and selected as valid candidates in other configurations (some of their inflectional variants, inserted in larger strings, etc.). For instance, *desde el punto de vista [de]* functions recurrently as a framing device (see Example 1), but the nominal expression *punto de vista* taken alone seems much more versatile in this respect, and not specialized in a given discourse function.

Example 1. Desde el punto de vista de *la comunicación, la conectividad permanente del móvil es su característica más relevante para diferenciarlo [...]*
'With respect to communication, mobile phones' permanent connectivity is the most relevant characteristic to distinguish them [...]'

Likewise, finite forms of *llevar a cabo* in the middle voice have been assigned the function of *Introducing the methodology*, since they can occur as the main verbs of sentences accounting for the methodological decisions of a study (Example 2). However, in the case of participles this is less clear (Example 3).

Example 2. Tal comprobación se llevó a cabo *a través de un estudio piloto de una muestra de [...]*
'Such checking was undertaken through a pilot study of a sample of [...]'

Example 3. Este debate y las investigaciones llevadas a cabo *sobre el tema evidenciaron la importancia [...]*
'This debate and the studies carried out on the subject evidenced the importance [...]'

In sum, high MI values seem to correspond to high quality phraseological expressions, but those expressions do not always meet the particular requirements of this study.

Qualitative examination can also provide clues as to the better performance of BTP with respect to MI. Some of the four word candidates with highest MI scores are fragmentary, even though their internal constituents are closely associated: e.g. *objetivo de este trabajo* 'aim of this paper', *objetivo de el presente* 'aim of the present', *muestran en la tabla* 'show in the table' (compare with *se muestran en la tabla* 'are shown in Table'). High scores of BTP, in contrast, assure the left-boundedness of candidates (e.g. *a lo largo de* 'through', *la mayor parte de* 'most', *a el mismo tiempo* 'at the same time', etc.) and thus their non-fragmentariness.

Right boundedness, on the other hand, has been much less relevant for the detection of good candidates. Some examples with low FTP scores can shed light in this respect. For instance, *en el fondo* 'in fact' has been selected by the annotators in spite of its low FTP. It is clear that the possible transitions for the string *en el* in the corpus are many, but this fact does not prevent that some of them are interesting for our purposes, while others are not.

Considering our results as a whole, it seems that the better performing association measures could alleviate the task of lexicographers, perhaps not by using thresholds, but by limiting the exam to a list of the n-best candidates. It must be noted that the AP50 of the best association measure for each type of bundle almost doubles the precision rate of randomly ordered lists (see Table 4). Nevertheless, even using association measures, precision rates are low, which suggests that a complete automation using unsupervised approaches seems, at least for now, unrealistic.

5   Conclusions

This paper has described the process of identifying and classifying recurrent word strings for their inclusion in an academic writing aid. The extraction of candidates has used frequency and dispersion thresholds in order to automatically identify lexical bundles. From the manual examination of these candidates it becomes apparent that the defining traits of bundles alone (i.e. frequency and dispersion) cannot ensure lexicographic relevance, especially if those bundles are destined to help lay users to write academic texts.

Association measures, particularly BTP and MI, alleviate the labour of lexicographers by promoting phraseological strings. However, the phraseological character of a string in itself does not guarantee that this particular string is interesting as a means to build the rhetoric structure of a text. Of course, these phraseological elements deserve treatment in a writing aid, but such treatment should be different from that given to routine word combinations associated to well-defined discourse functions. Likewise, the structure of collocations and certain idioms (not necessarily contiguous, with morphological variants; e.g. *realizar un análisis* 'perform an analysis', *llevar a cabo* 'undertake') require different strategies of extraction that should be addressed in future research.

Acknowledgments. Supported by Xunta de Galicia, through grant ED481D 2017/009, MINECO, through grant IJCI-2016-29598 and project FFI2016-78299-P, and by a 2017 Leonardo Grant for Researchers and Cultural Creators (BBVA Foundation).

Appendix: Sample of the Selected Most Frequent Bundles

Table 5. Most frequent bundles selected among bi-, tri- and four-grams

bi-gram	freq	tri-gram	freq	four-gram	freq
sin embargo	1340	a partir de	1105	en el caso de	511
ya que	1016	a través de	969	a lo largo de	355
respecto a	1001	por lo que	631	con el fin de	294
debido a	883	en cuanto a	560	a la hora de	225
mientras que	849	los resultados de	506	a el igual que	220
frente a	755	en la tabla	463	el punto de vista	161
por ejemplo	724	la mayoría de	462	a el mismo tiempo	150
es decir	707	en la figura	456	la mayor parte de	143
grado de	629	en función de	427	en la tabla 1	117
se realizó	615	con respecto a	419	a pesar de que	115
por tanto	587	a pesar de	407	en el presente estudio	110
se observa	445	por otro lado	376	con el objetivo de	102
en general	410	por otra parte	370	en el área de	96
no obstante	399	la necesidad de	343	es el caso de	96
sobre todo	358	de acuerdo con	339	a el final de	90
para que	356	se trata de	335	se llevó a cabo	88
por ello	333	por lo tanto	330	en el marco de	85
tamaño de	328	el objetivo de	309	en todos los casos	85
método de	324	a el menos	304	en el presente trabajo	84
no sólo	310	con el fin	303	en la tabla 2	84
si bien	302	en este caso	284	para el caso de	79
se debe	299	una serie de	273	para el desarrollo de	79
sino que	291	los resultados obtenidos	262	de el orden de	77
se utilizó	278	debido a que	258	para el análisis de	77
por último	271	en este sentido	250	en el ámbito de	73
es posible	268	en este trabajo	248	en la figura 2	72
superior a	266	la posibilidad de	247	en la figura 1	70
a continuación	259	por medio de	245	con la finalidad de	67
es necesario	259	en primer lugar	237	en el contexto de	67
puesto que	246	las características de	234	en la figura 3	62
igual que	237	en relación con	233	en la tabla 3	61
se presentan	226	el índice de	232	de el mismo modo	57
para ello	224	a su vez	225	en la figura 4	57
de hecho	215	en este estudio	214	teniendo en cuenta que	56
probabilidad de	204	el presente estudio	213	en lo que respecta	50
se refiere	204	los datos de	204	en el seno de	48

References

1. Alonso-Ramos, M., García-Salido, M., Garcia, M.: Exploiting a corpus to compile a lexical resource for academic writing: Spanish lexical combinations. In: Kosem, I., Tiberius, C., Jakubícek, M., Kallas, J., Krek, S., Baisa, V. (eds.) Electronic Lexicography in the 21st Century. Proceedings of eLex 2017 Conference, pp. 571–586. Lexical Computing CZ, Brno (2017). https://elex.link/elex2017/proceedingsdownload/

2. Appel, R., Trofimovich, P.: Transitional probability predicts native and non-native use of formulaic sequences. Int. J. Appl. Linguist. **27**, 1–20 (2017). https://doi.org/10.1111/ijal.12100. http://doi.wiley.com/10.1111/ijal.12100

3. Biber, D., Conrad, S., Viviana, C.: If you look at....: lexical bundles in university teaching and textbooks. Appl. Linguist. **25**, 371–405 (2004)

4. Cortes, V.: Lexical bundles in published and student disciplinary writing: examples from history and biology. Engl. Specif. Purp. **23**(4), 397–423 (2004). https://doi.org/10.1016/j.esp.2003.12.001

5. da Cunha, I., Montané, M.A., Hysa, L.: The arText prototype: an automatic system for writing specialized texts. In: Peñas, A., Martins, A. (eds.) Proceedings of the EACL 2017 Software Demonstrations, pp. 57–60. Association for Computational Linguistics (2017). https://doi.org/10.18653/v1/e17-3015

6. Durrant, P.: Lexical bundles and disciplinary variation in university students' writing: mapping the territories. Appl. Linguist. **38**(2), 165–193 (2017). https://doi.org/10.1093/applin/amv011. http://applij.oxfordjournals.org/cgi/doi/10.1093/applin/amv011

7. Evert, S., Uhrig, P., Bartsch, S., Proisl, T.: E-VIEW-alation - a large-scale evaluation study of association measures for collocation identification. In: Kosem, I., Tiberius, C., Jakubícek, M., Kallas, J., Krek, S., Baisa, V. (eds.) Electronic Lexicography in the 21st Century. Proceedings of eLex 2017 Conference, pp. 531–549. Lexical Computing CZ, Brno (2017). https://elex.link/elex2017/proceedingsdownload/

8. Ferrero, C.L., Renau, I., Nazar, R., Torner, S.: Computer-assisted revision in Spanish academic texts: peer-assessment. Procedia - Soc. Behav. Sci. **141**, 470–483 (2014). https://doi.org/10.1016/j.sbspro.2014.05.083

9. Grabowski, Ł., Juknevičienė, R.: Towards a refined inventory of lexical bundles: an experiment in the formulex method. Stud. Lang. **29**, 58–73 (2017). https://doi.org/10.5755/j01.sal.0.29.15327. http://www.kalbos.ktu.lt/index.php/KStud/article/view/15327

10. Granger, S., Paquot, M.: Electronic lexicography goes local design and structures of a needs-driven online academic writing aid. Lexicogr.: Int. Ann. Lexicogr. **31**(1), 118–141 (2015). https://doi.org/10.1515/lexi. http://hdl.handle.net/2078.1/166516

11. Grau, J., Grosse, I., Keilwagen, J.: PRROC: computing and visualizing precision-recall and receiver operating characteristic curves in R. Bioinformatics **31**(15), 2595–2597 (2015). https://doi.org/10.1093/bioinformatics/btv153

12. Hyland, K.: As can be seen: lexical bundles and disciplinary variation. Engl. Specif. Purp. **27**(1), 4–21 (2008). https://doi.org/10.1016/j.esp.2007.06.001

13. Kübler, N., Pecman, M.: The ARTES bilingual LSP dictionary: from collocation to higher order phraseology. In: Electronic Lexicography, pp. 187–210. Oxford University Press, November 2012. https://doi.org/10.1093/acprof:oso/9780199654864.003.0010

14. Mel'čuk, I.: Clichés, an understudied subclass of phrasemes. Yearb. Phraseol. **6**(1), 55–86 (2015). https://doi.org/10.1515/phras-2015-0005. http://www.deg ruyter.com/view/j/yop.2015.6.issue-1/phras-2015-0005/phras-2015-0005.xml
15. Montolío, E.: Mecanismos de cohesión (II). Los conectores. In: Montolío, E. (ed.) Manual de escritura académica y profesional, pp. 9–92. Ariel, Barcelona (2014)
16. Padró, L., Stanilovsky, E.: Freeling 3.0: towards wider multilinguality. In: Calzolari, N., et al. (eds.) Proceedings of the 8th International Conference on Language Resources and Evaluation (LREC2012), pp. 2473–2479. European Language Resources Association (ELRA) (2012). http://dblp.uni-trier.de/db/conf/lrec/lrec2012.html#PadroS12
17. Pecina, P.: Lexical association measures and collocation extraction. Lang. Resour. Eval. **44**(1–2), 137–158 (2010)
18. Pecina, P., Schlesinger, P.: Combining association measures for collocation extraction. In: Proceedings of the COLING/ACL on Main Conference Poster Sessions, pp. 651–658. Association for Computational Linguistics, July 2006
19. Pérez-Llantada, C.: Formulaic language in L1 and L2 expert academic writing: convergent and divergent usage. J. Engl. Acad. Purp. **14**, 84–94 (2014)
20. Salazar, D.: Lexical Bundles in Native and Non-native Scientific Writing: Applying a Corpus-based Study to Language Teaching. Studies in Corpus Linguistics. John Benjamins Publishing Company, Amsterdam (2014). https://books.google.es/books?id=9OJ4oAEACAAJ
21. Simpson-Vlach, R., Ellis, N.C.: An academic formulas list: new methods in phraseology research. Appl. Linguist. **31**(4), 487–512 (2010). https://doi.org/10.1093/applin/amp058
22. Sinclair, J.: Corpus, Concordance, Collocation. Oxford University Press, Oxford (1991). https://doi.org/10.2307/330144
23. Verdaguer, I., et al.: SciE-Lex. A lexical database. In: Verdaguer, I., Laso, N.J., Salazar, D. (eds.) Biomedical English: A Corpus-Based Approach, pp. 21–38. John Benjamins, Amsterdam/Philadelphia (2013)
24. Wei, N., Li, J.: A new computing method for extracting contiguous phraseological sequences from academic text corpora. Int. J. Corpus Linguist. **18**(4), 506–535 (2013). https://doi.org/10.1075/ijcl.18.4.03wei

Do Online Resources Give Satisfactory Answers to Questions About Meaning and Phraseology?

Patrick Hanks[1] and Emma Franklin[2(✉)]

[1] University of Wolverhampton, Wulfruna Street, Wolverhampton WV1 1LY, UK

[2] Lancaster University, Bailrigg, Lancaster LA1 4YW, UK
e.franklin@lancaster.ac.uk

Abstract. In this paper we explore some aspects of the differences between printed paper dictionaries and online dictionaries in the ways in which they explain meaning and phraseology. After noting the importance of the lexicon as an inventory of linguistic items and the neglect in both linguistics and lexicography of phraseological aspects of that inventory, we investigate the treatment in online resources of phraseology – in particular, the phrasal verbs *wipe out* and *put down* – and we go on to investigate a word, *dope*, that has undergone some dramatic meaning changes during the 20th century. In the course of discussion, we mention the new availability of corpus evidence and the technique of Corpus Pattern Analysis, which is important for linking phraseology and meaning and distinguishing normal phraseology from rare and unusual phraseology. The online resources that we discuss include Google, the Urban Dictionary (UD), and Wiktionary.

Keywords: Online dictionaries · Meaning · Phraseology · Phrasal verbs · Transitivity · Meaning change over time · Corpus Pattern Analysis

1 Introduction

As long ago as 1857, the English literary scholar and clergyman Richard Chenevix Trench (subsequently Archbishop of Canterbury) observed that a dictionary is an inventory of the words of a language. Trench pointed out that many words had been missed by the standard dictionaries of his day, including Johnson's. Compiling an inventory is harder than may at first sight appear. Trench's observations "on some deficiencies in our English dictionaries" [6] were a key element in the impetus that prompted the Philological Society to plan a new English dictionary, which many years later was published under a new name as the *Oxford English Dictionary* (OED). Over 100 years later the great American language teacher Bolinger [1], in a counterblast to the logical excesses of what was then called transformational grammar, emphasized the importance in language teaching of "getting the words in." But Bolinger went further, in that he started to ask questions concerning what should be said about each word – in a classroom by the teacher or in a dictionary by a lexicographer. An ardent advocate of common sense in language teaching, Bolinger emphasized "the enormous importance

© Springer Nature Switzerland AG 2019
G. Corpas Pastor and R. Mitkov (Eds.): Europhras 2019, LNAI 11755, pp. 159–172, 2019.
https://doi.org/10.1007/978-3-030-30135-4_12

of understanding the lexicon for its own sake", not merely as an appendage to the grammar.

Now, in the 21st century, the combined efforts of lexicographers, dialectologists, terminologists, and onomasticians have got us about as close as we can ever hope to get to a complete inventory of the lexicon of English. Now at last the research community can turn its attention to the neglected question of what should be said about each word and in particular the phraseology associated with each word in a language.

Constraints of space and paraphrasing, which bedevilled 19th- and 20th-century dictionaries, are no longer necessarily relevant. We argue that online dictionaries should say something not only about meaning but also about the stereotypical phraseology that characterizes each meaning of each word. Currently available online resources, being inherited from printed dictionaries, tend to say little or nothing about phraseology. They present word meaning in a way that supports the outmoded confusion of natural language with logic that was fashionable in the 19th century, having been inherited from the thinking of logicians such as Leibniz in the early 18th century. To make matters worse, many online resources reflect the traditional belief among old-fashioned lexicographers that the oldest meaning of any word is somehow more literal than its current meaning. The error of this belief can be illustrated with thousands of examples, of which we will give just one: the oldest meaning of the word *literal*, according to OED, is "of or relating to a letter or letters". But of course the literal meaning of a word or phrase is not the meaning of the letters of which it is composed.

As the use of online dictionaries and other Internet resources becomes ever more commonplace, we must put ourselves in the position of online dictionary users and ask, how useful are such resources? How well do they cater to the needs of English speakers and learners?

2   Trying to Find the Meaning of a Phrasal Verb

2.1   Wipe Out

Imagine you are a dedicated, intermediate-level learner of English. One of your English-speaking friends has shared the news article, *Climate Change may Wipe Out Bengal Tigers*. You want to know what the headline means. You know what a 'tiger' is, and you know what the verb 'wipe' means: it means to clean something, like your glasses. So *wipe + out* must mean 'clean out'. But how does something like climate change clean out a tiger? No, that can't be right. "Wipe out", you ask Google. The top result is a YouTube video from a band called *Surfaris*. The thumbnail is a picture of a surfer being pursued by a gigantic wave. "Okay," you say to yourself, rephrasing the Google search: "*wipe out definition*". Google Dictionary, by now a familiar sight to you, tells you that *wipe out*, a phrasal verb of *wipe*, means "INFORMAL be capsized by a wave while surfing". *Capsizing*, according to Google Dictionary, is something a boat does. Your mind races; what could be going on here? Are tigers being overwhelmed by the floods of climate chaos? Are they climbing into boats? You can't help but be reminded of that famous scene from *Life of Pi*, in which a man and a tiger are out at sea.

Thankfully, you find that an alternative sense is listed underneath: "NORTH AMERICAN fall over or off a vehicle". You check and find that, yes, the news story *is* from a North American website. And climate change *is* linked to vehicles, after all. This must be it. Google, the most used search engine in the world, would not be wrong about something as straightforward as this. And yet, this explanation is even less plausible than the first. Tigers falling off vehicles? From climate change? Bewildered, you turn to the next result in the list. This time it's from the *Cambridge English Dictionary*: "**Wipe out** US INFORMAL – phrasal verb with *wipe*: to lose control, especially in a vehicle, and have an accident." No further senses are listed. At this point you realize that you must have misunderstood some other part of the headline; what other explanation could there be? You decide to try one more dictionary, just to be sure. *Oxford Dictionaries dot com*, you type. "The World's Most Trusted Dictionary Provider," it replies. Search term: *wipe out*. "**Wipe out**, PHRASAL VERB *informal* 1. be capsized by a wave while surfing. 1.1 *North American* fall over or off a vehicle." Apparently, this is where Google gets its dictionary data from.

Baffled, but undeterred, you keep going. It must be a problem with *you*, the learner. You find the website for the *Oxford Advanced Learner's Dictionary* (OALD) and type in *wipe out*. This time, to your surprise, there are three senses available: (1) "**wipe out** (*informal*) to fall over, especially when you are doing a sport such as skiing or surfing"; (2) "wipe somebody↔out (*informal*) to make somebody extremely tired"; and (3) "wipe somebody/something↔out [often passive] to destroy or remove somebody/something completely". Clearly, the best fit here is sense number 3. But what a rare sense this must be! No wonder it was so difficult to find.

As a matter of fact, *wiping something out* is not rare at all, as we shall see. The problem is a well-known one in English language teaching, namely the moveable direct object of transitive phrasal verbs, which, by the way, is what the double-headed arrow in OALD is trying to explain. Unfortunately, not all intermediate students of English have been taught the difference between transitive and intransitive uses of verbs, and even those who have been taught this point of English grammar may not realize that this is the problem with Google's explanation: it explains only an intransitive meaning of wipe out, whereas the headline about Bengal tigers uses the phrasal verb transitively. By placing a rare intransitive sense before the much more common transitive senses, even the excellent OALD, with its ingenious presentation of the movable direct object, risks confusing the reader. The problem is, what governs what? If a noun phrase is found with a verb and a particle, does the verb govern the noun phrase as a direct object, or does the particle govern it as a prepositional object? For example, a well-known test for phrasal verbs is the example *run up a hill* vs. *run up a bill*. It is idiomatic to say *he ran up a large bill*, which alternates with *he ran a large bill up*. However, it is not idiomatic in English to say **he ran a large hill up*. This is because *a large hill* is a prepositional object governed by the particle *up*, whereas *a large bill* is the direct object governed by the verb and can occur before or after the particle.

2.2   Corpus Evidence

How does all this affect *wipe out*? The Corpus Pattern Analysis (CPA) project [4], carried out on a sample of the BNC, is being used to create the *Pattern Dictionary of*

English Verbs (PDEV). This is work in progress: as analysis of each verb is completed, an entry is published online (free of charge) at http://pdev.org.uk. Fortunately, a draft entry for **wipe** has been completed. For a detailed explanation of the concept of "patterns" as well as the full method and theoretical underpinnings of CPA, see [4], also summarized in [3].

PDEV records 10 patterns for the verb **wipe**; only one of them is for the phrasal verb **wipe out**. Perhaps surprisingly, the phrasal verb accounts for over 58% of all uses of the verb *wipe*; no intransitive uses of this phrasal verb are recorded as patterns in PDEV. The British National Corpus (BNC) was compiled in the 1990s. Perhaps intransitive uses of this phrasal verb have grown in frequency in recent years. An alternative explanation is that intransitive uses with a human subject (surfers or car drivers, as the case may be) are cognitively salient precisely because this is a rare usage. Cognitive salience (i.e. phraseology which is memorable or springs to mind easily) must be distinguished from frequency; the latter is precisely equivalent to social salience. For more on this, see [4].

It is well known that anyone attempting to generalize about the meaning of a word or phrase will likely encounter the problems of granularity: how fine-grained should an explanation be? It is comparatively easy to construct a paraphrase of a whole clause or sentence; much more difficult to construct a set of explanations that will explain all – or even most – future uses of a word or phrase outside of a particular context: contexts provide all sorts of clues to meaning, some of them unexpected and indeed unpredictable. The general sense of **wipe out** is "to completely remove or destroy". A more fine-grained analysis could distinguish a person or firm being driven into bankruptcy from a species of animal being eliminated from planet Earth. A further distinction could be made between these senses and the more metaphorical sense of causing a person to feel very tired. These distinctions could be expressed as three different patterns for the phrasal verb *wipe out*, thus:

1. [[Eventuality | Entity 1]] wipe out [[Entity 2 | Group]]
   Implicature: [[Eventuality | Entity 1]] completely removes or destroys [[Entity 2 | Group]].
   Examples:
   *If the situation continues unchallenged, not only will local populations of rare dolphins be **wiped out**, but the threat of extinction looms not far behind.*
   *Against that background, the minister seems intent on **wiping out** salmonella, but only in the egg-laying flocks.*
   *The feeling almost **wiped out** that terrible year as if it hadn't happened at all.*
2. [[Eventuality]] wipe out [[Human | Institution]]
   Implicature: [[Eventuality]] causes [[Human | Institution]] to go bankrupt
   Example:
   *If you had what I had, we'd have been totally—ah—bankrupt—well, **wiped out**.*
   *The breweries are providing by far the majority of cash flow with which to meet mounting debt payments, running at A$4million a day. A spokesman for Bond Corporation admitted the action could **wipe out** the entire group.*
3. [[Eventuality]] wipe out [[Human]]
   Implicature: [[Eventuality]] causes [[Human]] to feel very tired.

Example:
*People's energy levels vary: they may feel persistently **wiped out**.*

Additionally, an intransitive pattern of this phrasal verb is found, though it was very rare at the time when BNC was compiled, and is probably not much greater now (0.2% of all uses of **wipe** in the BNC sample; 0.4% of **wipe out**; 0.2% of all uses of **wipe** in a sample of the Corpus of Contemporary American English (COCA), 0.6% of **wipe out**).

4. [[Human = Surfer]] wipe out [NO OBJ]
    Implicature: [[Human = Surfer]] is capsized by a wave while surfing
    Example:
    *When I **wiped out**, it was like going through a car wash without a car.*

Pattern 1 above, which Internet dictionaries appear to suggest is unusual, actually accounts for 97% of a 250-line BNC sample for the phrasal verb **wipe out**. If we were to take a more fine-grained approach and split this pattern along the killing/non-killing divide, we could end up with two patterns: *[[Anything]] wipe out [[Human Group | Animal Group]]*, with the implicature, *[[Anything]] kills or causes to be killed all members of [[Human Group | Animal Group]]*; and *[[Anything]] wipe out [[Abstract Entity | Natural Landscape Feature]]*, with the implicature, *[[Anything]] erases or destroys [[Abstract Entity | Natural Landscape Feature]]*, with 45% and 52% shares of the sample, respectively. There are moral as well as semantic reasons for contemplating this split, but for now let's consider them all as belonging to one pattern.

Patterns 2, 3, and 4 comprise just 2%, <1% and <1% of the sample, respectively. Why, then, should a simple internet search using the most powerful search tools available to us produce such misleading results? Should it be down to the user, the possibly unsophisticated learner of English, to know how to differentiate transitive from intransitive uses of verbs? In their study of foreign-language learners' use of online dictionaries, Jin and Deifell [5] conclude that while learners consider such resources to be "essential" to their studies, they also experience a great disparity in the quality of online dictionaries, and generally need to consult several in order to reach a satisfactory answer. Deciding which answer fits best is, as demonstrated above, not always straightforward. Chun [2] notes that the multiple and non-specific definitions offered by online dictionaries can overwhelm lower-level learners. Evidently, there is a degree of skill that is required for the user to successfully sort through the piles of conflicting information presented online.

It is important to realize that the ontology used in CPA for analysis of verbs is intended to summarize stereotypes, not all possibilities. [[Group]] may be classed as a subset of [[Entity]], even if counterexamples are found. [[Group]] is specified as a direct object of the phrasal verb **wipe out** because we find that stereotypically groups of entities such as animals and humans are *wiped out*. This analysis of stereotypical cases is not invalidated by a handful of counterexamples. On the other hand, if many counterexamples are found, a different semantic type may be selected, as a large number of counterexamples is indicative of a norm that was not originally noticed.

At this point, we should note that bilingual dictionaries often give more information about phraseology than their monolingual counterparts. However, there is still much room for improvement and even simplification. To take just one example, the excellent (printed) Oxford-Hachette (1994) English-French Dictionary offers the following translations for this phrasal verb, which helpfully provides guidance for the prepositional object problem discussed in Sect. 2.1:

wipe out: – *out [sth]*, – *[sth] out* **1** *lit (clean)* nettoyer [container, cupboard]; **2** *Audio, Cin, Comput, Video* effacer; **3** *fig (cancel)* effacer [memory, past]; liquider [debt]; annuler [chances, inflation, gains, losses]; *(kill)* anéantir [species, enemy, population]; **4** ° *Sport (defeat)* lessiver°

The references here to the typical direct objects "species, enemy, population", with the gloss *(kill)*, shows that, at least in this context, the correct translation would be **anéantir**. Should this be prioritized over the other translations offered? Indeed, should all of them be there at all? Unfortunately, current trends in theoretical linguistics, for example in construction grammar, still tend to focus on the theoretically possible on the evidence of introspection, rather than on empirical analysis of actual usage. Corpus evidence is far more plentiful now than it was in the years leading up to publication of Oxford-Hachette in 1994 – and becoming ever more so – so it will be a challenge for future bilingual lexicographers to decide whether to prioritize this particular translation of this particular phrasal verb or even to remove some of the other theoretically possible but unusual translations, if corpus evidence shows them to be vanishingly rare. One would hope that newer dictionaries, as well as online adaptations of older printed dictionaries, would take this newly available data into account.

If we look at the online version of the more recent Oxford-Hachette (2012) Pocket English-French Dictionary, we find just two main senses listed for wipe out:

wipe out

a. nettoyer ‹container, cupboard›
b. annuler ‹inflation›; anéantir ‹species, enemy, population›

Similarly, in the online Collins English-French dictionary, we find:

wipe out, separable transitive verb

1. [*debt*] effacer
2. [*memory*] effacer
3. (= *destroy*) anéantir

Although both of these online entries are considerably slimmed down, we still have the same problem as before in terms of priority and level of generalisation: is the *wiping out* of inflation, debt or memory to be prioritized over the *wiping out* of a species? The student translating the "Bengal tigers" headline will once again be led to believe that the "kill" sense of *wipe out* is one of the rarest, rather than one of the most common. Evidently, both bilingual and monolingual lexicographers could improve the usefulness of online dictionaries by using corpus evidence to not only remove the clutter of rare but theoretically possible information, often lifted from printed dictionaries built on historical principles, but also to order the results in a more empirically defensible way.

2.3   A Phrasal Verb with Even More Complex Semantics and Phraseology: *Put Down*

Let's take a look at another example: the phrasal verb *put down*. When analysed using the CPA technique, a random sample of the BNC reveals 22 patterns for *put down*. Patterns and senses, it should be clarified, are not interchangeable concepts; multiple patterns can be used to convey the same sense. Most dictionaries, however, do not list patterns but senses. A Google search for *put down definition* returns six senses in the default Google Dictionary result. Google Dictionary automatically rephrases the query *put down* as the transitive *put something down*. It is not clear why Google decided not to apply the same principle (i.e. automatic rephrasing) to *wipe out*. Doing so would surely have helped the hypothetical puzzled dictionary user mentioned in an earlier section of this paper.

The six senses listed by Google for **put something down** are: (1) "Record something in writing" (with a sub-sense of "Make a recording of a piece of music"); (2) "Suppress a rebellion, coup, or riot by force"; (3) "Kill an animal because it is sick, injured, or old"; (4) "Pay a specified sum as a deposit"; (5) "Preserve or store food or wine for future use"; and (6) "Land an aircraft". Combined, these senses represent less than a quarter of the corpus lines that make up the BNC sample for *put down*. Because Google Dictionary specifies the query *put down* to refer to *put something down*, the entry does not include the senses of *put someone down*, nor is there a cross-reference to this entry. This results in a confusing entry for the naïve end user or learner of English.

Evidently, there is an issue with the consistency of entries derived using search algorithms. In the case of *wipe out*, we received a very specific, and intransitive, sense of the phrasal verb. For *put down*, we receive this time a transitive, but a similarly restrictive view of the verb's potential meanings. In practice, it turns out, *wipe out* and *put down* have similar transitive-to-intransitive ratios; in both cases, the intransitive senses (for *wipe out*, "to be capsized by a wave while surfing" and "to fall off or over a vehicle"; for *put down*, "(of a plane) to land") constitute <1% of their respective BNC samples. Whether or not such findings would bear out using samples from different reference corpora, the fact remains that the same lexicographical principles ought to be applied to all transitive phrasal verb search results.

Returning to *put down*, let's say that a learner of English encounters the phrase, *she put the phone down,* and is puzzled by it. So common is this phrase in English that native speakers will find little to be confused about: it means that she ended the telephone conversation. If I say that *she put the phone down on me*, the normal meaning – the default meaning – is that she ended the phone conversation before I had finished speaking (not that she assaulted me with a mobile phone as a weapon or that she used me as a repository for it). Supposing that the learner knows the very basic – and most common – sense of *put down*, i.e. "to stop holding something and place it somewhere in the immediate vicinity", they might deduce that the telephone itself was placed somewhere. Given that the use of mobile phones is gradually taking over as the norm of spoken interpersonal communication, in which no physical replacing of a receiver is required, to *put down the phone* is not necessarily obvious in meaning for a new learner of English. Idiomatic multiword entities such as these are especially important to include in online dictionaries, but they are often absent. In our analysis of a random sample from the BNC, "[[Human 1]] put {the phone} down" (with the optional adverbial of "on [[Human 2]]") was found to occur frequently. In fact, it is the fourth most common pattern out of 22 patterns found for *put down* in the BNC sample.

3   A Word That Has Undergone Dramatic Changes of Meaning: *Dope*

So far, we have considered the role of online dictionaries in the understanding of two commonly used phrasal verbs: **wipe out** and **put down**. Let us now take a different example, one that online dictionaries must handle differently. A word whose meaning has changed dramatically over the past century is *dope*. Apparently originating in America in the 19th century, the noun denoted a kind of thick, gooey porridge or a lubricant, traceable to the Dutch *doop* 'thick sauce for dipping things in', from *doopen* 'to dip'. The first dramatic change of meaning, which took place before the end of the 19th century, was to denote a stupid person. This sense has since come to be associated with the use of narcotics, though the history of this word's meaning development is not entirely clear.

In the early 20th century, a further change in meaning took place: *dope* came to be used as the word for a kind of varnish applied to the canvas fuselage of early aeroplanes. This sense is still found applied to model aeroplanes, which have canvas fuselages and where lightness of weight is all-important. The varnish was notorious as emitting intoxicating fumes, a fact that surely played a role in the development of two modern senses, namely: any of several kinds of stupefying drugs (variously marijuana, opium, or heroin, depending on the particular dialect or region of English); and, as found in both athletics and horse racing, a drug given to athletes, racehorses, and greyhounds, often illegally, either to enhance or inhibit performance. Later in the 20th century, two additional senses developed: 'important information', as in "give me the dope on this development"; and, most recently, a general term of approbation, as in "man, that suit is dope".

Someone using the Internet to decipher the meaning of *dope* will most likely begin in the usual place: with a Google search for "*dope definition*". As with all such searches, the default first result is the entry by Google Dictionary, licenced from OxfordDictionaries.com. It is reassuringly comprehensive. For the noun, there are four main senses:

1. INFORMAL a drug taken illegally for recreational purposes, especially cannabis

   - a drug given to a racehorse or greyhound to inhibit or enhance its performance
   - a drug taken by an athlete to improve performance

2. INFORMAL a stupid person
3. INFORMAL information about a subject, especially if not generally known.
4. a varnish formerly applied to fabric surfaces of aircraft to strengthen them and keep them airtight

   - a thick liquid used as a lubricant
   - a substance added to petrol to increase its effectiveness.

For the verb, three main senses are given:

1. administer drugs to (a racehorse, greyhound, or athlete) in order to inhibit or enhance sporting performance

   - INFORMAL, be heavily under the influence of drugs, typically illegal ones
   - treat (food or drink) with drugs
   - add drugs to, tamper with, adulterate, contaminate
   - INFORMAL, DATED regularly take illegal drugs

2. smear or cover with varnish or other thick liquid
3. ELECTRONICS add an impurity to (a semiconductor) to produce a desired electrical characteristic.

For the adjective just one sense is given:

1. very good.

Finally, an explanation of the phrasal verb **dope something out** is listed, with the meaning, "work out something".

Unlike our previous examples, in which the online dictionary entries were found to be inadequate, so that multiple resources needed to be consulted in order to find a relevant definition, this first available entry encapsulates every known meaning of the word *dope*.

3.1 Urban Dictionary

Our next Google result is not one of the usual contenders, such as *Cambridge English Dictionary, Oxford Dictionaries*, or *Merriam Webster*, but instead the *Urban Dictionary*, a website dedicated to defining slang terms not found in standard dictionaries. That this website ranks so highly in the search results for "dope definition" is a reflection of the heavily informal nature of *dope*.

Urban Dictionary (UD) is a collection of crowd-sourced definitions for terms that are typically not found in standard dictionaries or are controversial in some way. Entries are submitted by members of the public and can be 'upvoted' or 'downvoted' by fellow users, meaning that definition search results are in fact rankings of candidate entries for a given term based on the upvote-to-downvote ratio. Rather than being professionally produced by lexicographers, these are written by lay people, often featuring slang, jocular language. UD features 176 submitted entries for dope, suggesting that there is a degree of disagreement over meanings and nuance. The "top" entry for **dope** reads as follows:

Saying something is cool. Most heard in big cities. Or, a drug. (Ex. Cocane [sic]/ Mary J/Dope)".

Examples of usage are provided, presumably invented by contributors, as with almost all UD definitions: "'Yo that new shirt is dope!' Or 'Look! Some guy is selling dope!'". This has been voted the "top" definition presumably because users find it the most useful or, in their experience, accurate.

In the second-highest-ranking UD entry, *dope* is defined as "Old people definition: Marijuana. Southern definition: Meth. Northern definition Heroin. Also dope can mean awesome." This has been corroborated (upvoted) by 823 users, who seem to agree with this evaluation of the age and regional differences in the use of the term. The third entry, voted for by 18,757 users, also includes expressions of opinion, possibly based on observations of usage: "People who do not do drugs call Marajuanna [sic] Dope. People who do Marajuanna [sic] call Heroin Dope. Word has also been used to describe how good something [sic] is."

Despite the unconventional spelling and the absence of lexicographical etiquette – e.g. word class, register information, etymology and so on – these entries are both informative and interesting; they are also evidently popular, no doubt because they strike at the heart of the issue: *dope* is not a neutral term. Despite its positive connotations as an adjective, it tends to have a negative connotation when used as a noun. Entry number 3 even alludes to a kind of moral hierarchy of drug users: those who use no drugs at all, those who use cannabis, and those who use heroin.

How reliable are these entries? In a sample of the Contemporary Corpus of American English (COCA) for the lemma DOPE, we found that 73.5% was constituted by instances of the noun *dope,* denoting a stupid person. 9.2% of the sample was made up of examples of the positive adjective *dope.* The verb *dope,* perhaps surprisingly, has a very low frequency, constituting just 2.2% of the sample. In a sample taken from the BNC, for comparison, 75.5% of concordance lines featured the noun that refers to a drug; 6.1% referenced a stupid person; 11.2% featured the use of *dope* as a transitive verb; and 5.1% of the sample was concerned with the electronics sense of the term, as explained in the Google/Oxford definition above. The use of *dope* as an adjective is negligible in the BNC sample at just 1% – but it is slightly more frequent in COCA, a fact that suggests that this is a typically American use of the word.

4   Wiktionary

Next we asked ourselves, how good is Wiktionary as an online resource for questions about English phraseology and meaning? Like most online resources these days, it is free of charge, but that does not necessarily mean that it is any good.

We looked at the Wiktionary entries for the three cases that we have been studying – the phrasal verbs *wipe out* and *put down*, and the word *dope,* a word that is used both as a noun and a verb, and in recent years has also come to be used in slang as an adjective.

4.1   Phrasal Verbs: *Wipe Out* and *Put Down*

The first thing to say is that Wiktionary does not offer systematic cross-references from base verbs to phrasal verbs. In other words, the user has to already know that *wipe out*, *put down*, and many similar expressions are phrasal verbs in order to find the most common uses and meanings of these verbs, i.e. **wipe** and **put.** Wiktionary's failure to point the reader from the base verb to the phrasal verb means that it cannot be regarded as a reliable aid for intermediate students of English. It seems to be symptomatic of a false belief by the proprietors and software engineers of Wiktionary that the vocabulary of a natural language is more stable than it really is and that what online users of lexical resources really want are: (a) foreign-language equivalents of lexical items and (b) links to rare and unusual words. This supposition is borne out by the usual set of cross-references that are actually given at the verb *put,* including *forthput, input, puttable,* and the obsolete northern English dialect inflected form *putten.* In view of this bias, it is not surprising that, whereas Wikipedia has been enthusiastically adopted by almost everyone except a few pedants, its sister product, Wiktionary, is very much less popular.

Corpus evidence shows that by far the most common use of the verb **wipe** is in the phrasal verb *wipe out,* in the sense: "to destroy (a large number of people or things); to obliterate." A similar but more complicated story can be told about *put down.*

Having said that, we hasten to add that any readers who do manage to find the entries for the phrasal verbs are likely to find an excellent set of definitions – provided that the phrasal verb in question has not changed its meaning during the past 60 years. The reason for this is that most of Wiktionary's definitions are taken from an old edition (out of copyright) of *Merriam-Webster's Collegiate Dictionary,* which was compiled by professional lexicographers in the 1950s and 60s. Some more recent additions are accurate too (as in the case of sense 4 of **wipe out,** below). However, all too often Wiktionary's policy of allowing anybody to say anything leads to unsatisfactory results, as we shall see when we look at the entry for *dope.*

The Wiktionary entry for *wipe out* reads as follows:

1. (idiomatic) To destroy (a large number of people or things); to obliterate.
2. To physically erase something written.
3. To do away with; to cause to disappear.
4. (intransitive) To crash, fall over (especially in board sports such as surfing, skateboarding etc.)

As with *wipe out,* the entry for *put down* does not state explicitly that this is a phrasal verb, the base of which is the verb **put.** Instead, there are useful links to entries for *put down as, put down for, and put down to,* and the noun form *put-down,* meaning "an insult or barb; a snide or demeaning remark".

The entry for *put down* is comprehensive and well defined:

1. Used other than with a figurative or idiomatic meaning: see **put, down.**
   *Why don't you **put down** your briefcase and stay awhile?*
2. (idiomatic) To insult, belittle, or demean.
   *They frequently **put down** their little sister for walking slowly.*
3. (of money as deposit) To pay.
   *We **put down** a $1,000 deposit.*
4. To halt, eliminate, stop, or squelch, often by force.
   *The government quickly **put down** the insurrection.*
5. (euphemistic) To euthanize (an animal).
   *Rex was in so much pain, they had to **put** him **down.***
6. To write (something).
   ***Put down** the first thing you think of on this piece of paper.*
7. (of a telephone) To terminate a call; to hang up.
   *Don't **put** the phone **down.** I want a quick word with him, too.*

8. To add a name to a list.
   *I've **put** myself **down** for the new Spanish conversation course.*
9. To make prices, or taxes, lower.
   *BP are **putting** petrol and diesel **down** in what could be the start of a price war.*
10. (idiomatic) To place a baby somewhere to sleep.
    *I had just **put** Mary **down** when you rang. So now she's crying again.*
11. (idiomatic, of an aircraft) To land.
    *The pilot managed to **put down** in a nearby farm field.*
12. (idiomatic) To drop someone off, or let them out of a vehicle.
    *The taxi **put** him **down** outside the hotel.*
13. (idiomatic) To cease, temporarily or permanently, reading (a book).
    *I was unable to **put down** The Stand: it was that exciting.*

Our only serious criticism here is that the wording of sense 7 here is misleading. "Of a telephone" implies that *putting down* is something that a telephone does, rather than something that a person does to a telephone. This would certainly complicate things for our hypothetical learner who is trying to decode *she put the phone down on me* (see Sect. 2.3).

4.2   Dope

The Wiktionary entry for **dope** is clearly based on an old dictionary that is out of copyright, evidently an edition of *Merriam-Webster's Collegiate*. Here, the unsatisfactory nature of the policy of augmenting an old dictionary by crowdsourcing is evident. The definitions for the noun senses of this word are as follows:

1. Any viscous liquid or paste, such as a lubricant, used in preparing a surface.
2. (uncountable) An absorbent material used to hold a liquid.
3. (uncountable, aeronautics) Any varnish used to coat a part, such as an airplane wing or a hot-air balloon in order to waterproof, strengthen, etc.
4. (uncountable, slang) Any illicit or narcotic drug that produces euphoria or satisfies an addiction; particularly heroin.
5. (uncountable, slang) Information, usually from an inside source, originally in horse racing and other sports.
   *What's the latest **dope** on the stock market?*
6. (uncountable, firearms) Ballistic data on previously fired rounds, used to calculate the required hold over a target.
7. (countable, slang) A stupid person.
8. (US, Ohio) dessert topping

Wiktionary fails to say that senses 4 and 7 (and possibly 5) are the only ones that are in current usage, although sense 3 (a relic of the early days of aeronautics, when airplane fuselages were made of cloth, for the sake of lightness, then strengthened with varnish) still survives among makers of model planes. The label "aeronautics" is misleading, to say the least. *Dope* has not been an active term in mainstream aeronautics since before the Second World War.

Sense 6 appears to be a subsense of sense 5, presumably added by somebody with a specialist interest in firearms. It seems that no attention has been given to lexico-graphical principle getting the right level of generalization.

Sense 8 appears to have been added by someone living in Ohio, representing an unusual local sense of the word.

Worse is to follow. Wiktionary aims to be multilingual, but its translation equivalents are handled without linguistic sensitivity. To take just one example, the first French translation equivalent for sense 1 of *dope* is said to be *patine*, but this is glossed back into English as "patina, an oxidation like on bronze or similar effect."

The very principle that has made Wikipedia such a resounding success – an open forum in which anybody can contribute an article on subjects of which they have specialist knowledge – has contributed to the failure of Wiktionary. It is not a reliable resource. By attempting to satisfy everybody's linguistic needs, Wiktionary succeeds in satisfying nobody's.

The "welcome page" or blurb proudly announces, "Wiktionary is a multilingual **free dictionary**, being written collaboratively on this website by people from around the world. Entries may be edited by anyone!" In this paper, we have suggested that this policy is responsible for some bad results.

5 Conclusions

How reliable are these definitions? Where *dope* is concerned, analyses of samples from the BNC and the Corpus of Contemporary American English (COCA) suggested that most of the important senses are well covered by Oxford/Google at least. The same is true, up to a point, of the phrasal verbs, though the cross-referencing policy is in serious need of attention. The most common sense of *wipe out*, for example, is discoverable in online dictionaries but only for those who are determined to keep digging. Online dictionaries such as *Oxford Dictionaries*, which is now the default option offered by Google, do a pretty good job of explaining the contemporary and historical meaning of words in isolation, all things considered. However, this paper has drawn attention to two areas in which further work is desirable.

We suggest that Oxford and Google between them have not taken sufficient account of the difference between a printed dictionary and an electronic resource. This particularly affects questions about phraseology and in the case of phrasal verbs such as *wipe something out* or *wipe someone out*, results can be extremely confusing for a user who does not already know the meaning. On the printed page, *wipe something out* and *wipe someone out* can be clearly seen as part of the entry for **wipe**, but in an online resource these transitive phrasal verbs are hidden from view and may never be found by naïve users.

A first step towards remedying this deficiency would be for the software engineers in Oxford or Silicon Valley to introduce cross-references systematically for subentries that are not immediately visible in an online resource. More ambitiously, it would be desirable to distinguish the many rare, obsolete, and obsolescent senses of words from those that are still in common use today. This could only be done with reasonably reliable results by systematically sampling usage in a large corpus. Empirical analysis of phraseology by Corpus Pattern Analysis [3, 4] is necessary to distinguish normal, conventional uses words from unusual uses. Unusual uses include senses that are no longer current, but also freshly created metaphors and other exploitations of the normal patterns of word use. (It should be noted here that there are two kinds of figurative language, as found using CPA and detailed in [4], including metaphors: freshly created exploitations of normal phraseology; and conventional metaphors, which are secondary norms rather than examples of linguistic creativity.) Understanding the differences between norms and exploitations is key to providing relevant information on word meanings.

We also took a brief look at the *Urban Dictionary* and concluded that, while this is not to be taken seriously as a work of monolingual lexicography (an inventory of the words of English and their meanings) it allows people interested in contemporary usage (not professional lexicographers) to present some very interesting observations. It could even be seen as a beneficial application of the principle of crowd-sourcing. Unfortunately, the same cannot be said for *Wiktionary*, which falls between two stools. On the one hand it is basically an old dictionary, which was compiled in the 1950s or 60s. A policy of crowd-sourcing allows anyone to add anything to this base, often with unsatisfactory results, which are no help to anyone. We contrasted this with Wikipedia, where the crowd-sourcing principle allows people with specialist knowledge to contribute their expertise to the benefit of the whole community.

While the cases explored in this paper are necessarily few, they have demonstrated intrinsic problems with online lexicographic resources. Whether one begins with a Google search for "[word] definition", or whether one goes direct to the source, such as OxfordDictionaries.com or another online resource, the user will most likely be required to have relatively sophisticated linguistic knowledge to successfully navigate the results. Traditional printed dictionaries suffer with their own problems, but given the massive potential of the Web in terms of availability and richness of data, cross-referencing capability and lack of space constraints, online resources clearly have much room for improvement.

References

1. Bolinger, D.: Getting the words in. In: McDavid, R.I., Duckert, A.R. (eds.) Lexicography in English. New York Academy of Sciences, New York (1973)
2. Chun, D.M.: L2 reading on the web: strategies for accessing information in hypermedia. Comput. Assist. Lang. Learn. **14**(5), 367–403 (2001)
3. Hanks, P.: Corpus pattern analysis. In: Williams, G., Vessier, S. (eds.) Proceedings of the Eleventh EURALEX International Congress, EURALEX 2004, vol. 1, Lorient, France, 6–10 July 2004. Université de Bretagne-Sud (2004)
4. Hanks, P.: Lexical Analysis. MIT Press, Cambridge (2013)
5. Jin, L., Deifell, E.: Foreign language learners' use and perception of online dictionaries: a survey study. J. Online Learn. Teach. **9**(4), 515–533 (2013)
6. Trench, R.C.: On some deficiencies in our English dictionaries. Trans. Phil. Soc. **4**(2), 1–70 (1857)

Translating Manipulated Idioms (EN>ES) in the Word Sketch Scenario

Carlos Manuel Hidalgo-Ternero(✉)

University of Malaga, Malaga, Spain
cmhidalgo@uma.es

Abstract. This paper presents a teaching proposal for translation/interpreting undergraduate students. Following a corpus-based methodology, the main objective of this proposal is to train students on how to exploit the possibilities offered by Sketch Engine for the creation of *ad hoc* phraseological equivalences. More precisely, we will examine the potential of its functionality Word Sketch as a convenient tool in those cases where the manipulation of idioms and the absence of one-to-one phraseological correspondences may pose problems to translation. The experimental setting comprised an introductory seminar on the convergence of corpora, phraseology and translation, followed by a hands-on session, where trainee translators were presented with some case-studies for which they had to create *ad hoc* phraseological equivalents for the manipulated idioms in the source text (ST) and had to justify both the translation *process* and *product*. Overall, the insights gained from analysing the results obtained will allow us to determine to what extent trainee translators are able to translate manipulated idioms in the Word Sketch scenario.

Keywords: Teaching proposal · Translation · Word sketch · Idiom manipulation · *Ad hoc* phraseological equivalences

1 Introduction

The wealth of approaches and research topics on phraseodidactics illustrates a hectic activity in different linguistic disciplines such as second and foreign language teaching and learning (Meunier and Granger [14], Hallsteinsdóttir [8, 9], and González Rey [7]). However, phraseodidactics is still an *unexplored land* in the area of Translation Studies, notwithstanding the growing body of literature that acknowledges the difficulties phraseological units pose in the translation task (Corpas Pastor [3, 5], Colson, [1, 2], and Ladmiral [11], among many others). Against such a background, this study aims at opening up new avenues of research on the applications of phraseodidactics to translation training. We will follow a corpus-based methodology, and, for the sake of the argument, the focus will be on somatisms (idioms containing terms that refer to body parts) in Spanish and English.

In this regard, we present a teaching proposal for undergraduate students of the degree in Translation and Interpreting of the University of Malaga, Spain. The experiment was carried out as part of the syllabus of *Lengua y cultura "B" aplicadas a la Traducción e Interpretación (II) – inglés*, which is a first-year course on English

© Springer Nature Switzerland AG 2019
G. Corpas Pastor and R. Mitkov (Eds.): Europhras 2019, LNAI 11755, pp. 173–186, 2019.
https://doi.org/10.1007/978-3-030-30135-4_13

language and culture applied to Translation and Interpreting that is taught as part of the Bachelor's degree in Translation and Interpreting at the University of Malaga.

Against such a background, the overall structure of this study is as follows. Sections 2, 3, 4 and 5 are aligned with learning activities 1, 2, 3 and 4, respectively. The first learning activity includes an introductory seminar on the convergence of corpora, phraseology and translation. In the second learning activity we will delve into the notion of idiom manipulation and the problems it may pose to translation. The third learning activity commences by laying out the Sketch Engine tool Word Sketch and how it can be implemented in order to create *ad hoc* phraseological equivalents for manipulated idioms in the ST. Section 5 lays out the teaching proposal in which trainee translators will be presented with some translation scenarios comprising different types of idiom manipulation. Finally, the results concerning the trainees' translation proposals will be displayed in Sect. 6, and thoroughly analysed in Sect. 7.

2   Basic Notions on Corpus, Phraseology and Translation

The first learning activity included a theoretical seminar, in which the convergence of corpus, phraseology, phraseological units (and, more specifically, idioms) and translation was discussed. As a cornerstone procedure in the translation of phraseological units (and, more specifically, idioms), students had first been presented with the steps proposed by Corpas Pastor [5, pp. 213–223], i.e., the identification of an idiom, its interpretation in context as well as the search and establishment of its correspondences in the lexical, textual and discursive level. In this search for phraseological correspondences, translators can resort to a very effective documentation tool, namely text corpora. Along these learning activities we worked with both monolingual and parallel corpora. The latter can be defined as corpora conformed by source texts and their translations in one (*bilingual parallel corpora*) or several (*multilingual*) target languages (Teubert [16], Corpas Pastor [4], and Zanettin [18]).

In this regard, following a corpus-based methodology, trainee translators had recourse to both the parallel corpus OPUS 2, and monolingual corpora in Spanish (eseuTenTen) and English (enTenTen). OPUS 2 and the corpora belonging to the TenTen family are available through Sketch Engine, a language corpus management and query system with 500 corpora in more than ninety different languages. The corpora EsTenTen (over 17.5 billion words) and enTenTen (over 15 billion) belong to the TenTen corpus family and are compiled from texts retrieved from the Internet. These corpora are lemmatised and part-of-speech tagged. Finally, OPUS2 consists of parallel corpora which allow both bilingual and multilingual queries among forty different languages (Kilgarriff et al. [10]).

When effectively exploited, corpora can become an invaluable documentation source for translators. Given the phraseological anisomorphism across languages, a simple query in either a monolingual or a bilingual corpus does not usually suffice when searching for phraseological correspondences for manipulated idioms, let alone textual equivalents. In this regard, in the following sections we analysed the multiple applications of the corpus search engine Word Sketch when establishing *ad hoc* phraseological equivalents in those cases in which this manipulation of idioms and the absence of one-to-one phraseological correspondences may pose some problems to translation.

3   Idiom Manipulation and Translation

Before laying out Word Sketch functionalities, it will first be necessary to commence this second learning activity by framing the concept of *idiom manipulation* and by exploring the difficulties it may cause for the translation task. By *idiom manipulation*, also known as *idiom modification* or *idiom defamiliarisation*, it is meant 'different types of intentioned and easily recognisable modifications in the formal, semantic or discursive level of an idiom which aim at some specific illocutionary and perlocutionary effects, ranging from humour, irony, surprise and persuasion, inter alia' (ref. Zuluaga [19], Corpas Pastor [5], Mena Martínez [13], and Omazic [15]). In this context, Omazić [15, pp. 76–77] has extensively described the main steps in the recognition of manipulated idioms: "recognition of the modification, retrieval of the original, comparison of the original idiom and the modification, recognition of the communicative intent and understanding of idiom modification". These are consequently the main steps trainee translators must follow not only when identifying the idiom manipulation in the ST but also when creating an *ad hoc* phraseological equivalent for the TT.

In order to illustrate this procedure, let us analyse the following example: *I decided not to get a brain transplant, but then I changed my mind* (Fig. 1). Here it is possible to recognise the original idiom *change one's mind*, whose phraseological meaning is 'to adopt a different opinion or plan' (EOLD[1], [6]). In this context, both the image accompanying the sentence and, specially, the established scenario (*someone intending to undergo a brain transplant*) activate both the literal and the figurative interpretation of the unit and, hence, portray a paradoxical (and humorous) situation in which the speaker (figuratively) changed his mind about (literally) not changing his mind.

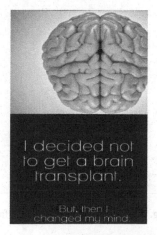

Fig. 1. Sample scenario (Image retrieved from this link: https://www.yourdictionary.com/slideshow/medical-puns)

---

[1] English Oxford *Living* Dictionaries (EOLD, [6]) are available through this URL address: https://en.oxforddictionaries.com.

When searching OPUS2 bilingual corpus for a primary correspondence of *change one's mind* into Spanish, some concordances can be retrieved with the expression *cambiar de opinión* (literally, 'to change one's opinion'). Nevertheless, through this idiom it would not be possible to preserve a similar manipulation to the one in the ST since *cambiar de opinión* is not a somatism and it could not hence display a literal interpretation referring to the body part. It is in this scenario that the trainee translator can have recourse to the Sketch Engine feature called Word Sketch in order to create an *ad hoc* phraseological equivalent that could accurately convey the pragmatic, semantic and discursive load of the ST idiom and, concomitantly, portray a similar manipulation to the one depicted in the ST. In the next section we will thoroughly analyse the array of possibilities the Sketch Engine feature Word Sketch can offer in this task of creating *ad hoc* phraseological equivalents for manipulated idioms in the ST.

4   Using Word Sketch to Create *Ad Hoc* Phraseological Equivalents

Before introducing the multiple applications of Word Sketch (Thomas [17]), it will first be necessary to display its interface and to describe the main components trainee translators can employ in their quests for translating manipulated idioms (Fig. 2).

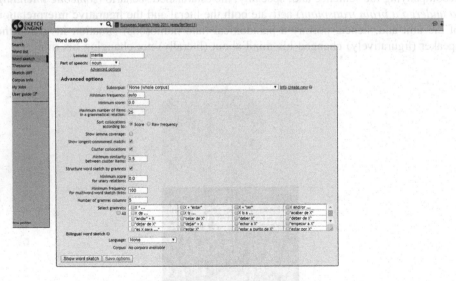

Fig. 2. Word Sketch query interface

As it can be observed, Word Sketch provides a complete and detailed search engine in order to refine the queries according to the users' needs. In our case, we will search for the grammatical and collocational behaviour of the Spanish primary correspondence for *mind* ('mente'), in order to detect whether there is any phraseological unit (be they idioms, collocations or any other kind of multiword unit) which could accurately convey an analogous semantic, pragmatic and discursive load to the idiom in the ST and, simultaneously, be subject to either internal or external manipulation. Our final objective will hence be to attain a similar perlocutionary effect as that of the idiom in the ST, i.e., to trigger the reader's laughter.

In this context, we will search for phraseological units containing the lemma *mente* with the POS tag *noun*. Among the advanced options, we will have the search engine sort collocates according to their collocation strength (*association score*) rather than their frequency (*raw frequency*), so that only significant collocates are retrieved. The option *Show longest-commonest match* will display the longest and the most frequent phrase including both the node and the collocate as a collocation example. We will also require the system to group collocates with related meanings (*Cluster collocation* option) with a minimum similarity of 0.5. In this way, it will be possible to cluster (partial) synonyms such as *pensar/creer* ('to think'/'to believe') or antonyms such as *abrir/cerrar* ('to open'/'to close'), expanding the range of manipulation possibilities. The option *Structure word sketch by gramrels (grammatical relations)* will allow us to group collocates according to their grammatical relation for easy retrieval and visualisation. Once these parameters have been set, this is the main view of Work Sketch interface displayed for the lemma *mente* (Fig. 3):

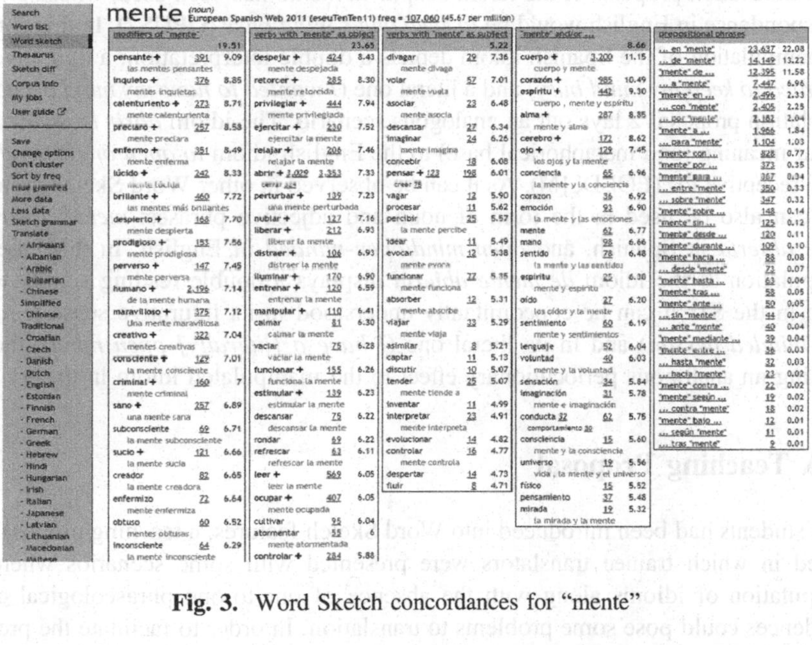

Fig. 3. Word Sketch concordances for "mente"

Besides these features, the search engine also enables the user to search for bilingual word sketches, whose results can be retrieved from a different corpus. For instance, this can be useful in case the trainee translator seeks to contrast the grammatical and collocational behaviour of *mente* in Spanish against *mind* in English. It would also be possible to refine the query by selecting only some specific *gramrels* such as *verbs with X as subject* or *verbs with X as object* in case the translator exclusively aims at retrieving items of verbs with *mente* either as a subject or as an object, which would facilitate data retrieval and visualisation.

Once the main features of Word Sketch have been explained, we will now analyse how they can be implemented to create *ad hoc* phraseological equivalents for manipulated idioms in the ST. In this context, returning to the ST *I decided not to get a brain transplant, but then I changed my mind*, it is possible to recognise that the manipulation of the idiom *change one's mind* displays a dylogy in which both the figurative (*change one's opinion*) and the literal (*replace one's brain*) interpretation are concomitantly present. When searching Word Sketch for phraseological units that could also depict an analogous dylogy, it is possible to perceive that *mente* can be modified by verbs such as *ocupar* (literally, 'to occupy'), *abrir* ('to open'), *liberar* ('to free'), *vaciar* ('to empty'), among others, whose manipulation could also activate a double reading, as it will be shown in the following translation proposals:

1. +Pero, tío, ¿por qué te has hecho un trasplante de cerebro?
   -Pues por tener la mente ocupada.[2]
2. +Pero, tío, ¿por qué te has hecho un trasplante de cerebro?
   -Sabes que soy una persona de mente abierta.[3]

In translation proposal 1, the idiom *ocupar la mente* has been used, whose primary correspondence in English would be *to keep one's mind busy* (OPUS2). In this context, the manipulation of the Spanish idiom depicts a double interpretation: a figurative one (*I wanted to keep my mind busy*) and a literal one (*I wanted to have my mind occupied*). Translation proposal 2 lays out an analogous scenario. The idiom *abrir la mente* has a similar meaning (and metaphorical base) to the English idiom *to open one's mind*, i.e., 'to be receptive to' (EOLD, [6]). As it can be observed in other Word Sketch gramrels, both can also be used in the form of noun and adjective phrases: *mente abierta/de mente abierta* in Spanish, and *open mind/open-minded* in English. In this case, the manipulation of the idiom *de mente abierta* displays a double reading similar to the idiom in the ST: it can be concomitantly understood in its figurative sense (*I am an open-minded person*) and in its literal one (*I have a [literally] open mind*), thereby attaining an analogous perlocutionary effect to the manipulated idiom in the ST.

5   A Teaching Proposal

Once students had been introduced into Word Sketch features, a teaching proposal was offered in which trainee translators were presented with some scenarios where the manipulation of idioms along with the absence of one-to-one phraseological correspondences could pose some problems to translation. In order to facilitate the process, students were provided with the following workflow structured in a sequence of

---

[2] +Hey, bro, why did you get a brain transplant? -Just to keep my mind busy.
[3] +Hey, bro, why did you get a brain transplant? -You know I am an open-minded person.

predefined and protocolised tasks in the form of heuristic strategies and steps to be implemented with the aid of corpora:

1. Detect the somatism in the ST and search for its meaning and usage in the English monolingual corpus enTenTen.
2. Analyse the somatism in the ST and determine what type of manipulation it has undergone and what two levels are portrayed by the idiom manipulation (the figurative and the literal one).
3. Access OPUS2 bilingual corpus and search it for primary phraseological correspondences of this somatism in the target language (TL) and examine whether it would be a textual equivalent not only in terms of conveying the same semantic, pragmatic and discursive load but also in being subject to an analogous manipulation.
4. If this primary correspondence does not fit those criteria, use Word Sketch in the corpus eseuTenTen in order to create an *ad hoc* phraseological equivalent.
5. Offer a translation proposal and justify both the *process* and the *product*.

After the presentation of this workflow, students were provided with some translation scenarios (Figs. 4, 5, 6, and 7), all of which included somatisms that had undergone any kind of manipulation with the perlocutionary effect of triggering the reader's laughter. For the completion this task, they were given the following instructions:

> Translate the following puns with body parts from English into Spanish (diatopic variety: European Spanish). Consider the image they are accompanied by. Justify both the *process* and the *product*.

In this context, trainee translators had to provide two types of answers: the first one consisted of the translation proposals for each ST and the second one included the steps they had followed in order to complete the task. In the following section, we will analyse how these incoming results can shed some light on the process of creating *ad hoc* phraseological equivalents for manipulated idioms in the ST through Word Sketch.

6   Results

Students' translation proposals were submitted in the form creation tool Googleform[4], which also allows an easy retrieval and visualisation of the results obtained. The main objective of the study was to analyse trainee translators' performance when searching Word Sketch for *ad hoc* phraseological equivalents for manipulated idioms in the ST. Therefore, results presenting morphological, syntactic, lexical and/or orthotypographic dissimilarities were unified within the same category as long as they included translation proposals with analogous idiom manipulation in the TT. Against such a background, we will now analyse the 35 submitted responses, in order to examine to what

---

[4] The form creation tool Googleform is available through the following link: https://www.google.es/intl/es/forms/about/.

extent trainee translators were able to create an *ad hoc* phraseological equivalent for the manipulated idioms in each translation scenario.

Translation scenario 1 (Fig. 4) presents the sentence "I've tried horse racing but I never seem to get a head", where it is possible to recognise the idiom *to get ahead,* whose figurative meaning is 'to overtake', in the context of a race. Nevertheless, its internal manipulation into *to get a head* along with the accompanying image of a headless rider provokes the polisemantisation of the sequence by also activating its literal meaning ('the horse rider never seems to get a head'). Considering the importance of attaining an equivalent effect in the TT, the results from the survey indicate that 34 trainee translators (i.e., 97%) were able to offer a manipulated somatism in the TT with the lemma *cabeza* ('head'). Among the most common proposals, it is possible to detect a wide array of manipulated idioms such as *perder la cabeza* o *írsele la cabeza* ('to lose one's head'); *jugarse la cabeza* ('to risk one's neck'); *(no) levantar cabeza* (lit., 'not to raise one's head', fig., 'to get back on one's feet again'); *con cabeza* (lit., 'with a head', fig., 'with a good head on one's shoulders'); *no tener ni pies ni cabeza* ('not to make head nor tail of something'), or *(no) asomar la cabeza* (lit., 'not to show one's head', fig., 'not to show up'), whose manipulation portrays an analogous double reading to that of the idiom in the ST, i.e., their own figurative meaning and concomitantly a literal interpretation alluding to the accompanying image of the headless rider.

Fig. 4. Translation scenario 1 (Image retrieved from the following link: https://memebase. cheezburger.com/puns/tag/head)

Scenario 2 (Fig. 5) displays the following setting: "you hang around, I'll go on ahead" with the image of a hat and a tie talking to each other. Here it is possible to detect a double idiom manipulation. Firstly, the scenario of the tie being told to *hang around* prompts a double reading of the idiom in its figurative meaning ('to wait around', according to EOLD, [6]) and in its literal one ('to hang around the neck'). Furthermore, the hat's statement "I'll go on ahead" provokes the polisemantisation of the sequence by activating a figurative interpretation ("I'll be at the lead") and a literal one ("I'll go on a head").

Fig. 5. Translation scenario 2 (Image retrieved from the following link: https://memebase. cheezburger.com/puns/tag/head)

Against such a background, for the first manipulated idiom *hang around* 22 trainee translators (63%) were able to provide different *ad hoc* phraseological equivalents in the TT, such as *dar vueltas* ('to turn around' and 'to walk around'), with 13 appearances (37%); *estar/quedarse colgado* (lit., 'to hang', fig., 'to be left in the lurch'), with 6 occurrences (17%); *enrollarse* (lit., 'to wind around'; fig., 'to chatter') and *ajustarse* (lit. 'to adjust oneself'; fig., 'to stick to [a plan]'), with 2 and 1 appearances (6% and 3%) respectively. For the second manipulated idiom in the ST, the results display a high rate of translation proposals with manipulated somatisms with the lemma *cabeza* in the TT: 26 out of 35 total answers (i.e., 74%). The main offered idiom manipulations were *(ir/ponerse) en cabeza/a la cabeza* ('in the lead of' or 'at the head of'), with 15 answers (43%); *(ir) de cabeza* ('[to rush] headlong'), with 5 occurrences (14%), and the verb *encabezar* ('to head', 'to lead'), with 2 answers (6%). Other translation proposals included the manipulation of idioms such as *traer de cabeza* ('to drive someone crazy' or 'to cause problems to someone'); *comer la cabeza [a alguien]* (lit., 'to eat someone's head', fig., 'to brainwash [someone]') or *(ir) una cabeza por delante* (lit., 'to be a head ahead'), among others.

Scenario 3 and 4 (Figs. 6 and 7 respectively) present the same manipulated idiom within two similar sentences (*I['ve] got your back*) but accompanied by different images. In the first one it is possible to observe a skeleton holding another skeleton's spine, which is why the latter is partially on the floor. In the second image, two stick men can be perceived, one of whom is holding the other's torso. In both of the scenarios it is possible to recognise the idiom *to get someone's back*, whose figurative meaning is 'to always be ready to defend or help someone' (MD[5], [12]). Nevertheless, the accompanying images of two characters without a torso simultaneously activate the literal reading of the sequence, i.e., 'to grab someone's back'. The objective of selecting two different images for the same idiom manipulation was to analyse whether

---

[5] McMillan Dictionary (MD, [12]) is available at the following link: https://www.macmillandictionary. com/.

the creation of *ad hoc* phraseological equivalents for the TT was mainly determined by the source text or by the source image, or both, which will be examined in the following Sect. 7 (*Analysis of the results*).

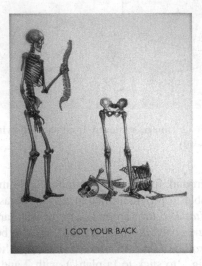

Fig. 6. Translation scenario 3 (Image retrieved from the following URL address: https://br. pinterest.com/pin/12596073944386237/?autologin=true)

Fig. 7. Translation scenario 4 (Image retrieved from this link: https://ahealthhouse.com/new-events/open-drop-in-vinyasayoga-2)

Against such a background, for translation scenario 3, 25 trainee translators (71%) were able to offer a manipulated idiom for the TT, 18 of which (51%) consisted of a manipulated somatism (15 with the lemma *espalda* ['back']). Among the most common proposals, it is possible to detect idioms such as *cubrir/guardar/cuidar las espaldas* ('to cover someone's back'), with 9 occurrences (26%); *respaldar [a alguien]* ('to back/endorse someone'), with 3 appearances (9%); *dar la espalda [a alguien]* ('to turn your back on someone'), with 2 answers (6%), or *(hacer algo) a las espaldas [de alguien]* ('to do something behind someone's back'), with 1 occurrence (3%). It is also possible to find a somatism manipulation with the lemma *espina* ('spine'): *dar mala espina* (lit., 'to give a bad spine'), with an analogous metaphorical meaning to the English idioms 'to have a bad feeling about something' or 'to smell fishy'.

In translation scenario 4, it is possible to perceive a higher rate of translation proposals with manipulated idioms (30, i.e., 86%), 26 of which (71%) included manipulated somatisms (25 with the lemma *espalda*). Similarly to scenario 3, the most frequent answers comprised idioms such as *cubrir/cuidar la espalda*, with 16 occurrences (46%); *respaldar*, with 4 appearances (11%); *dar la espalda*, consisting of 3 answers (9%); *a las espaldas [de alguien]* or *de espaldas* ('with one's back facing something'), with 1 occurrence each (3%). Other translation proposals included manipulations such as *¿qué pasa, tronco?* (lit., 'what's up, trunk?'; fig., 'what's up, mate?'), displaying a double interpretation to both a *friend* and a *(body) trunk*, and the verb *empalar* ('to impale'), whose internal manipulation through *inpalar* concomitantly portrays a literal meaning (*en palo*, 'in a stick'), directly referring to the accompanying image of the stick men.

7 Analysis of the Results

Once the results have been displayed, it is now necessary to examine their implications for the translation task. It is first important to mention that the phraseological anisomorphism between English and Spanish resulted in an impossibility of selecting the primary correspondences for the manipulated idioms in translation scenarios 1, 3 and 4. In these cases, it was hence necessary to search for *ad hoc* phraseological equivalents for each of them. Notwithstanding this 'phraseological obstacle', in the translation proposals most of the trainee translators were able to provide not only a manipulated idiom but more specifically a manipulated somatism for the TT (97% in translation scenario 1, 74% in scenario 2, 51% in scenario 3, and 71% in scenario 4). This accounts for the recursiveness of the body images in the phraseological repertoire of both languages and, thus, accentuates the existence of a wide range of translation possibilities when trying to create *ad hoc* phraseological equivalents for manipulated somatisms in the EN/ES combination.

When analysing trainee translators' responses on their translation process, it can be confirmed that the Sketch Engine tool Word Sketch has proved to be an effective documentation source in those cases in which the primary correspondence in Spanish for the manipulated idiom in English could not portray an analogous double reading considering the accompanying image (translation scenarios 1, 3 and 4) and it was hence necessary to create an *ad hoc* phraseological equivalent. In this regard, 32 trainee translators (91%) had recourse to Word Sketch for translation scenario 1; 18 respondents (51%) consulted Word Sketch for translation scenario 3, and 20 participants (57%) employed this feature for scenario 4. As it can be observed through these percentages, trainee translators encountered more difficulties when aiming at creating phraseological equivalents with the lemma *espalda* ('back') than with the lemma *cabeza* ('head'), which implies that the effectiveness of Word Sketch in the query process will chiefly depend, among other factors, on the recursiveness of every specific body image in the phraseological repertoire of the given language. Nevertheless, in order to overcome this obstacle, 5 trainee translators in translation scenario 3 (14%) and 7 respondents in scenario 4 (20%) were able to provide an *ad hoc* phraseological equivalent by exclusively employing a simple query on a parallel corpora, which means that a total of 23 trainee translators in scenario 3 (66%) and 27 in scenario 4 (77%) were capable of offering an *ad hoc* phraseological equivalent by having recourse to corpora, either consulting Word Sketch in the monolingual corpus eseuTenTen or the simple query in the parallel corpus OPUS2.

However, there is a specific case in which most trainee translators did not need the assistance of Word Sketch: translation scenario 2, where the manipulated somatism in the ST (*to go on a head*) holds a primary correspondence in Spanish (*ir en cabeza*) whose manipulation can portray an analogous double reading related to the accompanying image. In this context, only 8 trainee translators (23%) had recourse to Word Sketch in contrast with the 17 respondents (49%) who employed the simple query in the parallel corpus OPUS2 in order to provide a phraseological equivalent for the TT. These results suggest that trainee translators employ Word Sketch as a documentation tool only when the manipulated idiom in the ST does not possess a primary correspondence in the phraseological repertoire of the target language which may be subject to an analogous manipulation.

Finally, as it has been stated in the previous section, translation scenarios 3 and 4 presented the same manipulated idiom within two similar sentences (*I['ve] got your back*) but accompanied by different images. The objective of selecting two different images for the same idiom manipulation was to analyse whether the creation of *ad hoc* phraseological equivalents for the TT was mainly determined by the source text or by the source image, or both. Although 34 respondents (97%) offered different translation proposals for both scenarios, a closer analysis allows us to detect that only 5 trainee translators in translation scenario 4 (14%) and 2 participants in scenario 3 (6%) provided manipulated somatisms with different bases from *espalda* ('back'), which accounts for the dominant influence of the source text (above the source image) in the creation of *ad hoc* phraseological equivalents. Among these proposals, it is possible to observe manipulated somatisms with lemmas such as *columna* ('backbone'), with 2 occurrences (6%); *espina* ('spine'), and *hueso* ('bones'), with 1 occurrence each (3%), for translation scenario 3; and *tronco* ('trunk') or *palo* ('stick'), with 1 occurrence each (3%), for translation scenario 4, all of which reflect the two different accompanying images: the skeletons in translation scenario 3, and the stick men in scenario 4. In the light of these results, it is hence particularly important to teach trainee translators how not only the source text but also the source image can be of great assistance in the creation of *ad hoc* phraseological equivalents for the TT.

8   Conclusion

The shrewd digressions portrayed by manipulated idioms lay out a perfect symbiosis in which two readings (the literal and the figurative one) are concomitantly present, and hidden; both of them so softly depicted that they become unseen, but not unnoticed. It is in this scenario that the translator must be less of an impersonator and more of an impressionist.

This idiom manipulation, along with the crosslinguistic phraseological anisomorphism, should not cast a shadow on the translation task, but it should serve to give centre stage to a translator who must now (re-)create a parallel artwork with a symmetrical polysemy to the one evoked in the ST, so that both sides of the painting are faithfully depicted on the target canvas.

If, as Heinrich Heine once put it, "translating is dancing in chains"[6], rendering manipulated idioms into the TT can easily become dancing *in vain*, unless the translator is equipped with the appropriate garments. Our teaching proposal, comprising the search engine Word Sketch and a set of protocolised tasks, has thus been conceived in order to help trainee translators walk this balanced tightrope between literality and figurativeness in the manipulation of idioms for the TT.

Acknowledgements. This research has been funded by a FPU (Formación de Profesorado Universitario) contract, ref. FPU16/02032, awarded to Carlos Manuel Hidalgo Ternero by the Ministerio de Educación, Ciencia y Deporte (Spanish Ministry of Education, Science and Sport). Furthermore, this publication has been carried out within the framework of the thematic network TRAJUTEC and the teaching network "TACTRAD: aplicación de nuevas herramientas TAC para la enseñanza-aprendizaje de la traducción especializada" (ref. 719/2018) coordinated by the University of Malaga, as well as the research projects Interpreta 2.0 (PIE 17-015, type B), VIP (FFI2016-75831-P) and TERMITUR (HUM2754).

References

1. Colson, J.-P.: Cross-linguistic phraseological studies: an overview. In: Granger, S., Meunier, F. (eds.) Phraseology. An interdisciplinary perspective, pp. 191–206. John Benjamins, Amsterdam (2008)
2. Colson, J.-P.: Pratique traduisante et idiomaticité: l'importance des structures semi-figées. In: Mogorrón Huerta, P., Gallego Hernández, D., Masseau, P., Tolosa Igualada, M. (eds.) Fraseología, Opacidad y Traducción. Studien zur romanischen Sprachwissenschaft und interkulturellen Kommunikation (Herausgegeben von Gerd Wotjak) (2013)
3. Corpas Pastor, G. (ed.): Las lenguas de Europa, estudios de fraseología, fraseografía y traducción. Comares, Granada (2000)
4. Corpas Pastor, G.: Compilación de un corpus ad hoc para la enseñanza de la traducción inversa especializada. Trans: Revista de Traductología, **5**, 155–184 (2001)
5. Corpas Pastor, G.: Diez años de investigación en fraseología: análisis sintáctico-semánticos, contrastivos y traductológicos. Vervuert, Madrid (2003)
6. EOLD - Oxford University Press. English Oxford 'Living' Dictionaries. https://en.oxforddictionaries.com/. Accessed 22 Apr 2019
7. González Rey, M.I.: De la didáctica de la fraseología a la fraseodidáctica. Paremia **21**, 67–84 (2012)
8. Hallsteinsdóttir, E., et al. (eds.): Phraseodidaktik/Phraseodidactics. Linguistik online **47** (2011)
9. Hallsteinsdóttir, E.: Aktuelle Forschungsfragen der deutschsprachigen Phraseodidaktik. Linguistik online **47**, 3–31 (2011)

---

[6] "Übersetzen heißt in Ketten Tanzen".

10. Kilgarriff, A., et al.: The Sketch Engine (2003). Retrieved from. https://www.sketchengine. eu. Accessed 03 Apr 2019
11. Ladmiral, J.R.: La question phraséologique en traductologie. In: Mogorrón Huerta, P., Gallego Hernández, D., Tolosa Igualada, M. (eds.) Fraseología, Opacidad y Traducción, pp. 11–26. Peter Lang, Frankfurt (2013)
12. MD – Springer Nature Limited. McMillan Dictionary. https://www.macmillandictionary. com. Accessed 08 Apr 2019
13. Mena Martínez, F.: En torno al concepto de desautomatización fraseológica: aspectos básicos. Tonos. Revista Electrónica de Estudios Filológicos, 5 (2003)
14. Meunier, F., Granger, S.: Phraseology in Foreign Language Learning and Teaching. John Benjamins, Amsterdam (2008)
15. Omazić, M.: Processing of idioms and idiom modifications: a view from cognitive linguistics. In: Granger, S., Meunier, F. (eds.) Phraseology: An Interdisciplinary Perspective, pp. 67–79. John Benjamins, Amsterdam (2008)
16. Teubert, W.: Comparable or parallel corpora? Int. J. Lexicogr. 9(3), 238–264 (1996)
17. Thomas, J.E.: Word sketches. In: Discovering English with Sketch Engine (DESkE), pp. 161–176 (2015)
18. Zanettin, F.: Translation-Driven Corpora: Corpus Resources for Descriptive and Applied Translation Studies. Routledge, London (2012)
19. Zuluaga, A.: Análisis y traducción de las UF desautomatizadas. PhiN, 16, 67–83 (2001). http://www.fu-berlin.de/phin/phin16/p16t5.htm. Accessed 03 Apr 2019

Nominal Collocations in Scientific English: A Frame-Semantic Approach

Eva Lucía Jiménez-Navarro[✉]

Department of English and German, University of Córdoba, Córdoba, Spain
lucia.jimenez@uco.es

Abstract. In the last two decades, interest in the role played by phraseological units in the discourse of science has grown. Linguists have agreed that collocational frameworks help to structure the text and display a more restricted set of senses when used in this context. This paper aims at contributing to the study of collocations in the research article (RA). To this end, more than 400 collocations are analyzed in terms of Fillmore's Frame Semantics theory. Our methodology is corpus-based and explores adjective + noun open domain collocations extracted from the British National Corpus (BNC) in a specific corpus of more than three million words. The findings suggest that these collocations convey specific meanings when they are used in this genre, being the headword the element evoking the semantic frame of the combination and the collocate expressing a feature of the former. The frames evoked reflect the semantics of science and their combination shows the anatomy of the RA.

Keywords: Collocation · Corpus · Lexical unit · Research article · Semantic frame

1 Introduction

Phraseology is a broad term that encompasses numerous multi-word units, e.g. idiomatic expressions, lexical bundles, collostructions. This chapter is focused on collocations, a type of phraseological unit which is generally defined according to four aspects. First, the number of elements involved is at least two and they can be either two lexical words together (e.g. *crystal clear, have a go, strongly agree*) or one lexical word plus one grammatical word (e.g. *afraid of, research into, different from*). These two elements do not enjoy the same status given that the term under study is freely chosen and the accompanying word is determined by the first one. Second, these words need to recurrently co-occur in a language. Statistical measures can be used to know the significance of a combination of two words, such as Mutual Information, t-score and log-likelihood. Third, they are said to be arbitrary (there is not a linguistic motivation behind them), which makes them unpredictable. Fourth, they are normally semantically transparent, i.e., the meaning of the whole can be inferred from the meaning of its parts, although some headwords are more likely to be interpreted figuratively than literally.

© Springer Nature Switzerland AG 2019
G. Corpas Pastor and R. Mitkov (Eds.): Europhras 2019, LNAI 11755, pp. 187–199, 2019.
https://doi.org/10.1007/978-3-030-30135-4_14

However, collocations have been approached from different perspectives and have been given several definitions throughout history. On the one hand, authors like Firth [1], Halliday [2] and Sinclair [3] emphasized the frequency of co-occurrence of two elements to be regarded as a collocation. Therefore, any combination of two words which is usual in a language may be called a collocation. On the other hand, authors like Vinogradov [4], Cowie [5] and Howarth [6] were aware of the existence of various multi-word expressions, so they aimed at categorizing them considering their degree of compositionality and semantic transparency. Thus, according to this view, collocations are located along a continuum between idioms and free combinations, and they are usually compositional, i.e., their semantic interpretation is a compositional function of the elements of which it is composed, and almost semantically transparent, i.e., understanding the meaning of their constituent elements helps to unveil the meaning of the combination. Our approach is hybrid because we think that a combination of both can help to better understand what these phraseological units denote. For this reason, and for the purposes of this study, we state that collocations are compositional and (quite) transparent combinations of two lexical words, headword (main element) and collocate (dependent element), which hold a syntactic relationship and whose frequent co-occurrence can be demonstrated with the use of appropriate association measures.

Regardless of how many angles collocations have been considered from, linguists broadly agree that they are central to phraseological studies. This is because these associations of words are pervasive in every language, offering a basis to understand both its lexicon and structure. In addition, as we will show in the next section, they are genre-specific, which suggests that each type of text is characterized by a set of col-locations. In the last decades, corpus linguistics has proved itself to be a reliable method for the study of phraseology [7, 8], since it facilitates the exploration of authentic language from different perspectives by providing tools for searching, retrieving, annotating and analyzing it. In this respect, two different approaches can be developed: (1) corpus-based and (2) corpus-driven [9]. The basic difference lies in the moment in which the researcher produces a theory. Then, corpus-based research regards corpus linguistics as a methodology to confirm, refute or refine a theory or hypothesis that has been previously formulated. On the contrary, corpus-driven research analyzes the examples of a corpus first and, afterwards, proposes a theoretical statement that is fully consistent with the evidence obtained from the corpus.

As for the methodology in this investigation, it is corpus-based. Our hypothesis is that collocations convey specific meanings when they are examined in specialized discourse, specifically in scientific discourse. In order to prove this hypothesis, we will rely on corpus data compiled for this purpose. Therefore, the main aim of this paper is to give some insights into the relation between collocations and scientific genre, and the research questions to be addressed are the following ones:

(1) Can we establish a relationship between the most recurrent adjective + noun col-locations in the British National Corpus (BNC) [10] and the scientific discourse?
(2) What semantic role do these word combinations play in this genre?

The organization of the sections is as follows. We start with a broad overview of studies on collocations in scientific texts, with special reference to the semantics of these word associations (Sect. 2, 'Background'). Then, we describe our corpus and the methodology employed in this work (Sect. 3, 'Corpus and Methodology'). In Sect. 4 ('Results and Discussion'), we present the main findings of the study, so the quantitative results are shown and some examples from the corpus are discussed. Finally, Sect. 5 ('Conclusions') summarizes the conclusions drawn from this study, as well as answering our research questions and presenting some thoughts about further studies.

2 Background

Biber and Barbieri [11] recognize that "each register employs a distinct set of lexical bundles, associated with the typical communicative purposes of that register." In the last two decades, several studies on phraseological units in scientific texts have been conducted. The main conclusion reached is that, in accordance with Biber and Barbieri's statement, these expressions do play a crucial role in this specific genre. For example, Luzón Marco [12] analyzes the intermediate words, or collocates, included in a set of collocational frameworks in a corpus of medical research papers. She discovers that the choice of specific collocates within a framework is determined by the linguistic conventions of the genre and they help to structure the lexicon in the text. For example, she shows that collocates attracted by the framework *the ... of* express measure and quantification, such as *amount, degree, frequency* and *number*. Another example is the framework *be ... to* whose slot is filled with adjectives or past participles expressing probability, e.g. *likely, possible,* and cause/result, e.g. *due, related.*

Verdaguer and González [13] are more concerned with lexicography and run a project which is aimed at the creation of reference tools to facilitate the written production of scientific texts by non-native speakers of English. They concentrate on the verb *raise* and explain that this polysemous verb has a distinct semantic and combinatorial behaviour in scientific texts. To put it differently, this word shows specific collocational patterns and a more restricted set of senses which they think should be included in specialized dictionaries. In their analysis, they discover that this verb has four concrete meanings and one figurative meaning in this context. Thus, the most frequent meaning is 'to produce, cause to grow,' which appears with the collocates *antibody* and *antiserum*. On the other hand, its figurative meaning derives from its literal sense and, in this case, it collocates with plural nouns, e.g. *studies, results, findings, data.*

Other authors dealing with research articles (RAs) are Stuart and Botella [14], who aim at analyzing both lexical and grammatical collocations. Their corpus consists of more than 1,300 articles written by lecturers of the Universidad Politécnica of Valencia, Spain. Their starting point is the assumption that collocations are a system of preferred expressions of knowledge in scientific research. They create semantic networks by associating semi-technical terms with a high degree of frequency in the corpus with other technical terms to show how knowledge is organized and how it is produced by their academic discourse community. According to their semantic networks, their corpus deals with: results obtained in their experiments (e.g. *in agreement with the results*), models used for their experiments (e.g. *enterprise planning function descriptive model*), methods (e.g. *lax wendroff method*) and temperatures (e.g. *glass transition temperature*).

In contrast, Gledhill [15] focuses on the so-called 'colligations' of tenses in English in scientific articles, that is, the correlation between tenses and the lexico-grammatical patterns in which they occur. Additionally, he explores the correspondence between these two and the various sections of the genre and finds out that colligations are not serendipitous co-occurrences, but indicators of patterns of thought which are well-established in scientific discourse. For example, the present tense is used for qualitative and empirical expressions, e.g. *Another important matter is to prevent, standard practice is to use*, and the past tense is used for quantitative and research-oriented descriptions, e.g. *This analysis was performed*. Also, the past tense in the passive voice abounds in the 'Methods' sections of the RA to describe activities or observations. The author concludes that these constructions are highly delimited in this type of texts.

Menon and Mukundan [16] are more concerned with pedagogical aspects. They explore collocational and colligational patterns of selected semi-technical words found in a corpus of 12 science textbooks used by upper secondary students in Malaysia. They observe that the same word can be either the main element or the dependent element in the collocation, e.g. *reaction* in *nuclear reaction* or *reaction time*, respectively. In addition, they point out that some items do not carry a literal meaning when used in their collocations but an extended meaning more specific to the scientific field, e.g. *companion cell* where *companion* does not completely retain its original meaning of 'partner.' Likewise, they realize that some non-technical words are used as technical words when co-occurring in the text, e.g. *critical, fresh, dry*. Finally, they state that two-word combinations acquire specific meanings in the scientific discourse, e.g., *mass number* refers to the number of nucleons in an atomic nucleus of a particular nuclide.

The last author we will cover in this section is Pérez-Llantada [17]. She investigates the use of four-word lexical bundles in a corpus of more than 1,000 RAs according to three language variables: (1) English RAs written by English native speakers; (2) English RAs written by Spanish scholars; (3) Spanish RAs written by Spanish native speakers. These multi-word combinations are usually fully compositional, i.e., their meaning is retrievable from the meaning of their parts, and are used to express referential meaning, e.g. time (*at the end of*), place (*in the present study*), amount (*a large number of*), as well as to organize the text (e.g. *on the other hand*). In her opinion, formulaicity is a hallmark of academic written register across language variables and writers' choice of formulaic sequences is determined by the genre of the text.

3 Corpus and Methodology

Since this paper contributes to the study of collocational constructions in scientific genre, specifically in RAs, we created a corpus of more than 3,000,000 words (1,000 texts, each containing an average of 3,000 words) using the Sketch Engine tool [18]. The main criterion for choosing these journal articles was that they were written by leading members of the academic discourse community of the University of Córdoba, Spain, and published between 1996 and 2018 in more than a dozen research journals, such as *The American Journal of Clinical Nutrition, The Journal of Clinical Endocrinology & Metabolism* and *Oxford Journals*. The research papers belong to the fields of Medicine (40%), Veterinary (30%) and Biology (30%). Unlike previous works, we do not analyze collocations extracted from the specific corpus, but we match the most recurrent collocations in the BNC against our corpus and explore their semantics. For this reason, the procedure we adopted was the following one.

Firstly, we extracted 441 candidates for adjective + noun open domain collocations from all text types in the BNC. Dispersion measures (ranging 80% or over) were selected because we think highly dispersed two-word combinations can provide good candidates for these collocations, thus guaranteeing that they do not belong to a specific genre [Pęzik, personal communication]. Secondly, a thorough additional check was made to ensure that the syntactic category of these combinations was the one we were interested in. As a result, we discarded 15 combinations which belonged to longer lexical bundles, e.g. *only one* [+noun], [*on the*] *other hand*, [*in*] *other words*. Thirdly, we searched for the resulting set of collocations in our specialized corpus using Sketch Engine. This step allowed us to know which collocational strings from the BNC were the most recurrent ones in our RA corpus in terms of frequency per million; for so doing, no threshold was set. The span used was one word to the left of the headword, that is, there were no intervening words between the adjective and the noun. However, all the collocations did not occur in the corpus, so we discarded 14 combinations, e.g. *private life*, *black hair*, *front room*. Finally, they were classified into semantic frames according to the meaning of the headword to discover whether they revealed different senses in this discourse.

For the semantic analysis of the headwords, we followed the approach to the study of meaning developed by Charles J. Fillmore [19–21], known as Frame Semantics. In accordance with this theory, words do not relate to each other but to frames that provide speakers with the conceptual base to determine words' meanings. The author argues that the meanings of most words can best be understood on the basis of a semantic frame which entails the description of a type of event, relation or entity, and the participants in it, and he defines a frame as follows: "any system of concepts related in such a way that to understand any one of them you have to understand the whole structure in which it fits; when one of the things in such a structure is introduced into a text, or into a conversation, all of the others are automatically made available" [21].

From Frame Semantics we borrow the following terms. We will refer to the collocation headwords as 'lexical units' which are words that evoke a frame and all its components. Also, the categories, fields or domains evoked by the headwords will be called 'frames.' Furthermore, the 'frame elements' are inherent components in the frame, some of them are necessary ('core') and others are not ('non-core'). For example, the frame COMMUNICATION encompasses the following frame elements: a communicator, a message, an addressee, a topic and a medium. These elements are derived from the inherent properties of communication, that is, every act of communication involves an entity (communicator) conveying some information (message) about something (topic) to another entity (addressee) in a particular way (medium). In order to check our intuition with regards to the frames evoked by the selected nouns, we contrasted them with the information provided by the FrameNet project [22], a lexical database of English based on the theory of Frame Semantics. For deciding the frames evoked, the lexical units were considered in context.

4 Results and Discussion

In total, 412 different types of collocations, i.e. distinct collocations, were searched for in our corpus. We found 10,848 tokens, i.e. the total number of collocations including repetitions. It must be remembered that these numbers refer to collocations whose constituent elements co-occurred in immediate context. All the types of collocations were classified into frames according to the headword and grouped under 55 categories depending on the number of tokens per million (henceforth tokens p/m) in our specialized corpus. As a result, we got 4 groups: (1) more than or equal to 5.00 tokens p/m (5 semantic frames); (2) between 4.99 and 3.00 tokens p/m (7 semantic frames); (3) between 2.99 and 1.00 tokens p/m (4 semantic frames); (4) equal to or less than 0.99 tokens p/m (39 semantic frames). Table 1 summarizes these results.

As can be seen in Table 1, the most recurrent semantic frames according to the number of tokens p/m in our corpus are QUANTITY (21.88 tokens p/m), TIMESPAN (9.1 tokens p/m), PEOPLE (8.2 tokens p/m), EVALUATION (6.35 tokens p/m) and PLACE (5 tokens p/m). Additionally, it is important to realize that the number of types does not correlate with the number of tokens in some cases. For example, TIMESPAN is represented by 20 types of collocations whereas PEOPLE is represented by 47 types. However, TIMESPAN displays more tokens p/m than PEOPLE (9.1 vs. 8.2), which means that the types we find in the former are more frequently repeated than the types we find in the latter, making TIMESPAN a more recurring semantic frame. Also, we identify more different types of collocations in INSTITUTION (ranked eighth in our list) than in TIMESPAN (ranked second) (26 vs. 20), but the first semantic frame is represented by less than half the number of tokens which represent TIMESPAN (418 vs. 1,024), thus INSTITUTION is less characteristic of our genre than TIMESPAN.

4.1 Semantic Frames Represented by ≥ 5 Tokens p/m

As we have previously mentioned, five different semantic frames belong to this group: QUANTITY (21.88 tokens p/m), TIMESPAN (9.1 tokens p/m), PEOPLE (8.2 tokens p/m), EVALUATION (6.35 tokens p/m) and PLACE (5 tokens p/m). In the present subsection, we will explore the lexical units which evoke these frames and some examples from the corpus.

In the first place, QUANTITY is illustrated by 47 types of collocations, 2,457 tokens and 21.88 tokens p/m. According to this frame, nouns (headwords) denote quantities of a specified entity (a mass or individuals) and adjectives (collocates) are used as descriptors of these quantities. The most common lexical units that evoke this frame are *number, amount, part* and *level*, and some of their collocates are *large, low/lower, high/higher/highest, great/greater* and *small*. Some examples in context are:

(1) "Analysis of plasma FFAs revealed that homozygotes for the C allele showed *lower levels* of FFAs following the CHO and the Mediterranean diets, as compared with the saturated diet" (MED19).
(2) "Further, *higher amounts* of glycogen and TGs have been also found in muscles of rats after EOD conditions" (MED368).

Table 1. Semantic frames evoked according to the number of types, number of tokens and number of tokens p/m in our corpus

Semantic frame	# types	# tokens	# tokens p/m
QUANTITY	47	2,457	21.88
TIMESPAN	20	1,024	9.1
PEOPLE	47	909	8.2
EVALUATION	32	709	6.35
PLACE	32	566	5
SERVICE	15	517	4.53
TYPE	8	450	3.96
INSTITUTION	26	418	3.65
CALENDRIC_UNIT	18	399	3.55
MANNER	11	372	3.25
MEDICINE	7	357	3.17
SCOPE	6	343	3.04
DIRECTION	10	237	2.15
INFORMATION	11	220	1.9
CHANGE	9	156	1.38
CAUSATION	7	137	1.22
FUNCTION	3	112	0.99
LIFE	8	111	0.99
MATERIAL	5	108	0.96
DISTANCE	4	92	0.86
THING	10	98	0.84
INTEREST	5	82	0.74
AGE	3	82	0.72
NORM	5	78	0.69
PRICE	5	74	0.67
APPEARANCE	3	69	0.61
AWARENESS	3	68	0.56
NATURE	6	61	0.55
OPPORTUNITY	3	61	0.54
BODY	3	55	0.44
WORK	5	42	0.37
MONEY	4	37	0.33
INSTANCE	1	33	0.29
RELATION	2	32	0.29
ATTENTION	1	26	0.23
DIFFICULTY	2	25	0.23
EVIDENCE	1	24	0.21
SPEED	1	23	0.2
PROCESS	1	21	0.19

(*continued*)

Table 1. (*continued*)

Semantic frame	# types	# tokens	# tokens p/m
SOURCE	1	20	0.18
LUCK	3	14	0.13
CHARACTER	2	14	0.12
ENERGY	1	13	0.12
DURATION	2	12	0.11
STATE	1	12	0.11
EXPERIENCE	2	11	0.1
QUITTING	1	11	0.1
DIFFERENCE	1	10	0.09
GOAL	1	10	0.09
OPINION	1	10	0.09
ACCESS	1	7	0.06
COMMUNICATION	2	7	0.06
LEADERSHIP	1	7	0.06
PERCEPTION	1	3	0.03
MATTER	1	2	0.02

(3) "Studies in humans have shown different results, probably due to the *small number* of subjects involved in those studies" (BIO750).

Generally, the entity which is quantified is expressed, e.g. (1) "*lower levels* of FFAs," (2) "*higher amounts* of glycogen and TGs," (3) "*small number* of subjects." In addition, we can find the entities which these quantities refer to, e.g. (1) "homozygotes for the C allele showed *lower levels* of FFAs," (2) "*higher amounts* of glycogen and TGs have been also found in muscles of rats," (3) *small number* of subjects involved in those studies."

In the second place, TIMESPAN is illustrated by 20 types of collocations, 1,024 tokens and 9.1 tokens p/m. According to this frame, nouns (headwords) denote time references (in general or of a specific process) and adjectives (collocates) are descriptors and express a quality, the length or the specific moment of these references. The most common lexical units that evoke this frame are *term*, *time*, *period* and *stage*, and some of their collocates are *long/longer*, *short*, *entire* and *later*. Some examples in context are:

(4) "…our data further support the notion that *later stages* of normal follicular development in the human ovary are predominantly dependent on FSH…" (MED299).
(5) "No differences were found between witness and extenuated animals probably by the *short time* passed between extenuation and sacrifice" (VET526).
(6) "Triglyceride levels in large TRL particles remained significantly elevated over the baseline in X- subjects during the *entire period*" (MED220).

In some cases, the whole, understood as the larger moment in time of which the target is part, is included in the sentence, e.g. (4) *"later stages* of normal follicular development." In other cases, the collocation is introduced by a preposition, e.g. (6) "during the *entire period."*

In the third place, PEOPLE is illustrated by 47 types of collocations, 909 tokens and 8.2 tokens p/m. According to this frame, nouns (headwords) denote people and adjectives (collocates) present a quality that these people have. The most common lexical units that evoke this frame are *people/person, man, boy* and *friend,* and some of their collocates are *young/younger, old/older* and *close/closer/closest.* Some examples in context are:

(7) "Recently, the Brazilian Consumer Expenditure Survey (2002–2003) estimated that 16.7% of *young people* (10–19 yr) were affected by overweight" (MED135).
(8) "The APOC3 polymorphism at -640 has previously been studied in the Ashkenazi people, in whom homozygosity for the minor allele was over-represented in a cohort of *older persons"* (MED316).
(9) "Men who reported that talking with their *closest friend* or relative made things worse had 29% and 40% higher rates of short and long spells of absence, respectively, compared with those who reported positive support from this person" (BIO802).

Several frame elements are included in these examples. For instance, the age of the person, described as the length of time the person has been alive, is included in (7) *"young people* (10–19 yr)." Also, a characteristic related to this person that persists over time is expressed, e.g. (7) *"young people* (10–19 yr) were affected by overweight." Similarly, the ethnicity (religious, racial, national, socio-economic or cultural group) to which the person belongs can appear in the sentence, e.g. (8) "in the Ashkenazi people [...] was over-represented in a cohort of *older persons."*

In the fourth place, EVALUATION is illustrated by 32 types of collocations, 709 tokens and 6.35 tokens p/m. According to this frame, nouns (headwords) and adjectives (collocates) express a judgement about the amount, number or value of something. The most common lexical units that evoke this frame are *problem, factor* and *point,* and some of their collocates are *good, important, high/higher, main* and *major.* Some examples in context are:

(10) "...thereby suggesting that modulation of Rab18 production may represent an *important point* of control within the process of hormone secretion" (VET681).
(11) "Mononuclear cells play a major role in host defense and are one of the *main factors* responsible for the first step in the control of infection" (VET471).
(12) "Indeed, understanding how structures develop is one of the *major problem* areas in biology" (BIO740).

This frame can include the item which the evaluation is about and is realized as the subject, e.g. (10) "modulation of Rab18 production may represent an *important point,"* (11) "Mononuclear cells play a major role [...] and are one of the *main factors,"* (12) "understanding how structures develop is one of the *major problem* areas." Additionally, the location where the evaluation takes place can also appear in the sentence, e.g. (10) *"important point* of control within the process of hormone secretion," (11) "*main factors* responsible [...] in the control of infection," (12) "*major problem* areas in biology."

Finally, PLACE is illustrated by 32 types of collocations, 566 tokens and 5 tokens p/m. According to this frame, nouns (headwords) denote a place and adjectives (collocates) express a feature of this place. In some cases, this place may be accompanied by a preposition, e.g. *in*. The most common lexical units that evoke this frame are *area, country, door* and *world*, and some of their collocates are *far, main, Western* and *whole*. Some examples in context are:

(13) "The *main areas*, all closely related, in which biotechnology is being applied to plants are..." (BIO913).

(14) "A *major reason* for surrogacy arrangements in *Western countries* today has been to allow men in heterosexual couples to continue their 'bloodline' when their partners, the women, have fertility problems" (MED189).

(15) "The *whole world* is criss-crossed with causal arrows joining genes to phenotypic effects, far and near" (VET507).

4.2   Semantic Frames Represented by <5 Tokens p/m

In the previous subsection, we focused on semantic frames represented by more than or equal to 5 tokens of collocations per million. However, we think that some semantic frames represented by less than that are also relevant in the scientific genre. For this reason, we will describe them in the following lines.

Firstly, CALENDRIC_UNIT (ranked ninth, illustrated by 18 types of collocations, 399 tokens and 3.55 tokens p/m) displays different parts of the calendric cycle through collocations like *recent year* or *early morning*. The unit (headword) is normally accompanied by a relative time (collocate), and the combination is usually introduced by a preposition. Some examples in context are:

(16) "In *recent years*, it has been demonstrated that dietary fat may affect the endothelium and factors related to the arterial wall, such as type 1 plasminogen activator inhibitor and von Willebrand factor" (MED244).

(17) "All meals were administered in the *early morning*, usually between 0630 and 0900" (MED70).

Secondly, MANNER (ranked tenth, illustrated by 11 types of collocations, 372 tokens and 3.25 tokens p/m) is a frame which describes general or specific characteristics of an event in a given way. The headword of the collocation evokes this frame and the collocate tells how this manner is. For instance, *best way* describes the most appropriate manner of doing something. Likewise, an event may develop in *different forms*:

(18) "Concentrating on fat reduction in food is one of the *best ways* of ensuring a good weight loss" (MED117).

(19) "Since then the calculations have been repeated in a number of *different forms* by other people" (BIO835).

The last frame we will cover is CHANGE (ranked fifteenth, illustrated by 9 types of collocations, 156 tokens and 1.38 tokens p/m), evoked by collocations like *significant change, great increase* and *high decrease*. The headword in these combinations is the lexical unit which implies a change and the collocate gives some information about that. The change is caused or undergone by an entity, or it might happen on a scale:

(20) "As seen for MAP, <u>bicarbonate HD did not induce a</u> *significant change* <u>in CI</u> in control dogs, while in uremic dogs it caused only a moderate decrease in CI that did not reach statistical significance" (VET423).

(21) "Furthermore, we report an allele-specific response to fenofibrate intervention for the combined genotype, which suggests that subjects within the risk genotype group had a *higher decrease* <u>in plasma triacylglycerol concentrations</u> after treatment" (MED95).

5 Conclusions

This article has explored the presence and role of open domain adjective + noun collocations in the RA. These collocations were extracted from all text types from the BNC using dispersion measures and they were matched against a specific corpus of more than three million words. The first research question focused on the relationship between these word combinations and the scientific discourse. As Sinclair contends [3], "By far the majority of [specialized] text is made of the occurrence of common words in common patterns, or in slight variants of those common patterns." Table 1 above shows the results after grouping these collocations according to the semantic frame evoked by the headwords (nouns).

The second research question asked about the role they play in this sort of texts. After the frame-semantic analysis (see Fig. 1 below), it was proven that these word combinations need to be interpreted beyond their standard meaning since they express meanings integrally related to this genre. In other words, these phraseological units belong to the "syndromes, patterns of co-occurrence among features at one or another linguistic level [that] make it plausible to talk of 'the language of science'" [23]. The most compelling evidence is that the semantics of our selected collocation inventory from the BNC evokes the basic aspects of the scientific processes reported in RAs.

Overall, we can say that these semantic frames are also the semantic frames that constitute a RA. This is because the RESEARCH_ARTICLE frame concerns scientists performing experiments in a given period of time (TIMESPAN) where quantitative methods (QUANTITY) are used. Different subjects (PEOPLE) can participate in these experiments which are conducted in different places (PLACE). Finally, these experiments' results are assessed to know whether they were or not successful (EVALUATION). Additionally, information on the calendar may be included (CALENDRIC_UNIT), as well as some facts of the way in which the experiments were performed (MANNER) and the changes that occurred during the process (CHANGE).

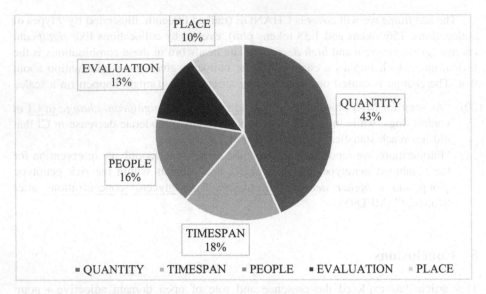

Fig. 1. Semantic frames represented by ≥ 5 tokens p/m

This study focused on adjective + noun collocations without intervening words in between. Future research may examine phraseology in wider spans, which might provide more tokens. In addition, the range of collocations may be expanded and other lexical types considered, such as verb + noun or verb + adverb collocations. Finally, the different sections in a RA may be explored separately to show the most characteristic collocational frameworks and their semantics in each of them.

References

1. Firth, J.R.: Papers in Linguistics, 1934-1951. Oxford University Press, London (1957)
2. Halliday, M.A.K.: Categories of the theory of grammar. Word **17**, 241–292 (1961)
3. Sinclair, J.: Corpus, Concordance, Collocation. Oxford University Press, Oxford (1991)
4. Vinogradov, V.V.: Izbrannye Trudy. Leksikologija i leksikografija. Nauka, Moscow (1947)
5. Cowie, A.P.: Phraseology: Theory, Analysis, and Applications. Clarendon Press, Oxford (1998)
6. Howarth, P.A.: Phraseology in English Academic Writing. Some Implications for Language Learning and Dictionary Making. Niemeyer, Tübingen (1996)
7. Evert, S.: Corpora and collocations. In: Lüdeling, A., Kytö, M. (eds.) Corpus Linguistics: An International Handbook, pp. 1212–1248. Walter de Gruyter, Berlin/New York (2008)
8. Pęzik, P.: Facets of Prefabrication. Perspectives on Modelling and Detecting Phraseological Units. Łódź University Press, Łódź (2018)
9. Tognini-Bonelli, E.: Corpus Linguistics at Work. John Benjamins Publishing Company, Amsterdam/Philadelphia (2001)
10. The British National Corpus, version 3 (BNC XML Edition). Distributed by Bodleian Libraries, University of Oxford, on behalf of the BNC Consortium (2007). http://www.natcorp.ox.ac.uk/. Accessed 15 Apr 2019

11. Biber, D., Barbieri, F.: Lexical bundles in university spoken and written registers. Engl. Specif. Purp. **26**(3), 263–286 (2007)
12. Luzón Marco, M.J.: Collocational frameworks in medical research papers: a genre-based study. Engl. Specif. Purp. **19**, 63–86 (2000)
13. Verdaguer, I., González, E.: A lexical database of collocations in scientific English: preliminary considerations. In: Williams, G., Vessier, S. (eds.) Proceedings of the Eleventh EURALEX International Congress, EURALEX 2004, pp. 929–934. Université de Bretagne-Sud, Lorient (2004)
14. Stuart, K., Botella, A.: Collocation and knowledge production in an academic discourse community. In: Neuman, C.-P., Plo Alastrué, R., Pérez-Llantada, C. (eds.) Proceedings of the 5th International AELFE Conference, pp. 238–245. Universidad de Zaragoza, Prensas Universitarias de Zaragoza, Zaragoza (2006)
15. Gledhill, C.: Colligation and the cohesive function of present and past tense in the scientific research article. In: Banks, D. (ed.) Les Temps et les Textes de Spécialité, pp. 65–84. L'Harmattan, Paris (2009)
16. Menon, S., Mukundan, J.: Analysing collocational patterns of semi-technical words in science textbooks. Pertanika J. Soc. Sci. Humanit. (JSSH) **18**(2), 241–258 (2010)
17. Pérez-Llantada, C.: Formulaic language in L1 and L2 expert academic writing: convergent and divergent usage. J. Engl. Acad. Purp. **14**, 84–94 (2014)
18. Sketch Engine. https://www.sketchengine.co.uk. Accessed 15 Apr 2019
19. Fillmore, C.J.: Frame semantics. In: Linguistic Society of Korea (ed.) Linguistics in the Morning Calm, pp. 111–137. Hanshin Publishing Company, Seoul (1982)
20. Fillmore, C.J.: Frames and the semantics of understanding. Quaderni di Semantica **6**(2), 222–254 (1985)
21. Fillmore, C.J.: Frame semantics. In: Geeraerts, D., Dirven, R., Taylor, J.R. (eds.) Cognitive Linguistics: Basic Readings, pp. 373–400. Mouton de Gruyter, Berlin/New York (2006)
22. FrameNet Project. https://framenet.icsi.berkeley.edu/fndrupal/. Accessed 15 Apr 2019
23. Halliday, M.A.K.: The Language of Science. Continuum, London (2004)

Effects of Statistical Learning Ability on the Second Language Processing of Multiword Sequences

Elma Kerz[1]([✉]) and Daniel Wiechmann[2]([✉])

[1] Department of English Linguistics, RWTH Aachen University, Aachen, Germany
elma.kerz@ifaar.rwth-aachen.de
[2] Institute for Logic, Language and Computation, University of Amsterdam,
Amsterdam, The Netherlands
d.wiechmann@uva.nl

Abstract. A substantial body of research has demonstrated that both native and non-native speakers are sensitive to the statistics of multiword sequences (MWS). However, this research has predominantly focused on demonstrating that a given sample of participants shows evidence of learning the statistical properties of MWS. Recent theoretical approaches to language learning and processing emphasize the importance of moving away from group-level analyses towards analyses that account for individual differences (IDs). Here, through a within subject design embedded within an IDs framework, we investigate whether and to what extent individual variability in the online processing of MWS are associated with the statistical learning (SL) ability of an individual. Second language learners were administered a battery of SL tasks in the visual and auditory modalities, using verbal and non-verbal stimuli, with adjacent and non-adjacent contingencies along with two online processing tasks of MWS designed to assess sensitivity to the statistics of spoken and written language. We found a number of significant associations between the SL ability and the two processing tasks: Individuals who performed better on an auditory verbal adjacent SL task demonstrated greater sensitivity to the statistics of MWS in the spoken language, whereas individuals with better performance on a visual, non-verbal sequence learning task demonstrated greater sensitivity to the statistics of MWS in the written language. We discuss the implications of these findings for the study of IDs in the processing of MWS.

Keywords: Individual differences · Multiword sequences ·
Statistical learning · Second language processing

G. Corpas Pastor and R. Mitkov (Eds.): Europhras 2019, LNAI 11755, pp. 200–214, 2019.
https://doi.org/10.1007/978-3-030-30135-4_15

1   Introduction

1.1   Emergentist Approaches and Statistical Learning of Multiword Sequences

Moving away from the traditional 'words-and-rules' approach, emergentist[1] approaches to language acquisition and processing have highlighted that compositional multiword sequences (MWS) are important building blocks of language use and development. MWS (also referred to as 'formulaic sequences') is a cover term often used to refer to various types of recurrent continuous or discontinuous sequences of words (see [4,57] for overviews). A substantial body of research has indicated that native language users (both children and adults) are sensitive to the statistics of MWS in their native language and rely on knowledge of such statistics to facilitate language processing and boost their acquisition (e.g., [2,8,32,55], for overviews, see [4,45]. A growing number of studies also suggest that such facilitatory effects extend to second language learners across different levels of proficiency (e.g., [22,24,38,49,52,56]). Very recently, it was found that language users are also capable of developing sensitivity to distributional statistics of MWS inherent in different (register-specific) spoken and written input types [25]. Many of these studies follow the threshold-approach that aims to determine whether and to what extent MWS are processed faster over less frequent counterparts. The stimulus material is typically derived from language corpora based on predefined frequency criteria. The carefully constructed stimulus material is often made up of pairs of MWS that differ only in one word and in overall frequency (high vs. low) but are matched for substring frequency, (e.g. high: *don't have to worry* vs. low: *don't have to wait*) (see, e.g., [2,22,24,25,55]). Participants' sensitivity to the statistics of MWS is determined by comparing response latencies and/or accuracy rates of higher a lower frequency items across a range of experimental designs and assessment methods. Emergentist approaches put forward an adequate mechanistic explanation for the observed MWS frequency effects. This broad class of approaches to language eschews the existence of innately specified knowledge (see 'universal grammar') and instead argue that language is learnable through general cognitive mechanisms. These approaches put the emphasis on usage and/or experience with language and assume a direct and immediate relationship between processing and learning, conceiving of them as inseparable rather than governed by different mechanisms ('two sides of the same coin'). In these approaches, language acquisition is viewed as learning how to process efficiently (see, 'learning-as-processing' assumption, [3]; see also 'language acquisition as skill learning', [5]).

Languages are abundant in statistical regularities. These statistical regularities are increasingly recognized as a key desiderata for explanatory theories

---

[1] Following the literature, we use the term 'emergentist' to refer to a family of models and approaches – including usage-based (a.k.a. experience-based) models, constraint-based approaches, exemplar-based models and connectionist models – that is becoming a mainstay of cognitive and psycholinguistic thinking as well as for theories of second language learning (see, [15,28], for a recent overview).

of language use, language learning and processing across theoretical orienta-
tions (see, [20], for a recent review of 'efficiency-based' accounts; see [7], for
an overview of the 'chunk-and-pass' account). Learning a language thus heavily
involves figuring out the statistics inherent in language input. This is supported
by a large body of evidence from the literature on statistical learning. Statistical
learning - defined as the mechanism by which language users discover the patterns inherent in the language input based on its distributional properties – has
been shown to facilitate the acquisition of various aspects of language knowledge,
including phonological learning (e.g., [33,53]), word segmentation (e.g. [39,41]),
learning the graphotactic and morphological regularities of written words (e.g.
[40]) and learning to form syntactic and semantic categories and structures (e.g.
[29,42,54]). Furthermore, an impressive body of evidence has been accumulating
over the last years indicating a close relationship between individual difference
(IDs) in statistical learning (SL) ability and variation in native language learning in both child and adult L1 populations (e.g., [9,27,35,47], and in adult L2
populations [17,19]). Thus, from an emergentist perspective, language acquisition is essentially an 'intuitive statistical learning problem' ([14], p. 376). Three
mechanisms that have been proposed to underpin frequency effects specifically in
learning word sequences are described as follows ([12]): [1] increased frequency
causes the strengthening of linguistic representations, [2] increased frequency
causes the strengthening of expectations and [3] increased frequency leads to
the automatization of chunks. The frequency with which building blocks of language occur is thus a driving force behind chunking and, all else being equal,
each exposure to a given sequence of words (sounds or graphemes) will affect its
subsequent processing.

But why is there a need for chunking? To ameliorate the effects of the 'real-
time' constraints on language processing imposed by the limitations of human
sensory system and human memory in combination with the continual deluge of
language input (cf., [6,7] for the 'Now-or-Never bottleneck'), through constant
exposure to (both auditory and visual) language input, humans learn to rapidly
and efficiently recode incoming information into larger sequences. The fact that
language is abundant in statistical regularities at multiple levels of language representations and that humans are able to detect such regularities via statistical
learning allows for such chunking to take place. The by-products of statistical
learning and chunking enable anticipatory language processing humans rely on
to integrate the greatest possible amount of available information as fast as possible. Processing a MWS as a chunk will minimize memory load and speed up
integration of the MWS with prior context (see, a chunk-based computational
model presented in a recent study by [34]).

1.2 Statistical Learning as a Predictor of Language Processing

Individual differences (henceforth IDs) are ubiquitous across the lifespan and
across the entire linguistic system both in first and second language (L2) acquisition. While IDs in native language attainment have effectively been ignored and

relegated to error variance (see, [28]), IDs in L2 learning have long been recognized spawned by Carroll's work dating back to 1959 (see, [11,13], for overviews). However, the impact of this line of research on L2 acquisition research at large, and on the development of second language acquisition theory, in particular, has been minimal due to its preoccupation with the search for universal characteristics, processes and developmental stages. This preoccupation may have inhibited the growth of IDs research [50].

With the increasing popularity of emergentist approaches, recent years have witnessed a renewed interest in accounting for the individual variability in language outcomes. It has been even argued that an adequate theoretical approaches to language acquisition and processing should be first and foremost constrained by empirical demonstrations of IDs and account for such differences in terms of variation in quantity and quality of linguistic input as well as cognitive factors ([28]). As mentioned above, a great deal of research has revealed a tight coupling between IDs in statistical learning (SL) ability and variability in native language and processing in both child and adult populations. This research is characterized by the use of within-subject experimental designs embedded in an individual differences framework. In such designs, participants perform an SL task, most often employing artificial grammar learning (AGL) and/or the sequence learning paradigms. In the AGL paradigm, participants first attend to a stream of auditory or visual items generated by a finite-state grammar that encodes some statistical regularity in terms of transitional probabilities (TP) among the items (familiarization phase). In a subsequent testing phase, participants are asked to classify new strings as grammatical or not, and their performance is often measured in terms of accuracy in two-alternative forced-choice decisions in distinguishing grammatical sequences from foils. In the sequence learning paradigm, participants are asked to react to each element of sequentially structured sequences of events in the context of a choice reaction task. Unknown to them, the sequence of successive stimuli is comprised of alternating blocks of item sequences that are governed by a set of (probabilistic) rules and blocks that are not. Learning has occurred when participants produce faster reaction times to possible (or probable) trials stimuli than to impossible (or improbable) stimuli. Depending on the aim of the study (e.g. explaining individual variability in sentence processing, vocabulary development, reading skills), participants' capacity in the respective linguistic domain is independently assessed through well-established language tasks. The participants' scores in SL tasks are used as predictors of their performance on a language task. Within this research program, SL tasks have been shown to be related to literacy skills (e.g. [1,43,51]), speech perception ([9]), vocabulary development ([44,48]), sentence processing ([26,27,35,36]). Compared to the available SL research in native language users – children and adults, attempts to investigate the role of statistical learning ability in adult second language learning and processing have been scarce (however, for exceptions, see, e.g. [17,19]).

1.3 The Present Study

An extensive body of research, as reviewed above, has shown that language users are sensitive to the statistics of multiword sequences (MWS) at the group level. To our knowledge, no attempt has been made to determine and account for the individual variability in the online processing of MWS (see, [24] for an exception). To fill this gap, this study examines whether and to what extent second language (L2) processing of MWS is affected by statistical learning (SL) ability, an individual differences (IDs) factor that has recently gained prominence in cognitive science research a predictor of language learning and processing. A group of L2 learners was tested in a within-subject design embedded in an IDs framework that included a series of SL tasks that monitored their ability to track statistical regularities, along with two MWS processing tasks from a written (academic) register and a spoken register.[2] We selected four tasks that have been consistently used in studies of SL. Three of these tasks come from the artificial grammar learning (AGL) paradigm – (1) Auditory-Verbal-Adjacent, (2) Auditory-Verbal-Nonadjacent, (3) Visual-Nonverbal-Adjacent – and (4) a probabilistic Serial Reaction Time (SRT) task, a task from the sequence learning paradigm. This variety of SL tasks enabled us to investigate the relations between different measures of SL ability and the two processing tasks.

2 Methods

2.1 Participants

Sixty advanced learners of English participated in this study (34 female and 26 male, M = 23.56 years, SD = 4.52). All participants were university students studying either towards an BA or an MA at the RWTH Aachen University at the time of testing. The L2 learners were classified as having a Common European Framework (CEFR) English proficiency level of upper intermediate (CEFR = B2) or lower advanced (CEFR = C1) based on their institutional status (educational background) and their scores on Lexical Test for Advanced Learners of English ([30]): an English vocabulary size test that is often used to estimate the CEF proficiency level. In addition, participants were asked to fill out the Language Experience and Proficiency Questionnaire (LEAP-Q, see, [30], a questionnaire used to obtain general demographic information and more specific information on self-rated proficiency for three language areas (reading, understanding and speaking) and self-rated current knowledge of L2 English and exposure to the L2. The tested L2 group reached an average LexTALE score of 72.78, supporting their classification as intermediate to advanced. Regarding their English acquisition, the L2 speakers started learning English around the age of 9 and reported to have acquired fluency at around 15 years of age. On

---

[2] This study was undertaken as part of a larger project designed to investigate the role of a range of cognitive and affective IDs factors on the L2 processing of MWS across several written and spoken input types (registers).

average, their current experience with English comes mainly from reading (mean score of 7.64 out of 10), watching TV (mean score of 7.64 out of 10), listening to music (mean score of 7.39 out of 10) and social media (mean score of 7.39 out of 10). Self-ratings of their English language proficiency based on a 10-point scale were relatively high (all mean scores greater 7.25).

2.2 Materials

Statistical Learning Ability. In the two auditory AGL tasks participants were presented with a 10 min stream of trisyllabic 'words' from an artificial language (52 repetitions of each 'word'). In the subsequent testing phase, participants were presented with 36 pairs of trisyllabic sequences each consisting of one item from the familiarization stream (a 'word') and one previously unseen variation of a word (a 'part-word') and had to decide which of the two items sounded more familiar to them. All stimuli were synthesized in PRAAT software (Boersma, 2001), at a fundamental frequency of 76 Hz, with a mean syllable duration of 290 ms. Performance on either task was assessed in terms of the total number of correct word identifications in the testing phase (0–36). The stimulus material in the Auditory-Verbal-Adjacent (AVA) AGL task was based on 12 'words' taken from [16], built from 18 CV syllables (e.g. *paseti, pamonu* or *munavo*). Items in the familiarisation stream were designed such that the transitional probabilities (TPs) between every two adjacent syllables within a word was 0.5 whereas the TP across words boundaries was only 0.187 on average. The detection of word boundaries in the familiarization stream was possible only in terms of this TP contrast. The stimulus material of the Auditory-Verbal-Nonadjacent (AVN) AGL also included 12 'words' (e.g. *pavegu, pavoga* or *pivega*). These words were built from three groups of consonantal patterns into which four different vowel combinations were inserted. In the testing phase, participant had to decide between 'legal words', i.e. items that were constructed from the consonantal patterns from which the words in the familiarization stream with novel vowels, and 'non-legal words', i.e. items that contained only one or two consonants from a given consonantal pattern and one or two from another pattern. To ensure that the only cue for extracting the underlying patterns of "words" in the familiarization stream was the non-adjacent TPs, the TPs between adjacent syllables was held constant, both between and within words.[3] The Visual-Nonverbal-Adjacent (VNA) task from [21] included 24 complex visual shapes that were randomly organized for each subject to create eight triplets. These triplets appeared immediately one after one another in a pseudorandomized order to create a 10-min familiarization stream in which each triplet appeared 24 times. Each shape appeared on the screen for 800 ms, with a 200 ms break between shapes. Participants were asked to attend to the stream, and were unaware that the stream was constructed of triplets. During testing, they responded to a total of 32 two-alternative forced

---

[3] The adjacent TPs between adjacent syllables within words were 0.5. To make the adjacent TPs across word boundaries equal to 0.5, each word could be followed by only one of four other words.

choice (2AFC) trials. In each trial participants were shown two groups of shapes: (1) 'true triplet' – three shapes that created a triplet during the familiarization phase (thus, the transitional probabilities between shapes were 1.0), and (2) 'foil' – made of three shapes that never appeared together in the familiarization phase (TPs = 0). Before the test phase, subjects were instructed that they would see in each trial two clusters of shapes and that their task would be to report which cluster, as a whole, is more familiar to them. As in the auditory AGL tasks, performance on this task was the percentage of correct identifications of triplets during the test phase. The probabilistic Serial Reaction Time (SRT) was taken from [23]. In each trial, participants saw an 'X' on the screen in one of four locations, and were asked to press a corresponding key on the keyboard. They were unaware that the order of stimuli was not random but, rather, governed by a probabilistic grammar that generated two possible sequences that occurred with different probabilities: 'probable sequences' that had a probability of 0.8, and 'improbable sequences' that had a probability of 0.15. The location of the X on the screen could be predicted implicitly given the previous two stimuli, based on the frequency of occurrence of the sequence from which it was taken. After a practice block of 16 trials, the task consisted of eight blocks, each containing 120 trials. The dependent variable of this task was the RT difference for the 'proba-ble' vs. 'improbable' trials, measured from block 3 to block 8 (i.e., based on the last 720 trials of the task). Error trials and outliers of three standard deviations above or below the subject's mean (less than 3% of trials) were removed.

Online Processing of Multiword Sequences. Participants' sensitivity to the statistics of MWS was computed from the results of the two of the four MWS decision tasks of [25]. In this task, participants had to judge if a four-word English MWS that appeared on the screen was a possible sequence in English or not. The materials used in the task consisted of pairs of four-word sequences that differed only in the final word and in overall MWS frequency (high vs. low) but were matched for substring frequency, e.g. *to let that happen* vs. *to let that stop*, from the spoken register, or *is beyond the scope* vs. *is beyond the boundaries*, from the academic register. The experimental items were constructed using the Corpus of Contemporary American English (COCA; [10]), a 560 million words corpus with approximately equal sized subcomponents representing the statistics of MWS from the two target registers: (1) spoken (118 million words) and (2) academic journals (112 million words). In a first step, all COCA text files were preprocessed using the sentence splitting (ssplit) and tokenization (PTNTok-enizer) components from the Stanford CoreNLP toolkit V.3.2.9 ([31]).[4] In a second step, the frequencies for all n-grams of orders 1 to 4 were extracted using Java scripts. N-grams with a frequency of one (so-called 'hapax legomena') were discarded. These two steps were performed on the RWTH Aachen University high-performance computing cluster. The experimental set of 60 pairs of MWS was randomly selected for each of the two registers. A total of 120 MWS for a given register was distributed across two lists that each contained one of the

---

[4] https://stanfordnlp.github.io/CoreNLP/.

two variants of a given pair, so that in a given experimental run participants would never see both variants of a pair. In addition to the experimental items, the lists also contained 60 ungrammatical items, which were incorrect due to scrambled word order. The log frequencies of the items ranged between 0.69 and 6.85 (spoken 0.69 − 6.07, academic 0.69 − 5.87). Each trial began with the presentation of a fixation point for 500 ms. MWS appeared at once in the middle of the screen and participants were instructed to indicate using the keyboard – as quickly and accurately as possible – whether the presented sequence of words was a possible English word sequence. The MWS was then presented and stayed visible on the screen until participants responded or until 3000 ms had passed. Error trials and outliers of three standard deviations above or below the subject's mean (less than 2% of trials) were removed. Response times were logged to reduce the skewness in their distributions. Performance on the MWS decision tasks was assessed by calculating the difference in their mean log reaction times to 'higher' and 'lower' frequency items (henceforth Δ log RT scores). To determine the optimal value to dichotomize the continuous MWS frequency variable we conducted a breakpoint regression analysis to find the breakpoint that best fits the data (the one where two models fit on either side of it have the maximum summed likelihood, Baayen, 2008). Break-point estimates were obtained using the algorithm implemented in the segmented function of the segmented library version 3.0 ([37]).

2.3 Procedure

Participants were administered the tasks during two sessions conducted on separate days (within a span of five to seven days apart). The order of tasks was the same for all participants with two statistical learning tasks being administered on each day (day 1: AVA, VNA; day 2: AVN, SRT) separated by intervening tasks assessing individual differences in L2 processing. All experimental tasks were run using PsychoPy v3.0 (Peirce, 2007).[5]

3 Results

Table 1 presents the means and standard deviations in performance in the various statistical learning and language processing tasks. Figure 1 presents the distribution graphs for all tasks. Shapiro-Wilk normality tests revealed no departures from normality for any of the performance variables.

For the three AGL tasks, average performance was not significantly above chance-level classification AVA: $t(59) = 1.02$, $p = 0.16$; AVN: $t(59) = 1.27$, $p = 0.10$; VNA: $t(59) = -0.49$, $p = 0.63$), meaning that the results of these tasks presented no evidence that our participants – as a group – were able to acquire the statistical regularities encoded in the respective input streams of the tasks. These results contrast with the findings in previous studies. For example,

---

[5] https://www.psychopy.org/.

Table 1. Descriptive statistics for the four statistical learning measures, the four proxy measures of L2 experience and the two L2 MWS processing dependent measures

		M (SD)	obs. range
Statistical learning			
AVA	Percent correct (of 36 2AFC items)	51.63 (12.11)	16.67–86.11
AVN	Percent correct (of 36 2AFC items)	51.95 (11.57)	33.33–80.56
VNA	Percent correct (of 32 2AFC items)	49.37 (9.69)	31.25–71.88
SRT	RT difference for probable vs. improbable trials (in sec)	0.04 (0.03)	−0.02–0.1
L2 processing			
MWS acad	Difference in log RT between higher and lower frequency MWS	0.06 (0.07)	−0.1–0.27
MWS spoken	Difference in log RT between higher and lower frequency MWS	0.07 (0.09)	−0.09–0.29

Siegelmann and Frost ([47]) reported successful implicit learning in all three AGL tasks ($M_{AVA} = 0.58$ ($SD = 0.16$); $M_{AVN} = 0.55$ ($SD = 0.13$); ; $M_{VNA} = 0.67$ ($SD = 0.17$)). The group tested in [35] exhibited even higher average performance levels on both AGL tasks (AVA, AVN) used in that study ($M_{AVA} = 0.62$ ($SD = 0.14$); $M_{AVN} = 0.60$ ($SD = 0.24$). However, as is evident in Table 2

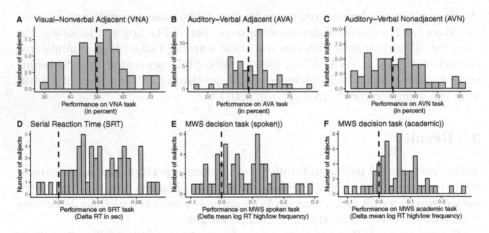

Fig. 1. Distribution of scores obtained in the four SL tasks (A, B, C, D) and the two L2 MWS processing tasks (E, F). In each plot, the dashed lines mark chance-level performance for a given task. For the AGL tasks this corresponds to an accuracy of 50% correct answers in the respective 2AFC task. For the SRT and the two MWS decision tasks this corresponds to an Δ RT of 0, i.e no difference in mean response times to probable and improbable trials in the SRT and no difference in mean logged reactions times to high or low frequency MWS, respectively.

and Fig. 1, consistent with a number of previous studies (e.g. [9,23,35,47]), there was considerable variance in the performance on all four statistical learning tasks with some participants reaching classification accuracy scores well past 70% correct ($max_{AVA} = 86.11\%$; $max_{AVN} = 80.56\%$; $max_{VNA} = 71.88\%$).

Our results further indicated that successful statistical learning has occurred in the probabilistic SRT task: the mean RT difference between probable and improbable trials was 39.7 ms (with a standard deviation of 29.7 ms), which is significantly higher than zero ($t(56) = 11.16$, $p < .001$). This difference is about twice as large as that found in [47] ($M_{SRT} = 18.4\,ms$; $SD = 34$). As in the original study ([23]), the change in reaction times to probable and improbable trials occurred from block 2 onward, in which RT became slightly slower, but the differences between responding to training and control trials became larger.

Turning to the results of the L2 MWS processing tasks, we found that – in the spoken register – participants were on average 90 ms faster to respond to high frequency items ($M_{high} = 1380\,ms$, $SD = 285$; $M_{high} = 1470\,ms$, $SD = 283\,ms$). The size of the MWS frequency effect (ΔRT high frequency – low frequency MWS) was thus slightly higher than those reported in previous studies based on spoken stimuli ([2] (L1 speakers): $\Delta RT = 60\,ms$; [22]: $\Delta RT = 50\,ms$; [24]: $\Delta RT = 80\,ms$ – both L2 speakers)). In the academic register, reaction times were slower on average relative to the spoken register ($M_{high} = 1500\,ms$, $SD = 233\,ms$; $M_{high} = 1590\,ms$, $SD = 241\,ms$) with an MWS frequency effect of 90 ms. Paired-sample t-tests revealed that the group tested in this study demonstrated sensitivity to the frequency of MWS in both registers (spoken: $t(59) = 6.16$, $p < 0.0001$; academic: $t(59) = 6.36$, $p < 0.0001$).

To investigate the interrelationship between statistical learning and the L2 processing of MWS, we first conducted correlational analyses assessing the bivariate relationships among all individual differences tasks and measures outlined above. The results of these analyses are shown in Table 2. Regarding statistical learning, AVA was positively associated with performance on the spoken MWS task ($r = 0.28$, $p = 0.037$) and negatively associated with performance on the academic MWS task ($r = -0.27$, $p = 0.04$). Furthermore, there was a significant positive correlation between performance on the SRT and performance on the academic MWS task ($r = 0.29$, $p = 0.031$). Scores on both the (AVN) and the (VNA) tasks were not correlated with any of the other measure. Consistent with previous studies (e.g. [35,47]), no correlations were found among the SL measures, suggesting that for a given individual, a relatively high capacity in detecting regularities in one domain does not imply high capacity in detecting regularities in another.

In a second step, to determine how well each SL measure predicted L2 processing of MWS, when controlling for the SL other predictors, we performed multiple regression analyses with stepwise variable selection. Separate models were fitted to the data obtained from the experiment on MWS from spoken English and academic English, respectively. In each case, we first fitted a full model in which participants' differences in mean logged reaction times to high and low frequency MWS (Δ log RT scores) were regressed onto the main effects

Table 2. Intercorrelations between task measures

	MWS processing		Statistical learning			
	Acad.	Spoken	AVA	AVN	VNA	SRT
MWS acad.	—					
MWS spok.	−0.14	—				
AVA	−0.27[a]	0.28[a]	—			
AVN	0.04	−0.11	0.06	—		
VNA	−0.12	0.19	0.23[b]	0.18	—	
SRT	0.29[a]	−0.21	−0.02	0.10	0.06	—

[a] $p < 0.05$ (two-tailed, N = 59).
[b] $p < 0.1$ (two-tailed, N = 59).

of all four statistical learning predictors (AVA, AVN, VNA, SRT). All variables were mean centered prior to being entered into the model. To obtain the most parsimonious – minimal adequate – model, a backward stepwise variable selection procedure was used. Covariates that did not improve the fit of the model – as assessed by Akaike's Information Criterion (AIC) – were removed. All models were fitted using the statistical software R (R Core Team, 2017). The results of the respective minimal adequate regression models are presented in Table 2. In both models, all variance inflation factor (VIF) values were less than 1.1, indicating the absence of multicollinearity. The models revealed that the significant associations among the indicators of statistical leaning ability and L2 MWS processing are still present after controlling for the effects of the covariates. Furthermore, the results indicated that performance on different statistical learning task make independent contributions to the L2 processing of MWS: In the case of spoken language, the full model was marginally significant and accounted for 15.4% of the variance in Δ log RT scores ($F(2.36, 52) = 2.15$, $p = 0.07$). The most the parsimonious model contained two of the four SL predictors (AVA, SRT) and was statistically significant ($F(2, 54) = 3.52$, $p = 0.04$). Better performance on the spoken MWS decision task was related to higher scores on the SRT sequence learning task and with lower scores on the AVA AGL task. The two significant predictors jointly accounted for 11.5% of the variance in Δ log RT scores. Performance on the AVA exerted a stronger effect (partial $r^2 = 0.7$) that that on the SRT task (partial $r^2 = 0.4$). For the academic register, the full model was marginally significant and accounted for 16% of the variance in Δ log RT scores ($F(4, 52) = 2.42$, $p = 0.09$). The most parsimonious model ($F(3, 53)$ $= 4.55$, $p = 0.01$) included the same two SL predictors as in the spoken model (AVA, SRT) – but with opposite influences. That is, better performance on the academic MWS decision task was related to higher scores on the SRT sequence learning task but with lower scores on the AVA AGL task. In this model, the two significant predictors jointly accounted for 14% of the variance in Δ log RT scores (SRT: partial $r^2 = 0.08$, AVA: partial $r^2 = 0.07$) (Table 3).

Table 3. Regression coefficients (with 95% confidence intervals) obtained from the minimal adequate multiple regression models fitted to the ΔRT scores of the spoken (left) and academic (right) language data.

	DV: Δ log RT high/low frequency MWS	
	Spoken language	Academic language
Constant	0.000 (−0.022, 0.022)	0.000 (−0.017, 0.017)
AVA	0.002* (0.0001, 0.004)	−0.001* (−0.003, −0.00003)
SRT	−0.604* (−1.369, 0.162)	0.659* (0.059, 1.260)
R^2	0.115	0.144
Adjusted R^2	0.083	0.113

Note: $^{*}p < 0.5$; $^{**}p < 0.01$; $^{***}p < 0.001$
Numbers in parentheses indicate 95% confidence intervals

4   Discussion and Conclusion

The goal of the present study was to determine whether and to what extent L2 speakers sensitivity to the statistics of multiword sequences (MWS) is mediated by their statistical learning (SL) ability. Using a within subject design embedded in a individual differences (IDs) framework, a group of 60 intermediate to advanced L2 learners of English were administered four separate widely used tasks in the field of SL research – tasks that involved the visual and auditory modalities, verbal and nonverbal stimuli with adjacent and non-adjacent dependencies from the artificial grammar learning and sequence learning paradigms. The participants' SL scores were then used as predictors of their performance on two online processing tasks designed to assess sensitivity to the statistics of MWS inherent in a written (academic) register and a spoken one.

Multiple regression modeling revealed differential effects of performance on the auditory verbal adjacent (AVA) artificial grammar learning task and the visual probabilistic serial reaction time (SRT) task on the two MWS processing tasks: While scores on the spoken MWS task were positively related to score on the AVA and negatively related to scores on the SRT, scores on the written MWS task were negatively related to score on the AVA and positively related to scores on the SRT. Taken together, these results provide additional evidence in support of the involvement of SL ability in language learning and processing and, to our knowledge, first evidence that the tight coupling between IDs in SL ability and variability in language outcomes observed in various linguistic domains extends to the realm of online processing of MWS. One of central issues in SL research is whether SL is a general unified capacity that is applied across different modalities and domains or whether it is a componential capacity with multiple facets ([18,46,47]). The lack of significant correlations among the four SL measures in this study is in line with the results of previous studies (e.g., [35,47]) and is thus consistent with the view that different tasks tap different mechanisms of SL (e.g. [47]). As already emphasized by [47] not all tasks are alike in terms of their efficiency in predicting IDs in SL ability. One of the key factors in this context is that the tasks varied in the standard deviation of their distribution. In our data, consistent with the results reported in [47], we found that the relative standard deviation – aka coefficient of variation (cv) – was largest in the VNA ($cv = 5.1$), followed by the AVN ($cv = 4.49$) and the AVA ($cv = 4.26$) and lowest in the SRT ($cv = 1.44$). The difference sizes of standard deviations of the four tasks indicates a fundamental difference between their psychometric quality.

In sum, the results of this study suggest a need for future research on MWS to move beyond group-level effects towards understanding the IDs in the processing of such sequences. More generally, explaining these differences is of central importance any adequate theory of language acquisition and processing must first and foremost constrained by empirical demonstrations of IDs as well as predict and account for meaningful IDs in terms of cognitive and experience-related factors (see, [28]).

References

1. Arciuli, J., Simpson, I.C.: Statistical learning is related to reading ability in children and adults. Cogn. Sci. **36**(2), 286–304 (2012)
2. Arnon, I., Snider, N.: More than words: frequency effects for multi-word phrases. J. Mem. Lang. **62**(1), 67–82 (2010)
3. Chang, F., Dell, G.S., Bock, K.: Becoming syntactic. Psychol. Rev. **113**(2), 234 (2006)
4. Christiansen, M.H., Arnon, I.: More than words: the role of multiword sequences in language learning and use. Top. Cogn. Sci. **9**(3), 542–551 (2017)
5. Christiansen, M.H., Chater, N.: Language as shaped by the brain. Behav. Brain Sci. **31**(5), 489–509 (2008)
6. Christiansen, M.H., Chater, N.: Creating Language: Integrating Evolution, Acquisition, and Processing. MIT Press, Cambridge (2016)
7. Christiansen, M.H., Chater, N.: The now-or-never bottleneck: a fundamental constraint on language. Behav. Brain Sci. **39**, e62 (2016)
8. Conklin, K., Schmitt, N.: The processing of formulaic language. Annu. Rev. Appl. Linguist. **32**, 45–61 (2012)
9. Conway, C.M., Bauernschmidt, A., Huang, S.S., Pisoni, D.B.: Implicit statistical learning in language processing: word predictability is the key. Cognition **114**(3), 356–371 (2010)
10. Davies, M.: The 385+ million word corpus of contemporary american english (1990–2008+): design, architecture, and linguistic insights. Int. J. Corpus Linguist. **14**(2), 159–190 (2009)
11. Dewaele, J.M.: Individual differences in second language acquisition. In: Ritchie, W.C., Bhatia, T.K. (eds.) The New Handbook of Second Language Acquisition, pp. 623–646. Emerald Insight Bingley, England (2009)
12. Diessel, H.: Frequency effects in language acquisition, language use, and diachronic change. New Ideas Psychol. **25**(2), 108–127 (2007)
13. Dörnyei, Z., Skehan, P.: Individual differences in second language learning. In: The Handbook of Second Language Acquisition, chap. 18, pp. 589–630. Wiley-Blackwell (2008)
14. Ellis, N.: The associative learning of constructions, learned attention, and the limited L2 endstate. In: Robinson, P., Ellis, N. (eds.) Handbook of Cognitive Linguistics and Second Language Acquisition, chap. 15, pp. 372–405. Routledge (2008)

15. Ellis, N.C.: Essentials of a theory of language cognition. Mod. Lang. J. **103**, 39–60 (2019)
16. Endress, A.D., Mehler, J.: The surprising power of statistical learning: when fragment knowledge leads to false memories of unheard words. J. Mem. Lang. **60**(3), 351–367 (2009)
17. Ettlinger, M., Morgan-Short, K., Faretta-Stutenberg, M., Wong, P.: The relationship between artificial and second language learning. Cogn. Sci. **40**(4), 822–847 (2016)
18. Frost, R., Armstrong, B.C., Siegelman, N., Christiansen, M.H.: Domain generality versus modality specificity: the paradox of statistical learning. Trends Cogn. Sci. **19**(3), 117–125 (2015)
19. Frost, R., Siegelman, N., Narkiss, A., Afek, L.: What predicts successful literacy acquisition in a second language? Psychol. Sci. **24**(7), 1243–1252 (2013)
20. Gibson, E., et al.: How efficiency shapes human language. Trends Cognit. Sci. **23**(5), 389–407 (2019)
21. Glicksohn, A., Cohen, A.: The role of cross-modal associations in statistical learning. Psychon. Bull. Rev. **20**(6), 1161–1169 (2013)
22. Hernández, M., Costa, A., Arnon, I.: More than words: multiword frequency effects in non-native speakers. Lang. Cogn. Neurosci. **31**(6), 785–800 (2016)
23. Kaufman, S.B., DeYoung, C.G., Gray, J.R., Jiménez, L., Brown, J., Mackintosh, N.: Implicit learning as an ability. Cognition **116**(3), 321–340 (2010)
24. Kerz, E., Wiechmann, D.: Individual differences in L2 processing of multiword phrases: effects of working memory and personality. In: Mitkov, R. (ed.) EUROPHRAS 2017. LNCS (LNAI), vol. 10596, pp. 306–321. Springer, Cham (2017). https://doi.org/10.1007/978-3-319-69805-2_22
25. Kerz, E., Wiechmann, D., Christiansen, M.H.: Tuning to multiple statistics: second language processing of multiword sequences across registers. In: Goel, A., Seifert, C., Freksa, C. (eds.) Proceedings of the 41st Annual Conference of the Cognitive Science Society. Cognitive Science Society, Austin (in press)
26. Kidd, E.: Implicit statistical learning is directly associated with the acquisition of syntax. Dev. Psychol. **48**(1), 171 (2012)
27. Kidd, E., Arciuli, J.: Individual differences in statistical learning predict children's comprehension of syntax. Child Dev. **87**(1), 184–193 (2016)
28. Kidd, E., Donnelly, S., Christiansen, M.H.: Individual differences in language acquisition and processing. Trends Cogn. Sci. **22**, 154–169 (2017)
29. Lany, J., Saffran, J.R.: From statistics to meaning: infants' acquisition of lexical categories. Psychol. Sci. **21**(2), 284–291 (2010)
30. Lemhöfer, K., Broersma, M.: Introducing lextale: a quick and valid lexical test for advanced learners of English. Behav. Res. Methods **44**(2), 325–343 (2012)
31. Manning, C., Surdeanu, M., Bauer, J., Finkel, J., Bethard, S., McClosky, D.: The stanford CoreNLP natural language processing toolkit. In: Proceedings of 52nd Annual Meeting of the Association for Computational Linguistics: System Demonstrations, pp. 55–60 (2014)
32. Matthews, D., Bannard, C.: Children's production of unfamiliar word sequences is predicted by positional variability and latent classes in a large sample of child-directed speech. Cogn. Sci. **34**(3), 465–488 (2010)
33. Maye, J., Weiss, D.J., Aslin, R.N.: Statistical phonetic learning in infants: facilitation and feature generalization. Dev. Sci. **11**(1), 122–134 (2008)
34. McCauley, S.M., Christiansen, M.H.: Language learning as language use: a cross-linguistic model of child language development. Psychol. Rev. **126**(1), 1 (2019)
35. Misyak, J.B., Christiansen, M.H.: Statistical learning and language: an individual differences study. Lang. Learn. **62**(1), 302–331 (2012)

36. Misyak, J.B., Christiansen, M.H., Tomblin, J.B.: On-line individual differences in statistical learning predict language processing. Front. Psychol. **1**, 31 (2010)
37. Muggeo, V.M.R.: Estimating regression models with unknown break-points. Stat. Med. **22**(19), 3055–3071 (2003)
38. Northbrook, J., Conklin, K.: Is what you put in what you get out?—Textbook-derived lexical bundle processing in beginner English learners. Appl. Linguist. (8) (2018). https://doi.org/10.1093/applin/amy027
39. Onnis, L., Waterfall, H.R., Edelman, S.: Learn locally, act globally: learning language from variation set cues. Cognition **109**(3), 423–430 (2008)
40. Pacton, S., Fayol, M., Perruchet, P.: Children's implicit learning of graphotactic and morphological regularities. Child Dev. **76**(2), 324–339 (2005)
41. Saffran, J.R., Aslin, R.N., Newport, E.L.: Statistical learning by 8-month-old infants. Science **274**(5294), 1926–1928 (1996)
42. Saffran, J.R., Wilson, D.P.: From syllables to syntax: multilevel statistical learning by 12-month-old infants. Infancy **4**(2), 273–284 (2003)
43. Seidenberg, M.S., MacDonald, M.C.: The impact of language experience on language and reading. Top. Lang. Disord. **38**(1), 66–83 (2018)
44. Shafto, C.L., Conway, C.M., Field, S.L., Houston, D.M.: Visual sequence learning in infancy: domain-general and domain-specific associations with language. Infancy **17**(3), 247–271 (2012)
45. Shaoul, C., Westbury, C.: Formulaic sequences: do they exist and do they matter? Ment. Lex. **6**(1), 171–196 (2011)
46. Siegelman, N., Bogaerts, L., Christiansen, M.H., Frost, R.: Towards a theory of individual differences in statistical learning. Philos. Trans. R. Soc. B: Biol. Sci. **372**(1711), 20160059 (2017)
47. Siegelman, N., Frost, R.: Statistical learning as an individual ability: theoretical perspectives and empirical evidence. J. Mem. Lang. **81**, 105–120 (2015)
48. Singh, L., Steven Reznick, J., Xuehua, L.: Infant word segmentation and childhood vocabulary development: a longitudinal analysis. Dev. Sci. **15**(4), 482–495 (2012)
49. Siyanova-Chanturia, A., Conklin, K., Van Heuven, W.J.: Seeing a phrase "time and again" matters: the role of phrasal frequency in the processing of multiword sequences. J. Exp. Psychol.: Learn. Mem. Cogn. **37**(3), 776 (2011)
50. Skehan, P.: Individual differences in second language learning. Stud. Second. Lang. Acquis. **13**(2), 275–298 (1991)
51. Spencer, M., Kaschak, M.P., Jones, J.L., Lonigan, C.J.: Statistical learning is related to early literacy-related skills. Read. Writ. **28**(4), 467–490 (2015)
52. Supasiraprapa, S.: Frequency effects on first and second language compositional phrase comprehension and production. Appl. Psycholinguist. **40**(4), 987–1017 (2019). https://doi.org/10.1017/S0142716419000109
53. Thiessen, E.D., Saffran, J.R.: When cues collide: use of stress and statistical cues to word boundaries by 7-to 9-month-old infants. Dev. Psychol. **39**(4), 706 (2003)
54. Thompson, S.P., Newport, E.L.: Statistical learning of syntax: the role of transitional probability. Lang. Learn. Dev. **3**(1), 1–42 (2007)
55. Tremblay, A., Derwing, B., Libben, G., Westbury, C.: Processing advantages of lexical bundles: evidence from self-paced reading and sentence recall tasks. Lang. Learn. **61**(2), 569–613 (2011)
56. Wolter, B., Yamashita, J.: Word frequency, collocational frequency, L1 congruency, and proficiency in L2 collocational processing: what accounts for L2 performance? Stud. Second Lang. Acquis. **40**(2), 395–416 (2018)
57. Wray, A.: Formulaic Language and the Lexicon. Cambridge University Press, Cambridge (2002)

Converse Phrasemes and Collocations in Czech: The Case of *dát* 'give' and *dostat* 'receive'

Marie Kopřivová(✉)

Charles University, Prague, Czech Republic
marie.koprivova@ff.cuni.cz

Abstract. The article focuses on lexical converse verbs which are part of phrasemes and collocations. Pairs of converse verbs express a lexical opposition, which however does not necessarily have to materialize within phrasemes, or can be restricted. One verb may have multiple opposites for a given type of collocation. This study builds upon the basic opposition between the two verbs which occur most frequently as part of phrasemes. In Czech, these verbs are *dát* 'give' and *dostat* 'receive'. The converseness analysis was performed on the current largest corpus of Czech written texts, SYN_v7, using a pilot version of phraseme annotation. Even though *dát* is polyfunctional, as evidenced by its large number of valency frames and collocation lemmas, the material yielded an abundant amount of instances of converse phrasemes and collocations. Some pairs showed notable differences in frequency distributions in texts, indicating a preference for one of the perspectives on the given situation in actual language use. Capturing this property in the lexicographical description of phrasemes and their annotation in corpus data could contribute towards a more accurate theoretical account of phrasemes, as well as practical applications in contrastive phraseology and phraseme teaching.

Keywords: Converse phrasemes · Phraseme annotation · Czech corpora

1 Introduction

This paper presents an analysis of phrasemes and collocations involving converse verbs which express lexical opposition through a different lexeme.[1] These verbs can preserve this property even within phrasemes and collocations and their valency slots can be occupied by the same lexical components. However, since these converse counterparts are not synonymous, but offer opposing views on the same situation, their relationship is captured neither in the dictionary nor in phraseme annotation in corpora. Yet this information could be very useful for learners encountering phrasemes in a foreign

---

[1] In other words, we do not pay attention to opposition expressed via other linguistic means, e.g. the passive (*porazit někoho* 'defeat sb' – *být někým poražen* 'be defeated by sb'). In studies of syntax, this topic is often introduced in the context of semantic diathesis alternations [1] and lexical-semantic conversions [2]. A comparison of several semantic diathesis alternations in Czech, Russian and Polish is provided by [3]. In the case of phrasemes however, there are numerous anomalies.

© Springer Nature Switzerland AG 2019
G. Corpas Pastor and R. Mitkov (Eds.): Europhras 2019, LNAI 11755, pp. 215–226, 2019.
https://doi.org/10.1007/978-3-030-30135-4_16

language, but also for annotating and further processing phrasemes. Last but not least, it is also an important aspect of the theoretical account of this phenomenon in each language. Obviously, there are many caveats, and the presence of the same components does not necessarily imply the description of the same situation from the opposite point of view. As everywhere in phraseology, but also in the semantics of linguistic expressions in general, meaning can shift to a lesser or greater extent. Even in confirmed cases of converseness, one of the verbs tends to be used more often. Additionally, polysemous verbs typically have multiple opposite counterparts which occur in different types of collocations.

This article attempts to demonstrate both the opportunities and the pitfalls presented by this approach on the example of the frequent ditransitive verbs *dát* 'give' and *dostat* 'receive'. The analysis is based on data extracted from the largest corpus of Czech written texts, SYN_v7, which features phraseme annotation FRANTA [4, 5]. Ideally, information about converseness relationships between pairs of expressions could be added to this annotation, as well as to a new database of multi-word lexical units, LEMUR [6].

2 Corpus Data and Phraseme Annotation

The SYN_v7 corpus is currently the largest corpus of contemporary Czech written texts (primarily spanning the period 1990–2017, and most of the data comes from 2004–2017). It is accessible to the public through the Institute of the Czech National Corpus. Version 7 was published in 2018 and contains 4.255 billion running words. While from a genre perspective, journalism dominates within the corpus, the texts are still very diverse, because the corpus subsumes four carefully balanced representative corpora [7]. This corpus also provides a pilot annotation of phrasemes and collocations. In spite of the bias due to the dominance of journalistic texts, which the user has to take into account, it appears that annotating phrasemes in large corpus data is both useful and important. Provided the data is varied, this scale pushes the number of attested types of phrasemes noticeably further (e.g. in comparison with the 100 million word corpus SYN2015, the number of different types of phrasemes and collocations with *dát* rose from 529 to 739, and with *dostat* from 307 to 455).

Phraseme annotation FRANTA [4, 6] in the CNC's written corpora is implemented using two attributes, the first one being the so-called *collocation lemma* (`col_lemma`), which represents the prototypical form of the phraseme or collocation (e.g. `dostat_se_k_moci` 'come to power'), i.e. basically a dictionary headword. The second attribute is the so-called *collocation type* (`col_type`), which further subdivides into two positions. The first position specifies the collocation type proper (e.g. verbal, proverb, etc.), the second one identifies the primary vs. secondary elements in the given phraseme instance. This distinction is mostly technical, its primary purpose is to allow for distinguishing between the number of occurrences of a phraseme as a whole vs. the number of occurrences of all of its components. In each occurrence of a phraseme or collocation, only one element is identified as the primary one, the remaining ones are tagged as secondary. Theoretically, a third position could be added to this attribute to indicate whether the given collocation has a converse counterpart.

By way of an example of what phraseme annotation looks like, let us consider the following sentence:

Mluví k vám váš kapitán, tak přestaňte dělat, co právě děláte, a dávejte/ dávat_pozor/VZ *pozor*/dávat_pozor/VH.

This is your captain speaking, so stop doing whatever it is you're doing and pay attention.

This means that the verb in the highlighted phraseme can come in different forms (in the collocation lemma, the infinitive is used: dávat_pozor); the collocation type indicates that the phraseme is verbal (V), the first component *dávejte* is labeled as secondary (Z) and the second component as primary (H). If we restrict our search using col_type = VH, we will therefore obtain a concordance with a single instance of this verbal phraseme.

3   Converseness

Converseness or the relation of conversion refers to pairs of words that display symmetry in their meaning; it is a type of antonymy. In the case of Czech, we follow the theoretical definition of Kováčová [8, 9]. Kettnerová [10] discusses the treatment of lexical-semantic conversions in the framework of a valency dictionary. Some of the theoretical groundwork of converseness was laid down as early as Apresjan [11]. Mel'čuk [12, 13] includes converseness as part of the description of lexical units in the dictionary. Our use of the term follows Lyons [14]. This phenomenon is also sometimes designated with different terms, e.g. Kuno [15] labels pairs of verbs of the type *give: receive* as "empathy verbs".

For the purpose of describing this property in phrasemes and collocations, we restrict ourselves to a narrower conception. Specifically, we understand converse verbs as verbs which describe the same situation using different linguistic meaning, which is also reflected in their lexical form. Between such pairs of verbs, the actants in valency slots are then re-arranged the other way around (cf. [9]). The dual perspective on a given situation is formally materialized when at least two valency patterns are available. This valency does not necessarily have to be listed as part of the collocation lemma, especially if it corresponds to the valency of a verb outside the phraseme. Conversely, violations of usual valency structure are understood as formal anomalies, often reflected in meaning shifts. In the new LEMUR database of multi-word units, valency will always be listed (cf. [6], 167). If converseness information is included in valency dictionary entries, it can be used as a starting point to ascertain whether it holds for phraseological units as well. It cannot be simply carried over though, especially not with phrasemes.

4 Verbs *dát* and *dostat* in Corpus Data

We will demonstrate converse phrasemes on the example of the verbs *dát:dostat*, which are very common in written Czech and often occur as phraseme components.

4.1 Lemma Frequency in Phrasemes and Collocations

According to Bartoň et al. ([16], 163), the verb *dát* is the 10th most frequent verb in written Czech, while the verb *dostat* comes in at the 14th place. Among the ditransitive verbs, it is the 3rd most frequent (after *říci* 'say' and *vědět* 'know'). The situation within phrasemes is somewhat different. In the SYN_v7 corpus [17], the most common verbs in phrasemes are *být* 'be' and *mít* 'have', both in terms of token and type counts (col_lemma); cf. Table 1. The verb *dát* and its converse counterpart *dostat* follow right behind in terms of raw token counts. As for a ranking based on number of different phraseme types according to col_lemma, *dostat* is overtaken by e.g. *jít* 'go' and *dělat* 'do' (cf. the last column in Table 1).[2]

Table 1. The most frequent verbs occurring in phrasemes in SYN_v7 corpus.

Rank	Verb		Number of occurrences	Number of collocation lemmas
1	být	be	4,068,756	3,444
2	mít	have	3,550,595	1,417
3	dát	give	1,093,526	739
4	dostat	get/receive	479,242	455
5	říci	say	446,865	228
6	jít	go	443,237	531
7	přijít	come	398,542	256
8	dělat	do	388,585	533
9	stát	stand	351,244	330
10	nechat	let/leave	344,686	216
11	dávat	give	340,594	220
169	dostávat	get	14,950	52

In contrast to the stative verbs *být* and *mít* [18], the verbs *dát* and *dostat* have aspectual (imperfective) counterparts: *dávat* and *dostávat*. Their ranking is however markedly different: while the verb *dávat* appears on the 11th place with 220 different collocation lemma types, the verb *dostávat* is only 169th, with 52 different collocation lemmas attested in the corpus.

---

[2] In the balanced corpus SYN2015, the ranking is different, with *dostat* demoted to the 12th place. This shift is due to the composition of the SYN_v7 corpus: *dostat* often occurs in verbonominal combinations, and these are very common in journalistic texts (cf. [19]).

4.2   Frequency Differences in Realizations of Collocation Lemmas

Both verbs are more common in the past tense, with 50% of occurrences of *dát* being in the past, and 75% of occurrences of *dostat*. The semantics of the verbs imply that the verb *dát* is encountered in the passive (the most common form being *dáno*) and the imperative (5% of occurrences). The imperative is attested for many phrasemes and collocations (427 collocation lemmas, compared to only 98 for *dávat*). The Czech imperative typically manifests aspect alternations (positive imperatives are formed from perfective verbs, negative imperatives from imperfective verbs, cf. [20], however, this tendency is subdued here. One phraseme with the perfective verb *dát* even preserves the historic 3rd person imperative form, *nedej Bůh* 'God forbid', which otherwise does not exist anymore in contemporary Czech. These differences affect the number of collocation lemmas and converseness patterns.

Another factor influencing the number of collocation lemmas is reflexivity: while the verb *dát* occurs in collocations with reflexive pronouns *si* and *se*, the verb *dostat* only occurs alongside *se*. The frequency breakdown of the different collocation lemmas for each verb is shown in Fig. 1, which make it clear that in the case of *dostat*, the collocation lemmas and text occurrences contribute more towards the overall frequency of phrasemes and collocations. Since reflexive pronouns take up one valency slot, the analysis of converse phrasemes and collocations is only based on collocation lemmas which did not involve any.

4.3   Valency

The differences between both verbs manifest also in the number of valency frames. The valency dictionary VALLEX 2.5 [21] captures valency frames jointly for both aspects, and separately for reflexive variants. The valency frames also attempt to give a summary of typical collocations and phrasemes (Table 2).

All of the data listed above indicate a higher degree of grammaticalization of *dát*, which also occurs more frequently in light verb constructions [22]. In spite of this, many cases of converseness occur even in phrasemes and collocations.

5   Analysis of Converse Phrasemes and Collocations of the Verbs *dát* and *dostat*

The analysis was based on manual comparisons, because having the same lexical items in the corresponding slots does *not* guarantee that the meaning of the collocation is the same. Via this method, we identified 215 collocation lemmas with the same lexical items, the same meaning, and differing only in having either *dát* or *dostat* as verb, i.e. in the perspective from which the situation is viewed. This set comprises 43% of the collocation lemmas (without reflexive pronouns) of *dát*, and as much as 68% in the case of *dostat*. We will now take a closer look at these lemmas and consider their valency types, semantic groups and frequency.

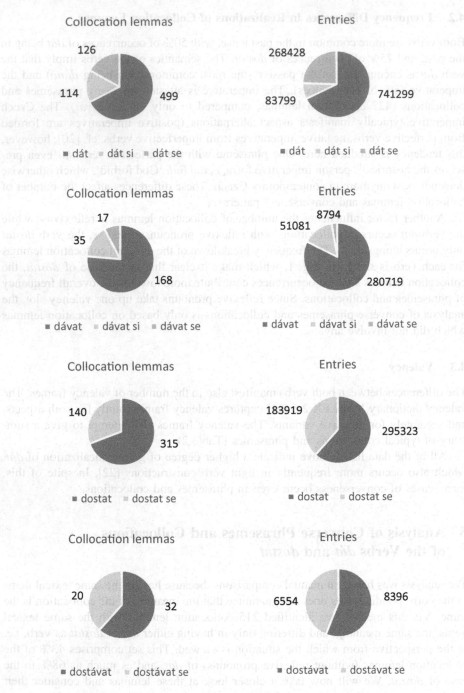

Fig. 1. Distribution of verbs in phrasemes and collocations.

Table 2. Number of valency frames for the verbs *dát* and *dostat*.

Verb	Num. of valency frames	Verb	Num. of valency frames
dát, dávat	28	dostat, dostávat	10
dát se, dávat se	6	dostat se	7
dát si, dávat si	4		

5.1 Valency Types

Formally, the accusative and prepositional valencies were predominant (101 and 102 collocation lemmas, respectively), as shown in Table 3. Prepositional constructions are listed in the table under the respective prepositions only; in the case of the preposition *pod* 'under', there is one construction with the accusative and two with the instrumental. The most frequent prepositions *na* 'on' and *přes* 'over' combine with body parts (cf. 5.2).

Table 3. Valency of collocation lemmas with the verbs *dát* and *dostat*.

Valency	Preposition		Number of collocational lemmas
Accusative			103
Instrumental			6
Preposition			98
	do	to/into	13
	k	to	3
	na	on	36
	po	after	7
	pod	under	3
	pro	for	1
	přes	over	21
	za	behind	13
	od	from	1
Verb			1
Adverb			6

5.2 Semantic Groups

The set of converse phrasemes and collocations is dominated by expressions related to violence – mostly physical, but also psychological (103 collocation lemmas in total). Body parts are often referenced, sometimes using vulgar equivalents – mostly the head (*dát/dostat přes kebuli* 'give/receive a smack on the noggin') or its parts (*dát/dostat za uši*, lit. 'give/receive behind the ears'), the rear (*dostat na zadek* 'get spanked'), the stomach (*dostat do držky*). Some of them occur in variants featuring different prepositions (*dát/dostat přes hubu /na hubu /po hubě /do huby*). Alternatively, these somatic idioms can also encode the body part which is being used to perform the violent act:

dát/dostat ránu pěstí 'give/receive a punch with the fist'). If one of the components is *ruka* 'hand' or *prst* 'finger', the meaning tends to be figurative and therefore related to non-physical violence or warnings (*dostat přes ruku/prsty* 'receive a slap on the hand/fingers'). Other categories include items of clothing (*dát/dostat na frak*, lit. 'give/receive on the tuxedo'), words expressing physical violence (*dát/dostat facku* 'give/receive a smack'), or possibly just a count (*dát/dostat pětadvacet/nepočítaných*, lit. 'give/receive twenty-five/uncountable [blows]'). Phrasemes occasionally feature non-compositional combinations (*dát/dostat čočku/kapky*, lit. 'give/receive lentils/drops') or combinations with monocollocable words (*dát/dostat na pamětnou*, lit. 'give/receive a remembering's worth').

A second, substantially smaller group consists of expressions related to meting out punishment (22 collocation lemmas), e.g.: *dát/dostat doživotí* 'life sentence', *provaz* 'death sentence', lit. 'the rope', *flastr* 'fine', lit. 'band-aid', *domácí vězení/zaracha* 'house arrest'. Even fewer collocation lemmas were related to rewarding (10), including e.g. *dát/dostat metál/frčku/za odměnu* 'give/receive a medal/epaulette/reward'.

A semantic group related to finances comprises 12 collocation lemmas, with phrasemes having to do with bribes (*dát/dostat bakšiš* 'give/receive baksheesh'), acquiring goods cheaply (*dát/dostat za babku/pakatel* 'sell/buy for a penny') or cash (*dát/dostat peníze na dřevo* 'to be paid in cash', lit. 'give/receive money on the wood').

Another group, similar in size, concerns expressions related to responsibility (12 collocation lemmas), including e.g. *dát/dostat na starost /na triko /za úkol* 'give/receive as a responsibility/task'. The last larger group (8 collocation lemmas) consists of expressions describing the transmission of a message, e.g. in the form of a warning or preliminary information (*dát/dostat avízo* 'give/receive a heads up'), information about a good deal (*dát/dostat echo* 'give/receive a tip') or an official confirmation (*dát/dostat něco černé na bílém* 'give/get it in writing', lit. 'give/receive it black [writing] on white [paper]').

Other areas are only represented by solitary phrasemes; an honorable mention should perhaps be made of phrasemes related to job termination like *dát/dostat padáka* 'give/receive the boot'. If the job termination is accompanied by a generous bonus, then the expression *dát/dostat zlatého padáka* 'give/receive a golden parachute' is used.

5.3   Frequency Comparison

41% of the converse phrasemes and collocations with *dát* and *dostat* belong among highly frequent collocations, with a combined frequency for both verbs higher than 200 occurrences (Fig. 2). The top of the frequency distribution, with frequencies over 10,000 hits, is occupied by collocations like *dát/dostat gól* 'score/concede a goal', *dát/dostat za pravdu* 'prove /be proven right', *dát/dostat trest* 'give/receive punishment', *dát/dostat najevo* 'make it clear', *dát/dostat k dispozici* 'put at one's disposition', *dát/dostat za úkol* 'set/receive a task', *dát/dostat zpět* 'give/receive back'. The frequency of some of the collocations, particularly *dát/dostat gól/góly* and *dát/dostat trest*, is undoubtedly influenced by the composition of the corpus with a predominance of journalistic texts, which prominently feature sports news. The singular occurs more commonly with *dostat*: *dostat gól* 'concede a goal', whereas the plural typically collocates with *dát*: *dát*

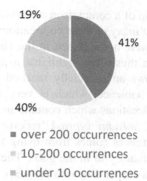

Fig. 2. Frequency distribution of converse phrasemes.

góly 'score goals'. The other most frequent collocations also show a marked preference for one of the verbs: *dát: za pravdu, najevo, k dispozici*; *dostat: trest, zpět*.

The phrasemes *dát za pravdu* 'prove right' and *dát najevo* 'make it clear' are considered invariant and exclusively related to the verb *dát*. However, the corpus data show that the verb *dostat* is also used here, although marginally. Apparently, this happens under the influence of the semantic relationship of these verbs. It appears in modal constructions (*měl dostat za pravdu* 'he was supposed to be proved right', *musí dostat najevo* 'it must be made clear to him') and in contexts where it would be necessary to use passive construction (*I v této sezóně dostal najevo, že se s ním pro NHL nepočítá.* 'Even this season, it was made clear to him that they don't count on him for the NHL.').

The first collocation with similar proportions of the overall frequency attributable to both verbs is *dát facku* 'give a smack' (3865 hits) and *dostat facku* 'get a smack' (3393 hits). Other such cases include e.g. *dát pěstí* 'hit with fist' (1978) and *dostat pěstí* 'get hit with fist' (1623), *dát za vyučenou* 'teach a lesson' (712) and *dostat za vyučenou* 'to be taught a lesson' (891). The most balanced proportion was recorded for the collocation *dát do tlamy* 'hit in the gob' (51 hits) and *dostat do tlamy* 'get hit in the gob' (52 hits). In most cases, the collocation with *dostat* is the most frequent one.

About 40% of the phrasemes achieve very low frequencies, occurring fewer than ten times with both verbs combined. This may be partially due to the fact that not all instances were identified by the automatic annotation procedure, but given the size of the corpus, it is unlikely that the numbers would increase by an order of magnitude if they had been.[3] This is the group whose annotation could be cross-checked and

---

[3] In its pilot version, the FRANTA tool for automatic annotation of phrasemes and collocations is configured to maximize precision. This means that if the encountered form of a phraseme candidate is the same as a more frequent literal word combination, the candidate is not labeled as a phraseme. In our data set, this affects e.g. the collocation *dát přes ústa*, which often continues with an object like *kapesník* or *masku*, and therefore is not an instance of the phraseme 'give a smack on the gob', but simply means 'put a handkerchief/mask over one's mouth'. Another similar case is the collocation *dát pětadvacet* 'give twenty-five', which is often followed by various nouns, e.g. *tisíc* 'thousand' (referring to money), *let* 'years', *bodů* 'points', again invalidating the phraseme reading ('give twenty-five [blows]').

possibly extended with the help of a comparison of converse verbs in collocations and phrasemes. The problem is that many of these collocations were not attested in older or smaller corpora, and so they were not included in the annotation.

The frequency comparison thus often highlights a preference for one of the two verbs. One group which shows an especially marked preference for *dostat* is the semantic group connected to violence, which is very large. The most pronounced difference can be found in collocations which contain an intensifying adjective: *dostat pořádnou/pěknou nakládačku, pořádný výprask* 'receive a hefty/substantial/etc. beating'. Another source of occurrences comes from using these collocations as a threat, e.g. *dostaneš přes hubu* 'I'll smack you in the gob'. The 2nd pers. pl. form is the 12th most frequent one. However, a deeper dive into the texts would be needed to elucidate these patterns in more detail.

6 Conclusion

The article attempts an analysis of the converse verbs *dát* and *dostat* in Czech phrasemes and collocations. The material consists of written Czech texts, mostly journalistic, annotated with the pilot version of the FRANTA tool for annotating phrasemes and collocations, as used in the SYN_v7 corpus. This manual analysis showed that converse phrasemes and collocations are relatively frequent. However, it also showed that the frequency breakdown between the individual verbs is often uneven. This part of the analysis could be complemented with possible converse phrasemes featuring a different verb, which might be preferred under certain circumstances. This analysis was fairly restricted and based only on the two mentioned verbs. By going into more detail and covering additional types of verbs, it might be possible to ascertain which perspective on a given situation is typically emphasized in verbal accounts.

This analysis also leads to a suggestion to capture the existence of converse counterparts in the annotation of collocations in Czech corpora. This property could also be recorded within the LEMUR database of multi-word units. Adding this information might be laborious and demand human intervention, but it could have several positive consequences for the present annotation. In the current pilot version, the collocation lemmas are very detailed, and analysis showed the possibility of merging some of them; this is currently technically implemented in the LEMUR database by a possibility to mark some phraseme components as potential/optional. In order to capture this variability, the previously used detailed lemmas could be merged (in order to indicate that they are related) while preserving information about the variants.

This overview also indicates that some types of phrasemes and collocations can only be found in very large corpora, and even so, only in small amounts. As evidenced by the analysis, a collocation can have a very low frequency with one (or both) of the converse verbs. Checking for the existence of a converse collocation thus helps capture lesser used phrasemes. It makes it possible to discover cases which typically occur with only one of the verbs and the other variant has not yet been recorded in the dictionary, but it *has* occurred in the corpus.

Since the analysis targeted verbs that are highly frequent, i.e. somewhat anomalous in terms of the scope and typicality of the collocations (the verb *dát* is undergoing grammaticalization), a subsequent analysis should ideally focus on a different type of converse verbs and cover more lexical items. When determining whether a phraseme is converse or not, one additional problem has to be taken into account: there can be multiple verbal counterparts which act as converses in specialized contexts. For the verb *dát*, it can be e.g. the verb *brát/vzít* 'to take impf./pf.' (e.g. *dát někomu dovolenou* lit. 'to give sb a vacation' – *vzít si dovolenou* lit. 'to take a vacation'); alternatively, verbs with more generic meanings can function as synonyms (e.g. *prodat/dát* – *koupit/dostat za babku* 'sell/give – buy/get [sth] for a penny'). However, the individual types can have varying frequencies, and minor semantic differences. All of these issues should be taken into account in future analyses.

Acknowledgments. This paper resulted from the implementation of the Czech National Corpus project (LM2015044) funded by the Ministry of Education, Youth and Sports of the Czech Republic within the framework of Large Research, Development and Innovation Infrastructures.

References

1. Karlik, P., Nekula, M., Rusínová, Z. (eds.): Handbook of Czech Grammar (in Czech). NLN, Praha (1995)
2. Panevová, J., et al.: Grammar of contemporary Czech. Syntax of Czech based on annotated corpus (in Czech). Karolinum, Praha (2014)
3. Skwarska, K.: Semantic diatheses in Czech and other Slavic languages (in Czech) In: Čmejrková, S., Hoffmannová, J., Klímová, J. (eds.) Čeština v pohledu synchronním a diachronním. Stoleté kořeny Ústavu pro jazyk český, Karolinum, Praha, pp. 621–627 (2012)
4. Kopřivová, M., Hnátková, M.: From dictionary to corpus. In: Jesenšek, V., Grzybek, P. (eds.) Phraseology in Dictionaries and Corpora, Filozofska fakulteta Maribor, Maribor, pp. 155–168 (2014)
5. Čermák, F., et al.: Dictionary of Czech phraseology and idiomatics I–IV (in Czech). Praha, Leda (2009)
6. Hnátková, M., Jelínek, T., Kopřivová, M., Petkevič, V., Rosen, A., Skoumalová, H., Vondřička, P.: Eye of a needle in a haystack. In: Mitkov, R. (ed.) EUROPHRAS 2017. LNCS (LNAI), vol. 10596, pp. 160–175. Springer, Cham (2017). https://doi.org/10.1007/978-3-319-69805-2_12
7. Hnátková, M., Křen, M., Procházka, P., Skoumalová, H.: The SYN-series corpora of written Czech. In: Proceedings of the Ninth International Conference on Language Resources and Evaluation (LREC 2014), pp. 160–164. ELRA, Reykjavík (2014)
8. Kováčová, K.: The relation of conversion as a system relation. (Konverzívnost jako systémový vztah. Disertační práce) FF UK, Praha (2005)
9. Marková, K.: Semantic and grammatical parameters of conversive lexems (illustrated on Czech nouns victory and slaugher (in Czech). Slovo a slovesnost **60**, 102–106 (1999)
10. Kettnerová, V.: Lexical semantic conversions in a valency lexicon. (in Czech). Karolinum, Praha (2015)
11. Apresjan, J.D.: Lexical Semantics: Synonymous Language Means. Nauka, Moskva (1974). (in Russian)

12. Mel'čuk, I.A., Pertsov, N.V.: Surface Syntax of English. A Formal Model within the Meaning-Text Framework. Benjamins, Amsterdam (1987)
13. Mel'čuk, I.A.: Polguère: A Formal Lexicon in the Meaning-Text Theory (or How to Do Lexica with Words). Comput. Linguist. **13**, 261–275 (2002)
14. Lyons, J.: Semantics. Cambridge University Press, Cambridge (1977)
15. Kuno, S.: Functional Syntax: Anaphora, Discourse and Emphaty. University of Chicago Press, Chicago (1987)
16. Bartoň, T., et al.: Statistics of Czech Language (in Czech). NLN/ÚČNK, Praha (2009)
17. Křen, M., et al.: Corpus SYN, version 7 from 29. 11. 2018. Ústav Českého národního korpusu FF UK, Praha (2017). http://www.korpus.cz
18. Čermák, F.: Czech and General Phraseology. Karolinum, Praha (2007)
19. Kopřivová, M.: Variability of Czech verbal phrasemes: case study of *dát* (to give). (in print)
20. Karlík, P., Nübler, N.: Negation and mode of the Czech imperative (in Czech). In: Karlík, P., Krčmová, M. (eds.) Jazyk a kultura vyjadřování, pp. 159–166. Masarykova univerzita, Brno (1998)
21. Lopatková, M., Žabokrtský, Z., Kettnerová, V.: VALEX 2.5. Valency Lexicon of Czech Verbs. http://ufal.mff.cuni.cz/vallex. Accessed 5 Oct 2019
22. Kettnerová, V., Kolářová, V., Vernerová, A.: Deverbal nouns in Czech light verb constructions. In: Mitkov, R. (ed.) EUROPHRAS 2017. LNCS (LNAI), vol. 10596, pp. 205–219. Springer, Cham (2017). https://doi.org/10.1007/978-3-319-69805-2_15

Automatic Identification of Academic Phrases for Czech

Dominika Kováříková[1(✉)] and Oleg Kovářík[2(✉)]

[1] Institute of the Czech National Corpus, Charles University,
Prague, Czech Republic
dominika.kovarikova@ff.cuni.cz
[2] Datamole, Banskobystrická 2080/11, 160 00 Prague, Czech Republic
oleg.kovarik@gmail.com

Abstract. The aim of this study is to automatically extract academic phrases in Czech using data-mining techniques as a first step towards creating a dictionary of academic words and phrases targeting university-level students (L1 and L2). The decision to use data mining was based on excellent results of data mining in automatic recognition of single-word and multi-word terms [10]. This method has identified various types of academic phrases: structurally incomplete lexical bundles with specific functions in texts (e.g. *na druhou stranu – on the other hand*), collocations (e.g. *podrobná analýza – detailed analysis*) or combinations of a content word and a typical function word (e.g. *zaměřený na - focused on; podobný jako - similar to*). The final list of automatically identified academic phrases is quite extensive and consists of 7,300 bigrams. Manual evaluation of the output data sample showed that precision of the automatic identification method is more than 72% and recall is 81%. The list of identified academic phrases is a very good starting point for the planned dictionary because the majority of the extracted bigrams constitute collocations typically used for academic texts. Such collocations are useful for the target audience, that is, university students interested in academic writing.

Keywords: Academic phraseology · Academic phrase list · Automatic identification

1 List of Czech Academic Phrases

The aim of this research is to create a list of multi-word expressions (MWE) typically used in academic texts (hereafter referred to as academic phrases) in Czech language that would contain various types of salient MWEs. This list is inspired by the creation of similar lists of academic phrases for English; for example, Academic Formulas List [14] or Academic Collocation List [1], as well as research on academic texts and

This paper has been, in part, funded by the Ministry of Education, Youth and Sports of the Czech Republic within the framework of Large Research, Development and Innovation Infrastructures (Czech National Corpus project, LM2015044). It was also supported by the European Regional Development Fund-Project "Creativity and Adaptability as Conditions of the Success of Europe in an Interrelated World" (No. CZ.02.1.01/0.0/0.0/16_019/0000734).

© Springer Nature Switzerland AG 2019
G. Corpas Pastor and R. Mitkov (Eds.): Europhras 2019, LNAI 11755, pp. 227–238, 2019.
https://doi.org/10.1007/978-3-030-30135-4_17

terminology [10]. The submitted research is part of a larger project that aims to compile a dictionary of phrases and words to be used in academic texts. The dictionary is intended as an academic writing aid for university students, as well as foreign students for whom Czech is a second language.

Following empirical research and extraction of phrases from previous research (e.g. Simpson-Vlach and Ellis [14] and others), we further develop the idea of using the automatic extraction method for academic phrases based on different linguistic, frequency, distribution and co-occurrence features. A novel contribution of this study is the introduction of data mining, which has proved useful in linguistic research (e.g. automatic extraction of single- and multi-word terms, [10]). By using data mining, it is possible not only to extract a list of academic phrases, but also to assess the importance of the individual features used. Data mining[1] is defined as the (semi)automatic process of discovering patterns in substantial quantities of data [16]. The requirement for a "useful" pattern is that it allows us to make nontrivial predictions on new data; for example, we can predict which n-grams in a text are or are not academic phrases based on a specific combination of attributes.

The resulting list includes word combinations that are significantly more frequent in academic texts than non-academic texts, that are distributed across a large number of academic disciplines and that are strong collocations (see more detailed description of specific features in Table 2).

2 Background

Over the past 15 years, many English for Academic Purposes (EAP) studies have demonstrated the importance of identifying multi-word combinations typical for academic texts ([1, 3, 4, 6, 8, 14, 15] and others) that would enhance the existing lists of individual academic words (e.g. Academic Word List [5]). Such academic phrases are essential for fluent production of expert-level academic texts such as research articles, as well as for student academic writing such as research papers or theses [4, 9].

One of the problems of identifying MWEs in academic texts is the diversity of these units, both semantic and formal. Some studies search for high-frequency **lexical bundles,** that is, extremely common sequences of words that are usually structurally incomplete and are not idiomatic in meaning [3, 9]. Such word sequences (*na základě – based on; v rámci – within; bez ohledu na – regardless of*) often contain a high frequency of grammatical words and have specific functions in the texts (e.g. stance expressions, discourse organisers, referential expressions [3].

On the opposite side of multi-word units relevant for the list of academic phrases are combinations of content words (adjective+noun, noun+noun, noun+verb, adverb +adjective/verb), examined among others by Ackermann and Chen [1]. These

---

[1] Data mining is a discipline partially overlaping with machine learning. In this study, we choose to use data mining terminology, because we are searching for useful information in vast amounts of language data. However, we recognize that this terminological preference is just a matter of a point of view.

combinations form a different type of multi-word expression: **collocations**[2] as meaningful and structurally complete word sequences. Collocations in academic texts are usually non-idiomatic, although there are some exceptions (*jít ruku v ruce – to go hand in hand; úhelný kámen – cornerstone; zlatý věk – golden age of*).

Collocations are the basis for a list of academic phrases: they are salient and very common and are thus particularly useful for pedagogical purposes. Most of the collocations relevant for the list of academic phrases are non-terminological (e.g. *výsledky experimentu – experiment results; pozitivně hodnotit – to evaluate positively; podrobná analýza – detailed analysis*). However, there are also numerous weakened multi-word terms originally specific to one discipline, such as philosophy of science or statistics, but which are currently used in a large number of disciplines (e.g. *analytická metoda – analytical method; přírodní vědy – natural sciences*).

Another type of multi-word unit that may be particularly useful for non-native (L2) students at university-level are specific combinations of **content words with a typical function word**, such as a preposition or conjunction (*platit pro – to apply to; řešit pomocí – to solve by; definovaný jako – defined as*).

In addition to non-terminological collocations (or widely used terminological collocations with weakened terminological validity, see above), there is one more significant type of collocation in academic texts: **multi-word terms** (MWT) specific to individual academic disciplines or smaller groups of related disciplines (*infarkt myokardu – myocardial infarction; oxid uhličitý – carbon dioxide; eukaryotní buňka – eukaryotic cell; sériový port – serial port; hrubý domácí produkt – gross domestic product*). MWTs constitute a substantial portion of academic texts, and according to Kováříková [10], MWTs account for almost 15% of academic texts. MWTs should not be included in general academic phrase lists, but rather in specific terminological dictionaries.

Automatic extraction of some of the multi-word unit types can be methodologically quite straightforward (find all 4-grams with a certain frequency, find all adjective+noun combinations with a certain frequency, etc.). It is much more problematic to extract several different types at once, because each type has unique frequency, distributional or other characteristics. Data-mining methods are useful for this kind of complex task because they can detect intricate relationships among various linguistic, frequency, distributional and co-occurrence of word-combination characteristics[3]. Various combinations of the following features have been used in previous research:

- **Frequency in academic texts.** Only phrases with sufficient frequency are of interest to the target audience, that is, students [1, 2].
- **Frequency ratio in academic text and general texts.** We are only looking for phrases that are typical of academic texts, that is, they occur with significantly higher frequency in academic than non-academic texts [14].

---

[2] By collocation we mean a meaningful combination of frequently co-occurring words, cf. e.g. McEnery and Hardie [13].

[3] As these characteristics are mostly based on frequency or distribution, it can be assumed that similar values will allow automatic identification of academic phrases in other languages, e.g. English.

- Occurrence in a large number of academic disciplines, resulting in a broad **distribution**. Phrases that occur only in one discipline are more likely to be discipline specific MWTs and are therefore not of interest for general academic phrase lists [1].
- **Dispersion in texts.** As opposed to distribution, an even dispersion identifies phrases that are used in many disciplines with relatively consistent frequency [9].
- **Co-occurrence.** Several types of association measures can be used to assess the collocation strength of the phrase, for example, MI score, logDice, log-likelihood or t-score among others [14].
- Preference for certain **parts of speech** (POS) or combinations of POS [11].

3   Data and Method

The corpus used for the research of Czech academic phrases, SYN2015 [12], contains contemporary written Czech and it is part of the Czech National Corpus. It contains 120 million words (with punctuation) and is divided into three balanced parts: fiction, non-fiction (including academic, technical and professional texts) and journalism. Calculations of some of the characteristics depend on comparison of different types of texts, namely academic texts versus non-academic, non-professional texts such as fiction and journalism. For that reason, two subcorpora were created: a corpus of academic texts and a reference corpus of fiction and journalism (see Table 1). The number of academic disciplines in the academic corpus is 24, consisting of various social sciences, humanities, natural sciences, and technical and formal sciences. (List of disciplines based on National Library of the Czech Republic: anthropology, arts, biology, chemistry, economy, pedagogy, geography, history, information technologies, library and information science, linguistics and literature, law, mathematics, medicine, music, philosophy, physics, political science, psychology, sport and recreation, sociology, engineering, theatre.)

Table 1. Size of the corpus of academic texts and size of the reference corpus of journalism and fiction.

Type of text	Number of tokens (incl. punctuation)
Academic texts	13 million
Journalism and fiction	81 million

The present research is aimed at automatic identification of academic phrases only within bigrams[4]. Longer n-grams will be studied in the next stages of the project (see Future plans). Some English-language authors recommend working with longer n-grams, especially 3-grams and 4-grams (e.g. Biber and Barbieri [3] use 4-grams to find

---

[4] We only use lemmas, because they have proved to be more effective in previous research [10]. The reason for this is due to the rich morphology of the Czech language.

lexical bundles). However, as current research by Cvrček et al. (in print) shows, due to the typological differences between the two languages, bigrams in Czech behave in a similar way to 3-grams in English, and 3-grams in Czech have similar characteristics to 4-grams in English. It therefore certainly makes sense to study Czech bigrams.

For practical reasons, the number of academic corpus bigrams was limited to 48,000 using the following criteria: bigram must be twice as frequent in the academic corpus as in the reference corpus of non-academic texts and must occur in at least one third of academic disciplines (8 out of 24 disciplines). This step removed most of the general (non-academic) phrases as well as discipline-specific multi-word terms.

The identification of academic phrases as well as the evaluation of their specific attributes was provided by the data mining tool Weka (Waikato Environment for Knowledge Analysis, [7]). The tool identifies relevant multi-word units based on input training data using 10-fold cross validation to prevent overfitting.

The training data consist of 1,000 bigrams manually labelled either as academic phrases or as bigrams that are not academic phrases. To each of the bigrams, eleven linguistic, frequency, distributional and co-occurrence attributes were assigned (see Table 2). The features were chosen based on extensive previous research on multi-word expressions in Czech academic texts [10].

Table 2. Features used in the automatic identification process.

Feature	Abbreviation
Part of speech of the first lemma	POS1
Part of speech of the second lemma	POS2
Relative frequency in academic corpus (instances per million, ipm)	RFQ_SCI
Relative frequency in reference corpus (ipm)	RFQ_GEN
Ratio of relative frequency in academic and reference corpus	RFQRFQ
Distribution in disciplines	DIST_SCI
Dispersion in academic corpus	DISPERSION_SCI
Association measure logDice	logDice_SCI
Association measure log-likelihood	logLikelihood_SCI
Association measure MI-score	MI_SCI
Association measure t-score	T_SCI

The testing dataset consists of 1,000 bigrams (different from the training data). The testing data were labelled as academic phrase and "other bigrams" both automatically and manually and the accuracy of the automatic identification was established (see Table 4).

With respect to the data-mining methodology, we used an interesting feature: model ensembling, i.e. voting of several different decision tree models[5] trained by WEKA. Voting makes the output more reliable because we are accounting for only those bigrams that have been identified as academic phrases by at least two of the three used methods. The example of a simple decision tree is in Fig. 1.

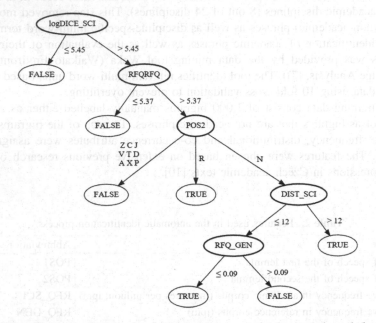

Fig. 1. Figure shows an example of a simple decision tree trained on unbalanced classes. Each decision progresses towards an individual leaf (end node) which shows the final outcome of the decision path (true = academic phrase, false = is not academic phrase). (POS: N = noun, A = adjective, P = pronoun, V = verb, D = adverb, R = preposition, J = conjunction, T = particle, C = numeral, Z = punctuation, X = unknown)

Manual labelling of training data is a critical component of the research because the quality of the output—in our case a list of automatically identified academic phrases—depends on the quality of the input. As this is the first large-scale project focused on academic phrases in the Czech language[6], we have faced two major problems related to the manual analysis: first, manual labelling of data is to some extent subjective [14], unless we have some reliable source of information, such as an existing academic

---

[5] We used J48 decision tree models. These were selected as the most suitable method for automatic extraction of terms and non-terms in Kováříková [10]. Different pre-processing was chosen for each model: (1) unbalanced classes (phrases and non-phrases), (2) class balancer, and (3) resampling..

[6] With the exception of a study that launched our interest in academic phrase list [11].

phrase list[7]. In the future, the manually labelled data should be compared with some of the available lists (namely lists in English: AFL, ACL, AWL etc.). Second, unless we have a clear idea of all the types of phrases we are looking for, it is hard to identify them with certainty in the training data. Therefore, the next step should involve detailed analysis of the automatically identified phrases and their classification.

4 Results

Of the 48,000 bigrams originally examined, 7,300 bigrams were automatically identified as academic phrases. The total number of occurrences of these bigrams in the corpus of academic texts is 616,000 (see Table 3), which is 47,000 tokens per million.

Table 3. Number of bigrams examined and bigrams automatically identified as academic phrases.

Bigrams	Number
Bigrams in academic texts (RFQRFQ >= 2, DIST >= 8)	48 000
Academic phrases (types)	7 300
Academic phrases (tokens in 13 million corpus of academic texts)	616 000
Academic phrases (tokens per million)	47 000

The success rate of automatic data labelling is assessed by statistical measures such as precision and recall[8]. For that purpose, 1,000 randomly selected bigrams (testing dataset, see above) automatically labelled as academic phrases and "other bigrams" were manually evaluated by a linguist. Out of 1,000 cases, 104 bigrams were labelled as academic phrases by both data-mining methods and a person (true positive TP), 833 were labelled as other bigrams by both data-mining methods and a person (true negative TN). 24 academic phrases were incorrectly labelled as other bigrams (false negative FN) and 39 other bigrams were incorrectly labelled as academic phrases (false positive FP). Precision of the automatic academic phrase identification is 72.2% and the recall is 81.3%, whereas the percentage of correctly automatically labelled bigrams is 93.7% (see summary in Table 4).

The number of automatically identified academic phrases was unexpectedly large. The manual evaluation (or precision rate) shows that thousands of bigrams can indeed be considered a type of academic phrase. If the aim of the project was to produce a concise list of extremely frequent academic phrases for pedagogical purposes, the resulting list would need to be radically scaled down by selecting only a few hundred of the most frequent, the most widely distributed or the most evenly dispersed items from

---

[7] Currently, there is only one such list for Czech language, Akalex, that is limited in terms of size and completeness, cf. www.korpus.cz/akalex [2].

[8] Precision is fraction of relevant instances among the retrieved instances, recall is fraction of relevant instances that have been retrieved over the total amount of relevant instances.

Table 4. Success measures of the automatically labelled bigrams.

n=1000		Predicted	
		NO	YES
Actual	NO	TN = 833	FP = 39
	YES	FN = 24	TP = 104

Measure	Value
correctly labelled bigrams	(TP+TN)/(TP+TN+FP+FN) = 93.7%
precision	TP/(TP+FP) = 72.2%
recall	TP/(TP+FN) = 81.3%

the automatically extracted list. The difficulty is in selecting the best criterion because the differently ordered lists can vary greatly, as shown in the following table (Table 5).

However, as already mentioned, the aim of the project is not to create a concise list of academic phrases but a more extensive dictionary of academic words and phrases. A crucial element of such a dictionary requires an inventory of the most important collocates to selected headwords (single words typical for academic texts, see Table 6). The output of the present study provides such collocates, produced from a very large list of automatically selected academic phrases. The advantage of the collocations derived from the list is that they have already met the criteria of adequate frequency and dispersion. In Table 6 we present collocates for noun *analýza* (*analysis*), adjective *odlišný* (*different/distinct*) and verb *ovlivňovat* (*to affect/influence*).

POS Combinations of the Identified Academic Phrases. The list of automatically identified academic phrases contains almost 50 types of POS combinations. The most prominent among them is the **adjective+noun** combination – it constitutes 34% of the entire list. There are three main groups within this type: typical collocations, such as *relevantní informace – relevant information; vzájemné vztahy – interrelationship*; weakened MWTs, such as *vědecká teorie – scientific theory; kvantitativní metody – quantitative methods*; and parts of larger lexical bundles, such as *(do) jisté míry – (to a) certain degree; (v) různé míře – (to) varying degrees, (v) širším smyslu – (in a) broader sense*.

Very similar groups are formed within the second most common type, **noun+noun** (8% of the list): typical collocations, such as *řešení problému – solution to a problem; zpracování tématu – topic processing*; weakened MWTs, such as *analýza dat – data analysis; definice pojmu –definition of a concept*; lexical bundles, such as *(na) základě * (studia/analýzy/zkušeností* etc.) *– based (on) * (study/analysis/experience* etc.).

Combinations of **noun or verb with a typical preposition** constitute 10% of the list (5% each type). An inventory of such combinations is especially helpful for non-

Table 5. Table presents examples of the top 15 entries in lists of all automatically labelled academic phrases that have been ordered by frequency, dispersion and frequency ratio (in the academic and reference corpus) respectively. The first and second column containing mostly lexical bundles overlap to some degree, while the third list is different because it mainly consists of combinations of content words (collocations and weakened multi-word terms).

15 academic phrases with the highest frequency in corpus of academic texts (RFQ_SCI)	15 academic phrases most evenly dispersed in corpus of academic texts (DISPERSION)	15 academic phrases most frequent in corpus of academic texts in comparison with reference corpus (RFQRFQ)
je možné *(it) is possible*	*na rozdíl (od)* *as opposed to*	*viz kapitola* *see chapter*
v rámci *within*	*vycházet z* *based on*	*viz tab.* *see Fig.*
na základě *based on*	*spojený s* *associated with*	*nezávisle proměnných* *independent variables*
vzhledem k *relative to*	*všechny tyto* *all of these*	*studijní cíle* *learning objectives*
v oblasti *in area*	*z hlediska* *in terms of*	*vyjádřit vztahem* *express by relationship*
považovat za *consider as*	*(ve) srovnání s* *(in) comparison with*	*obecné řešení* *general solution*
z hlediska *in terms of*	*lze říci* *can be said*	*korelační koeficient* *correlation coefficient*
být nutný *be necessary*	*podobně jako* *similar to*	*sociální normy* *social norms*
(v) současné době *currently*	*další vývoj* *other developments*	*kde n* *where n*
na obr. *in Fig.*	*lze předpokládat (, že)* *can be assumed (that)*	*regresní analýzy* *regression analysis*
jedná (se) o *this is*	*v důsledku* *due to*	*zkoumaných jevů* *examined phenomena*
(bez) ohledu na *regardless of*	*je založena (na)* *is based (on)*	*lineární závislost* *linear relationship*
(na) rozdíl od *(as) opposed to*	*dvě základní* *two basic*	*velikost vzorku* *sample size*
vycházet z *based on*	*důležitou roli* *important role*	*pojmový aparát* *conceptual apparatus*
et al. *et al.*	*charakterizovat jako* *characterize as*	*schematicky znázorněn* *schematically depicted*

native university students: *vztah mezi – relationship between; odpověď na – answer to, lišit se od – be different than.*

Most of the three other relatively common types (adverb+verb, adverb+adjective, verb+noun, each category represents 4% of the list) are typical collocations: *poměrně malý – relatively small, relativně vysoký – relatively high, poněkud odlišný – slightly*

Table 6. Examples of automatically identified collocates for noun *analýza* (*analysis*), adjective *odlišný* (*different/distinct*) and verb *ovlivňovat* (*to affect/influence*).

Collocates for *analýza*	Collocates for *odlišný*	Collocates for to *ovlivňovat*
analýza dat data analysis	*diametrálně odlišné* vastly different	*faktory ovlivňují* factors influencing
analýza ukázala analysis showed	*kvalitativně odlišné* qualitatively different	*možnost ovlivňovat* possibility to influence
analýza vztahů relationship analysis	*poněkud odlišné* somewhat different	*navzájem ovlivňují* influence each other
detailní analýza detailed analysis	*zásadně odlišné* fundamentally different	*negativně ovlivňuje* negatively affects
prostřednictvím analýzy through analysis	*odlišné druhy* different types	*přímo ovlivňuje* directly affects
provedena analýza conducted analysis	*odlišné od* different from	*výrazně ovlivňuje* significantly affects
předmětem analýzy subject of analysis	*odlišný přístup* different approach	*ovlivňuje chování* affects behavior
statistické analýzy statistical analysis	*odlišné typy* different types	*ovlivňuje kvalitu* affects quality
vědecké analýzy scientific analysis	*odlišné závěry* different conclusions	*ovlivňuje vývoj* affects development
výsledky analýzy results of analysis	*odlišným způsobem* different way	*ovlivňovat dění* influence events

different, negativně ovlivňovat – to influence negatively, podstatně lišit – to differ significantly, zaměřit pozornost – to concentrate on, definovat pojem – to define a concept.

These POS combinations constitute almost two thirds of the automatically extracted list of academic phrases. The other third consists of almost 40 much less common combinations.

5 Future Work

The present research is part of a larger project (dictionary of English academic words and phrases), so naturally there are plans for future work. The next step is to automatically search for academic phrases in the list of trigrams and longer n-grams using data mining.

At the same time, we need to address the problems of the manual labelling of the training and testing data. Relevant academic phrases should be labelled as objectively as possible, based on existing lists (including those in English) and steady rules that should be derived from a detailed analysis of the different types of multi-word units typical for academic texts. Also, relevance of the individual n-grams should be evaluated by several experts independently. This will increase the quality and reliability of the input as well as output data.

Last, but not least, is the production of the intended dictionary itself, including definitions as well as a list of collocates to a selected headword.

6 Conclusion

The aim of this research was to create a list of academic phrases in Czech language that would contain various types of multi-word expressions, the ultimate goal being to compile a dictionary of academic phrases and words.

The automatic extraction method identified 7,300 common academic phrases in the corpus of academic texts. The number of occurrences of these bigrams in the corpus of academic texts is 47,000 per million tokens. The success rate of automatic data classification was estimated by statistical measures precision and recall. The testing data (1,000 bigrams) were labelled manually as well as automatically, and the results were compared. Precision of the automatic academic phrase identification was 72.2% and the recall was 81.3%, and the percentage of correctly automatically labelled bigrams was 93.7%.

The number of automatically identified academic phrases is quite large - for an extensive dictionary of academic words and phrases it is an adequate quantity, especially because a substantial number of extracted bigrams are frequent collocates of words typically used in academic texts. For a more concise list of very frequent academic phrases, this large number of identified phrases would have to be reduced based on frequency, dispersion and/or frequency ratio in academic and reference corpus.

The most prominent POS combinations are adjective+noun (34%), noun+noun (8%), noun+preposition (5%) and verb+preposition (5%). The four main types of multi-word expression within the prominent POS combinations are typical collocations, weakened multi-word terms (discipline-non-specific), lexical bundles and combinations with a typical preposition.

The study met the expectations: the method was able to identify a large number of academic phrases with sufficient success rates. In addition, it provided a list of collocations typically used in academic texts valuable for the planned dictionary.

References

1. Ackermann, K., Chen, Y.-H.: Developing the academic collocation list (ACL) – a corpus-driven and expert-judged approach. J. Engl. Acad. Purp. **12**(4), 235–247 (2013)
2. Akalex 2018: Lexikon akademické češtiny. Akalex 2018: A Lexicon of Academic Czech (in Czech) (2018). https://korpus.cz/akalex. Accessed 15 May 2019
3. Biber, D., Barbieri, F.: Lexical bundles in university spoken and written registers. Engl. Specif. Purp. **26**, 263–286 (2007)
4. Chen, Y.-H., Baker, P.: Lexical bundles in L1 and L2 student writing. Lang. Learn. Technol. **14**, 30–49 (2010)
5. Coxhead, A.: A new academic word list. TESOL Q. **34**(2), 213–238 (2000)
6. Durrant, P.: Investigating the viability of a collocation list for students of English for academic purposes. Engl. Specif. Purp. **28**, 157–169 (2009)

7. Frank, E., Hall, M.A., Witten, I.H.: The WEKA Workbench. Online Appendix for Data Mining: Practical Machine Learning Tools and Techniques, 4th edn. Morgan Kaufmann, Burlington (2016)
8. Granger, S.: Academic phraseology: a key ingredient in successful L2 academic literacy. Oslo Stud. Engl. **9**(3), 9–27 (2017)
9. Hyland, K.: Bundles in academic discourse. Ann. Rev. Appl. Linguist. **32**, 150–169 (2012)
10. Kováříková, D.: Kvantitativní charakteristiky termínů. Quantitative Characteristics of Terms (in Czech). LN, Praha (2017)
11. Kováříková, D., Lukešová, L.: Extracting multi-word expressions for the Czech academic phrase list (conference presentation)
12. Křen, M., et al.: SYN2015: Representative Corpus of Written Czech. Institute of the Czech National Corpus, FFUK, Prague (2015). http://www.korpus.cz. Accessed 15 May 2019
13. McEnery, T., Hardie, A.: Corpus Linguistics: Method, Theory and Practice. John Benjamins, Amsterdam (2012)
14. Simpson-Vlach, R., Ellis, N.: An academic formulas list: new methods in phraseology research. Appl. Linguist. **31**(4), 487–512 (2010)
15. Vincent, B.: Investigating academic phraseology through combinations of very frequent words: a methodological exploration. J. Engl. Acad. Purp. **12**, 44–56 (2013)
16. Witten, I.H., Frank, E.: Data Mining: Practical Machine Learning Tools and Techniques. Elsevier, Amsterdam (2005)

Translation Correspondences of Digressive Discourse Markers in English and Spanish: A Corpus-Based Study

Julia Lavid López(✉) ⓘD

IULMYT - Universidad Complutense, 28040 Madrid, Spain
lavid@ucm.es

Abstract. The present study is work-in-progress in the context of a larger project aimed at the creation of a bilingual (English-Spanish) corpus annotated with discourse markers (DMs) as part of the activities derived from the Textlink Cost Action. Focusing on two of the most frequent digressive discourse markers (DDMs) in English –*by the way* and *incidentally*- and their Spanish counterparts –*por cierto* and *a propósito* –as a case study, the paper addresses the following research questions: is it possible to construct semantic fields of DDMs in English and Spanish on the basis of their translation correspondences? Is it possible to establish core and non-core meanings? Four parallel corpora are used for the study: the MULTINOT corpus (Lavid et al. 2015), the EUROPARL corpus (Koehn 2005), the OPUS2 Corpus and the OPEN Subtitles Corpus (Tiedemann 2009). The analysis reveals that these DDMs are semantically underspecified and have a large number of different translations which can be grouped into semantic fields on the basis of their closeness of meaning. It also shows that translations can make explicit certain meanings which are less obvious from a monolingual syntagmatic analysis. It is expected that the methodology and the results of this analysis can be useful for contrastive and translation research on discourse markers as well as for the bilingual annotation of parallel corpora for computational tasks.

Keywords: Digressive discourse markers · English · Spanish · Parallel corpus

1 Introduction

1.1 Background and Motivation

The study of discourse markers (DMs) in the context of translation is considered a crucial task for several reasons: first, the idiomatic nature of these structures (Aijmer 2007; Beeching 2013); second, their frequent polysemy; third, their significant role in the coherence and readability of a text: if a wrong connective is used in translation, the target text can be fully incomprehensible or produce a different meaning as the one expressed in the source text. However, their study has been usually carried out from a monolingual perspective and, to date, there are no systematic studies which address their cross-language behavior in the context of translation between English and Spanish. However, translation is "one of the very few cases where speakers evaluate

© Springer Nature Switzerland AG 2019
G. Corpas Pastor and R. Mitkov (Eds.): Europhras 2019, LNAI 11755, pp. 239–252, 2019.
https://doi.org/10.1007/978-3-030-30135-4_18

meaning relations between expressions not as part of some kind of metalinguistic, philosophical or theoretical reflection, but as a normal kind of linguistic activity" (Dyvik 1998: 51). The translator is, therefore, an ideal linguistic 'informant' and a corpus of translations can be used for "empirically testing one's intuitions (or hypotheses) about the semantics of linguistic forms that is complementary to the systematic exploitation of the circumstantial evidence provided by monolingual corpora" (Noël 2003). Accordingly, translations of DMs into one or more languages can help us to get a better picture of their meaning and of their correspondences (Aijmer 2007).

This paper presents a corpus-based analysis of the translation correspondences of two of the most frequent digressive discourse markers (DDMs) in English and their Spanish counterparts, using bilingual and bidirectional English-Spanish parallel samples as dataset. The aim is to investigate the core meanings of DDMs in English and Spanish and to set up semantic fields for DDMs on the basis of their translation equivalents.

The paper is organised as follows: after the review of some relevant monolingual studies of the most frequent DDMs in English and Spanish (Subsect. 1.2), the data and the analysis methodology used for this study are described (Sect. 2). This is followed by the presentation of the analysis results (Sect. 3) and the summary and pointers for the future (Sect. 4).

1.2 Monolingual Studies

DDMs have not received much attention from a cross-lingual perspective, although there exist some monolingual studies which have examined some of their main features in English and Spanish. These are briefly described in the following subsections.

English Studies

The English DDMs *by the way* and *incidentally* have been studied by Traugott from a diachronic perspective (in press). According to this author, *by the way* and *by the by(e)* may originally have been conceptualized as a subset of *spatial expressions* and both were used as metatextual adverbials in the metaphorical sense of ARGUMENT IS A JOURNEY. By 1900 or so, *by the by(e)* was obsolescing, while *incidentally* and *parenthetically*, both originating as metatextual adverbs and both indexing *an aside*, "were presumably attracted to the schema and used in some of the ways characteristic of *by the way*, especially clause-initial use as a topic-shift marker" (ibídem). She concludes that "the four DDMs form a schema, albeit a fairly loose and changing one" (ídem).

Fraser has also studied what he calls "topic orientation markers", among which he includes *by the way* and *incidentally* as expressing digression from the current theme (2009: 895).

Spanish Studies

The Spanish DDMs *por cierto* and *a propósito (de)* have been studied by different Spanish scholars both from a diachronic and a synchronic perspective (Mateo Rodríguez 1996; Acín Villa 2000; Martín Zorraquino and Portolés 1999; Estellés Arguedas 2011, to mention a few), but no general consensus exists as to their nature and functions (see Pons and Estellés Arguedas 2009). Acín Villa (2000) classifies DDMs into several subtypes:

(A) those indicating a parenthesis, i.e., spontaneous information which interrupts the discourse and permits to get back to it once it is finished. These are sequences highly related to the previous one or to the main one which introduce a new element or comment on what has been said immediately before or an added, brief and related information. They are usually marked by *por cierto* and other less frequent markers such as *dicho sea de paso, entre paréntesis.*

(B) those indicating a marked digression with a higher syntactic and thematic rupture with respect to the previous discourse; these are usually marked by *a propósito (de)*, *hablando de, a todo esto*, etc.

(C) those indicating a topic shift or mark a new discourse topic, typically expressed by markers such as *por otro lado, en otro orden de cosas, por otra parte.*

2 Data and Methodology

2.1 Data

The data used for analysis consists of four parallel datasets, as described below:

(1) The MULTINOT corpus, a half-a-million-word sentence-aligned, and linguistically annotated parallel corpus for the language pair English-Spanish (Lavid et al. 2015).

(2) The EUROPARL7 corpus, a parallel corpus created from the European Parliament Proceedings in the official languages of the EU (Koehn 2005). For this paper a subset of English and Spanish files was selected, consisting of about 60 million words per language.

(3) The OPUS2 corpus, a large collection of freely available parallel corpora completely aligned at the sentence level for all possible language pairs (Tiedemann 2009). The English-Spanish subset used for this study consists of 1440 million words.

(4) The Opensubtitles corpus, which consists of movie subtitles and contains of 826 million words.

2.2 Analysis Method

The analysis methodology used in this study is inspired in Dyvik's approach to meaning (1998; 2004; 2005), more specifically, on his theory of 'semantic mirrors', but complementing his approach with a study of the functions of the DDMs in monolingual contexts. Dyvik starts from the assumption that the meaning of words becomes visible in translation and that the translation mirrors the meaning of a word. In his own words: "The anatomy of meaning emerges in the translational tension between languages" (Dyvik 2005: 7). He proposes the following steps in the translation analysis: first, a set of translations of a word from the source language is identified in a parallel corpus. This set is called a t-image. Afterwards, the words from that t-image are translated back into the original language, and this second set is called an inverted t-image. Finally, by observing the distribution of words and overlapping translations of two images, it is possible to identify their different senses.

In this study the following steps were taken for the analysis of the translation correspondences of DDMs in English and Spanish:

1. A monolingual revision of the meanings/functions of *by the way* and *incidentally* in English and of *por cierto* and *a propósito* in Spanish was carried out.
2. The EN-ES translation correspondences were identified in the parallel corpora and the different frequencies and their meanings –as revealed by the translation preferences– were used as the basis for establishing semantic groupings (first mirroring).
3. The back-translation correspondences from ES-EN were identified (second mirroring) in order to find out if there are any other items which along with the initial English DDMs create a semantic field. Semantic fields containing the DDMs from English and Spanish are then considered to form corresponding translation lexical domains (TLDs).

3   Analysis Results

This section presents the results of the analysis of the translation correspondences of the English and the Spanish DDMs. This is done in two steps: first, the results of the first mirroring are described, focusing on the Spanish translations of *by the way* and *incidentally* and grouping them into semantic domains; in a second step, the most frequent translations of these two English DDMs, i.e., *por cierto* and *a propósito* are back-translated into English and grouped into semantic domains.

Translation Correspondences of *by the way.* As shown in Table 1, *by the way* is translated into Spanish in many different ways in all four parallel datasets: the most frequent translation is the Spanish DDM *por cierto*, with a total frequency of 2174 occurrences (0.93 per million words), followed by *a propósito*, with a total of 591 occurrences (0.25 per million words). These two highly frequent translations are followed by other less frequent ones, such as *(dicho sea) de paso* (0.05 p.m/w/w), *además* (0.04 p.m/w/w), *por lo demás* (0.03 p.m/w/w), and *por otra parte* (0.02 p.m/w/w), among others.

Table 1. Distribution of translations of *by the way* into Spanish in four parallel corpora

ENGLISH Original	SPANISH Transl.	FREQUENCY IN CORPORA				
		M-NOT	OPEN SUBT.	EUROPARL7	OPUS2	TOTAL
	Por cierto	1 (1m)	1366 (**1.67** per m) (826 mill)	119 (**1.96** per m) (60 million)	689 (0.48 per million) (1440 million)	2174 (**0.93 p.m**)
	Por lo demás	0	0	45 (**0.74** per m)	27 (0.02 per million)	72 (0.03 p.m)
	(Dicho sea) de paso	0	43 (0.05 per million)	28 (**0.46** per m)	67 (0.05 per million)	135 (0.05 p.m)
	Por otra parte	0	0	33 (0.54 p.m)	22 (0.02 per million)	55 (0.02 p.m)
BY THE WAY	Además	0	43 (0.05 per million)	22 (0.36 per m)	39 (0.03 per million)	104 (0.04 p.m)
	A propósito	0	226 (0.28 p.m)	18 (0.3 per m)	347 (0.24 per million)	591 (**0.25 p.m**)
	En este caso	0	0	12 (0.2 per m)	0	10 (0.004 p.m)
	Dicho al margen	0	0	2 (0.03 per m)	0	2 (0.0008 p.m)
	Entre paréntesis	0	0	1 (0.02 per m)	3 (less than 0.01)	3 (0.001 p.m)
	A este respecto	0	0	0	6 (less than 0.01)	6 (0.002 p.m)

The translation correspondences of *by the way* and their preferred meanings/functions can be grouped into semantic fields or sets, as graphically shown in Fig. 1 below:

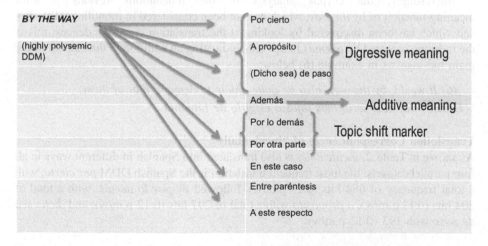

Fig. 1. Semantic groupings of *by the way* on the basis of translation equivalents

In English, the most frequent meaning/function of *by the way* is to express *a digression from the current topic* (Fraser 2009: 895), as in examples (1), (2) and (3) below:

(1) By the way, Maastricht is not a strange city, Mrs Frassoni, it is a very exciting city.
(2) By the way the few independent papers that do exist are hard to come by in the provinces.
(3) By the way, the law was also severely criticised by Amnesty International, which says that the demilitarisation and demobilisation have not actually taken place.

The Spanish translations show this by using the DDMs *por cierto*, *a propósito* and *dicho sea de paso*, with clear digressive functions in Spanish, as well as the less frequent *entre paréntesis* (Acín Villa 2000, Mateo Rodriguez 1996). The Spanish DDM *por cierto* is the most frequently used and can replace any of the other ones in the same contexts.

The second most frequent meaning/function of *by the way* is to express a topic shift, as illustrated in examples (4) and (5):

(4) By the way, I totally agree with Mr Lipietz when he says that what is at stake in Paraguay is not just General Oviedo, but human rights as a whole.
(5) By the way, an irritating error has crept in to the erratum.

The Spanish translations capture this meaning/function through the use of markers such as *por otro lado* and *por otra parte*, which are typically used as topic-shift markers in Spanish.

Interestingly, the corpus analysis of the translations reveals a third meaning/function of *by the way*, which has not been considered in monolingual studies and which has been discovered by looking at the translation correspondences: this is the meaning captured by *además* in Spanish, indicating an addition to the content of the main message, as in example (6) below:

(6) It would, by the way, also be quite unfair to demand that of them.
(Transl.) Además, sería muy injusto exigirlo de Lituania...

Translation Correspondences of "incidentally"
As shown in Table 2, *incidentally* is also translated into Spanish in different ways in all four parallel datasets: the most frequent translation is the Spanish DDM *por cierto*, with a total frequency of 684 hits (0.29 p.m/w), followed by *por lo demás,* with a total of 304 hits (0.13 p.m/w), *a propósito* with a total of 297 hits (0.12 p.m/w), and *dicho sea de paso* with 193 (0.12 p.m/w):

Table 2. Distribution of translations of *incidentally* into Spanish in four parallel corpora

ENGLISH Original	SPANISH Transl.	FREQUENCY IN CORPORA				
		M-NOT	OPEN SUBT.	EUROPARL7	OPUS2	TOTAL
	Por cierto	1 (1m)	190 (0.23 per million) (826 mill)	118 (**1.94** per million) (60 million)	375 (0.21 per million) (1440 million)	684 (**0.29** p.m)
	A propósito		95 (0.12 per million) (826 mill)	48 (0.79 million) (60 million)	154 (0.11 per million) (1440)	297 (**0.12** p.m)
	Por lo demás		0 (826 mill)	150 (2.47 per million) (60 million)	154 (0.11 per million) (1440)	304 (**0.13** p.m)
	(Dicho sea) de paso	1 (1m)	16 (0.02 per million) (826 mill)	76 (1.25 per million) (60 million)	101 (0.07 per million) (1440)	193 (**0.12** p.m)
INCIDENTALLY	Además		0 (826 mill)	61 (1 per million) (60 million)	70 (0.05 per million) (1440)	131 (**0.05** p.m)
	casualmente		0 (826 mill)	0 (60 million)	39 (0.03 per million) (1440)	39 (**0.01**)
	A este respecto		0 (826 mill)	7 (0.12 per million) (60 million)	10 (0.01) (1440)	17 (**0.007**)
	Por otra parte	1(1m)	0 (826 mill)	66 (1.09 per million) (60 million)	0 (1440)	66 (**0.02**)
	De forma accesoria		0 (826 mill)	5 (0.08 per million) (60 million)	0 (1440)	5 (**0.0004**)
	Sin duda		0 (826 mill)	0 (60 million)	9 (0.01 per million) (1440)	9 (**0.003**)

As in the case of *by the way*, the translation correspondences of *incidentally* can be grouped into semantic sets, as graphically shown in Fig. 2 below:

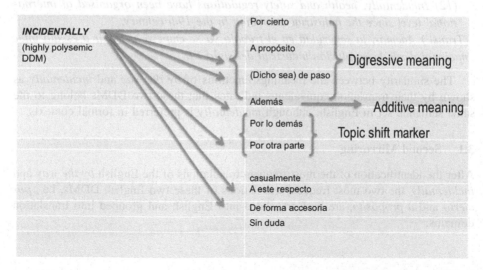

Fig. 2. Semantic groupings of *incidentally* on the basis of translation equivalents

As in the case of *by the way*, the most frequent meaning/function of *incidentally* is to express *a digression from the current topic* (Fraser 2009: 895), as in examples (7), (8) and (9) below (English DDM in red):

(7) Incidentally, in Belgium, we are all too familiar with this.
(8) Incidentally, the largest and most successful firms in America and in the world - Fidelity is a good example - are exactly of this type.
(9) Japan, incidentally, ties its debt relief to responsibility to buy Japanese ex ports.

The Spanish translations also show this by using the DDMs *por cierto, a propósito* and *dicho sea de paso*, with clear digressive functions in Spanish. As in the case of *by the way*, the Spanish DDM *por cierto* is the most frequently used and the most lexicalized of all.

The second most frequent meaning/function of *incidentally* is to express a topic shift, as illustrated in examples (10) and (11). The Spanish translations capture this meaning/function through the use of markers such as *por otro lado* and *por otra parte*, which are typicaly topic-shift markers in Spanish (in blue):

(10 Incidentally, this must be done through dialogue with the candidate coun tries, as the Savary report rightly stresses.
(Transl.) Por lo demás, será preciso dialogar con los países candidatos, esto lo acentúa con razón el informe de nuestro colega, el Sr. Savary.
(11) That was my position from the outset, incidentally.
(Transl.) Ésta fue, por otra parte, mi posición desde el principio.

As in the case of *by the way*, the corpus analysis of the translations reveals a third meaning/function of *incidentally*, which has not been considered in monolingual studies and which has been discovered by looking at the translation correspondences: this is the meaning captured by *además* in Spanish, indicating an addition to the content of the main message, as in example (12) below:

(12) Incidentally, health and safety regulations have been organised at interna-tional level since the industrial revolution in the 19th century.
(Transl.) Además, la seguridad en el trabajo ya se empezó a definir a escala inter nacional desde la revolución industrial del siglo XIX.

The similarity between the meanings/functions of *by the way* and *incidentally* as shown by their translation equivalents, indicates that these two DDMs belong to the same semantic set in English, although *incidentally* is preferred in formal contexts.

3.1   Second Mirroring

After the identification of the most frequent translations of the English *by the way* and *incidentally*, the two most frequent translations of these two English DDMs, i.e., *por cierto* and *a propósito*, are back-translated into English and grouped into translation domains.

Translation Correspondences of *por cierto*. As shown in Table 3, *por cierto* is back-translated into English by a wide variety of English forms in all four parallel datasets: the most frequent translation is the English DDM *by the way*, with a total frequency of 3,243 occurrences (2.16 p.m/w). This is no surprise, given the fact that *por cierto* is the most lexicalized of all Spanish DDMs and the most frequent as well, similar in many uses to the most frequent English DDM *by the way*.

Table 3. Distribution of translations of *por cierto* into English in four parallel corpora

Spanish Original	English Transl.	FREQUENCY IN CORPORA				
		M-NOT	OPEN SUBT.	EUROPARL7	OPUS2	TOTAL
POR CIERTO	By the way	1 (1m)	0	119 (1.96 p.m) (60 million)	3,123 (3.59 p.m) (1440 million)	3,243 (2.16 p.m)
	indeed		0	0	418 (0.48 p.m)	418 (0.48 p.m)
	Incidentally		0	118 (1.94 per million)	375 (0.43 p.m)	493 (0.32 p. m)
	Certainly		0	9 (0.15 per million)	309 (0.35 p.m)	318 (0.21 p.m)
	In fact		0	119 (1.96 p.m)	84 (0.1 p.m)	203 (0.13 p.m)
	Moreover		0	8 (0.13 p.m)	45 (0.05 p.m)	53 (0.03 p.m)
	Furthermore		0	8 (0.13 p.m)	34 (0.04 p.m)	42 (0.028 p.m)
	actually		0	9 (0.15 p.m)	0	9 (0.15 p.m)
	In addition		0	4 (0.07 p.m)	0	4 (0.07 p.m)
	For the rest		0	2 (0.03 p.m)	0	2 (0.03 p.m)
	True		0	1 (0.02 p.m)	0	1 (0.02 p.m)
	In a nutshell		0	1 (0.02 p.m)	0	1 (0.02 p.m)
	I must say / I might say		0	1 (0.02 p.m)	0	1 (0.02 p.m)
	As a brief aside		0	2 (0.03 p.m)	0	2 (0.03 p.m)
	For the record		0	1 (0.02 p.m)	0	1 (0.02 p.m)
	It is certain that		0	1 (0.02 p.m)	0	1 (0.02 p.m)

This is followed at quite a distance by *incidentally*, with a total frequency of 493 (0.32 p.m/w), *indeed*, only used in the spoken domain with a frequency of 418 hits (0.48 p.m/w).

These highly frequent translations are followed by other less frequent ones, such as *certainly* (318 hits, 0.21 p.m/w), *in fact* (203, 0.13 p.m/w), *moreover* (53 hits, 0.03) and *furthermore* (42 hits, 0.028 hits), among others. These less frequent translations, however, are indicative of the different meanings/functions that *por cierto* fulfills in different contexts.

Thus, along with the digressive function mirrored in the preferred translations into English, the Spanish *por cierto* is a highly polysemic marker with a variety of meanings/functions which become apparent when one looks at their translation equivalents. Translations by items such as *certainly, in fact, indeed* or *true* point to epistemic and verificative meanings which can be diachronically traced back to previous stages of the language, and that still survive in certain contexts, as referenced by the Spanish DRAE dictionary (Real Academica Española 2001).

Other translations such as *moreover* or *furthermore* point to an additive meaning which has not been detected by monolingual studies, but which also belongs to the meaning potential of the Spanish DDM.

On the basis of these translation correspondences it is possible to establish the semantic groupings which are graphically presented in Fig. 3 below:

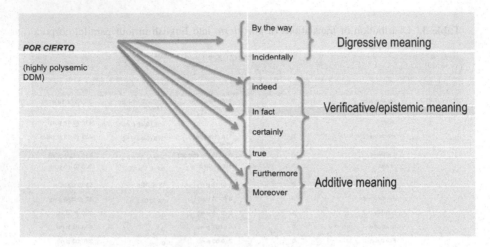

Fig. 3. Semantic groupings of *por cierto* on the basis of translation equivalents

The most frequent meaning/function of *"por cierto"* is to express *a digression from the current topic and to introduce a new one,* as most Spanish studies have identified (Acín Villa 2000; Estellés Arguedas 2011). This is illustrated by example (13) below:

(13) Por cierto, ¿con qué derecho imponen los Estados Unidos sus condiciones a los países en vías de desarrollo si ellos mismos incumplen todos los acuer dos internacionales?

(Trans.) By the way, what gives the US the right to make demands from developing countries if the US itself flouts all international agreements?

However, as the translation corpus analysis has shown, *por cierto* can also be used with an epistemic/verificative meaning, as shown by the use of *certainly, in fact* and *indeed*, in examples (14), (15) and (16):

(14) Por cierto, podemos ser cautelosos.

(Trans) Certainly we can be cautious

(15) Por cierto, el mismo fenómeno se produce en el ámbito fiscal.

(Trans) In fact, the same phenomenon occurs in tax law.

(16) ¿Quién, por cierto, quisiera que le gobernasen ministros de economía únicamente?

(Trans) [..], and indeed who would wish to be governed solely by a government of Finance Ministers?

In addition, *por cierto* has an additive meaning, as shown by the use of *moreover* and *furthermore* in the English translations, as illustrated by (17) and (18):

(17) Este excelente principio debería por cierto aplicarse también dentro_de la Unión Europea.
(Trans) This excellent principle should, moreover, be applied within the European Union as well.
(18) Es una pena, por cierto, que el Consejo no dé ninguna continuidad a esta propuesta de ciudadanía y de residencia.
(Trans) Furthermore, it is a pity that the Council has not followed up this pro posal of citizenship and residence.

This additive meaning, which has also been detected for the English DDMs, has not been previously detected in monolingual studies and it has been discovered through the translation corpus analysis.

Translation Correspondences of *a propósito*. This is the second most frequent DDM in Spanish and it is translated into English by a wide variety of English forms in all four parallel datasets: the most frequent translation is the English DDM *incidentally*, with a total frequency of 67 hits (0.04 p.m/w), followed by *with regard to* with a frequency of 49 hits (0.03 p.m/w) and *by the way* with a total frequency of 28 (0.018 p.m/w). The rest of the translations are rather infrequent, as shown in Table 4:

Table 4. Distribution of translations of a propósito into English in four parallel corpora

Spanish Original	English Transl.	FREQUENCY IN CORPORA				
		M-NOT	OPEN SUBT.	EUROPARL7	OPUS2	TOTAL
	By the way	0		18 (0.03 p.m) (60 million)	10 (0.01 p.m) (1440 million)	28 (0.018 p.m)
	Incidentally	0		48 (0.79 p.m)	19 (0.02 p.m)	67 (0.04 p.m)
A PROPÓSITO	Moreover	0		2 (0.03 p.m)	1 (less than 0.01 p.m)	3 (0.002 p.m)
	With regard to	0		42 (0.69 p.m)	7 (0.01 p.m)	49 (0.03 p.m)
	As regards	0		6 (0.01 pm)	0	6 (0.004 p.m)
	Regarding	0		6 (0.01 pm)	0	6 (0.004 p.m)
	Talking about	0		1 (0.02 p.m)	1 (less than 0.01 p.m)	2 (0.001 p.m)
	In relation to	0		2 (0.03 p.m)	0	2 (0.001 p.m)
	On the subject of	0		16 (0.26 p.m)	1 (less than 0.01 p.m)	17 (0.01 p.m)
	As far as	0		2 (0.03 p.m)	3 (less than 0.01 p.m)	5 (0.003 p.m)

The most frequent meaning/function of *a propósito* is to express *a digression from the current topic* as in example (19) below (Spanish DDM in red):

(19) *A propósito, -y la Sra. Grossetête se ha referido a ello- en la prensa han aparecido recientemente especulaciones sobre una posible tercera vía de*
infección *a través de la hierba contaminada por material fecal.*
(Transl.) Incidentally - and Mrs Grossetête referred to this - there has been recent press speculation about a third possible infection route through grass contaminated by faecal material.

This meaning is also captured by *by the way*, a less frequent translation in the four parallel corpora.

The second most frequent translation is *with regard to*, with a thematizer function. In this function, *a propósito* is followed by the preposition "*de*", as illustrated in example (20):

(20) *A propósito de la diversidad cultural, asimismo, se habla mucho de lenguas minoritarias;*
(Trans) With regard to cultural diversity, moreover, much is spoken about minority languages.

One final residual meaning is the additive one, as captured by *moreover*, but its frequency is very low in the four parallel corpora.

On the basis of these translation correspondences it is possible to establish the semantic groupings which are graphically presented in Fig. 4 below:

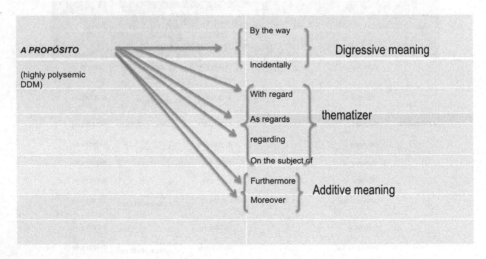

Fig. 4. Semantic groupings of *a propósito* on the basis of translation equivalents

4 Summary and Pointers for the Future

The present study has shown that it is possible to construct semantic fields of DDMs in English and Spanish on the basis of translation equivalents. DDMs, like many other DMs, are semantically underspecified and have a large number of different translations representing different senses and implicatures. Different items are indeed related to each other on the basis of closeness and remoteness of meaning; some are closer to each other than others, and translations show this.

As the present study has shown, the translation correspondences of these DDMs can make explicit certain meanings which are less obvious from a monolingual syntagmatic analysis: this is the case of *by the way*, a highly polysemic DDM with three different meanings, revealed through the translation analysis: (a) digressive meaning (translated by *por cierto, dicho sea de paso*), (b) topic shift marker (translated by *por lo demás, por otra parte*), and (c) additive meaning (translated by *además*). The last meaning was not previously identified in the existing monolingual analysis.

Similarly, the analysis of *por cierto*, the most lexicalized DDM in Spanish, and a highly polysemic one, has shown that it is possible to distinguish three different meanings/semantic fields, revealed through the translation correspondences: (a) an epistemic/verificative meaning (translated by *indeed, in fact, certainly*); (b) a digressive meaning (translated by *by the way, incidentally*); and (c) and additive meaning (translated by *furthermore, moreover*).

It is expected that the findings of this study can be used not only for translation research and teaching, but can guide the annotation of parallel corpora so that they can be used as training data for computational tasks such as, for example, Machine Translation. Further translational analysis of other DMs in English and Spanish as well as in other languages will confirm the explanatory power and the usefulness of the translation method for the study of the meanings of DMs from a cross-linguistic perspective.

References

Acín Villa, E.: 'Por cierto' 'a propósito' y otros digresivos. In: Lengua y discurso. Estudios dedicados al profesor Vidal Lamíquiz, Madrid, Arco Libros, pp. 59–72 (2000)

Aijmer, K.: Translating discourse particles: a case of complex translation. In: Incorporating Corpora: The Linguist and the Translator, pp. 95–116. Multilingual Matters, Clevedon (2007)

Beeching, K.: A parallel corpus approach to investigating semantic change. In: Advances in Corpus-Based Contrastive Linguistics. Studies in honour of Stig Johansson, pp. 103–125. John Benjamins, Amsterdam (2013)

Dyvik, H.: A translational basis for semantics. In: Johansson, S., Oksefjell, S. (eds.) Corpora and Crosslinguistic Research: Theory, Method and Case Studies, pp. 51–86. Rodopi (1998)

Dyvik, H.: Translations as semantic mirrors: from parallel corpus to worldnet. In: Language and Computers, Advances in Corpus Linguistics. Papers from the 23rd International Conference on English Language Research on Computerized Corpora (ICAME 23), Göteborg, 22–26 May 2002, pp. 311–326. Rodopi, Amsterdam (2004)

Dyvik, H.: Translations as a semantic knowledge source. In: Proceedings of the Second Baltic Conference on Human Language Technologies, Tallin, Estland, pp. 27–38 (2005)

Estellés Arguedas, M.: Gramaticalización y paradigmas: Un estudio a partir de los denominados marcadores de digresión en español. Peter Lang Verlag, Frankfurt (2011)

Fraser, B.: Topic orientation markers. J. Pragmat. **41**, 892–898 (2009)

Koehn, P.: EuroParl: a parallel corpus for statistical machine translation. In: Proceedings of the Machine Translation Summit, Phuket, Thailand, pp. 79–86 (2005)

Lavid, J., Arús, J., DeClerck, B., Hoste, V.: Creation of a high-quality, register-diversified parallel corpus for linguistic and computational investigations. In: Current Work in Corpus Linguistics: Working with Traditionally- conceived Corpora and Beyond. Selected Papers from the 7th International Conference on Corpus Linguistics (CILC2015). Procedia - Social and Behavioral Sciences, vol. 198, pp. 249–256 (2015)

Martín Zorraquino, M.A., Portolés, J.: Los marcadores del discurso. In: Gramática descriptiva de la lengua española, Madrid, Espasa Calpe, Chap. 63 (1999)

Mateo Rodriguez, J.E.: Los marcadores digresivos. Estudio especial de 'por cierto' en español actual. In: Scripta Philologica in Memoriam Manuel Taboada Cid. Universidade da Coruña, La Coruña (1996)

Noël, D.: Translations as evidence of semantics: an illustration. Linguistics **41**(4), 757–785 (2003)

Pons, S., Estellés Arguedas, M.: Expressing digression linguistically: do digressive markers exist? J. Pragm. **41**, 921–936 (2009)

Real Academia Española: Diccionario de la lengua española [Dictionary of the Spanish Language], 22nd edn., Madrid, Spain (2001)

Tiedemann, J.: News from OPUS - a collection of multilingual parallel corpora with tools and interfaces. In: Recent Advances in Natural Language Processing, vol. V, pp. 237–248. John Benjamins, Amsterdam/Philadelphia (2009)

Traugott, E.C.: The development of digressive discourse topic-shift markers in English. J. Pragmat. (in press). https://doi.org/10.1016/j.pragma.2019.02.002

Context-Induced Reinterpretation of Phraseological Verbs

Phrasal Verbs in Late Modern English

Ljubica Leone[✉]

University of Salerno, 84084 Fisciano, SA, Italy
ljubical@libero.it

Abstract. The aim of the present study is to examine the semantic changes affecting phraseological verbs, and specifically phrasal verbs (hereafter PVs), during the Late Modern English period (1750–1850). In particular, the objective is to describe cases of context-induced reinterpretation and the related phenomena of lexicalization and/or idiomatization. Semantic changes undergone by PVs to date have mainly been linked to metaphoric and metonymic processes and to analogical thinking (Brinton 1988). However, they have never been examined following a phraseological perspective (Sinclair 1991, 2004), and considering the "extended" context of use (Stubbs 2002) as catalyst for change. In this view, if the meaning of a single word is the result of its interaction with the immediate context (Bublitz 1996), then the semantic evolution of PVs should be seen as the result of their context-induced reinterpretation. The present research has been conducted on the Late Modern English-Old Bailey Corpus (1750–1850), a corpus compiled by drawing texts from the Proceedings of the Old Bailey, London Central Criminal Court, and annotated with the Visual Interactive Syntax Learning interface (VISL). The findings reveal that the lexical environment has played a major role in the semantic renewal of PVs: they were affected by the development of aspectual properties in some cases, in others, they were instead characterized by the intensification of the already acquired aspectual features, both driven by processes of lexicalization and idiomatization.

Keywords: Phrasal verbs · Reinterpretation · Context · Late Modern

1 Introduction

The present study aims to describe the semantic evolution of phraseological verbs during the Late Modern English (LModE) period (1750–1850). Specifically, the objective is to examine the lexical environment of PVs and to describe context-induced changes and the related phenomena of lexicalization and/or idiomatization. Common to most works on PVs, they are phraseological verbs resulting from the analytic tendency of English in its historical development and emerging as segmentalized structures complex in constituency (Brinton 1988, 1996; Thim 2012) as they are formed by a verb + an adverbial particle (e.g. *to come in, to set up, to take up, etc.*) which exhibit the lexeme status (Quirk et al. 1985; Biber et al. 1999). Semantically, PVs are

© Springer Nature Switzerland AG 2019
G. Corpas Pastor and R. Mitkov (Eds.): Europhras 2019, LNAI 11755, pp. 253–267, 2019.
https://doi.org/10.1007/978-3-030-30135-4_19

characterized by a different degree of idiomaticity and set on a semantic cline ranging from literal to aspectual[1] (i.e. verbs denoting durative or telic aspect), and idiomatic verbs (Dixon 1982; Thim 2012), overall behaving as "more or less cohesive unit[s]" (Brinton 1996: 188).

This complex characterization is the result of historical paths endorsed by the members of this verb group, having emerged as a result of processes of grammaticalization, lexicalization and idiomatization[2] (Brinton and Traugott 2005; Rodríguez-Puente 2013) and as the effect of interactive factors linked to foreign influence, both Scandinavian and Latin, or to "purely language-internal" changes (Claridge 2000: 87), along with the mechanisms working to the conventionalization of diverse meanings. Semantic changes affecting PVs, in particular, have mainly been studied by means of metaphoric and metonymic processes (Brinton 1988; Rodríguez-Puente 2013), and by highlighting the role of conversational inferences and analogical thinking. However, in no cases have they been approached by adopting a phraseological perspective (Sinclair 1991, 2004), and considering the potentiality of "extended" context of use (Stubbs 2002), i.e. the node and its surroundings, as catalyst for change. This would entail the need to embrace an approach devoted to the study of "meaning is use" which "tends to emphasize that the units of meaning are not individual words, but longer multi-word units, collocations and extended phrasal units of various kinds" (Stubbs 2007: 317).

This is the spot where the historical perspective to the study of change affecting PVs meets the Neo-Firthian approach claiming that language is a system of relations (Sinclair 1991, 2004), and the syntagmatic relations existing between the various "co-occurring" elements *create* the basis to new interpretations that would also "be derived from the contextual conditions of a word's use" (Murphy 2003: 20). At the same time, the overall effect of this is to *stimulate* the renewal of meaning of the node, here consisting of verbs that are complex in shape, given that it is context which allows us "to map the word to a concept or set of concepts" (Murphy 2003: 20). From this perspective, if "meaning resides not in a single word but in several words", and that "the word adopts semantic features from an adjacent item"[3] (Bublitz 1996: 9,11, cited in Stewart 2010: 9), then it is possible to conceptualize the diachronic evolution of linguistic elements as context-induced phenomena that potentially could affect a single item, simple or phraseological in its shape. This is no more than to say that diachronically the use of a word can be influenced by the lexical environment and it may be "colored" accordingly (Bublitz 1996) thanks to specific "prosodies" of the context. Semantic prosody is here a concept that departs from its conceptualization as "evaluation" and linked to the "attitude (...) to certainty or obligation or desirability or any of a number of other sets of values" (Thompson and Hunston 1999: 5). Lexical context is interpreted as the means of a speaker's emotional attitude toward a situation

---

[1] Aspectual PVs contain particles which mark the *aktionsart* of the verb (Thim 2012: 16–19). *Aktionsart* is "an indication of the intrinsic temporal qualities of a situation" (Brinton 1988: 3).

[2] Grammaticalization is "the change whereby (...) [an] item may become more grammatical", whereas lexicalization is intended as the change "that results in the production of new lexical/contentful forms" (Brinton and Traugott 2005: 99, 96). Idiomatization is the linguistic process prompting increasing demotivation.

[3] I am borrowing here the concept coined by Bublitz (1996) in his investigation on semantic prosody.

(Stewart 2010: 21), and it is able to convey positive or negative associations, rather than, as is the case here, as a "discourse phenomenon [which] hinges so critically on the immediate lexical environment" (Stewart 2010: 56). Seen in this way, semantic prosody should be related to "the overall communicative function of the unit of meaning" (Philip 2011: 60) and touches areas linked to lexical semantics and connotative values, and in this scenario, the neighboring context may be conceived as able first to add nuances and then to affect the whole connotation.

If this notion is then associated with the semantic evolution of PVs over the LMod era, then it naturally follows that also here the neighboring context should be taken into account to evaluate the phenomena of semantic shifting and idiomatization. The immediate implication from this is that PVs are multi-word units that should be analyzed as single lexemes, them being phraseological in nature when following the traditional approach to phraseology of the Soviet school (Cowie 1998). At the same time, they need to be analyzed by accounting for the more recent phraseological approach based on Sinclair's pioneering works (1991, 2004), which considers the immediate context of use as a leading factor in the interpretation of the meanings, in this way moving behind a narrow definition of "meaning" to embrace the extended notion of "connotation" (Murphy 2003): the basic idea is that "in natural language different aspects of a word's meaning potential are activated by different collocations" (Hanks 2017: 54). On the other hand, this also relates to the idea commonly associated with the creation of a new grammatical meaning where contextual variation is "a powerful tool" in the understanding of "strategies of meaning transfer" (Heine 2002: 83, 96), a concept that can be extended to grammaticalized and lexicalized forms like PVs as well.

Following these principles and adopting a corpus-based methodology, the present research aims to examine whether and the extent to which the lexical context promoted semantic changes in PVs, trying to define the path the single instances followed. The present study has been undertaken on the Late Modern English-Old Bailey Corpus (LModE-OBC), a corpus compiled by drawing texts from the Proceedings of the Old Bailey (https://www.oldbaileyonline.org), London Central Criminal Court, and annotated with the Visual Interactive Syntax Learning interface (VISL) (https://www.beta.visl.sdu.dk). The corpus covers the century 1750–1850 and thus focuses on part of the LMod era which is the period that, in my opinion, due to its similarity and temporal proximity to Present Day English (PDE),[4] and the consistent number of already formed PVs, is more than any other the privileged area where the phenomenon of semantic shifting took place: the basic idea is that once a new coinage has been established, this may undergo further changes affecting its semantic substance.

This paper is organized as follows: Sect. 2 introduces the theoretical background while Sect. 3 describes the present study and provides details on the data and methodology used. Section 4 is devoted to the discussion of the findings and the evaluation of the role of context in semantic shift of PVs dating back to the LModE era (1750–1850).

---

[4] The LModE period is linked to the latter end of the standardization process and, linguistically speaking, is characterized by many features common to PDE but also by still ongoing changes (Tieken-Boon van Ostade 2009; Hundt 2014).

2   Theoretical Background

PVs are multi-word verbs composed of a base verb and an adverbial particle (Biber et al. 1999: 403), e.g. *to come by, to go on, to set up, to take up,* which behave semantically and syntactically as a single lexical unit (Quirk et al. 1985: 1150).

Syntactically, they are set "at an interface of syntax and morphology" (Thim 2012: 32) and considered as lexemes complex in structure exhibiting specific linguistic behavior derived from the phraseological constituency, as in the case of transitive PVs that allow two diverse complementary distributional properties, named by their post-particle and mid-position order, where the object is placed after the adverbial particle or set in the middle between the verb and the particle (Biber et al. 1999: 932–935).

With respect to semantics, PVs are characterized by different degree of compositionality with some instances literal in meaning, others semi-compositional and aspectual, others idiomatic (Thim 2012), and in the majority of the cases substitutable with "a polysyllabic verb of Romance origin, with very similar meaning" (Dixon 1982: 3, 4) further proving their unitary phraseological status. PVs are, indeed, not "words" in the general sense supported within the frameworks which account for a morphologically defined word class (Quirk et al. 1985: 1150), but rather phraseological units classified as "referential phrasemes" conveying a content message (Granger and Paquot 2008: 43; cf. Gries 2008: 7).

The tripartite semantic characterization leading from literal to semi-compositional, and then to non-compositional PVs, is a leading aspect in their semantic treatment. In addition to the items where the meaning is the result of the combinatory effect of the base verbs and the following particles as in *to carry out, to come in,* there are, at the extreme pole, verbs including *to get by, to give up,* whose connotation is not easily conceivable as the sum of their parts (Thim 2012: 11–20; cf. Rodríguez-Puente 2012: 71–90). In the middle, between them, there is one group that is considered to be semi-compositional, which includes aspectual PVs, where the base verb combines with particle marking aspect and the whole combination conveying aspectual meaning, as in *to finish up, to go on, to use up* (Brinton 1988: 168; Thim 2012: 17). Particles in this case contribute to the meaning of the string which turns out to be similar to other kinds of verbs behaving as aspectualizers as, for example, could be the case with *to begin, to continue, to start,* and thus, the whole combination conveys a durative or telic connotation (Brinton 1988: 168). Overall, this has inspired the idea that PVs are semantically set on a *continuum* where "the meanings range on a cline from purely compositional to highly idiomatic" (Thim 2012: 11).

A common position shared by many historical works (Brinton 1988; Rodríguez-Puente 2013) is that PVs are the result of diachronic processes often interacting each other. Indeed, these verbs have been examined on the basis of phenomena linked to the processes of grammaticalization prompting the decategorialization of linguistic items to the adverbial status and its lexicalization intended as univerbation (Brinton and Traugott 2005: 48) of particles with the preceding base verbs. PVs underwent a gradual process of change also due to the contribution of phenomena associated with syntactic reanalysis, direct formation and analogical generalization, a process of change that started in the Middle English period and that continued during the LMod era (Denison

1981; Claridge 2000; Rodríguez-Puente 2013; Leone 2016a). At the same time, idiomatization led to the coinage of new phraseological meanings, along with the development of aspectual connotation and renewal of already formed instances. More specifically, further changes affected the new lexeme creating the basis now to the semantic shift from locative/spatial literal meaning to aspectual connotation or to the idiomatic one (Brinton 1988; Rodríguez-Puente 2013), now even to the semantic reanalysis of the meanings and the intensification of the already acquired properties, resulting in the increase of idiomaticity. This implies that complex paths characterized PVs with the passage of time. In this respect, the existing literature is rich, and PVs have been extensively examined (Brinton 1988; Thim 2012; Rodríguez-Puente 2013), but without tying in directly the question of the role of lexical context in semantic shift and increasing idiomatization. This means that the description of the context of use of these verbs[5] and the dependence of connotative features upon the lexical environment has not been an object of analysis to date.

On the basis of these considerations, a major role is expected here to be that of lexicalization not intended as the change leading to "UNIVERBATION, of a syntactic phrase or construction into a single word" (Brinton and Traugott 2005: 48) but rather as resulting in the modification of the extant connotation and increasing internal cohesion of constituents in phraseological items; at the same time, it is likely that an invaluable contribution should be that of the process of idiomatization, identified with what comes after the emergence of the aspectual from literal meaning, which may withstand the intensification of the already acquired aspectual connotation and increasing non-compositionality. In all the cases, semantic changes could have been hypothetically promoted by contextual factors and by the lexical environment, which is the issue under investigation here.

3   The Present Study

3.1   Aims

The present study is ongoing research which aims to examine the role of context in the phenomena of semantic shift and idiomatization of PVs during the LModE period and in particular over the years 1750–1850. My intention is to contribute to the knowledge of the semantic evolution of PVs, and in particular I will focus my attention on literal/aspectual verbs, which are more prone to change than idiomatic ones, and the area majorly characterized, in all likelihood, by increasing idiomatization. It is possible to hypothesize that further changes affected already established PVs gathering new connotative properties and that this could be due to the co-occurrence of specific lexical environment, in some cases modifying their non-compositionality as the effect of a reinterpretation driven by context-specific factors. In particular, the aims are:

---

[5] The importance of the lexical environment has been mentioned by Leone (2016b) but not extensively examined.

- To study the semantic evolution of literal/aspectual PVs over the years 1750–1850 taking a phraseological perspective;
- To examine whether and the extent the lexical environment promoted the semantic reinterpretation of literal/aspectual PVs by means of lexicalization and idiomatization.

3.2   The Corpus

The corpus used to undertake the present research is the Late Modern English-Old Bailey Corpus (LModE-OBC), a corpus of 1,008,234 tokens covering the century 1750–1850.

The corpus has been compiled taking a selection of texts from the Proceedings of the Old Bailey, London Central Criminal Court, which are easily accessible online at https://www.oldbaileyonline.org/, and that constitutes an important source of spoken data from the period predating audio recording technology (Huber 2007). Indeed, the LModE-OBC contains recordings of speech from the past, specifically belonging to the genre of trials. The LModE-OBC is divided into five subcorpora each containing 200,000 words and covering a span of two decades: Subcorpus-1 (1750–1769), Subcorpus-2 (1770–1789), Subcorpus-3 (1790–1809), Subcorpus-4 (1810–1829), and Subcorpus-5 (1830–1849).

The LModE-OBC has been annotated by means of the parser called VISL (Visual Interactive Syntax Learning) interface (https://www.beta.visl.sdu.dk), which enriched the data with POS tags, including V (verb), ADV (adverb) followed by both @ADVL (free adverbial not attached to verb) and @MV < (main verb-attached particle), which are those of major interest in the present study.

3.3   Procedure

The extraction of PVs and the selection of the immediate lexical context has been conducted on both the annotated and unannotated version of the corpus.

In the first case, I have selected the tags marking verbs followed by non-verbal elements that could have been potentially adverbial in nature, differentiating the free combinations from those instances that are proper PVs; in the second case, instead, the attention has been on the selected PVs and their immediate context in order to evaluate the possible phenomena of lexicalization and idiomatization determined by the context. The data retrieval has been undertaken in both cases by using concordancers, here the ConcApp4, and WordSmithTools 6.0 (Scott 2013) that allow the selection of the node (=the single PVs) and whatever else occurs in the selected span of 3:3, which is then evaluated following a phraseological perspective. The data have been treated statistically by means of raw frequencies (Rf) and percentages.

The findings also benefit from a comparison with data selected from the ARCHER corpus (legal section) dating back to the years 1750–1850 (https://www.alc.manchester. ac.uk/archer), and from the eminent Oxford English Dictionary (OED), both used for reference purposes.

4 Results and Discussion

The analysis of the data reveals that, while some PVs emerged as aspectual verbs shifting from literal combinations, others which were already conventionalized as aspectual forms during the LMod era, only undertook a process leading to the intensification of their idiomatic properties transferring occasionally their meaning to other domains in consequence of the metaphoric extension of the original connotation. In other words, while some PVs moved from the group of literal to that of semi-compositional, a number of semi-compositional PVs became more opaque in meaning even preserving their original extant aspectual connotation.

At this point, the question is whether these two paths were in some ways promoted by context-induced factors and, if so, the way the lexical environment has created the condition to exploit new more idiomatic nuances. The limited space here does not permit an extensive evaluation of instances but I have selected some verbs (i.e. *to take away, to throw away* and *to lock up*), which can be considered as case studies to the comprehension of processes of innovation as well as to the evaluation of the role of context in such changes.

4.1 Three Case Studies of Context-Induced Changes

Examples of the path typically leading from a literal connotation to an aspectual meaning, include verbs like *to take away* which, during the years 1750–1850, was used as a literal PV and also started to enrich its semantic properties advancing along the cline of idiomaticity and acquiring an aspectual telic connotation. Specifically, its occurrence in the literal connotation of "to take elsewhere" (OED) exhibits well established features in the LModE as proven by many examples in both the LModE-OBC, as in (1)–(3), and the ARCHER, as in (4):

(1) *I was before Justice Scott, the Monday after Christmas; there James Grief produced some of my goods which <u>were taken away</u> (1750s).*

(2) *The prisoner said he had a knife in his hand, and tumbled down; I staid till the body <u>was taken away</u> on a shutter - the prisoner was then at her own door, holding a light (1810s).*

(3) *Nothing was taken out; a table-cloth was removed, but <u>not taken away;</u> the corner was drawn out of the window as far as they could draw it (1790s).*

(4) *That, by another charter, of they were made a county-borough, and the two bailiffs <u>taken away</u>, and two sheriffs appointed in their room (ARCHER 1756phil_14b).*

This is a kind of connotation which, as reported in the OED, first attested in 1372, as in (5), and that it is still used in PDE:

(5) *Mi bodi dey3et for mannis sake, Senful soules in helle lake—To hem i go <u>awey to take</u> (OED - 1372 in C. Brown Relig. Lyrics 14th Cent. (1924) 86).*

However, beyond this stability, this verb gradually changed over the years, and this was due to context-induced reinterpretation of the extant meaning. In addition to the well-established and concrete objects of *things, money, coat, clothes, key, bundles,* the use of this verb with collocates belonging to different semantic fields and characterized by different degree of abstractness turned out to be the switching context, intended as context characterized by ambiguity (Heine 2002: 83–101), to the semantic reinterpretation of its meaning: it shifted from the meaning of "to take elsewhere", to that of "to take elsewhere and completely", and then "to deprive physically" of something. In particular, it was since the 1750s that the verb started to be followed by the collocate *life*, as in (6), and to exhibit the aspectual connotation of "to take elsewhere and completely/to deprive physically". From then on, and especially from the 1790s, it extended its context of use and enriched its collocational profile with, for example, collocates such as *senses, sight, breath,* as in (7)–(9), further reinforcing the new interpretation:

(6) *He got hold of me and knocked me down upon the stones, and ran a chissel into my cheek, with intent to take my life away (1750s).*

(7) *You thought you could got some of this man's money, you liked it well enough when you won, and you would have liked to have got his forty pounds well enough? - I believe my senses were taken away by what was in the drink (1790s).*

(8) *When I received a violent blow at the back part of my head I did not fall it stunned me it confused my senses and took my sight away (1830s).*

(9) *I received a blow on my side, which took my breath away, till I got about six houses off (1810s).*

Thus, the variation of the collocates and the inclusion of words such as *senses, sight, breath,* as in (7)–(9) above, makes semantic innovation inevitable. The syntagmatic relation existing between the PV and the context promotes the movement from a former literal meaning to the renewed aspectual/figurative one.

Looking at the distribution across the decades of both the meanings, as shown in Table 1 below, it becomes evident that, despite the low frequency of occurrence of *to take away* with abstract collocates, - which are also those which promote the idiomatization of the literal meaning, - these results are likewise significant. Indeed, the comparison between the first and the second column reveals that the use in abstract contexts is gradually attested at a higher level in terms of percentages when compared with the other extant use, especially in 1830s.

Table 1. To take away.

To take away	Literal meaning/Concrete collocates		Aspectual meaning/Abstract collocates	
	Rf	%	Rf	%
1750s	44	93.6%	3	6.3%
1770s	40	81.6%	9	18.3%
1790s	24	82.7%	5	17.2%
1810s	40	88.8%	5	11.1%
1830s	21	77.7%	6	22.2%

The point is that the use of *to take away* with abstract collocates gradually, though barely detectably, moved into the territory of the literal use and inspired an interpretation which would have been incompatible with that attested in the case of concrete lexemes: it overall forced a new mapping of the extant meaning and a sort of "adaptation" of it to the new context. In this regard, the image of space in "to take elsewhere" may be regarded as mapped on a more abstract level and seen as referring to the figurative connotation of "to take elsewhere and completely" and, then, to that of "to deprive physically of something". In particular, when considering this change in terms of lexicalization and idiomatization, of course, connotation is here renovated and the whole string can be seen as characterized by both processes: this verb undergoes idiomatization since the collocational patterns reactivate in a more idiomatic sense the already existing connotation, and motivate a metaphoric shift and the creation of the mental picture of "deprivation" on the basis of the semantic associations between the PV and its object; at the same time, it is affected by lexicalization since it increases its internal cohesion, and this, for the reasons reported above, could be linked to context-induced factors.

Moreover, since then, this verb started to refer to the changing status of somebody when "deprived of the liberty", which, overall, prompted the intensification of the aspectual features and gave rise to the more idiomatic connotation of "to confine", as in (10)–(11):

(10) *What were the mob about as you were taking him to the station? A. We expected they would* take the prisoner away. *They hallooed out, "*Take him away, take him away*" (1830s).*

(11) *They were in King-street, somewhere by Grosvenor-street - the officer found them there and* took them away *- I took the prisoner into custody (1830s).*

This latter case is a kind of meaning that is not attested before the 1830s where there are even 14 tokens matching this use, a number which is undoubtedly very low, but if one imagines that this new interpretation first takes hold in those years, of course, it would follow that this should be seen as the incipit of something new. This interpretation seems, however, to be inspired by the whole context rather than specifically induced by collocates, and it opens another area of investigation namely the semantic renewal of PVs which is linked to analogical thinking. Indeed, this latter case is a case of idiomatization which is not linked to the context, but rather the contrary is true: the context is adapted to this new meaning, and the verb is idiomatized as the effect of other factors such as analogical thinking and pragmatic matters. Thus, it is possible to suppose the existence of a bidirectional process of change: one is that set from collocates to the node which comes to be influenced by them; another that sees the verb as able to select its collocates according to its new connotative features.

Overall, the major aspect in the evolution of *to take away* is that it underwent both metaphorization intended as "a metaphoric shift from movement in space to movement in time" (Eckardt 2006: 35) and increasing non-compositionality, but the resulting meaning of "to deprive" even being opaque, cannot be seen as totally idiomatized. The reason is that the relationship between the original literal connotation is not totally destroyed as in proper idiomatization, but rather it is still present despite it being more idiomatic and the whole connotation shifted along the cline of idiomatization.

These considerations also apply to other PVs, which during the century 1750–1850 underwent idiomatization/lexicalization such as *to throw away, to lock up,* which generalized their well-established aspectual telic features transferring their meaning to other domains in consequence of the extension of the original connotation. In particular, these instances, unlike verbs of the kind of *to take away,* were already used as aspectual PVs from the beginning of the LModE age. Thus, they did not shift to idiomatic and aspectual telic from literal meaning but, instead, they only went further along the cline of idiomaticity via the intensification of aspectual properties and increasing idiomatization.

As for *to throw away,* for example, it has the meaning of "to cast away" and the more opaque of "to waste", as the OED reports, established in 1530 and 1653 respectively, as in (12)–(13), and they were well conventionalized in use during the following years as witnessed by occurrences conveying these meanings in the data, as in (14)–(15):

(12)   *I throwe awaye, as we do thynges that we care nat for.., je deguerpis,..je desjecte (OED 1530 J. PALSGRAVE Lesclarcissement 756/2).*

(13)   *We are pleased to throw away our time (OED 1653 BP. J. TAYLOR Ενιαυτος: Course of Serm. I. xxii. 294).*

(14)   *The pawnbroker said he would not give him five shillings for it; and then he gave him half-a-crown, and he was going to throw away the ticket (1790s).*

(15)   *I believe to be the money he threw away. I found it wide from the other, in the way that he threw it. (1770s).*

Proof of this acquired stability is that instances of *to throw away* conveying this meaning also occur in the reference corpus, i.e. the ARCHER, a fact that suggests that this semi-compositional form should be regarded as fossilized and stably stored in the mental lexicon:

(16)   *No, no, madam, you shall throw away no more sums on such unmeaning luxury. (ARCHER 1777sher_d4b).*

In particular, the occurrence of *to throw away* with this meaning is inevitable when used in collocation with words such as *the money, time, the ticket, the stockings* as emerging from the examination of the data. This of course is something that is not conceivable when the collocates instead belong to another semantic field, as it is the case of *a great deal* and *the raisings* as in (17)–(18):

(17)   *"That is a great deal too much to throw away at present; it is quite a speculative thing" Bouch said, "I will take 35 l. for it" after we had talked the thing over some little time (1830s).*

(18)   *I heard of the robbery, and went home, and threw the raisings away. I have been thirty-six years in the parish and fourteen in His Majesty's service (1830s).*

Overall, this implies that, while well-established in its aspectual connotation, it experienced further innovation on the semantic level revealing once again the role of phraseological context in determining semantic renewal: the extension of the semantic collocability of the verb led to the enrichment of the semantic nuances of the PV, which was surrounded by different entities belonging to a higher level of abstractness. In other words, in addition to the previous collocates which included items belonging to the material sphere such as *the knife, silver pieces*, or *tickets* and *money*, others characterized by an abstract referent established after the 1810s, such as *a great deal* and *the raisings*, as in (17)–(18) above. It follows that the well-established much more frequently used meanings of "to cast" and "to waste" were gradually followed by examples indicating the reinforcement of aspectual features, and moving toward the acquisition of the more abstract meaning of "to neglect", which better fits, in semantic terms, with more intangible objects. It is this, not a conceptual shift, since the referent is preserved and it is the whole context to inspire this interpretation, where only the extant traits are intensified, giving in this way further support to the idea, very common within the phraseological approach to the study of language, that "word and context are inseparable" (Stubbs 2002: 100), and that this can evolve over time operating as catalyst for change.

The path which *to throw away* followed was that from aspectual to idiomatic meaning as a result of the metaphoric shift of the original aspectual meaning to an opaque connotation where, similarly to the case of *to take away*, the derivational relationship is not totally destroyed. It is worth highlighting that, as suggested above, *to throw away* takes distance from the verb *to take away* due to an important element, which is the former case underwent only a shift from the stage "from aspectual" to that of "to more aspectual" during the years 1750–1850, giving proof of its stability in the aspectual more idiomatic meaning of "to waste" since 1653. At the same time, similar to the other case, it was involved in lexicalization in so far as it increased in term of lexicality and internal cohesion, and idiomatization which provoked a kind of metaphoric shift, which makes the lexeme non-compositional in meaning, reaching the status that is often considered as among the core feature of phraseological forms (Svensson 2008). The new meaning of course did not emerge *ex nihilo*, but rather the semantic traits of the environment were those which determined the semantic reinterpretation and the reanalysis of the components. Intended in this way, thus, over the years 1750–1850 this PV first moved along the cline of idiomaticity as the effect of "contagion" undergoing further idiomatization, and it then lexicalized once again: if increasing idiomatization is a sign of internal cohesion (Brinton and Traugott 2005: 94), and the more cohesive the more lexicalized, this verb is obviously lexicalized, in addition to being idiomatized.

The same considerations can be extended to the verb *to lock up* which occurred at first with the meaning of "to confine in a room" in 1568 (OED), as in (19)–(20), and then around 1790 with that of "to imprison", as in (21)–(22):

(19) *I have a warrant against you; and took him and put him in a room and locked him up, and went after Holderness. (1750s).*

(20) *What did you do with the sheep? - I left the sheep locked up, and took the key with me; they were the same sheep that were in the cart (1770s).*

(21) *I took them to the cage, and locked them up; I had not locked them up two minutes, before I thought I would search them again (1790s).*

(22) *Did I not tell you where they were? A. Yes: he was locked up for re-examination - I went to him and asked him where they were, and he told me without hesitation (1830s).*

The major feature is that this PV gradually increased in use in collocation with diverse referents which, unlike the verbs analyzed above, were not characterized by increasing abstractness, but rather belonging to other spheres: the previous collocates denoting objects such as *his tools, the sheep, things, a desert spoon, the house*, were set side by side with others denoting humans such as *the boy, the prisoner*. In this latter case, the verb *to lock up* started to be interpreted as "to imprison" as the effect of the lexical environment. Thus, a new image schemata was created and the new sense set among the potential phraseological realizations of it.

The trajectory of change followed by this verb is especially evident in the occurrence with the meaning of "to imprison" that is used with increasing frequency over the years 1750–1850. Table 2 shows the distribution of these two meanings over the years.

Table 2. To lock up.

To lock up	To confine in a room		To imprison	
	Rf	%	Rf	%
1750s	3	100%	/	0%
1770s	7	100%	/	0%
1790s	13	92.8%	1	7.1%
1810s	7	70%	3	30%
1830s	3	33.3%	6	66.6%

What is worthy of note here is that the second interpretation is not attested in the years 1750–1770, where the first meaning is the sole connotation with 10 tokens, but from then on the second seems gradually to establish itself. It shifted from a 7.1% in 1790 to that of 30% and 66.6% in 1810 and 1830 respectively, indicating this as the ongoing conventionalization of this meaning and related use within the linguistic community. The telicity of the particle *up* underwent once again a semantic reanalysis via idiomatization as would be the case of the examples reported in (21)–(22) above.

This overall proves that *to lock up* was affected by means of "contagion" by the immediate neighboring context, and it started to occur with the acquired meaning, that is it exhibits semantic nuances that are the result of context-induced changes occurring over time and causing the conventionalization of the new connotation. It was undoubtedly metaphor the driving force of this semantic renewal but, at the same time, following a phraseological approach, the hidden hand could be that of semantic relations which would "be derived from the contextual conditions of a word's use" (Murphy 2003: 20).

If sharing the idea reported above (see Sect. 1) that "through the context, we figure out how to map the word to a concept or set of concepts" (Murphy 2003: 20), then the immediate consequence is that the renovated connotations discussed so far are determined by the context, and that the new senses arise by the "flexibility of meaning" known as one of the causes of semantic change (Crespo 2013: 77), here intended as the ability of meaning to vary according to the context. In this respect, an indication of the changing status of PVs is that they developed polysemy, with the older meaning existing side by side with the new one, and this clearly fits the assertion whereby "words have no fixed number of senses" (Murphy 2003: 19) and that this can evolve over a long term period (Murphy 2003: 27–28). Indeed, this has been the case.

5   Conclusion

The analysis of a selection of PVs reveals that the development of aspectual/figurative meaning was still ongoing during the LMod period and characterized by a two-fold process: (1) Some PVs emerged as aspectual verbs shifting from literal combinations; (2) Others which were already conventionalized as aspectual forms only undertook a process leading to the intensification of their idiomatic properties transferring occasionally their meaning to other domains in consequence of the metaphoric extension of the extant connotation. The findings reveal that the lexical environment has created the condition to exploit new more idiomatic nuances and to favor the semantic shift and anchor the PV to a more abstract level, in some cases modifying their non-compositionality as the effect of a reinterpretation driven by context specific factors. The semantic renewal was the result of processes of lexicalization promoting the modification of the extant connotation and increasing the internal cohesion of constituents, and idiomatization which promoted the intensification of the already acquired connotation. The results reached so far highlight the necessity of further research on this topic by extending the area of investigation to other PVs trying to examine further context-induced changes affecting the semantic substances and to elucidate possible interrelation with the lexical environment.

Acknowledgements. I would like to thank Professor Rita Calabrese for her professional support.

References

Biber, D., Johansson, S., Leech, G., Conrad, S., Finegan, E.: Longman Grammar of Spoken and Written English. Pearson Education Limited, Harlow (1999)

Brinton, L.J., Traugott, E.C.: Lexicalization and Language Change. Cambridge University Press, Cambridge (2005)

Brinton, L.J.: The Development of English Aspectual System. Aspectualizers and Post-verbal Particles. Cambridge University Press, Cambridge (1988)

Brinton, L.J.: Attitudes toward increasing segmentalization. Complex and phrasal verbs in English. J. Engl. Linguist. **24**(3), 186–205 (1996)

Bublitz, W.: Semantic prosody and cohesive company: *somewhat predictable*. Leuvense Bijdragen: Tijdschrift voor Germaanse Filologie **85**(1–2), 1–32 (1996)

Claridge, C.: Multi-word Verbs in Early Modern English. A Corpus-Based Study. Rodopi, Amsterdam, Atlanta (2000)

Cowie, A.P. (ed.): Phraseology: Theory, Analysis, and Applications. Oxford University Press, Oxford (1998)

Crespo, B.: Change in Life, Change in Language. A Semantic Approach to the History of English. Peter Lang, Frankfurt am Main (2013)

Denison, D.: Aspects of the history of English group-verbs, with particular attention to the syntax of the ORMULUM. Ph.D. Dissertation, University of Oxford, Oxford (1981)

Dixon, R.M.W.: The grammar of English phrasal verbs. Aust. J. Linguist. 2(1), 1–42 (1982)

Eckardt, R.: Meaning Change in Grammaticalization. An Enquiry into Semantic Analysis. Oxford University Press, Oxford, New York (2006)

Granger, S., Paquot, M.: Disentangling the phraseological web. In: Granger, S., Meunier, F. (eds.) Phraseology. An Interdisciplinary Perspective, pp. 27–49. John Benjamins Publishing Company, Amsterdam, Philadelphia (2008)

Gries, S.T.: Phraseology and linguistic theory: a brief survey. In: Granger, S., Meunier, F. (eds.) Phraseology. An Interdisciplinary Perspective, pp. 3–25. John Benjamins Publishing Company, Amsterdam, Philadelphia (2008)

Hanks, P.: Mechanisms of meaning. In: Mitkov, R. (ed.) EUROPHRAS 2017. LNCS (LNAI), vol. 10596, pp. 54–68. Springer, Cham (2017). https://doi.org/10.1007/978-3-319-69805-2_5

Heine, B.: On the role of context in grammaticalization. In: Wischer, I., Diewald, G. (eds.) New Reflections on Grammaticalization, pp. 83–101. John Benjamins Publishing Company, Amsterdam, Philadelphia (2002)

Huber, M.: The Old Bailey Proceedings, 1674–1834. Evaluating and annotating a corpus of 18th- and 19th-century spoken English. In: Meurman-Solin, A., Nurmi, A. (eds.) Studies in Variation, Contacts, and Change in English, vol. 1, Annotating Variation and Change (2007). http://www.helsinki.fi/varieng/journal/volumes/01/huber/

Hundt, M. (ed.): Late Modern English Syntax. Cambridge University Press, Cambridge (2014)

Leone, L.: Phrasal verbs and analogical generalization in Late Modern Spoken English. ICAME J. 40, 39–62 (2016a)

Leone, L.: Aspectual and idiomatic properties of the particle on in Late Modern Spoken English. Top. Linguist. 17(1), 64–80 (2016b)

Murphy, M.L.: Semantic Relations and the Lexicon. Antonymy, Synonymy, and Other Paradigms. Cambridge University Press, Cambridge (2003)

Oxford English Dictionary (OED). http://www.oed.com

Philip, G.: Colouring Meaning. Collocation and Connotation in Figurative Language. John Benjamins Publishing Company, Amsterdam, Philadelphia (2011)

Quirk, R., Greenbaum, S., Leech, G., Svartvik, J.: A Comprehensive Grammar of the English Language. Longman, London (1985)

Rodríguez-Puente, P.: The development of non-compositional meanings in phrasal verbs: a corpus-based study. Engl. Stud. 93(1), 71–90 (2012)

Rodríguez-Puente, P.: The development of phrasal verbs in British English from 1650 to 1990: a corpus-based study. Ph.D. Dissertation, Universidade de Santiago de Compostela, Santiago de Compostela (2013)

Scott, M.: WordSmith Tools Manual. Version 6.0. Lexical Analysis Software Ltd (2013). https://lexically.net/downloads/version6/wordsmith6.pdf

Sinclair, J.: Corpus, Concordance, Collocation. Oxford University Press, Oxford (1991)

Sinclair, J.: Trust the Text. Language, Corpus and Discourse. Routledge, London, New York (2004)

Stewart, D.: Semantic Prosody. A Critical Evaluation. Routledge, London, New York (2010)

Stubbs, M.: Notes on the history of corpus linguistics and empirical semantics. In: Nenonen, M., Niemi, S. (eds.) Collocations and Idioms, pp. 317–329. Joensuu Yliopisto, Joensuu (2007)

Stubbs, M.: Words and Phrases. Corpus Studies of Lexical Semantics. Blackwell Publishing, Malden, Oxford (2002)

Svensson, M.H.: A very complex criterion of fixedness: non-compositionality. In: Granger, S., Meunier, F. (eds.) Phraseology. An Interdisciplinary Perspective, pp. 81–93. John Benjamins Publishing Company, Amsterdam, Philadelphia (2008)

The ARCHER Corpus. https://www.alc.manchester.ac.uk/archer

The Proceedings of the Old Bailey. https://www.oldbaileyonline.org

Thim, S.: Phrasal Verbs. The English Verb-Particle Construction and its History. Walter De Gruyter Mouton, Berlin, Boston (2012)

Thompson, G., Hunston, S.: Evaluation: an introduction. In: Hunston, S., Thompson, G. (eds.) Evaluation in Text. Authorial Stance and the Construction of Discourse, pp. 1–26. Oxford University Press, Oxford, New York (1999)

Tieken-Boon van Ostade, I.: An Introduction to Late Modern English. Edinburgh University Press, Edinburgh (2009)

Visual Interactive Syntax Learning (VISL). https://www.beta.visl.sdu.dk

Adjectivation of Attributive Nouns in French and Spanish: A Corpus-Based Study of NOUN +clé/clave and NOUN+éclair/relámpago Expressions

François Maniez[✉]

CRTT, Université Lumière-Lyon 2, Lyon, France
francois.maniez@univ-lyon2.fr

Abstract. N1 + N2 expressions in Romance languages have been studied extensively in the past few decades, among others by Noailly (1990), Arnaud (2018) and Van Goethem and Amiot (2019) for French, and García-Page (2011), Buenafuentes (2014) and Fernández-Domínguez (2019) for Spanish, to name but a few. The use of such expressions is spreading in Romance languages and occasionally leads to their lexicalization. They often result from ellipsis of a preposition (*code à barres > code barre(s)*, *estrella de mar > estrella mar*) and the shortened versions of these expressions gradually replace the full forms. However, semantic relations between the two nouns vary considerably, and some N2s seem to take on the role of an adjective (*rôle clé*, *solution miracle*). In this article, we study constructions in which N2s combine with various N1s in several corpora. The POS-tagged version of the *Chambers-Rostand Corpus of Journalistic French* is queried for N1 + N2 expressions, and we study some of their most productive N2s (*clé, culte, fantôme, fétiche, miracle, phare, record, vedette*) and we document their increased use in the second half of the twentieth century with the Ngram Viewer interface of the Google Books corpus. Using French and Spanish examples drawn from various corpora (Leipzig University Corpus, BYU Spanish corpora), we mostly focus on two characteristics of some of these N2s that testify to their growing adjectival function, namely agreement in number (*postes clés /puestos claves*) and predicative use (*ma visite a été éclair /mi visita fue relámpago*). Our data suggest that adjectivation of attributive N2s distinguishes them from relational adjectives, whose predicative uses are rare, although some scholars have compared such adjectives to the N2s of binominal expressions.

Keywords: Adjectivation · Attributive nouns · Binominal compounds · Corpus · Relational adjectives

1 Introduction

N1 + N2 French constructions have been the subject of numerous studies in recent decades, notably by Noailly (1990). In her frequently cited study on attributive nouns, she mentions the proliferation of sequences such as "événement minceur" or "cadeau saveur". Sablayrolles (2002), points to the recent use of nouns in attributive (*il est*

© Springer Nature Switzerland AG 2019
G. Corpas Pastor and R. Mitkov (Eds.): Europhras 2019, LNAI 11755, pp. 268–282, 2019.
https://doi.org/10.1007/978-3-030-30135-4_20

canon) or adverbial structures (*furieusement tendance*). Such sequences are common to many Romance languages (Fabre 1996, Villoing 2002, Savary 2004, Montermini 2008) and it seems that their use (which became widespread in the second half of the twentieth century) tends to increase.

French constructions of the N1 + N2 type are often interpreted as the result of an ellipsis of the preposition that separates the two nouns in the original formulation of the noun phrase. The preposition frequently disappears, especially in oral use, in phrases such as *version (sur) papier*, *études (de) marketing* or *allocations (de) chômage*. Use of such abbreviated versions is gradually increasing. Figure 1 shows how the expression *code à barre(s)* has been superseded in recent usage by an abbreviated version of the term that does not include the preposition *à*, *code barre*.

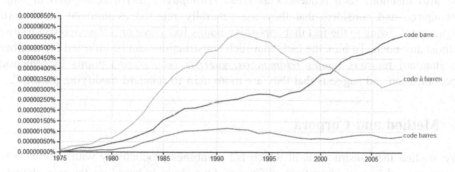

Fig. 1. Use of the expression *code (à) barre(s)* in Google Books between 1975 and 2008.

The literature on the subject emphasizes the number of different semantic relations that may exist between the two nouns (Arnaud 2001). Thus, *code barres*, *code client* and *code couleur* can respectively be paraphrased by expressing the diversity of the semantic links involved. *code (constitué de) barres*, *code (attribué à un) client*, *code (associant une) couleur (à une caractéristique donnée)*. However, in many cases, such noun phrases do not result from the ellipsis of a preposition, as N2 may have an attributive value (Arnaud 2018) reflecting a hyponymic (ISA) relation (*solution miracle*, *présentateur vedette*). N1 N2 structures may be analyzed in two ways: some consider them to be the product of an N + N composition, while others rather see them as the result of the syntactic combination linking a noun with another noun that was converted into an adjective. Since N2 often has basic adjectival properties, especially in cases where there is a hyponymic relationship between N1 and N2, some scholars have gone as far as considering N2 as an adjectival modifier (Martinho 2013).

In Spanish, García-Page (2011) describes such expressions as *hombre clave*, *viaje relámpago*, *velocidad límite* or *personaje estrella* as appositional noun phrases (*sintagmas nominales en aposición*). Among differences with compounds such as *hombre rana*, he mentions the possibility of appreciative suffixation (*hombrecito clave* vs. **hombrecito rana*) while considering that N2 plural agreement is usually not possible in either category (**viajes relámpagos*, **hombres ranas*). On this last point, he mentions the fact that some N2s in appositional noun phrases do allow for pluralization so that there is indeed variation in such sequences as *hombres clave(s)*, *velocidades límite (s)* and *proyectos modelo(s)*.

Buenafuentes (2014) also mentions the possibility to pluralize N2 in expressions belonging to both categories (*relojes despertador(es), palabras clave(s)*) while considering the pluralization of N2 as not acceptable in **productos estrellas*. She also points out that depending on the degree of institutionalization in appositive structures within an attributive environment, such N2s may or may not agree in the plural when used predicatively (i.e. in so-called copulative structures), considering *Estos momentos son claves para el país* as acceptable while **Estos productos son estrellas para la empresa* is not.

Fernández-Domínguez (2019) also points out that certain formations can be seen as compounds but also as phrases followed by an apposition, and mentions cases in which N2 inflection is attested in more colloquial registers (*perros policías, muebles-bares*). He also mentions such sequences as *visita relámpago, guerra relámpago* or *viaje relámpago* and considers that they are generally rejected as nominal multi-word expressions owing to the fact that appositive nouns like *clave* or *relámpago* can follow almost any noun. To him, the fact "that such constructions can be inflected for number in standard registers (*viajes relámpagos, guerras relámpagos*) points to semantic specialization and suggests that they are more akin to standard modifying phrases".

2 Method and Corpora

We studied the constructions in which N2 combines productively with various N1s (*assurance chômage, allocations chômage*). Our study is based on the use of three corpora. The *Chambers-Rostand Corpus of Journalistic French* (henceforth CJF) can be downoaded at http://ota.ox.ac.uk/desc/2491, and its design was described in Chambers (2005). We used it in its part-of-speech tagged version to retrieve all N1 + N2 structures. It is a relatively small corpus (just under a million words) made up of articles published in 2002 and 2003 in three French-language dailies (Le Monde, L'Humanité and La Dépêche du Midi). Using the list of the most commonly used N1 + N2 structures, we analyzed the expressions with the most productive N2s (*clé, culte, fantôme, fétiche, miracle, phare, record, symbole, vedette*).

We also used the French Corpus made available by the University of Leipzig (henceforth WFC, the acronym for *Wortschatz French corpus*), from which we retrieved the N1s that were most frequently used in combination with the N2s we had selected in the CJF using the method described above. This corpus, which contains over 37 million sentences (about 700 million words), is composed of articles drawn from French-language newspapers (which account for half of the corpus), pages crawled from various Web sites (just under a third of the corpus), and pages from Wikipedia (15% of the corpus). It can be queried at http://wortschatz.uni-leipzig.de/ws_fra/.

Finally, we examined recent evolution in their use with the Ngram Viewer interface (https://books.google.com/ngrams), which makes it possible to query the Google Books corpus (henceforth GB). The corpus, which Google claims contains about 500 billion words (thus accounting for 4% of the books published in the year 2010), was created by digitizing books in eight languages, but the distribution between these languages is not precisely known. The Ngram Viewer interface, as we shall see, is a convenient tool for diachronically oriented lexicological studies and seems to be a fairly good indicator of general language use, although some recent publications (Pechenick et al. 2005) have pointed to a certain degree of overrepresentation of scientific language in the English part of the corpus.

As an example, we reproduce below a selection of the results of a query of the WFC for collocates of the singular and plural forms of the word *clé*.

Significant Left-hand Collocates for *clé*:

élément (9266.84), rôle (8512.3), mot (8397.14), facteur (3150.36), moment (1270.03), personnage (1254.24) [...]

Significant Left-hand Collocates for *clés*:

mots (29468.4), Mots (15437.9), éléments (4163.79), chiffres (3273.52), postes (3123.66), moments (2969.83), secteurs (2629.83), points (2504.89), facteurs (2017.69), [...]

The N1s that most often precede *clé* in the WFC are the following in decreasing order of frequency: *élément, rôle, mot, facteur, moment, personnage, étape, acteur, point, témoin, secteur, poste*. The statistics provided by the WFC notably allow for the study of N2 number agreement when N1 is a plural form (see Part 4).

3   Diachronic Study of French N2S Using the NgramViewer

For each of the above-mentioned N2s, the ten most frequent N1s listed in the WFC were selected. For the sake of clarity, only the four most common nouns are displayed in the following graphs. We chose 1950–2008 as the default time range, and we extended it to previous decades in a few cases.

The graphs in Figs. 2, 3, 4 and 5 show some variety in the dates for the first attributive uses of these N2s. Indeed, some of them (e.g. *fantôme*) go back to the 1880s. The English word *record*, which entered the French language in 1882 according to the Trésor de la langue française (henceforth TLF), began to be used after a noun in the 1910s (although the TLF mentions an occurrence of the compound *courses-records* in 1884). The words *miracle* and *symbole* were first used as N2s in the 1950s, followed by *clé* and *fétiche* in the 1960s, while the most recently observed forms are *vedette* (1950s), *culte* and *phare* (1980s).

In many cases, the graphs suggest that a specific N1 N2 combination whose curve is growing rapidly (*élément clé, solution miracle, produit phare, chiffre record*) may have served as a model after which similar expressions were coined, allowing for its combination with other N1s through paradigmatic substitution and thus helping to promote the adjectival function of the noun at hand.

4   N2 Agreement in Number

Having observed that number agreement seemed to increase for most of the N2s in our original selection, we studied once again the displays provided by the GB Ngram Viewer interface for those N2s.

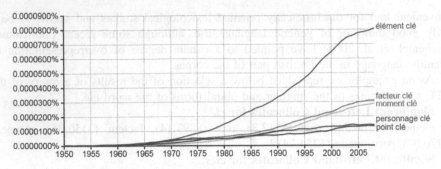

Fig. 2. N1-clé expressions in GB (1950–2008).

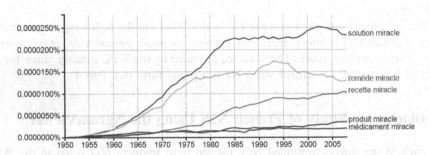

Fig. 3. N1-miracle expressions in GB (1950–2008).

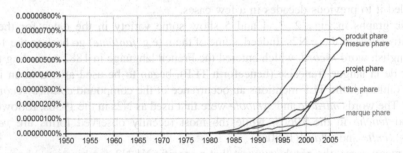

Fig. 4. N1-phare expressions in GB (1950–2008).

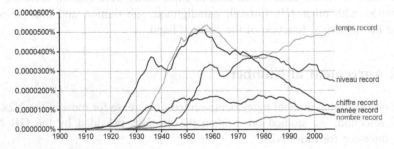

Fig. 5. N1-record expressions in GB (1900–2008).

These various displays reveal discrepancies between the numbers of plural forms, which could be due to gender constraints related to either N1 or N2. Thus, *record* seems to agree more often in number when associated with masculine N1s. The ratio between the numbers for *profits records* and *profits record* was thus 2,5 in 2008 (the last year for which Google Books data are available) while *ventes records* and *ventes record* had the same counts for that year. This could be due to the fact that some French speakers still perceive *record* as a Word borrowed from English, as plural agreement is not systematic for such loanwords (Saugera 2012). The case of the adjective *standard* also supports the hypothesis that gender might play a role, as the curves for the N1s *produits* and *modèles* are alike, whereas the spelling *méthodes standard* is now more widely used than *méthodes standards*.

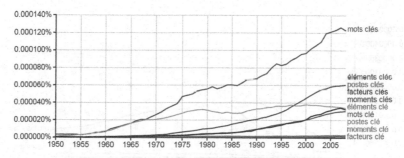

Fig. 6. Use of the N2 *clé(s)* in GB.

Figure 6 shows that when *clé* is used as an N2 (here, with the most frequent N1s in descending order of frequency, i.e. *mots*, *éléments*, *postes*, *facteurs* and *moments*), plural agreement is systematically much more frequent, with the curves corresponding to the five singular forms all merging into one at the bottom of the graph). Contrary to what could be observed in the case of the word *record*, agreement in number for *clé* is much more frequent with feminine N1s (about ten times more frequent for *questions*, *notions* and *étapes*), which may be due to the fact that *clé* is a feminine noun. The same phenomenon is observed when the N2 *miracle* is combined with N1s such as *solution*, *recettes* and *remèdes*.

Plural agreement is almost systematic for the other N2s we selected (*fantôme*, *fétiche*, *vedette*, *phare* and *culte*). Again, the fact that they all end in *-e* might foster agreement in number with feminine N1s.

However, there is a lack of agreement in number for other N2s not included in our selection such as *crédit* in expressions like *risques crédit* or *assurances crédit*. Generally speaking, plural agreement seems more likely when the semantic link between N1 and N2 is akin to a hyponymic relationship (N1 ISA N2), which is the case for *présentateurs vedettes* (*a talk show host* ISA *star*), but not for such expressions as *risques crédit*. For the same reasons, perhaps combined with French speakers' apparent reluctance to make English borrowings agree in number, this also seems to be true of N2s ending in *-ing* (*stratégies marketing*, *plans marketing*, *services marketing*).

5   N2 Agreement in Number for *N1 clé(S)/clave(S)* Compounds in French and Spanish

The selection method used for our sample in the CJF identified sequences consisting of two names separated by a space, which made any comparison with hyphenated compound names formed with the same constituents impossible. Our queries in the GB corpus led us to the hypothesis that certain binominal sequences first appear as hyphenated compounds until the hyphen gradually disappears from use. In the case of *postes clés* (Fig. 7), the four possible spellings were still used in 2008, but there are comparatively very few occurrences of *clé* in the singular, and the unhyphenated form in the plural (*postes clés*) was already more prevalent than the hyphenated form by the end of the 1960s.

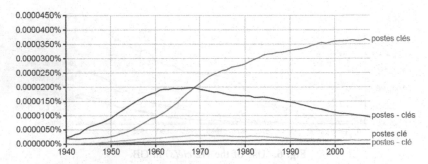

Fig. 7. Alternate spellings of *postes(-)clé(s)* on GB between 1940 and 2008.

The same evolution was observed for other N1s used in combination with *clé* (*éléments, facteurs, moments*), again with higher frequencies for the unhyphenated version since the 1960s. The most notable exception is *mots clés*, for which the prevalence of the unhyphenated spelling is more recent (late 1990s), perhaps because it was lexicalized at an earlier stage. It it worth noting that the spelling *mots(-)clefs* is very rarely encountered (between six and eight times less), whether it is hyphenated or not, and that it is the only compound in which this particular spelling is consistently used.

In English (a language in which adjectives do not agree in number), *key* has been used as a noun modifier for over a century. On GB, there are occurrences of *key word*, (also spelled *key-word* or *keyword*) as early as the 1890s, although the word was mainly used in a military context and not in a scientific one. However, the entry for *key* does not list it as an adjective in the 1913 version of Webster's Revised Unabridged Dictionary (http://machaut.uchicago.edu/websters), which only includes technically oriented compound nouns (*key bed, key seat, key wrench*). The current metaphorical uses do not appear until much later.

The first occurrences of *mot clé* date back to the 1920s in French (first in the form *mot clef*), so we can safely assume that it is a literal translation of the English *key-word*. In Spanish, *palabras claves* (more frequently used than *palabras clave* until the late 1980s on GB) has been in use since the 1930s.

A query of the Spanish corpus of the University of Leipzig (spa_newscrawl_2011, over 391 million words, hence WSC) retrieves the three nouns *momentos, puntos* and *piezas* as the main left-hand collocates for *clave* (the fact that the verb form *son* is also another of its frequently used left-hand collocates is proof of the predicative uses of *clave*) (Fig. 8).

Close examination of the results obtained for plural agreement of expressions using these three nouns followed by *clave* in the singular and plural reveals that the use of *claves* was much more frequent in the second half of the 20th century (about twice as frequent in 1990). But a reverse trend seems to have emerged recently, as the number of occurrences in the singular (*clave*) and plural (*claves*) is almost identical for *piezas* and *momentos*, and the trend has been very clearly reversed since the mid-1990s for *puntos*. In the GB Spanish corpus as a whole, use of *N1 claves* expressions has consistently increased since the 1950s, with fewer than 1,400 occurrences in the 1940s as opposed to over 20,000 both in the 1990s and 2000s.

Queries conducted on the search engine Google (14/03/2019) reveal that current usage still favors the use of *clave* in the singular form by a ratio of about two to one, as shown in Table 1, although the difference does not seem to be statistically significant in the case of *aspectos clave(s)*.

A similar search carried out in the NOW Corpus del Español (6,8 billion tokens from the 2012–2019 period) yields very similar results (Table 2). The nineteen N1-N2 expressions with *claves* as an N2 with over 500 occurrences in the corpus (column 1) are paired with the equivalent expressions in which the singular form (*clave*) is used (column 3). Once again, the ratio between plural and singular forms for *clave* (column 5) is consistently below 1 except for the expression *piezas claves*.

The ratio observed here should not be considered as the norm, since only the most frequent forms of *N1 claves* expressions were used as a basis for calculation. Using the most frequent forms of *N1 clave* expressions as a basis for calculation yields a ratio of 0.57 (with almost twice as many forms without plural suffixation).

The stratification of data according to the twenty countries featured in the NOW Corpus suggests that plural suffixation may be higher in Central and South America than it is in peninsular Spanish. For *N1 claves* phrases, frequency is over twice as high in Central and South America than it is in peninsular Spanish (13.3 as opposed to 6.15 occurrences per million words). Venezuela, Guatemala and Nicaragua have over 0.20 per million occurrences of *N1 relámpagos* phrases, whereas peninsular Spanish has only 0.01. For *N1 estrellas* phrases, frequency is also higher in Central and South America, but to a lesser degree (1.21 as opposed to 1.08), but for some recent uses, the ratio may be a lot higher. For instance, the phrase *jugadores estrellas* (star players), which was rarely ever used in 2012 (8 occurrences) quickly gained currency in the following years (279 occurrences in the next five years), but mostly in South America, as peninsular Spanish only recorded a total of 27 occurrences for that same period. The field of sports generally seems to provide a higher number of such expressions with plural affixation for N2 in the South American variant, with for instance a ratio of over 6 to 1 for the use of the expression *jugadores claves* when compared to peninsular usage.

276   F. Maniez

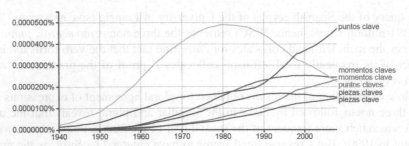

Fig. 8. Occurrences of *clave(s)* after *momentos, piezas* and *puntos* in GB (1940–2008).

Table 1. Google search results for frequent *N1 clave(s)* expressions in Spanish.

N1 clave	Frequency	N1 claves	Frequency	Plur./Sing. ratio
palabras claves	33 200 000	palabras clave	149 000 000	0,2
aspectos claves	1 700 000	aspectos clave	1 470 000	1,2
puntos claves	1 370 000	puntos clave	3 520 000	0,4
elementos claves	1 140 000	elementos clave	2 370 000	0,5
factores claves	775 000	factores clave	1 390 000	0,6
momentos claves	722 000	momentos clave	1 430 000	0,5
puestos claves	210 000	puestos clave	239 000	0,9
sectores claves	164 000	sectores clave	533 000	0,3
posiciones claves	52 900	posiciones clave	71 800	0,7
				(average) 0,58

Table 2. Search results for *N1 clave(s)* expressions in the NOW Corpus del Español.

N1 clave	Frequency	N1 claves	Frequency	Plur./Sing. ratio
puntos claves	4230	puntos clave	7148	0,6
piezas claves	3717	piezas clave	2943	1,3
momentos claves	3394	momentos clave	4246	0,8
elementos claves	1994	elementos clave	2781	0,7
aspectos claves	1655	aspectos clave	2077	0,8
temas claves	1597	temas clave	2192	0,7
jugadores claves	1574	jugadores clave	1827	0,9
puestos claves	1526	puestos clave	1779	0,9
palabras claves	1469	palabras clave	3433	0,4
factores claves	1323	factores clave	2379	0,6
sectores claves	1282	sectores clave	1686	0,8
actores claves	1012	actores clave	1436	0,7
figuras claves	935	figuras clave	1329	0,7
áreas claves	858	áreas clave	1633	0,5

(continued)

Table 2. (*continued*)

N1 clave	Frequency	N1 claves	Frequency	Plur./Sing. ratio
partidos claves	823	partidos clave	582	1,4
datos claves	728	datos clave	945	0,8
fechas claves	637	fechas clave	952	0,7
testigos claves	601	testigos clave	563	1,1
hombres claves	579	hombres clave	920	0,6
estados claves	533	estados clave	1198	0,4
				(average 0,76)

6 Predicative Uses of N2

Agreement in number for some N2s probably contributes to their being perceived as adjectives, which has led to their increasingly frequent use in predicative structures in recent decades. Noailly (1999: 24) described this phenomenon as still relatively rare at the turn of the twentieth century:

> «On a noté, à propos des substantifs épithètes, qu'il n'était pas courant de les rencontrer en position attribut, même pour ceux dont l'adjectivation est la plus aboutie. On dira bien *ta réflexion est limite, nos pâtés sont maison*, et peut-être *son voyage fut éclair*, on le fait aussi avec les substantifs utilisés pour décrire les propriétés des couleurs et des formes [...] mais guère ailleurs».[1]

Sablayrolles (2002) drew attention to the increase in the use of such structures for nouns such as *cliché, canon* or *tendance* («c'est pas un peu *cliché*, non !», «il est trop *canon*», «slogan furieusement *tendance*»). Querying GB does not make it possible to conclusively state whether plural agreement (*ils/elles sont canons*) predominates in that corpus, but it is likely that such predicative structures are still considered too colloquial to figure significantly in a corpus primarily composed of printed books (on the Web, however, the sequence featuring plural agreement *ils/elles sont canons* is used twice as frequently as *ils/elles sont canon*).

In the GB corpus, the first predicative use of *record* dates back to 1985 (*Le taux de participation est record*) and its first plural agreement to 1992 (*[...] dans un pays où les taux de syndicalisation sont records*). Given the scarcity of documents published on the Web before the early 1990s, it is difficult to say with certainty when such predicative uses first appeared in oral use before they came to be consistently used in writing.

---

[1] Concerning attributive nouns, many have remarked that they are rarely used in predicative structures, including those that behave as adjectives in many other ways. While people do say *ta réflexion est limite, nos pâtés sont maison* (or perhaps *son voyage fut éclair*) and may use predicative structures involving nouns that describe colors or shapes [...], this hardly ever occurs anywhere else.

6.1   Predicative Uses of *éclair* and *Relámpago*

The examples cited by Noailly deserve further examination. If the first two can easily be paraphrased by adding prepositional groups that reveal their elliptical nature (*ta réflexion est (à la) limite (de l'acceptable), nos pâtés sont (faits à la) maison),* the third clearly implies a metaphor that could be paraphrased as an ISA-type relation (*son voyage fut (tel un) éclair*).

There are currently just over 90,000 occurrences of predicative structures combining a form of the verb *être* with the noun *éclair* in a past context on the Web, a figure obtained by adding the results for the sequences "fut éclair" and "a été éclair" (Google search, 28/03/2019).

Based on data from the GB (Fig. 9), the attributive use of *éclair* was probably facilitated by French translation of the German *Blitzkrieg* by *guerre éclair* (even though the term *fermeture éclair* had been in use since the 1920s). The expressions *voyage éclair, visite éclair* and *passage éclair* appeared in that order in the 1940s, but it was not until the 21 st century that attributive structures described as still relatively rare by Noailly in 1999 started gaining currency. The following examples are taken from the WFC:

(1) Alors que l'audition du prévenu [...] a duré près de cinq heures, celle de l'ancien ministre du Budget, très attendue, **fut éclair**.

(2) Elle *a été "éclair"* et s'est déroulée en moins de cinq minutes. Les agresseurs étaient au nombre de quatre, habillés de gilets pare-balles.

The presence of quotation marks in the second example is typical of emerging forms whose acceptability may yet be doubtful at the time of publication. The predicative uses of *éclair* most currently observed on the Web mainly concern the N1s *passage* and *visite,* and to a much lesser degree *voyage* (Fig. 9).

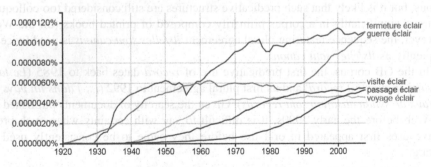

Fig. 9. Occurrences of *Noun + éclair* expressions on GB between 1920 and 2008.

In Spanish, in addition to *guerra,* which was used as an N1 preceding *relámpago* in the 1920s with usage peaking in 1950, there are a wide variety of N1s (in decreasing order of frequency in 2008: *viaje, visita, mítines, ataque, operación, campaña*). As far as predicative uses are concerned, in 2019 there were a total of more than 9,500 Google results for the two sequences *fue relámpago* and *sido relámpago.* The sequence *visita fue relámpago*, with over 2,500 results is much more frequently encountered on the Web than its French counterparts *visite a été éclair* and *visite fut éclair*. Examples (3) and (4) are taken from the Web, where quotation marks are seldom used for this expression, which might mean that attributive uses of *relámpago* (which first appeared in the GB corpus in 1985) developed before those of *éclair* in French:

(3) La modalidad delictiva *fue relámpago*, en menos de cinco minutos los mal-vivientes lograron su cometido, indicó Radio La Voz.

(4) El romance *fue relámpago*. En 8 meses se pusieron de novios, se compro-metieron y se casaron.

However, the number of occurrences of such structures does not seem to be increasing very quickly in the NOW corpus, with under 10 occurrences per year between 2014 and 2016, and fewer than 20 between 2017 and 2019.

6.2 Predicative Uses of *clé*, *key* and *clave*

The first predicative use of *clé*, in the GB corpus dates back to 1994:

(5) Dans les trois cas, les relations avec l'exportateur *sont clés*.

However, such predicative structures are scarce in this corpus, since only two occurrences of the bigram *sont clés* were used between 2004 and 2008. In comparison, the use of *key* in this type of construction happens much earlier in English. It is first documented in structures that seem to be the result of ellipsis of the definite article in an abbreviated style that is typical of the titles used for newspaper articles or classified ads, such as that of Example (6), published in 1929 in the American magazine *Popular Mechanics* :

(6) You can do it. Aviation *is key* to success. Build planes, repair engines, make real ribs and struts [...].

As early as the 1930s, *key* is used predicatively in structures where it is followed by a prepositional phrase introduced by *to:*

(7) A study of the emotions *is key* to an understanding of man and his work.

The last step in this adjectivation process occurs when *key* is used without a complement, as the last word of a clause, which can be observed as early as the 1950s:

(8) Again, it is the sense that it is time slowly acting on human lives which *is key*.

In Spanish, the WSC gives many examples of recent predicative uses of *claves*:

(9) Las elecciones legislativas de 2005 **han sido claves** para la evaluación de la gestión de gobierno y una verificación de qué fuerzas políticas emergían y cuáles sucumbían.

(10) [...] 90 m y 18 puntos) y la ex Guadalajara, Silvia Lara (15 puntos), **fueron claves** para evitar la caída de Space Tanit.

(11)   Es un premio grande que nos merecemos hace tiempo", destacó Suárez, quien
        junto al arquero Fernando Muslera y el defensor y capitán Diego Lugano **fueron
        claves** en el desempeño del conjunto charrúa.
(12)   El trabajo y las buenas relaciones **han sido claves** en la carrera del nuevo
        Procurador [...].

In the NOW Spanish corpus, the use of predicative structures in which a form of the
verb *ser* is followed by *claves* has slowly but steadily increased since 2012 (1.7 per
million words) to reach 2.3 in 2019. A similar increase can be observed for the singular
form *clave*, with much higher frequencies (respectively 11.2 and 16.0 per million
words), which shows that the singular/plural usage ratio in such structures is still about
tenfold.

6.3   Two Recent Examples in French: Predicative Uses of *culte* and *référence*

Following the emergence of attributive uses of *culte* since the early 1980s in expressions such as *film culte*, *livre culte* or *série culte* (Fig. 10), predicative uses are
becoming more and more prevalent on the Web (several thousand results for each of
the sequences *répliques sont cultes* and *films sont cultes*).

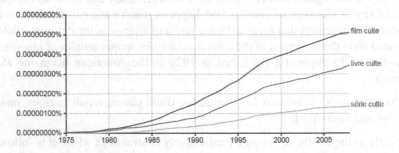

Fig. 10. Occurrences of *film culte*, *livre culte* and *série culte* on GB between 1975 and 2008.

Since such predicative uses are relatively recent, it is not currently possible to
document their evolution by using the NGram Viewer, which generates graphs based
on the GB corpus only up to the year 2008, but the WFC corpus returns a very large
number of N1s that can precede *culte* used as N2, shown here in decreasing order of co-
occurrence probability:

émission, groupe, livre, film, objet, jeu, chanson, album, réalisateur, roman, saga, personnage,
œuvre, réplique, trilogie, cinéaste, statut, télésérie, BD, série, phrase, feuilleton, manga, héros,
figure, ourson, artiste, road-movie, comédie, polar, sitcom, lieu, scène, auteur, disque.

The first predicative use of *culte* that is documented on the GB corpus goes back to
the year 2000:

(13)   Cerise sur le gâteau : leur goût pour la reprise. Comme celles de Sonic Youth
        [...] les leurs **sont cultes**.

It should be noted that all the N1s that can precede *culte* belong to the semantic field of culture, as expressions like *livre culte* and *film culte* probably served as a model for later uses. Recent use of the superlative *cultissime* is yet another proof of the new adjectival function of *culte*, which is attested in the WFC corpus by sequences such as *cultissime série/film/émission/groupe*, with *cultissime* preceding the noun in most cases. In the same corpus, we find instances of *culte* after various forms of the verb *devenir* and after such adverbs as *désormais* or *instantanément*, which also confirms its recently acquired adjectival function:

(14) Bref, l'émission dans sa version française était **devenue culte** pour nous aussi.

(15) [...] vous aurez toutes les raisons pour passer une soirée inoubliable dans ce lieu **désormais culte** et incontournable.

Similar structures seem to be appearing in the field of sport, following the recent appearance of the expression *match référence* (following the pattern of other pre-existing collocations using the noun *référence*, such as *décision référence, espace référence* or *personne référence*):

(16) On a déjà gagné par plus de buts [d'écart] mais ce match **est référence** pour les barrages.

(17) Les deux joueurs sont très sérieux, et [même] dans une possible défaite, je considère que le match **est référence** pour Richard.

7 Conclusion

The signs of N2 adjectivation in French and Spanish which we have examined (agreement in number and use in predicative structures) have multiplied in writing over the past five decades. The phenomenon also seems to be increasing on the Web, especially in the colloquial register used on blogs and forums.

However, tracking the appearance of such binominal forms is a difficult lexico-graphical task. Identification of neology by conversion is indeed difficult even with tools as powerful and user-friendly as the GB Ngram Viewer, since it allows for part-of-speech specification for only one word of a given expression (although the search module does allow the display of the ten most frequent bigrams including a given noun.). It is thus difficult to document the first uses of such binominal expressions, as their frequency usually is under the threshold that triggers the production of a graph, which is the case for emerging expressions such as *match référence, espace référence, décision référence* or *personne référence* in French.

While we have examined only two criteria for adjectivation of N2s, many more have been studied by other scholars (notably Van Goethem 2012). Among others, the increasing use in the press of intercalated adverbs (*cette période est réellement char-nière /un évènement désormais phare /el invitado inesperado, y por lo tanto estrella*) between N1 and N2 both in predicative and attributive structures seems to be yet another sign of N2 adjectivation worth investigating.

References

Arnaud, P.J.-L.: Relations sémantiques N1-N2 dans les composés timbre-poste. In: Paugam-Moisy, H., Nyckees, V., Caron-Pargue, J. (eds.) La Cognition entre individu et société, pp. 105–117. Hermès-Sciences, Paris (2001)

Arnaud, P.J.-L.: Bateau phare, magasin phare: composés [N1N2] N et séquences syntaxiques N1 + N2 à N2 adjectivé. Travaux de linguistique, (1), 7–26 (2018)

Buenafuentes, C.: Compounding and variational morphology: the analysis of inflection in Spanish compounds. Borealis–An Int. J. Hispanic Linguist. **3**(1), 1–21 (2014)

Fabre, C.: Interprétation automatique des séquences binominales en anglais et en français. Application à la recherche d'informations, thèse de doctorat, Université de Rennes (1996)

Fernández-Domínguez, J.: Compounds and multi-word expressions in Spanish. In: Finkbeiner, R., Schlücker, B. (eds.) Complex Lexical Units: Compounds and Multi-Word Expressions, vol. 9, pp. 189–219 (2019)

García-Page, M.: Hombre clave, hombre rana, ¿un mismo fenómeno? In: Verba: Anuario galego de filoloxia, vol. 38 (2011)

Martinho, F.: Noms épithètes dans les expressions binominales. Lingüística: Revista de Estudos Linguísticos da Universidade do Porto, vol. 8, pp. 39–67 (2013)

Montermini F.: La composition en italien dans un cadre de morphologie lexématique. In: Amiot, D. (ed.) La composition dans une perspective typologique. Etudes linguistiques, Artois Presses Université, pp. 161–187 (2008)

Noailly, M.Le: Substantif épithète. PUF, Paris (1990)

Noailly, M.: L'adjectif en français. Editions Ophrys, Paris (1999)

Pechenick, E.A., Danforth Christopher M., Dodds, P.S.: Characterizing the Google books corpus: strong limits to inferences of socio-cultural and linguistic evolution. PLOS One, 0137041 (2015). http://journals.plos.org/plosone/article?id=10.1371/journal.pone

Sablayrolles, J.-F.: Fondements théoriques des difficultés pratiques du traitement des néologismes. In: Revue française de linguistique appliquée 1/2002, vol. VII, pp. 97–111 (2002)

Saugera, V.: How English-origin nouns (do not) pluralize in French. Lingvisticae Investigationes. **35**(1), 120–142 (2012)

Savary, A.: Recensement et description des mots composés – méthodes et applications, Thèse de doctorat en Informatique Fondamentale, Laboratoire d'Automatique Documentaire et Linguistique, Université Paris, vol. 7 (2004)

Van Goethem, K.: Le statut des séquences "N+N à N2 productif": le cas de N-clé. Lingvisticae Investigationes 35(1), 76–93 (2012)

Van Goethem, K., Amiot, D.: Compounds and multi-word expressions in French. In: Finkbeiner, R., Schlücker, B. (eds.) Complex Lexical Units: Compounds and Multi-Word Expressions, vol. 9, 127–151 (2019)

Villoing, F.: Les mots composés [VN] N/A du français: réflexions épistémologiques et propositions d'analyse, thèse de doctorat, Paris-X Nanterre (2002)

Corpora

Chambers-Rostand Corpus of Journalistic French: http://ota.ox.ac.uk/desc/2491. Accessed 06 May 2019

Google Books Ngram Viewer: https://books.google.com/ngrams/. Accessed 06 May 2019

Leipzig University Corpora Collection: https://corpora.uni-leipzig.de/. Accessed 06 May 2019

NOW Corpus del Español: https://www.corpusdelespanol.org/now/. Accessed 06 May 2019

MBLA Social Corpus

Multipurpose Multidimensional Corpus on Cyber-Language

Álvaro L. Maroto Conde(✉) [ID] and Manuel Bermúdez Vázquez(✉) [ID]

University of Córdoba, Córdoba, Spain
amaroto@gmail.com, manuel.bermudez@uco.es

Abstract. Technological advances have made it possible for areas such as Corpus Linguistics and Computational Linguistics to advance exponentially. However, the basic evolution followed by corpora, as an essential tool in these areas, has been fundamentally in size. Proof of this is the Google nGram project, which has digitized a vast number of books from 1505 to the present day, allowing studies to be carried out on corpora. However, and as a result of the continuous evolution of new communication media and social networks, we have witnessed the birth of a new genre, called cyber-language, situated between orality and textuality, of which there are no specialized corpora. Our proposal is to design a tool to create a large multidimensional corpus based on the social network Twitter and a set of specific tools to generate subcorpora, conduct quantitative studies and visualize the stored information, from the perspective of bigdata manipulation.

Keywords: Cyber-Language · Twitter · Corpus · Bigdata · Social network

1 Introduction: Theoretical Background

Since technological improvement has helped to improve Corpus Linguistics, the development and creation of corpora have experienced a tremendous growth in the last decades. Also, new methodological areas of analysis have been created, such as Computational Linguistics, Natural Language Processing and other branches of artificial intelligence and data mining. These areas have been applied to different aspects of analysis, classification, and automatic and semi-automatic translation. Yet, if we examine the different traditionally-used corpora, we will find that they fundamentally focus on two areas of language: orality and textuality. One of the most significant examples of recent years is Google Ngram technology [1, 2], which contains millions of digitized books from 1505 to the present day, allowing searches on n-grams (for $0 < n < 6$), as well as enabling the download capacity of the information used by the engine to perform studies based on that corpus. This basic but no less impressive example has allowed experts to carry out diachronic studies on the evolution and use of both words and Phraseological Units (PUs) over the last few centuries.

However, nowadays, and mainly due to the emergence and boom of telecommunication networks and virtual communication, a new genre has appeared within

© Springer Nature Switzerland AG 2019
G. Corpas Pastor and R. Mitkov (Eds.): Europhras 2019, LNAI 11755, pp. 283–298, 2019.
https://doi.org/10.1007/978-3-030-30135-4_21

language: that of cyber-language [3], which finds its natural means of development in social networks. This concept is described by different authors and is framed within a continuum existing between orality and textuality. Because of the non-existence of current telecommunication media infrastructure, it does not have a sophisticated methodological research development, although there are some interesting projects that help the researcher to manipulate data gathered from social networks [4]. Being this new communication environment an essentially dynamic and massively adopted medium, it is interesting to consider it as a starting point for the elaboration of a corpus that allows the analysis of the state of language use from any perspective including (and not limited to) the study of phraseology.

An important characteristic of this new communication environment lies within its universal access and its natural means of diffusion formed by social networks. Mobile devices, tablets, computers, and even the so-called IoT[1] generate enormous quantities of information provided in multiple dimensions, such as authorship, geographic information of production, the precise instant of creation, and other metadata that can enrich the contextualization of this information not only from a linguistic point of view, but also from a social and even political perspective. In addition, social media and networks, such as WhatsApp, Facebook, Twitter, Instagram, etc., are already part of the daily life of the human being and have become a constantly active communication channel that replaces the classic support of paper and sound. Therefore, the purpose of this study is to develop a tool to generate a corpus based on the production of cyber-language in social networks, which incorporates enriched information (metadata) and allows the study of this new linguistic reality located between orality and textuality from a corpus linguistics and phraseological perspective.

The next step to continue with the development of research will be to determine which social network or networks will form part of the source of information to create the desired corpus. After a previous analysis, Instagram and WhatsApp are initially discarded, since the former is mainly focused on the image and the latter on private conversations, making external access to textual production not possible. For the same reason, Facebook is excluded, as privacy does not allow a balanced access to information. Still, we find the social network Twitter as the perfect representation of open communication source. In addition, it uses cyber-language in a vehicular way and its characteristics of privacy and public access to information allow a simple management of textual production. Also, the massive international implantation of the network and the size of production make it a perfect source of information to use in the generation of a corpus of the desired characteristics.

1.1 Twitter Social Network

Twitter is a micro-blogging system based on small messages called tweets that are posted by users along the world. These messages were initially limited to 140 characters when the social network was created in 2006, but since 2018 that length has been doubled, allowing a maximum of 280-character message. This message can also

---

[1] More information on https://www.ibm.com/internet-of-things.

include links to articles, images and videos. The main idea that lies in Twitter is the immediacy. For that reason, tweets are called 'statuses'. These statuses try to show what the user is doing at any moment, updating that information to friends and relatives, but nowadays the vast amount of users is pushing the concept to new dimensions, quite different from the original purposes for which twitter was designed.

Table 1. Twitter demographics (Source: https://www.omnicoreagency.com/twitter-statistics/)

Twitter Demographics	
Total number of monthly active Twitter users	326 million
Percentaje of Twitter users on mobile	80%
Number of Twitter daily active users	100 million
Internet users that use Twitter	45%
International Twitter users outside US	261 million
Twitter users inside US	69 million
Daily Twitter users	49%

Added to that, Twitter allows its users to spread messages in a fast way: for public awareness campaigns and information-sharing, to communicate with large audiences, to follow or cover events in real-time, to engage with followers and non-followers, among others. Furthermore, Twitter allows people to follow each other based on their interests and the content of their tweets. To put it differently, this tool has evolved into a community of people with specific interests where anyone can follow another person, even a total stranger, independently of their social or economic status (e.g. artists, writers, politicians, actors). Figure 1 and Table 2 below show and describe some items of information found in a tweet:

Fig. 1. Structure of a tweet

Table 2. Data shown on a tweet.

Field name	Description
Avatar	The image associated to the profile
Account name	The name of the account
Handle/user id	The username (unique in the social network)
Timestamp	The date of creation of the tweet
Tweet text	Main text of the tweet
Reply	Button that allows to write a tweet in reply to another
Mention	A citation to a twitter user
Retweet	Button that allows to copy a tweet from another user
Hashtag	A descriptive Word that tags the tweet in order to facilitate searches
Like	A button that allows to show a positive sentiment from the user that read the tweet
Direct message	A button that allows to write a private message to an user
Link	A link to an internet resource

Although this data is the one that a common user can see when using the official app or site, there is more information inside a tweet which becomes particularly important to our context. This is called "tweet metadata" and is listed in Table 3 below:

Table 3. Metadata inside a tweet

Language	The language of a tweet (autodetected)
Country	Country of creation of the tweet
Coordinates	Exact geolocation information (lat/lon)
No. of likes	The language of a tweet (autodetected)
No. of mentions	Country of creation of the tweet

This metadata will enrich the corpus because not only will it be able to be used to analyze texts from a linguistic point of view, but it will also permit researchers to place results of their investigation in social, geographic and even political contexts.

2 Methodology: MBLA Social Corpus

Considering all the aforementioned, we designed a multidimensional social corpus which contained selected data from each tweet produced by Twitter, as listed in Table 4:

Table 4. Selected fields for
the MBLA Social Corpus

Fields
User ID
Tweet Text
Timestamp
Language
Country
Coordinates

2.1   Tasks

Once the subject of the investigation was raised, we identified three tasks:

1.- Data acquisition, indexing and storing;
2.- Data selection and exportation;
3.- Data visualization (for background information).

In order to perform these tasks, three modules were developed, which are described in detail below.

2.2   MBLA SC Acquisition Engine

Architecture

Twitter provides an Application Programming Interface (API)[2] that enables developers to design custom applications that gather information directly from the social network in different ways. One of these allows the extraction of the tweets that are sent to the microblogging service in runtime. This endpoint provides any custom app registered with Twitter with tweets from the social network. Afterwards, information can be filtered and processed to create the desired corpus in a structured manner. For small samples, the system is efficient without indexing, but regarding big data, as the length of data acquired grows quickly, it is completely necessary to implement an indexing system that enables the user to make searches and selections using different criteria. The simplified structure of the MBLA SC acquisition engine is shown in Fig. 2:

---

[2] An API is a set of commands, functions, protocols, and objects that programmers can use to create software or interact with an external system. It provides developers with standard commands for performing common operations, thus they do not have to write the code from scratch.

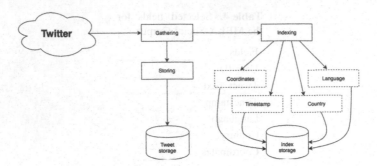

Fig. 2. MBLA Social Corpus acquisition engine

The engine connects to Twitter using Twitter real-time filter (API endpoint)[3] with registered credentials and gathers all the information in runtime. These tweets represent 1% of the total Twitter production, but the social network guarantees that the sample is statistically valid. Also, the extrapolation of that geotagged sample has been evaluated [5] against the whole set, concluding that the data gathered maintains the same proportions.

While tweets are being captured, the process splits into two tasks. First, each tweet is simplified and data that is not relevant to the corpus is discarded. Then, the new tweet is recreated and stored in the repository. Simultaneously, the tweet metadata is analyzed and a set of information is also split into the aforementioned four fields: coordinates, language, timestamp and country. These fields are stored in dedicated indexes that speed up the responsiveness of the search system, linking these categories to the tweets that meet the required criteria.

In order to provide researchers with statistical data, the engine also calculates a detailed breakdown of the tweets processed in runtime from a quantitative point of view. This set of data contains information about language distribution for each country, amount of tweets processed in each language grouped by country, and vice versa, country tweets grouped by language, and a set of common data traditionally associated to corpus linguistics [6], such as token and type statistics and frequencies, which are always classified according to the date, location (country and coordinates) and language. This approach outperforms the traditional corpus technology, as the system enables the access to the information of the corpus associated with the sociopolitical context (i.e. comparative linguistic analysis between countries, or even in the same country, in different times of the year, etc.).

Data Format
The MBLA acquisition engine stores all the information (tweets and indexes) in JSON standard format. This choice has been made for the sake of compatibility because this format is widely used in data handling and manipulation, being interchangeable between XML, and easily adaptable to be dumped as a relational SQL database, or even as a flat text. Also, this format allows the repository to be used-as-is as a data

---

[3] More information on https://developer.twitter.com/en/docs/api-reference-index.

```
{
    "country": "US",
    "date": "20170309",
    "id": "839930008248262656",
    "id_user": "827759148",
    "lang": "en",
    "lat": 47.614817,
    "lon": -122.3306025,
    "text": "Lovely food out here",
    "timestamp_ms": "1489089893768",
}
```

Fig. 3. JSON payload example

source in non-structured NoSQL databases, like MongoDB, specifically designed for bigdata tasks. A sample JSON payload of the MBLA Social Corpus engine is shown in Fig. 3 and the selected fields for the payload are described in Table 5 below:

Table 5. Selected fields for the MBLA Social Corpus and standard format

Field	Description	Format
country	Country of creation of the tweet	ISO 3166-1 alpha 2
Date	Date of creation in year/month/day format	Human readable
Id	ID of the tweet	Twitter internal
id_user	ID of the user that create the tweet	Twitter internal
Lang	Language of the tweet	ISO 639-1 alpha 2
Lat	Latitude	Decimal degrees
Lon	Longitude	Decimal degrees
Text	Text of the tweet	Unicode UTF-8
timestamp_ms	Date of creation in Unix time	Unix Epoch/POSIX

2.3   MBLA-SC Selection and Exporting

Once the tweet engine acquires and stores the tweets, the main goal is to provide a way the researcher can access the data that meets the requirements of the study. This point is crucial because such an oversized corpus can be heavy and hard to process as a raw sample, and in all probability much of the data will become irrelevant to specific research, rendering it even harder to be processed. Hence, additionally the MBLA Social Corpus engine implements a set of scripts that enables the researcher to create subcorpora from the main corpus with the criteria specified. Basically, these criteria refer to the indexes specified above in the engine description, plus word selection, enabling to filter the main corpus also by content.

The result of these scripts is delivered to the user in a wide range of formats, including annotated JSON, plain JSON, XML, CSV, TSV, and plain text files, max-imizing the compatibility of the data with any other corpus engine, programming language or data representation software. The scripts are in experimental state at the time of writing this paper, privately accessible via web or by using the server console directly and are divided into two groups. The first one enables the researcher to obtain quantitative statistical data from the main corpus or data from a sample that meets the criteria applied. These criteria cover language, country, date, coordinates and text. Examples of data that can be retrieved using these scripts are listed in Table 6:

Table 6. Data selection examples of the MBLA-SC selection and exporting module

Quantitative data selection examples
Number of tweets between two dates around the world
Number of tweets between two dates in one language around the world
Number of tweets between two dates in any language in a city of a country
Number of tweets between two dates in two languages in one country
Number of words in one language in one country used between two dates
Number of tweets that use a word in any language in two countries
Number of tweets in a date that used a word in one language in one country
Wordlist used in a country between two dates in one language with frequencies

The second one allows the researcher to create subcorpora from the main MBLA Social Corpus that meet criteria similar to the presented above in the statistical data. The use of regular expressions as a matching engine over the text enables the system to make advanced selections that cover PUs, like n-grams, multi-word units, complex word patterns, etc. Examples of subcorpora that can be created with these scripts are listed in Table 7:

Table 7. Subcorpora selection examples of the MBLA-SC selection and exporting module

Subcorpora data selection examples
Subcorpus of tweets between two dates in one language in a country
Subcorpus of tweets in a date in ten languages in ten countries
Subcorpus of tweets in any language around the world matching the word "Trump"
Subcorpus of all tweets that matches the expression "She sa[id|ys] me [yes|not]"
Subcorpus of tweets in any language in a determined street in a city of a country

The obtained subcorpora can be easily imported to any corpus management tool due the wide range of formats the scripts allow to export. The diagram that shows the structure of this module can be found in Fig. 4:

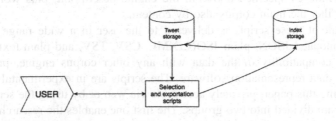

Fig. 4. MBLA Social Corpus selection and exporting module

2.4   MBLA-SC Data Visualization

Although the purpose of this project is to create a multidimensional social corpus, considering the huge size of the data it becomes essential to design a tool that enables the researcher to represent data in a visual context, apart from the subcorpus properly. For accomplishing this mission, a new set of web scripts has been developed, enabling the user to quickly visualize the subcorpora data in an intuitive way. The web scripts are built on solid web standards using PHP language and well-known/well-supported open source graphs and charting libraries, as well as custom graphic libraries developed specifically for this purpose, which are able to represent bigdata accurately.

The MBLA-SC data visualization module can interface directly with the MBLA-SC acquisition engine and the MBLA-SC selection and exporting module, so, from the point of view of the researcher, obtaining visualizations directly from the system is a nearly-transparent process. Taking into account that a researcher can create a subcorpus and process it using external (standard or custom) tools, this module also accepts uploadable JSON data with the format shown in Fig. 3.

Furthermore, the MBLA-SC Data Visualization module takes data in runtime from the MBLA-SC Acquisition Engine, as a consequence, the researcher can have a brief quantitative understanding of the data being acquired in a 24-hour time window for each variable the system can categorize. The graphs and charts include a map-type image, rendered with colored by lang dots that represent each tweet gathered in the last 24 h, as shown in Fig. 5:

Fig. 5. Map displaying last 24 h' tweets gathered by MBLA Social Corpus engine

Also, the data visualization module can extract the world language usage in the last 24 h, grouped by hour. This line chart can be configurated to filter any captured language, as seen in Fig. 6:

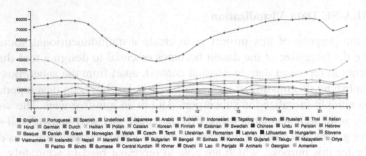

Fig. 6. World language production on Twitter by hour

This data, without being classified into hours, can be aggregated by the module and shown as a global usage chart. Figure 7 is an example of this:

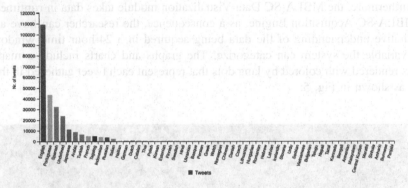

Fig. 7. World language production by day

This module has the following architecture, represented in Fig. 8:

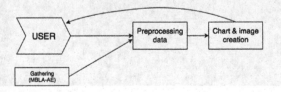

Fig. 8. MBLA Social Corpus Visualization module

Finally, the full system diagram is shown in Fig. 9 below:

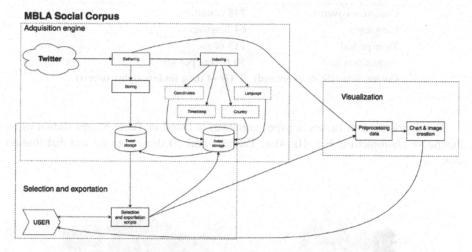

Fig. 9. MBLA Social Corpus general architecture

3 Implementation and Results

3.1 Deployment

The engine has been built and deployed in a custom server hosted in Paris with a permanent and high bandwidth connection to Internet in order to minimize service disruptions. This system has been running continuously from Feb 13, 2017 to June 6, 2017, gathering, storing and indexing tweets in runtime. The software has been designed using a map-reduce[4] philosophy in order to obtain the best scalability performance because of bigdata concerns. Currently, it processes queries using 16 core parallel processing, speeding up data handling significatively.

3.2 MBLA Social Corpus Global Statistics

The statistical breakdown of data acquisition is shown in Table 8:

---

[4] More information on https://www.ibm.com/analytics/hadoop/mapreduce.

Table 8. Statistical breakdown of data acquisition

Corpus size	Total 419,137,014 tweets
Countries covered	248 countries
Languages	64 languages
Time period	113 days
Acquisition rate	50 tweets per sec
Corpus size (JSON annotated)	7 TB of data (indexes plus tweets)

The distribution of tweets between countries is listed in Table 8, and shown as an illustrative choropleth in Fig. 10. Also, Tables 9 and 10 show country and distribution data:

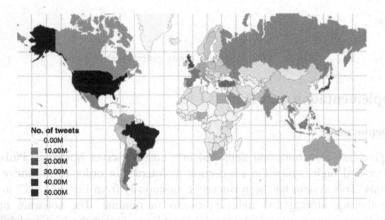

Fig. 10. Choropleth of MBLA Social Corpus tweet production by country

Table 9. Tweet distribution per country

United States	127,822,349	Mexico	8,253,327	Venezuela	3,151,509
Brasil	61,673,545	Indonesia	8,168,209	Australia	3,014,029
Japan	25,225,502	Thailand	7,205,411	Chile	3,013,077
Great Britain	21,786,656	Russia	6,464,788	Germany	2,849,349
Phillippines	13,891,581	Canada	5,891,391	Portugal	2,592,756
Argentina	12,923,330	Saudi Ar.	5,600,413	Nigeria	2,553,098
Turkey	12,512,662	India	5,538,515	Netherlands	2,255,436
Spain	9,623,705	Italy	3,993,934	Egypt	2,218,683
Malaysia	8,957,690	Colombia	3,832,086		
France	8,314,663	Zambia	3,687,087	Others	36,122,233

Table 10. Tweet distribution per language

English	180,732,824	Chinese	435,640	Bengali	40,728
Portuguese	54,834,984	Danish	383,910	Marathi	39,562
Spanish	43,467,924	Romanian	335,251	Gujarati	28,080
Undefined	31,382,996	Czech	315,608	Malayalam	25,202
Japanese	24,619,407	Greek	314,793	Sinhala	13,164
Indonesian	13,598,138	Basque	313,755	Kannada	10,092
Turkish	10,990,788	Norwegian	310,773	Telugu	10,084
Arabic	10,525,178	Ukrainian	263,206	Panjabi	5,185
Tagalog	8,874,692	Welsh	262,233	Oriya	3,875
French	8,154,779	Persian	260,114	Armenian	3,336
Russian	6,631,456	Latvian	233,659	Kurdish	3,042
Thai	5,638,646	Urdu	231,347	Lao	2,320
Italian	3,471,165	Hungarian	206,410	Georgian	2,294
Deustch	2,127,118	Lithuanian	182,126	Pashto	2,223
Dutch	2,073,119	Vietnamese	179,390	Burmese	1,816
Korean	1,303,776	Hebrew	156,463	Sindhi	1,680
Polish	1,169,722	Slovenian	132,254	Khmer	911
Hindi	1,065,532	Tamil	125,712	Amharic	732
Haitian	979,770	Nepali	123,226	Divehi	262
Estonian	848,276	Icelandic	114,556	Tibetan	151
Swedish	743,339	Bulgarian	77,062	Uighur	109
Finnish	690,279	Serbian	60,761	n/a	9

Sample Statistics from Generated Subcorpora

In order to test statistical data acquisition from the MBLA Social Corpus, we have done some data extraction using the MBLA-SC selection and exporting scripts.

Comparison of lexical availability of Spanish language in four countries. We have extracted all words from Spanish language in Spain, Mexico, Venezuela and the United States, in order to see the lexical availability of Spanish speakers in each country. The data exposed in Table 11 corresponds to the full timeframe stored in the corpus. It shows the number of types of the Spanish subcorpora in each country, plus the total number of tweets in any language, and specifically the tweets produced in Spanish, including a calculated ratio of types per tweet.

Table 11. Types, tweets, Spanish tweets and ratio of lexical availability on tweets

Country	No. of types	Total tweets	Spanish tweets	Types/tweet
Spain	4.128.757	9.623.705	6.755.783	0,61
Mexico	3.542.734	8.253.227	6.478.375	0,49
Venezuela	1.526.955	3.151.509	2.665.134	0,57
United States	1.512.229	127.822.349	2.066.081	0,73

Although lexical availability is a widely studied topic, we are moving into a new context, such as cyber-language. So, in this case, and taking into account the huge size of the subcorpora, we can see that in the United States the tweets produced show better lexical availability than the other countries, probably caused by the influence of the English language in the form of neologisms and anglicisms. It should be a good starting point of research, but it will not be covered in this paper. By the same token, comparing Spanish types and token frequencies against English subcorpora in the US might shed some light on the proposal.

Count and distribution of tweets containing 'Make America Great Again' versus 'Make America [any word other than Great] Again' in the US.

For this experiment, it has been selected the regular expression '/make america (\b +) again/i', which extracts a list of words that matches that pattern. The modifier 'i' after the slash instructs the engine to match PUs in case insensitive mode.

Once the script analyzes all the tweets and creates a wordlist with the matched unit, it creates a type/frequency list. The results are described in Tables 12 and 13. Furthermore, as the tweets are geolocated, the subcorpus obtained has been split into two subcorpora, one including the 'great' word, and the other one containing the remaining tweets. These corpora will be displayed in a map (Fig. 11 below) to get a geopolitical insight and association to the words matched.

Table 12. Quantitative results on tweet search matching the specified criteria

Sample phraseological unit	Tweets	Color
Make America Great Again	5218	Orange
Make America [any word other than Great] Again	2169	Green

Table 13. Types/cases of the words found in the PU

Type	Cases	Type	Cases	Type	Cases
Great	5218	Corinne	32	Polluted	17
White	128	Green	29	Healthy	16
Safe	118	Grate	27	Proud	16
Sick	86	Dumb	27	Skate	15
Hate	80	Sane	26	Broke	15
Golf	74	Think	26	Gag	14
Smart	66	Kind	22	Laugh	14
Covfefe	60	Corrine	20	Gleesh	13
Gay	56	Strong	20	Read	13
Emo	34	Stupid	19	Mexico	13

Fig. 11. Distribution of selected subcorpora tweets in the United States

4 Conclusion and Future Work

It has been demonstrated that Twitter is suitable to be chosen as a datasource for creating a social corpus of cyber-language. In addition, this corpus has been enriched with metadata, extending it in a multidimensional manner, which enables the researcher to extrapolate linguistic results to sociological [7] or political events [8].

The corpus represents 1% of the total of Twitter production; yet it is statistically valid. Moreover, this 1% of the total Twitter production is vast enough to be considered as a bigdata source, involving specific methodology for handling, manipulation, and data storage. At the time of writing this paper, the second version of MBLA Social Corpus is being processed, with extended metadata (retweets, likes and 'in response to' tag), and extended in time, covering from January 1, 2018 to December 31, 2018 (complete year), as the storage scheme has been optimized to handle more data without limiting accessibility. This second version of MBLA Social Corpus handles more than 1,500 million of tweets, four times bigger than the first version.

Twitter is fully UTF-8 compliant, as MBLA Social Corpus is. This implies that there is full support to the new emoji characters, allowing to extend the research of PUs to emoji symbols by providing a solid data resource to do so. Also, sentiment analysis can be applied to text and emojis, offering a new dimension for phraseological research.

As textual information from Twitter comes in plain text, there is not part-of-speech tagging by default. The future work comprises the adaptation of the NLTK Toolkit[5] to automatically make PoS-tagging of the text. This will enable the corpus to be searched in an advanced manner, more suitable for PUs, and will enrich the exportation features to other external corpus manipulation engines and tools.

Finally, as there are many console scripts intended to make selections of data in order to create subcorpora, it seems necessary to deploy a full web-based user interface to facilitate the research tasks. That user interface will enable to use the tool on-the-go from any type of device.

---

[5] More information on http://www.nltk.org/ .

References

1. Michel, J., Shen, Y., et al.: Quantitative analysis of culture using millions of digitized books. Science **331**(6014), 176–182 (2011)
2. Zieba, A.: Google books Ngram viewer in socio-cultural research. Res. Lang. **16**, 357–376 (2018). https://doi.org/10.2478/rela-2018-0015
3. Naveed, A., Aziz, S., Mehfooz, M.: Analysis of cyber language: identifying gender boundaries. Eur. Acad. Res. **II**(7), 9706–9724 (2014)
4. Anthony, L., Hardaker, C.: FireAnt (1.1.3) [Computer Software]. Waseda University, Tokio (2019). http://www.laurenceanthony.net/. Accessed 06 July 2019
5. Morstatter, F., Pfeffer, J., Liu, H., Carley, K.: Is the sample good enough? Comparing data from Twitter's Streaming API with Twitter's Firehose. Association for the Advancement of Artificial Intelligence arXiv:1306.5204 (2013)
6. Church, K.: Corpus methods in a digitized world, pp. 3–15 (2017). https://doi.org/10.1007/978-3-319-69805-2_1
7. Maroto, A.: Big Data, Twitter and Music: New paths in research. https://www.researchgate.net/publication/331479188. Accessed 14 Jan 2019
8. Maroto, A.: El metadiscurso en las redes sociales: Una extensión multidimensional. Análisis de cinco dirigentes políticos de la coalición Ahora Podemos a través de la red social Twitter. https://www.researchgate.net/publication/331479188. Accessed 14 Jan 2019

A Cognitive Modeling Approach on Ironical Phraseology in Twitter

Beatriz Martín Gascón[(✉)] [iD]

University of Córdoba, 14071 Córdoba, Spain
z82magab@uco.es

Abstract. The development and growth of social networks evidence human creativity via the use of figurative language including irony. Recent studies on modeling irony and irony detection in social media have looked at it from a traditional perspective and have focused primarily on developing natural language processing systems, thus ignoring the mental processes the participants experience during ironic speech acts. As a result, irony has been misinterpreted and mixed by the experimental literature with other disparate phenomena, such as jokes, understatements or banter. On the other hand, scholars from the field of Cognitive Linguistics have studied the cognitive processes operating in the creation of ironic remarks. With regard to this, Ruiz de Mendoza's [9] development of the echoic account focuses on ironic discourse and categorizes verbal irony. Yet, no study to date has explored ironical phraseology in terms of cognitive modeling based on bigdata. This study, therefore, aims to examine how Spanish-speakers conceptualize and express irony in Twitter. Results revealed that irony was frequently misconceived and, as a consequence, additional cues such as explicit ironic hashtags prevented readers from interpreting the message literally, especially in explicit-echoic ironic cases. A more frequent interaction between text-hashtag as compared to text-emoji was also evinced for all potentially ironic linguistic signs. It is expected that our findings contribute to research on Spanish as a foreign language (ELE in the native-language acronym) teaching by enhancing the intercultural sensitivity in the learner, as well as to the field of computational linguistics in adding feature types.

Keywords: Social media · Echoic account · Ironical phraseology · Cognitive modeling · Twitter · ELE · Intercultural sensitivity

1 Introduction

According to Ghosh et al. [3] the development and growth of social webs have enhanced the use of figurative and creative language, including irony. Following this line of reasoning, recent studies on modeling irony and irony detection in social media [8, 11] have looked at irony from a traditional perspective, thus conceiving it as a rhetorical device or literary trope that arises from the discrepancy between what the speaker conveys and what is actually the case. Furthermore, studies within the field of

© Springer Nature Switzerland AG 2019
G. Corpas Pastor and R. Mitkov (Eds.): Europhras 2019, LNAI 11755, pp. 299–314, 2019.
https://doi.org/10.1007/978-3-030-30135-4_22

computational linguistics that follow machine learning-based approaches to detect irony have focused primarily on developing automatic natural language processing systems[1] rather than on understanding the mental processes the participants experience during an ironic speech act. The notion of cognitive model, which is essential for a proper interpretation of ironic statements, has been thus disregarded. As a result, irony has been related with a range of disparate phenomena, such as hyperbole, jokes, understatements, and banter, for these have been commonly treated as forms of irony in the experimental literature.

Yet, ironic language use is ubiquitous and is part of everyday communication. It is also a highly pervasive aspect of texts in social media, which renders irony-grasping an arduous task due to the lack of face-to-face contact and of other suprasegmental aspects such as vocal intonation. In this line, scholars and theorists from the field of Cognitive Linguistics (CL) have studied ironic speech as a cognitive mechanism displaying socio-pragmatic outcomes [4] and have examined the cognitive processes operating in the creation of ironic remarks [10]. From a cognitive perspective, understanding the mental mechanisms that underlie irony enhances our comprehension of how we reason and convey our thoughts and beliefs. Besides, since social media is increasingly becoming more "social," irony detection will eventually be a pressing problem: user-generated content is hard to analyze because of the absence of context and lack of paralinguistic cues. On the other hand, most studies on irony have focused their attention on the English language. Still, since Spanish is a language in constant growth and one of the most studied foreign languages with over 21 million learners, efforts must be invested in research on ELE irony teaching. The potential socio-cultural component that emerges from irony renders it an efficient tool to enhance ELE learners' intercultural sensitivity, boosting their communicative competence.

The aim of the study is thus to fill in this literature gap by examining ironical segments in terms of cognitive modeling, paying special attention to Phraseological Units (PUs), these latter conceived here as pairings of words or word-groups that are ready-made recurrent units in communication through social media and are stable at the phraseological level. More specifically, we attempt to elucidate how irony is conceptualized and expressed by Spanish-speakers using Twitter in Spanish territory by collecting authentic data and associating text-hashtag and text-emoji in order to understand the complexities of irony and to show ecologically-valid examples to ELE learners. We aim at answering the following research questions:

1. To what extent do Spanish-speaking users of Twitter conceptualize and use Verbal Irony in a proper manner?
2. How is Verbal Irony conveyed, through explicit or non-explicit echo? Are the ironic utterances positive or negative?
3. Is explicit and non-explicit echoic irony mostly hashtag-induced or emoji-induced? And positive and negative utterances?
4. Which Phraseological Units are related to the expression of Verbal Irony? How are they constructed, hashtag or emoji-induced?

---

[1] Yet, it is not within the purposes of the present study to conduct a fully-automated analysis of irony, for tweets were extracted semi-automatically via linguistic anchors.

2 Irony: An Important Communicative Phenomenon

The CL notion of irony departs from the rhetorical view that conceives it as a figure of speech or a literary trope in which speakers utter the opposite of what they intend to convey. This ground-breaking cognitive approach to language contends that irony is a figure of thought and a conceptualization of the world, of how we reason and feel, thus it is part of the everyday language used by ordinary people, like metaphor or metonymy [2, 5]. In order for irony to fulfil its purposes, the speaker needs to accomplish a series of cognitive operations to have the hearer reconstruct the opposite of the literal meaning and receive the message correctly. These operations can be defined as mental mechanisms used to generate conceptual representations that are articulated linguistically, that is, any conceptual mechanism contributing to the inferential processes that are required to derive a semantic representation out of linguistic signs or any other non-linguistic element (i.e. emojis, hashtags) so as to make it meaningful in the context in which it is to be interpreted [9].

Ruiz de Mendoza's [9] account of cognitive operations for explaining ironic discourse and analyzing its components aims at unifying inferential pragmatics and cognitive semantics. His cognitive approach complements pragmatic accounts of irony, which focus on meaning effects to the detriment of cognitive mechanisms. In his theory, Ruiz de Mendoza contends that Verbal Irony (hereinafter VI) is the result of mental operations, for both speaker and hearer need background knowledge to create and interpret the ironic utterance. He creates his own development of the echoic account from a cognitivist perspective in which two organizational forms for cognitive operations are distinguished: **A IS B** and **A FOR B**. In the case of VI, this adopts the former pattern: **A IS B,** which involves understanding aspects of concept A in terms of aspects of concept B, and more specifically, it is based on the cognitive operation of echoing in combination with contrasting.

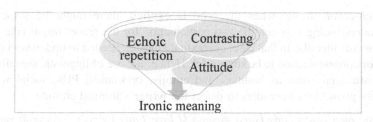

Fig. 1. Cognitive operations involved in irony

Echoing consists of repeating someone's thoughts or beliefs –or social stereotypes– and needs another cognitive operation that triggers the ironic effects, which is contrasting. This latter is an operation that involves creating an opposition or clash between an echoed thought and someone's actual or attributed thoughts. Therefore, according to his echoic account, irony consists of an echoed opinion and of a blatant clash between an observed and an echoed scenario, which are integrated in the ironist's mind, suggesting that the situation is the opposite of the described one and adding an attitude [9]. This echoic use allows speakers to humorously complain about a state of affairs that seemed to be different. The previous utterance or echoed thought clashes and is cancelled out by the speaker's real belief on a matter. Also, this clash displays her skeptical and ironical attitude, directing the hearer's attention to reconstruct the opposite of the literal meaning (*Vid. Fig. 1*). This latter needs to share with the speaker the same situational model[2] in order to understand the irony. Communication includes not only the information that the writer of a written text aims to convey, but also information about her intention to tell the reader her purpose. In line with this, depending on how the echo is constructed, this echoic account classifies VI into two main types:

1. *Non-explicit-echoic irony*: if the echo is non-explicit, it is easier for the reader to interpret irony, and background information is not needed, for the intention is carried within the linguistic material. In other words, the echo is formed at a linguistic level and the echo itself is the most important element. However, in order for the utterance to be considered ironical, previous context is sometimes required.

   a. *Me encanta ir al cajero y que no funcione [I love going to withdraw money and finding a broken ATM]*

Example[3] *a.* constitutes an ironic statement where the reader is required to derive an implication: by uttering "Me encanta ir al cajero," it is understood that what comes next will be something positive. The irony here relies on the contrast which arises when the reader processes the remaining fragment. That is, the echo is put to work as soon as the reader processes the observable scenario or context, which is the opposite of what anyone, by world knowledge, would want: an ATM that works. At this exact point, a contradiction is produced and the ironical effects emerge. The echo cancels the implicated meaning and that contrast between the echoed scenario and the real scenario has irony emerge. Depending on the degree of irony detectability, the ironist might use non-linguistic signs to emphasize the echo.

2. *Explicit-echoic irony:* when the echo is explicit, there might be some sort of misunderstanding between the two participants, for the reader might take the writer's words literally. In that case, contextual cues are needed to understand the irony and for communication to be successful. Hence, the use of linguistic signaling (non-linguistic signs such as hashtags and emojis, or ironical PUs) social webs like Twitter gives clues to readers to detect the writer's ironical attitude.

   b. *Qué bien canta Lady Gaga #ironía [I love Lady Gaga's singing #irony]*
   c. *Adoro la primavera, claro que sí☺[I love springtime, oh, yeah☺]*

In example *b.*, we need to think of a twitter user who either thought or heard someone saying that Lady Gaga was a good singer, but then a video came out in which

---

[2] A situational model offers all the stored information in relation to a specific situation.

[3] Examples a-c are made-up utterances created for clarity and explanatory matters.

she was out of tune. **A** stands for the real state of affairs (the singer being off pitch), which contradicts a previous thought by the speaker or someone else. **B**, by echoing that prior thought, presents the situation as the opposite, showing the user's ironical or skeptical attitude. For both examples (*b.*, *c.*) the reader first processes the utterance without the observable scenario, and is required to derive an implication: if speaker likes (2) how Lady Gaga sings and springtime, that implies a positive emotion. Furthermore, the conventional series of events (situational models) allow the reader to adjust the conceptual representation to reality, which may vary across cultures, but in this case denotes positive scenarios (Lady Gaga is a renowned singer and springtime is related to love, blossom and animals awaking). Still, since these are instances of explicit-echoic irony, the utterance itself is not sufficient for readers to perceive it, and additional information is thus needed.

Normally, VI is reinforced by suprasegmental features, such as stress, intonation and facial expressions. Attardo et al. [1] propose these latter as markers of irony and sarcasm. In written text, however, these suprasegmental non-verbal cues normally present in face-to-face communication are not feasible to be analyzed. Hence the relevance of analyzing the linguistic signs (PU: *claro que sí*) along with non-linguistic signs, such as hashtags and emojis (*#ironía*, ☺) to evoke a metonymic frame via a lexical unit whose polarity is incoherent with the speech event scenario. Among such linguistic signs, certain PUs become crucial for the writer to convey irony and for the reader to elucidate the ironic intention underlying the utterance. Hence, in the case of the above-mentioned explicit-echoic utterances, PUs such as *qué bien* + #ironía and *claro que sí* + ☺ are used to express irony. Regarding non-explicit-echoic irony (*a.*), since the echo is constructed at a linguistic level, the use of hashtags and/or emojis is not strictly required; yet we can identify potential PUs denoting irony, e.g. *me encanta* (experiencer + verb). In all cases, when readers process the whole utterance, they realize that the linguistic signs have been manipulated and it is that new information contrasted by the previous one what modifies the reader's knowledge. Hence, the relevance of PUs as powerful linguistic signs to express irony in written text.

3 Twitter: A Data Genre for Irony Detection

In examining irony in Spanish, many difficulties might arise when we look at standard linguistic corpora (i.e. CREA, CORPES, CORDE), for VI is constrained by context and culture. Such a limitation highlights the need of computerized tools capable of supplying a large database of irony, which, in turn, are able to identify the location and the speaking community producing those ironic utterances. In this line, Twitter, for it is easily accessible and constitutes a big sample of data, becomes a potential source and a fast instrument to come across potential ironic tweets by looking at hashtags that tend to coappear with VI. Furthermore, irony is part of everyday language and is mostly conveyed in informal dialogue types. In this sense, Twitter, as the world-wide social web by excellence to express one's beliefs and thoughts in an informal way, becomes an online mine for irony data. It constitutes, furthermore, a bridge data genre between spoken and written language, with the advantages of interacting, being informal, adding emotional context from the former and with the offline characteristics from the latter.

Previous research on the processing of semantic and pragmatic content of emojis have succeed at showing that emoji-generated irony is processed in a similar manner to word-generated irony [12]. These can be related and automatically annotated to later be manually selected in order to obtain potential instances of VI. This last procedure, where linguists intervene, is a vital step of data triangulation to gather valid ironic utterances. Yet, to our knowledge, this final phase has been so far neglected by the literature targeting at irony detection in social media.

4 Methodology

The methodological approach followed for this study responded to a cognitive approach to ironical phraseology and was based on the analysis of authentic data collected from social media, more specifically from Twitter. Our instrument of analysis[4] [6, 7] was designed so as to retrieve information through computational elements to analyze a large and non-biased sample, since, contrary to other means of data collection (i.e. surveys, interviews, observation), the subjects here were not aware of their tweets being analyzed. The corpus was based on a specific application that retrieved from this social platform all tweets in real time and distributed them according to certain criteria, such as user, body text, date, language and geographic coordinates. The dataset consisted of a total of 419,137,014 tweets[5] from 248 countries and 64 different languages written within a period of 113 days.[6] The corpus was built retrieving 1,793 tweets from Spanish-speaking users in the Spanish territory. The sample was considerably reduced since it automatically annotated those using the "irony" hashtag as information source. This feature type, previously targeted in studies on irony detection in English [11] was extended to the word *ironía* in its different forms (singular and plural, with and without the accent, with and without hashtag). This information source allowed us to retrieve those tweets where users explicitly showed their ironic attitude, but also a sample of non-ironic ones.

Subsequently, data were manually analyzed and codified to identify real ironical utterances and gain a deeper understanding of how irony is conveyed at a written linguistic level. This manual annotation was carried out by two experts and a non-linguistic connoisseur as means of data triangulation to increase the validity of the sample. Hence, corpora analysis departed from a mixed paradigm for our research was of an exploratory-quantitative-interpretative nature. Only tweets presenting an echo that involved a contrast with reality and revealed the ironist's attitude were selected. Furthermore, the already-filtered sample was further categorized into explicit and non-explicit echoic irony, as well as classified into positive or negative emotion utterances. Since echoing implies repeating someone's words or thoughts, that is, context is frequently necessary to have VI, one important aspect that our tool of analysis had

---

[4] Research tool implemented in previous studies of bigdata applied to the field of politics and music impact.

[5] This result is derived from calculating an average of 50 tweets PS, which becomes 4,320,000 tweets QD.

[6] The dataset was created from tweets from 13 February to 6 June, 2017.

incorporated was the option to have access to the timeline for each tweet. All instances of VI were also examined looking at the contrast between elements within each utterance: text-hashtag and text-emoji. We considered these combinations as PUs instances of hashtag-or-emoji-induced irony.

5   Results and Discussion

5.1   To What Extent Do Spanish-Speaking Users of Twitter Conceptualize and Use Verbal Irony in a Proper Manner?

From a total of 1,793 tweets written in Spain by Spanish-speakers, only 448 were retrieved and considered as instances of VI after manual codification (*Vid. Fig. 2*). The remaining sample ($n = 1,348$) were not instances of ironic utterances and were not thus considered for further analyses. Yet, the discarded tweets allowed us to gain a deeper understanding of how VI is frequently misused and misconceived. Examples *d.-f.* below evidence the users' wrong perception of irony (normally attributed to the traditional view of irony as a literary trope), for it is understood as opposed to the truth. This clashes with the cognitive perspective which contends that ironists always convey a true message, and it is the shared knowledge and the upcoming contrast what have irony arise. This wrong perception extends to how some users conceive irony as something you can *do: hacer ironía [do irony]* meaning *to be funny* or *to be kidding* (examples *g.* and *h.* below).

d. *La ironía, esa verdad poliédrica [irony, a multifaceted reality]*
e. *No es ironía, es la realidad [it's not irony, it's reality]*
f. *Se nota la ironía, aprende a mentir [you can tell the irony, learn how to lie]*
g. *(...) Me ha hecho ironía [it was funny]*
h. *Estaba haciendo ironía [I was kidding]*

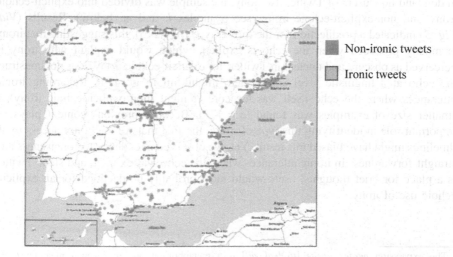

Non-ironic tweets
Ironic tweets

Fig. 2. Map of total tweets manually codified

In line with this, a wide range of comments explicitly evinced how users find it a rather arduous task to express ironical tweets and how they even reflect on the use of linguistic markers, such as emojis, interjections or *ironía on* and *off*, for clarification (examples *i.* and *j.* below). In this respect, some texts followed by emojis, which would normally be derived as ironic utterances, might not be interpreted as so by the literally-minded. In such cases, the presence of the hashtag might be necessary to transmit the intended message. Furthermore, not all utterances including the word "irony" were ironic (i.e. instances of *ironía off*), so they were not contemplated for later analyses. Another common pattern that we found was a list of Situational Irony tweets; however, since it departed from the focus of our study, it was casted off (*k.* below). This, along with the above-mentioned cases and the fact that occasionally it was not possible to access the timeline because of suspended twitter accounts, resulted in a final database of 445 tweets. Still, the sample was large enough to illustrate the characteristics of explicit and non-explicit echoic irony, as well as to do a typology of the PUs that highlight the ironic nature of a message. Besides, the non-ironic tweets helped us gain a better understanding of how irony is conceptualized in Twitter by Spanish-speakers.

i. *Voy a tenerle que poner a todas las ironías un* 😄 *detrás porque si no no se entienden [I will need to write* 😄 *after using irony, because my messages are not coming across]*

j. *El wao es para de alguna forma dar a entender que es 100% ironía [The "wow" is to show somehow that it's irony 100%]*

k. *Que el autobús homófobo de Hazte Oír pierda aceite es una gran ironía de la vida [The homophobic bus from Hazte Oír leaking oil[7] is irony of life]*

5.2 How Is Verbal Irony Conveyed, Through Explicit or Non-explicit Echo? Are the Ironic Utterances Positive or Negative?

A final corpus of 448 tweets served as a basis for our analysis on VI. In an attempt to understand how users of Twitter use irony, the sample was divided into explicit-echoic irony and non-explicit-echoic irony (see examples *l.* and *m.* below). Results (*Vid. Fig. 3*) indicated a predilection for the former type (*n* = 275), this suggesting that irony is mostly produced when the echo is explicit, which would explain why irony is perceived as obscure and unclear in Twitter, for explicit-echoic irony does not construct the echo at a linguistic level and readers might fail to grasp it. Regarding ironic utterances where the echo itself was the core element (non-explicit-echoic irony), a smaller size of examples was found (*n* = 173). Because previous context plays an important role in identifying this type of irony, the fact that we could not access to all timelines might have biased this result. Yet, we observed a tendency to conciseness and straight-forwardness in ironic utterances where the echo was explicit, and since Twitter is a place for brief thoughts, users would most probably be declined for an explicit-echoic use of irony.

---

[7] The expression *perder aceite* [*to leak oil*] is a metaphorical one in Spanish meaning *to be homosexual.*

l. Non-explicit: *Otro peligroso fascista que defiende la libertad de expresión (ironía)* *[Another dangerous fascist defending freedom of speech (irony)]*

m. Explicit: *Otro rojo peligroso (#ironía) [Another dangerous red (#irony)]*

Fig. 3. Explicit and non-explicit-echoic irony tweets

With regard to positive and negative utterances, we looked only at the linguistic sign (*n.* below) in the case of explicit-echoic irony, and for non-explicit-echoic irony (*o.* below) we analyzed the first section of the utterance, that is, the part that the reader is required to process first. When the ironist wrote a tweet and the utterance contained positive words or carried out an optimistic or pessimistic message at the beginning and then there was a polarity or emotional change caused by either hashtags, emojis or the continuation of the utterance, that clash indicated that it was indeed ironic. Whether irony was made through positive or negative phrases, it described the opposite psychological process.

n. *Qué vida más guay tenngoooo #ironía [what a niceee life #irony]* (positive and explicit)

o. *Qué malo es esto de* ir a formarse (modo ironía on) *[how bad it is to get an education -irony on]* (negative and non-explicit)

p. *Feminismo en estado puro (ironía)* 😆 *[Feminism in its pure state (irony) 😆]*

As a result, positive utterances denoted the ironist's negative attitude on the matter and negative ones were used to convey positive thoughts. This semantic incoherence and changes in emotional scenarios have been used in computational linguistics as a feature or information source to detect irony in English [8]. Results from our analysis indicated that Spanish-speaking users of Twitter tended to significantly use positive utterances (n = 138) in comparison to negative ones (n = 42), which led us to deduce that irony is mostly used for conveying negative attitudes rather than positive emotions. This could be explained by the fact that in our culture complaining about something

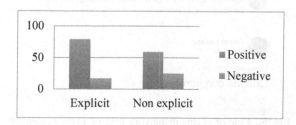

Fig. 4. Relation between echoic types of VI and positive/negative linguistic signs

meaning that you are not happy with it or that you do not agree in a straight-forward and direct manner is not that common or well accepted in social media. Furthermore, only those tweets that were clear examples of positive or negative scenarios were selected and, as a result, utterances not incorporating ironic linguistic signs showing positive or negative emotions were excluded ($n = 265$) (see example $p.$).

Considering all these variables together, we wanted to explore whether there was a difference in the use of positive or negative utterances depending on the echoic type (*Vid. Fig. 4*). As for explicit-echoic irony, a significantly higher amount of positive linguistic expressions was found ($n = 79$) in comparison to negative ones ($n = 17$). Similarly, users expressing irony in a non-explicit-echoic manner used more positive utterances to convey negative attitudes ($n = 59$) in comparison to negative linguistic expressions ($n = 25$). The analysis also yielded a worth-mentioning finding that sheds light on the echoic typology of irony, for results showed a tendency towards higher uses of negative utterances in non-explicit-echoic irony ($n = 25$) compared to ironical instances where the echo was explicit, that is, not formed at a linguistic level. This finding is in agreement with our previous results and seems to suggest that when the echo is present within the utterance, normally in longer and more obscure tweets, the linguistic markers employed by the ironist tend to be negative.

5.3   Is Explicit and Non-explicit Echoic Irony Mostly Hashtag-Induced or Emoji-Induced? and Positive and Negative Utterances?

Our next analysis aimed at examining whether each of the previously-explored values —explicit-echoic and non-explicit echoic irony, and positive and negative utterances— were constructed by tagging the message with the hashtag #*ironía* (and its variants) or with emojis, in order to understand which non-linguistic signs interact the most along with potential ironic texts. Findings from a qualitative analysis evidenced the importance of adding extra-elements, especially when there was explicit-echoic irony. Figure 5 shows how the use of either an emoji or hashtag would have allowed the reader to interpret *reciente [recently]* as ironic, with no need for ironic clarification: *que iba con ironía [it was ironic].*

Fig. 5. Line of tweets displaying lack of irony perception

Results from a quantitative analysis of the total number of ironic tweets showed a major use of hashtag utterances (n = 499) in comparison to emoji-generated ironic ones (n = 129). These findings can be interpreted as users having a preference to be clear about their tweet being ironical, for as previously discussed, ironical attitudes frequently remain just intentionally ironical in social media, but not linguistically or tend to fail to be grasped by obtuse addressees. A higher use of hashtags might also be related to users' will to increase their reach, as it is easier to have a tweet liked or retweeted when using a hashtag. Furthermore, this finding was found to be mirrored in each subcategory of irony (*Vid. Table 1*). Hence, explicit-echoic irony was mostly produced with hashtags (n = 216; 78,54%) as compared to utterances using emojis (n = 59; 21,45%); non-explicit-echoic irony also showed more instances of hashtag ironic utterances (n = 140; 80,92% vs n = 33; 19, 07%); similarly, positive utterances were found to be more hashtag-induced (n = 112; 81,15%) than emoji-induced (n = 26; 18,84%); and finally, negative utterances also evinced more hashtags (n = 31) than emojis (n = 11) to form irony, but the difference was found to be smaller (73,8% vs 26,19%).

Table 1. Emoji vs hashtag in %

Type	Hashtag	Emoji
Explicit-echoic	78,54%	21,45%
Non-explicit-echoic	80,92%	19, 07%
Positive	81,15%	18,84%
Negative	73,8%	26,19%

With regard to the findings for explicit-echoic irony, since the echo is explicit there is a high probability that the reader interprets the words literally. In this case, cues such as hashtags, which were found to be the generally-preferred markers to highlight irony in Twitter, were also significantly higher for this subtype. As for non-explicit irony, these results corroborated our hypothesis that since echo is the most relevant element and it is observed at a linguistic level, the "text" itself could be sufficient to grasp irony and thus peripheral elements such as emojis or the hashtag would not be so prevalent.

5.4   Which Phraseological Units Are Related to the Expression of Verbal Irony? How Are They Constructed, Hashtag or Emoji-Induced?

The last research question examined the different cues within the text, that is, the expressions or linguistic markers that are productive in conveying ironic implicatures. A qualitative analysis of the selected data (n = 448) was conducted so as to understand how irony is created linguistically. All tweets containing VI were explored paying attention to the contrast between elements in each utterance: text-hashtag and text-emoji. Apart from these latter, we also found a large list of PUs within the "text" regardless of them being part of a larger PU (see example *q.* below).

$$q. \underline{\text{Claro que sí #ironía [yeah, sure #irony]}}$$
$$\underline{\text{PU}}$$
$$\text{Text + hashtag= PU}$$

A classification of the different expressions potentially conveying irony was first done by looking at the utterance and disregarding the non-linguistic signs (hashtag and emoji). Thus, tweets were first codified and categorized by subject or theme on which they had the irony constructed. Three main categories were identified: users' emotional status, politics (including the inter-governmental conflicts between Spain and Catalonia as a major subtopic) and football. Results from a quantitative analysis (*Vid. Fig. 5*) showed that irony was mostly used when tackling emotions and feelings, and there was a significant tendency to mark this type of tweets through hashtags (n = 247) compared to emojis (n = 33). Politics, particularly comments on the actions undertaken by the four main parties and on the Catalan independence movement, was the second most discussed topic, with 72 ironic tweets formed by text-hashtag and only 9 with emojis. The last big topic of ironic use in Twitter was football, which, contrary to the other two subjects, was found to build up the irony using more emojis than hashtags (n = 27 vs n = 20). This could be explained according to our previous results on hashtag and emoji-generated irony, for this latter seems to be more obscure. Because football is more of an informal topic compared to politics or expressing one's feelings, users might not mind being ambiguous. We included as "other" a list of tweets targeting at a wide variety of topics, including TV programs, such as Big Brother, or the weather.

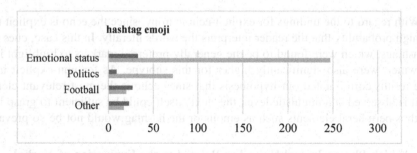

Fig. 6. Topics related to hashtag or emoji-induced irony

A second categorization was done looking first at the type of "text" and second at each possible combination: text-hashtag and text-emoji. Regarding the text, the linguistic signs were classified into two main categories: (1) features closer to orality, for they could potentially evoke distinctive tones or stress, or even inform of bodily and facial expressions, and (2) features common to written text not displaying any non-verbal direct inference. With regard to the first set of features, after codification, six subcategories were identified:

– Interjections (*oh, eh, uh; ¡anda! [come on!], viva [hurrah!], enhorabuena [con-gratulations!], gracias [thanks], vaya [okay]*; PUs: *vaya + noun [what a + noun], menos mal [thank god], qué va [no way]*);
– Punctuation marks (quotation marks, ellipses, exclamation marks, interrogation marks);
– Vowel enlargement (*maravilloooooso [amaaazing]*);
– Uppercases (*VAMOS [COME ON]*);
– Derivational suffixes: diminutive (i.e., *[cosilla little thing]*), augmentative (i.e., *queridísima [dearest]*) and pejorative (i.e., *sueldazo [fat salary]*);
– Laughter typing (*jaja [haha], jeje [hehe], jiji [hihi], jojo [hoho]*).

Results from a quantitative analysis of each subcategory indicated that uppercases and punctuation marks were the features that correlated the strongest with irony formation, with a total of 334 ironic tweets using hashtag and only 45 using emojis, for uppercases (*Vid. Fig. 6*), and 201 tweets with hashtag and 42 with emoji for punctuation marks. These were followed by the use of interjections (especially the PU *vaya + noun*) along with hashtags ($n = 67$) and emojis ($n = 11$). Laughter typing accounted for a total of 29 hashtag-generated ironic utterances compared to a smaller size containing emojis ($n = 6$). Fewer instances of irony formed through vowel enlargement and derivational suffixes were found (22 and 14 respectively along with hashtag, and 7 and 1 respectively for emojis), yet they were still clear examples of segmental features that influenced suprasegmental ones such as the stress of the word and intonation of the sentence, thus reinforcing the ironic nature of the utterance (*Vid. Fig. 7*).

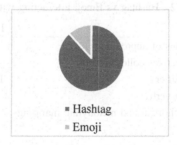

■ Hashtag
▪ Emoji

Fig. 7. Hashtag vs Emoji with uppercases

Moving now to the second category, which was formed by a diverse variety of PUs, we identified five subcategories: (1) fixed expressions of approval (i.e., *claro que sí [yeah sure)*, (2) collocations with qualitative adjectives (adj + noun: *dramática muerte [drastic death]* or noun + adj: *error garrafal [terrible mistake]*), (3) intensifiers in the form of collocations (adv + adj/adv: *tan divertido [so* funny] or *mazo guay [super cool]/tan bien [so good]* or *qué pena [what a shame]*; det +noun: *qué año [what a year]*, (4) psych-verbs (experiencer + verb + stimulus: *me encantan los lunes [I love Mondays]*), and last but not least (5) expressions with metaphorical and metonymic mappings used in everyday language (*el próximo sábado culés y leones como un solo hombre [next Saturday culés and leones as one man]*; (...) *son los más honrados de la galaxia [they are the most honored ones in the galaxy]*, as an example of metaphoric hyperbole).

A quantitative analysis of these linguistic expressions yielded similar results to the ones obtained for features connected to orality with regard to the use of hashtag or emojis to form irony. Hence, each subcategory of the five above-mentioned showed greater co-occurrences of text-hashtag as compared to those of text-emoji. Table 2 shows the number of expressions used along with either hashtag or emojis to generate irony. In the case of approval fixed expressions, 12 linguistic expressions were found to appear with hashtags and 3 were emoji-induced. Regarding collocations composed by noun + qualitative adjectives, these also evinced greater connections to hashtags than to emojis (20 and 5, respectively). PUs containing intensifiers were by far the most used expressions, also showing significantly higher co-occurrences with hashtags than with emojis (115 and 9). Also PUs where the nucleus was a psych-verbs and PUs with metaphorical or metonymic mappings were found to coappear with hashtags more frequently than with emojis (hashtags, 39 and 17 respectively; emojis, 14 and 2). This common pattern observed for these two categories leads us to infer that even though the linguistic cues are considered as markers of irony, they are still missing suprasegmental cues present in face-to-face communication. As a result, for clarification matters, they mostly incorporate the hashtag in order for readers to not miss on no account the writer's ironic attitude.

Table 2. Hashtag vs Emoji interacting with PUs

Type	Hashtag	Emoji
Fixed expressions of approval	12	3
Qualitative adjectives collocations	20	5
PUs with intensifiers	115	9
PUs with psych-verbs	39	14
PUs with metaphorical and metonymic mappings	17	2

6   Conclusions

The findings in the present study have contributed to gain a better understanding of how Spanish-speakers conceptualize and express linguistically irony in one of the most-used social platforms nowadays. Results suggest that VI tends to be misused and misconceived by Twitter users and, thus, adding external non-linguistic signs, such as hashtags, indicating that the statement is ironical averts misunderstandings, especially in explicit-echoic ironic cases. When users made use of irony in an efficient manner, a higher use of both explicit-echoic irony and positive linguistic expressions was found to the detriment of non-explicit-echoic and negative tweets. In the same vein, a major co-occurrence between text-hashtag as compared to text-emoji was evinced for all potentially ironic linguistic signs (uppercases, PUs in interjections, etc.). Results also underline the main topics to which users recur for irony, being these the user's emotional state, politics and football.

This is the first study to our knowledge which has investigated ironical phraseology in terms of cognitive modeling based on the analysis of a big dataset that departed from near 5 million tweets from 64 different languages. Narrowing our sample down, data were collected from Spanish-speaking users of Twitter who used it to convey ironical attitudes in Spanish territory within a period of four months. This authentic corpus of ironic statements that reveals how irony is formed linguistically through PUs becomes then an ecologically-valid and useful pedagogic tool in the ELE classroom. Because VI is expressed differently across languages, it is fundamental to teach potentially ironic PUs at early stages of acquisition in order for the student to acquire these as indivisible units that express a single notion. Likewise, the teaching of irony can enhance the development of intercultural sensitivity in the learner, resulting in this latter being closer to become a social-agent and an intercultural and autonomous speaker in the foreign language. We expect these results to not only have implications within the field of didactics in ELE, but to also contribute to the area of computational linguistics in the categorization of feature types by incorporating information from the explicit and non-explicit-echoic typology, as well as from the PUs categorization presented in this study.

Acknowledgments. The research presented in this paper was supported by an FPU grant from the Spanish Government. A special thanks goes to Álvaro Maroto for access to his bigdata corpus of Twitter. The author thanks Prof. Antonio Barcelona and Prof. Olga Blanco for their guidance and continuous support, and Prof. Francisco J. Ruiz de Mendoza for his invaluable help and enlightening conversations on verbal irony.

References

1. Attardo, S., Eisterhold, J., Hay, J., Poggi, I.: Multimodal markers of irony and sarcasm. Humor **16**(2), 243–260 (2003)
2. Barcelona, A.: On the plausibility of claiming a metonymic motivation for conceptual metaphor. In: Barcelona, A. (ed.) Metaphor and Metonymy at the Crossroads. A Cognitive Perspective, pp. 31–58. Mouton de Gruyter, Berlin (2000)
3. Ghosh, A., Li, G., Veale, T., Rosso, P., Shutova, E., Barnden, J., Reyes, A.: SemEval-2015 task 11: sentiment analysis of figurative language in Twitter. In: Proceedings of the 9th International Workshop on Semantic Evaluation, Denver, Colorado, pp. 470–478 (2015)
4. Gibbs, R.W., Colston, H.L.: The future of irony studies. In: Gibbs, R.W., Colston, H.L. (eds.) Irony in Language and Thought: A Cognitive Science Reader, pp. 581–593. Lawrence Erlbaum Associates Publishers, Mahwah (2007)
5. Lakoff, G., Johnson, M.: Metaphors We Live By. University of Chicago press, Chicago (1980)
6. Maroto, A.: Big Data, Twitter and Music: New paths in research. https://www.researchgate.net/publication/331479188. Accessed 14 Jan 2019
7. Maroto, A.: El metadiscurso en las redes sociales: una extensión multidimensional. Análisis de cinco dirigentes políticos de la coalición Ahora Podemos a través de la red social Twitter. https://www.researchgate.net/publication/331479188. Accessed 14 Jan 2019

8. Rosenthal, S., Farra, N., Nakov, P.: SemEval-2017 task 4: sentiment analysis in Twitter. In: Proceedings of the 11th International Workshop on Semantic Evaluation, Vancouver, Canada, pp. 502–518 (2017)
9. Ruiz de Mendoza, F.J.: Metonymy and cognitive operations. In: Benczes, R., Barcelona, A., Ruiz de Mendoza, F.J. (eds.) Defining Metonymy in Cognitive Linguistics, pp. 104–123. John Benjamins, Amsterdam/Philadelphia (2011)
10. Ruiz de Mendoza, F.J., Masegosa, A.G.: Cognitive modeling: a linguistic perspective. John Benjamins Publishing Company, Amsterdam (2014)
11. Van Hee, C., Lefever, E., Hoste, V.: SemEval-2018 task 3: irony detection in English tweets. In: Proceedings of the 12th International Workshop on Semantic Evaluation, New Orleans, LA, USA, pp. 39–50 (2018)
12. Weissman, B., Tanner, D.: A strong wink between verbal and emoji-based irony: How the brain processes ironic emojis during language comprehension. PloSone 13(8), e0201727 (2018)

Profiling Idioms:

A Sociolexical Approach to the Study of Phraseological Patterns

Sara Može[✉] and Emad Mohamed[✉]

Research Institute of Information and Language Processing (RIILP),
University of Wolverhampton, Wolverhampton, UK
{S.Moze,E.Mohamed2}@wlv.ac.uk

Abstract. This paper introduces a novel approach to the study of lexical and pragmatic meaning called 'sociolexical profiling', which aims at correlating the use of lexical items with author-attributed demographic features, such as gender, age, profession, and education. The approach was applied to a case study of a set of English idioms derived from the Pattern Dictionary of English Verbs (PDEV), a corpus-driven lexical resource which defines verb senses in terms of the phraseological patterns in which a verb typically occurs. For each selected idiom, a gender profile was generated based on data extracted from the Blog Authorship Corpus (BAC) in order to establish whether any statistically significant differences can be detected in the way men and women use idioms in every-day communication. A quantitative and qualitative analysis of the gender profiles was subsequently performed, enabling us to test the validity of the proposed approach. If performed on a large scale, we believe that sociolexical profiling will have important implications for several areas of research, including corpus lexicography, translation, creative writing, forensic linguistics, and natural language processing.

Keywords: Idiom · Phraseology · Sociolexical profiling · Gender · Corpus linguistics

1 Introduction

The field of lexicography has undergone dramatic changes over the past three decades, mainly as a direct result of the latest technological developments in Computer Science and the emergence of Corpus Linguistics as the predominant methodology in the compilation of modern dictionaries and lexical resources. This has important implications for the study of language and meaning, as scholars are now able to study large numbers of observed uses of each word in order to discover how it is normally used. Furthermore, the Internet now offers plentiful evidence for word use and word meaning, with billions upon billions of words of text in machine-readable form being readily available to linguists and Natural Language Processing (NLP) specialists alike. The opportunities are seemingly limitless – and with a large portion of the general population being increasingly active on social media, the amount and type of linguistically relevant information that can be harvested from blogs, tweets, and other

G. Corpas Pastor and R. Mitkov (Eds.): Europhras 2019, LNAI 11755, pp. 315–329, 2019.
https://doi.org/10.1007/978-3-030-30135-4_23

publicly available online texts can help shed new light onto previously undiscovered patterns of linguistic behaviour.

Another multidisciplinary field that has greatly benefitted from Corpus Linguistic research is Forensic Linguistics, with corpus stylometry techniques being increasingly used to study the linguistic habits and patterns of both individuals and groups. Authorship profiling and attribution, in particular, are two such tasks where major breakthroughs have been made (cf. Grieve 2007; Juola 2008; Stamatatos 2008; Argamon et al. 2009; Savoy 2015). Computational methods are now being extensively used to determine which sets of textual features can be used to distinguish between the writing styles of different authors, enabling researchers to study their stylistic signatures in a similar way a detective would analyse a suspect's fingerprint, and to determine how common characteristics such as, for instance, age, gender, level of education, profession, and socioeconomic background are reflected in the choices we make as authors of texts (cf. Oakes 2014).

In this paper, we propose a new approach to the study of lexical items, which we call *sociolexical profiling.* In a similar way to how forensic linguists approach the study of authorial fingerprints, we advance that researchers can profile lexical items (including phraseological units) by correlating their use with author-attributed demographic features. As far as we are aware, this approach has not been attempted anywhere before. In the present study, we decided to apply the technique to the study of English idioms in order to test the validity of our approach.

Existing English dictionaries provide a wealth of information on a word's semantics and, to some extent, phraseological units in which it participates, however, they very often fail to explain how the user is supposed to distinguish one sense from another, or provide them with sufficiently detailed information on a word's collocational preferences. To address these inadequacies, Hanks (2013) advocates for a new generation of 'context-sensitive' dictionaries, i.e. corpus-driven pattern dictionaries, which disambiguate between the different senses of a word based on the phraseological patterns in which it typically occurs. Whilst pattern dictionaries provide an innovative solution to the word sense disambiguation problem, enabling lexicographers to list verb senses in a systematic and empirically well-founded way, there are currently still some limitations as to the type of semantic information they provide. More specifically, a word's meaning typically also incorporates fine-grained semantic and pragmatic distinctions that cannot be captured from its local linguistic context. In dictionaries, usage information is typically limited to domain and register labels, with semantic prosody only sporadically being encoded (e.g. through the use of labels such as 'pejorative' and 'offensive'), and general monolingual dictionaries typically do not encode detailed demographic information, profiling lexical items or word senses in terms of the gender, age, profession, or level of education of their prototypical users. The reason for this is relatively simple – speaker profiles are not meaning-determining features, hence they are not covered in dictionaries. We propose that using sociolexical profiling to enrich existing dictionaries could benefit a range of users from language professionals (e.g. translators, writers), linguists, to NLP researchers, and if such information can be integrated in a user-friendly, visually appealing way (e.g. interactive pop-ups, graphs etc.), it could help attract a wider pool of non-expert dictionary users.

The paper is structured as follows: Sect. 2 provides a detailed description of the Pattern Dictionary of English Verbs (PDEV), the primary lexical resource used to compile the initial list of idiom candidates to be examined in the study. Section 3 is dedicated to the practical experiments undertaken in this paper: the corpus and methodology (Sect. 3.1) used in the case study are described, and the results of both the quantitative and qualitative analysis are presented and summarised (Sect. 3.2). Finally, the main findings of the study are discussed (Sect. 4), alongside potential applications and future directions for our research.

2 Pattern Dictionary of English Verbs

The Pattern Dictionary of English Verbs (PDEV) (Hanks, in progress) is an online lexical resource that aims to describe the full variety of phraseological patterns exhibited by English verbs. PDEV is a corpus-driven resource compiled using the methodological apparatus of Corpus Pattern Analysis (CPA) (Hanks 2004, 2013), which allows linguists to disambiguate between a word's senses by mapping meaning onto specific lexicogrammatical patterns exhibited by a verb in a given context. Underpinned by the Theory of Norms and Exploitations (TNE) (Hanks, 2013), CPA aims at identifying 'norms', i.e. semantically motivated syntagmatic patterns of normal usage, including literal and domain-specific uses, conventional metaphors, phrasal verbs, and idioms, and exploring the way these patterns are creatively exploited in language through detailed, labour-intensive lexical analysis of large corpus samples.

The core idea behind TNE is that whilst words are hopelessly ambiguous, lexicogrammatical patterns are unambiguous and can therefore serve as a powerful tool for word sense disambiguation. TNE focuses on real language use rather than preconceived speculations about language typical of introspection-driven theories of meaning, thus providing a window into the every-day phraseology, an area of study often overlooked by traditional linguists who, for a very long time, favoured atypical and marginal linguistic phenomena over prototypical patterns of language use. Due to this focus, CPA and TNE are particularly well-suited to both lexicographic projects and meaning-focused Natural Language Processing (NLP) tasks.

In CPA-based pattern dictionaries, the different senses of a verb are presented as combinations of specific syntactic structures, lexical collocates, and semantic types representing the typical nominal slot fillers for each syntactic argument. Consider the verb *bark* shown in Fig. 1. According to PDEV, this verb exhibits four patterns, which correspond to four separate verb senses. Pattern 1, which occurs in more than two thirds (67.68%) of the annotated sample, describes a situation where an animal, usually a dog, fox, seal, or baboon, emits one or more sharp cries. This is also the most cognitively salient sense of *bark*, meaning that this is the primary, core meaning associated with the verb. This meaning of the verb is extended in pattern 2, in which *bark* is coerced into being a reporting verb by the monotransitive construction, in which either a noun phrase (e.g. *The platoon commanders barked their orders to dismount*) or a quote (e.g. *'BY TOMORROW THEN!' he barked back, and slammed down the receiver*) occurs in the direct object slot. In this case, parts of the verb's core semantics relating to the utterance of sharp noises is preserved, whilst the aggressive aspect of barking is foregrounded to indicate that the human's behaviour is perceived to be highly unpleasant (negative semantic prosody). The capitalised words displayed between double square brackets ([[Human]], [[Dog]], [[Speech_Act]]) are not lexical items, but 'semantic types', i.e. mnemonic labels that best describe the semantic features shared by the nouns that typically occur in a given argument slot. Pattern 4 is not relevant for our discussion, as it refers to an etymologically unrelated sense of the verb (homonymy). Pattern 3, on the other hand, features a well-known idiom, i.e. *bark up the wrong tree* (to pursue a misguided course of action or line of thought), which clearly originated from pattern 1. This type of patterns are the focus of the present paper and case study. Each observed sense of the verb *bark*, including the idiom *bark up the wrong tree,* can only be activated by this specific combination of obligatory syntactic arguments (subject, direct object, adverbial) and their corresponding semantic types or nominal slot fillers called lexical sets (e.g. *the wrong tree*).

For each verb in PDEV, a random corpus sample consisting of at least 250 concordance lines is extracted from the British National Corpus (Leech 1992) using Sketch Engine (Kilgarriff et al. 2014), and tagged with numbers corresponding to the pattern each concordance line exemplifies. When analysing high frequency and phraseologically complex verbs, e.g. light verbs such as *take*, *make*, or *blow*, the sample is normally augmented to 500, 1,000, or more lines so as to ensure that all phraseological patterns exhibited by the analysed verb are covered. Patterns are identified mainly through lexical analysis of corpus lines, complemented by information obtained through the 'word sketch' functionality in the Sketch Engine, which allows users to automatically generate a list of statistically relevant collocates and syntactic structures from a selected corpus. Patterns are then recorded and described in the CPA Editor (Baisa et al. 2015), our customized dictionary writing system, using CPA's shallow ontology of semantic types (Ježek and Hanks 2010), which is shared across all CPA projects (for a detailed commentary on cross-linguistic adaptations of the ontology, see Nazar and Renau 2015). For each pattern, one or more implicatures are also added; the pattern's primary implicature (dark blue font) functions as its definition, whilst secondary implicatures (light grey font), which are optional, are added to semantically complex patterns that require further contextual information (situational, historical, or cultural) to be interpreted correctly (e.g. *'Typically, [[Dog]] does this as a warning'* in Pattern 1 – see Fig. 1). Domain (e.g. Medical, Law, Biology, Journalism) and register labels (e.g. Slang, Informal, Archaic) are added to each pattern individually, as are idiom and phrasal verb labels. Finally, each pattern is linked to the corresponding semantic frame in FrameNet (Ruppenhofer et al. 2006), with the aim of linking the two complementary lexical resources. PDEV entries also include quantitative information: for each separate pattern, a percentage is listed based on the pattern's frequency of occurrence in the manually annotated corpus sample.

Currently, PDEV contains over 1,700 completed dictionary entries, covering about one third of all lexical verbs in the English language. Similar pattern dictionaries are currently being compiled for Spanish (Renau and Nazar, in progress), Italian (Jezek et al. 2014), and Croatian, *inter alia.*

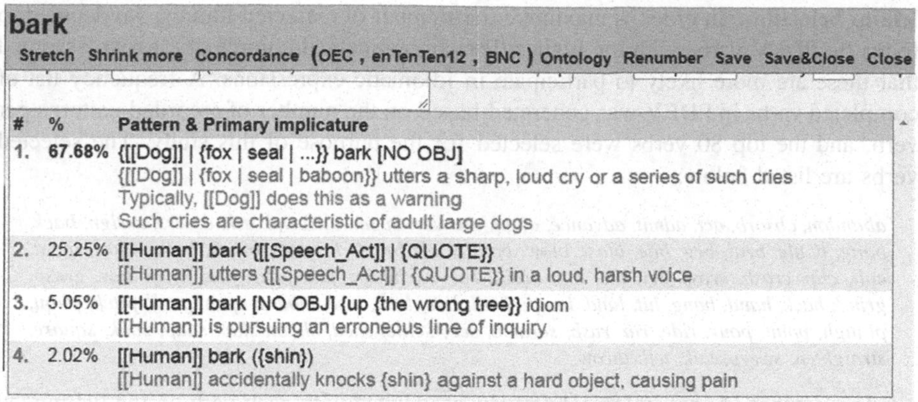

bark

Stretch Shrink more Concordance (OEC , enTenTen12 , BNC) Ontology Renumber Save Save&Close Close

#	%	Pattern & Primary implicature
1.	67.68%	{[[Dog]] | {fox | seal | ...}} bark [NO OBJ] {[[Dog]] | {fox | seal | baboon}} utters a sharp, loud cry or a series of such cries Typically, [[Dog]] does this as a warning Such cries are characteristic of adult large dogs
2.	25.25%	[[Human]] bark {[[Speech_Act]] | {QUOTE}} [[Human]] utters {[[Speech_Act]] | {QUOTE}} in a loud, harsh voice
3.	5.05%	[[Human]] bark [NO OBJ] {up {the wrong tree}} idiom [[Human]] is pursuing an erroneous line of inquiry
4.	2.02%	[[Human]] bark ({shin}) [[Human]] accidentally knocks {shin} against a hard object, causing pain

Fig. 1. The PDEV entry for the verb *bark.*

3 Case Study: Profiling PDEV Idioms

3.1 Corpus and Methodology

Corpus. The primary objective of this study was to investigate whether there are significant differences in the way men and women use idioms in every-day communication. For this purpose, we decided to use a subset of the Blog Authorship Corpus (BAC) (Schler et al. 2006; Argamon et al. 2009) comprising 681,288 blogs written by 19,230 bloggers, with a total of over 140 million words. BAC includes metadata about the bloggers' gender, age, occupation, and zodiac sign, which enabled us to generate gender usage statistics for our selected PDEV idioms. The subcorpus was selected so as to include an equal number of male and female bloggers, all aged between 13 and 47, as shown in Table 1 below.

Table 1. Age distribution in the BAC subcorpus.

Age group	Number of blogs
13–17	8,240
23–27	8,086
33–47	2,994

In order to test our core assumption that significant differences can be observed between speakers of different genders, we ran a preliminary experiment in which we trained a machine learning classifier to predict the gender of the blog writer. A precision and recall score of 0.72 was obtained in the experiment, indicating that the difference between the two genders is not random. In the experiment, we used the FastText classifier (Joulin et al., 2017) with a training set of 500,000 documents and a test set of 81,285 documents. The classifier used lemmatized bigrams as features and was not optimized for prediction, as our only goal was to determine whether there are quantifiable linguistic differences between male and female bloggers.

Idiom Selection. In order to maximize the number of extracted idioms, we decided to focus on PDEV verbs with the highest lexicogrammatical complexity, as we assumed that these are more likely to participate in idiomatic expressions. A frequency list of completed verbs in PDEV was generated based on the number of recorded patterns per verb, and the top 80 verbs were selected for the purpose of this study. The selected verbs are listed below:

abandon, absorb, act, admit, advance, align, answer, appear, ascend, ask, assess, assign, back, bang, battle, beat, beg, bite, blast, blow, boil, book, break, breathe, brush, build, burn, burst, call, clip, crash, cross, cry, die, dig, drain, eat, exchange, fail, filter, fire, fly, follow, grasp, grind, hack, hand, hang, hit, land, laugh, lead, live, lock, lose, mount, open, pack, pitch, plant, plough, point, pour, ride, rip, rush, scratch, see, settle, shed, shoot, slap, snap, soak, square, straighten, sweep, talk, tell, throw

The number of phraseological patterns associated with each verb on the list ranged from 83 (*break*) to 11 (*grasp*). As mentioned in Sect. 2, idioms are considered as separate patterns in PDEV and are explicitly labelled; this enabled us to automatically extract all idioms found in the 80 PDEV entries with relative ease. The list was then manually checked and validated; for the purpose of this study, we decided to focus on idioms that are relatively fixed in terms of their lexical and syntactic behaviour so as to facilitate computational processing. As a result, idioms exhibiting a high number of lexical alternations or word order configurations (e.g. non-projective structures, particles) were removed from the list. The procedure yielded a final list of 106 idiom candidates to be extracted from the BAC Corpus.

Idiom Extraction. A cascaded set of regular expressions was used to process the corpus data and extract the idioms from BAC. The procedure can be broken down into the following steps:

Data pre-processing: this step involved cleaning the corpus by separating punctuation from words, normalizing spaces, and handling encoding issues in order to ensure that the corpus is encoded in UTF-8.

Morphological processing: for each selected idiom, a list of all potential word form combinations was generated. For example, the idiom *blow one's head* is conjugated in the following forms:

a. *blow one's head, blew one's head, blown one's head, blowing one's head;*
b. *blow his head, blow her head, blow their heads, blow my head, blow our heads, blow your head, blow your heads;*
c. *blew his head, blew her head, blew their heads, blew my head, blew our heads, blew your head, blew your heads;*
d. *blown his head, blown her head, blown their heads, blown my head, blown our heads, blown your head, blown your heads;*
e. *blowing his head, blowing her head, blowing their heads, blowing my head, blowing our heads, blowing your head, blowing your heads.*

The generation of these forms required writing rules and lists of word form alternations.

Statistical analysis: the generated list of word form combinations was used to extract all instances of the selected idioms in the BAC subcorpus, recording the number of occurrences in texts written by male and female authors, and these were then ranked to check their relative frequency per gender.

Manual Validation. The extracted information was manually examined to ensure that the results were valid and could be meaningfully used in the analysis. Out of the initial list of idiom candidates, 101 were found in the corpus; one (*lose it*) was removed from the list due to ambiguity issues (most extracted sentences were instances of literal and not idiomatic use). Idiom candidates with a frequency lower than 5 in the subcorpus were also removed from the list in order to ensure that the results of the analysis were statistically significant. The process resulted in a finalized list of 85 idioms with 37 different verb bases, i.e. *abandon, act, answer, battle, beat, beg, bite, blow, break, breathe, burn, burst, call, cry, die, dig, eat, fly, follow, grasp, grind, hang, hit, laugh, live, lose, open, pack, point, pour, scratch, shoot, snap, soak, sweep,* and *throw*.

Data Analysis. A qualitative analysis of the extracted idioms and the quantitative data was carried out in order to identify differences and similarities in the use of idioms between the two genders. Idioms were manually clustered into semantic classes based on semantic prosody, source and target domain (e.g. weapon and communication idioms), and other fine-grained semantic components.

3.2   Results

Two major conclusions can be drawn from the results obtained in the experiments: (1) some idioms appear to be predominantly used by one gender over the other, and (2) these tendencies do not necessarily correlate with the use of the verb lemma alone. Figure 2 shows the gender ratio of all 85 idioms in the BAC subcorpus, sorted from left to right in descending order by male percentage, with the symmetrical curve in the middle demonstrating a healthy distribution between the two genders. Whilst a significant portion of idioms appearing in the middle of the graph appears to be equally associated with both male and female speakers, idioms appearing at the two extremities, which tend to be used predominantly by male (left) and female (right) speakers, constitute just as significant a portion of the examined idiomatic expressions.

Tables 2 and 3 list the top 20 idioms predominantly used by men and women respectively. Although some of the relative frequencies listed in the tables are still relatively low,[1] the results do seem to point out to significant differences in the use of idioms between the two genders, with most idioms listed in the two tables being used by one of the genders in over two thirds of the corpus examples. A more detailed look into the two lists helped uncover further differences and similarities, enabling us to cluster idioms into semantically motivated groups and draw conclusions based on their gender profiles, as shown in the following subsections.

---

[1] This is not surprising; idioms are known to generally occur with very low frequencies in most corpora.

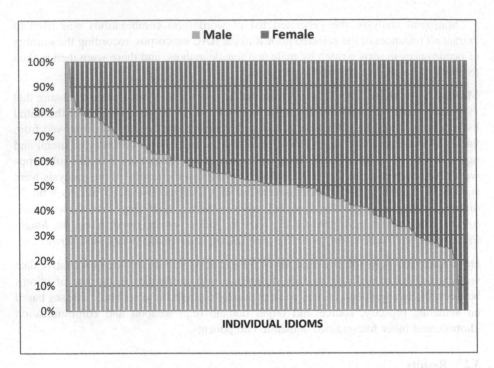

Fig. 2. Gender distribution of idioms in the subcorpus.

Verb Base. The idioms were first grouped according to their verb base, and basic statistics were generated in order to explore whether any meaningful distinctions can be made in the use of idioms by male and female bloggers. The results seem to indicate that men tend to prefer verb bases that express physical actions (e.g. *pack, grind, abandon, call, follow, answer, open, plant, grasp, pour, beg*), some of which are particularly forceful or violent (e.g. *shoot, hit, battle, beat, break*). Conversely, women typically use idioms whose verb base denotes basic life actions and bodily functions, e.g. *breathe, laugh, cry, live*, and *act*. Only two verb bases associated with women speakers encode some sort of force dynamics, i.e. *throw* and *blow*. However, *throw* typically appears in idiomatic light verb constructions (e.g. *throw a tantrum/fit/wobbly*) and is therefore delexicalised, hence the forceful aspect of its primary meaning is mostly not preserved.

In order to further explore the relationship between the analysed idioms and their verb bases, we extracted the total frequencies of occurrence of the 39 verb lemmas in the BAC subcorpus and compared them against their corresponding idioms. The new data showed that there are no statistically significant differences in the use of verb lemmas between the two genders, which clearly contrasts with their use in idiomatic expressions. Figure 3 compares the gender profiles of idioms predominantly associated with male bloggers with their corresponding verb lemmas. The verbs *abandon, point, grant,* and *pack* are used more or less equally by men and women; however, the data shows a strong male bias in the use of their corresponding idioms *abandon ship, point*

Table 2. The top 20 idioms predominantly used by male bloggers.

	Idiom	Frequency			Percentage	
		Male	Female	Total	Male	Female
1	*hit the headlines*	6	0	6	**100.00%**	0.00%
2	*throw the baby out with the bathwater*	6	1	7	**85.71%**	14.29%
3	*call the tune*	9	2	11	**81.82%**	18.18%
4	*answer the call of nature*	4	1	5	**80.00%**	20.00%
5	*grind to a halt*	28	8	36	**77.78%**	22.22%
6	*pour cold water on*	7	2	9	**77.78%**	22.22%
7	*pack a punch*	7	2	9	**77.78%**	22.22%
8	*bite the hand that feeds*	16	5	21	**76.19%**	23.81%
9	*hang in the balance*	23	8	31	**74.19%**	25.81%
10	*point the finger at sb*	30	11	41	**73.17%**	26.83%
11	*abandon ship*	17	7	24	**70.83%**	29.17%
12	*call a spade a spade*	13	6	19	**68.42%**	31.58%
13	*lose ground*	28	13	41	**68.29%**	31.71%
14	*call the shots*	30	14	44	**68.18%**	31.82%
15	*shoot oneself in the foot*	27	13	40	**67.50%**	32.50%
16	*breathe new life*	8	4	12	**66.67%**	33.33%
17	*follow suit*	128	66	194	**65.98%**	34.02%
18	*open the floodgates*	9	5	14	**64.29%**	35.71%
19	*hard to beat*	42	25	67	**62.69%**	37.31%
20	*plant the seed*	15	9	24	**62.50%**	37.50%

a finger at somebody, grind to a halt, and *pack a punch.* Furthermore, our analysis of *call* idioms uncovered significant differences in their gender profiles, with the percentage associated with men ranging from slightly over the 50% mark to as high as 81.82%. All of this seems to indicate that sociolexical profiling is indeed pattern-specific, which means that the different senses of a given word (physical, metaphorical, and domain-specific), as well as idioms, phrasal verbs, or other phraseological units, would theoretically require separate profiles.

Emotion Idioms. Significant differences have been detected in the use of idioms that express intense emotional states and attitudes. In the analysed sample, 15 such idioms were identified, and based on overall and individual frequency data, we can conclude that this type of idioms are used significantly more often by women. More specifically, over two thirds of all occurrences (69.41% or 776 out of 1118) were attributed to female bloggers, with all of the individual idioms on the list showing a strong bias towards female usage, as shown in Fig. 4.

Control and Aggression. Idioms expressing aggression were found to be evenly distributed, with a minor bias towards male usage (54.96%). Nonetheless, a minor difference can be observed in the type of aggression that is expressed by the idioms in

Table 3. The top 20 idioms predominantly used by female bloggers.

	Idiom	Frequency			Percentage	
		Male	Female	Total	Male	Female
1	*lose one's heart to*	0	7	7	0.00%	**100.00%**
2	*throw a wobbly*	0	5	5	0.00%	**100.00%**
3	*blow hot and cold*	2	8	10	20.00%	**80.00%**
4	*throw a fit*	28	87	115	24.35%	**75.65%**
5	*fly off the handle*	9	27	36	25.00%	**75.00%**
6	*burst into laughter*	55	163	218	25.23%	**74.77%**
7	*cry one's heart out*	47	130	177	26.55%	**73.45%**
8	*throw a tantrum*	12	32	44	27.27%	**72.73%**
9	*throw caution to the wind*	13	34	47	27.66%	**72.34%**
10	*breathe a word*	2	5	7	28.57%	**71.43%**
11	*act one's age*	19	46	65	29.23%	**70.77%**
12	*laugh one's head off*	39	85	124	31.45%	**68.55%**
13	*breathe a sigh of relief*	21	42	63	33.33%	**66.67%**
14	*not know whether to laugh or cry*	4	8	12	33.33%	**66.67%**
15	*live a double life*	3	6	9	33.33%	**66.67%**
16	*bite one's tongue*	50	96	146	34.25%	**65.75%**
17	*throw in the towel*	31	54	85	36.47%	**63.53%**
18	*pour one's heart out*	23	39	62	37.10%	**62.90%**
19	*soak up the sun*	16	27	43	37.21%	**62.79%**
20	*bite one's head off*	17	28	45	37.78%	**62.22%**

question: the only idiom expressing psychological aggression (bullying), i.e. *throw one's weight around,* was used slightly more frequently by women, although the frequencies extracted from the corpus are too low to make this observation conclusive. Conversely, male bloggers seem to have a slight preference for idioms that have a stronger physical component, with *pack a punch* and *battle it out* in particular being associated by male speakers (77.78% and 57.41% respectively), as shown in Fig. 5.

Control was another semantic component shared by a significant portion of the analysed idioms. Whilst the overall distribution of idioms expressing lack of control (e.g. *throw in the towel, hang by a thread, lose ground, bite off more than one can chew, abandon ship, eat humble pie*) was surprisingly even, this was not the case with idioms expressing highly assertive behaviour. More specifically, both *call the shots* and *call the tune* were found to be predominantly used by men, with 68.18% and 81.82% respectively. Both idioms have positive semantic prosody, indicating that speakers perceive the described act of taking control over a situation as proactiveness rather aggressive behaviour. This contrasts with the above mentioned *throw one's weight around,* which has decisively negative semantic prosody and is slightly more biased towards female usage.

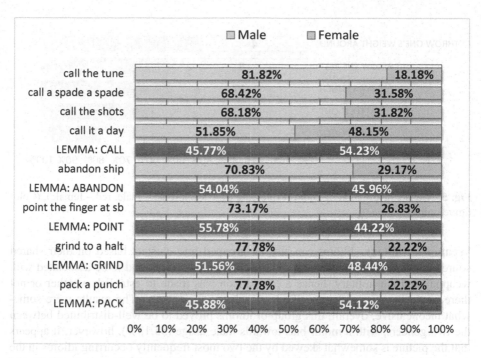

Fig. 3. Gender analysis of predominantly 'male' idioms and their corresponding verb lemmas.

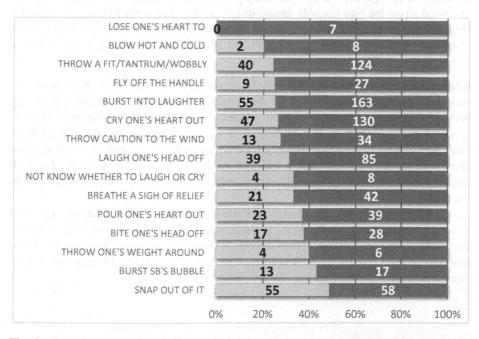

Fig. 4. Gender analysis of idioms incorporating a strong emotional component (blue – male; red – female). (Color figure online)

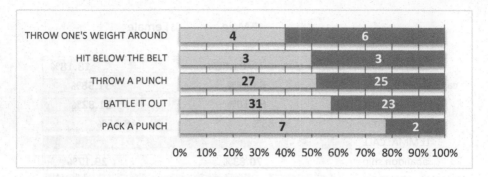

Fig. 5. Gender distribution of idioms expressing aggression (blue – male, red – female). (Color figure online)

Weapons, Military. Idioms can also be grouped into clusters based on their shared source domain(s). For instance, six idioms on the list were found to be associated with weapons and the military, hence a comparison was made to establish whether or not there might be any gender-specific tendencies in their usage. The results were somewhat inconclusive; overall, this group of idioms proved to be well-distributed between the two genders, with a minor bias towards male usage (55.13%), however, it appears that the picture is somewhat skewed by the two most frequently occurring idioms in the group, i.e. *hit the ground* and *bite the bullet,* which exhibited equal distribution between the two genders. It is worth noting that none of the six idioms in this group exhibited a positive bias towards female usage, whilst three other idioms, i.e. *abandon ship, call the shots,* and *shoot oneself in the foot,* were all found to be significantly more often used by male bloggers, with 70.83%, 68.18%, and 67.5% respectively, as shown in Fig. 6.

Communication. Several idioms loosely related to communication were identified and analysed in the study. Based on the results, these idioms constitute a relatively homogenous group in terms of their gender distribution (male bloggers: 47.45%, female bloggers: 52.55%). Nonetheless, it is worth noting that the only two idioms there were found to be predominantly used by women, i.e. *breathe a word* and *bite one's tongue,* are both associated with not speaking up or keeping silent. No such idioms were found among those that are evenly distributed or predominantly used by males.

An antonymous pair of idioms was also identified in the analysis, i.e. *beat around/about the bush – call a spade a spade,* which are used to describe one's style of communication (i.e. evasive versus direct). Whilst *beat around/about the bush* was found to be used equally by both genders, *call a spade a spade* was found to be used more frequently by men (see Fig. 7).

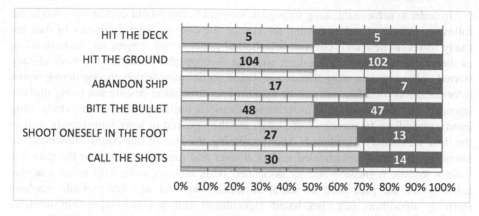

Fig. 6. Gender distribution of idioms originating from the Military/Weaponry domain (blue – male, red – female). (Color figure online)

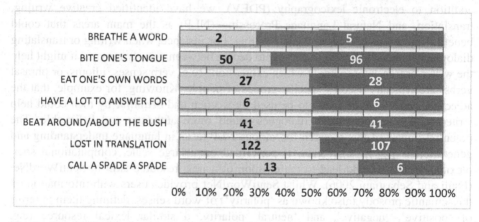

Fig. 7. Gender distribution of communication idioms (blue – male, red – female). (Color figure online)

4 Conclusion

In this paper, we presented a novel approach to the study of lexical and pragmatic meaning called sociolexical profiling. The results of our case study on idiom usage clearly demonstrated that there are significant differences in the way speakers of different genders use idioms, and that verb lemmas and phraseological units in which they are found do not necessarily share the same gender profile. This led to the conclusion that sociolexical profiling is pattern-specific. In the future, we intend to extend our approach to all other types of patterned language, generating a wide range of demographic profiles (gender, age, profession, *inter alia*) for all patterns in PDEV, including those corresponding to core senses, conventional metaphors, and other types of phraseological units such as phrasal verbs and proverbs.

In order to achieve this long-term goal, we plan to extend our current research in the following directions: (i) increasing the size of the corpus: large quantities of data are likely to reveal new undiscovered behavioural patterns and deepen our understanding of the correlation between language use and demographic features. We have already started collecting data using distant annotation techniques, which encode demographic information as metadata that can be exploited as annotation despite not being initially intended for this purpose; (ii) using more advanced statistical tests: in this study, only lemma and idiom frequencies were used, and they proved to work surprisingly well as the data was evenly distributed. After increasing the size of our corpus, however, we intend to use more sophisticated statistical tests and methods to explore the data, i.e. mainly logistic regression and its associated odds ratio measure; (iii) using machine learning for the prediction of social attributes: we will use interpretable machine learning algorithms (e.g. tree-based algorithms) and not-so-interpretable machine learning (e.g. neural network methods) to classify documents as belonging to one demographic class or another based on their linguistic features.

Several potential areas of application have been envisioned for our research; in addition to electronic lexicography (PDEV), we have identified creative writing, translation, and Natural Language Processing (NLP) as the main areas that could benefit from research in sociolexical profiling. For instance, when writing or translating dialogue between characters and trying to decide between near-synonyms, it might help the writer or translator to know which expressions (e.g. verb senses, idioms, or phrasal verbs) are typically used by specific groups of people. Knowing, for example, that the adjective *pretty* is more likely to be used by women and *beautiful* by men could help writers and translators make dialogues sound more authentic and believable. The potential impact of this research for various NLP tasks in language understanding and generation is just as significant. If performed on a large scale, computational sociolexical profiling could lead to the creation of a new resource akin to SentiWordNet (Esuli and Sebastiani 2006). Whilst SentiWordNet provides users with information on the semantic prosody (also known as 'polarity') of word senses, defining them in terms of 'positive', 'negative', and 'neutral' polarity, a similar lexical resource (e.g. 'SocioWordNet') that profiles lexicogrammatical patterns in terms of various demographic features could be compiled using sociolexical profiling as working methodology. Such a resource could be used in various NLP tasks. For instance, sociolexical profiles could be used as an additional feature in authorship attribution and profiling to improve the accuracy of existing systems, which currently still rely on relatively simple features such as word and character n-grams.

References

Argamon, S., Koppel, M., Schler, J., Pennebaker, J.: Automatically profiling the author of an anonymous text. Commun. ACM **52**(2), 119–123 (2009)

Baisa, V., El Maarouf, I., Rychlý, P., Rambousek, A.: Software and data for corpus pattern analysis. In: Horák, A. et al. (eds.) RASLAN, pp. 75–86. Tribun EU (2015)

Esuli, A., Sebastiani, F.: SENTIWORDNET: A Publicly Available Lexical Resource for Opinion Mining (2006). http://citeseer.ist.psu.edu/esuli06sentiwordnet.html

Grieve, J.: Quantitative authorship attribution: an evaluation of techniques. Lit. Linguist. Comput. **22**(3), 251–270 (2007)

Hanks, P.: Corpus pattern analysis. In: Williams, G., Vessier, S. (eds.) 11th Euralex International Congress, Proceedings, pp. 87–97. Université de Bretagne-Sud, Lorient (2004)

Hanks, P.: Lexical Analysis: Norms and Exploitations. MIT Press, Cambridge (2013)

Ježek, E., Hanks, P.: What lexical sets tell us about conceptual categories. Lexis: E-J. Eng. lexicol. 7–22 (2010). 4: Corpus Linguistics and the Lexicon

Ježek, E., Magnini, B., Feltracco, A., Bianchini, A., Popescu, O.: T-PAS: a resource of corpus-derived typed predicate argument structures for linguistic analysis and semantic processing. In: Proceedings of the Ninth International Conference on Language Resources and Evaluation (LREC'14), pp. 890–895. ELRA (2014)

Joulin, A., Grave, E., Bojanowski, P., Mikolov, T.: Bag of tricks for efficient text classification. In: Proceedings of the 15th Conference of the European Chapter of the Association for Computational Linguistics: Volume 2, Short Papers, pp. 427–431 (2017)

Juola, P.: Author attribution. Found. Trends Inf. Retr. **1**(3), 233–334 (2008)

Kilgarriff, A., et al.: The sketch engine: ten years on. Lexicography **1**(1), 7–36 (2014)

Nazar, R., Renau, I.: Ontology population using corpus statistics. In: Papini, O. et al. (eds.) Proceedings of the Joint Ontology Workshops 2015 Co-located with the 24th International Joint Conference on Artificial Intelligence (IJCAI 2015) (2015)

Leech, G.: 100 million words of English: the British National Corpus (BNC). Lang. Res. **28**(1), 1–13 (1992)

Oakes, M.: Literary Detective Work on the Computer. John Benjamins, Amsterdam/Philadelphia (2014)

Renau, I., Nazar, R.: Verbario. http://www.verbario.com. Accessed 14 May 2019

Ruppenhofer, J., Ellsworth, M., Petruck, M.R., Johnson, C.R., Scheffczyk, J.: FrameNet II: Extended Theory and Practice. ICSI, Berkeley (2006)

Savoy, J.: Comparative evaluation of term selection functions for authorship attribution. Lit. Linguist. Comput. **30**(2), 246–261 (2015)

Stamatatos, E.: A survey of modern authorship attribution methods. J. Am. Soc. Inf. Sci. Technol. **60**(3), 538–556 (2008)

Schler J., Koppel, M., Argamon, S., Pennebaker, J.: Effects of age and gender on blogging. In: AAAI Spring Symposium: Computational Approaches to Analyzing Weblogs, pp. 199 –205. AAAI (2006)

Typical Phraseological Units in Poetic Texts

Frequent Concepts in Works of Poetry and How MWUs Lack Synonyms

Michael Pace-Sigge[✉]

University of Eastern Finland, Joensuu, Finland
michp@uef.fi

Abstract. This paper looks at a corpus of British and US poetry, uncovering phraseological units which, through their frequency, are indicators of key concepts. *Multi-word units* (MWUs) have been discussed extensively with reference to corpus-based research, for example by Sinclair (1996) [2004], Biber and Conrad (1999), or, referred to as *formulaicity* by Wray (2002); O'Keefe *et al.* (2007), Greaves and Warren (2010) and Pace-Sigge (2015) describe MWUs preferred in different spoken and written genres. So far, however, there has been very little research in how far MWUs appear in the sub-genre of imaginative writing, namely, poetry. A commonly held view is that poetry by definition should not be yielding patterns- it subverts every pattern linguistically speaking that it can. Through focus on the main themes surfacing in multiword units, this research looks at usages found in poetic texts in-depth and compares sets of words found with their occurrence patterns in prose literature.

Keywords: Poetry · Common themes · Multi-word units · Synonymy

1 Introduction

This paper looks at a corpus of British and US poetry, focusing on the main themes surfacing and investigates the usages of sets of words that form multi-word units found and compares the occurrence patterns surfacing with those found in prose literature.

A commonly held view is that poetry by definition should not be yielding patterns- it subverts every pattern linguistically speaking that it can. Thus, poetry is defined by the linguist Sara Thorne [1] as follows: "[p]oetry is perhaps the most distinctive literary genre in terms of its (...) often unexpected approach to language and syntax." According to A.E. Houseman, a poet himself as well as a scholar of the classics, poetry defies rational definition (cf. [2]). This notwithstanding, the lexis and lexical patterns a poet employs cannot exist in a vacuum: while there might be idiosyncratic divergence from conventions seen as 'normative' or 'natural', the poet, nevertheless has to strive for a level of convergence in order to fulfil a communicative need. This crucial point as described by Hutchings: "[a]rt is communicative. Although art emerges from an individual's mind and senses, it is **not merely subjective** or expressive of one set of personal feelings. Were it to be so, it would remain **comprehensible only to its creator**" [2] (highlights are mine). A piece of poetry must, there- fore, remain within the bounds of a broadly agreed level language use. While an argument can be made that

© Springer Nature Switzerland AG 2019
G. Corpas Pastor and R. Mitkov (Eds.): Europhras 2019, LNAI 11755, pp. 330–344, 2019.
https://doi.org/10.1007/978-3-030-30135-4_24

density or level of opacity could be equated with artistic skill, this would always be an oversimplification: every poetic text remains an act of human communication. As Louw [3] has demonstrated, poets do not necessarily use uncommon words: they use words readers are familiar with, albeit in more frequent ways and with nesting patterns that are less familiar. This, in turn, can be expanded: the 'nesting of these uncommon words' are, amongst other things, chunks including the same: formulaic multi-word units. A more detailed background can be found in Pace-Sigge [4].

1.1   Research Aim and the Corpora Used

This paper looks at patterns that are salient across large swaths of poetic writing. To start with, there are a relatively small number of key themes that key re-occurring over a period of several hundred years and regardless whether the producers were British or American English speakers.As such, it aims to highlight the words and their use in MWUs that are *key* to poetic writing, following from that, a comparison of the nesting of these target words and sets of words with prose fiction of the time when majority of the poetry corpus material has been written, namely the 19th century.

This research utilises a corpus built from volumes of poetry found on Gutenberg. org. This particular Gutenberg Poetry Corpus (GPC) is considerably larger than the BNC poetry sub-corpus. Unlike Parrish's *Gutenberg Poetry Corpus* [5], which has been extracted using filters, this corpus has been revised by hand.

Table 1 gives an overview of possible corpora for a project like this. It can be seen that the BNC poetry sub-corpus has only 30 files cannot be seen as representative enough. The second corpus is very large and should therefore be a lot more representative – at least for out-of-copyright works of poetry. However, the Parrish Corpus also caries secondary text, in particular, literary criticism, annotations and comments written in prose as well as and non-English material. After surveying these options, the author made the decision to create another Gutenberg Poetry Corpus (GPC hereafter) as described above. In order to reveal keywords and key concepts in the poetry corpora, Patterson's 19C British full-text prose fiction corpus [6] (hereafter 19C) is employed. This prose corpus is employed as a viable comparator, reflecting that the majority of the GPC material has been produced in the 19th century.

Table 1. Corpora considered (white) and used (grey)

CORPUS	BNC-Poetry	Gutenberg Poetry Corpus	GPC	19C Brit fiction
N FILES	30	n/a	168	100
N TOKENS	226,367	19,223,679	4,203,894	13,933,715

2   Key Concepts in the Gutenberg Poetry Corpus

This section describes the method to find and select a select number of salient themes addressed by the poets in the GPC corpus. The initial investigation, focussed looking at highly frequent (ranked 1 to 500) words and sets of words, calculating GPC key- words in reference to 19C British fiction. The method employed for this research is similar to the work undertaken by other corpus linguists and NLP researchers who have worked on poetic language (see, for example, O'Halloran [7] or McIntyre and Walker [8]).

In order to uncover the salient themes found in the GPC corpus, word lists and then word-cluster lists were created and then WordSmith Tools 7 [9] was employed to create keyword and keycluster lists to make the key concepts visible. Further comparisons to check for log-likelihood have been undertaken employing the Excel-based tool developed by Rayson [10]. Log-likelihood (LL) as a tool to test for statistical significance was chosen for a number of reasons. Firstly, the 19C corpus is about four times as large as the GPC and LL is works very well for corpora of different sizes. Secondly, the corpora produce word-counts an n-gram counts that are relatively low. Again LL is widely seen as a preferable measurement for relatively low occurrence numbers.

The first step of this piece of research was to create wordlists of highly frequent words and sets of words (2–4 gs) for the GPC. *Wordsmith Tools* was em- ployed in order to create the wordlists. Frequently occurring words in these two word- lists were initially highlighted as they seemed to point towards a number of salient themes that kept re-occurring. As a next step, wordlists of single and 2–4 gram sets of words were created for the 19C corpus. Based on that, the GPC keywords in comparison to the 19C British fiction material were calculated. These lists were then com- pared, using *keywords*. After conducting these two moves, it became clear that there are a select number of salient themes that the poets have addressed in their writings.

A large number of themes as shown in Table 2 – in particular, *love* (most highly key word) – are widely seen as prototypical themes dealt with in poetic texts.

Table 2. Salient themes in the GPC

THEME	(I) World	(II) Sky	Time	Love	God	Nature	Colour	Song	Death
	world	sky	day	love	god	tree	golden	song	dead
	earth	sun	night	sweet	soul	flower	gold	sing	(heaven)
	sea	air	(dark)	heart	praise	bird	green	sound	(hell)
Realisation	land	wind	old	joy	glory	doe	gold	sing	
	ground	stars	morn/ing	(soul)	muse				
	hills	moon	spring		hell				
	snow	heaven	winter						

Themes (1) (2) and (3) were originally chosen as they were represented by the largest amount of single keywords. However, for reasons of space, this paper can only focus on Themes (1) and (2) and here only the highlighted items *world, earth, sea* as well as *sun* and *stars*. It remains important, however, to investigate the empirical evidence beyond mere introspection, as Louw [3] highlights: "As corpus linguistics reveals a greater and greater mismatch between the products of introspection about language and those of direct observation, it is easy to become blasé as we receive these new facts about language".

3   Analysis: What the Concepts Aim to Express

3.1   Introduction

Sardinha [11] describes in his study groups of correlated collocations repeatedly found in texts, and highlights parameters underlying the variation of these collocations across the registers, and his findings underpin the idea that "the collocation dimensions reflect the corpus upon which they are based". This is supported by O'Halloran [7] who quotes Moon: "[a] large corpus provides evidence of typical formulaic sequences. It thus provides a form of evidence for typical language usage (...). Typical language schemata, naturally enough, are associated with typical world schemata (...). Indeed, for Moon [12] typical phrases trigger "agglomerates of cultural information".

3.2   Usage Study I: *World* and *Earth*

Introduction. *World* and *earth* appear about as often as each other in the GPC. As Table 3 makes clear, these two terms are substantially less frequent in 19C prose fiction. Another important difference is the proportional usage differential between *world* and *earth* in 19C. The raw proportional figures already hint that the two items are more relevant to the writers of poetry than to those of prose in the corpora compared.

Table 3. Frequencies for *world* and *earth* in GPC & 19C

Term	N	%	per 100,000w
GPC 'world'	3,973	0.09	94.5
GPC 'earth'	3,801	0.09	90.4
19C 'world'	7,384	0.05	53.0
19C 'earth'	2,553	0.02	18.3

Of all the pairs investigated here, these two words are semantically most closely related. The most frequent collocates appear to be the same. Divergence becomes apparent when focussing on lexical words, even if these are found to collocate with both words: in other words, the modifiers of the nouns. There are two phrases which are equal in their proportional frequency – *our world/our earth* and *of the world/of the earth*. There are only a set of bigrams with the following determiners which is equally used for *world* and *earth*: *the, this, another* and *a/an*. All of these are significantly more frequent for *world* in comparison to *earth*; all other collocates that are highly frequent are different for these two items.

World. *World* is the more frequent of the two terms, markedly so in 19C. Bigrams of a frequency with no statistical difference are the following: *another world, great world, little world, other world* and *that world*. A first review of frequent chunks is presented in Table 4, which gives the and trigrams that have been tested for statistical significance (cf. [10]) where no differences have been found.

Table 4. *World* bigram and trigram MWUs that are of similar proportional frequency

trigram WORLD	N 19C	N GPC
all the world	464	249
to the world	158	76
the whole world	101	65

Table 4, therefore, represents both the grammatical forms and descriptive phrases that are so formulaic as to not change even in poetical setting. Thus, we see the multi-word-expressions "all the world" and "to the world". It must be noted that trigram descriptors for this category are more frequent, and that the bigram "whole world" almost always is preceded by the definite article in both corpora. This produces the MWU "the whole world" – another element in stressing its formulaicity.

The results shown in Table 5 are interesting where the bigram "that world" is considered: mostly 19C has *world* preceded by the definite determiner *the*: yet "that world" can be found in equally frequent use in GPC.

Table 5. *World* trigrams significantly more frequent in 19C

trigrams	observed frequencies		expected frequencies		Log Likelihood
	19C	**GPC**	**19C**	**GPC**	
in this world	240	42	183.35	98.65	57.51
of the world	1001	340	871.88	469.12	57.58
in the world	1663	142	1173.56	631.44	735.60

Furthermore, there is the bigram "outer world" in 19C is almost exclusively "the outer world": a metaphorical description of the life outside the known circle of family or friends. By contrast, one of the four uses in GPC speaks of "the outer world that was before this earth". "Outer world" in 19C also seems to be standing in contrast to "little world" which is often *her/our* little world. Yet in GPC the personal pronoun appears only once while definite determiners ("hath borne me from this little world") prevail.

Table 6. *World* bigrams significantly more frequent in GPC

bigram	observed frequencies		expected frequencies		Log Likelihood
	19C	**GPC**	**19C**	**GPC**	
my world	10	21	20.16	10.84	13.74
old world	58	62	78.02	41.98	13.96
round world	1	14	9.75	5.25	22.92
a world	199	206	263.32	141.68	42.75
world is	196	211	264.62	142.38	48.33

As Table 6 shows, the bigram "world is" stands out as being strongly key. While usually followed by an adjective, adverb or verb, GPC appears to have a greater number of verbs, some nouns ("the world is night") fewer complete clauses and notably stronger usage of metaphors. Further bigrams are discussed briefly below:

"World of" appears structurally different – followed by nouns or short NPs in GPC, yet complex NPs or full clauses in fiction prose.

That "New World" is key in GPC reflects the amount of US poets represented in GPC – 19C usually does not employ this as reference to the Americas. Both corpora, otherwise, use "old world" and "new world" in the sense of the fossilized metaphor; again, it the semantic range is far wider in poetry.

"Round world" is an example of stress: that is the usage of this tautological phrase. In 19C, 'round' is usually employed as a way of describing a journey (voyage/run/sail) [a]round the world occurs 76 times. Yet it is used only 36 times in GPC – only 2.5 times as often as the descriptive phrase for the globe.

The marked use of personal pronouns also indicates that poets see the use of *world* as a container for something more private.

Earth. When it comes to *earth*, the 19C and GPC share the same top ten collocates; the most frequent lexical word is *heaven* – within the 20 most frequent collocates in both corpora. And yet: with *earth*, much more prominently than with *world*, there are signal divergences when bi- and trigrams are investigated.

Table 7. *Earth* trigrams significantly more frequent in 19C

n-gram	observed frequencies		expected frequencies		LL
	19C	GPC	19C	GPC	
nothing on earth	45	4	37.64	11.36	7.72
face of the earth	35	2	28.42	8.58	8.74
what on earth	108	5	86.81	26.19	30.62

Table 7 shows that the simple type of description which employs the preposition 'on' are very typical of 19C literature, yet appear significantly less in use in GPC. The rather formulaic MWUs "nothing on earth" and "face of the earth" are rare in poetic writing and the exclamation "what on earth", typical of spoken exchanges, is recorded in poetical writings, yet is significantly more often found as part of spoken conversation sections of 19C fiction.

In direct comparison to *world, earth* in GPC is very strongly marked by its use with the definite article as Table 8 shows. We can see, for example, that "on earth" (key in 19C) has the definite article to expand the bigram into the trigram "on the earth" (key in GPC). This explains why "on earth" is significantly more used in 19C – GPC has "on the earth" as equivalent.

The linked-noun-group phrase "heaven and earth" appears significantly more frequently in GPC than 19C and is, furthermore, of interest because of its semantic divergence. In 19C, it is typically employed as the tired metaphor (e.g. "Gilbert moved

Table 8. *Earth* n-grams significantly more frequent in GPC

n-gram	N GPC	N 19C	LL
the earth	1083	782	321.01
earth and heaven	32	11	50.46
on the earth	91	77	74.96
all the earth	56	15	98.43
heaven/heav'n and earth	89	46	111.28
of the earth	224	247	133.40
the ends of the earth	12	11	9.05

heaven and earth") whereas, in poetry, it is literal, often describing works of saints or gods (e.g. "For but now did heaven and earth divide"). This, too, is mostly also the case for the inverse form "earth and heaven".

Furthermore, the colligational structure *earth* + conjunct is preferred in GPC compared to 19C.

Thus, the chunk "earth and" appears, apart from "earth and heaven", often in "earth and sky" or "earth and sea". A substantial amount is accounted for by line breaks as in "When I go back to earth/And all my joyous body".

In 19C, *earth* almost always ends a clause (and is followed by a comma). "Earth and air", is a frequent linked noun group (LNG) whereas GPC shows a preference for the LNG "earth and sky; "earth and sea" occurs in 19C too, yet is significantly less frequent.

"Earth with", however, marks the strongest contrast. Typically, in 19C, this is found a blandly descriptive, as in "we heard him come to the earth with a thud". In GPC, however, the uses and usage pattern vary between each concordance line. "Go back to Earth with a lip unsealed" is a prime example of the metaphorical, figurative and image-laden language employed for this form.

Crucially, the key references to *earth* are entirely different in GPC. While 19C strongly focuses on items "on earth", GPC is extremely varied. Thus, for example, "to earth" which can relate to religion ("heaven to earth", "descend to earth", "earth to earth") as much as the descriptive phrase "down to earth" – yet the biblical contexts are the dominant usage. Yet more pregnant are the forms "of earth"/"of the earth". The former is employed often with biblical references, literal uses ("soil of earth") yet mostly figurative forms like "poetry of earth", "gladness of earth" etc.; while the latter covers a range of references: space ("ends of the earth"), or metaphors ("bottom/delights/nectar of the earth"). Proportionally, references to (human) beings dominate: "son/daughter/brother/king/masters/wealthy of the earth". This explains why "of the earth" is key in GPC while "face of the earth" is key in 19C: the former links this trigram to a number of different themes; the latter has a single majority use, namely the 4-gram "the face of the earth", which appears in 34 of 35 instances of "face of the earth". All the other 5-grams are similarly concerned with a (slightly) metaphorical description which refers to spatial matters: "the bowels of the earth" (14 occurrences), "the ends of the earth" (11) as well as "the surface of the earth" (6). As can be seen at the bottom of Table 9, "the ends of the earth" is, to a degree, significantly more in use in GPC. It is, however, the only spatial reference in the poetry corpus. This confirms the claim that "of the earth", in 19C, typically refers only to space (using a variety of descriptions) while it is one (not the most relevant one) type of expression occurring in the GPC which displays a wide range of semantic links.

Overall, the investigation of *world* and *earth* shows that these two items are a lot more than synonyms referring to the planet we live on. It is clear that *earth* as in *soil* is a less preferred meaning in both GPC and 19C. Both *world* and *earth* are part of metaphorical phrases: these MWUs are very distinct both for the different words and are found to be employed, with their proportional and statistically significant higher frequencies, in different ways in poetry and prose texts.

3.3   Usage Study I: *Sea*

Sea stands, semantically, in clear contrast to the land-definition of earth. It is larger part covering the globe. While still quite frequent in GPC, it is slightly less frequent than either *world* or *earth;* it occurs, proportionally, four times as often in GPC than 19C, as Table 9 shows.

Table 9. Frequencies for *sea* in GPC & 19C

word	N	%	per 100,000w
GPC 'sea'	3,578	0.08	85.1
19C 'sea'	3,320	0.02	23.8

A first comparison of *sea* in the two comparator corpora shows little difference: both have grammatically fitting prepositions as frequent collocates; the most frequent tri- gram clusters are the same. Yet when applying the log-likelihood statistics, the main bigrams are significantly more frequent in GPC. In fact, a significant difference for being more prominent in 19C is only detected for the following bi- and trigrams: "sea was" and "open sea" as well as "in the sea", "into the sea", "out to sea". The most obvious divergence is "the new sea" which occurs 75 times in 19C but only once in GPC. All other bi- and trigrams are significantly more frequent in GPC.

As Table 10 shows, *sea* in GPC is very significantly more frequent for a wide range of trigrams. Therefore, in poetry this can be seen as a set number of short chunks with *sea* appear with such a high frequency they are almost formulaic. Table 10 highlights two trigrams that appear innocently non-poetic yet are significantly overused in the GPC: "by the sea" and "of the sea". Yet the usage seems to be not different for the former: often, it is a 'place by the sea'. The latter, however, displays different qualities: In 19C appear phrases like "bottom of the sea", "edge of the sea" or, indeed, "smell of the sea" – apart from very rare exceptions ("Queen of the sea", "hear, you pigs of the sea") these are prosaic in being merely descriptive. The opposite is true for GPC: either descriptions are far more evocative (e.g. "the lustrous dusk of the sea") or there are names like "daughter/son of the sea", "wanderer of the sea". Furthermore, there are forms of redundant information: "dolphins of the sea" or "(lean) fish of the sea". Lastly,

Table 10. *Sea* trigrams significantly more frequent in GPC

trigram	observed frequencies		expected frequencies		Log Likelihood
	19C	GPC	19C	GPC	
sea-like	3	10	9.99	3.01	16.78
sea to sea	8	15	17.67	5.33	18.36
like a sea	8	18	19.97	6.03	24.75
sea and land	13	26	29.96	9.04	33.23
from the sea	68	61	99.10	29.90	35.77
across the sea	14	30	33.80	10.20	40.06
land and sea	20	37	43.79	13.21	44.86
and the sea	78	73	116.00	35.00	45.42
to the sea	119	96	165.17	49.83	47.87
by the sea	40	65	80.66	24.34	71.60
of the sea	318	275	455.56	137.44	152.83

like in the example of the poet Henly, it appears to make use of alliteration- "… the shining, sensitive silver of the sea".

Looking at the trigram chunk "sea to sea" in GPC, it can be found that it occurs, in 8/10 of all uses, as "from sea to sea" and it refers to either movement ("he traverses from sea to sea") or geographical spread (noise of war shall cease from sea to sea"). Two poets (Swinburne and Whittier) do indeed, 'wed sea to sea' – a poetic turn of phrase hardly to be expected in prose literature.

It must also be noted that the one simile, "like the sea" appears to be only slightly more commonly used in poetry than in 19C fiction. Other ways of employing the simile are, however, significantly stronger. Therefore, we find "sea-like" as typical of poetical texts and likewise the indefinite comparison "like a sea". And, while Alfred Noyes speaks of "sea-like sound" twice in one poem, and Swinburne says "sea-liked soun-ded", there is no further discernible pattern here.

It can be seen that the LNG "land and sea" is both more frequent and more significantly different in use than "sea and land" in the GPC. Table 11 gives some indica- tion that 'land' is preferred as the first referent as people tend to be land-based. This appears strongest in the cluster "the seeds *of land and sea*" or the wonders *of land and sea*"; even movement and travel show a preference to name land first "like swallows *over land and sea*", whereas the "wandered she *o'er sea and land*" appears to invert this in order to present the correct metre of that line.

Looking on the MWUs that are significantly more frequent in the former there are clear indications that, while basic grammatical forms appear both in prose and poetry, these are integrated into longer, more varied and more flowery language in poetic material. As the discussion in the preceding paragraph indicates, a swap of nouns in a trigram where "land" and "sea" are linked can originate in the poet's desire to keep the required rhythm and metre.

Table 11. *Sea* 4-n skipgram with *land* in GPC

4n first item	land and sea	%	sea and land	%
the-	7	19.4	4	15.4
by-	5	13.5	4	15.4
on-	3	8.0	2	7.7
of-	4	10.8	1	3.8
both-	0	0.0	2	7.7
o'er/over-	5	13.5	2	7.7

3.4 Usage Study II: *Sun* and *Stars*

Introduction. As Table 12 shows, both the items *sun* and *stars* are markedly less used in prose texts than in poetic works. In fact, *stars* is so rare in 19C that almost no useful data can be garnered from the 665 occurrences of the word. As a consequence, this (brief) investigation into the words usage will be focussed on the data the GPC presents.

Table 12. Frequencies for *sun* and *stars* in GPC & 19C

Word	N	%	per 100,000w
GPC 'sun'	3,462	0.08	82.4
GPC 'stars'	1,558	0.04	37.0
19C 'sun'	2,513	0.02	18.0
19C 'stars'	665	<0.01	4.8

Sun. The use of *sun* has a near collocate-structure points towards a colligational difference. The most frequent L1 collocates – usually a pre-modifying adjective ('rising') or a timing marker ('morning') – are the same for both corpora. The second most frequent ones have definitely a stronger positive prosody in the GPC. However, the R1 collocates are different. Verb forms dominate in 19C whereas GPC seems to have verbs as well as prepositions following.

Looking at the most frequently occurring trigrams and 4-grams in GPC and 19C is revealing. The cluster MWUs that are highly frequent in 19C occur with frequencies that bore no statistically significant difference to the ones found in GPC: thus "the sun shone", "the sun was shining", "the sun rose" or "the sun was setting" are on par for both text types. However, the most frequent MWU clusters in GPC are all significantly more frequent when contrasted to the prose texts. Table 14 shows the formulaic phrases that are significantly overused in GPC. Furthermore, that table will highlight a number of other trigrams and 4-grams that predominate in the poetry material.

As Table 13 makes quite clear, the use of *sun* is quite prosaic: descriptive and either a location marker ("beneath the sun"). Yet even the raw figures in the bottom two rows give a clear indication of difference. "In the sun" remains the most frequently found

MWU, followed by "of the sun (and …)". The most interesting finding here is that "beneath the sun" and "the sun goes down", though in their semantics nor structure different to "the sun was setting" or "the sun went down" are markedly more frequent in their use in GPC rather than equal to 19C.

Table 13. Frequencies for *sun* 3-grams and 4-grams most overused in GPC

3-gram / 4-gram	observed frequencies		expected frequencies		Log Likelihood
	19C	GPC	19C	GPC	
the sun in heaven	3	6	6.91	2.09	7.67
the sun goes down	7	11	13.83	4.17	11.80
from sun to sun	0	10	7.68	2.32	29.24
the sun and moon	2	16	13.83	4.17	35.28
sun and moon	11	41	39.95	12.05	72.02
beneath the sun	7	40	36.11	10.89	81.09
like the sun	10	44	41.48	12.52	82.18

The use of antonyms is clearly stronger in GPC as "(the) sun and moon". These are very rare in 19C yet appear in a wide range of nestings in GPC, of the 41 occurrences of "sun and moon", nine also make reference to "stars" and a further three to "other planets".

The repetition formats "the sun the sun" (4 occurrences) and "from sun to sun" are not even found in the prose corpus. The first is mostly an exclamation, while, in one case, the repeat happens over two lines:

"An ague doubt comes creeping in the sun,

The sun himself shudders, the day appals," (L. Abercrombie).

However, the phrase "from sun to sun" was used by Pope, Burns and Frost amongst others and always denotes time (from sunrise to sunset) as in the following lines:

"Why, of two brothers, rich and restless one

Ploughs, burns, manures, and toils from sun to sun" (W. Trumbull).

It is therefore rather surprising that such a phrase should not appear even once in the much larger corpus of 19C prose. It should be noted that this 4-gram has the same colligational structure as "from sea to sea" (see above). It can be argued that this particular construction, at least as a way of referring to the natural world, is typical of poetical writing.

Also rather unexpected is the finding that the use of *sun* as a simile, "like the sun" occurs quite frequently in GPC, yet is hardly recorded in 19C. Clare, Rossetti, Thomas, Tennyson and Vaughan all make liberal use of the simile, at times preceded by "shining". The whole colligational set-up is very different in the few lines in 19C where the simile is followed frequently by a post-modification: "like the sun through a mist", "like the sun in a tempest" or "like the sun that warms". Such a structure, however, is not at all to be found in any of the poems.

As a complete phrase, "the sun goes down" will be found acceptable, while trigrams like "stars and the", will be seen as 'chunks' – sets of words that might crop up repeatedly yet which seem devoid of completeness. This points to possible doubts whether trigrams like "in the sun" or "of the sun" are phraseological. These are, however, grammatically complete and, as we have seen, formulaic in their usage. Pace-Sigge [13] points out that typical prepositional phrases can be seen as MWUs that specific to text type and, indeed, the circumstances of use: they do not follow blind grammatical rules. Thus, for example "(the pale sickle) of the moon" can be expected – whereas "(still stood there basking) in the moon" appears a deliberate inversion of "still stood there basking) in the sun". It can therefore be argued that MWUs – and in particular how they are employed divergently in different genres – should include not merely idiomatic phrases but must also take account of meaningful clauses and clause-fragments.

Looking at the usage patterns for *sun* overall, it must be highlighted that there are 3,462 instances of *sun* in GPC. The most frequent meaningful trigram where *sun* is included, "in the sun" accounts for less than 1/10 of that, and other trigrams are substantially less frequent. It can be assumed, therefore, that the overall low numbers in trigrams and 4-grams indicate a fairly free, creative use of the word, non-formulaic and hardly ever as a frequent, meaningful MWU.

Stars. Table 12 above shows that the item is extremely rare in its use in 19C. Quite often the MWUs found are similar to the format found for *sun* there are "the stars and" being almost exactly as frequent as "and the stars". Likewise, we see the parallel with the construction found for *sun* in GPC where "the stars and" is the clearly dominant form of the two. Significantly, however, amongst the very few observed trigram MWUs, the divergence is even more stark than found with *sun*: even fairly simple descriptive forms ("the stars were") are in the prose but only rarely found in the poetry corpus. Likewise the present-tense equivalent "the stars are" have a place in GPC but not 19C.

Table 14 presents an interesting vista with regards to the usage of *stars*. Less than 10 per cent of all uses are in the trigram "of the stars" – which also happens to be the most frequent trigram in GPC. We can find indeed a large number of parallels to the term *sun*, not unexpected as *sun* and *star* are even closer synonyms than *earth* and *world*. Very similar to the patterns of *sun*, we find that "the stars shone" and "under the stars" appear with similar proportional frequencies. However, "beneath the stars" or "the stars shine" are significantly more frequent in the GPC. One interesting difference is the comparison of "sun of heaven" and "stars of heaven". Above, we have seen 19C records none of the former – clearly, for writers of 19C prose this archaic form is, however, acceptable with reference to stars in general, if not to the star closest to our own planet. A significant difference can be found when looking at "(and) all the stars". In half the cases in 19C, this MWU is at the start of a new clause. As Table 14 shows, in just under a quarter of its occurrences, it follows the connector *and*. The usage appears to be the same for poetry and prose for the 4-gram "of all the stars" as in.

"...for she might have been heiress to the throne *of all the stars*, without mounting any higher than she already was with me" (R.D. Blackmore),
or "Rise to the crest *of all the stars* and see/
The ways of all the world as from a throne?" (J. Drinkwater)

Table 14. Frequencies for *stars* 3-n/4-n overused in GPC

trigrams & 4- grams	observed frequencies		expected frequencies		Log Likelihood
	19C	GPC	19C	GPC	
beneath the stars	3	8	8.45	2.55	12.08
moon and stars	17	19	27.66	8.34	14.72
among the stars	7	15	16.90	5.10	20.03
and all the stars	0	8	6.15	1.85	23.39
sun and stars	2	14	12.29	3.71	29.93

One has to take into account the low total number of occurrences for *stars* in 19C which can be seen as making a clear-cut comparison rather difficult: too often, trigrams occur less than 5 times. A brief comparison between the usage patterns of "beneath the sun" vs "beneath the stars" and "sun and moon" vs "moon and stars". As to the former, "beneath the sun" appears in at least four out of 40 concordance lines that appear to be of religious poetry or (in the case of Lord Byron) linked to religion: like A.C. Swinburne's lines: "What for us hath done/Man *beneath the sun,*/What for us hath God?" Additionally, while there are negative associations ("he has no consolation beneath the sun", "everyone is vanity beneath the sun"), mostly this MWU is linked to positive values, as represented through words like *benefactions, fair, glittering, glory, loved* etc.

Both "beneath the sun" and "beneath the stars" are linked to geographical expanse ("the vast moors stretch beneath the sun"/"*beneath the stars* the roofy desert spreads") – yet only *stars* are linked to the idea of 'journey' as in the example of Amy Lowell: "A single vessel waited, shadowy;/All night she ploughed her solitary way/*Beneath the stars*, and through a tranquil sea."

Furthermore, two of the eight concordance lines of "beneath the stars" refer to dancing. When it comes to semantic prosodies, the overall positive expression found with *sun* is not present for *stars*. Instead, there are collocates like *bare, barren, crazy, death, farewell, lost, glint, solitary, unheeding,* and *vacant:* all these are negative sematic prosodies.

As far as "sun and moon" and "moon and stars" are concerned, this seems to be a pragmatic reflection of experiential realities: the life-giving sun is seen as ever- present, whereas the phases of the moon render it a secondary referent. Similarly, the moon is closer, brighter, bigger to those observing from planet earth than any star. Overall, "sun and moon" appear to be used several times in reference to travels, while "moon and stars" makes several references to the presence (or absence) of light. Three of the 17 concordance lines present "when the moon and stars" which gives it a descriptive feel – a time marker. For "sun and moon" no such use is recorder, however there is "for whom the sun and moon + *verb*" which presents a collocation and colligation not found for the other LNG.

The in-depth discussion of these MWUs with the similar grammatical and lexical structure, with a key term that is a near synonym demonstrates how the use and nesting of *sun* here diverges from the use of *stars* in lines of poetry to a very high degree.. Looked at side by side, these two similar phrases reveal that semantic prosodies, word-fields and points of reference are different to a degree that the idea of 'synonymy', in this particular use, does not at all apply.

4   Findings

We have seen that a corpus of UK and US poetry, written between 1600 and 1900 where a number of referents that are key to this corpus in comparison to British fic- tion written in the 19th century. What has become apparent is that both poetry and prose show frequently recurrent chunks that include high-frequency words from these tropes. As poets still need to be able to communicate their thoughts, this should not come as a surprise. More often than not, these multi-word units differ significantly in their number of occurrences where GPC is compared to 19C. Furthermore, the level of greater creativity (and therefore few re-occurring MWUs) is mainly found in the extensions to the frequent chunks uncovered.

It can be seen that the idiom "nothing on earth" is typical of 19C fiction; the linked-noun-group "heaven and earth", by contrast, is preferred in GPC. Likewise, "in this world" is preferred in 19C; "the outer world" in GPC. However, *world* also provides a certain degree of overlap in the use of tri-grams, for example, "the whole world", whereas "world" seems typically used with personal references in GPC and only bigrams can be found with any degree of repeated frequency. This presents a stark contrast to *earth* which presents a range of trigrams that are entirely different in the GPC in contrast to prose fiction. While 19C strongly focuses on items "on earth" itself, GPC is extremely varied. Thus, for example the strong inclination towards religious themes.

A brief look at the idea of *sea* indicated that both the LNG "land and sea" and the colligation format **Prep**-*the sea* is significantly more frequent in poetry than prose texts. Therefore, "from the sea", "across the sea" etc. were found to be typical MWUs that are in preferred use in 19C.

Moving on to *sun* and *stars* however demonstrates the limits of Sardinha's framework in reference to poetry. While 3-n chunks can be found, they are exceedingly rare in relation to the total number of occurrences for the head-words. This seems to indicate that such words are employed with a far higher degree of freedom and cre-ativity: chunking or MWUs are therefore few in number. Interestingly, we saw that purely descriptive forms like "the sun rose" or "the sun was setting" are used equally in GPC and 19C while another descriptive MWU like "the sun goes down" is preferred in poetic texts. Similarly, "beneath the sun/beneath the stars" are highly key in GPC while, for example "under the stars" appears similar in both corpora.

One very important finding, which is in line with Sinclair's "idiom principle" theories, is that both sets of near-synonyms – *world/earth* as well as *sun/stars* have been shown to be employed in very different semantic relations. As a consequence, after MWUs forming key phrases in GPC were investigated in greater detail, each of these items appears to have shown to have some qualities typical of near-synonyms. However, within the nesting of 3-grams or 4-grams, the usage, in particularly in the poetic corpus, appears far more divergent both in meaning and in prosody. This can be interpreted as evidence how a synonym loses its semantic profile within fixed strings of words. As far as the author is concerned, there are few examples where one MWU can be seen as a likely synonym for any given other MWU, nor is the author aware of any research in that particular area.

References

1. Thorne, S.: Mastering Poetry. Red Globe Press, Houndmills (2006)
2. Hutchings, W.: Living Poetry. Palgrave Macmillan, Houndmills (2012)
3. Louw, B.: Irony in the text or insincerity in the writer? The diagnostic potential of semantic prosodies. In: Text and Technology: In Honour of John Sinclair, pp. 240–251 (1993)
4. Pace-Sigge, M.: Typical phraseological units in poetic texts. A case study on some frequent concepts in works of poetry. J. Res. Des. Stat. Linguist. Commun. Sci. (Forthcoming)
5. Parrish, A.: A Gutenberg Poetry Corpus (2018). https://github.com/aparrish/gutenberg-poetry-corpus. Accessed 09 Nov 2018
6. Patterson, K.J.: The analysis of metaphor: to what extent can the theory of lexical priming help our understanding of metaphor usage and comprehension? J. Psycholinguist. Res. (2014). https://doi.org/10.1007/s10936-014-9343-1. Accessed 08 May 2019
7. O'Halloran, K.: Corpus-assisted literary evaluation. Corpora 2(1), 33–63 (2007). https://doi.org/10.3366/cor.2007.2.1.33
8. McIntyre, D., Walker, B.: How can corpora be used to explore the language of poetry and drama? In: O'Keefe, A., McCarthy, M. (eds.) The Routledge Hand-Book of Corpus Linguistics, pp. 544–558. Routledge, London (2010)
9. Scott, M.: Wordsmith Tools version 7. Stroud: Lexical Analysis Software (2004). www.lexically.net. Accessed 02 July 2019
10. Rayson, P.: Log-likelihood and effect size calculator. Excel spreadsheet. (2016)
11. Sardinha, T.B.: Lexical Priming and Register Variation. In: Pace-Sigge, M., Patterson, K. J. (eds.) Lexical Priming: Applications and Advances, pp. 189–230. John Benjamins, Amsterdam (2017)
12. Moon, R.: Sinclair, lexicography, and the Cobuild project: the application of theory. Int. J. Corpus Linguist. 12(2), 159–181 (2007)
13. Pace-Sigge, M.: The Function and Use of TO and OF in Multi-word Units. Palgrave Macmillan, Basingstoke (2018)

Semantic Prosody in Middle Construction Predicates: Exploring Adverb + Verb Collocation in Middles

Macarena Palma Gutiérrez[✉][iD]

University of Córdoba, Córdoba, Spain
182pagum@uco.es

Abstract. The aim of this paper is to explore the collocation Adverb + Verb in the English middle construction in the particular cases of four of the most productive predicates found in the construction (*cut, drive, handle,* and *sell*) [Levin 1993] in combination with Facility, Time and Quality-oriented adverbs/adverbial phrases [Heyvaert 2001, 2003; Davidse and Heyvaert 2007]. The data collection process is conducted through a corpus of contextualized examples taken from three different sources, and aiming at the compilation of a trustful catalogue of instances which includes formal and textual, as well as written manifestations of spoken conversations, and even cyber language. The sources used are the BNC, the COCA, and the MBLA-SC [Maroto 2019]. The total number of instances examined is 207. The data analyzed reveals that Adverb + Verb collocations in middle constructions which include the predicates and the adjuncts previously mentioned possess a chiefly positive semantic prosody [Oster and van Lawick 2008]. Such positive semantic prosody is provided by the semantics of the adverb/adverbial phrase in question, not by the semantics of the verb or the noun. Moreover, the productiveness of middle Adverb + Verb collocations involving a positive semantic prosody is assumed as a clear indication of the connection between this grammatical structure and its use in both real life and literature, mainly found in contexts which embroil the promotion or foregrounding of the inherent qualities and selling skills of a given product, as it happens in the field of advertisement.

Keywords: Semantic prosody · Adverb + verb collocation · Middle construction

1 Introduction

Traditionally, the English middle construction is thought to be elaborated on the basis of the following core aspects: (i) transitive verbal predicates used as one-argument intransitives [4]; (ii) implied and unexpressed non-agentive Subject referents fulfilling the role of Patient, which involve restricting the types of verbs accepted as middle-forming just to transitives with an affected object [4, 9]; (iii) the need of an adjunct [4]; (iv) non-eventive situations which lack a specific time reference and which profile features of the Subject entity [1]; and (v) certain facilitating and letting properties [4, 8, 9]. An example of a prototypical middle, according to these core aspects, is illustrated in *This book reads easily* [4].

© Springer Nature Switzerland AG 2019
G. Corpas Pastor and R. Mitkov (Eds.): Europhras 2019, LNAI 11755, pp. 345–359, 2019.
https://doi.org/10.1007/978-3-030-30135-4_25

On the lexicalist approach advocated by authors like Levin [9] and Fagan [4], it is possible to identify a set of middle-forming verbs simply because of their lexical and aspectual properties. However, according to Yoshimura [15], the semantics of the middle construction is found in the formula [X (by virtue of some property P) ENABLES ACT]. The author assumes that "the use of verbs is sanctioned only to the extent that they instantiate the semantics of the middle construction" [15].

In this paper we aim at exploring the semantic alignment existing among the three main elements found in the middle construction: Noun – Verb – Adverb. That is to say, first, we analyze the relation found in middle collocations of the type Adverb + Verb, and then, we explore the semantic connection between the noun and the verb.

On the one hand, we analyze the syntactic realization of lexical collocations which follow the structure Adverb + Verb, which would combine a predicative lexeme functioning as the base – i.e. the verb – and its argument working as the collocator (also called collocate in Bosque [2]) – i.e. the adverb. Such combination of Adverb + Verb in the middle construction is characterized by possessing a positive/negative semantic prosody in middle verbs depending on the semantic nature of the adverbs, given that the middle construction is understood as denoting a value judgment of the qualities of the nominal from the perspective of the speaker, expressed through the positive/ negative semantic prosody of the verb. In this paper, we will explore the semantic relation between the middle verb and the adverb by means of Heyvaert's [6, 7] and Davidse and Heyvaert's [3] semantic typology of middles.

We start from the premise and assume that the majority of middles which involve a positive value judgment of the noun working as Subject of the sentence are connected to a Positive Semantic Prosody in the verb, as expressed by their adverb/adverbial phrase. And this is not because the verb itself possesses a positive connotation, but due to the semantics of the adverb. Thus, in this paper we explore the connection between a positive value judgment and a positive semantic prosody when the middle expression refers to the promotion of a given product or object in the world of advertisement.

This paper is organised as follows: Sect. 2 deals with the methodology used in this project; Sect. 3 is devoted to the exploration of the type of collocation found in the middle construction, following the pattern Adverb + Verb, as well as referring to the definition of semantic prosody; Sect. 4 presents the results obtained from the analysis of the data, and the last section draws some concluding remarks.

2 Methodology

This project is based on a corpus study of contextualized examples to examine which are the most frequent Adverb + Verb combinations, by using four given bases: *cut, drive, handle*, and *sell*. These four verbs have been selected for the study because they are some of the most productive predicates found in the English middle construction, as attested in the literature [3, 4, 9, 14, 15]. The different collocates, in this case, adverbs/adverbial phrases, combined with the four verbs chosen for the study belong to three different groups, basically, facility, time and manner/quality adverbs, as explained in Sect. 3.

The sample of instances analyzed in this project conform a total of 207 items, taken from three different corpora in order to agglutinate examples from distinct registers: (i) the BNC, which includes textual, formal examples; (ii) the COCA, which consists of both textual-formal instances and also written manifestations of spoken conversations as interviews, and finally (iii) the MBLA-SC [10, 11], which explores the cyber language used in the colloquial context of Twitter within a limited timeframe, from 2017/02/13 to 2017/06/06.

The total of 207 instances analyzed in this project, last accessed 2019/05/15, have been obtained after a detailed search in the corpora by means of the application of two main restrictions in the searching tools, as listed below: (i) 3rd person Present Simple affirmative uses of the verbs *cut, drive, handle*, and *sell*, and this involves leaving aside sentences expressed in the negative form, because the purpose of this project aims at exploring the positive/negative semantic prosody found in the adverb, independently from the semantics of the verb, and (ii) the election of inanimate entities working as Subjects of the middle instances, as this type of nouns are more frequently found in middles [15].

3   Adverb + Verb Middle Collocations: Exploring Semantic Prosody

Gries [5] defines the term collocation as the co-occurrence of two elements, "a form or a lemma of a lexical item" and "one or more additional linguistic elements of various kinds", as long as such combination of elements "functions as one semantic unit in a clause or sentence" and its "frequency of co-occurrence is larger than expected on the basis of chance" [5].

The middle alternation in English is constructed on the basis of three elements, Noun – Verb – Adverb. In this section, we deal with the relation between the middle predicate and its adjunct, understood as a collocation because of the restricted list of possible adverbs found in the middle construction. As Bosque puts it, "restricted adverbs are collocates" [2].

Using corpus linguistics terminology, we can assume that most middle predicates possess a negative/positive semantic prosody [13], depending on the semantic nature of their adverbs. The concept of semantic prosody is close to that of semantic preference; however, according to Oster and van Lawick [12], semantic preference is defined as "the semantic field a word's collocates predominantly belong to", whereas the authors restrict the concept of semantic prosody to "a more general characterization of these collocates, chiefly in terms of a positive or negative evaluation" [12]. The authors go on to argue that semantic prosody refers to a combination of two aspects, "semantic field and pragmatic realization" [12]. Thus the Adverb + Verb combination in the middle construction reflects an underlying pattern of semantic selection by which the collocation of the middle adverb is in accord with the positive/negative prosody of the verb, i.e. the middle construction follows a pattern of semantic prosody rather than a pattern of semantic preference regarding the relation Adverb - Verb.

The middle construction is understood as denoting a value judgment of the qualities of the nominal from the perspective of the speaker, expressed by the positive/negative semantic prosody of the verb. In other words, the speaker utters a grammatical structure which comprises the semantic charge of a given adverb/adverbial phrase in order to denote a positive or a negative evaluation on the way the process is carried out due to the inherent features of the nominal. Hence we could group middle instances into two distinguishing sets: (i) those middle expressions which denote a positive semantic prosody in their verbs followed by a positive adverb; (ii) those middles which indicate a negative semantic prosody when analyzing their verbs followed by adverbs containing a negative semantic charge.

As Bosque argues, "since collocates are taken to be predicates, they are expected to restrict their arguments (= bases) on semantic grounds" [2]. Therefore, drawing on Heyvaert's [6, 7] and Davidse and Heyvaert's [3] typology, we explore the semantic grounds by which adverbs restrict middle verbs as indicated in the following groups of middles:

(i)   Facility-oriented middles are said to comment on the ease or difficulty with which the process is carried out, e.g. *The valve opens easily* (COCA).

(ii) Quality-oriented middles focus on the way the process can be carried out and they normally include an adverbial conveying a quality judgment, e.g. [about a car] *On the road it handles well* (BNC), or express a comparison of quality, e.g. [about water and corn flour] *A thick mixture of the two pours like a liquid* (Now corpus).

(iii) Time-oriented middles rely on the time the process takes to be carried out, e.g. *The house sells fast* (COCA).

(iv) Feasibility-oriented middles focus on whether the inherent properties of the Subject entity allow the process to be carried out and they are adjunctless, e.g. *This car doesn't drive, it tours* (WebCorp).

(v)   Destiny-oriented middles include a Subject entity working as a Locative oblique participant either focused on where it has to be placed to make it function, e.g. *Adventure Time Jewelry wraps around your neck* (WebCorp), or where it can be stored when not needed, e.g. *A bedstead that folds up into a cabinet when it's not being slept in* (COCA).

(vi) Result-oriented middles refer to the result of carrying out a certain process onto the Subject entity, e.g. [about a car washing product] *Rinses away clean* (Linguee).

In this paper, we mainly concentrate on Facility, Quality and Time-oriented middles in order to restrict the adverbs that occur more frequently in these constructions in English. Thus we leave the other – sometimes less prototypical – types of middles aside because of several reasons: (i) Feasibility-oriented middles are adjunctless and in this paper we explore collocations of the type Adverb + Verb in the middle construction; Destiny-oriented middles are construed on the basis of adjuncts with a Locative meaning, but they are formed by complex adverbial phrases which hinder the task of restricting the frequency of appearance of such phrases in a project focused on phraseology, and (iii) Result-oriented middles do not normally contain an Adverb but an Adjective with an adverbial function commenting on the result of carrying out the process onto the Subject entity.

In the literature referred to in this paper, some of the most common adverbs/adverbial phrases found in Facility, Quality and Time-oriented middles are listed below:

(i)   Adverb(ial)s within Facility-oriented middles: *easily, with ease, (only) with (great) difficulty, with difficulties.*

(ii) Adverb(ial)s within Time-oriented middles: *rapidly, fast, quickly, slowly, within 2 days* (or any other time reference).

(iii) Adverb(ial)s within Quality-oriented middles: *well, badly, superbly, smoothly, neatly, better than* +comparison, *worse than* +comparison, *like* +comparison.

Potentially, a greater number of adverbs or adverbial phrases could occur in these three groups, but the truth is that the middle construction employs a limited set of them, as shown in the following section by the instances found in the corpora used here.

4   Data Collection and Results

In this section we present the data analyzed. The information is divided into four tables, each one focused on a different verb from the ones chosen for the study (*cut, drive, handle,* and *sell*). Each table explores the following elements: (i) the corpus source from which the date is taken and the number of instances per source; (ii) the semantic typology of the middles found, according to their respective adverbs and the number of examples in each case; (iii) the most frequent types of Subjects occurring in the examples, expressed with both number of instances as well as percentage; and (iv) the distinction between those middles involving a positive and a negative semantic prosody, expressed with both number of instances as well as percentage. After every table, the list of middle instances found in the different corpora is instantiated.

Table 1 below shows the results obtained regarding middles which include the verb *cut* and its respective adverbs:

Table 1. Middles with *cut* (abbreviations included after items).

Corpus source	Semantic typology and adverb(ial)s	Most frequent Subjects (%)	Semantic prosody (%)
BNC *(B)* [5]	Facility *(F)* [4]: *Easily* (4)	Type of *instrument* to cut *(I)* [17] – (62.96%)	Positive *(+)* [19] – (70.37%)
COCA *(C)* [20]	Time *(T)* [0]		Negative *(-)* [8] – (29.63%)
MBLA-SC *(M)* [2]	Quality *(Q)* [24]:	Type of *object* which is cut *(O)* [10] – (37.04%)	
	Well (11) *Smoothly* (2)		
TOTAL (27)	*Like* (10)		

The 27 middle instances which include the verb *cut* referred to in Table 1 above and their corresponding adverbials of positive and negative semantic prosody are listed below. Respectively, instances 1–5 are taken from the BNC, instances 6–7 from the MBLA-SC, and instances 8–27 from the COCA. All of them possess a Positive Semantic Prosody except for examples 18–20, 22, 24-27, which have a Negative Semantic Prosody:

1. [About *a type of soil*] Dark, rich, moist and *cuts well. (B/Q/O/+)*
2. [About *a chocolate cake*] With lots of cherries and *cuts well. (B/Q/O/+)*
3. [About *a woman's hair*] good colour, *cuts well. (B/Q/O/+)*
4. *A neat shape* that *cuts well. (B/Q/O/+)*
5. *The cake cuts well. (B/Q/O/+)*
6. *A virtuous knife cuts well. (M/Q/I/+)*
7. *A sharp razor blade. Cuts easily. (M/F/I/+)*
8. [About *a mowing*] *This machine cuts well. (C/Q/I/+)*
9. [About *a mowing*] And it *cuts well. (C/Q/I/+)*
10. [About *a mowing*] It's *a solid machine* that *cuts well. (C/Q/I/+)*
11. Think sensual, tropical romance, and you have *ginger lily. It cuts well. (C/Q/O/+)*
12. [About *a type of adhesive stickers*] *it cuts well* with … linoleum tools. *(C/Q/O/+)*
13. [About *a blade*] If *it cuts easily*, you're done. *(C/F/I/+)*
14. *The foam "wood" cuts easily* with plastic tools. *(C/F/O/+)*
15. [About *a brand of snow-skis' tip*] *Cuts easily* through crud. *(C/F/I/+)*
16. [About a gas saw] *Cuts smoothly. (C/Q/I/+)*
17. [About *a hoe blade*] It *cuts smoothly. (C/Q/I/+)*
18. *A jagged white light cuts like a branching vein. (C/Q/I/−)*
19. *Status cuts like a straight razor. (C/Q/I/−)*
20. [About *wind*] *Cuts like a frigid knife through hot butter. (C/Q/I/−)*
21. *The mower* cuts and *cuts like a yowling knife. (C/Q/I/+)*
22. It's always raining and *the wind cuts like a knife. (C/Q/I/−)*
23. *Coat lean cuts like filet mignon* with a very light layer of olive oil. *(C/Q/O/+)*
24. That *water* hits the back of your neck and it *cuts like a knife. (C/Q/I/−)*
25. It's five below zero, and *the air cuts like a knife. (C/Q/I/−)*
26. *The lock cuts like butter* and the steel door is yanked open. *(C/Q/O/−)*
27. *The war* that *cuts like a jagged wound. (C/Q/I/−)*

The 39 middle instances which include the verb *drive* referred to in Table 2 above and their corresponding adverbials of positive and negative semantic prosody are listed below. Respectively, instance 1 is taken from the BNC, instances 2–2 from the MBLA-SC, and instances 13–39 from the COCA. All of them possess a Positive Semantic Prosody except for examples 33, 35 and 36, which have a Negative Semantic Prosody:

Table 2. Middles with *drive* (abbreviations included after items).

Corpus source	Semantic typology and adverb(ial)s	Most frequent Subjects (%)	Semantic prosody (%)
BNC *(B)* [1]	Facility *(F)* [0]	Road vehicles *(R)* [36] – (92.31%)	Positive *(+)* [36] – (92.3%)
COCA *(C)* [27]	Time *(T)* [3]:		Negative *(-)* [3] – (7.7%)
	Fast (2)		
	Rapidly (1)		
MBLA-SC *(M)* [11]	Quality *(Q)* [36]:	Water vehicles *(W)* [1] – (2.56%)	
	Well (12)		
	Smoothly (2)		
	Better than (1)		
TOTAL (39)	Like (21)	Miscellaneous items *(M)* [2] – (5.13%)	

1. *Every green bus drives fast. (B/T/R/+)*
2. [About *a car*] It's clean literally he cleans it everyday, *drives well. (M/Q/R/+)*
3. [About *a car*] Lift kit looks good and *drives well. (M/Q/R/+)*
4. [About *a car*] For sale - Clean interior, AUX cord, *drives well. (M/Q/R/+)*
5. blah *my car* is only A Ford CD2 platform. *Drives well. (M/Q/R/+)*
6. Anyone have *an really old, dry RV* that *drives well? (M/Q//R/+)*
7. [About *a car*] I hear that *it drives well. (M/Q/R/+)*
8. If it *drives well*, it *drives well*. What kind of *car* is it? *(M/Q/R/+)*
9. Same but i gotta wait a few hours and hopefully *the car drives well. (M/Q/R/+)*
10. Wow has it been 2 years already? *Time drives fast! (M/T/M/+)*
11. My *car drives smoothly* for the first time in MONTHS! 😊💫 *(M/Q/R/+)*
12. [About *a car*] *Midnight Thunder drives smoothly. (M/Q/R/+)*
13. *Land Rover* ... # *Overall: *Drives well*, looks smart, roomy up front. *(C/Q/R/+)*
14. [About *a car*] Overall: Seductive. Looks cool, *drives well. (C/Q/R/+)*
15. [About *a car*] If it *drives well* and it looks good, that's the main thing. *(C/Q/R/+)*
16. *This mid-size carlike sport-ute* ... rides and *drives well. (C/Q/R/+)*
17. *A black Toyota 4X4* ... *drives rapidly* off. *(C/T/R/+)*
18. *H2 drives better than any other full-size GM truck. (C/Q/R/+)*
19. [About *a technological device to synchronize data across your PC and mobile phone*] *Synology's NAS drives like the DiskStation DS418. (C/Q/M/+)*
20. [About *a Jaguar car*] It *drives like something much smaller. (C/Q/R/+)*
21. Now even *the lowliest Golf drives like an Audi* in disguise. *(C/Q/R/+)*
22. And *the Mazda6 drives like a sports car. (C/Q/R/+)*
23. Above 10 mph, *the Jetta Hybrid drives like any other Jetta*–peppy, with taut steering and direct throttle response. *(C/Q/R/+)*
24. The 11-pound, camera-equipped *Sand Flea drives like an R/C car. (C/Q/R/+)*
25. That is *a real car*. It *drives like a livery car*, and that's the point. *(C/Q/R/+)*

26. [About *a car*] It's in no way a sporting machine, but it performs and *drives like any other roomy and practical hatchback. (C/Q/R/+)*

27. [About *a car*] You know, *it drives like a real car. (C/Q/R/+)*

28. [About a boat] *The 310 BR … drives like one as well. (C/Q/W/+)*

29. [About *a car*] It *drives like a new car*, absolutely silent. *(C/Q/R/+)*

30. [About *a car*] It *drives like you took it off the showroom floor. (C/Q/R/+)*

31. *Nissan Pathfinder*: Midsize SUV drives like the rugged truck that it is. *(C/Q/R/+)*

32. *Subaru Forester* BASE MSRP: $22,390 WHY WE LIKE IT: It *drives like a car, but hauls cargo like an SUV. (C/Q/R/+)*

33. If *another new car drives like yours*, then consider installing … *(C/Q/R/−)*

34. It's *a well-positioned vehicle*. It looks sporty but *drives like a sedan. (C/Q/R/+)*

35. *The BMW drives like, well, a BMW, while the Ducati is all Ferrari. (C/Q/R/−)*

36. [About *a car*] It looks *like a regular Civic*, and it *drives like one too. (C/Q/R/−)*

37. *JEEP JEEPSTER*: This one *drives like a sports car on the road. (C/Q/R/+)*

38. *Mercedes-Benz C280*: ($ 34,900) *Drives like it's made from one solid part rather than 1,000 different pieces. (C/Q/R/+)*

39. *The blue Ford 1320*, which looks and works like a regular farm tractor and *drives like a small sports car. (C/Q/R/+)*

The 58 middle instances which include the verb *handle* referred to in Table 3 below and their corresponding adverbials of positive and negative semantic prosody are listed below. Respectively, instances 1–4 are taken from the BNC, instances 5–6 from the MBLA-SC, and instances 7–58 from the COCA. All of them possess a Positive Semantic Prosody except for examples 6 and 36, which have a Negative Semantic Prosody:

Table 3. Middles with *handle* (abbreviations included after items).

Corpus source	Semantic typology and adverb(ial)s	Most frequent Subjects (%)	Semantic prosody (%)
BNC *(B)* [4]	Facility *(F)* [3]: Easily (3)	Road vehicles *(R)* [36] – (62.07%)	Positive *(+)* [56] – (96.55%)
COCA *(C)* [52]	Time *(T)* [1]: Fast (1)	Water vehicles *(W)* [6] – (10.34%)	Negative *(-)* [2] – (3.45%)
MBLA-SC *(M)* [2]	Quality *(Q)* [54]:	Weapons *(We)* [6] – (10.34%)	
	Well (22)	Golf clubs *(G)* [3] – (5.17%)	
	Smoothly (2)	Cameras *(C)* [2] – (3.45%)	
	Superbly (2)	Miscellaneous items *(M)* [5] –	
	Better than (3)	(8.62%)	
TOTAL (58)	Like (25)		

1. *The paint* is soft, *handles well* and is easily thinned with water, though of course it is waterproof when dry. *(B/Q/M/+)*

2. [About *a car*] On the road it *handles well. (B/Q/R/+)*

3. [About *a car*] And it *handles well on independent coil suspension. (B/Q/R/+)*

4. *BMW ... handles better* and is more fuel efficient. *(B/Q/R/+)*
5. *Ford Explorer.* Runs great and *handles well.* *(M/Q/R/+)*
6. About *an artifact called Pedal Tavern; i.e. a tavern in which people sit and pedal all together]* This *handles well in ¾. (M/Q/R/−)*
7. [About *a golf club*] The nimble wedge *handles well at low speeds* and lets confident players command delicate shots. *(C/Q/G/+)*
8. *The car handles well in corners,* does 0 to 60 in 5.5 s. *(C/Q/R/+)*
9. [About *a rifle*] The 5.15-pound Ultralight *handles well* and is easy to shoot, even with 150- grain magnum loads. *(C/Q/We/+)*
10. [About *a rifle*] The MR7 *handles well,* balancing almost neutrally when gripped and during follow-through. *(C/Q/We/+)*
11. [About *a rifle*] *The Craftsman handles well,* has reasonable power and offers excellent visibility of the cut line. *(C/Q/We/+)*
12. Though the weight capacity is only 300 lb, *this boat handles well on milder rivers* and is well suited for most lakes. *(C/Q/W/+)*
13. [About *a car*] It *handles well* and has a competent powertrain. *(C/Q/R/+)*
14. [About *an archery weapon, i.e. a bow*] The Highlander kicks when you shoot, but the 36-in. length *handles well.* *(C/Q/We/+)*
15. [About *a bike*] *The KM40* fits and *handles well when you're in the full aero position.* *(C/Q/R/+)*
16. *His car handles well,* making it nearly impossible for it to be passed. *(C/Q/R/+)*
17. [About *a car*] The *few mid-size SUVs* with third-row seating, and it's fast, prestigious and *handles well.* *(C/Q/R/+)*
18. [About *a boat*] *The 45 handles well in all conditions.* *(C/Q/W/+)*
19. [About *a car*] It's fast and it *handles well.* *(C/Q/R/+)*
20. [About *a car*] It *handles well* ... the most grip on the skidpad. *(C/Q/R/+)*
21. [About *a skis brand*] Smooth flex. *Handles well in fairly varied conditions.* *(C/Q/M/+)*
22. [About *a car*] It *handles well;* nice pickup. *(C/Q/R/+)*
23. [About *a car*] It is relatively efficient, *handles well,* looks good. *(C/Q/R/+)*
24. [About *a climbing rope*] It *handles easily* and is very flexible. *(C/F/M/+)*
25. [About *a boat*] It planes quickly and *handles easily.* *(C/F/W/+)*
26. *The dough handles easily* and is very forgiving. *(C/F/M/+)*
27. And criterium geometry means *the bike handles fast.* *(C/T/R/+)*
28. [About *a painting*] It holds brushstrokes but *handles smoothly.* *(C/Q/M/+)*
29. [About *a boat, a craft*] In all, the 360 delivers livable accommodations in *a craft* that performs well and *handles smoothly.* *(C/Q/W/+)*
30. *A fast car that handles superbly.* *(C/Q/R/+)*
31. [About *a car*] And despite its bulk, it handles superbly. *(C/Q/R/+)*
32. [About *a car*] *Handles better than truck-based vehicles.* *(C/Q/R/+)*
33. *The Cherokee* rides and *handles better than before.* *(C/Q/R/+)*
34. [About *a golf club*] Feels and *handles like a blade.* *(C/Q/G/+)*
35. [About *a golf club*] *The Pro handles like an iron.* *(C/Q/G/+)*
36. [About *a car*] Handles like a truck, and parking lots are not its friend. *(C/Q/R/−)*
37. [About *a car*] Yes,... it goes and *handles like mad.* *(C/Q/R/+)*
38. [About *a car*] *The BRZ handles like it's your personal road therapist.* *(C/Q/R/+)*

39. He loves *the car. Handles like a dream*, he says. *(C/Q/R/+)*
40. With a center of gravity near its midline, *the bow handles like a European sports car. (C/Q/R/+)*
41. *The Fusion* rides and *handles like the big sedan it is. (C/Q/R/+)*
42. You know, *it handles like a sports* car and it's quite fast. *(C/Q/R/+)*
43. [About *a shotgun*] *Handles like a dream. (C/Q/We/+)*
44. On the road, *the car* is tight and *handles like most Hondas. (C/Q/R/+)*
45. [About *a shotgun*] *It handles like a British best* but sells for a price that many ordinary uplanders can afford. *(C/Q/We/+)*
46. [About *a camera*] *DCR-TRV38*, shown above, is not the most compact, but it looks and *handles like a movie camera. (C/Q/C/+)*
47. *Cayenne Turbo sport-utility vehicle … handles like a Porsche*-at $89,000. *(C/Q/R/+)*
48. *The product of Kawasaki's racing experience … handles like a quarter horse. (C/Q/R/+)*
49. It was a calm day when I drove *the 43. She handles like a sports car. (C/Q/R/+)*
50. *The DeVille handles like a sports car. (C/Q/R/+)*
51. [About *a car*] *It handles like Michael Andretti's CART racer. (C/Q/R/+)*
52. *The 56 handles like a sportboat*, quickly and firmly responding. *(C/Q/W/+)*
53. [About *a boat*] *The Queen Mary handles like a dream. (C/Q/W/+)*
54. *The 53-pound BMW handles like a sport bike half size. (C/Q/R/+)*
55. [About *a car*] *It handles like a slot car. (C/Q/R/+)*
56. [About *the KODAK DC40 DIGITAL CAMERA*] Better still, it *handles like a stylus* and works on any surface. *(C/Q/C/+)*
57. [About *a car*] *It handles like a sports sedan. (C/Q/R/+)*
58. *The Nissan built four-seater handles like a sports car. (C/Q/R/+)*

The 83 middle instances which include the verb *sell* referred to in Table 4 below and their corresponding adverbials of positive and negative semantic prosody are listed below. Respectively, instances 1–6 are taken from the BNC, instances 7–29 from the MBLA-SC, and instances 30–83 from the COCA. All of them possess a Positive Semantic Prosody, except for example 19, which has a Negative Semantic Prosody:

1. [About *an electric bike brand*] And if *Sir Clive Sinclair's Zike sells well* he has ambitions to get into this new market. *(B/Q/S/+)*
2. [About *a painting*] *Sells well at the art society exhibition. (B/Q/C/+)*
3. If you write *a song* that *sells well enough to reach the top 50 in the albums or singles chart* you are eligible automatically. *(B/Q/C/+)*
4. [About *a complete history of the mountain, entitled Eiger, Wall of Death*] It still *sells well in the Grindelwald. (B/Q/B/+)*
5. [About *artists' works of art*] *Their work sells well. (B/Q/C/+)*
6. The third is *his London trilogy*, which *sells better than his others. (B/Q/B/+)*
7. y'all we need to like figure out how to promote *Malibu so it sells well. (M/Q/C/+)*
8. Pre-ordering *Crash Bandicoot trilogy* because 1. If it *sells well*, maybe Activision will give us HD Spyro and 2. Never played Crash before. *(M/Q/S/+)*
9. Naw I think they'll remaster another Street fighter game if *USF2 sells well. (M/Q/S/+)*
10. I don't like *Ambers* much. But *this stuff sells well* so I finally got one. *(M/Q/M/+)*
11. *Apocrypha anime sells well …* we might get stuff for Karna and Sumanai. *(M/Q/T/+)*

Table 4. Middles with *sell* (abbreviations included after items).

Corpus source	Semantic typology and adverb(ial)s	Most frequent Subjects (%)	Semantic prosody (%)
BNC *(B)* [6]	Facility *(F)* [0]	Cultural products *(C)* [14] – (16.87%)	Positive *(+)* [82] – (98.78%)
COCA *(C)* [55]	Time *(T)* [7]: Fast (4) Quickly (3)	Software products *(S)* [7] – (8.43%) Book-related objects *(B)* [9] – (10.84%)	Negative *(-)* [1] – (1.2%)
MBLA-SC *(M)* [22]	Quality *(Q)* [76]:	TV-related products *(T)* [10] – (12.05%)	
	Well (60) Better than (11)	Food-related products *(F)* [7] – (8.43%) Housing *(H)* [5] – (6.02%)	
TOTAL (83)	Like (5)	Abstract items *(A)* [10] – (12.05%) Miscellaneous items *(M)* [21] – (25.3%)	

12. [About *a book on Ethics*] If it *sells well*, he's going to write a book about Kent as well. *(M/Q/B/+)*

13. *Alex Primeau painting sells well above estimate!* *(M/Q/C/+)*

14. a band dude asked on facebook "what's *merch* that *sells well*" and someone said "press on nails" hahahkfjekfk. *(M/Q/M/+)*

15. *Bomberman* is cool if *game sells well*. *(M/Q/S/+)*

16. *Taking 880 billion out of Medicaid to give that much in tax cuts to you and your friends sells well* to who? *(M/Q/A/+)*

17. [About *a TV series*] I was sad to see it end. It still *sells well* too. *(M/Q/T/+)*

18. If it *sells well* enough I might write another *porno;)* Keep your fingers crossed! *(M/Q/B/+)*

19. *Hate no longer sells well* Sirs. *(M/Q/A/-)*

20. No wonder *the new CEO* is from Coca Cola. (…) *Sells well.* *(M/Q/F/+)*

21. [About *a vegan pizza*] on the article i read they said until september but if it *sells well* it'll be permanent. *(M/Q/F/+)*

22. [About *a TV show*] Gotta make sure it *sells well* next month. *(M/Q/T/+)*

23. If *Panda Go Panda sells well on Blu-Ray*, maybe go for Shirokuma Cafe next? *(M/Q/T/+)*

24. [About *a house*] Hoping it *sells fast!* ☺ *(M/T/H/+)*

25. [About *a house*] awesome! Hope it *sells fast.* *(M/T/H/+)*

26. Trying *this drink* because it was on sale and *sells quickly.* Verdict: Pretty good *(M/T/F/+)*

27. t's #openhouse day for us, hoping *our house sells quickly* and at a great price! *(M/T/H/+)*

28. Beautiful *home!!* Hope it *sells quickly!!!* *(M/T/H/+)*

29. Honey. You're so talented. *Your art sells well,* and for a lot of money. *(M/Q/C/+)*

30. [About *TV programs*] Said Mum, "But if there's one person who knows *what sells well* it's my Katherine. She was the TV host of Fakes & Treasures. *(C/Q/T/+)*

31. There is a lot of *art* out there that does not display virtuosity that *sells well*, because some sort of buzz surrounds the artist. *(C/Q/C/+)*

32. [About *a car*] *Sells well* and legitimately feels like nothing else on the road. *(C/Q/M/+)*

33. *The Iron Lion T-shirt* he wears on game day, even in freezing weather, *sells well*. *(C/Q/M/+)*

34. *Type of music*: Anything that *sells well* enough to fill a giant outdoor amphitheatre. *(C/Q/C/+)*

35. [About *windmill stuff*] If that one *sells well* after tonight, the next time you order it, it may be coming from G.E. *(C/Q/M/+)*

36. *Local food sells well. (C/Q/F/+)*

37. Once *a product sells well on TV*, Khubani will get the product into stores. *(C/Q/T/+)*

38. *His work sells well* – the artist captures nature's dynamism on paper. *(C/Q/C/+)*

39. "You see yourself as *a good product* that sits on a shelf and *sells well*", Princess Diana said in a confessional BBC TV interview in 1995. *(C/Q/M/+)*

40. Of course, in a global economy, *the "exotic" sells well* too. *(C/Q/A/+)*

41. *The same black velvet gown* that *sells well* in London will also play in South Carolina. *(C/Q/M/+)*

42. So if *the video sells well*, they get a double payday. *(C/Q/T/+)*

43. [About *a type of hook for alpinists*] Still *sells well* today. *(C/Q/M/+)*

44. If *the book* ...*sells well*, Mr. Ecker says, each could receive up to $ 6,000 more. *(C/Q/B/+)*

45. [About *Princess Di portrait in a magazine's cover*] But I know that something like that obviously *sells well*. *(C/Q/M/+)*

46. [About *a set of golf clubs*] Set of three woods and eight irons *sells well* at Golf-smith. *(C/Q/M/+)*

47. [About *a book*] The author's precocity ensure that *the Bestiary sells well. (C/Q/B/+)*

48. If *an image sells well* – and forever – it's going to be very lucrative over time. *(C/Q/C/+)*

49. [About *a type of valentine card*] *Sells well. (C/Q/M/+)*

50. *Metal* remains a viable force that *sells well. (C/Q/M/+)*

51. [About *HBO movies*] Ebert said that just because *a product sells* well doesn't mean it meets community standards for decency. *(C/Q/T/+)*

52. [About *cultural contributions by celebrities*] *What sells well*, will be construed as what is essentially superior. *(C/Q/C/+)*

53. If *the album sells well*, look for a U.S. tour in 1997 or' 98. *(C/Q/C/+)*

54. [About *stronger and more expensive environmental regulation*] It is *an idea* that *sells well* back in Washington. *(C/Q/A/+)*

55. If *the map sells well*, it therefore immediately goes out of print. *(C/Q/M/+)*

56. *Anything with garlic* – like garlic mashed potatoes – *sells well. (C/Q/F/+)*

57. [About athletes' endorsement merchandise] We cut contracts with a minimum number of autographs and an option to keep going if *the merchandise sells well*. *(C/Q/M/+)*

58. *Educational software* has grand intentions and often *sells well. (C/Q/S/+)*

59. [About *a perfume for men, Baryshnikov Pour Homme*] *Sells well. (C/Q/M/+)*

60. He is using that knowledge to buy the *conservative, traditional furniture* he's discovered *sells well at auctions. (C/Q/M/+)*
61. [About *violence on TV*] They are looking for *a formula* that *sells well.* It so happens that this is *violence. (C/Q/T/+)*
62. "Consultants are pushing the hell out of *reengineering*", says one of their brethren, "because *it sells well* and it's very labor-intensive". *(C/Q/M/+)*
63. *The first soup sells well, the first salad sells well, the first entree sells well. (C/Q/F/+)*
64. [About *Microsoft products*] If it's *a good product*, it *sells well. (C/Q/S/+)*
65. *Mosbacher's message about economy sells* well in Kansas City. *(C/Q/A/+)*
66. *The best known of all his works*, it has been translated into fifteen languages, has gone through numerous reprintings, and still *sells well. (C/Q/B/+)*
67. He plans to stay in his old house until the work is done, but *the house sells fast.* *(C/T/H/+)*
68. [About *a book*] It won't be something that *sells fast*, but over a long time. *(C/T/B/+)*
69. [About *a WWE fighter's promo*] *Vince McMahon* also *sells better than anyone.* *(C/Q/T/+)*
70. [About *a funded project for black kids' education*] *Sells better than it does coming from a bunch of grayhairs. (C/Q/M/+)*
71. *Fake sells better than real. (C/Q/A/+)*
72. *Funny sells better than sappy in a recession. (C/Q/A/+)*
73. AJ is convinced that *curing a problem sells better than preventing one. (C/Q/A/+)*
74. But *the light blue sells better than the dark blue. (C/Q/M/+)*
75. Of course *Stephen King (…) sells better than his Revolutionary forefather. (C/Q/B/+)*
76. *The official Atlanta Ballet Nutcracker ($20) sells better than anything. (C/Q/C/+)*
77. Today, *guava fruit sells better than posters of Osama bin Laden. (C/Q/F/+)*
78. *White gold sells better than yellow. (C/Q/M/+)*
79. [About *a Punk album*] It just *sells like crazy. (C/Q/C/+)*
80. *Everything that smacks of the unexplained and the sensational sells like hot buns.* *(C/Q/A/+)*
81. [About *a DVD*] *Sells like hotcakes. (C/Q/S/+)*
82. [About *the Maxwell Street flea market* collecting merchandise*] Each summer it's something unbelievable that *sells like hot queques. (C/Q/M/+)*
83. Always look' em in the eye. (to the camera) *Nothing sells like sincerity. (C/Q/A/+)*

5 Conclusions

The most productive corpus source in this study is the COCA, from which a total of 154 out of 207 instances have been taken. The most frequent semantic type of middle analyzed in this project is that of Quality-oriented middles, with 190 instances belonging to this group, out of the total 207 examples of the sample. In addition, within the group of Quality-oriented middles, the most productive Adverb + Verb collocations found in the corpora contain the adverb *well* and adverbial phrases starting with *like. Well* collocations account for 105 instances, while *like* collocations appear in 61 examples. The adverb *well* provides a productive collocate for bases such as *cut, drive, handle* and *sell* as a natural consequence of its very definition 'in a good, right or acceptable way.' Similarly, adverbial phrases starting with *like* also provide collocates for such bases due to its flexibility in terms of semantic motivation.

The key information revealed in this study concerns the issue of semantic prosody. As shown in Tables 1, 2, 3 and 4 above, the selected bases *cut, drive, handle,* and *sell* are chiefly followed by a positive semantic prosody in the English middle construction, and just a residual minority of cases involves a negative one. Specifically, in the case of the base *cut,* more than 70% of the instances analyzed possess a positive semantic prosody; regarding the base *drive,* the percentage would be in this respect more than 92%; in the case of the base *handle,* it would be more than 96%; and finally, regarding the base *sell,* it would be more than 98%. Such positive semantic prosody is provided by the semantics of the adverb/adverbial phrase in question, not by the semantics of the verb or the noun. This idea is fundamental to understand the semantics of the type of middle construction analyzed here, one which deals with the foregrounding of the inherent properties of a given inanimate entity, a product, by means of a value judgment uttered by the speaker in the form of a collocation of the type Adverb + Verb. The fact that positive semantic prosody is so productive in the middle construction is assumed as a clear indication of the connection between this grammatical structure and its use in both real life and literature, mainly found in contexts which involve the promotion, foregrounding of the inherent qualities and selling skills of a given product, as it happens in the field of advertisement.

References

1. Ackema, P., Schoorlemmer, M.: The middle construction and the syntax semantics interface. Lingua **93**, 59–90 (1994)
2. Bosque, I.: On the conceptual bases of collocations: restricted adverbs and lexical selection. In: Torner Castells, S., Bernal, E. (eds.) Collocations and other lexical combinations in Spanish: theoretical, lexicographical and Applied perspectives, vol. 1, pp. 9–20. Routledge, London (2016)
3. Davidse, K., Heyvaert, L.: On the middle voice: an interpersonal analysis of the English middle. Linguistics **45**(1), 37–83 (2007)
4. Fagan, S.: The Syntax and Semantics of Middle Constructions: A Study with Special Reference to German, 1st edn. Cambridge University Press, Cambridge (1992)
5. Gries, S.: Phraseology and linguistic theory: a brief survey. In: Granger, S., Meunier, F. (eds.) Phraseology: An Interdisciplinary Perspective, vol. 1, pp. 3–25. John Benjamins, Amsterdam (2008)
6. Heyvaert, L.: A Cognitive-Functional Approach to Nominalization in English, 1st edn. Mouton de Gruyter, Berlin (2003)
7. Heyvaert, L.: Nominalization as an interpersonally-driven system. Functions Lang. **8**(2), 283–324 (2001)
8. Kemmer, S.: The Middle Voice, 1st edn. John Benjamins, Amsterdam (1993)
9. Levin, B.: English Verb Classes and Alternations: A Preliminary Investigation, 1st edn. The University of Chicago Press, Chicago (1993)
10. Maroto, A.: Big Data, Twitter and Music: New paths in research. http://www.researchgate.net/publication/331479188. Accessed 15 May 2019

11. Maroto, A.: El metadiscurso en las redes sociales: Una extensión multidimensional. Análisis de cinco dirigentes políticos de la coalición Ahora Podemos a través de la red social Twitter. http://www.researchgate.net/publication/331479188. Accessed 15 May 2019
12. Oster, U., van Lawick, H.: Semantic preference and semantic prosody: a corpus-based analysis of translation-relevant aspects of the meaning of phraseological units. In: Translation and Meaning, vol. 8, pp. 333–344. Hogeschool Maastricht, Amsterdam (2008)
13. Sinclair, J.: Lexical grammar. Naujoji Metodologija **24**, 191–203 (2000)
14. Yoshimura, K., Taylor, J.: What makes a good middle? The role of qualia in the interpretation and acceptability of middle expressions in English. Engl. Lang. Linguist. **8**(2), 293–321 (2004)
15. Yoshimura, K.: Encyclopedic structure of nominals and middle expressions in English. Kobe Pap. Linguist. **1**, 112–140 (1998)

Classification of the Combinatorial Behavior of Verbs in the Marketing Domain

Ivanka Rajh[1](✉) and Larisa Grčić Simeunović[2](✉)

[1] Zagreb School of Economics and Management, Jordanovac 110,
10000 Zagreb, Croatia
irajh@zsem.hr
[2] University of Zadar, Mihovila Pavlinovića 1, 23000 Zadar, Croatia
lgrcic@unizd.hr

Abstract. The aim of this article is to provide a description of verbs in the specialized domain of marketing by focusing on their syntactic-semantic behaviors. Using a methodology based on combinatorial properties and paradigmatic relationships, we describe the essential syntagmatic profile of verbs that belong to different verb classes. The hypothesis is that each verb is associated with its particular argument scheme from which it is possible to identify its specialized meaning and establish correlations with a series of predicates with which it shares a set of linguistic properties.

The research was done in the domain of marketing, which is a very dynamic field, also underlined in the definitions, which use terms such as *activity, process, mechanism, adaptation, strategy, techniques*, all designed to satisfy the needs of the customer for the benefit of the company [1].The domination of lexical units describing processes motivated us to explore verbs, as the main words used to express actions, with the help of the Sketch Engine tool, so as to determine their terminological nature and their role in expressing marketing dynamics.

Keywords: Verbs · Syntagmatic profile · Selectional preferences · Specialized French monolingual corpus · Marketing domain

1 Introduction

In the context of language for special purposes, many authors have studied verbs and adjectives as secondary elements in terminology description. Since noun forms are primarily considered as the denominations of concepts, verbs and adjectives are described as part of phraseological information, that is, they are considered of secondary importance in the terminological entry.

We maintain that linguistic knowledge about the syntactic behavior of terms can have an important role for understanding and acquiring knowledge of a specialized domain. From a theoretical point of view, we follow a distributional approach based on the premise that lexicon, syntax, and semantics cannot be separated. If the semantic and syntactic properties of a word are inseparable, the use of a word is defined by the

© Springer Nature Switzerland AG 2019
G. Corpas Pastor and R. Mitkov (Eds.): Europhras 2019, LNAI 11755, pp. 360–374, 2019.
https://doi.org/10.1007/978-3-030-30135-4_26

distribution of its contexts. From this perspective, describing a language means conducting an organized identification of all the uses it contains [3].

In specialized languages that describe a discourse of a certain domain, co-occurrences offer important information for understanding specialized concepts. Corpus methodology has opened the way to analyze selectional preferences which enable us to list typical occurrences of lexical or terminological units. These are called patterns and are defined as "an argument structure with semantic values for the arguments – i.e. semantic types – populated by lexical sets, e.g. paradigmatic sets of words occupying the same syntagmatic position [7, p. 8].

Patterns of usage can be described on the basis of an analysis of actual usage in a corpus. Nevertheless, the Corpus Pattern Analysis (CPA) introduced by Hanks [6] considers that patterns are only indirect evidence for meanings. In order to determine the meaning, it is necessary to summarize the syntagmatic profiles that consist of "various different syntactic and collocational patterns in which the word regularly participates" [5, p. 79].

The lexico-grammatical approach proposed by the French scholars Gross [2, 4] and Le Pesant [8] follows the same point of view that acknowledges the relationship between the meaning of the verb and its syntactic behavior. The authors suggest a methodology that allows classifying lexical units based on the predicate-argument structure. This kind of syntactic-semantic classification applies distributional criteria in order to describe the lexicon by means of two major semantic classes: semantic classes of predicates and semantic classes of arguments. Each of them regroups together units that share common syntactic and semantic features. The advantage of this approach is that it provides a systematic model for representing the interplay between syntactic behavior and semantic features. Apart from making the lexical selection explicit, this model includes syntactic sub-categorization of the predicate and its semantic classification by representing hierarchical relations between classes.

In this paper, we report on the preliminary results of a corpus-based investigation of verb forms in the French monolingual corpus of the marketing domain. The domination of lexical units belonging to the category of processes, in the corpus of the marketing domain, motivated us to explore the verbal predicates and their arguments. We consider that knowledge about verbs is especially important because verbs convey specialized meaning in sentences.

According to the distributional methodology, we carried out an analysis of verbal predicates from the point of view of the semantic types of their arguments. We therefore assumed that each verb had its own particular argument scheme from which it is possible to identify its specialized meaning.

For this reason, the arguments have been listed and grouped in paradigmatic terminological sets in order to be able to determine the verbs' syntagmatic profiles. This kind of analysis allowed us to make links to other predicates that share the same semantic combinatorial features.

2 Methodology

2.1 The Field of Marketing and the Corpus

Marketing is a very dynamic field, its activity concentrating in six main areas, which are the study of markets and consumer behavior, product policy, pricing policy, distribution policy, and communication or promotion policy. The specialized corpus analyzed for the purpose of this research consisted of one million words from three types of texts in the field of marketing written in French: manuals for university marketing courses, scientific and professional articles, and working or management documents prepared for companies by marketing specialists (Table 1).

Table 1. Composition of the French marketing corpus

Text type	Number of texts	Tokens
University textbooks, chapters and theses	18	721,260
Scientific and professional articles	29	226,663
Working or management documents	5	63,498
Total	**52**	**1,007,792**

2.2 The Pilot Phase

The description of a verb's syntagmatic profile involved several complementary steps. First, the key terms of the domain were identified using the frequency list. Afterwards these terms became seed words that were used for direct verb searches. At this point, certain lexical-semantic criteria were used for validating verb candidate terms for the marketing domain.

In the pilot phase of the research, we used three key terms in the marketing domain, the nouns *marché*, *produit* and *prix*, as the starting point for the analysis since nouns are the word class that most typically appear as terms. Furthermore, these three terms belong to three different categories of concepts: market being a **place** where supply meets demand; products being tangible or intangible **goods** offered for consumption, and price being a monetary **value** of goods or services. We used the SketchEngine tool to analyze the distribution of these terms, with special attention given to verbal syntagmatic patterns. A comparison of the word sketches for the three terms showed that the verbs that combine with those nouns as objects are not only more numerous, but terminologically more interesting than those verbs that combine with them as subjects. For example, there were on average 25 verbs cited with those nouns as object against 3 to 6 verbs where the noun is the subject, including modal verbs such as *pouvoir* and *devoir* (Table 2).

A more thorough analysis of the word sketch for the noun *marché*, and the word sketches of the verbs it combines with, showed that among verbs listed with that noun as object, there were many verbs that appeared with *marché* as attributes, in the form of past participles, rather than as predicates, as presented in Table 3. Furthermore, some of

Table 2. Word Sketch for the noun *marché*

	Total number of verbs	Verbs and their frequencies
Verbs with *marché* as object	27	segmenter 43, orienter 18, définir 18, cibler 17, détenir 11, viser 11, élever 12, approcher 9, comprendre 9, servir 8, donner 8, créer 7, saturer 7, élargir 7, découper 6, composer 6, constituer 6, desservir 5, dominer 5, étudier 5, produire 5, connaître 5, pénétrer 4, mondialiser 4, diviser 4
Verbs with *marché* as subject	6	pouvoir 6, cibler 5, exister 4, atteindre 3, connaître 3, consister 3

the listed verbs proved to be synonyms of the terminologically more interesting verbs, e.g. *viser* as a synonym of *cibler* and *découper* as a synonym of *segmenter*.

Table 3. Verbs combining with the noun *marché* and their arguments

Verbs	Frequency	Arguments
segmenter	43	marché 43
		population 2; public 1
cibler	17	clients 12 (client ciblé 6); clientèle 10 (clientèle ciblée 5); population 5 (population ciblée 4); public ciblé 7
		marché 17 (marché ciblé 2); segment 9 (segment ciblé 4); subvention ciblée 7; offre 5 (offre ciblée 4); opération 4; pays/publicité/recherche/communication 3
viser *syn. of* cibler	11	cible visée 30; segment 15 (segment visé 13); marché 11 (marché visé 9); public 6 (public visé 3); clientèle 6 (clientèle visée 3); position 6 (position visée 4); consommateur visé 6; client visé 6; femme/personne 3
servir	8	client 10 (client servi 1); marché (marché servi 4); besoins 4
saturer	7	marché saturé 7
découper *syn. of* segmenter	6	marché 6

Taking into account the findings of the pilot phase, that is, the fact that terminologically interesting verbs more frequently appear with terms as objects and that many listed verbs actually behave as attributes, in the second research phase we focused on an analysis of the syntactic pattern verb + noun in the object function.

2.3   The Second Research Phase: Validation of Verb Candidate Terms

Since our aim was to study verbs, as the main words used to describe actions, an initial analysis was necessary to determine those with some terminological value (primary verbs). In order to determine the terminological value of the verbs, we used several criteria provided by L'Homme [9, 11] and Žele [12].

In the first phase, we considered the lexical-semantic criteria proposed by L'Homme [11]. According to the first criterion, a lexical item may be a term if its meaning is related to the domain; secondly, if its arguments are considered terms (according to criterion 1); thirdly, if its morphological derivations are considered terms themselves (according to criteria 1 and 2) and the lexical item shares a semantic relation with some of them; and lastly, if there is another paradigmatic relation to other terminological units from the domain.

The second and third criteria are also postulated by Žele [12] who distinguishes between primary and secondary verbal terms. Primary verbal terms are specialized verbs, which are mostly derived from nouns, while secondary verbal terms are actually primitive or basic verbs which, in combination with highly-specialized arguments, acquire a certain degree of terminologization.

In order to extract the syntagmatic patterns that we were interested in, we applied the frequency criterion and searched for combinations of verbs and their arguments by using CQL (Corpus Query Language) and the part-of-speech tagset. We looked for all the verbs that appear in the corpus in the verb+determiner+noun structure. The search of the corpus with the "[tag="VER.*"][tag="DET.*"][tag="NOM.*"] tagset resulted in syntagmatic patterns containing definite articles (*le, la, les*) and the indefinite article (*un, une*), but failed to retrieve combinations with the indefinite article in the plural (*des*). Therefore, an additional search was made with the [tag="VER.*"][tag="PRP: det"][tag="NOM.*"] tagset, which not only gave the previously missing combinations, but also those where the noun complement is necessarily preceded with the prepositions *à* or *de* (*au, du, aux, des*).

Next, we used the above-mentioned criteria as a starting point for the selection of verbs. Firstly, we applied the morphological criteria which allowed us to recognize the so-called primary verbs that share the same morphological and semantic relation with the noun term and we checked their definition [13–16] in the field. Secondly, we eliminated all combinations with auxiliary and modal verbs, as well as all combinations with a frequency smaller than three. Finally, by applying the semantic criterion, we eliminated those combinations where arguments were not terms or heads of complex terms. Some results of the application of the above criteria can be seen in Table 4.

3   Proposed Approach

3.1   Sub-categorization of Arguments

Once the key verbs were identified, we grouped together their arguments, i.e. terminological sets occupying the same syntagmatic position. After analyzing terminological sets of different verbs, we realized that the arguments belong to different conceptual categories (Table 5), which needed to be defined with respect to specificities of the

Table 4. Sample of results after the application of the two criteria

Syntagmatic combinations (Frequency)	Nominal terms related to the verb	Arguments
évaluer la valeur (6)	évaluation activité du vendeur, évaluation post achat	valeur perçue, valeur vie client
accepter un prix (4)	acceptation par le marché	prix, prix prédateurs
adopter un comportement (11)	adopteurs précoces; adoption des produits nouveaux	comportement du consommateur, comportement d'achat
développer une offre (11)	développement du produit	offre, offre de réduction
gérer une gamme (11)	gestion de la relation client	gamme (de produits)
lancer un produit (10)	lancement produit	produit, produit dérivé
mesurer la performance (3)	mesure d'exposition publicitaire	performance marketing; marketing à la performance
promouvoir un produit (3)	promotion	produit, produit générique
satisfaire le client (11)	satisfaction	client actif/inactif
utiliser la matrice (6)	utilisateur	matrice BCG

marketing domain. It was then necessary to attribute semantic value to the arguments in order to create semantic types that correspond to conceptual categories for the marketing domain.

Table 5. Arguments of different semantic types

Verb	Arguments Semantic type A	Arguments Semantic type B	Arguments Semantic type C
segmenter	marché	population	public
cibler	marché	clients	segment
servir	marché	client	besoins

As Jezek and Hanks [7] point out, the lexical sets in general language do not necessarily map the conceptual categories. We were interested to investigate this problem in a specialized language and to see to what extent the distributional terminological sets could be mapped into semantic types. For this reason, we combined the onomasiological and semasiological approach to map the two systems, the conceptual and semantic ones. Once the syntagmatic behavior of verbs and terminological units in this specialized corpus was analyzed, experts were consulted in order to create a valid semantic type system for the marketing domain.

Our starting point was the conceptual classification proposed by Sager (1990) which distinguishes 4 types of concepts: (a) Entities (material or abstract);

(b) Processes or Activities (performed by Entities); (c) Qualities or Attributes (of the Entities); and (d) Relations (hierarchical, participatory, associative).

In order to adapt this general classification to the field of marketing, we consulted a marketing expert who presented us with a diagram of marketing activities (Fig. 1).

Fig. 1. Diagram of the marketing process

The marketing of services and products is described as a 6-phase process. First of all, there is the analysis of the market (**Entity/Place**), which is in reality an abstract place where demand meets supply (**Entity/Object**). The market analysis includes both the micro and macro environment. Micro-level participants are consumers (**Entity/Human**), companies, distributors, competitors, etc. Macro-environmental analysis provides information (**Result**) on political, economic, social, technological, ecological, and legal factors. The second phase includes the segmentation (**Process/Activity**) of the market according to the desires and needs (**State**) of consumers. The third phase consists of choosing the target market, while the fourth phase represents the process of positioning and of defining value (**Attribute**) for consumers. The fifth phase defines the marketing mix through its four classic components: decisions related to the product, its price, its promotion, and its distribution in different places or channels of distribution. For services, the marketing mix contains three additional elements: personnel, processes, and physical evidence (the physical environment). The sixth phase is the implementation of controls and monitoring of all these processes.

This description and the consultations with a marketing expert helped us classify the arguments found after the second phase of research in the corpus. These arguments or terminological sets are considered as elementary distributional units to the extent that they define the semantic type system of terminological units as well as the uses of the verbs they combine with. Apart from the types of concepts proposed by Sager (1990), we added some others such as Result, Measure, *Modus operandi*, and State, while entities were divided into Human Entities, Objects, Abstract Entities and Places (Table 6).

The semantic types were defined with the help of marketing experts while the definitions were found in specialized dictionaries [13–16], and both procedures proved to be quite challenging. While domain experts do not think about their field of expertise in the same categories as linguists or terminologists, terminological dictionaries differ in the number and choice of terms. Furthermore, some terms contain several definitions under the same entry, or different definitions exist in different dictionaries, which makes the classification of the term difficult. Consider, for example, definitions of the term *positionnement* in three different dictionaries (Table 7):

Looking at the definitions below, *positionnement* could be classified as [[Attribute]] (of a brand or a product), [[Process]] (activities undertaken to obtain the positioning),

Table 6. Semantic type system in the marketing domain

Semantic types	Terminological sets
Entity/Human	prestataire, équipe, client, clientèle, segment, entreprise, consommateur
Entity/Object	produit, offre, stocks, gamme, solution, ensemble
Entity/Abstract	concept, connaissance
Entity/Place	marché, réseau
Attribute	valeur, marque, qualité, potentiel (de profit, de croissance, de développement), proposition (de valeur), prix, notoriété, identité, image, ambiance, disponibilité, nom, position, comportement
Process/Activity	développement, suivi, processus (de vente), campagne, marketing, relations (publiques), veille, vente, action, promotion, gestion, effort, bouche-à-oreille, achat, communication, publicité, positionnement
Result	performance, impact, donnée, réponse, objectif,
Measure	coût, capacité, efficacité, rentabilité, chiffre, nombre, taux; panier, vente, écart, nombre, retombée
Modus operandi	stratégie, circuit, programme, parcours, technique, démarche, méthode, outil, matrice
State	besoin, demande, risque, sensibilité

Table 7. Definitions of term *positionnement*

Dictionary	Definition
www.definitions-marketing.com	Le positionnement est un terme marketing dont **la définition peut varier** selon le contexte d'usage. Dans son usage dominant, le positionnement correspond à **la position** qu'occupe un produit ou une marque dans l'esprit des consommateurs face à ses concurrents sur différents critères (prix, image, caractéristiques, etc.). Dans une logique volontariste, le positionnement peut désigner **le positionnement recherché par l'entreprise** et non celui perçu par les consommateurs. Enfin, dans une optique d'action (usage rare), le terme peut désigner **l'ensemble des actions** entreprises pour obtenir la position souhaitée dans l'esprit des consommateurs
www.ledicodumarketing.fr	Définit **la manière** dont on souhaite que le produit soit perçu par rapport aux produits concurrents, en fonction des différents critères de marché (prix, mode de vente, publicité....)
www.mercator-publicitor.fr	**Choix stratégique** des éléments clefs d'une proposition de valeur, qui permet de donner à son offre une position crédible, attractive et différente sur son marché et dans l'esprit des clients. Le positionnement a deux dimensions: **identification** à une catégorie de produit et **différenciation** au sein de cette catégorie

[[Result]] (of that process) and [[*Modus operandi*]] (strategy of obtaining certain positioning).

L'Homme [10] identified a similar problem with computing terminology and terminological dictionaries and emphasized the importance of contexts for the classification or grouping of terms with similar characteristics. Her analysis led her to conclude that verbs (and adjectives) provide clues to the meaning of noun terms. The above reasoning is an example of the difference between how linguists and domain specialists consider the concepts and related terminology. When presented with different definitions, and after the initial hesitation, our marketing expert clearly opted for positioning as a [[Process]], which does not mean that another expert would not consider some other conceptual category.

The categorization of the arguments allowed us to illustrate the syntactic behavior of verbs as well as their meaning potential. According to Hanks [5], "the semantics of each verb in the language are determined by the totality of its complementation patterns". This approach suggests that several meaning potentials co-exist and that they are contextually determined.

Table 8 illustrates the meaning potentials for three different verbs: *évaluer, développer* and *satisfaire*. In combination with arguments from the semantic type [[Attribute]] and [[State]], the verb *évaluer* conveys the meaning of assessing, which is more of a qualitative approach, while in combination with the [[Result]] it denotes appraisal or measuring, which is a quantitative approach. *Développer* in combination with [[Entity/Objects]] conveys the meaning of building or creating, while in combination with [[*Modus operandi*]] and [[Process/Activity]], it conveys the meaning of elaboration, which is more abstract than building. The arguments affect the verb's meaning, which becomes even more obvious when translated into another language. For example, the English equivalent of the verb *satisfaire* in combination with [[State]] would be "to meet", while in combination with [[Human Entity]], it would be "to satisfy".

Table 8. Syntagmatic profile of verbs

Verb	Semantic type	Terminological set
évaluer	Attribute	valeur, marque, qualité, potentiel (de profit, de croissance, de développement), proposition de valeur
	Result	performance, efficacité, impact
	State	risque
	Entity/Place	marché
	Entity/Human	prestataire
développer	Entity/Object	produit, offre
	State	demande
	Modus operandi	programme, stratégie
	Process/Activity	vente, relation, veille
satisfaire	State	demande, besoin
	Entity/Human	client, consommateur

3.2   Sub-categorization of Verbs

Having categorized the verb's arguments, we were interested to see which verbs combine with the terms from the same semantic type. Overall, ten such tables were produced for verbs combining with each of the semantic types specific for the field of marketing. Table 9 exemplifies the verbs that combine with arguments from the semantic type [[Process/Activity]].

Table 9. Verbs + [[Process/Activity]]

Verbs	Terms from the semantic type [[Process/Activity]]
créer	relations publiques
concevoir	campagne
considérer	marketing
développer	veille, vente
mesurer	opération
réaliser	étude, enquête, recherche
utiliser	marketing, communication, publicité, positionnement
renforcer	veille
développer	relation
guider	action
lancer	promotion
optimiser	gestion
stimuler	effort, bouche-à-oreille, achat, vente

Further analysis of the verbs grouped together as in the Table above showed that they can be categorized into five following classes (Table 10), which seem to be recurrently used in the marketing domain. The verbs were categorized depending on the meaning of their nominal forms and the arguments they combine with.

As the definition of verb classes depends on the arguments they combine with, sometimes it was difficult to categorize a verb as belonging to one or another class. For instance, *servir* combines with arguments such as *besoin* [[State]] and *client* [[Entity/Human]] and could thus be categorized as both a verb of complex processes and a verb for dealing with people. A similar ambiguity exists with the verb *utiliser* which combines with the arguments *méthode* [[*Modus operandi*]] and *produit* [[Entity/Object]], which may be categorized as a verb of complex processes or a verb for handling objects.

Bearing in mind that each verb's behavior expresses its specific meaning potential, we investigated to what extent the members of the same verb class share the same combinatorial potential. However, our results showed that no fixed terminological sets are possible as verbs from the same class tend to share a subset of arguments within a certain semantic type but not necessarily all of the members. This problem was already indicated by Jezek and Hanks [7] who state that "the internal composition of sets changes when one moves from verb to verb" because "their membership has a loose semantic unity".

Table 10. Verb classes and their members

Verb class	Verbs
Verbs of cognition/analysis	analyser, comprendre, concevoir, connaître, considérer, découvrir, décrire, définir, évaluer, identifier
Verbs of complex processes	accepter, adopter, apporter, approcher, assurer, augmenter, capter, collecter, commercialiser, contrôler, couvrir, créer, développer, distribuer, échanger, enrichir, fixer, fournir, gérer, lancer, mesurer, minimiser, offrir, optimiser, partager, positionner, prévoir, promouvoir, proposer, réaliser, réduire, relancer, renforcer, satisfaire, segmenter, servir, stimuler, tester, utiliser
Verbs for handling objects	utiliser, essayer, stocker
Verbs for dealing with people	fidéliser, inciter, aider, animer, attirer, impliquer, influencer, satisfaire, servir
Verbs of communication	communiquer, représenter, formuler

We continued our analysis by evaluating the combinatorial profile of a verb class that regroups verbs of cognition.

The results given in Table 11 illustrate the meaning potential of the verbs in the marketing domain. For instance, the verb *évaluer* is present in several subsets because it combines with arguments from four different semantic types [[State]], [[Attribute]], [[Entity]] and [[Results]]. This kind of information can be used for the disambiguation of a verb's meaning, as well as to illustrate its meaning potential. Taking into account that a verb's specialized meaning depends on the arguments and is context dependent, its polysemy becomes visible as soon as we introduce synonyms or apply a bilingual perspective. Thus, with the arguments from the subsets [[State]], [[Attribute]], and [[Entity]], the meaning of the verb *évaluer* refers to measuring qualitative features and could be an equivalent of the English *assess*, while with the subset [[Results]], it focuses on quantitative features and could be translated into English as *estimate*.

3.3   Correlation Between Semantic Types of the Arguments and Verb Classes

After categorizing key verbs of the marketing domain and the semantic types of their arguments, we compared the correlation between them. As can be seen from the results, each semantic type has its own selection preferences. Certain semantic types combine with the same verb class, but not with the same set of verbs within that class. For instance, arguments from both semantic types [[Processes]] and [[Attributes]] combine with verbs of complex processes, but the verb *stimuler* combines only with the arguments *vente* and *bouche-à-oreille* from the [[Processes]] type. Similarly, both [[Attributes]] and [[States]] arguments combine with the verbs of cognition, but the verb *prévoir* combines only with the argument *demande* from the [[State]] type. Table 12 shows that the most important verb classes in the direct object function in the marketing domain are those of complex processes and cognition as they combine with nine out of

Table 11. Syntagmatic profile of verbs of cognition

Verbs of cognition	Semantic type of the arguments	Terminological set
évaluer, analyser, comprendre, connaître, prévoir	State	besoin, demande, risque
évaluer	Attribute	valeur, marque, qualité, potentiel (de profit, de croissance, de développement), proposition (de valeur)
comprendre, évaluer, regrouper	Entity/Human	prestataire, client
évaluer, analyser, mesurer, valider	Result	performance, impact, donnée, réponse, efficacité, résultat
concevoir, developer, analyser, comprendre, valoriser	*Modus operandi*	stratégie, processus, programme

ten semantic types of arguments. In contrast, there are three verb classes that combine with only one semantic type of arguments: verbs of communication combine only with [[Attributes]], verbs for handling objects only with [[Entity/Object]], while verbs for dealing with people combine only with [[Entity/Human]].

4   Results

In order to describe verbs used in the marketing domain, several criteria were used. Firstly, lexico-semantic and morphological criteria were applied so as to determine which verbs have terminological value in the domain. Secondly, the pattern verb + direct object was chosen as the starting point and the first step in the analysis of the verbal syntagmatic patterns. By using this method, we obtained 190 combinations with more than 3 occurrences in the corpus. The semantic analysis of the predicate-argument structure enabled us to determine 5 different classes of verbs and 10 semantic types of arguments. Out of the total number of 64 verbs, roughly 39 of them were classified as verbs of complex processes, 10 as verbs of cognition, 3 as verbs for handling objects, 9 as verbs for dealing with people and 3 as verbs of communication. Around 80 different nouns were classified into the following 10 semantic types: Entity/Human, Entity/Abstract, Entity/Object, Entity/Place, Attribute, Process, Result, Measure, *Modus operandi* and State. The most significant type by the number of different arguments was that of [[Process]], followed by the semantic types [[Attribute]], [[Measure]] and [[*Modus operandi*]].

The analysis of patterns showed different selectional preferences for each verb class. Verbs of complex processes combine with all semantic types of terminological sets apart from [[Human entities]], where they are replaced with verbs for dealing with people. Verbs of cognition do not combine with the arguments from the semantic type

Table 12. Correlation between semantic types of arguments and verb classes

Semantic type of arguments	Verb class	Verbs from the corpus
Processes/Activities	verbs of complex processes	créer, concevoir, réaliser, développer, lancer, optimiser, stimuler, mesurer
Attributes	verbs of cognition	évaluer, contrôler, valider, analyser
	verbs of communication	communiquer, représenter
	verbs of complex processes	créer, enrichir, mesurer, renforcer, accepter, adopter, apporter, capter, augmenter, réduire, fixer, offrir, utiliser
State	verbs of complex processes	créer, développer, minimiser, réduire, relancer, satisfaire, server, tester, renforcer
	verbs of cognition	évaluer, analyser, comprendre, connaître, découvrir, prévoir
Entity/object	verbs of complex processes	concevoir; créer; développer, lancer, positionner, promouvoir, commercialiser, réaliser,
	verbs for handling objects	stocker, utiliser, vendre, acheter, essayer, gérer, regrouper
Entity/place	verbs of cognition	évaluer, comprendre
	verbs of complex processes	segmenter, approcher
Result	verbs of cognition	évaluer, analyser, mesurer, valider
	verbs of complex processes	réaliser, réduire, fixer
Measure	verbs of complex processes	réduire, augmenter, couvrir, répartir, supporter, renforcer
	verbs of cognition	valider, renforcer, comprendre
Entity/abstract	verbs of cognition	valoriser
	verbs of complex process	utiliser

(continued)

Table 12. (*continued*)

Semantic type of arguments	Verb class	Verbs from the corpus
Entity/Human	verbs for dealing with people	fidéliser, inciter, animer, satisfaire, aider, servir, impliquer
	verbs of cognition	comprendre, évaluer, regrouper
Modus operandi	verbs of cognition	analyser, comprendre, valoriser
	verbs of complex processes	optimiser, adopter, réclamer, utiliser, concevoir, développer

[[Process/Activities]], which may be due to a method of classification of particular verbs (e.g. *concevoir* – can be considered as a verb of process or cognition). Verbs of communication appear only with the semantic type [[Attribute]], showing their importance in presenting products to the target market, that is, consumers or buyers. Even though the analyzed verbs tend to keep the meaning from the general language, this kind of analysis shows their meaning potential, i.e. nuances of meaning that become obvious in combination with different semantic types of arguments.

5   Conclusion

This research has enabled us to identify essential verbs for writing texts in the field of marketing, to establish semantic categories of predicates and their arguments, as well as to organize the uses of these verbs according to the semantic types of their arguments. We believe that a linguistic analysis focusing on the syntactic-semantic behavior of terms can provide a means of organizing the uses but also reveal the specific meanings of terminological units.

The application of lexico-semantic criteria for the purpose of determining the verb classes of verbs and semantic types of arguments allows for a more precise definition of different nuances of the meaning of words, which may have implications not only for the acquisition of a language, but also for lexicography and translation. In this particular case of language of the marketing domain, this method enabled us to detect verbs that may be considered terms or that have higher terminological value due to the arguments they combine with, and as such merit special attention both in terminographic work and in the development of translation tools. Further research should focus on refining the proposed classification, especially regarding the verb class of complex processes. In addition, an analysis of other syntagmatic patterns containing verbs may reveal further terminologically significant combinations.

Acknowledgments. This work has been supported in part by the Croatian Science Foundation under the project UIP-2017-05-7169.

References

1. Barth, I.: L'Histoire intellectuelle du marketing. Du savoir-faire à la discipline scientifique. Market Manag. Mark. Commun. **6**(2), 76–107 (2006)
2. Gross, G.: Une sémantique nouvelle pour la traduction automatique : les classes d'objets. La tribune des Industries de la Langue et de l'Information électronique 17-18-19, Paris (1995)
3. Gross, G.: Manuel d'analyse linguistique: approche semantico-syntaxique du lexique, Presses Universitaires du Septentrion (2012)
4. Gross, G.: Classes d'objets et description des verbes. Langages **115**, 15–30 (1994)
5. Hanks, P.: Contextual dependency and lexical sets'. Int. J. Corpus Linguist. **1**(1), 75–98 (1996)
6. Hanks, P.: Lexical Analysis. Norms and Exploitations. MIT Press, Cambridge, MA (2013)
7. Jezek, E., Hanks, P.: What lexical sets tell us about conceptual categories. Lexis **4**(7), 7–22 (2010)
8. Le Pesant, D.: Principles for a Semantic Classification of Verb Predicates. Language Research, Special Issue, pp. 21–38 (2003)
9. L'Homme, M.-Cl.: Définition du statut du verbe en langue de spécialité et sa description lexicographique. Cahiers de lexicologie **73**(2), 125–148 (1998)
10. L'Homme, M.-Cl.: What can verbs and adjectives tell us about terms? In: Proceedings Terminology and Knowledge Engineering (TKE), pp. 65–70 (2002)
11. L'Homme, M.-Cl. : La terminologie : principes et techniques. Les Presses de l'Université de Montréal (2004)
12. Žele, A.: Stopnje terminologizacije v leksiki (na primerih glagolov). In: Humar, M. (ed.) Terminologija v času globalizacije, pp. 77–91. Založba ZRC SAZU, Ljubljana (2004)

Dictionaries

13. Bathelot, B.: Définitions marketing. https://definitions-marketing.com/. Accessed 10 May 2019
14. Le Dico du Marketing. http://www.ledicodumarketing.fr/. Accessed 10 May 2019
15. Lexique marketing et publicité. https://www.mercator-publicitor.fr/Lexique-du-marketing-livre-Mercator-Dunod-Editeur. Accessed 10 May 2019
16. Richard-Lanneyrie, S.: Le Dictionnaire français du marketing. Le Génie des Glaciers Editeur, Chambéry (2014)

"You Took the Word Out of My Mouth":
A Morphosyntactic and Semantic Analysis
of a Phraseological Lexicon of Colombian
Spanish

José Luis Rojas Díaz[1]([✉]) [iD] and Juan Manuel Pérez Sánchez[2]([✉]) [iD]

[1] NHH Norwegian School of Economics, Helleveien 30, 5045 Bergen, Norway
jose.diaz@nhh.no
[2] University of Antioquia, Calle 67 # 53-108, Medellín, Colombia
jmanuel.perez@udea.edu.co

Abstract. Phraseology has been widely studied in Linguistics. However, to date, the representation of phraseological units (Henceforth PUs) in lexicographic resources of dialectal Spanish variants has not been explored in detail. This paper addresses this issue through an analysis of PUs in a phraseological lexicon of Colombian Spanish. In order to perform this analysis, a database was compiled with more than 4,000 entries from the *Lexicón de fraseología del español de Colombia* (henceforth LFEC) (Mora Monroy 1996). The database was tokenized, lemmatized, and tagged; and then morphosyntactic and semantic patterns were extracted. The contribution of this paper is three-fold, (i) It presents a sample of the most frequent syntactic patterns (e.g. V Det N = *agachar la cabeza*) extracted from the LFEC, (ii) it describes how semantic patterns can be extracted through semantic tagging using the UCREL semantic analysis system (USAS) (Archer et al. 2002), and (iii) it presents a frequency analysis of some lexical components of the extracted PUs that can shed light on some of the basic tenets of Cognitive Semantics. More than 700 morphosyntactic patterns and more than 1,300 semantic patterns were identified from the database. This collection of both syntactic and semantic patterns, along with an analysis of their co-occurrence, may help enhance the scripts and tools used nowadays for the extraction of PUs in general and specialized languages.

Keywords: Phraseology · Lexicography · Cognitive semantics ·
Morphosyntatic patterns · Semantic patterns

1 Introduction

The study of phraseology in Spanish has been a matter of interest for many scholars since the mid-20th century, starting with the work of Casares (1950). That work, as many others in Spanish, was a lexicographic study in which this author set the principles for the study of PUs and their indexation in dictionaries.

The way PUs are represented in dictionaries along with recommendations on how those units should be treated by lexicographers are two of the main topics covered by

© Springer Nature Switzerland AG 2019
G. Corpas Pastor and R. Mitkov (Eds.): Europhras 2019, LNAI 11755, pp. 375–390, 2019.
https://doi.org/10.1007/978-3-030-30135-4_27

the many studies that comprehend the close bond between phraseology and lexicography. This "scientific marriage" offers more than 1,700 bibliographic references related to both lexicography and phraseology (Leroyer 2006, p. 183). For instance, Penadés (2006) addresses the recurrent problem of marking PUs in dictionaries, Mellado (2008) presents a series of theoretical-practical issues of indexing PUs in dictionaries, while Paquot (2015) deals with how PUs lack consistency and accuracy when comparing dictionaries.

However, this relationship between phraseology and lexicography has barely been explored in the Colombian dialectal variety of Spanish. Therefore, two important questions arise, (i) How are PUs represented in the lexicographic resources available for Colombian Spanish? (ii) What are the semantic and morphosyntactic characteristics of the PUs indexed in the *Lexicón de fraseología del español de Colombia* (Henceforth LFEC) in particular?

In an attempt to answer those questions, the present work has been devoted to analyzing the LFEC in detail both from a semantic and a morphosyntactic point of view. In order to do so, some central concepts must be clarified first.

2 Phraseology: Denomination Issues and Definition

Firstly, the denomination of phraseology is a matter of discussion among theorists and researchers. Some authors suggest that Western structuralist linguists coined the term originally; others state that phraseology –as a discipline– appeared in linguistic theories in the 1940s as part of Soviet linguistic studies. Carneado Moré (1985) states that phraseology is indeed influenced by Bally's (1909) "exact combination of words" but also recognizes that it was Vinogradov who set the "fundamental concepts of phraseology" (1985, p. 7). Nevertheless, Zuluaga (1980) points out that, before Bally's work, there were three other authors (Paul 1880; Bréal 1897; von der Gabelentz 1901) who dealt with phraseology with forefather denominations for the concept we now know as phraseology (Zuluaga 1980, pp. 31–37).

Now, defining phraseology is the same as defining its object of study, i.e. the PU. Delimiting phraseology is central because this denomination has been used with very different meanings not only as a term in the field of Linguistics, but also as a word in the general language, carrying no technical meaning (Sciutto 2015, pp. 286–287).

We opted to adopt the definition of phraseology provided by Corpas (1996, p. 20) as a starting point. According to Corpas, a PU is a plurilexical unit that is frequently used, which causes it to be fixed in the language; its component forms tend to co-occur, and, in most cases, it has a figurative meaning. Those three characteristics (plurilexicality, fixation, and idiomaticity) are shared by many other scholars when describing what a PU is, like Mellado Blanco (2004, p. 17), Gries (2008, p. 6), and Mel'čuk (2012).

This definition and the characteristics attached to it fit the entries of the LFEC, which constituted the database for the present study, and which will be presented later in this text.

3   Cognitive Semantics and Embodiment: A Very Brief Introduction

Secondly, as mentioned above, along with analyzing the morphosyntactic character-istics of the units being studied in this paper, we also intend to analyze those units from a semantic point of view. In order to do this, some terms and concepts need to be clarified and delimited beforehand.

Cognitive Linguistics in general, and Cognitive Semantics in particular have been around for quite a while –at least from the late 1970s– and they have gained ground during the last decades as a plausible –perhaps the most plausible– way to explain how we express our thoughts through language. In the best known and probably the most cited work on Cognitive Linguistics –Metaphors We Live By (1980)–, George Lakoff and Mark Johnson set the bases for this at-the-time-revolutionary view of language, thought, and of the interaction between them.

Among the many groundbreaking insights introduced by Lakoff and Johnson in their work, one that stands out is that "we typically conceptualize the nonphysical in terms of the physical, that is, we conceptualize the less clearly delineated in terms of the more clearly delineated." (1980, p. 59) That claim is, in turn, based on the assumption that our conceptualization of the nonphysical in terms of the physical is mediated by our own physiological and cultural experience of the world. Thus, what we make of the world depends highly on how our body interacts with that world, or, in the words of Valenzuela et al. (2016):

> "Language does not reflect facts based on an objectivist outer world, totally independent from what people perceive, but language reflects conceptual structures built by people through their more or less common experiences and knowledge about their own surrounding world and culture." (p. 37)

Thus, one of the basic tenets of Lakoff and Johnson's theory is that our bodily and cultural experience are at the heart –no pun intended– of our understanding of not-so-physical experiences, and that we tend to express that understanding linguistically mainly through the use of metaphors. Those metaphors, in turn, tend to resort to physical, familiar, close-to-our-perception words or expressions –called vehicles in the metaphor-related literature– to talk about more abstract, vague, or not-so-close-to-our-perception concepts –called tenors–.

Some years later, in his book The Body in the Mind (1987), Mark Johnson elab-orated further on the role of our bodily experience in our understanding of reality, and, subsequently, in the way we express that understanding. Johnson's ideas contributed greatly to what has come to be labelled as the embodiment hypothesis, i.e. that most conceptual metaphors –the term Lakoff and Johnson used to refer to supra-linguistic metaphorical relationships– "draw primarily on domains stemming from bodily experience, and that these bodily source domains do the vast majority of the work of structuring more abstract human concepts." (Rohrer 2006, 125)

With the passing of time, the embodiment hypothesis has grown as to cover many aspects of our perception, including even fine-grained neural mechanisms that are at play in our conceptualization of the world (e.g. Lakoff and Johnson 1999).

However, although much of the current work leading to further developments in Cognitive Linguistics in general, and in embodiment in particular, is being done through their interaction with neuroscience, it is still linguistic instantiations that provide researchers with the biggest amount of data for analyzing the real influence of embodiment on our perception and expression of reality.

Nonetheless, one of the main criticisms traditionally made about the embodiment hypothesis and about Cognitive Linguistics has to do with their relying mainly on introspection, and not on large-scale empirical, corpus-based linguistic studies, and, most importantly, on cross-linguistic and cross-cultural research.

Additionally, much work in Cognitive Linguistics has dealt with linguistic phenomena such as semantic change, grammaticalization, and monolexical-level semantics, mainly in English. In contrast, very few works have dealt with the interaction of Cognitive Linguistics and phraseology, even less work has dealt with that interaction in the Spanish language, and, to the best of our knowledge, none of it has dealt with that interaction in the Colombian variety of that language by means of a large-scale lexicon-size corpus. Thus, one of this paper's main goals is to analyze the semantic characteristics of the LFEC from a Cognitive Semantics point of view, and, more precisely, examining the phraseological instantiations of the bodily basis of reasoning and understanding in Colombian Spanish.

4   Data Characterization and Analysis

For the analysis intended here, a lexicon compiled by Siervo Mora Monroy and published by the Caro y Cuervo Institute (1996) was used. Studies of this kind have not come under the spotlight of Hispanic Linguistics due to the lack of phraseological information and lexicographic repositories from Spanish-speaking countries other than Spain. In Colombia, in particular, there have been some phraseological-data gathering and PU collection works like those by Sierra García (1990), García and Muñoz (1996), and Soto Posada (1997). However, most of those works index entries closer to sayings and proverbs than to idioms and collocations, being the latter group of PUs the one of interest in the present paper.

The work by Mora Monroy (1996) is, in his own words, "a motivation for other researchers to do larger-scale studies [on phraseology] (p. 13)." In the instructions section of his dictionary, the lexicographer explicitly states that the LFEC uses the selection criteria and typologies developed by Casares (1950, p. 170) and later regrouped by Tristá (1988, p. 29).

The following section includes some of the lexicographic information retrieved from the LFEC's mega, macro, and microstructure.

4.1   Lexicographic Information: Megastructure, Macrostructure and Microstructure

According to Hartmann and James (1998), the megastructure "includes the macrostructure and the outside matter" (p. 93); the macrostructure, for these authors, is, in turn, "the overall list structure which allows the compiler and the user to locate information" (p. 91); lastly, they define the microstructure as "the internal design of a reference unit" (p. 94).

Regarding its megastructure, the LFEC consists of 225 pages, and the first part of the book includes the presentation and the introduction. The introduction sets the bases for the lexicographic work, and it presents a rich description of the criteria for the selection of the indexed PUs. This section also presents the sources and the references from where the entries were taken. Finally, the author explains that some of the PUs of the dictionary cannot be directly defined, therefore, in those cases, he has chosen to describe their use (see Table 1).

Table 1. Definition examples taken from the LFEC (Mora Monroy 1996, p. 38)

Type of definition	Entry	Definition
Direct	*sacar la mano*	*Averiarse*
Context of use	*arderle las orejas*	*se usa para señalar que alguien habla, generalmente mal de uno*

The LFEC's macrostructure and microstructure share some features, related mainly with the lack of marking. There is no evidence of a clear distinction between idioms (known in Spanish as *locuciones*) and collocations. Thus, the lexicon does not include any list of abbreviations such as the ones included in the works by García and Muñoz (1996, p. xxvii) and by Seco et al. (2004, pp. xxvii–xxviii).

In regard to the lemmatization and indexation of entries, PUs in the LFEC are listed alphabetically by the first letter of the first orthographic word of the PU (see Table 2).

Table 2. Examples of the first three entries indexed under letter A

Order of the entry	Entry
1	*a boca de jarro*
2	*a boca llena*
3	*a brazo partido*

The LFEC's lexicographic articles and their microstructure are reduced in their content. They do not contain any comments on the entries (spelling, pronunciation, or grammar) and each entry only includes the source from where it was taken, followed by its definition (see Table 3).

Table 3. Examples of lexicographic articles and their microstructure

Entry	Source (abbreviation)	Definition
coger patas	*Al.*	*desaparecer*
mano a mano	*	*confrontación de destrezas*
picar el ojo	*T., Al.*	*guiñar en señal de advertencia*

4.2   Data Selection and Database Compilation

In order to carry out this analysis, a database including all the entries that make up the LFEC was compiled. 4006 PUs composed by 13,701 tokens (grammar words, lexical words, and punctuation marks) were extracted. Then, this data set was filtered by excluding expressions such as Latin idioms, compound words, or expressions including question marks, among others (see Table 4).

Table 4. Expressions excluded from the LFEC during the database compilation process

Categories	Examples	# of expressions excluded
Latin idioms	*ab aeterno, de iure*	126
Exclamation marks	*¡eso faltaba!, ¡Dios quiera!*	43
Commas	*lo pasado, pasado*	13
Question marks	*¿no se le hace?, ¿y qué?*	11
Compound words	*a rajatabla, a quemarropa*	5
No registry	*ful y soda*	2
Total		200

The decision to exclude those expressions was based on the following criteria: (i) expressions that included non-Spanish words or words the meaning of which, as a lexical unit, could not be found (ii) expressions that used punctuation marks that could not be tagged properly syntactically and semantically (commas, question marks, and exclamation marks), and (iii) expressions that did not appear in other resources or corpora (CORDE[1]) (CREA[2]) consulted. After the exclusion of those expressions, the resulting number of entries in the database amounted to 3806.

The initial idea, after having the resulting 3806 entries was to tag every single component of them in order to check the frequency of morphosyntactic patterns. To do so, a Part-of-Speech (Henceforth POS) tagging software called TreeTagger (1994), developed in the University of Stuttgart by Helmut Schmid, was used. Those patterns allowed us to classify each PU by function. In order to do so, we chose the typology used in the *Diccionario Fraseológico Documentado del Español Actual* (Seco et al. 2004, pp. xxvii–xxviii). After checking the POS tagging and the phraseological marking manually, the PUs extracted from the lexicon were counted and classified (see Table 5).

As it can be observed in Table 5, more than two thirds of the resulting PUs were classified as verbs (68.58%), while PUs classified as adverbs amounted to 20.07% of the total number of units. That is, those two categories together amount to 88.65% of the whole number of PUs.

We also wanted to verify the plurilexicality of PUs in the LFEC. In that regard, frequency tended to decrease in proportion to the number of components, i.e. the more

---

[1] *Corpus diacrónico del español* (CORDE).

[2] *Corpus de referencia del español actual* (CREA).

Table 5. Frequency and classification of the resulting PUs extracted from the LFEC

Category	Frequency	%	Cumulative % in the DB
Verb	2610	68.58%	68.58%
Adverb	764	20.07%	88.65%
Adjective	169	4.44%	93.09%
Formulaic	136	3.57%	96.66%
Noun	74	1.94%	98.61%
Construction/collocation	17	0.45%	99.05%
Comparative	12	0.32%	99.37%
Pronominal	10	0.26%	99.63%
Adjective/adverb	5	0.13%	99.76%
Interjectional	3	0.08%	99.84%
Conjunctional	3	0.08%	99.92%
Prepositional	2	0.05%	99.97%
Adverb/conjunctional	1	0.03%	100%

tokens a PU had, the lesser its number of occurrences. However, that was not the case with two-token expressions, the number of which was smaller than that of three-word expressions (see Fig. 1).

There is not enough conclusive evidence as to explain why two-token expressions do not follow the overall frequency tendency. It would be necessary to resort to other lexicographic resources in order to corroborate if this behavior is reiterative. Nevertheless, we think there are two possible reasons for this to happen; either (i) the consulted sources did not contain a big number of these expressions or (ii) it was a decision taken by the lexicographer motivated by the discussion whether some of these units

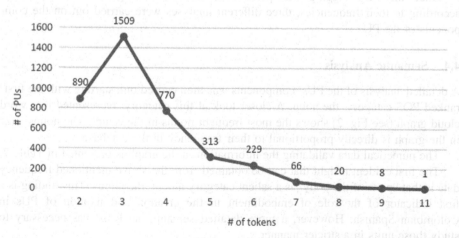

Fig. 1. Frequency of occurrence by number of tokens

were compounds or PUs, which is a very well-known delimitation problem in phraseology (Granger 2005, p. 165).

4.3 Lexical Analysis

Having all the units annotated in the database, the resulting number of component words (tokens) in the database was 13,031. Subsequently, a query was made to see the percentage distribution of the PUs' component words according to their POS tag (see Table 6).

Table 6. Percentage distribution of tokens by POS tags in the database

POS	Frequency	%	Cumulative % in the DB
Noun	3,395	26.05%	26.05%
Verb	3,106	23.84%	49.89%
Adjective	999	7.67%	57.56%
Adverb	665	5.10%	62.66%
Past participle	242	1.86%	64.52%
Present participle	32	0.25%	64.76%
Grammar words	4,592	35.24%	100.00%

The category grammar words (listed last in Table 6) includes all the words that were tagged as conjunction, contraction, demonstrative, determiner, interjection, preposition, or pronoun. Something noteworthy while crossing information was that although most of PUs were marked functionally as verbs, verbal components only ranked second as individual lexical units, being the category "Noun" the most common in the database.

Once the POS tagging was performed, and POS categories were classified according to their frequencies, three different analyses were carried out on the components of the PUs.

4.4 Semantic Analysis

A detailed analysis of the PUs' components was then carried out, starting with the first-ranked POS category: the noun. A closer look at this category, represented in a word cloud graph (see Fig. 2) shows the most frequent nouns in the center. The nouns' size in the graph is directly proportional to their frequency in the database.

The numerical data validating the information in the graph is presented in Table 7.

The first evident insight that can be obtained from the above-mentioned frequency data is that "parts of the body" is a salient category among the nouns. This finding is a first indicator of the role of embodiment in the creation and fixation of PUs in Colombian Spanish. However, a more detailed semantic analysis was necessary to study those units in a stricter manner.

Fig. 2. Word cloud graph of the POS tag category noun in the LFEC

Table 7. Frequencies of the top 10 nouns in the LFEC

Word	Frequency	%	Cumulative % in nouns
mano (hand)	75	2.2%	2.2%
ojo (eye)	51	1.5%	3.7%
paso (step)	42	1.2%	4.9%
palabra (word)	37	1.1%	6.0%
cabeza (head)	35	1.0%	7.1%
pie (foot)	28	0.8%	7.9%
boca (mouth)	25	0.7%	8.6%
cara (face)	23	0.7%	9.3%
diablo (devil)	22	0.6%	10.0%
vida (life)	21	0.6%	10.6%

Although in recent years researchers have been increasingly exploring the semantic aspect of phraseology, especially in phraseological studies related to language for specific purposes (LSP) (Patiño 2017) (Grčić Simeunović and de Santiago 2016), it is quite common to find studies where syntactic tagging and annotation is used to explore PU patterns (Gries 2008); therefore, this study was intended to try to find a correlation between syntactic and semantic patterns.

Firstly, the UCREL semantic analysis system was employed in order to tag the PUs in the LFEC semantically. UCREL is a semantic tagset based on the work of McArthur (1981) and contains "21 major discourse fields expanding into 232 category labels" (Archer et al. 2002, p. 2), one of those discourse fields being "body and the individual" [(B) See Table 9].

For this study, all the forms of the database were tagged using the UCREL tagset, thus creating three layers or bands: (i) one with the forms, (ii) one with POS tag, and (iii) one with a semantic tag, allowing us to see the information from several perspectives. This allowed us to observe the morphosyntactic pattern or the conceptual or semantic categories that each token belonged to (as exemplified in Table 8).

Table 8. Sample database tagging

| | Forms and tags | | | |
	a	*cuerpo*	*de*	*rey*
Part-of-speech	Prep	N	Prep	N
Category level (descriptive)	Z5 Grammatical bin	B1 Anatomy and physiology	Z5 Grammatical bin	S2.2 People: male
Discourse field (descriptive)	Z Names and grammatical words	B Body and the individual	Z Names and grammatical words	S Social actions, states, and processes

Some insights could only be obtained when the semantic tagging was applied to the data. For instance, if one considers the information from Fig. 2 and Table 7, one can say that there is a tendency for parts of the body to be very frequent nouns in the PUs being studied. However, the figures in Table 9 indicate that "body and the individual" is the fourth most frequent category in the database after "movement, location, travel, and transportation."

Table 9. Distribution of discourse field tags in the database

Discourse field	Frequency	%	Cumulative % in nouns
Names and grammar (Z)	5138	39.4%	39.4%
General and abstract terms (A)	1925	14.8%	54.2%
Movement, location, travel, and transportation (M)	1362	10.5%	64.7%
Body and the individual (B)	864	6.6%	71.3%
Substances, materials, objects, and equipment (O)	671	5.1%	76.4%
Numbers and measurement (N)	604	4.6%	81.1%
Psychological actions, states, and processes (X)	401	3.1%	84.1%
Other	2066	15.9%	100.0%

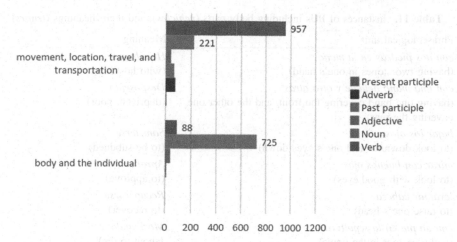

Fig. 3. Distribution of POS tags according to discourse field tags in the database

Table 10. Distribution of semantic categories inside discourse fields

Categories	Examples	Frequency
Anatomy and physiology	*barba* (beard), *sangre* (blood)	605
Clothes and personal belongings	*capa* (cape), *vestidura* (clothing)	92
Disease	*ampolla* (ampoule), *roña* (scabies)	19
Medicines and medical treatment	*píldora* (pill), *pomada* (ointment)	7
Without clothes	*descosido* (burst seam)	1
Health and disease	*salud* (health)	1
Total		725

However, as shown in Fig. 3, nouns are more frequent in the discourse field "body and the individual" than in any other semantic category, while the field "movement, location, travel, and transportation," for example, contains mostly verbs.

Next, a closer look at the distribution of categories inside the discourse field "body and the individual" shows that, by far, nouns related to body parts were the most frequent in that discourse field (see Table 10).

After establishing that "body parts" is indeed the most common semantic category containing nouns in our database, a second stage in the semantic analysis of the LFEC units was entered. That stage consisted in describing the figurative use of body parts in the LFEC's PUs. In that stage, both the PUs and their contextual meanings were necessary in order to identify the kind of semantic relationship between them. As it can be observed in Table 11, PUs in the LFEC tend to use body parts as vehicles in order to refer to abstract tenors (target concepts).

Although, at first sight, most semantic relationships between vehicles and tenors seem to be metaphorical in nature, a closer look would reveal that several cases are also metonymical, but that kind of analysis is beyond the scope of the present work.

Table 11. Instances of PUs including body parts (*vehicles*), and their meanings (*tenors*)

Phraseological unit	Meaning
con dos piedras en la mano (having two stones in one's hand)	*Hostilmente* (with hostility)
con una mano delante y otra atrás (having one hand covering the front, and the other one covering the rear)	*Desposeído* (deprived, poor)
bajar los ojos (to look down/to send one's eyes down)	*Someterse* (to be subdued)
mirar con buenos ojos (to look with good eyes)	*Aprobar* (to approve)
levantar cabeza (to raise one's head)	*Recuperarse* (to recover)
con un pie en la sepultura (with one foot in the grave)	*Moribundo* (about to die)
a boca llena (with a full mouth)	*Claramente* (clearly)
quitar la palabra de la boca (to take the word out of someone's mouth)	*Anticiparse a decir* (to anticipate what someone is going to say)

However, and as already stated above, the extraction of morphosyntactic patterns is very common in phraseological studies, but does it make any difference if one adds semantic information?

4.5   Morphosyntactic Analysis

728 morphosyntactic patterns were extracted from the LFEC, 277 (38.04%) of them with two or more instantiations. Moreover, it was also possible to extract 1330 semantic patterns, 464 (34.88%) of them with two or more instantiations.

Table 12. Top five morphosyntactic patterns that include a word from the category "anatomy and physiology"

Morphosyntactic pattern	Frequency of the pattern	Example
V Det N	142	*salvar el **pellejo***
V Prep Det N	44	*quedarse en los **huesos***
V N	36	*echar **lengua***
V Det N Prep Det N	26	*quitarle la palabra de la **boca***
V Prep N	22	*conocer de **cara***
V Adj N	14	*abrir tamaña **boca***

When combining both variables, it was possible to make a query allowing to consult the morphosyntactic and semantic patterns linked to expressions including a word related to "anatomy and physiology." With this selection of variables, 177 patterns were extracted, 68 of them with two instantiations or more. The top five of these verb idiom patterns or collocations are evidenced in Table 12.

It was also possible to nest the semantic categories with morphosyntactic patterns, which made it possible to find nouns related to body parts, as well as verbs related to physiological processes. In Table 13, some examples of the semantic patterns extracted from the most frequent morphosyntactic pattern are shown. Each of the letters of the semantic patterns correspond to one of the discourse field tags previously presented in Table 9.

Table 13. Example of pattern nesting of semantic tags in morphosyntactic patterns

Morphosyntactic pattern	Semantic pattern	Example
V Det N	M Z B	*agachar la **cabeza***
	F Z B	*comerse las **uñas***
	B Z O	***morder** el anzuelo*
	B Z W	***tragárselo** la tierra*

It is also possible to look for semantic patterns and see the morphosyntactic patterns that follow a specific semantic combination (see Table 14).

Table 14. Example of pattern nesting of POS tags in semantic patterns

Semantic pattern	Morphosyntactic pattern	Example
M Z B	V Det N	*parar las **orejas***
	V Prep N	*meter en **cintura***
	V Contr N	*salirle del **corazón***
	V Prep V	*poner a **parir***

5 Discussion

On the one hand, a rather simple frequency analysis of nouns present in the PUs contained in the LFEC is in agreement with some of the most important tenets of Cognitive Semantics, and of the embodiment hypothesis, namely that we tend to resort to our bodily experience in order to understand and to express reality; and this, in turn, is done through the use of metaphor (and/or metonymy).

On the other hand, in addition to commonly extracted morphosyntactic patterns, chains of semantic categories can also be created, which can be nested, thus creating semantic patterns. Then, it is possible to use this annotation to extract PU candidates from corpora. The main limitations for that extraction methodology have to do with the tools that are currently available for semantic annotation and their level of accuracy. However, having corpora annotated with both syntactic and semantic tags opens a completely new set of options not only for the analysis of PUs but for their extraction.

The next step must be a dialectal comparison of PU syntactic and semantic patterns in Spanish (Colombian and Peninsular) from lexicographic resources. This will give us a Gold Standard of morphosyntactic and semantic characteristics to compare between dialectal variants.

Recent works on phraseology and corpora are using mutual information score as a measurement of word combination association and as an indicator of productivity (Paquot 2017). It is true that the sole factor of frequency cannot be seen as an indicator of productivity. Nevertheless, the combination of these methods could shed light on the improvement of PU recognition techniques, and, consequently, on the enhancement of lexicographic resources.

We would like to continue our research by testing semantic patterns, and by comparing the results of the extraction based on different combinations of morphosyntactic and semantic patterns.

References

Archer, D., Wilson, A., Rayson, P.: Introduction to the USAS category system. Benedict project report (2002)

Bally, C.: Précis de Stylistique. C. Winter, Heidelberg (1909)

Bréal, M.: Essai de sémantique (Semantics: Studies in the Science of Meaning). Hachette, Paris (1897). (in French)

Carneado, Z., Trista, A.: Estudios de Fraseología. Academia de Ciencias de Cuba. Instituto de Literatura y Lingüística, La Habana (1985)

Casares, J.: Introducción a la lexicografía moderna (An Introduction to Modern Lexicography). CSIC, Madrid (1950). (in Spanish)

Corpas, G.: Manual de fraseología española (Handbook of Spanish Phraseology). Gredos, Madrid (1996). (in Spanish)

von der Gabelentz, G.: Die Sprachwissenschaft, ihre Aufgaben, Methoden und bisherigen Ergebnisse (Linguistics, Its Tasks, Methods, and Results So Far). C. H. Tauchnitz, Leipzig (1901). (in German)

García, C., Muñoz, C.: Refranero antioqueño: diccionario fraseológico del habla antioqueña (Antioquia Proverb Collection: A Phraseological Dictionary of Antioquia's Speech). Editorial Universidad de Antioquia, Medellín (1996). (in Spanish)

Granger, S.: Pushing back the limits of phraseology. How far can we go? In: Cosme, C., Gouverneur, C., Meunier, F., Paquot, M. (eds.) Proceedings of the Phraseology 2005 Conference, pp. 165–168. University of Leuven, Leuven (2005)

Grčić Simeunović, L., de Santiago, P.: Semantic approach to phraseological patterns in karstology. In: Proceedings of the XVII Euralex International Congress, pp. 685–693. Ivane Javakhishvili Tbilisi State University, Tbilisi (2016)

Gries, S.: Phraseology and linguistic theory: a brief survey. In: Granger, S., Meunier, F. (eds.) Phraseology: An Interdisciplinary Perspective, p. 6. John Benjamins, Amsterdam (2008)

Hartmann, R.R., James, G.: Dictionary of Lexciography. Routledge, New York (1998)

Johnson, M.: The Body in the Mind: The Bodily Basis of Meaning, Imagination, and Reason. University of Chicago Press, Chicago (1987)

Lakoff, G., Johnson, M.: Metaphors We Live By. University of Chicago Press, Chicago (1980)

Lakoff, G., Johnson, M.: Philosophy in the Flesh: The Embodied Mind and Its Challenge to Western Thought. Basic Books, New York (1999)

Leroyer, P.: Dealing with phraseology in business dictionaries: focus on dictionary functions - not phrases. Linguist. Online 27(2), 183–194 (2006)

McArthur, T.: Longman Lexicon of Contemporary English. Longman, London (1981)

Mel'čuk, I.: Phraseology in the language, in the dictionary, and in the computer. In: Kuiper, K. (ed.) Yearbook of Phraseology, vol. 3, pp. 31–56. De Gruyter Mouton, New York (2012)

Mellado Blanco, C.: Fraseologismos somáticos del alemán (Somatic Phraseologisms in German). Peter Lang, Frankfurt am Main (2004). (in Spanish)

Mellado, C.: Colocaciones y fraseología en los diccionarios (Collocations and Phraseology in Dictionaries). Peter Lang, Frankfurt am Main (2008). (in Spanish)

Mora Monroy, S.: Lexicón de fraseología del español de Colombia (Phraseology Lexicon of Colombian Spanish). Instituto Caro y Cuervo, Santafé de Bogotá (1996). (in Spanish)

Paquot, M.: Lexicography and phraseology. In: Biber, D., Reppen, R. (eds.) The Cambridge Handbook of English Corpus Linguistics, pp. 460–477. Cambridge University Press, Cambridge (2015)

Paquot, M.: The phraseological dimension in interlanguage complexity research. Second Lang. Res. 35(1), 121–145 (2017)

Patiño, P.: Description and representation in language resources of Spanish and English specialized collocations from Free Trade Agreements. Ph.D. thesis, The Norwegian School of Economics, Department of Professional and Intercultural Communication, Bergen (2017)

Paul, H.: Prinzipien der Sprachgeschichte (Principles of Language History). Max Niemeyer, Halle (1880). (in German)

Penadés, I.: La información gramatical sobre la clasificación de las locuciones en los diccionarios (Grammar information related to locution classification in dictionaries). In: Alonso, M. (ed.) Diccionarios y fraseología (Dictionaries and Phraseology), pp. 249–259. Universidade da Coruña, La Coruña (2006). (in Spanish)

Real Academia Española: Corpus Diacrónico del Español (CORDE) (Diachronic corpus of the Spanish language (CORDE)). (in Spanish). http://corpus.rae.cs/cordenet.html. Accessed 26 Apr 2019

Real Academia Española: Corpus de Referencia del Español Actual (CREA) (Reference corpus of present-day Spanish (CREA)). (in Spanish). http://corpus.rae.es/creanet.html. Accessed 26 Apr 2019

Rohrer, T.: Three dogmas of embodiment: cognitive linguistics as a cognitive science. In: Kristiansen, G., Achard, M., Dirven, R., de Mendoza Ibañez, F.J.R. (ed.) Cognitive Linguistics: Current Applications and Future Perspectives, pp. 119–146. Mouton de Gruyter, Berlin (2006)

Schmid, H.: Probabilistic part-of-speech tagging using decision trees. In: Proceedings of the International Conference on New Methods in Language Processing, pp. 44–49. UMIST, Manchester (1994)

Sciutto, V.: Apuntes historiográficos de la fraseología española (Historiographic Annotations on Spanish Phraseology). Lingue Linguaggi 15, 285–303 (2015). (in Spanish)

Seco, M., Andrés, O., Ramos, G.: Diccionario fraseológico documentado del español actual (Documented, Present-Day Spanish Phraseology Dictionary). Aguilar, Madrid (2004). (in Spanish)

Sierra García, J.: El refrán antioqueño en los clásicos (Antioquia's Proverbs in Classical Works). Ediciones Autores Antioqueños, Medellín (1990). (in Spanish)

Soto Posada, G.: La sabiduría criolla: refranero hispanoamericano (Creole Wisdom: Hispanic American Proverb Collection). Veron, Barcelona (1997). (in Spanish)

Tristá, A.: Fraseología y Contexto. Editorial de Ciencias Sociales, La Habana (1988)

Valenzuela, J., Ibarretxe-Antuñano, I., Hilferty, J. (eds.): Lingüística Cognitiva (Cognitive Linguistics). Anthropos, Barcelona (2016). (in Spanish)

Zuluaga, A.: Introducción al estudio de las expresiones fijas (An Introduction to the Study of Fixed Expressions). Peter Lang, Frankfurt (1980). (in Spanish)

Translating Emotional Phraseology:
A Case Study

J. Agustín Torijano[✉] and Maria Ángeles Recio[✉]

University of Salamanca, Salamanca, Spain
{torijano, recio}@usal.es

Abstract. This paper focuses on the classic problem of how to deal with the translation of Phraseological Units (PU) linked to emotion, and contemplates a threefold path: their omission –when the translator/interpreter does not feel capable of rendering them into another language–; the relentless search for a functional equivalence that perfectly fulfills the role of PUs in the target language (TL); and, finally, the semantic-pragmatic neutralization of phraseologism as a less compromising and more practical option.

For this purpose, we will first devote a few lines to reviewing some references that could be considered classical and current works in the area of a transversal nature and specifically focused on emotional concepts such as fear. Later, we will analyze metaphorization and metonymy from the point of view of Cognitive Grammar and the Conceptual Metaphor Theory (CMT), as a strategy for the translation of emotions in PU, as well as the false universality of phraseological representations related to emotions. This will provide us with the theoretical support to conduct a case study, which will be presented in Sect. 5. Finally, we will draw some conclusions from the findings of our research.

Keywords: Phraseology · Emotions · Metaphors · Translations · Cognitive linguistics

1 Introduction

This paper aims to analyze the presence of emotions, such as fear, in some phraseological units and their translation, particularly those linked with the more idiomatic aspects of a language. For this, we will first review the existing literature on the topic and then we will carry out a comprehensive analysis with specific examples and a discussion of the problems that may derive from them. Faced with this problem, translators will have to choose from the three options of omission, equivalence and neutralization. More specifically, the phraseological unit "ser un gallina" [literally: being a hen] as a paradigmatic example of the emotion of fear with the use of metaphors with animals as *source domain*.

In an attempt to discuss this topic in greater depth, we will analyze some phraseological units related to fear in languages such as German, English, French, Italian, Portuguese and even Latin, among others.

Finally, we will try to determine the degree of universality that apparently underlies the formation of metaphors and metonymies generated by phraseological units.

© Springer Nature Switzerland AG 2019
G. Corpas Pastor and R. Mitkov (Eds.): Europhras 2019, LNAI 11755, pp. 391–403, 2019.
https://doi.org/10.1007/978-3-030-30135-4_28

2   A Brief Literature Review

There are many authors who have devoted excellent works, not only to phraseology itself (something that, fortunately, is improving exponentially), nor merely to the phraseology of emotions (which we could already categorize as a subgenre of phraseology), but also to problems of translation posed by the combination of both aspects, since phraseology is one of the areas that presents more difficulties when rendering one language into another. Furthermore, the emotions we are talking about emerge from the depths of each language, in what has been called "the DNA of language". In this sense, Eberwein *et al.* (2012: 5) contend that "cada lengua constituye un universo emotivo propio"[1]. In their opinion, PUs are magnificent elements for the communication of emotional circumstances, due to their characteristic vagueness and difficult delimitation, but also to their rhetorical processes.

Regarding Spanish/German translation, many authors[2] have carried out research works which constitute a great sample of the advances in the translation of phraseology of emotions, studied from very different perspectives and problems, such as the problem of establishing a lexicographic encoding of the emotions conveyed through PUs or the emotional factor in the use of PUs in advertising and their translation, as well as the translation of emotions in children's literature, to mention just a few.

Along with many other works addressing other languages or with a more general scope (such as the emblematic studies by G. Corpas, A. Pamies or M. García-Page), or applied to didactics –subsumed or not under phraseodidactics– (M.I. González del Rey, I. Penadés, A. Szyndler, C. Navarro, J.D., Mendoza Puertas, or A.I. Cernuda), these works make up a rigorous and motivating bibliographic corpus in order to continue moving forward in this practically infinite –but at the same time passionate– universe of emotions in phraseological units within their intercultural dimension.

As Aznárez and Santazilia (2016: 6–8) suggest, it is worth highlighting, from the numerous studies that have addressed the phraseology of emotions or feelings in different languages, those that have been considered seminal for more than 30 years (Kövecses 1986; Lakoff and Johnson 1980; Lakoff 1987) and set out to conceptualize some emotions in language. Thereafter, and following the subsequent research by Kövecses (2000), the studies have exhibited a broadening or, more exactly, a deepening, insofar as phraseology no longer only studies how people talk about emotions, but also what they know or what they think about them, what is now known as "popular psychology", which results in the so-called "popular theory of emotions". According to this, as established by Lakoff and Kövecses (1987) and Lakoff (1987: 389), speakers verbalize their ideas linked to emotions starting from the way they express themselves when having certain feelings. According to these authors, there is a metonymic principle, based on that popular theory of emotions, that considers that the physiological effects of an emotion represent that emotion. "Mediante este principio",

---

[1] 'Each language creates its own emotional universe'.

[2] H. Burger, S. Geck, L. Luque, B. Ahrens, L. Amigot, U. Becker, A. Torrent, L. Uría, J. Beßler, P. Eberwein, M. Marín, A. Grutschus, C. Grümpel, N. Iglesias, C. Mellado Blanco, M. Recio, R. Sánchez, R. Schröpf, or M. Soliño.

points out Comşa (2012: 154), "es como los hablantes entienden cómo se forman las proyecciones metafóricas"[3].

For Stepień (2007: 393), both the metaphorical basis of thought and the physical basis of human cognition, as well as the relationship between the conceptual and semantic structure, are the key. Therefore, a cognitive categorization of phraseology – as we will analyze later– allows us to establish a series of criteria that can assist greatly in addressing PUs and their translation.

3 Phraseology in Language Learning and Proficiency

In previous studies[4], we have already drawn attention to the suitability of PUs to express emotions, inasmuch as they are the still picture of feelings and meaning, that is to say, they reflect the emotion experienced. In this sense, we agree with Schröpf's opinion (2012: 221), for whom emotions and language are intrinsically linked. For this author, the prosody, as well as everything related to the polysemiotic, play a fundamental role.

We endorse Mellado Blanco's (1997: 288) idea: "el pensamiento humano se sirve de mecanismos cognitivos universales a la hora de expresar verbal y figuradamente determinadas emociones"[5]. There are even scholars such as Hudson (1984: 34 and ss.), for whom there is no "clara línea divisoria entre el conocimiento lingüístico y el conocimiento del mundo"[6]. This explains the reason why the greater knowledge of the world a speaker has, the easier it will be to acquire certain linguistic structures or elements, as is the case of phraseology.

In this regard, it is essential to promote those "cognitive mechanisms" that are specific for a language in the students of that language and, consequently, of that culture, and particularly in future translators/interpreters. To do so, the goal should be trying to put the functional capacities of both brain hemispheres on the same level, considering that it seems that in mother tongue acquisition, the left cerebral hemisphere is involved while, from a certain age, language learning and therefore cognitive processes take place in the right hemisphere. For Grümpel (2012: 109), the right hemisphere is dominant when it comes to musical and emotional aspects.

In Mora's opinion (2013: 17), "una buena educación produce cambios en el cerebro que ayudan a mejorar el proceso de aprendizaje"[7]. By becoming aware of the plasticity of the brain, we will have the tools to intervene and improve the learning process.

It is undeniable, with regard to the topic of study discussed here, that hose specific cognitive mechanisms can find an answer in the learning process of the expression of

---

[3] 'It is through this principle that speakers understand how metaphoric projections are formed'.

[4] Recio (2012).

[5] 'The human thought uses universal cognitive mechanisms when expressing some emotions verbally and figuratively'.

[6] 'There is no clear border between linguistic knowledge and knowledge of the world'.

[7] 'A good education induces changes in the brain that help to improve the learning process'.

feelings, because they are part of one of the most idiomatic aspects of each language and each culture.

3.1 "Fear" in Phraseology

In this regard, at the beginning of the 90s, Dobrovol'skij (1992: 281) discovered that concepts typically expressed through phraseology are negative: stupidity, fear, death, etc., and constitute domains of great phraseological productivity. This tendency is associated with the idea that phraseology designates the subjectively relevant phenomena of the objective world. This principle has been confirmed by other authors in the lexical field of feelings (Marina and López Penas 1999) and more specifically in the phraseological field (Mellado Blanco 1997 or Torrent-Lenzen 2008).

In this same line, we may highlight the study carried out by Mellado Blanco (1997: 383) on German and Spanish phraseologisms in the field of emotions. She considers that "una particularidad del significado fraseológico en contraposición con el de los lexemas libres, se refiere al predominio del componente connotativo sobre el denotativo"[8]. It is even more so in the case of phraseologisms related to emotions.

In this regard, she states that "fear" is represented in German and in Spanish by means of a set of situational invariables: the act of defecation, which she illustrates with *Hose (n) voll haben* ('*estar cagado de miedo*'[9]); feeling of physical weakness (*weiche Knie haben, 'temblarle a alguien las piernas'*[10]); paralysis of the body (*jm erstarrt/gefriert/gerinnt/stockt das Blut in den Adern, 'helársele a alguien la sangre [en las venas]'*[11] and, finally, the act of fleeing (*jm würde (vor Angst) am liebsten in ein Mauseloch kriechen*, which refers in Spanish to '*alguien se metería de buena gana en una ratonera*'[12], which, in turn, may be interpreted as '*no saber dónde meterse*' ('*not know which way to turn*'). However, we believe that this translation does not seem the most appropriate, given that '*no saber dónde meterse*' (and the English PU) is not necessarily linked to fear, but to embarrassment, since this expression is often used to refer to embarrassment, sometimes second-hand embarrassment, which may be felt at a certain moment.

The *embodiment* hypothesis is attested by various studies by showing that emotions have been conceptualized in different languages based on their physiological effects, because it is essentially in the body where emotions manifest themselves. By the same token, as Aznárez and Santazilia (2016) summarize it, an emotion such as fear is conceptualized from its physiological effects, such as the decrease in body temperature, in the expressions "to have cold feet" in English, (*jemandem*) *gefriert das Blut in den Adern* in German, *se glacer le sang* in French, *sentirsi gelare il sangue nelle vene* in

---

[8] 'One particular feature of the phraseological meaning when compared with the meaning of free lexemes is that there is in the former a predominantly connotative component, rather than a denotative one'.

[9] In English 'to be scared shitless'.

[10] 'Someone's knees are knocking'.

[11] In English 'someone's blood froze [in their veins]'.

[12] 'Someone would willingly jump into the fire'.

Italian or *helársele a alguien la sangre (en las venas)* in Spanish (Pamies and Iñesta 2000: 43–79).

We could consider the body as the first sphere of knowledge of human beings. While animals would constitute, along with home or family, the second sphere. This sphere comprises a perfect symbolic system to create emotional metaphors that crystallise in phraseology, because it belongs to the most intrinsic sphere of language, where the expression of the most intimate, most spontaneous, most visceral and personal feelings have a perfect place, which is equivalent to saying, despite the oxymoron, more universal. From all the so-called source domains, the predominance of some features of any animal serves, by metonymy, to express feelings, thanks to the simple comparison of body parts, shapes, colours, functions or attitudes of animals and people. This means that, for example, *ser un gallina* serves to represent fear, while *ser un gallo* is used almost entirely as the opposite[13].

4 Cognitive Grammar and Conceptual Metaphor Theory

From the point of view of Cognitive Grammar (CG), for example, the semantic structure must be seen in terms of conventionalized conceptual structure, i.e., this conception of grammar emphasizes the capacity for conceptualization: the ability to allocate mental images to linguistic meaning. This term refers to how a certain situation is conceived, the mental image that it evokes. There seems to be a need to define more exhaustively the description and content of CG for didactic purposes, albeit in this work, for reasons of space, we cannot delve into this topic. However, we believe that this can be extrapolated to phraseology, thus it would be necessary to reflect on a fundamentally holistic and integrative approach when dealing with the translation of emotions in phraseology.

According to Stępień (2007: 393–395), Cognitive Linguistics has offered a theoretical-practical apparatus that allows rigorous linguistic analysis. An example of this is the Theory of the Conceptual Metaphor (TCM), proposed by Lakoff and Johnson (1980), developed by Lakoff and Turner (1989) and improved by Lakoff himself (1993), which is based –as Moreno (2005: 645) points out– on "la noción de correspondencias entre conceptos de diferentes dominios"[14].

This theory directly addresses the question of figurative meaning, so it is convenient to analyse idiomaticity, by means of three major principles:

1. the metaphorical nature of thought,
2. the bodily basis of human cognition, and
3. the connection between the semantic structure and the conceptual structure.

---

[13] In Spanish, there is a large number of animals' names in masculine and feminine that, apart from sexist interpretations, appear in phraseological units of many languages and represent not only different but opposite values: gallo/gallina, toro/vaca, perro/perra, lagarto/lagarta, gato/gata, caballo/jaca, liebre/conejo, etc.

[14] 'The notion of a correspondence between concepts from different domains'.

The TCM describes a set of correspondence relations between two sources that provide meaning: the categories of thought and the categories of language. A cognitive experimental basis relates, on the one hand, the words to their meaning and, on the other, the concepts of mind to their meaning. That is to say, throughout his life, and through the perception of an infinite number of images and concepts, often based on stereotypes, the human being forms a system of conceptual relations of which he is not always aware, because, among other reasons, many of them are inherited and consubstantial to the same language. Consequently, linguistic forms are acquired in relation to these same concepts in such a way that it is possible to infer a prototypical or literal semantic value for a great number of words.

The cognitivist approach is fundamental in this sense, due to the pivotal role that metaphors usually play in the conceptual processes of the individual, as we noted above. In other words, it is therefore undeniable that Cognitivism and its precepts may be provide a useful contribution to the phraseology of emotions and, more specifically, of fear. In this regard, Domínguez Chenguayen (2013: 65) claims that metaphorical language (based on Lakoff and Johnson 1980), both from the point of view of metaphor and metonymy, is linked to the way thought is articulated, and therefore to our conceptualization of the world.

For Zimovets and Komanova (2016: 8) the world around us is fundamentally represented in three ways:

a. real image of the world;
b. cultural or conceptual image of the world and,
c. linguistic image of the world.

The real image of the world refers to the objective perception of it, whereas the cultural image indicates the perception or conception based on the reflection of the real image through the prism of the concepts created on the basis of personal impressions, both collective and individual. As far as the linguistic image of the world is concerned, it reflects reality precisely through the cultural image of the world. These authors believe that the individual is able to label objects or phenomena that surround him or her and, thereby it is possible to determine to which culture a person belongs through the study of PUs: "phraseological units help to define which historical, intellectual and emotional significance this or that culture contains", as Gutiérrez (2010: 71) puts it:

> En muchas ocasiones, es la propia cultura la que nos ayuda a captar el significado metafórico de una expresión. Por ejemplo, en la metáfora "él es un gallina", [as we will discuss later in this study], relacionamos inmediatamente la gallina con la cobardía, y no con la falta de fortaleza. Por tanto, muchos conceptos o proyecciones metafóricos son puramente culturales y son el fruto de la tradición, la educación y el folklore.[15]

Although we believe that the progress in the research on automatic translation – which is growing exponentially and may provide solutions in the future that are

---

[15] 'It is often the culture itself which helps us to understand the metaphorical meaning of an expression. For example, in the metaphor "él es un gallina" [he is a hen], we immediately associate the hen with cowardice, rather than with a lack of strength. Therefore, many metaphorical projections or concepts are purely cultural and are the result of tradition, education and folklore'.

currently unknown– is a positive fact, we consider that automatic translators have not yet demonstrated the capability of achieving that with fairly acceptable results in the translation of emotions.

4.1 Phraseology and Translation

With regard to phraseology in translation, it should be noted that we must speak in terms of equivalence. Torrent-Lenzen (2011: 190), for instance, emphasises the fact that "(...) el cotexto y el contexto intervienen de manera decisiva a la hora de buscar una equivalencia traductora"[16]. This author believes that it is necessary to speak fundamentally of a translation unit in the field of phraseology, inasmuch as its meaning is usually interpreted "(...) sobre la base de implicaturas convencionales y de connotaciones (...)"[17], hence "una teoría dinámica que parta de la unidad de traducción (...)"[18] should be considered.

Regarding translation, it is worth quoting the opinion of García Álvarez (2011: 25), who states that "la analogía que lleva a cabo el traductor a la hora de establecer los inputs que componen los referentes de las distintas culturas (...) depende a su vez de la percepción sensorial del traductor"[19].

We are aware of the need to delve in greater depth into this issue; however, it would lead us along paths that, for reasons of space, we cannot cover in this paper, but that we will certainly develop in future work.

5 A Case Study

5.1 Idiosyncratic Nature of PU

An ancestral coexistence of domestic animals with human beings –today limited to pets– has encouraged the establishment of the symbolic system we are discussing, which has helped for generations to explain to children, for example, concepts such as death, procreation, family, beauty, ugliness, cruelty, paternal/maternal instinct, intelligence, ignorance, courage or fear. In this study, we will focus on fear, verbalised in the phraseologism *ser un gallina*, with the aim of illustrating what has been explained up to now.

The PU *ser una gallina* is deeply rooted in the history of Spanish language, since we can trace it back to the reign of the Roman emperor (from 218 to 222) Varius Avitus Bassianus (Syria, c. 203 - Rome, 222), under the title of Marcus Aurelius Antoninus Augustus. When he was young, he served as a priest of the god El-Gabal in his hometown, Emesa (Homs, Syria), this is why long after his death he was known as Heliogabalus. Apparently, according to the historian Dio Cassius, Heliogabalus imposed drastic changes in Roman religion, including circumcision (and even castration

---

[16] '(...) the context and cotext play an essential role in the search for equivalence in translation'.

[17] '(...) on the basis of conventional implicatures and connotations (...)'.

[18] 'a dynamic theory based on the translation unit'.

[19] 'the analogy proposed by the translators when they establish the inputs that make up the references from different cultures (...) depends, in turn, on the sensory perception of the translator'.

in some cases), which led the Praetorian Guard, who had never supported the new Asian emperor, to start defaming him to reveal his supposed cowardice. Even a play on words with the name of the emperor spread, and was immortalized by some writers of the time, who told how the phrase *Non Helioga(ba)llus sed Heliogallina* ('It is not Helioga(ba)llo but Heliogallina') started to appear painted in Rome. This circumstance may have originated or reinforced the association of the bird with cowardice or fear.

However, the first reference that we find in our literature appears in Juan de Salina's *Poesías*[20], although it is not until Lope de Vega's *Nacimiento de Ursón y Valentín, reyes de Francia* (1604) that the expression combines the reference to the ridicule of warrior ardour and eschatological jokes, with a double sexual meaning, starring a woman and a soldier:

[SOL 2] Caminaré diligente / por el campo diez y veinte. / ¿Veinte? ¡Qué digo, y mil leguas!

[MUJER] ¡Mal hayan estas treguas! / Y el hombre que las consiente / debe de ser *un gallina*[21].

More than a century later, Don Sebastian de Covarrubias included the expression in his *Dictionary of Authorities* (1726) and it is defined as follows:

GALLINA. Por analogía se llama al que es cobarde, pusilánime y tímido. Dixose assí aludiendo a la cobardía que tiene esta ave. Latín. *Timidus. Iners.* INC. GARCIL. Part. 1. Lib. 9. Cap. 23. Hai entre los Indios el mismo refrán que los Españoles tienen, de llamar a un hombre *gallina* para notarle de cobarde. [...][22]

It is worth noting that Covarrubias chooses an *authority* like the Inca Garcilaso, who in his "*Comentarios reales de los incas*" provides very valuable information about the sociolinguistic transference of phraseologisms. He points out that the same PU is used in two very different cultures. However, if we continue reading, the author describes the following:

[...] El refrán de llamar a un hombre *gallina*, por motejarle de cobarde, es que los indios lo han tomado de los españoles, por la ordinaria familiaridad y conversación que con ellos tienen; y también por remedarles en el lenguaje [...].[23]

In other words, it is a phraseological loan, which the *Indians* had adapted to their culture, despite the fact that they had other ways of calling a man a coward.

---

[20] Dated ca. 1585. Henry Bonneville, *Poesías humanas*, Madrid: Editorial Castalia, 1987.

[21] '[SOLDIER 2] I shall walk diligently / through that field for ten and twenty... / twenty? What am I saying! for a thousand leagues!

[WOMAN] Damn these truces! / Any man who consents to them / must be a hen'. In: *Nacimiento de Ursón y Valentín, reyes de Francia*: http://buscador.clemit.es/ficheros/El%20nacimiento%20de% 20Urs%C3%B3n%20y%20Valent%C3%ADn.pdf.

[22] 'HEN: Used as an analogy to refer to somebody who is a coward, fainthearted or shy. The term alludes to the cowardice of this bird. Latin. *Timidus. Iners.* INC. GARCIL. Part. 1. Book 9. Chap. 23. Indians have the same saying as Spaniards, in which they call a man a hen when they want to call him a coward. [...]'

[23] '[...] The proverb in which a man is referred to as a *hen* when he is accused of being a coward is something that Indians have adopted from Spaniards due to the familiarity and the conversations they have, and also in an attempt to mimic their language. [...]'

5.2   Translation Problems

It seems that what might be deemed a universal in the attribution of cowardice to the laying bird, is actually not so. A cursory comparison of the PU in neighbouring languages shows that, although the phraseologism may be understood in other languages, it is not a formula shared by all cultures. On the contrary, the form of the PU can be misleading when trying to recognise it or identify it with other similar existing in different languages. As it was already stated in previous works (Torijano and Recio 2017):

> El problema es la superficialidad, es decir, cuando el aprendiz o el traductor no trasciende la superficie de la expresión sin tener en cuenta su evolución y su más que posible evolución divergente. La mayoría de las veces esta evolución se debe a que pertenecen a fraseologismos completamente idiomáticos cuyo origen es de cada lengua en sí, su historia y evolución, así como su cultura.[24] (p. 53)

Let us illustrate this with an example: although in Portuguese you can use *ser uma galinha*, being *uma galinha choca*, that is, 'broody', means practically the opposite: 'enraged, hostile, aggressive, irreducible, indomitable, rude', etc. This would pose a serious problem of communication and translation. To further complicate the issue of two seemingly close languages, in Brazilian Portuguese the expression *homem-galinha*, defined as 'mulherengo, conquistador, galanteador' or as 'homem que corteja várias mulheres'[25], could be translated into English as 'playboy, womanizer' or, more vulgarly, 'masher'[26], which in Spanish is much closer to 'gallito', characterized by its bravado, than to a hen, the symbol of cowardice or fear.

On the other hand, in another Latin language such as French, and documented since 1680[27] –almost at the same time as in Spanish–, we find *être une poule mouillée* ('to be a chicken'), having the same phraseological value as its Spanish counterpart ('ser una gallina mojada'). While in Italian the object of metonymy becomes a "rabbit", instead of *gallina*, "*fare il coniglio*", because the attribution of fear changes the animal, which is perfectly acceptable by the mere observation of reality before the trembling image of these animals[28].

---

[24] 'The problem here is the superficial nature of the expression, that is, when the apprentice or the translator does not go beyond the surface of the expression and does not take into account its evolution and the fact that this transformation has very likely been divergent. Most of the times this development is due to the fact that they belong to utterly idiomatic phraseologisms whose origins are part of each language in itself, as well as of their history, their evolution and their culture.'

[25] DLP: 1. Que ou o que gosta de namoriscar ou namorisca várias mulheres; que ou o que anda sempre metido com mulheres./ Someone who likes to flirt with several women; someone who is always surrounded by women.

[26] Wordreference: s.v. mulherengo. / A womanizer.

[27] In the *Dictionnaire français contenant les mots et les choses*, by Pierre Richelet.

[28] In the 17th century, the *Diccionario de Autoridades* (1726–1739) includes the term *lebrón*, which Covarrubias defines as follows:
LEBRÓN. It is used metaphorically to refer to someone who is shy and cowardly, and it alludes to the timidity and suspicion of hares. Latín. *Timidissimus*. […] (IV Volume, 1743).

As far as English is concerned, the metaphorical figure is considerably close to that of Spanish, as there exists "to be a chicken" (*Don't be a chicken!*) –apart from other phraseologisms such as *Don't be a sissy* or *Don't be a wuss*–, in which *gallina* becomes a chicken. As we can observe, the chicken reference is closer than the rabbit, in the case of Italian, despite the fact that the latter is a supposedly closer language to Spanish. Nevertheless, in English it can also become a *cat* in *to be a scaredy-cat*.

With regard to German, the option we consider most valid for translating the PU is *ein Angsthase sein*[29], which reflects the pragmatic value of the Spanish PU, although there is not the slightest reference to **eine Henne sein*. Once again, the arbitrary nature of languages underlies the fact that the symbolic animal that represents fear in German (in addition to many other values[30]) is the hare (*'der Hase'*), undeniably related to the Italian *coniglio*, despite them being two languages from different families and with distant systematic features.

In a standard approach to the understanding of the PU, it does not seem difficult to discover that the metaphorical image is complemented by the compositional element *die Angst*, which accompanies the nuclear noun in adjective function, a sort of conceptual hyperonym of dozens of terms semantically linked with 'fear', under which nouns, verbs and adjectives could be grouped ranging from *Abneigung, Angstgefühl* or *Ängstlichkeit* to *Schrecklichkeit, Unruhe, Unterdrückung* or *Zwang*[31]. In this case, the German speaker has reinforced the chosen trait of the hare by adding the noun to emphasise the idea that it is a fearful hare, a kind of unnecessary but very expressive epithet, as if in Spanish we were saying "eres un gallina miedoso".

The term, present in German as early as the 8th century, has its roots in the Proto-Indo-European **angú-*, having the same value as the Latin *angŭstĭa, -æ* ('narrowness, difficulty'), still present in *angosto*, for instance.

As mentioned above, our understanding of phraseologism is based on a standard approach. As further proof of the complexity and depth that characterizes the interpretation and study of phraseology, it is likely that the hare in the PU (related to the English, Norwegian and Swedish *hare* or the Dutch *haas*) is not such and has nothing to do with the metonymy of the flight instinct of the hare, but with something very different. There are many scholars who do not rule out the hypothesis that it actually is an alteration of a possible **Angsthose* form, from *Hose* (i.e. 'trousers'). This would lead us to transfer the source domain of domestic animals to that of clothing, another

---

[29] It would also be valid, according to the contexts, *sich ins Hemd machen*, which would lead us to the Spanish analogous *no llegarle a uno la camisa al cuerpo*, for example.

[30] For *ser un perro viejo*, German uses *ser una liebre vieja* [to be an old hare] (*ein alter Hase sein*), in which wisdom based on experience is praised, while apparently the same animal is the protagonist of the PU *Mein Name ist Hase*, which we could freely translate as *A mí que me registren / Yo no tengo ni idea / Yo no sé nada* or *Yo pasaba por aquí* [You can search me / I don't know what is going on here / I don't know anything / I was just passing by]. Although the origin actually goes back to a student of Heidelberg, Karl Victor von Hase, involved in a duel in 1854 and stripped of his identity card so as not to be arrested.

[31] 'aversion, anxiety or anxiety horror, restlessness, oppression or coercion', respectively.

area also related to sensations due to their physical proximity to the body. This can be noticed in the German PU that we mentioned before: *sich ins Hemd machen* or in the colloquial constructions *sich in die Hose(n) machen* or *die Hose(n) voll haben*, conceptually identical to the English to *shit one's pants*, and, of course, to the Spanish *cagón* or to the phraseologisms *cagarse en los pantalones* or, in their euphemistic forms, *hacérselo en los pantalones* or *hacérselo encima*[32].

A deep understanding of the PU, its historical-cultural location, and the exhaustive knowledge of the language are indispensable premises for a correct interpretation and, therefore, a correct rendering of the phraseologism. In order to achieve this, a good translator will draw heavily on various strategies (equivalence, omission, translation, explanation and neutralization)[33], which should be employed according to the demands of the text and the given pragmatics.

6 Conclusions

In this study, we set out to show a brief overview of the great interest that the treatment of phraseology arouses, and more precisely the phraseology of emotions, especially from the field of translation studies, which represents a threefold challenge, due to the subjective nature of the former and the susceptibility to error of the latter. The professional translator must face not just a linguistic form, but the crystallization of feeling, culture, the understanding of the universe by the source language and the idiosyncrasy of the text underlying phraseological units.

A correct rendering of PUs of emotion requires being able to recreate the metaphorical potential of the linguistic community to which they belong and to unavoidably complement linguistic knowledge with socio-cultural sentiment. So far, automatic translators have not demonstrated the capability of achieving that with fairly acceptable results.

The acquisition, or more accurately, the apprehension of the way in which thought is articulated and the conceptualization of the world (symbolized in metaphor and in metonymy in its linguistic expression) from which the original text is born is the only way to approach a translation with a certain guarantee of success. Additionally, in our opinion, only through cognitive grammar, the professional translator will be able to use those three images which Zimovets and Komanova (2016) formulate: real, conceptual and linguistic.

References

Aznárez, M., Santazilia, E.: Un acercamiento a la conceptualización de algunas emociones en el patrimonio fraseológico del euskera y del castellano. Huarte de San Juan. Filología y Didáctica de la Lengua 16, 13–33 (2016)

---

[32] Or to regionalism *die Bangbüxe* (from *Bang*, 'coward' and *Büxe*, a less frequent variant of *Buxe*, 'pants'), very similar to the Dutch *bangebroek*.

[33] Toury (1995: 82).

Comşa, A.: La traducción del miedo. Breve estudio de las metáforas españolas y rumanas. In: XIII Encuentros (III): Telar de traducción especializada. Centro Virtual Cervantes (2012). https://cvc.cervantes.es/lengua/iulmyt/pdf/telar_traduccion/13_comsa.pdf. Accessed 10 May 2019

DA = Real Academia Española (1726–1770): Diccionario de la lengua castellana [Autoridades] (edición facsímil en Academia Española, 2001). Accessed 10 May 2019

DLP = Porto Editora Dicionário da língua portuguesa. com Acordo Ortográfico – Infopédia (2013). https://www.infopedia.pt/dicionarios/lingua-portuguesa/mulherengo. Accessed 10 May 2019

Dobrovol'skij, D.: Phraseological universals: theoretical and applied aspects. In: Kefer, M., Auwera, J. (eds.) Meaning and Grammar, Cross-Linguistic Perspectives, pp. 279–301. De Gruyter, Berlin (1992)

Domínguez Chenguayen, F.J.: Las emociones en las unidades fraseológicas del castellano limeño: patrones de interacción conceptual. In: Martos y Flores (ed.) Actas del «VIII Congreso Internacional de Lexicología y Lexicografía enhomenaje a Martha Hildebrandt Pérez Treviño», pp. 63–82. Fondo Editorial de la Academia Peruana de la Lengua, Lima (2013)

Eberwein, P., Torrent, A., Uría Fernández, L. (eds.): Kontrastive Emotionsforschung. Spanisch-Deutsch. Shaker Verlag, Aachen (2012)

García Álvarez, A.M.: Aprendiendo a agudizar la percepción para la comprensión y traducción de referentes culturales, gastronómicos alemanes: un enfoque cognitivo en el aula. In: Roiss, S., et al. (eds.) En las vertientes de la traducción e interpretación del/al alemán, pp. 25–38. Frank & Timme, Berlin (2011)

Garcilaso de la Vega, E.I.: Primera parte de los Commentarios Reales, qve tratan del origen de los Yncas, reyes qve fveron del Perv, de sv idolatria, leyes y gouierno en paz y en guerra: de sus vidas y conquistas, y de todo lo que fue aquel Imperio y su Republica, antes que los Españoles passaran a el.... Biblioteca Virtual Miguel de Cervantes, Alicante; Biblioteca Nacional, Madrid 2009 (1609). http://www.cervantesvirtual.com/obra/primera-parte-de-los-commentarios-reales-qve-tratan-del-origen-de-los-yncas-reyes-qve-fveron-del-perv-de-sv-idolatria-leyes-y-gouierno-en-paz-y-en-guerra-de-sus-vidas-y-conquistas-y-de-todo-lo-que-fue-aquel-imperio-y-su-republica-antes-que-los-espanoles-p/. Accessed 10 May 2019

Grümpel, C.: Spracherwerb L2-Affekte, Gefühle und Motivationen bei der Wissenskonstruktion kognitiver Prozesse. In: Eberwein, P., Torrent, A., Uría Fernández, L. (eds.) Kontrastive Emotionsforschung. Spanisch-Deutsch, pp. 107–117. Shaker Verlag, Aachen (2012)

Gutiérrez Pérez, R.: Estudio cognitivo-contrastivo de las metáforas del cuerpo. Análisis empírico del corazón como dominio fuente en inglés, francés, español, alemán e italiano. Peter Lang, Frankfurt am Main (2010)

Hudson, R.: Word Grammar. Blackwell, Oxford (1984)

Kövecses, Z.: Metaphors of Anger, Pride and Love: A Lexical Approach to the Structure of Concepts. John Benjamins Publishing, Amsterdam (1986)

Kövecses, Z.: Metaphor and Emotion: Language, Culture, and Body in Human Feeling. Cambridge University Press, Cambridge (2000)

Lakoff, G.: Women, Fire and Dangerous Things: What Categories Tell Us About the Mind. University of Chicago Press, Chicago (1987)

Lakoff, G.: The contemporary theory of metaphor. In: Ortony, A. (ed.) Metaphor and Thought, 2nd edn, pp. 202–251. Cambridge University Press, Cambridge (1993)

Lakoff, G., Johnson, M.: Metaphors We Live By. University of Chicago Press, Chicago (1980)

Lakoff, G., Kövecses, Z.: The cognitive model of anger inherent in American English. In: Holland, D., Quinn, N. (eds.) Cultural Models in Language and Thought, pp. 195–221. Cambridge University Press, Cambridge (1987)

Lakoff, G., Turner, M.: More than Cool Reason. A Field Guide to Poetic Metaphor. University of Chicago Press (1989)

Marina, J.A., López Penas, M.: Diccionario de los sentimientos. Anagrama, Barcelona (1999)

Mellado, C.: Fraseologismos alemanes y españoles del campo de las emociones. Paremia 6, 383–388 (1997)

Moreno Lara, MªÁ.: Metáfora primaria y lenguaje político periodístico: el caso de Clichy-sous-Bois. In: Moreno Lara, MªÁ. (ed.) La metáfora conceptual y el lenguaje político periodístico: configuración, interacciones y niveles de descripción. Doctoral Dissertation, Universidad de La Rioja (2005). http://www.unirioja.es/servicios/sp/tesis/tesis28.shtml. Accessed 10 May 2019

Pamies, A., Iñesta, E.M.: El miedo en las unidades fraseológicas: enfoque interlingüístico. Lang. Des. J. Theor. Exp. Linguist. 3, 43–79 (2000)

Recio Ariza, M.Á.: Der emotionale Faktor beim Gebrauch der Phraseologie in der deutschen und spanischen Werbung und ihre Übersetzung. In: Eberwein, P., Torrent, A., Uría Fernández, L. (eds.) Kontrastive Emotionsforschung. Spanisch-Deutsch, pp. 197–206. Shaker Verlag, Aachen (2012)

Schröpf, R.: Zur Darstellung von Emotionen in der Filmuntertitelung am Beispiel "Wut". Ein Beitrag zur konstruktiven Emotionsforschung Spanisch – Deutsch. In: Eberwein, P., Torrent, A., Uría Fernández, L. (eds.) Kontrastive Emotionsforschung. Spanisch-Deutsch, pp. 221–233. Shaker Verlag, Aachen (2012)

Stępień, M.A.: Metáfora y metonimia conceptual en la fraseología de cinco partes del cuerpo humano en español y polaco. Université de Perpignan Via Domitia, Anuario de Estudios Filológicos XXX, pp. 391–409 (2007)

Torijano Pérez, J.A., Recio, M.Á.: La Traducción en Fraseología: el caso de los falsos amigos. In: Mellado Blanco et al. Discurso repetido y fraseología textual (español y español-alemán), pp. 41–54. Iberoamericana, Madrid; Vervuert, Frankfurt am Main (2017)

Torrent-Lenzen, A.: Fraseología y comunicación de emociones. In: XV Congreso Internacional de la Asociación de Lingüística y Filología de América Latina, Montevideo (2008). www.epb.bibl.th-koeln.de/frontdoor/index/index/docId/169. Accessed 02 Apr 2019

Torrent-Lenzen, A.: Extensión y estructura de la unidad de traducción en la fraseología. In: Roiss, S., et al. (eds.) En las vertientes de la traducción e interpretación del/al alemán, pp. 189–200. Frank & Timme, Berlin (2011)

Toury, G.: Descriptive Translation Studies. John Benjamins, Amsterdam (1995)

Zimovets, N.V., Komanova, A.Y.: Phraseological units with the elements of colour denomination. In: Trends in the Development of Modern Linguistics in the Age of Globalisation. Belarusian State University, Prague (2016)

The Difficult Identification of Multiworld Expressions: From Decision Criteria to Annotated Corpora

Agnès Tutin[1](✉) and Emmanuelle Esperança-Rodier[2](✉)

[1] Université Grenoble Alpes, LIDILEM, 38000 Grenoble, France
agnes.tutin@univ-grenoble-alpes.fr
[2] Univ. Grenoble Alpes, CNRS, Grenoble INP (Institute of Engineering Univ. Grenoble Alpes), LIG, 38000 Grenoble, France
emmanuelle.esperanca-rodier@univ-grenoble-alpes.fr

Abstract. Multiword expressions (MWEs) are known to be widespread in most languages, but how can we actually identify them in texts? How can we account for the diverse nature of these multiword expressions with a consistent typology? This paper aims to address this topic by carrying out two tasks: (1) conducting a small survey with expert linguists on several types of MWEs; (2) building an annotated corpus which includes several genres incorporating a large panel of multiword expressions. The results show that experts can reach a consensus and that the annotation task can be performed satisfactorily, as long as the typology is not overly complex and clear guidelines are provided. Finally, a useful application of the annotated corpus for statistical machine translation is presented, showing significant differences among multiword expressions considered in the study.

Keywords: Typology of multiword expressions · Annotated corpora · Statistical machine-translation

1 Introduction

It is now common to consider that language is largely prefabricated and that phraseology plays a major role. "Tout est idiomatique dans la langue" [all is idiomatic in language] claims Hausmann (1997). Sinclair's (1991) idiom principle and interest in formulaic language (Wray 2009) seem to attract a growing number of followers. Many consider that a large part of texts are prefabricated, if not the majority (for example, Altenberg 1998). But what exactly is the proportion of MWEs in corpora? Where do multiword expressions (now MWEs) begin and end? Can they be easily delineated and can we apply consistent criteria easily to develop a typology?

This paper aims to address these issues. Beyond the convenient prototypes presented in the articles (*heavy smoker* and *spill the beans*), it seemed essential to us to better understand the phraseological phenomenon in all its diversity. In this perspective, two tasks were carried out in order to clarify the issue. The first was a small survey with expert linguists to measure the degree of agreement among them to classify a set of expressions using the Explanatory and Combinatorial Lexicology model (Mel'čuk

G. Corpas Pastor and R. Mitkov (Eds.): Europhras 2019, LNAI 11755, pp. 404–416, 2019.
https://doi.org/10.1007/978-3-030-30135-4_29

et al. 1995; 2012). The second one was an annotation task, based on a typology of MWEs that we consider "realistic".

This work had several objectives: (1) determining whether or not there were prototypes on which everyone could agree; (2) refining the delimitation criteria among MWEs and proposing "realistic" criteria for linguists and NLP scholars; (3) providing an annotated corpus with MWEs in order to illustrate the phenomena for linguistics, NLP and lexicography.

2 A Small Expert Survey: To What Extent Do Linguists Agree on a MWE Typology?

Multiword expressions, which we define here as lexical bundles perceived as preconstructed, are a very diverse class of elements (Cowie 1998; Granger and Paquot 2008; Heid 2008; Mel'čuk 2012). However, for linguistic and NLP applications, we think it is essential to propose a typology which takes into account the diversity of this heterogeneous group of elements.

Nevertheless, while this variety is essential (pragmatic expressions such as *see you later* have little in common with grammatical multiword expressions such as *insofar as*), how far shall we go in the typology of MWEs? It is advisable that such a typology should be both detailed enough but not too complex, on the one hand, and consistent among linguists, on the other hand.

Through a small survey with expert linguists, we wanted to evaluate to what extent a consensus could be reached among specialists. Another aim of this survey was to highlight prototypes among MWE classes.

2.1 The Typology, Experts, and Questionnaire

For this survey, the typology used the Explanatory and Combinatorial Lexicology (now ECL) (Mel'čuk *et al.* 1995, 2012). This model was chosen because it is, in our opinion, one of the most mature and detailed approaches to MWEs. It also has the merit of having been applied to a large subset of expressions treated in the volumes of the Explanatory and Combinatorial Dictionary (Mel'čuk et al. 1992, 1994, 1996, 1998) and more recently, as part of the electronic dictionary *Réseau Lexical du Français* (Polguère 2014).

The 7 consulted experts[1] are all linguists experienced in phraseological issues and familiar or experts in the ECL model. Three are non-native French speakers, but all have an excellent level of French or are perfectly bilingual.

In order to simplify the task, the survey did not cover all types of MWEs, but only idioms (semi or weak idioms), collocations or free expressions in French. The definitions of these elements, taken from Mel'čuk (2013[2]), were provided to the experts.

---

[1] Special thanks to (in the alphabetic order): Margarita Alonso Ramos, Cristelle Cavalla, Francis Grossmann, Véronika Lux, Salah Mejri, Igor Mel'čuk, Alain Polguère.

[2] See Mel'čuk (2012) for definitions in English.

They were asked to determine the types of 23 MWEs in French, all taken from the Zola's novel *Thérèse Raquin* and presented in a large context, among the following options:

1. **Full idiom** (e.g., *'by heart'*, *'black sheep'*). The meaning of the idiom does not include any meaning of its components.
2. **Semi-idiom**, for example *'sea anemone'*. The idiom includes the meaning of one element but not the other.
   or
   weak idiom, for example *'barbed wire'*. It includes the meaning of the components but also an additional meaning. The two types were merged in our survey because of their semantic proximity.
3. **Collocations**, such as *seriously injured*, or *heavy smoker*, which are lexical phrases with a combinatorial restriction.
4. **Other cases**, with possible comments from the authors.

These different types of MWEs can easily be classified according to their "degree of frozenness" (Fraser 1970; Gross 1996; Moon 1998; Granger and Paquot 2008), from the most compositional (free phrases) to the least compositional or more fixed (full idioms), as shown in the diagram below (Fig. 1).

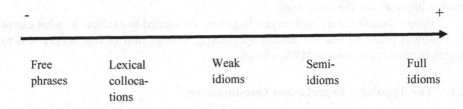

Fig. 1. Continuum scale among MWEs

The survey was conducted by email sent to the 7 experts, with a list of 23 expressions[3] for which, the experts had to decide the type. Table 1 presents an excerpt of this survey with some examples:

2.2 Analysis of the Results

For lack of space, we will not go into detail here about the analysis of the results, but we observed that the distinction between weak/semi-idioms and strong idioms was particularly hard to make and this fine-grained difference did not reach a very satisfactory agreement. When merging all types of idioms (full, weak and semi idioms), the

---

[3] The complete list of expressions is: *becs de gaz, vert bouteille, à angle droit, beaux jours, en face de, le long de, tablier de travail, coup d'œil, lampes funéraires, clair-obscur, de haut en bas, de l'autre côté, sans doute, en forme de, d'ordinaire, taches de rousseur, un peu de, vieille dame, en même temps, pendant ce temps, au fond de.*

Table 1. Excerpts of the questionnaire sent to the expert linguists

MWEs	Context	Full idiom	Weak idiom or semi-idiom	Collocation	Other (comment)
bec de gaz	Le soir, **trois becs de gaz ['gaslight']**, enfermés dans des lanternes lourdes et carrées, éclairent le passage				
Vert bouteille	Il y a quelques années, en face de cette marchande, se trouvait une boutique dont les boiseries d'un **vert bouteille ['bottle green']** suaient l'humidité par toutes leurs fentes				

results appear to be more satisfactory. Given the small number of expressions analyzed, we did not use inter-annotator measures commonly used in NLP. For analyzing the results, we distinguished three main types of values to evaluate the agreement between experts: a very good agreement (above 70% agreement), a fairly good agreement (above 50%) and a bad agreement (below 50%). In Fig. 2, we set out the values distributed according to this classification, with the predominant type.

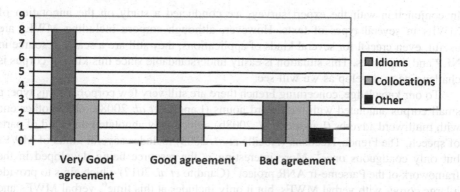

Fig. 2. Expert judgments on the type of MWEs

In line with our expectations, the less consensual types have a higher proportion of adverbs (*pendant ce temps* 'meanwhile' lit. 'during that time'; *sans doute* 'probably' lit. 'without any doubt') and prepositions (*au fond de* 'at the bottom of'). This type of grammatical expression seems to be far more difficult to analyze semantically (grammatical MWEs are really poor cousins of phraseology and have not been much studied). One expert even wishes to treat grammatical MWEs in a specific way, different from other classes of words:

"For many prepositional phrases, I would like to consider them as full idioms, even if they include the meaning of one or several of their components."

These hesitations were confirmed by an evaluation performed on the annotation of collocation (see Sect. 3), which led us to use a specific class for grammatical words. There was also a weak agreement between expressions such as *pays développé* ['developed country'], which can be considered according to the point of view as an idiom (a "developed country" is a type of country) or as a collocation. Fortunately, the agreement was very satisfactory for several MWEs, such as *coup d'œil* ['quick look', lit. 'stroke of eye'], which are clearly non-compositional, or for some expressions which have a very unusual syntactic structure such as *çà et là* ['here and there'] and *clair-obscur* ['half-light', lit. 'light-dark'].

This first survey of experts seems to validate the notion of a continuum along the degree of frozenness. It also shows that a typology with too fine-grained semantic distinctions (full vs. weak idioms) appears difficult to exploit, even with experts. By tightening the types, we obtain a fairly satisfactory degree of agreement, which can be improved by providing more discriminating criteria for grammatical words and adverbs. This survey also confirmed that an annotation of MWEs was a feasible task as long as the typology uses clear and not too complex criteria.

3 Annotation of Multiword Expressions

In conjunction with the expert survey, we conducted a study on the annotation of MWEs in several types of texts. However, although corpora including MWEs are useful, even crucial for several kinds of applications, they still are a scarce resource in NLP and linguistics. This situation is easily understandable since this kind of corpus is challenging to develop as we will see.

To our knowledge, concerning French there are still very few corpora of this type: a small corpus annotated with multiword nouns (Laporte *et al.* 2008a) and another one with multiword adverbs (Laporte *et al.* 2008b), which only annotated one kind of parts of speech. The French Treebank (Abeillé *et al.* 2003) includes several kinds of MWEs but only contiguous ones[4]. More interesting is the resource being developed in the framework of the Parseme-fr ANR project[5] (Candito *et al.* 2017) which aims to provide a large corpus with verbal MWEs, but it only includes at this time[6], verbal MWEs and excludes collocations (except light verb constructions) and pragmatic MWEs, contrary to our annotation scheme, which are very interesting phenomena. In English, more corpora are available. Among them, it is worth mentioning Schneider *et al.* (2014) a

---

[4] It means that discontinuous verbal expressions, for example in *j'ai pris cela en compte* ['I took that into account'] are not included.

[5] http://parsemefr.lif.univ-mrs.fr/.

[6] A larger set of MWEs is being annotated in the framework of this project (https://gitlab.lis-lab.fr/PARSEME-FR/PARSEME-FR-public/wikis/Guide-annotation-PARSEME_FR-chapeau). It will include all kinds of frozen idiomatic expressions but exclude collocations, pragmatic expressions and routine formulae. For example, expressions such as *force est de constater* ['it must be noted'], *il n'y a pas de quoi* ['you're welcome'] or *célibataire endurci* ['confirmed bachelor'] are not included in the PARSEME annotation project. However a major interest of the PARSEME project is the association with a syntactic annotation.

social web corpus with MWE annotations, which distinguishes between strong and weak MWEs, but does not provide a detailed typology.

3.1 Typology of Multiword Expressions and Annotation Process

Typology of MWEs. Our typology of MWEs (see Table 2), inspired by several linguistic typologies (Granger and Paquot 2008; Heid 2008; Tutin 2010; Mel'čuk 2012), is fairly broad and includes 8 types of MWEs, ranging from most compositional MWEs such as collocations (e.g., *heavy smoker, pay attention*) to fully frozen expressions such as *insofar as* or *black sheep* and oral expressions with pragmatic constraints (e.g., *see you later! Thank you. You're welcome*). We thought it was important to include more compositional expressions such as collocations because they are known to be crucial in NLP applications such as text generation (Lareau et al. 2011) or Machine Translation (Liu et al. 2010; Ramisch 2017).

The robustness of this typology has been evaluated. We computed the inter-annotator agreement on a sub-corpus (2,000 words in the literary text and 2,000 words in the scientific text) (Cf. (Tutin et al. 2015)). It provided acceptable results (Fleiss kappa of 0.683 for the literary text and 0.741 for the scientific report) with a good agreement on functional MWEs, performing slightly less well with collocations and idioms, which brought us to provide more detail and formal criteria in our annotation guidelines.

Table 2. Typology of multiword expressions in PolyCorp.

Multiword expressions	Examples
Idioms[a]: frozen multiword expressions	*cul de sac* (fr)/*dead end, prendre en compte* (fr)/*take into account*
Collocations: preferred binary association, including light verb constructions	*gros fumeur* (fr)/*heavy smoker; faire une promenade* (fr)/*to take a walk*
Functional Multiword Expressions: functional adverbs, prepositions, conjunctions, determiners, pronouns	*c'est pourquoi* (fr)/ *that is why; d'autre part* (fr)/*on the other hand; insofar as*
Pragmatic MWEs: Multiword expressions related to specific speech situations	*de rien* (fr)/*You're welcome; à plus tard* (fr.)/*see you later*
Proverbs	*Pierre qui roule n'amasse pas mousse* (fr)/*A rolling stone gathers no moss*
Complex terms	*Natural Language Processing*
Multiword named entities	*Université Grenoble Alpes; the European Union*
Routine formulae: routines generally associated with rhetorical functions	*force est de constater* (fr)/*it must be noted*

[a]Idioms include compounds in our typology.

Annotation Scheme and Annotation Process. The annotation scheme is a surface annotation, where each token included in a MWE is annotated with an identifier, the grammatical category of the whole expression, the part of speech of every element of the MWE, and the type of MWE as a whole (idiom, collocation ...). Cases of overlapping MWEs, i.e., when some parts of the MWEs belong to several MWEs, as in the example *We paid close attention,* where we can have two collocations (*close attention* and *pay attention*), are dealt with.

The annotation process has been performed semi-automatically with the help of an NLP tool, NooJ (Silberztein 2016), and a large dictionary of 5,000 frequent MWEs. This dictionary, which provides the morpho-syntactic and the type of each MWE, has been compiled from several resources, including the *Dictionnaire Électronique des Mots* (Dubois and Dubois Charlier 2010), *Wiktionary* or the *DELAC* (Courtois et al. 1997). About 35% up to 50% of MWEs are semi-automatically annotated. The automatic annotation has been completed and checked manually with the help of guidelines by at least two skilled annotators[7] (some texts have been annotated by three persons). Moreover, a Perl script has been used to ensure the consistence of the annotation. It allowed to spot and to correct some errors, when the various elements of 1 MWE had been labeled with different tags of part of speech.

Figure 3 provides an example of annotated text extracted from *Thérèse Raquin*.

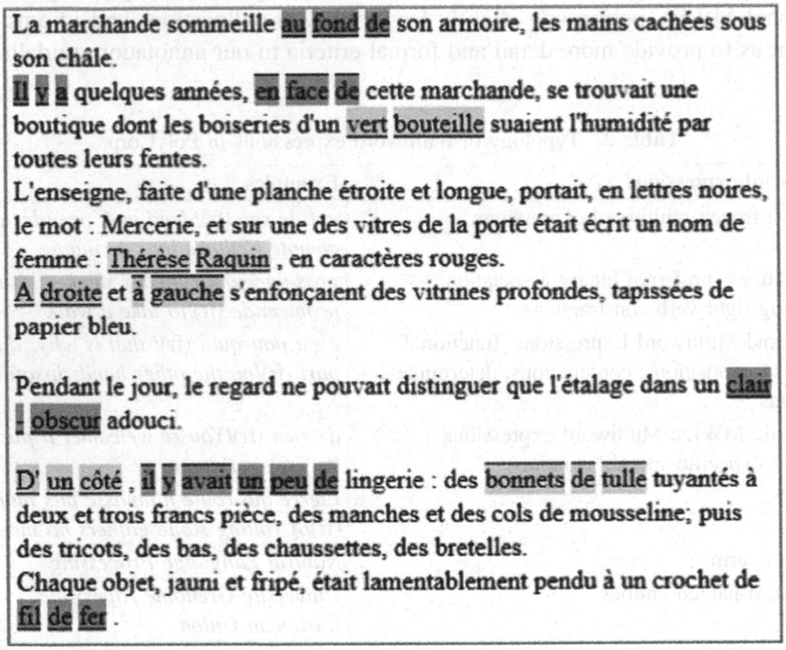

La marchande sommeille au fond de son armoire, les mains cachées sous son châle.
Il y a quelques années, en face de cette marchande, se trouvait une boutique dont les boiseries d'un vert bouteille suaient l'humidité par toutes leurs fentes.
L'enseigne, faite d'une planche étroite et longue, portait, en lettres noires, le mot : Mercerie, et sur une des vitres de la porte était écrit un nom de femme : Thérèse Raquin , en caractères rouges.
A droite et à gauche s'enfonçaient des vitrines profondes, tapissées de papier bleu.

Pendant le jour, le regard ne pouvait distinguer que l'étalage dans un clair
- obscur adouci.

D' un côté , il y avait un peu de lingerie : des bonnets de tulle tuyantés à deux et trois francs pièce, des manches et des cols de mousseline; puis des tricots, des bas, des chaussettes, des bretelles.
Chaque objet, jauni et fripé, était lamentablement pendu à un crochet de fil de fer .

Fig. 3. An example of annotated text (*Thérèse Raquin*) with a stylesheet (collocations, idioms, named entities, functional words) (Color figure online)

---

[7] Master's degree students and scholars in computational linguistics.

3.2 Some Tricky Cases

The annotation process is not trivial. The annotators encounter two main kinds of problems: delimiting boundaries of MWEs and choosing the right type of MWE. Due to the lack of space, we will only address some examples.

Delimiting boundaries of MWEs is generally trivial for functional words (e.g. *in order to*) or nominal idioms (e.g. *point of view*). It is far more complicated for verbal MWEs. As a rule, we decided to exclude the annotation of grammatical words that are not essential in the MWE. For example, in the following example,

Il faut <u>faire</u> un <u>effort</u> ['we have to <u>make</u> an <u>effort</u>]

we do not include the determiner in the MWE annotation, since it is highly variable (*faire <u>l'</u>effort, <u>des</u> efforts, <u>cet</u> effort*). Conversely, in some MWEs, the determiner is fixed and should be included:

Je ne veux pas <u>passer l'</u> éponge là-dessus. [I don't want to <u>wipe the slate</u> clean on that']

Nor do we include it within the prepositions that are subcategorized by the MWE verbs (e.g.: *to give a talk <u>to</u>*). Including or not including the grammatical words strongly depends on the type of MWE, and often requires corpus queries in order to make the right decision.

Selecting the right type of MWE is also tricky. Some MWEs such as functional MWEs and Named entities are less prone to inter-annotator disagreement than other ones such as decision between collocations and frozen expressions (we will see that they are also the most tricky cases for statistical Machine Translation). Clear-cut decisions along this continuum of "frozenness" can be considered somewhat arbitrary. However, providing syntactic and semantic criteria in the guidelines can help to ensure consistency during the annotation process and enables us to refine the annotation process. For example, we decided to include expressions such as *developed country* as collocations. These expressions can be considered as kinds of "hyponymic collocations" (the collocation refers to a subtype of the head noun. A *developed country* is a kind of *country*). We also included binomials (e.g., *I work <u>day and night</u> for this project*) in the class of collocations.

4 A Corpus Annotated with Multiword Expressions: Some Results

4.1 The PolyCorp Corpus

Our annotated corpus with MWEs (see Table 3), the PolyCorp corpus, reaches the size of almost 70,000 tokens and includes several freely available corpora. Except EIIDA, all texts have an English equivalent, which enabled some studies on MT (see Sect. 4.4).

Table 3. Types of textual genres included in the PolyCorp corpus

Sub-corpus	Textual genre	Number of tokens
BAF Citi 1 (Baf corpus)	Scientific writing	14,500 tokens
Thérèse Raquin (Emile Zola)	Literary novel	7,260 tokens
News	"Journalese"	17,400 tokens
Film Le fabuleux destin d'Amélie Poulain	Film dialogues (subtitles)	9,900 tokens
TED talks	Talks in science popularization	8,160 tokens
EIIDA French corpus (scientific talks)	Scientific talks	12,630 tokens

The corpus is diverse since it includes 3 oral texts (film dialogues, scientific talks, TED talks) and 3 written texts (scientific report, news, literary novel) in several fields[8]. This diversity of textual genres is useful to better understand the linguistic properties of MWEs.

In this corpus, 5.560 MWEs have been annotated. Some interesting results could be computed from this annotated corpus.

4.2 Phraseological Density

The phraseological density is the ratio of tokens included in MWEs. For example, in the following sentence

Nous avons <u>pris</u> ce problème <u>en</u> <u>compte</u>.

[we have <u>taken</u> this problem <u>into</u> <u>account</u>]

our ratio is 3/8. The phraseological density for the whole corpus is 20.45%, which is quite close to that of Schneider et al. (2014). These results show that although MWEs are widespread, they are far from being as frequent as simple words. In French, phraseological density would greatly increase if we included compound tenses (e.g. *j'ai mangé* 'I have eaten') and discontinuous negation, which can be considered as a kind of MWE (e.g. *je ne mange pas*).

With regard to the kind of text, we can observe that phraseological density is quite stable from each textual genre to another (between 17.40% and 27.88%). The differences between the genres are not as important as we could have expected, but it seems that oral transcriptions, especially scientific talks, contain more MWEs than the other written genres (e.g. journalese and scientific writing) (Fig. 4).

---

[8] The criteria for selecting the texts were the following ones: diversity of genres and availability of aligned bilingual corpora.

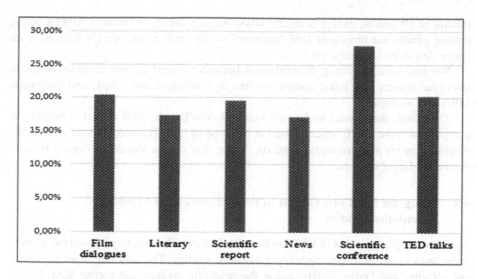

Fig. 4. Phraseological density across genres

4.3 Distribution of MWEs Across Textual Genres

More interesting is the distribution of MWEs across textual genres (Fig. 5). We notice that some expressions are stable across all kinds of texts: collocations, idioms and functional words. As is often claimed in literature, collocations are more frequent than

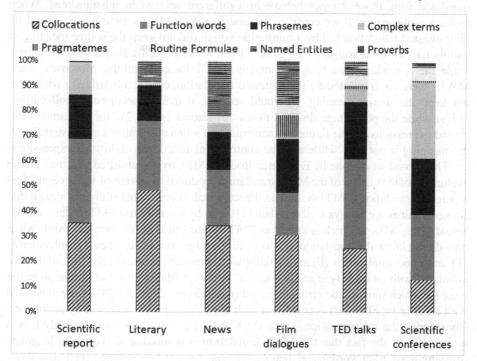

Fig. 5. Distribution of MWEs across textual genres

idioms in all genres, except scientific talks. Among the most frequent MWEs across textual genres, we obviously find functional words such as *un peu* ('a little bit'), *au cours de* ('over the course of'), ...

We also observe strong dissimilarities between textual genres: complex terms in scientific reports and talks, named entities in journalese and films, and pragmatic MWEs in dialogues.

Therefore, there seem to be two kinds of MWEs: the first ones fall within the category of "core MWE lexicon" used in any type of text. The second ones are specific to given genres and pragmatic contexts. These first results should obviously be confirmed on larger corpora.

4.4   Using the PolyCorp Corpus in the Framework of Machine Translation Studies

An interesting application in NLP has been performed. The corpus obtained has already been used in two translation-quality evaluation studies. The first one done by Esperança-Rodier and Didier (2016), using the scientific writing sub-corpus BAF Citi 1, demonstrated that most (actually 80%) of MWEs in French were translated into equivalent MWEs in English. This interesting result shows that there is a high structural and lexical similarity between two close languages such as English and French. Furthermore, the study showed that when an idiom, a collocation or a functional multiword expression was well translated, it was translated by its attested translation in more than 95% of the occurrences. Nevertheless, even if there is consistency when translated well, those 3 types behave in a different way when mistranslated. When looking at the errors, if we consider the case in which MWEs were not translated by their attested translation but by a translation which did not keep the source meaning, it mainly happened for roughly 41% of functional MWEs against almost 19% of idioms, while the percentage rose to approximately 32,7% for collocations. Moreover, when MWEs were not translated by their attested translation, but by a translation which did not keep the source meaning, we could see that it mainly occurred in collocations (13%) while the percentage dropped to 8% for idioms and to 2% for functional multiword expressions. These figures demonstrate that when collocations are mistranslated, the meaning is not kept while it is the contrary for functional multiword expressions.

The second work done by Esperança-Rodier (2019, to be published), focuses on the evaluation of the quality of the MWE translation produced by a state-of-the-art Statistical Machine Translation (SMT) system on the same sub-corpus. This study has shown that Named Entities are always well translated (100%) by the in-house SMT system, named hereafter Lig-Moses, which is logical as SMT systems provide the original words when they do not know the translation of a word in the target language. Then Technical terms (T) and Functional words (F) are partially well translated (respectively 15% of T were annotated with an error type and 8% of F.). Finally, Collocations and idioms were the ones for which most of the errors occurred (respectively 23% and 24% were annotated with an error type), which is consistent with the difficulties encountered by annotators. Considering the mistranslation, when the MWEs were not translated correctly it was mainly due to the fact that the MWE translation was missing in the target language (missing word, filler words), and then the fact that the MWEs were incorrectly translated (incorrect word sense, wrong lexical choice or incorrect disambiguation).

5 Conclusion and Perspectives

These experiments on French MWEs show that experts can reach a consensus and that an annotation task with a panel of multiword expressions can be performed satisfactorily, as long as the typology is not overly complex and clear guidelines are provided. The annotation of various texts provides interesting results concerning MWEs, which are prevalent but not as numerous as often claimed. The phraseological density is quite stable across textual genres. The lexicon of MWEs falls into 2 broad types: (a) core MWE lexicon including function words, collocations and idioms; (b) specific MWE lexicon including named entities, complex terms, pragmatic MWEs, and to a lesser extent, routines formulae and proverbs. The annotated corpus has been used to evaluate statistical machine translation, showing interesting differences among multiword expressions considered in the study.

This work needs to be extended to bilingual annotation (including the English version of this parallel corpus) and extended to other corpora in order to confirm these first results and better understand the nature and diversity of multiword expressions.

Acknowledgements. Internships for the corpus annotation have been funded by the Pôle Cognition (http://www.grenoblecognition.fr/) (Université Grenoble Alpes). Special thanks to the interns and students who contributed greatly to this project: Doriane Simonnet, Pauline Soutrenon, Manolo Iborra, Justine Reverdy, Zied Elloumi, Johan Didier.

References

Abeillé, A., Clément, L., Toussenel, F.: Building a treebank for French. In: Abeillé, A. (ed.) Treebanks. Text, Speech and Language Technology, vol. 20, pp. 165–187. Springer, Dordrecht (2003). https://doi.org/10.1007/978-94-010-0201-1_10

Altenberg, B.: On the phraseology of spoken English: the evidence of recurrent word-combinations. In: Cowie, A.P. (ed.) Phraseology: Theory, Analysis and Applications, pp. 101–122. Clarendon Press, Oxford (1998)

Candito, M., et al.: Annotation d'expressions polylexicales verbales en français. In: 24e conférence sur le Traitement Automatique des Langues Naturelles (TALN), pp. 1–9 (2017)

Courtois, B., et al.: Dictionnaire électronique DELAC: les mots composés binaires. Technical report 56, University Paris 7, LADL (1997)

Cowie, A.P. (ed.): Phraseology: Theory, Analysis, and Applications. OUP, Oxford (1998)

Dubois, J., Dubois-Charlier, F.: La combinatoire lexico-syntaxique dans le Dictionnaire électronique des mots. Les termes du domaine de la musique à titre d'illustration. Langages **179**(3), 3–56 (2010)

Esperanca-Rodier, E., Didier, J.: Translation Quality Evaluation of MWEs from French into English Using an SMT System (2016). Translating and the Computer 38 © AsLing, The International Association for Advancement in Language Technology (2015). www.asling.org

Esperança-Rodier, E.: Analyse de la qualité des traductions automatiques du français vers l'anglais, d'Expressions Poly-Lexicales (EPL) à partir d'un corpus parallèle – Quelles sont les erreurs les plus fréquentes par type d'EPL? In: LTT 2018 (2019, to be published)

Fraser, B.: Idioms within a transformational grammar. Found. Lang. 2242 (1970)

Granger, S., Paquot, M.: Disentangling the phraseological web. In: Granger, S., Meunier, F. (eds.) Phraseology: An Interdisciplinary Perspective, pp. 27–49. John Benjamins, Amsterdam (2008)

Gross, G.: Les expressions figées en français: noms composés et autres locutions. Ophrys, Paris (1996)

Hausmann, F.J.: Tout est idiomatique dans les langues. In: Martins-Baltar, M. (ed.) La locution entre langue et usages, pp. 19–52. ENS Editions, Fontenay-Saint-Cloud (1997)

Heid, U.: Computational phraseology. An overview. In: Granger, S., Meunier, F.: Phraseology. An Interdisciplinary Perspective, pp. 337–360. Benjamins, Amsterdam (2008)

Koehn, P., et al.: Moses: open source toolkit for statistical machine translation. In: Proceedings of the 45th Annual Meeting of the Association for Computational Linguistics, pp. 177–180 (2007)

Laporte, E., Nakamura, T., Voyatzi, S.: A French corpus annotated for multiword nouns. In: Language Resources and Evaluation Conference. Workshop Towards a Shared Task on Multiword Expressions, pp. 27–30 (2008a)

Laporte, E., Nakamura, T., Voyatzi, S.: A French corpus annotated for multiword expressions with adverbial function. In: Language Resources and Evaluation Conference (LREC). Linguistic Annotation Workshop, pp. 48–51 (2008b)

Lareau, F., Dras, M., Börschinger, B., Dale, R.: Collocations in multilingual natural language generation: lexical functions meet lexical functional grammar. In Proceedings of ALTA 2011, pp. 95–104 (2011)

Liu, Z., Wang, H., Wu, H., Li, S.: Improving statistical machine translation with monolingual collocation. In: Proceedings of the 48th Annual Meeting of the Association for Computational Linguistics, pp. 825–833 (2010)

Mel'čuk, I., et al.: Dictionnaire explicatif et combinatoire du français contemporain. Recherches lexico-sémantiques 1, II, III, IV, Les Presses de l'Université de Montréal, Montréal (1984, 1988, 1992, 1998)

Mel'čuk, I.: Tout ce que nous voulions savoir sur les phrasèmes, mais… Cahiers de lexicologie 102, 129–149 (2013)

Mel'čuk, I.: Phraseology in the language, in the dictionary, and in the computer. Yearbook of Phraseology 3(1), 31–56 (2012)

Moon, R.: Fixed Expressions and Idioms in English: A Corpus-Based Approach. Oxford University Press, Oxford (1998)

Polguère, A.: Principles of lexical network systemic modeling (Principes de modélisation systémique des réseaux lexicaux). In: Proceedings of TALN 2014 (Volume 1: Long Papers), pp. 79–90 (2014). (in French)

Potet, M., Esperança-Rodier, E., Besacier, L., Blanchon, H.: Collection of a large database of French-English SMT output corrections. In: LREC 2012, Istambul, 21–27 May 2012, pp. 4043–4048 (2012)

Ramisch, C.: Putting the horses before the cart: identifying multiword expressions before translation. In: Computational and Corpus-Based Phraseology - Second International Conference, Europhras 2017, London, UK, pp. 69–84 (2017)

Schneider, N., et al.: Comprehensive annotation of multiword expressions in a social web corpus. In: Proceedings of LREC, Reykjavík, Iceland, pp. 455–46 (2014)

Silberztein, M.: Formalizing Natural Languages: The NooJ Approach. Wiley, London (2016)

Sinclair, J.: Corpus, Concordance, Collocation. Oxford University Press, Oxford (1991)

Tutin, A., Esperança-Rodier, E., Iborra, M., Reverdy, J.: Annotation of multiword expressions in French. In: European Society of Phraseology Conference (EUROPHRAS 2015), pp. 60–67 (2015)

Wray, A.: Identifying formulaic language: persistent challenges and new opportunities. In: Corrigan, G., Moravcsik, E., Ouali, H. (eds.) Formulaic Language, vol. I. Benjamins, Amsterdam (2009)

The Portrait of Dorian Gray: A Corpus-Based Analysis of Translated Verb + Noun (Object) Collocations in Peninsular and Colombian Spanish

M.ª Victoria Valencia Giraldo[1](✉) and Gloria Corpas Pastor[2,3](✉)

[1] University of Salamanca, Salamanca, Spain
victoriavalencia@usal.es
[2] University of Malaga, Málaga, Spain
gcorpas@uma.es
[3] University of Wolverhampton, Wolverhampton, UK

Abstract. Corpus-based Translation Studies have promoted research on the features of translated language, by focusing on the process and product of translation, from a descriptive perspective. Some of these features have been proposed by Toury [31] under the term of *laws of translation*, namely the law of growing standardisation and the law of interference. The law of standardisation appears to be particularly at play in diatopy, and more specifically in the case of transnational languages (e.g. English, Spanish, French, German). In fact, some studies have revealed the tendency to standardise the diatopic varieties of Spanish in translated language [8, 9, 11, 12]. This paper focuses on verb + noun (object) collocations of Spanish translations of *The Portrait of Dorian Gray* by Oscar Wilde. Two different varieties have been chosen (Peninsular and Colombian Spanish). Our main aim is to establish whether the Colombian Spanish translation actually matches the variety spoken in Colombia or it is closer to general or standard Spanish. For this purpose, the techniques used to translate this type of collocations in both Spanish translations will be analysed. Furthermore, the diatopic distribution of these collocations will be studied by means of large corpora.

Keywords: Corpus-based translation studies · Diatopic variation · Collocations · Standardisation

1 Introduction

Corpus-based Translation Studies have promoted research on the features of translated language, by focusing on the process and product of translation, from a descriptive perspective. Some of these features or regularities have been proposed by Toury [31] under the term of laws of translation, namely the law of growing standardisation and the law of interference. According to Toury's law of growing standardisation [31], "in translation, source-text textemes tend to be converted into target-language (or target-culture) repertoremes". In other words, the complicated textual relations established in

© Springer Nature Switzerland AG 2019
G. Corpas Pastor and R. Mitkov (Eds.): Europhras 2019, LNAI 11755, pp. 417–430, 2019.
https://doi.org/10.1007/978-3-030-30135-4_30

the source text are replaced in the target text by more common ones in the target discursive-textual community. Thus, translated texts tend to be more conventional and standardised than non-translated texts. Another related notion was introduced by Baker [2, 3] under the umbrella term 'translation universals' in order to encompass several common features of translated texts (simplification, explicitation, normalisation, convergence and transference). Based on Toury's law, some research has been carried out on the tendency to standardise the diatopic varieties of Spanish in translated language by means of collocations and other phraseological units [8, 9, 11, 12]. In general, it can be inferred from those studies that the richness of the different Spanish national varieties is not reflected in translated language, nor in the existing bilingual dictionaries. However, to the best of our knowledge, no study has already determined whether the translation of collocations in a literary work reflects a specific Spanish variety or whether it is closer to general or standard Spanish[1].

In this paper, we argue that the translation of verb + noun (object) collocations found in the first two chapters of *The Portrait of Dorian Gray* by Oscar Wilde [32] in a translation into Colombian Spanish appears closer to general or standard Spanish than to the Spanish variety of Colombia. In order to demonstrate this, the techniques used to translate this type of collocations in a translation into Peninsular Spanish[2] [34] and in another one into Colombian Spanish [33] will be analysed. Moreover, the diatopic distribution of these Spanish collocations will be studied by means of large corpora. As a convenient theoretical background, we endorse Toury's laws, as well as previous studies on standardisation of diatopic varieties of Spanish in translation.

2 Translation of Collocations and Diatopic Varieties of Spanish

The term collocation is understood as the property of language by which speakers tend to produce certain combinations of words among a large number of possible combinations [16]. From a linguistic point of view, collocations are phraseological units which are free syntagms generated from rules, although, at the same time, they show different ranges of combinatorial restriction conditioned by use [14]. A full discussion on the notion of collocation is beyond the scope of this work. We will present the main features we took into consideration to conduct this study.

Collocations are considered composite units and conventionally restricted structures, in which both collocates have a different semantic status [18]. For example, in *to make a decision* and *tomar una decisión*, nouns constitute the autosemantic bases, while *to make* and *tomar* are collocates, i.e., the meanings of these depend entirely on their respective bases.

---

[1] General or standard Spanish is understood here as 'global' or 'unified' Spanish spoken/written all over the Spanish-speaking world [27].

[2] The term Peninsular Spanish will be used to refer to Spanish from Spain, including the islands, Canary and Balearic Islands, Ceuta and Melilla.

As far as verb + noun (object) collocations are concerned, verbs (as collocates) in these combinations exhibit a variety of ranges of collocability: from practically unlimited to practically fixed with intermediate categories [14]. In the first type, we find collocations which share collocates and a base of the same semantic field, for instance *desempeñar un cargo, una función* or *un papel,* in Spanish. On the opposite extreme of the spectrum, we find practically fixed or very restricted collocations, such as *conciliar el sueño, acariciar una idea, grind one's teeth,* or *shrugh one's shoulders,* whose collocates exhibit a figurative meaning or have a narrow or specific meaning [21]. Among the intermediate cases (*asumir una responsabilidad,* for example), a homogeneous group is formed by a delexical verb (or, rather, a verb used in a delexical sense, [21]), almost grammaticalised, and a noun, generally deverbal, which provides the fundamental meaning. Delexical verbs are highly polysemous verbs, such as *dar, tomar, hacer,* or *poner;* and *take* and *make,* etc., in English.

Collocations express typical relations between components, as can be observed in noun + verb and verb + noun collocations [24]. *Tocar la guitarra* and *rasguear la guitarra* are collocations, due to the typical relation between its components [24]. On the contrary, *limpiar la guitarra* and *guardar la guitarra* are not considered collocations, because the noun *guitarra* can only express a typical relation as a musical instrument [24].

By repeating a combination of words, speakers recognise it as familiar and use it as if it were a prefabricated fragment [13]. One way to determine whether a certain sequence is sufficiently frequent or salient to be considered conventionalised, habitual or typical is to count its occurrences in a corpus, as suggested by Manning and Schütze [25]. A large number of occurrences is enough to consider that a collocation is frequent, and therefore entrenched in the mind of speakers. Although, a significant collocation could be considered typical and cognitively salient (entrenched), even if it might not strike as particularly frequent [12, p. 6].

As Koike [24] points out, lexical units that form a collocation do not necessarily have to be followed one after the other in a text. In some cases, one or more words appear in the middle of them. Some authors [23, 30] have proposed the concept of *collocational span* of four words before and after the keyword or node, but there are collocations in which constituent elements are separated from each other by more than four words [24].

Collocations tend to be semantically transparent, but not always predictable [9, 12]. Unlike idiomatic phraseological units (idioms), collocations generally do not pose comprehension problems, but mainly in production, especially in second language learning, languages for academic/specific purposes, translation, and interpretation [9, 10].

Collocations are not only peculiar to a particular language, but they also reveal variation in their collocational patterns when it comes to a particular text or literary style [17], an author style [20], domain-specific genres and registers [5, 11, 15, 35, etc.]. They are also useful to characterise linguistic change over time [19], and diatopic variation [12].

The translation of collocations into the target language is often characterised by the anisomorphism of languages when it comes to choosing collocates [9, 12]. While bases are usually translated literally, collocates vary enormously. For example, *to pay* *homage* cannot be translated into Spanish as **pagar homenaje*, but, generally, as *rendir homenaje*. In general, the translator should try to make that the translation of collocations sounds as natural as possible in the target language, except, of course, when the function of a collocation is precisely generating surprise or draw the attention of the recipients, as frequently occurs in poetry, advertising and humour [4].

In the case of transnational languages, such as English or Spanish, the rendering becomes even more complicated, since it is necessary to choose the language variety into which to translate [12]. Let us illustrate this again with the collocation *to pay homage*. Spanish offers a wide range of collocates on a scale of formality and grammaticalisation, the most frequent of which are: *dar/hacer un homenaje* (informal), *rendir/tributar/brindar un homenaje* (formal). However, this list is further restricted if diatopic variation is taken into consideration. For instance, *dar* y *brindar* are not plausible verbal collocates for *homenaje* in Nicaraguan Spanish; in Mexican and Argentinean Spanish *dar* is not used, but *hacer* as delexical verb with homenaje. Dominican Spanish only allows collocations with *rendir* and *tributar*; in Honduran Spanish the only option is *rendir*, etc., [12].

Translating diatopy is not a small or trivial task, and bilingual dictionaries are not of much help either, as they tend to maintain a simplified and conventional approach to the translation of collocations. In fact, there is currently no Spanish-English bilingual collocations dictionary [9, 10], and in those where equivalents of collocations are included, e.g. Collins, Larousse and Oxford, *rendir homenaje* is offered as the only translation equivalent of *to pay homage* [12], which does not at all reflect the richness of the Spanish language. However, according to Corpas Pastor [12], the varieties of transnational languages, like Spanish, should be taken into consideration in order to increase the fluency and naturalness of translated texts.

The tension between standard Spanish and transnational Spanish (pluricentric) has consequences for the type of Spanish (transnational variety) used in translation. For commercial reasons, the translation industry has adopted the presumed neutral Spanish, as opposed to the Spanish located for a specific market (diatopic variety) [8]. But this variety, far from being neutral, is loaded with a positive sociocultural value and prestige, in opposition to other diatopically marked varieties.

In the following section, the corpora used in this study case are described. Then, the analysis of the translation of collocations and their diatopic distribution in corpora are presented.

3   Choice of Corpora

There are some diachronic corpora of Spanish documents on the web nowadays, such as *Corpus del Español* (CE)[3], *Corpus de Documentos Españoles Anteriores a 1800* (CODEA)[4], *Corpus Biblia Medieval* (BM)[5], *Corpus Hispánico y Americano en la Red:*

---

[3] Available online through: http://www.corpusdelespanol.org/.

[4] Available online through: http://corpuscodea.es/.

[5] Available online through: http://corpus.bibliamedieval.es/.

Textos Antiguos (CHARTA)[6], *Corpus Diacrónico del Español* (CORDE) [29] and *Corpus Diacrónico y Diatópico del Español Americano* (CORDIAM) [1]. For this study, the following diachronic corpora have been selected: the Corpus Diacrónico del Español (CORDE)[7], (Diachronic Corpus of Spanish), which contains American Spanish varieties and Peninsular Spanish (available through the Spanish Royal Academy); and the Corpus Diacrónico y Diatópico del Español de America (CORDIAM)[8] (Diachronic and Diatopic Corpus of American Spanish), which is accessible through the Mexican Academy of the Language.

CORDE was created by the Royal Spanish Academy in the late 1990s. It was the first historical corpus of Spanish. It is a corpus of texts from the all places where Spanish is spoken (23 countries): Argentina, Bolivia, Chile, Colombia, Costa Rica, Cuba, Ecuador, El Salvador, USA, Spain, Philippines, Guatemala, Honduras, Mexico, Nicaragua, Panama, Paraguay, Peru, Portugal, Puerto Rico, Dominican Republic, Uruguay, Venezuela. Due to its historical perspective, CORDE allocates a total of 74% to Peninsular Spanish and 26% to the remaining 22 varieties. Additionally, there are records of Spanish from all periods, from its beginnings to 1974. CORDE currently contains 250 million words (approximately) from texts pertaining to various subjects (fiction, didactics, science and technology, press, religion, history, law and legal). The CORDE interface allows narrowing searches to specific places, periods of time, and domains.

The Corpus Diacrónico y Diatópico del Español de América (CORDIAM) is divided into three subcorpora: CORDIAM-Documents, which contains chronicle, administrative, legal texts and letters; CORDIAM-Literature, where narrative, poetry, prose (satire, dialogues, first manifestations of modern essay, etc.) and theatre are found; and CORDIAM-Press, which is constituted by documents written exclusively in American Spanish from the 19 Latin American countries, besides Southern and Western United States, Jamaica, Haiti and Guyana (former territories of the Spanish crown). CORDIAM-Press contains only texts from the eighteenth and nineteenth centuries because the press exists in America from the eighteenth century. CORDIAM covers texts from four centuries, the oldest dating from 1494 and the most recent from 1905. It is a relatively small corpus containing 4,475,759 words in 6,058 texts (4,178 documents, 15 literature and 1,865 newspapers).

In this study, the searches in CORDIAM were not restricted to any particular type of text or genre, because the portion of literary texts in CORDIAM is too small. However, they were narrowed to the nineteenth century (chronological criterion).

We have chosen to work with CORDE and CORDIAM for the following reasons: both corpora offer users the possibility of performing query searches by using geographical and chronological filters; both contain a wide variety of genres and a large number of words.

In this study, the searches for verb + noun (object) collocations in CORDE have been restricted geographically for obtaining individual results from Colombia, Spain

---

[6] Available online through: http://www.corpuscharta.es/.

[7] *Corpus Diacrónico del Español* (CORDE): http://corpus.rae.es/cordenet.html.

[8] *Corpus Diacrónico y Diatópico del Español de América* (CORDIAM): http://www.cordiam.org/.

and also from general Spanish. Due to the fact that *The Portrait of Dorian Gray* was published in 1890, the chronological restriction here has been established between 1850 and 1950, because we consider this to be a reasonable period of time to observe the use of the language of that time, which must be also reflected in the target texts.

4   Rendering of Collocations

Collocations were extracted manually from the source text (ST), as well as their corresponding translation equivalents from the two selected target texts, one from Colombia [33] and the other one from Spain [34]. The translation techniques used in the rendering of collocations into Spanish were identified and analysed in the selected texts, based on the classification of techniques proposed by Hurtado Albir [22].

First, all verb + noun (object) combinations of the first two chapters of the ST and their corresponding translation equivalents in the target texts (TT) were extracted manually. Then some were eliminated until a list of 60 collocations was obtained. The criteria to discard some combinations of this type were typicality and frequency of use, hence the selected collocations express typical relations between their components and present high frequency of use. Among the combinations that were discarded are to *cause excitement, preach the importance, return to the ideal, etc.* In cases where there was doubt, some dictionaries and resources were consulted, namely, the monolingual dictionary *Oxford Collocations* [26], the corpus EnTenTen13[9] (Word Sketch through *Sketch Engine*), which indicates collocations or word combinations for any lemma queried, the *Diccionario Combinatorio Práctico del Español Contemporáneo* [6], the EsTenTen11 (see footnote 9) and the diachronic corpora CORDE and CORDIAM. This was done with caution, since these resources do not take into account the diachrony of language, except for CORDE and CORDIAM.

4.1   Translation Techniques

It can be clearly observed that in the Colombian Spanish target text (hereafter CO_SP_TT) (see Table 1) a great variety of techniques were applied in the translation of verb + noun (object) collocations, while in the Peninsular Spanish target text (hereafter PEN_SP_TT) fewer techniques were used (see Table 2). Established equivalence was the preferred option in both target texts.

77% of collocations were translated using the **established equivalence** technique in the CO_SP_TT. In this category, we group those collocations that were translated as other collocations recognised (by usage or by the dictionary) in the target language (TL), and which, therefore, constitute the established equivalents.

In the CO_SP_TT, for instance, the translation of *to catch the gleam* as *ver el brillo*, or *to elevate one's eyebrows* as *arquear las cejas*; and the translation in both TT of *to close one's eyes* as *cerrar los ojos* and *to tell the truth* as *decir la verdad*. The

---

[9] Available through Sketch Engine: https://www.sketchengine.co.uk/. (Subscription required).

Table 1. Translation techniques identified in the rendering of collocations in the CO_SP_TT

Technique	CO_SP_TT	Percentage
Established equivalent	47	77%
Linguistic compression	6	10%
Modulation	2	3%
Transposition	2	3%
Literal translation	1	2%
Discursive creation	1	2%
Linguistic amplification	1	2%
Reduction	1	2%

Table 2. Translation techniques identified in the rendering of collocations in the PEN_SP_TT

Technique	PEN_SP_TT	Percentage
Established equivalent	53	89%
Linguistic compression	5	8%
Literal translation	1	2%
Reduction	1	2%

collocation *to exhibit a picture* was translated using two established equivalents: *exponer un retrato* and *exhibir un retrato*.

In the vast majority of cases, the base was translated literally and the collocate did vary. In just one case the base was changed in the collocation, as in the translation of *to bear the burden* as *soportar el peso*.

Similarly, the **established equivalent** was the most frequently used technique in the translation of collocations in the PEN_SP_TT (see Table 2). For example, the collocations *to make a success* translated as *tener éxito* or *to play the piano* as *tocar el piano*. It would not make any sense to translate literally *to make a success* as *hacer un éxito*, hence it must be translated using the established equivalent in Spanish: *tener éxito*.

Only in one case, the **literal translation** technique was applied in both target texts. Many collocations in the English language are transparent, not only in terms of comprehension but also of production, which permits a word-for-word translation into Spanish, although this does not always imply that the resulting translation is a typical and frequent collocation in the TL, that is, the established equivalent. For instance, the collocation *to think (...) thoughts* translated as *pensar (...) ideas* in the PEN_SP_TT and *pensar con pensamientos* in the CO_SP_TT.

On the other hand, the **linguistic compression** technique was applied in the translation of collocations as single verbs in the TL, instead of as other collocations, resulting in a synthesis of linguistic elements. Most of these cases occur with collocations formed by delexical, almost grammaticalised verbs, and a generally deverbal noun, which provides the main semantic load [14, p. 69]. Some collocations that illustrate this are: *to have no appreciation*, translated as *no apreciar*, in both CO_SP_TT and PEN_SP_TT; *to make no answer* translated as *sin responder* and *no* *contestar*, in the CO_SP_TT and in the PEN_SP_TT, respectively. Whereas in the PEN_SP_TT, we find: *to make a difference* translated as *distinguir*. Likewise, as an example of the use of this technique, we include collocations that were translated as more general verbs, like *to ring the bell* and *llamar* (in both TT).

Other techniques were used less frequently in the translations analysed. In the CO_SP_TT, for instance, a change of point of view (**modulation**) can be observed in the translation of *to keep one's promises* as *faltar a sus promesas* and *to break one's promises* as *no cumplir sus promesas*. Additionally, a change of grammatical category is noticed in the translation of *to cure the soul* as *remedio para el alma* (**transposition**). In this same TT, a linguistic amplification is employed in the translation of the collocations *to frame [a portrait]* as *poner en marco [el retrato]*; and an ephemeral equivalence (**discursive creation**) is established for the collocation *to convey the sense* translated as *plasmar la velocidad*, which is not a frequent collocation in Spanish. Also, the reduction technique is clearly used in the omission of the collocations *to have a romance* in the PEN_SP_TT and *to give a definition* in the CO_SP_TT.

Not all collocations from the source language were translated as other collocations in the target language. Some of them were translated as free combinations of verb + noun, ephemeral equivalents (**discursive creation**), as verbs that contain all the semantic load, or they were simply omitted. Most of these instances were observed in the CO_SP_TT and others, such as the discursive creation, were pinpointed exclusively in this TT.

The English collocations found in the ST were consulted in some popular bilingual online dictionaries too, namely the *Oxford Dictionary*[10], *Collins Dictionary*[11], *Cambridge Dictionary*[12], and the *Linguee Dictionary*[13], with the aim of observing the repertoire of translation (English-Spanish) options they offer for collocations. Undoubtedly, the treatment of collocations in bilingual dictionaries is now extremely poor compared to that in monolingual dictionaries [9], and their approach to the translation of collocations is usually very simplified. In general, the *Linguee dictionary* is the one that provides the highest number of possible equivalents for collocations, for example, *to produce an effect* is rendered into Spanish as *causar un efecto, tener un efecto, generar un efecto* and *producir un efecto*; the latter is the one that has more instances. In the *Collins Dictionary* this collocation is translated as *producir un efecto* and *surtir efecto*. Conversely, in the other two bilingual dictionaries analysed no translation equivalent is found for this same collocation. Another example is *to yield to (a) temptation*, whose only equivalent in the *Collins* and *Oxford dictionaries* is *ceder a (la) tentación*, whereas in *Linguee* the following are also retrieved: *rendirse a la tentación, caer en la tentación, sucumbir a la tentación*.

The English collocation *to exhibit the picture/portrait* is included in the *Collins* and *Cambridge dictionaries* with the verb *exponer* as the only translation equivalent, albeit

---

[10] *Oxford English-Spanish Dictionary* <https://es.oxforddictionaries.com/> (Accessed: 01-04-19).

[11] *Collins English-Spanish Dictionary* <https://www.collinsdictionary.com/> (Accessed: 01-04-19).

[12] *Cambridge English-Spanish Dictionary* <http://dictionary.cambridge.org/es/diccionario/ingles-espanol/> (last accessed: 01-04-19).

[13] *Linguee English-Spanish Dictionary* <http://www.linguee.es/> (last accessed: 01-04-19).

in some Latin American countries the verb *exhibir* is a more common collocate for the nouns *cuadro/pintura*. Regarding the collocation *to pay attention*, its only translation equivalent found in these dictionaries is *prestar atención*, despite the fact that the verb *poner* is also a very frequent collocate used in American Spanish.

It is evident that bilingual dictionaries do not reflect the diatopic variation of Spanish, but rather favour general Spanish as regards the translation of verb + noun (object) collocations. These results support those obtained by Corpas Pastor [9, 12]. In the following section, the results of the search for collocations in CORDE and CORDIAM are presented.

4.2   Searching Collocations in CORDE and CORDIAM

After identifying and analysing the techniques used in the translation of collocations in chapter 1 and 2 of *The Portrait of Dorian Gray*, it was necessary to discard those that are not considered collocations in the target language, in order to carry out the analysis in the Spanish corpora (CORDE and CORDIAM), whose results are presented in this section.

A total of 50 collocations were extracted from the PEN_SP_TT, out of which 23 (46%) were also found in the CO_SP_TT, which means that both target texts share a high percentage of collocations. With respect to the results yielded by the large corpora, 44 (88%) collocations out of those 50 also occurred in general Spanish (GEN_SP) from CORDE. 47 (94%) out of these collocations appeared in Peninsular Spanish (PEN_SP) from CORDE and 3 (6%) were not found in CORDE or CORDIAM. Whereas in CORDIAM, only 9 (18%) collocations out of the total 50 were found in the GEN_SP and only 3 (6%) collocations in the Colombian Spanish (CO_SP) from CORDIAM: *producir un efecto*, *decir la verdad* and *prestar atención*.

On the other hand, a total of 48 collocations were found in the CO_SP_TT, out of which 23 (47.91%) were also found in the PEN_SP_TT. As for large corpora, 46 (95.83%) collocations out of those 48 appeared in the GEN_SP from CORDE, and 29 (95.83%) out of these also occurred in the CO_SP from CORDE, 2 (4.16%) were not found in CORDE or CORDIAM, and all of these collocations occurred in the PEN_SP (100%) from CORDE. As we can observe, a high percentage of the collocations which occur in the Colombian Spanish target text are used in Peninsular Spanish and in many other diatopic varieties.

Regarding CORDIAM, only 11 (22.91%) collocations out of 48 were found in the GEN_SP. Only 2 (4.16%) collocations occurred in the CO_SP. This is due to the small size of CORDIAM and the fact that the queries were restricted to the 19th century, which further reduced the chances of finding occurrences in this corpus.

The results retrieved from CORDIAM were very poor, mainly those concerning Colombian Spanish. Furthermore, the larger proportion of Peninsular Spanish words contained in CORDE is justified by the fact that this is a historical corpus of Spanish from all the countries where Spanish has been spoken, thus the documents from Spain outnumber those from elsewhere.

The data reveals that the translation of collocations in the CO_SP_TT is closer to general Spanish than to Colombian Spanish, inasmuch as this TT and the PEN_SP_TT share a high percentage of collocations. Those collocations that were found only in the

CO_SP_TT occurred in the corpora in other varieties too, especially in Peninsular Spanish, which indicates that none of these collocations are diatopically restricted to Colombian Spanish. For example, the collocations *arquear las cejas, exhibir el retrato, sentir placer*, etc., despite appearing in the CO_SP_TT, were not found in the Colombian Spanish from CORDE or CORDIAM, albeit they were retrieved from other national varieties of CORDE.

However, no occurrences of the collocations *crear (un) efecto* and *ganar (un) empuje*, extracted from the CO_SP_TT, were observed in any of the corpora, suggesting a very low frequency of use of such collocations in Spanish between 1850–1950. In the case of the collocation *crear (un) efecto*, as in the vast majority, it was necessary to check each of the concordances and discard some of them for not complying with the syntactic function we expected to find in the corpora.

It is also noteworthy that there were no instances in CORDE or CORDIAM of four collocations extracted from the PEN_SP_TT: *captar (el) efecto, despilfarrar (el) oro, captar (el) significado* y *enmarcar (un) retrato*. This may be due to several factors: first, these collocations are neither very frequent nor very typical in the language; second, generally collocations allow the variation of at least one of their components without affecting the meaning of the others, for instance *despilfarrar el oro*, where the noun *oro* could be replaced by *dinero/fortuna/recursos*, etc. *Despilfarrar dinero* does have occurrences in CORDE, although not in Colombian Spanish. As for the absence of the collocations *captar (el) significado* and *enmarcar (un) retrato* from both corpora, it could be attributed to a rare use of them in the period of time consulted.

The established equivalent was the most used technique in the translation of collocations in both target texts, which results in more conventional and standard translations, and less creative and experimental target language. Although a greater number of techniques were applied in the Colombian Spanish target text, besides the established equivalent, this TT reflects a general Spanish. In other words, it does not exhibit specific features of the Colombian Spanish variety, as regards collocations, but, on the contrary, it is more similar to general Spanish.

On the other hand, the bilingual dictionaries consulted are characterised by maintaining this tendency to standardise translated language, listing only one or two translation equivalents for certain collocations. These dictionaries are indeed far from reflecting the reality of the diatopic variety of a transnational language like Spanish. In most cases, the collocations that we looked up in these dictionaries were not even listed. This is evidence of standardisation in translated language and, at the same time, can be a contributing factor for maintaining standardisation in translated language since dictionaries are one of the translators' essential tools. Other important tools are translation memories and machine translation. According to Pym [28], the use of translation memories reinforces standardisation because they offer consistency in terminology and phraseology. By the same token, we consider that corpus-based machine translation tools (statistical machine translation and Neural machine translation) also reinforce standardisation because, broadly speaking, they rely on huge parallel corpora, which results in more usual and standard translated language and less creative and unusual one.

Additionally, Pym [28, p. 325] argues that standardisation is a strategy used by translators to reduce communicative risk. Translators tend to select more frequent and typical collocations that are recognised and accepted by most of the Spanish-speaking community as the prestigious variety, rather than select a diatopically marked variety that might sound odd and incorrect to the majority. Furthermore, standardisation practices may also take place during the editing process carried out by publishing houses, as Bush [7, p. 129] puts it: "In the English, Spanish and Portuguese-speaking worlds, for example, there will be issues of different dialects and editors who will only accept their variety of standard [...]. The editor's reading, however, need not simply be a threatening and standardizing project".

Today, research by means of diachronic and diatopic Spanish corpora face numerous limitations. In this study, we had to deal with the fact that CORDE and CORDIAM are neither lemmatised nor grammatically annotated, which implies a slower data extraction process. Therefore, it was necessary to check each of the results yielded by the corpora to verify that these actually reflected the linguistic phenomenon we intended to analyse. To illustrate this, let us give the example of the query *mezcl* dist/5 color**, which yielded instances containing adjectives like *mezclado*, nouns such as *mezcla*, and verb + noun (subject) collocations, but these were ruled out as being beyond the scope of this study.

The total size of the subcorpus of Colombia, or that of any particular national variety, is not specified in either of the corpora. For this reason, it was not possible to establish the normalised frequency of each collocation. This, in turn, prevented us from comparing objectively the frequency of use of the collocations in different countries (subcorpora), in order to determine whether each collocation was more typical of and more frequent in one national variety or another – which is what was intended, generally speaking, in this research. Another disadvantage of CORDE is that in order to be able to check the concordances resulting from a given query, the maximum number of these cannot exceed 2,000. Consequently, it is necessary to formulate query searches as specific as possible so that all results are shown.

As far as CORDIAM is concerned, its size is much smaller than that of CORDE. Therefore, when query searches in CORDIAM are narrowed using geographical and chronological criteria, the results are very poor, or even zero. Furthermore, this corpus is composed mainly of legal, administrative, private documents and chronicles. Only a small percentage of the total corpus is made up of literary texts, which largely conditions the results of queries.

5 Conclusions

Generally, translated language tend to exhibit more features of standardisation than non-translated language. In the case of translated Spanish, we observe a tendency to avoid the use of diatopically marked phraseological units and, on the contrary, favour those that correspond to general or standard Spanish. In this paper, we argue that the rendering of verb + noun (object) collocations into Colombian Spanish of the first two chapters of *The Portrait of Dorian Gray* by Oscar Wilde is indeed closer to general Spanish than to the Colombian Spanish variety. The data reveal that the most frequently applied technique in the rendering of collocations in both target texts was the established equivalent. The Colombian Spanish target text shares 23 out of the 48 collocations (47.91%) with the peninsular Spanish target text. Secondly, the results of the analysis of the diatopic distribution of the collocations in CORDE show that 46 out of the 48 collocations (95.83%) found in the Colombian Spanish target text are also used in general Spanish and 100% of these in Peninsular Spanish. Moreover, no diatopically restricted collocations to Colombian Spanish variety were found.

The evidence presented in this study also reveals that bilingual dictionaries (English-Spanish) show a general and simplified approach to translation since they usually list only one or two translation equivalents, or even none, for certain collocations. This may indicate that the reality of diatopic varieties of Spanish, as a transnational language, is not taken into consideration. In conclusion, these findings support the starting hypothesis of this study, and they contribute to the research on standardisation of national varieties of Spanish in translated texts, insofar as they provide evidence on translated literature from English into Spanish. This could be explained by many factors, including, but not limited to, commercial interests of the translation industry, the use of translation memories, machine translation tools, and bilingual dictionaries (English-Spanish), risk-aversion translators' performance, editing process in both countries, among others. In any case, it will be necessary to delve deeper into other publishing-related, socio-cultural, and even cognitive variables involved in the tendency towards standardisation, to be able not only to describe translation behaviour, but also to explain it.

However, a note of caution is order at this point. The limitations of this study could have affected the distributional results obtained from CORDE and CORDIAM as to frequency and diatopy. Moreover, these conclusions are also limited by the fact that this study only deals with two translated texts. Further studies of this nature for Spanish and other types of phraseological units are badly needed in order to reveal 'true' regularities in translated language. A first step will be to revise and expand the existing diachronic and diatopic Spanish corpora, by size increase and annotation enrichment (particularly at the morphosyntactic level).

Acknowledgements. M.ᵃ Victoria Valencia Giraldo is supported by Banco Santander–Universidad de Salamanca International Ph.D. Scholarship.

References

1. Academia Mexicana de la Lengua, Corpus Diacrónico y Diatópico del Español de Ámerica (CORDIAM). Accessed 20 Apr 2019
2. Baker, M.: Corpus linguistics and translation studies: implications and applications. Text and technology: in honor of John Sinclair. In: Baker, M., Francis, G., Tognini-Bonelli, E. (eds.), pp. 233–250. John Benjamins, Amsterdam (1993)
3. Baker, M.: Corpus-based translation studies: the challenges that lie ahead. In: Somers, H. (ed.) Terminology, LSP and Translation, pp. 175–186. John Benjamins, Amsterdam (1996)
4. Baker, M.: In Other Words: A Coursebook on Translation. Routledge, London (2011)
5. Biber, D., Conrad, S.: Register, Genre, and Style. Cambridge Textbooks in Linguistics. Cambridge University Press, Cambridge (2009)
6. Bosque, I. (dir.): Redes. Diccionario combinatorio del español contemporáneo. Ediciones SM, Madrid (2004)

7. Bush, P.: Literary translation practices. In: Baker, M. (ed.) Routledge Encyclopedia of Translation Studies, 1st edn, pp. 127–130. Routledge, London (1998/2001)
8. Corpas Pastor, G.: Laughing one's head off in Spanish subtitles: a corpus-based study on diatopic variation and its consequences for translation. In: Mogorrón, P., Martines, V. (eds.) Phraseology, Diatopy and Translation, Collection IVITRA Research in Linguistics and Literature, pp. 54–106. John Benjamins, Amsterdam (2018)
9. Corpas Pastor, G.: Collocations in e-bilingual dictionaries: from underlying theoretical assumptions to practical lexicography and translation issues. In: Torner, S., Bernal, E. (eds.) Collocations and Other Lexical Combinations in Spanish. Theoretical and Applied Approaches, pp. 139–160. Routledge, London (2017)
10. Corpas Pastor, G.: Collocations dictionaries for English and Spanish: the state of the art. In: Orlandi, A., Giacomini, L. (eds.) Defining collocations for lexicographic purposes: from linguistic theory to lexicographic practice. Series 'Linguistic Insights', pp. 173–208. Peter Lang, Frankfurt (2016)
11. Corpas Pastor, G.: Register-specific collocational constructions in English and Spanish: a usage-based approach. J. Soc. Sci. **11**(3), 139–151 (2015)
12. Corpas Pastor, G.: Translating English verbal collocations into Spanish: on distribution and other relevant differences related to diatopic variation. Lingvisticæ Investigationes **38**(2), 229–262 (2015)
13. Corpas Pastor, G.: En torno al concepto de colocación. Euskera **1**, 89–108 (2001)
14. Corpas Pastor, G.: Manual de fraseología española. Gredos, Madrid (1996)
15. Gledhill, C.: Collocations in Science Writing. Gunter Narr, Tübingen (2000)
16. Haensch, G., Wolf, L., Ettinger, S., Werner, R.: La lexicografía. De la lingüística teórica a la lexicografía práctica. Gredos, Madrid (1982)
17. Hardy, D.E.: The Body in Flannery O'Connor's Fiction: Computational Technique and Linguistic Voice. University of South Carolina Press, Columbia (2007)
18. Haussmann, F.J.: Le dictionnaire de collocations. In: Haussmann, F.J., Reichmann, O., Wiegand, H.E., Zgusta, L. (eds.) Wörterbücher, Dictionaries, Dictionnaires, vol. 1, pp. 1010–1019. De Gruyter, Berlin (1989)
19. Hilper, M.: Distinctive collexeme analysis and diachrony. Corpus Linguist. Linguist. Theory **2**(2), 243–257 (2006)
20. Hoover, D.: Frequent collocations and authorial style. Lit. Linguist. Comput. **18**(3), 261–286 (2003)
21. Howarth, P.A.: Phraseology in English Academic Writing. Some Implications for Language Learning and Dictionary Making. Max Niemeyer Verlag, Tübingen (1996)
22. Hurtado Albir, A.: Traducción y traductología: Introducción a la traductología. Cátedra, Madrid (2001)
23. Jones, S., Sinclair, J.M.: English lexical collocations. A study in computational linguistics. Cahiers de Lexicology **24**, 15–61 (1974)
24. Koike, K.: Colocaciones léxicas en el español actual: estudio formal y léxico-semántico. Universidad de Alcalá/Takushoku University, Alcalá de Henares (2001)
25. Manning, C.D., Schütze, H.: Foundations of Statistical Natural Language Processing. The MIT Press, Cambridge (1999)
26. Oxford collocations dictionary for students of English. Oxford University Press, Oxford (2002)
27. Paffey, D.: Language Ideologies and the Globalisation of 'Standard' Spanish. Bloomsbury, London (2012)
28. Pym, A.: On Toury's laws of how translators translate. In: Pym, A., Shlesinger, M., Simeoni, D. (eds.) Beyond Descriptive Translation Studies, pp. 311–328. John Benjamins, Amsterdam (2008)

29. Real Academia Española: Data Bank (CORDE). Corpus Diacrónico del Español. http://www.rae.es. Accessed 20 Apr 2019

30. Sinclair, J.: Beginning the study of lexis. In: Bazell, C., Catford, J., Halliday, M., Robins, R. (eds.) In Memory of J.R. Firth, pp. 410–430. Longman, London (1966)

31. Toury, G.: Descriptive Translation Studies and Beyond, 2nd edn. John Benjamins, Amsterdam (1995/2012)

32. Wilde, O.: The Picture of Dorian Gray. Penguin Classics, London (1985). (Original work published 1890)

33. Wilde, O.: El retrato de Dorian Gray. Panamericana, Bogotá (1994)

34. Wilde, O.: The Portrait of Dorian Gray. Translated by J. López Muñoz. El Mundo, Madrid (1999)

35. Williams, G.: In search of representativity in specialised corpora – categorisation through collocation. Int J. Corpus Linguist. 7(1), 43–64 (2002)

Phraseological Sequences Ending in *of* in L2 Novice Academic Writing

Kateřina Vašků[1]([⊠]) [iD], Gabriela Brůhová[2] [iD],
and Denisa Šebestová[2] [iD]

[1] Department of English Language and ELT Methodology, Charles University,
nám. J. Palacha 2, Prague, Czech Republic
katerina.vasku@ff.cuni.cz
[2] Charles University, Prague, Czech Republic

Abstract. This study explores the use of recurrent four-word sequences ending in *of* in English L2 novice academic writing. Our aim is to identify to what extent and in what ways the use of phraseological patterns differs in academic texts written by L2 novice academic writers from texts authored by professional L1 academic writers. Both actual four-word sequences and structural patterns are investigated. The results show that Czech novice academic writers in the field of English literature are able to use a wide range of multi-word sequences and patterns. The frequency of the main structural patterns is very similar in the two corpora, with the prepositional sequence [prep det N *of*] representing by far the most frequent type, followed by nominal sequences [det adj/num N *of*], and verbal sequences [V det N *of*]. However, it is the prepositional type that displays most differences between the learners and native speakers, especially the use of complex prepositions. The functional analysis of the sequences has shown that the discourse functions of sequences are similar in both languages; nevertheless, Czech L2 novice academic writers tend to overuse sequences containing less advanced lexical items with transparent meaning. Pedagogical applications of the results should include improvements of pedagogical tools by increasing emphasis on advanced and semantically more complex phraseological sequences.

Keywords: Learner corpus · Phraseology · Multi-word sequences · *Of* ·
Structural patterns · Functions

1 Introduction

This study explores the use of multi-word sequences in L2 novice academic writing. Although recurrent multi-word sequences have been referred to by many different terms in literature, e.g. clusters (Scott 1996), recurrent word combinations (Altenberg 1998), lexical bundles (Biber et al. 1999; Cortes 2004) and n-grams (Granger and Bestgen 2014; Rayson 2015), all these approaches share the common idea that the use of multi-word sequences is crucial in language production. In other words, language users rely relatively heavily on "combinations of words that customarily occur" (Kjellmer 1991: 112). It has been demonstrated that the usage of multi-word sequences "unmistakably distinguishes native speakers of a language from L2 learners" (Granger and Bestgen 2014; cf. also

© Springer Nature Switzerland AG 2019
G. Corpas Pastor and R. Mitkov (Eds.): Europhras 2019, LNAI 11755, pp. 431–443, 2019.
https://doi.org/10.1007/978-3-030-30135-4_31

Pawley and Syder 1983; Ebeling and Hasselgård 2015). Similarly, Hyland (2008: 4) points out that "[m]ulti-word expressions are an important component of fluent linguistic production and a key factor in successful language learning".

The focus of this study is on four-word sequences ending in *of* in L2 novice academic writing. Our aim is to identify to what extent and in what ways the use of phraseological patterns differs in academic texts written by L2 novice academic writers from texts authored by professional L1 academic writers. Previous research has suggested that language produced by advanced L2 speakers can be influenced by their limited lexical and phraseological choices (Granger 2017: 9). Hence, the present study intends to contribute towards developing a phraseology-informed approach to language instruction.

Generally, L2 language users show the tendency to use a less varied repertoire of multi-word sequences in comparison with L1 speakers, employing the same sequences more frequently (Garner 2016: 33), and in contexts where native speakers would favour a different expression. This may be explained by the fact that L2 speakers tend to feel less certain when using a foreign language, and therefore "regularly clutch for the words [they] feel safe with" (Hasselgren 1994: 237). Hasselgren describes the words favoured by L2 speakers as "lexical teddy bears", while Ellis introduces the term "phrasal teddy bears" for "[h]ighly frequent and prototypically functional phrases like *put it on the table, how are you?, it's lunch time*" (Ellis 2012: 29). Hasselgård (forthcoming) proposes the term "phraseological teddy bears" for multi-word units "used more frequently and in more contexts" in the language of L2 speakers when compared with those used by native speakers.

2 Material and Method

In our analysis we employ a custom-made corpus of essays written by students of English at Charles University whose L1 is Czech (here referred to as the L2 corpus).[1] These essays are credit assignments written in a literary studies seminar. As a reference corpus, we have compiled a corpus of papers published in academic journals written by professional literary critics who were native English speakers (the L1 corpus). The size of the English corpus is 234 877 tokens; the Czech corpus contains 106 668 tokens, being approximately half the size of the L1 corpus (see Table 1). While it may be argued that the two corpora under examination differ markedly in the authors' language proficiency as well as the amount of professional experience and training that they have likely received, we base our approach on the assumption that the university students are in fact aspiring to become proficient users of academic English in the field of literary studies. Our study seeks to identify differences between L1 and L2 writers' writing, aiming to use the results to inform future language instruction. Therefore, our L1 corpus represents the students' target register, providing a reasonable tertium comparationis for our analysis.

---

[1] This collection is part of the VESPA corpus, currently under construction at the Department of English Language and ELT Methodology, Faculty of Arts, Charles University. For more information about the VESPA project see https://uclouvain.be/en/research-institutes/ilc/cecl/vespa.html.

Table 1. The two corpora used for the analysis

Corpus	L1 corpus	L2 corpus
Tokens total	234877	106668
Texts total	48	34
Four-word sequences retrieved	233	152
Four-word sequences excluded	19	41
Four-word sequences analyzed	214	111
Tokens of four-word sequences in the sample	669	295

A keyword analysis (using AntConc 3.5.8; Anthony 2019) of the L1 corpus (with the L2 corpus as a reference corpus) has revealed that one of the most underused words in the L2 corpus is the preposition *of* (the log-likelihood value is significant at the level of $p < 0.05$). As pointed out by Groom (2010: 63), "*of* constitutes an excellent test-bed for the claim that closed-class keywords are tractable to qualitative semantic analysis". We have therefore decided to focus on four-word sequences containing *of*, limiting our research to four-word sequences having *of* as their final element[2]. We investigate both actual four-word sequences and the structural patterns (i.e. general structures of the retrieved sequences based on a word-class analysis of their constituents). It may be expected that some sequences and structural patterns will be underused or overused in the L2 corpus.

In the present study, we focus on four-word sequences "because they are far more common than 5-word strings and offer a clearer range of structures and functions than 3-word bundles" (Hyland 2008: 8). Recurrent four-word sequences ending in the preposition *of* were automatically extracted by means of Antconc 3.5.8 and then analyzed both quantitatively and qualitatively. Four-word sequences that were considered "specific to particular topics or tasks" (Hasselgård, forthcoming) were excluded, as it is unlikely that they would occur in other kinds of texts (e.g. *The decision of the trial in The Merchant of Venice*... the L1 corpus). 19 four-word sequences were excluded from the L1 corpus and 41 from the L2 corpus.

First, the sequences were categorized structurally, i.e. in terms of their grammatical pattern. Next, the sequences were analyzed functionally. On the basis of previous classification proposed by Biber et al. 2004 we distinguish three primary discourse functions performed by four-word sequences[3]: referential sequences, discourse organizers and stance sequences. Referential sequences "make direct reference to physical or abstract entities, or to the textual context itself" in order to identify the entity or describe some particular attribute of the entity as especially important (Biber et al. 2004: 384). Four subtypes of referential sequences can be distinguished: identification/focus, imprecision

---

[2] As pointed out by Hunston (2008: 272), the study of these "small words" may prove useful in that they reveal characteristic features of "specialised corpora", while also playing an important role in structuring the text, being involved in grammar patterns.

[3] Biber et al. (2004) use the term *bundle* for what we describe as sequences. The term *lexical bundles* is defined in Biber et al. (1999: ch. 13) as the most frequent recurring word combinations in a given register, their minimum frequency being 10 IPM (ibid.: 989).

indicators, specification of attributes, time/place/text reference. Discourse organizers "reflect relationships between prior and coming discourse" (ibid.). Stance bundles "express attitudes or assessments of certainty that frame some other proposition" (ibid.).

3 Analysis

Sequences obtained by the search were classified according to the formal pattern of the sequence based on word classes.

Table 2. Structural classification of four-word sequences

Formal pattern	L1 corpus					L2 corpus				
	Types		Tokens			Types		Tokens		
	Raw freq.	%	Raw freq.	Freq. per 100k	%	Raw freq.	%	Raw freq.	Freq. per 100k	%
prep det N of	146	68.2	499	212.5	74.6	57	51.4	174	163.1	59.0
det adj/num N of	36	16.8	90	38.3	13.5	22	19.8	53	49.7	18.0
V det N of	15	7.0	38	16.2	5.7	14	12.6	28	26.2	9.5
conj det N of	8	3.7	19	8.1	2.8	2	1.8	4	3.7	1.4
other	9	4.3	23	9.8	3.4	16	14.4	36	33.7	12.2
Total	**214**	100	**669**	284.8	100	**111**	100	**295**	276.6	100

As follows from Table 1, the most frequent pattern in both corpora is the prepositional type [prep det N of] with 68% in the L1 corpus and 51% in the L2 corpus (ex. 1), followed by the nominal type [det adj/num N of] with 16.8% in the L1 corpus and 19.8% in the L2 corpus (ex. 2–3). The third most common is the verbal type [V det N of], which appears to be more prominent in the L2 corpus (13%) compared with 7% in the L1 corpus (ex. 4). The less common pattern [conj det N of] is illustrated by example 5.

(1) The moral deprivation of the lyric voice **at the end of** the second group of poems is followed by three translations from Horace, Catullus and Seneca. (L1 corpus)
(2) **A close examination of** the language of the two plays reveals that Shakespeare and Jonson frequently employ similar metaphors. (L1 corpus)
(3) Yet **the second half of** the couplet which closes the scene registers his pride in his own skill… (L1 corpus)
(4) That **is the case of** e.g. Lorenzo and Jessica when they confess their love for each other. (L2 corpus)
(5) This poem portrays the change **and the end of** a relationship between two lovers. (L2 corpus)

The remaining group of patterns (marked as *other* in Table 1) contains instances of patterns which occurred only once in either corpus, for instance *point of view of* or *not a sign of*. It is noteworthy that the L2 corpus contains a significantly larger proportion of such instances (14% in L2 vs. 3% in L1), which might suggest that learners of English tend to rely on the open choice principle rather than on the idiom principle (cf. Sinclair 1991). The following sections focus on the three most frequent patterns, exploring similarities and differences between the use of phraseological sequences by L1 and L2 speakers of English.

3.1 Prepositional Type

As follows from Table 2, the prepositional type is by far the most common type of four-word sequences in the two corpora. The most frequent prepositions in the pattern are represented by *in* (38 sequences in the L1 corpus, 21 in the L2 corpus), *as* (22 sequences in L1, 10 in L2), *at* (12 sequences in L1, 5 in L2) and *of* (12 sequences in L1, 5 in L2).

Table 3 lists twenty-two most commonly used prepositional sequences in both corpora in decreasing order of frequency, with the number of tokens for each sequence

Table 3. The most frequent prepositional sequences

L1 corpus	Raw freq.	Per 100k	L2 corpus	Raw freq.	Per 100k
at the end of	24	10.2	**at the end of**	16	15.0
at the heart of	17	7.2	**at the beginning of**	9	8.4
in the context of	15	6.4	**as a way of**	7	6.6
in the face of	15	6.4	**in the case of**	7	6.6
at the beginning of	12	5.1	as a means of	5	4.7
as a form of	11	4.7	in the course of	5	4.7
as a kind of	10	4.3	**in the form of**	5	4.7
at the expense of	8	3.4	for the purposes of	4	3.7
at the hands of	8	3.4	in the end of	4	3.7
on the part of	8	3.4	in the eyes of	4	3.7
as a result of	7	3.0	of the idea of	4	3.7
by the end of	7	3.0	with the exception of	4	3.7
in the form of	7	3.0	as a symbol of	3	2.8
in the world of	7	3.0	as an act of	3	2.8
as a sign of	6	2.6	**by the end of**	3	2.8
in the history of	6	2.6	for the sake of	3	2.8
in the wake of	6	2.6	in a number of	3	2.8
as a way of	6	2.6	in the beginning of	3	2.8
as the basis of	5	2.1	**in the world of**	3	2.8
in the case of	5	2.1	on the role of	3	2.8
in the light of	5	2.1	with the use of	3	2.8
on the side of	5	2.1	within the structure of	3	2.8

(absolute frequency). As regards the frequencies of the most common prepositional sequences, they roughly correspond to each other (given that the L1 corpus is approximately twice as large as the L2 corpus). The items occurring in both corpora are marked in bold. The lists share only seven sequences: *at the end of, at the beginning of, by the end of, in the form of, in the world of, as a way of* and *in the case of.*

Perhaps more interesting are instances which either occur in one of the corpora only or are significantly underused in the second corpus. The following are the most prominent sequences from the L1 corpus which are underrepresented in the L2 corpus: *at the heart of, in the context of, in the face of, at the expense of, as a sign of.* It appears that these sequences commonly used in the L1 corpus may not be stored as phraseological units in L2 speakers' mental lexicon. Interestingly, the head nouns in these expressions are all used in the abstract, often metaphorical, sense, which even advanced learners of English may find difficult to use (ex. 6–8).

(6) But at the same time, our critical task must be to uncover the fissures, paradoxes, and contradictions that lie **at the heart of** that economy. (L1 corpus)
(7) Authors use these surrogates, who resist the violent father/master, to solve the problem of wifely obedience **in the face of** murder. (L1 corpus)
(8) …when the speaker embraces present pain **as a sign of** future pleasure… (L1 corpus)

Similarly, the L2 corpus contains several sequences which are underrepresented in the L1 corpus. The most significant instances are: *in the end of, in the beginning of, in the eyes of, of the idea of.* The first two sequences *in the end of* or *in the beginning of* represent a common error of L2 speakers, who may often confuse the preposition *at* with *in.* Apart from such instances of language errors, the list of the most frequent sequences overused in the L2 corpus contains *in the eyes of,* which occurs four times in the L2 corpus, but only once in the L1 corpus and its overuse in L2 is thus statistically significant ($p < 0.05$). Since there is a corresponding phrase in Czech, *v očích* + $N_{genitive}$, the higher frequency in the L2 corpus might reflect a possible influence of the first language[4] (cf. Hyland 2008: 20).

All prepositional sequences were checked for their discourse function based on the classification proposed by Biber et al. (2004). Both samples contain only sequences with the referential function (see Table 4).

On the basis of previous research (Biber et al. 2004: 398; Hyland 2008: 16) the high distribution of the referential function was expected, but the fact that discourse organizers and stance sequences were not attested in our corpora at all was surprising. This may be due to the nature of sequences containing the *of*-phrase fragment, which tend to be used "to focus readers on a particular instance or to specify the conditions under which a statement can be accepted, working to elaborate, compare and emphasise aspects of an argument" (Hyland 2008: 16). Out of the four possible subtypes of referential expressions mentioned by Biber et al. (2004), our analysis revealed that prepositional sequences in academic writing display predominantly two functions,

---

[4] The Czech idiom *v očích* + $N_{genitive}$ has a frequency of 6.76 i.p.m in the Czech corpus syn2015 as opposed to 3.76 i.p.m. of *in the eyes of* in the BNC.

Table 4. Functions of prepositional sequences

Subtypes of referential sequences	L1	%	L2	%	Examples
Identification/focus	0	0	1	2	*as the one of*
Specification of attributes	115	79	36	63	*as a way of, for the purposes of*
Time/place/text reference	31	21	20	35	*at the end of, at the hands of*
Total	**146**	**100**	**57**	**100**	

namely specification of attributes (79% in the L1 corpus and 63% in the L2 corpus) and time/place/text reference (21% in the L1 corpus and 35% in the L2 corpus).

The most common function of prepositional sequences, i.e. specification of attributes, is to "identify specific attributes of the following head noun" (Biber et al. 2004: 395). Some of the sequences specify quantity or amount, e.g. *in a range of* or *into a set of* (ex. 9), the size and form of the following head noun, abstract characteristics or logical relationships in the text, e.g. *in the case of, as a means of, as a result of, as a way of, in the form of*[5] (ex. 10–12). The last subtype expresses abstract characteristics of the following noun or specifies logical relationships in the text, and it is by far the most common function of referential expressions in both corpora. Hyland (2008) describes sequences with this function as "framing signals", used "to frame arguments by highlighting connections, specifying cases and pointing to limitations" (Hyland 2008: 16).

(9)   Amor appears **in a range of** conflicting characterizations external to the speaker... (L1 corpus)

(10) However, the reader always gains insight into the relationship between the two and, **in the case of** Petrarch and Spenser, the main focus falls on the power dynamics therein. (L2 corpus)

(11) **As a result of** this invention, alchemy could be studied by any literate person. (L2 corpus)

(12) Thus he pretends to be at the point of death **as a way of** convincing himself of his own immortality. (L2 corpus)

Both corpora also contain a significant number of prepositional sequences expressing location in time, place or the text. Due to the genre of our sample texts, however, we do not attempt to distinguish temporal, locative and textual reference, as many of the prepositional sequences of this type refer to the location of some point in a play, where the distinction between the situational and textual location is irrelevant. The most common sequence in both corpora is *at the end of* (ex. 13). Surprisingly, *at the beginning of* is the second most common sequence of this type only in the L2 corpus (ex. 14), while occupying the fifth position in the L1 corpus.

---

[5] Biber et al. (2004) include the sequence *in the form of* among "tangible framing attributes" (i.e. expressions specifying the size and form of the following head noun). However, in our corpus this sequence is used only in its abstract meaning; therefore, we classified *in the form of* as an "intangible framing attribute" describing the abstract characteristics of the following noun (e.g. *in the form of restrictions/a trust/retrospection/his own mortality*).

(13) *To read Kate's speech as an ironic performance of submission should also take into account the continued intellectual acuity and physical power Petruchio retains at the end of the play. (L1 corpus)*

(14) *The poet tells his addressee at the beginning of the poem... (L2 corpus)*

Some authors focus on the status of prepositional sequences as formally and functionally fixed phraseological units and emphasize their grammatical function. Granger and Paquot view them as textual phrasemes, "typically used to structure and organize the content (i.e. referential information) of a text or any type of discourse" (Granger and Paquot 2008: 42) describe them as complex prepositions, "grammaticalized combinations of two simple prepositions with an intervening noun, adverb or adjective" (ibid.: 44).

Similarly, Klégr (1997; 2002) regards some of the prepositional sequences that "tend to be fixed in form" (Klégr 1997: 62) as complex prepositions. Based on a set of syntactic criteria (e.g. restricted variability of form, replaceability with a lexicalized primary or secondary preposition, inability to function as an independent clause element), Klégr lists over 400 complex prepositions. When comparing our samples of prepositional sequences with Klégr's list, we identified the following complex prepositions:

Table 5. Complex prepositions in the corpora

L1 corpus (23 instances)	L2 corpus (15 instances)
in the context of, at the expense of, on the part of, as a result of, in the form of, as a sign of, in the wake of, in the case of, in the light of, on the side of, in a state of, in the absence of, on the basis of, at the cost of, for the sake of, in the midst of, in the service of, on the verge of, from the point of, in the aftermath of, in the hands of, in the matter of, with the exception of	*in the case of, in the form of, in the eyes of, with the exception of, for the sake of, during the time of, for the purpose of, from the point of, in the hands of, in the manner of, in the middle of, in the space of, on the basis of, on the side of, with the help of*

If we compare Table 5 with the list of most frequent prepositional sequences (Table 3), we can notice a different distribution of complex prepositions in the two corpora. While complex prepositions in the L1 corpus show a stronger tendency to occur among the most frequent prepositional sequences (10 instances of complex prepositions among the items in Table 3, cf. ex. 15), the L2 corpus contains only 5 types of complex prepositions among the most frequent sequences, each of the remaining 10 types occurring only twice. We can therefore conclude that this type of prepositional sequences is underused in the L2 corpus.

(15) Portia's suitors are judged not **on the basis of** their wealth or goods, but in terms of personal and moral qualities, and it must be said, racial prejudice.

The overall results of the analysis of the prepositional sequences suggest that this type is indeed underused by L2 learners of English compared with the L1 corpus, where the range of different lexemes used as nouns within the prepositional sequences is much broader, with many highly advanced vocabulary items (ex. 16–19). In addition, some of the most common prepositional sequences found in the L1 corpus, although not included in the list compiled by Klégr (1997), could be also considered instances of complex prepositions, e.g. *at the heart of* and *in the face of.*

(16) **In the wake of** extensive critical discussion revolving around the analysis of sonnet sequence personae, this, too, seems self-evident. (L1 corpus)

(17) **In the midst of** this spatial dissonance, the presence of the island-mountain shows how the mythology of The Faerie Queene depends on examples taken from the poet's life in Ireland. (L1 corpus)

(18) Her findings should be viewed **against the backdrop of** the rising number of women involved in litigation more generally... (L1 corpus)

(19) In both versions of this origin myth, the island is a geographically peripheral place **on the cusp of** the known world. (L1 corpus)

As has been pointed out by Hasselgård (forthcoming), the reason for the underuse of these prepositional sequences may be that "most learners simply do not know them, or [...] they belong to a style level that the learners are not fully familiar with."

3.2 Nominal Type

The nominal type [det adj/num N of] is the second most common type of four-word sequences in both corpora. Especially in the L1 corpus, there is a significant drop between the frequency of the prepositional and nominal type (see Table 1). The type includes sequences with a determiner followed by an adjective/numeral, a noun and the preposition *of.* In the L1 corpus, 30 sequences contain an adjective (ex. 20) and 6 sequences contain a numeral (ex. 21), while in the L2 corpus, 18 sequences contain an adjective and 4 sequences contain a numeral.

(20) For Volumnia, martial honour is **the logical outcome of** maternal nurture. (L1 corpus)

(21) **The first instance of** role-playing in the play is Jessica's dressing as a page. (L2 corpus)

The raw frequencies of nominal sequences are considerably lower than those of prepositional sequences, especially in the L1 corpus, where only three sequences reach the level of at least four occurrences in the corpus: *the second half of* (six occurrences), *the very act of* (five occurrences) and *a close examination of* (four occurrences). Since four occurrences in the L1 corpus should roughly correspond to two occurrences in the L2 corpus (given the size of the two corpora), all 22 nominal sequences in the L2 corpus have the corresponding frequency. This discrepancy between the L1 and L2 corpus may be caused by a limited vocabulary of English learners, or by the effect of "phraseological teddy bears" (cf. Hasselgård forthcoming). However, due to the low numbers of raw frequencies in both corpora these conclusions should be viewed as tentative.

All nominal sequences found in both corpora can be classified as referential. However, the sequence *a close examination of* (L1 corpus) could alternatively be classified as a discourse organizer, which is used to "provide overt signals [...] that a new topic is being introduced" (Biber et al. 2004: 391). As follows from Table 6, sequences in the sample either contribute to the specification of attributes or express time, place or text reference. The table also shows that the latter type is more prominent in the L2 corpus than in the L1 corpus.

Table 6. Functions of nominal sequences

Subtypes of referential sequences	L1 corpus	%	L2 corpus	%	Examples
Specification of attributes	26	72.2	13	59.1	*the first instance of, the individual features of, the very act of, a good deal of*
Time/place/text reference	10	27.8	9	40.9	*the second half of, the final act of, the very end of*
Total	**36**	**100**	**22**	**100**	

Similarly to the distribution of prepositional sequences (cf. Table 4), the most common function of specifying nominal sequences is to specify abstract characteristics or logical relationships in the text (ex. 22–23). In addition, our L1 corpus revealed 5 sequences specifying quantity (ex. 24). Two of them (*a good deal of, a great deal of*) can be seen as lexicalized phraseological units corresponding to the single-word quantifier *many*. Apart from these two sequences, the L1 corpus also contains the sequences *a wide range of* (three occurrences), *a particular set of* (two occurrences) and *the same set of* (two occurrences). By contrast, there are no sequences of this type in the L2 corpus.

(22) Readers are advised imaginatively to invent (literally, to reinvent) the making of the poem, to reconstruct the conceptual design of its fictional landscape in order to profit in **the very act of** so doing, from its teaching. (L1 corpus)

(23) "Sonnet 130" does the opposite: the focus is on **the individual features of** the lover, however, it does not serve to emphasize her beauty but rather to draw attention to her imperfections. (L2 corpus)

(24) They also foster **a wide range of** quasi-religious or magical beliefs about the malevolent agency of objects that are not properly exchanged. (L1 corpus)

(25) He is named as such **at the very end of the play** by the advocates... (L2 corpus)

It appears that L2 users tend to use more frequently sequences which refer to time, place or location in the text. Similarly to the corresponding function within the prepositional type, it is impossible to distinguish temporal, locative and textual reference, as many of the nominal sequences of this type refer to the location of some point in a play or its part (ex. 25).

3.3   Verbal Type

The analysis of four-word sequences revealed that the verbal type is represented by 15 sequences in the L1 corpus and 14 instances in the L2 corpus, but the overall distribution is very low since the vast majority of sequences is only represented by two occurrences. What is characteristic of the verbs in this pattern is that they are semantically empty, the most frequent verb being the copular *be* (ex. 26), see Table 7.

Table 7.   Verbal sequences in the corpora

L1 corpus (15 instances)	L2 corpus (14 instances)
is a form of, are a number of, is a figure of, is a kind of, is a parody of, is a sign of, is the body of, is the product of, is the site of, takes the form of, emphasizes the importance of, suggests the presence of, becomes a sign of, had the effect of, occupies the place of	*is a cycle of, is a part of, is a way of, is an example of, is the case of, is the climax of, is the subject of, is the use of, adopts the role of, assume the role of, keep a memory of, playing the role of, share a number of, uses a metaphor of*

(26)   For Augustine idolatry **is a form of** forgetting, a failure to notice and honor this indicative relationship: a failure to interpret properly. (L1 corpus)

(27)   While it might initially seem that time **is the subject of** many of these poems it is in fact just as much, if not more, the mutability or inherent inconstancy produced by it. (L2 corpus)

(28)   She thinks that [...], which to her **is a sign of** Antony's regression.

As for the function of the verbal sequences, almost all function as referential expressions specifying attributes of the following noun. With the exception of two sequences expressing quantity, *are a number of* (L1 corpus) and *share a number of* (L2 corpus), all these sequences specify a form (ex. 26), abstract characteristics (ex. 27) or logical relationships (ex. 28). There are two instances of referential expressions referring to time, place or location in the text (*is the site of, occupies the place of*).

4   Conclusions

The present study explored four-word sequences ending in the preposition *of* in L2 novice academic writing in order to identify to what extent and in what ways the use of these multi-word sequences differs in academic texts written by L2 novice academic writers from texts written by professional L1 academic writers. The sequences were analyzed both from the structural and functional point of view.

The study has shown that the language of novice L2 academic writers and professional L1 writers displays both similar features and differences. Generally, the L2 corpus analysis proved that Czech novice academic writers in the field of English literature are able to use a wide range of multi-word sequences and patterns. As far as the use of structural patterns is concerned, it can be concluded that the frequency of the main structural patterns is very similar in the two corpora under examination, with the prepositional sequence representing by far the most frequent type. At the same time, it is the prepositional type that displays the most differences between learners and native speakers. Our findings have shown that the most formally fixed prepositional sequences, i.e. complex prepositions, tend to be underused by Czech learners of English. Although some complex prepositions are found in the L2 corpus, the range of different lexemes used as nouns within the prepositional sequences is much narrower, with few advanced vocabulary items and predominantly with transparent meaning. The nominal and verbal type of sequences were considerably less frequent in both corpora, but the drop between the prepositional and nominal/verbal types is considerably more striking in the L1 corpus than in the L2 corpus. Our L2 corpus contains significantly more structural patterns that we included in the category "other" (14.4% of sequences in L2 corpus vs. 4.3% in L1 corpus), which may suggest that structural patterns are less fixed in the language of learners than in the language native speakers and that learners tend to rely rather on the "open-choice principle" than on the "idiom principle" (cf. Sinclair 1991).

The functional analysis of four-word sequences ending in the preposition *of* revealed that their typical discourse function is referential, discourse organizers and stance sequences being not at all attested in our corpora. It is argued that this is due to the nature of sequences containing the *of*-phrase fragment, which describes "some attribute of the object being discussed" (Garner 2016: 40). A closer examination of the referential expressions showed that regardless of the structural type, the examined sequences display predominantly two functions, namely specification of attributes and time/place/text reference.

Our findings have confirmed that Czech learners indeed do underuse some phraseological sequences. Differences between native and non-native language production on the phraseological level tend to be rather subtle, yet they present an interesting challenge and room for development even for advanced L2 speakers, especially so for students aiming to become language professionals. As pointed out by Granger (2017: 9), general academic vocabulary (i.e. words and sequences typical of academic discourse in general, not limited to a particular discipline) tend to be difficult for learners to master, mainly because they "are not particularly salient and tend to pass unnoticed". Pedagogical applications of the results should include improvements of pedagogical tools by increasing emphasis on advanced phraseological sequences.

Acknowledgements. This study is a result of the research funded by the Czech Science Foundation as the project GA CR 19-05180S "Phraseology in English academic texts written by Czech advanced learners: a comparative study of learner and native speaker discourse", and by the Faculty of Arts, Charles University within the project "Specifický vysokoškolský výzkum - Jazyk a nástroje pro jeho zkoumání".

References

Altenberg, B.: On the phraseology of spoken English: the evidence of recurrent word-combinations. In: Cowie, A.P. (ed.) Phraseology, Theory, Analysis, and Applications, pp. 101–124. OUP, Oxford (1998)

Anthony, L.: AntConc (Version 3.5.8) (Computer Software), Waseda University, Tokyo (2019). http://www.laurenceanthony.net/

Biber, D., Conrad, S., Cortes, V.: *If you look at* ... Lexical bundles in university lectures and textbooks. Appl. Linguist. **25**, 371–405 (2004)

Biber, D., Johansson, S., Leech, G., Conrad, S., Finegan, E.: Longman Grammar of Spoken and Written English. Longman, London (1999)

Ebeling, S.O., Hasselgård, H.: Learner corpora and phraseology. In: Granger, S., Gilquin, G., Meunier, F. (eds.) The Cambridge Handbook of Learner Corpus Research, pp. 207–230. Cambridge University Press, Cambridge (2015)

Ellis, N.C.: Formulaic language and second language acquisition: Zipf and the phrasal teddy bear. Annu. Rev. Appl. Linguist. **32**, 17–44 (2012)

Garner, J.R.: A phrase-framed approach to investigating phraseology in learner writing across proficiency levels. Int. J. Learn. Corpus Res. **2**(1), 31–68 (2016)

Granger, S.: Academic phraseology. A key ingredient in successful L2 academic literacy. In: Fjeld, H., Henriksen, J. (eds.) Academic Language in a Nordic Setting – Linguistic and Educational Perspectives. Oslo Studies in Language, vol. 9, no. 3, pp. 9–27. Olsen & Prentice (2017)

Granger, S., Bestgen, Y.: The use of collocations by intermediate vs. advanced nonnative writers: a bigram-based study. Int. Rev. Appl. Linguist. Lang. Teach. **52**(3), 229–252 (2014)

Granger, S., Paquot, M.: Disentangling the phraseological web. In: Granger, S., Meunier, F. (eds.) Phraseology. An Interdisciplinary Perspective, pp. 27–50. John Benjamins, Amsterdam (2008)

Groom, N.: Closed-class keywords and corpus-driven discourse analysis. Keyness Texts **41**, 59–78 (2010)

Hasselgård, H.: Phraseological teddy bears: frequent lexical bundles in academic writing by Norwegian learners and native speakers of English. In: Mahlberg, M., Wiegand, V. (eds) Corpus Linguistics, Context and Culture. De Gruyter Mouton, Berlin (forthcoming)

Hasselgren, A.: Lexical teddy bears and advanced learners: a study into the ways Norwegian students cope with English vocabulary. Int. J. Appl. Linguist. **4**, 237–259 (1994)

Hunston, S.: Starting with the small words. In: Römer, U., Schulze, R. (eds.) Patterns, Meaningful Units and Specialized Discourses (2008). Int. J. Corpus Linguist **13**(3), 271–295

Hyland, K.: As can be seen. Lexical bundles and disciplinary variation. English Specific Purposes **27**(1), 4–21 (2008)

Kjellmer, G.: A mint of phrases. In: Aijmer, K., Altenberg, B. (eds.) English Corpus Linguistics, pp. 111–127. Routledge, London (1991)

Klégr, A.: English complex prepositions of the prepositional phrase type. Acta Universitatis Carolinae–Philologica. Prague Stud. English **22**(5), 51–78 (1997)

Pawley, A., Syder, F.H.: Two puzzles for linguistic theory: nativelike selection and nativelike fluency. In: Richards, S.C., Schmidt, R.W. (eds.) Language and Communication, pp. 191–226. Longman, London (1983)

Rayson, P.E.: Computational tools and methods for corpus compilation and analysis. In: Biber, D., Reppen, R. (eds.) Cambridge Handbook of English Corpus Linguistics. CUP, Cambridge (2015)

Scott, M.: Wordsmith Tools 4. Oxford University Press, Oxford (1996)

Sinclair, J.: Corpus, Concordance, Collocation. OUP, Oxford (1991)

Author Index

Printed in the United States
By Bookmasters